Industrial Locomotives of North Wales

INDUSTRIAL LOCOMOTIVES of NORTH WALES

Compiled by V J Bradley

Series Editor: R K Hateley

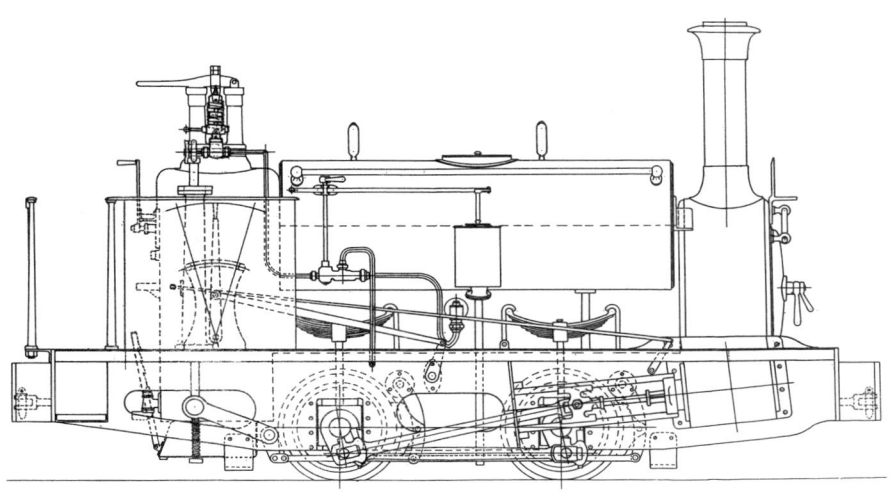

Hunslet 409 of 1886, VELINHELI, at Dinorwic Quarries (p.235)
- Drawing by D. H. Townsley

INDUSTRIAL RAILWAY SOCIETY

Published by the INDUSTRIAL RAILWAY SOCIETY

at 47 Waverley Gardens, LONDON NW10 7EE

© **INDUSTRIAL RAILWAY SOCIETY 1992**

ISBN 0 901096 72 5   (Hardbound)

ISBN 0 901096 73 3   (Softbound)

Note: The original artwork for the maps was produced by Philip Hindley, but we would like to acknowledge the help of Map-X Visuals of Kilkhampton (0288 82591) in finalising and expediting the production of these maps

Printed by Clifford Ward Ltd, Bridlington

This book is copyright under the Berne Convention. Apart from any fair dealing for the purposes of private study, research, criticism, or review, as permitted under the Copyright Act 1911, no portion may be reproduced by any process without the written permission of the publisher

CONTENTS

INTRODUCTION & SCOPE		6
EXPLANATORY NOTES:	Arrangement of book	7
PRESENTATION OF DATA:	Format of Entries	9
LOCOMOTIVE BUILDERS		13
ACKNOWLEDGEMENTS & SOURCES		16
	Index to Journals	17
	Index to Books	19
SOME CLUES FOR FURTHER RESEARCH		27

LOCOMOTIVE LISTINGS:

SECTION 1 : Non-Static Loco Fleets	33
SECTION 2 : Public Railways & Associated Contracts	59
SECTION 3 : Industrial & Contract Railways	177

INDEXES	Locomotives - identities	424
	Locomotives - names	479
	Sites & Operators	487

INTRODUCTION & SCOPE

This volume, one of a series of Handbooks covering Great Britain, had its origins in 'Pocket Book No.5' published in 1950, and the updated and expanded 'Pocket Book F' published in 1968. At the time these books were published, the Industrial Railway Society was known as the Industrial Locomotive Information Section of the Birmingham Locomotive Club.

The first series of Pocket Books were slim volumes, restricted to brief listings of the locomotives then known to have been used at industrial Locations; in the 1968 edition coverage was expanded to include minor public railways, and the limited number of contracts then researched. This third edition embodies a very considerable quantity of additional information which has become available over the past two decades - thanks to the co-operation of many individual researchers, who have often enjoyed access to sources of data quite inaccessible until recent times. This has resulted in an expanded layout resulting, hopefully, in a volume both more "readable" and of wider appeal.

Space limitations, however, have resulted in a restriction of coverage to the "true" North Wales - defined by the present-day counties of Gwynedd and Clwyd. The former Mid-Wales counties of Cardigan, Radnor and Montgomery, included in the 1968 edition, have since been amalgamated into new counties which impinge on the South Wales industrialised area; thus these will now to be dealt with by other Handbooks in the series.

Almost all of the information in this new edition has been obtained from fresh research into basic sources, or from a re-examination of sources that had been used before. It is not simply an up-date of the 1968 edition.

Whilst every effort has been made to keep typesetting errors to a minimum, it is impossible to guarantee a total freedom from such. Also, by its very nature, research is an on-going activity, thus no claim is made that this book tells the complete story. I will therefore be very pleased to hear from any reader who is able to offer additional information, comment or constructive criticism, with a view to the periodic circulation of up-date Bulletins, and incorporation in a future revised edition of this book.

Up-date Bulletins are circulated free of charge to members of the Industrial Railway Society. Non-members may purchase copies as they are issued and, if interested, non-members should send a stamped-addressed envelope marked "North Wales Bulletin" on the rear of the envelope, to the address below. The envelope will then be used to send details of available Bulletins in due course.

The address for correspondence is:
V.J.Bradley, Gilfachddu, Llanberis, Gwynedd, LL55 4TY.

IMPORTANT

It is strongly recommended that all readers, and particularly those familiar with the Handbook series, should carefully study the Explanatory Notes and Presentation of Data details on the following pages, as the format and detail of this edition differs in some respects from previous books in the series.

EXPLANATORY NOTES

SCOPE OF BOOK

All railways that are known to have used locomotives are included, other than miniature and model railways of less than 350mm (13¾") track gauge.

All locomotives known to have been used on such railways are included, other than locomotives in the fleets of the major "Main Line" railway Companies.

Occasionally locomotives are stored at non-railway premises - sites which would not normally attract visitors when the locomotives were not there. Such "Private Stores" are not listed as "Locations" in their own right, but are referred to in the footnotes of the previous/later Locations of the locomotives as appropriate.

Museums which contain locomotives are included in the listings; and details are given of any displayed locomotives which have had a commercial history within North Wales.

ARRANGEMENT OF BOOK

The locomotives, and their railways, recorded in this book have been classified into three "Sections", each dealing with a specific type of railway. This is not in accordance with the usual Handbook format but, in a book such as this which covers just two Counties, it is a more convenient arrangement, and deals with the area as a cohesive unit.

Section One - Non-Static Locomotive Fleets

This Section details the limited number of privately-owned fleets of locomotives based - or belonging to owners based - within the area, but which were not actually used at their base Locations. It is a convenient Section in which to summarise the locomotives known to have been owned by various North-Wales-based dealers and contractors. Where such locomotives are recorded as having also been used within North Wales, they are also listed under the appropriate headings in Sections 2 or 3.

Section Two - Public Railways & Associated Contracts

This Section lists all the Public Railways in North Wales, arranged generally in chronological order of the dates on which they were first opened. One purpose of this Section is to provide a framework for the listing of the contractors' locomotives used for their construction, reconstruction (and demolition where appropriate), and has the advantage that any as-yet undiscovered information is more readily apparent than would be the case if, as hitherto, these contracts were scattered throughout a general listing of entries under a County title. A listing is also given of the locomotives used for the actual operation of these railways up to, but NOT including, 4' 8½" gauge locomotives within the stock of a Major Railway Company. In this context, and within this book, the Major Railway Companies are defined as British Railways, LMSR, LNWR, LNER, GCR, MS&LR, GWR and Cambrian Railways (Cam.Rys.).

The ownership of each Public Railway is listed under its title; in order to save constant repetition the ownership is detailed only so far as to a Major Railway Company, after which ownership would take the normal national course of 1923 Grouping and 1948 Nationalisation

For inclusion in this Section, a "Public Railway" is defined as being a railway to which people (maybe only Companies) - other than the owners of the railway - had a "right" of access for the carriage of passengers and/or freight. There are, however, a few difficult cases; like the Port Penrhyn branch - classified as Public (because it was operated by LNW/LMS/BR) despite the fact that it carried freight for only one user. Whilst the Wrexham Trading Estate Railway, which served many users, is excluded; appearing instead in Section 3 because of its pure "industrial" origins.

Each Public Railway is referenced by a "PR/n" number which is used for cross-reference purposes throughout this Handbook. A diagrammatic index to the Public Railways appears at the start of Section Two, and the Railways' titles and owners' names are included in the comprehensive Index at the end of the book.

Section Three - Locomotive Operated Industrial & Contract Railways.

This Section is a listing of all Locations where locomotives are known, or believed, to have been used (other than those included in Section 2). As such, it conforms to the usual Handbook layout, except as follows:

a) Entries are sorted alphabetically by the name of the Location, and not by the name of the last or current owner/operator.

In an essentially rural area such as North Wales, most sites are best known by the name of the site (quarry, mine, works, etc.) and this is a more convenient form of listing, avoiding the necessity of re-listing in different alphabetical order when ownership changes. Should this ever present a difficulty to the reader, the comprehensive Index at the rear of the book will assist.

b) The alphabetical sorting is done without regard to Counties within the area. However, each Location is identifed by a National Grid reference number by which it may be located on the more recent editions of Ordnance Survey (etc.) maps. In this Handbook, these reference numbers are shown with a prefix which indicates both the present and former Counties in which the Location falls, as follows:

    Cd   : Clwyd ex Denbighshire/Sir Ddinbych

    Cf   : Clwyd ex Flintshire/Sir Fflint

    Cfd   : Clwyd ex Flintshire Detatched/Fflint a Maelor

    Cm   : Clwyd ex Merioneth/Sir Feirionnydd

    Ga   : Gwynedd ex Anglesey/Ynys Mon

    Gc   : Gwynedd ex Caernarfonshire/Sir Gaernarfon

    Gm   : Gwynedd ex Merioneth/Sir Feirionnydd

c) Each Location has been given a reference code in the form "Xn", where 'X' is the alphabetical initial of the Location, and 'n' a serial number within that alphabetical group. These reference codes are used for cross-reference purposes elsewhere within this Handbook, and on the Index Maps. As published here, only "even" numbers are used for these codes, leaving "odd" numbers for allocation to any further Locations that may be discovered.

PRESENTATION OF DATA

FORMAT OF ENTRIES

Most entries in Section 3 follow a standard format - as follows - and entries in Sections 1 and 2 follow a similar arrangement sometimes modified to suit the nature of the entry in question.

Location title/reference code/County code and Grid Reference.

List of known owners/operators at this Location.
     reg   - date company registered
     £xK   - INITIAL authorised capital (thousands of £)
     liq   - date or period of liquidation of company
     vol.liq- date company entered into voluntary liquidation

This is followed by a brief description of the Location with sometimes a suggestion for further reading, "[Read: reference code/s]", where some additional information of a general nature may be found if desired. Such references may, however, contain information which differs from the details given in this Handbook, as this frequently incorporates updated data not available when the suggested references were written.
For an explanation of the reference codes used, see "Sources".

The Gauge of the railway system at the Location is then given.
Frequently smaller quarries have used locomotives of different gauges (such as 1'11½", 2'0" and 600mm) without alteration and such systems are given as '2ft' gauge - an approximate measurement, as distinct from 2'0" gauge. The actual gauges of individual locomotives, as manufactured, are given in the Locomotive Index at the rear of this book.

Number and/or Name carried by the locomotive whilst at this Location.
A number or name formerly carried whilst at this Location is shown '(in brackets)', though in the case of a secondhand locomotive any former number or name, carried on arrival but removed before the loco entered service, is usually given only within the source footnote. The removal of numbers/names, after withdrawal from service but prior to disposal, is generally ignored. A name officially used but not actually carried by the loco is shown in " " inverted commas, and a dash '-' indicates that no identity was carried. This column is left blank in cases where it is not known whether a title was carried or not.

Type of Locomotive.
The Whyte system of wheel classification is used except when the driving wheels were not coupled by external rods but by other means such as chains (as in 'Sentinels' and many non-steam locos). These are indicated by abbreviations such as '4w' (four-wheel), '6w' (six wheel) etc. The abbreviation '2w-2' is used for certain very light internal combustion (etc) units which had only one driven axle.

When quoting from sources (particularly advertisements) which used the terms "four wheels coupled" "six wheels coupled" etc, the form '4wc', '6wc' (etc) is used. Note that "four wheels coupled" (etc) was sometimes applied to locos that had further wheels (eg, 2-4-0, 0-4-2, 0-4-4, etc) and therefore '4wc' may not necessarily indicate '0-4-0' (etc).

The wheel classification is terminated with a code describing the locomotive as follows:

STEAM LOCOMOTIVES

- **T**   Side Tank, or similar: a tank positioned externally and largely fastened to the frame, including such variants as Wing Tanks.
- **gt**   Garratt articulated 'tank and tender' loco.
- **IT**   Inverted Saddle Tank - a combination of T and WT.
- **PT**   Pannier Tank - side tanks wholly above the level of the frame.
- **ST**   Saddle Tank.
- **UT**   Undertank - tank beneath the boiler but on top of chassis.
- **WT**   Well Tank - tank located within the chassis.
- **VB**   Vertical Boilered locomotive.
- No code - a tender loco.

- **F**   Fireless steam loco, having steam reservoir in lieu of boiler.

- **C**   (in conjunction with any above) - loco fitted with a crane.
- **G**   (in conjunction with any above) - geared transmission between cylinders and wheels.
- **t**   (in conjunction with any above) - a tank and tender loco.
- **tdr**   (usually in source references) - a loco with a tender.
- **tk**   (usually in source references) - a tank loco of unknown sort.

NON-STEAM LOCOMOTIVES

- **DM**   Diesel locomotive; Mechanical transmission
- **DE**   Diesel locomotive; Electric transmission
- **DH**   Diesel locomotive; Hydraulic transmission
- **PM**   Petrol or Paraffin locomotive; Mechanical transmission
- **PE**   Petrol or Paraffin locomotive, Electric transmission

- **BE**   Electric locomotive; Battery powered
- **RE**   Electric locomotive; live-Rail powered
- **WE**   Electric locomotive; overhead-Wire powered

- **r**   (in conjunction with any above) - "railcar"; a vehicle primarily designed to carry people rather than haul vehicles

Position of Cylinders (Steam Locomotives):
- **IC**   Inside Cylinders - located within the chassis
- **OC**   Outside Cylinders
- **VC**   Vertically mounted Cylinders
- **3C**   Three Cylinders (normally two OC plus one IC)
- **4C**   Four Cylinders (two OC plus two IC)
- **4OC**   Four Outside Cylinders

- **S**   (in conjunction with some above) - Single cylinder

In the case of Non-Steam locomotives, the nominal horsepower (when known) is given in the "cylinder" column.

Locomotive Builder: Abbreviations used are listed on Page 13.

Builders' Number and date built:
The first column lists the Builders' Serial Number ("Works Number") and the second column the building date which appeared on the works plate or, if no date shown on the plate, then the date the loco was built. More precise "ex-works" dates, where known, are listed in the Locomotive Index at the rear of this Handbook.

Rebuilding Details:
Information is given regarding "rebuilding" which either resulted in major alteration to the appearance of the locomotive, or was recorded on plates fixed to the locomotive. Other minor "rebuilds" (often in fact only complete overhauls) are not listed.

Origin of Locomotive:
"New" indicates that the locomotive arrived at this Location direct from the Builder - a "month/year" arrival date is given where this is known and space permits; "ex-works" dates can usually be found in the Locomotive Index at the rear of this Handbook.
The origin is otherwise keyed to a "footnote".

Disposal of Locomotive:
Disposal to another Location is keyed to a "footnote".
In other cases, the following abbreviations are used:
    Scr : broken up on site as scrap metal (on date shown if known)
    s/s : scrapped or sold; no details known

Existing locomotives, where appropriate, are noted as:
    OOU : Out Of Use; intact (or largely so) but not fit for use, and likely to remain thus for some considerable time.
    Dsmt : Dismantled - OOU and not intact for a considerable time.

Footnotes:
Footnotes in this Handbook conform to a new standard of accuracy, intended to eliminate the errors and confusion caused by the hitherto indiscriminate use of pre-fixes "ex" and "to" - "ex" often meaning nothing more than that the origin Location quoted is the last-known Location of the locomotive, with no evidence to show that a direct transfer took place. Indeed, such footnotes have frequently ignored a timespan of very many years. Likewise, "to" footnotes have been similarly deficient.

This Handbook adopts a more systematic approach to the problem, and in general the following footnote prefixes are used:

    tdx: "Transferred Direct Ex/From" (previous Location).
                  Used ONLY when a Direct Transfer has been established.

    wfw: "Was Formerly With" (a former Location).
                  If this is the FIRST entry, it quotes the LAST KNOWN Location of the locomotive.
                  If NOT the first entry (ie, if following a "tdx" or a "wfw"), it details A PREVIOUS Location for information only.
    Such secondary "wfw" notes may assist in tracing the locomotive in another Handbook.

    wfw(tdx?): is used to indicate that "wfw" certainly applies, and
                    there is good reason to believe that "tdx" could apply.

Disposal footnotes accord with the same system:

    tdt: "Transferred Direct To" (next Location).
    wlw: "Was Later With" (a subsequent Location).
    wlw(tdt?): "wlw" and believed "tdt" could apply.

Where details regarding origins and disposals remain unresolved, the footnotes have been expanded and frequently discuss both facts and suggestions. The temptation to publish editorial opinion as "fact" has been carefully avoided; the reader is thus free to consider the evidence and, hopefully, to provide clarification from other sources.

"Transfers for Fun":
In recent times it has become fairly common for locomotives (particularly narrow-gauge) to be moved from site to site, for short visits, "just for fun". Such transfers are not listed in this Handbook. To qualify for listing, it must be clear that there was a genuine commercial requirement for the transfer to take place.

General Abbreviations:
    c   "circa" - about the date given
    f   "formerly"
    GR   Grid Reference
    Reb   Rebuilt
    NCB National Coal Board
    ROF Royal Ordnance Factory
    WD   War Department
And the recognised abbreviations for main-line railway companies.

Otherwise, the use of abbreviations, particularly in footnotes, has been avoided; indeed, in many cases and where space permits, these listed abbreviations have been expanded.

Dates:
Many historians are apparently satisfied with transfer (etc) dates correct to the nearest month [eg, 6/1952] and, where such dates are unknown, to settle for an assumed mid-point date within a known timespan [eg; here 2/1952, gone 12/1952, therefore moved "c7/1952"]. In this Handbook, dates are quoted to the precise day if possible; otherwise the timespan is quoted and no presumptions made. Hence the preferred format adopted in this example is: "after 16/2/1952 by 20/12/1952". However, with sometimes only "month" parameters in the records, this format becomes "after 2/1952 by 12/1952". Obviously this can be misleading, as the transfer may have taken place not only between but also during either of the months stated, and therefore, pending fuller details of dates being (hopefully) ascertained, it must be presumed that the transfer may have occurred both during and between the parameter months given.

Notwithstanding the foregoing, entries may still be found herein of the "c1952" nature; indicating that in these cases it has as yet proved impossible to ascertain any trustworthy parameters.

In "disposal" footnotes ("tdt") the date is the date of departure; because of travelling time, this may not of course be the date of arrival at the next Location as listed elsewhere.
Likewise in "tdx" origin footnotes the date is the date of arrival.

Square Brackets:
Throughout this book, 'square brackets [ ]' are used to surround data which is either (obviously) a data source reference; or else is an editorial comment. The inclusion of a question mark [?] indicates an editorial suggestion. The presentation of editorial opinion as "fact" has been eliminated.

Railway, Tramway and Tramroad:
These terms, particularly in connection with narrow-gauge lines, tend to be somewhat confused, with no distinct differences. In this Handbook it is presumed that:
RAILWAY is a line worked (in whole or part) by locomotives.
TRAMWAY is a line laid (in whole or part) in or beside a highway.
TRAMROAD is a Railway not worked by locomotives.
PLATEWAY is a primitive form of Tramroad.
But, of course, there are some that defy such categorisation !

Language:
One inevitable problem when writing anything concerning Wales, and particularly North Wales, arises from the extensive use of the Welsh language within the area. Clearly, cost alone must preclude the complete bilingual publication of a specialist book of this nature. However, the correct Welsh spellings for most place names (particularly so in Gwynedd) are used, rather than persist with the anglicised spellings used widely in times past, with the exceptions of:-
> The titles of Companies, which are spelled as in the documents of those companies.
> Where the Welsh language name of a Place differs considerably from the form which persists in everyday use, the latter, more familiar form, is used. This approach is necessary in view of the extensive use of archives in a work of this nature.

It is hoped that no offence will be taken (for assuredly none is intended) for the often difficult decisions made in this context.

LOCOMOTIVE BUILDERS

Extended details, including full titles, of the locomotive builders referred to in this Handbook, are given in the Locomotive Index at the rear of this book. The following abbreviated list is intended for quick reference only:

AB	Andrew Barclay, Kilmarnock	BH	Black Hawthorn
AD	Austro Daimler, Austria	BL	Bassett Lowke
AE	Avonside Engine, Bristol	BLW	Baldwin Loco Works, USA
	Stothert Slaughter	BP	Beyer Peacock
	Slaughter Gruning	Bs	Barclays & Co, Kilmarnock
AH	A.Horlock, Northfleet	Bton	Brighton Loco Works
ALCo	American Locomotive Co	Bury	Edward Bury & Co
AP	Aveling & Porter		Bury Curtiss & Kennedy
AtW	Atkinson Walker, Preston	CE	Clayton Equipment Co Ltd
AW	Armstrong Whitworth		Clarke Chapman Ltd
Barber	Trevor Barber	Ch	Alexander Chaplin
Barnes	A.Barnes, Rhyl	Chance	Chance Manufacturing, USA
BE	Brush, Loughborough	CoedTalon	
BEV	British Electric Vehicles		Coed Talon Colliery
Bg	Baguley, Burton on Trent	Cromford	Cromford & High Peak Rly
	McEwan, Pratt & Co	Cross	James Cross, St.Helens
	(post-1913)	Cwe	Crewe Loco Works

DA	Daniel Adamson, Dukinfield	HL	Hawthorn Loco Works
DB	Duffield Bank (Heywood)		R & W Hawthorn
DC	Drewry Car Co		Hawthorn Leslie
DCL	David Curwen Ltd	HoL	Hawthorns of Leith
Derby	Derby Loco Works		R & W Hawthorn
DeW	DeWinton, Caernarfon		Hawthorns & Co
DK	Dick Kerr, Kilmarnock	Hor	Horwich Loco Works
Dodds	Dodds & Son, Rotherham	HRM	Hardy Rail Motors, Slough
Dtz	Deutz (Otto), Germany		Four Wheel Drive Lorry Co
Dub	Dubs, Glasgow	HU	Robert Hudson, Leeds
EAV	Edison Accumulator Vehicles	HVF	Owen Hughes, Valley Foundry
EBW	E.B.Wilson, Leeds	Hz	Hohenzollern, Dusseldorf,
	Shepherd (& Todd)		Germany
	Fenton Craven	IWB	Isaac Watt Boulton, Ashton
EE	English Electric	JF	John Fowler, Leeds
	Stephenson Works - EES	Jones	Jones (Newton le Willows)
	Vulcan Foundry - EEV		Jones (Liverpool)
Ellis	H & J Ellis, Salford		Jones, Turner & Evans
Fbn	William Fairbairn		Jones & Potts
FE	Falcon Works, Loughborough		John Jones
	Hughes & March	Jung	Arn. Jung, Jungenthal, Germany
	Henry Hughes	Kellow	Moses Kellow, Croesor
	Hughes Loco & Tram	Kirtley	Kirtley & Co, Warrington
	Falcon Engine & Car	Kit	Kitson Locomotives, Leeds
FH	Planet Locomotives		Todd, Kitson & Laird
	Kent Construction		Kitson & Laird
	F.C.Hibberd		Kitson, Thompson, Hewitson
	Butterley Co		Kitson & Hewitson
FJ	Lowca Works, Whitehaven		Kitson & Co
	Tulk & Ley	KS	California Works, Stoke-on-Trent
	Fletcher Jennings		
	Lowca Engineering		Hartley & Arnoux
	New Lowca Engineering		Hartley, Arnoux & Fanning
FRCo	Festiniog Railway Co		Kerr Stuart
FW	Fox Walker	L	Lister Locomotives
GB	Greenwood & Batley		R & A Lister & Co
GE	George England		Lister Blackstone
	Fairlie Engine & Carriage	LAdB	Les Ateliers de Bondy
GECT	G.E.C.Traction, Vulcan Works	Lane	Claude Lane, Barnet
	GEC Industrial Locos		Lancaster Electrical Co
GUEST	Guest Engineering Works	LIL	Lilleshall Co, Oakengates
	G & S Light Engineering	Llechwedd	
	Guest Engineering &		Llechwedd Slate Quarries
	Maintainance	LMM	Logan Mining Machinery, Dundee
HC	Hudswell, Leeds		
	Hudswell Clarke	MH	Muir Hill Engineers
	Hudswell Clarke & Rodgers		E.Boydell & Co
	Hudswell Badger	MR	Motor Rail Simplex Locos
HE	Hunslet Engine Works, Leeds		Motor Rail & Tram Car
	Hunslet Barclay, Leeds		Motor Rail Ltd
HEN	Henschel, Kassel, Germany		Simplex Mechanical Handling
HICK	Hick Locomotives, Bolton	MW	Manning Wardle, Leeds
	Benjamin Hick		
	Hick Hargreaves		

N	Neilson Locomotives, Glasgow	SG	Slaughter Locomotives, Bristol
	Kerr, Neilson		Henry Stothert
	Neilson & Mitchell		Stothert Slaughter
	Neilson & Co		Slaughter Gruning
	Neilson, Reid & Co	SIG	Schweizerische Industrie Gesellschaft
NB	North British Locomotives, Glasgow	SL	Severn Lamb Ltd
NBICo	New British Iron Co	SLM	Schweizerische Lokomotiven, Winterthur
OK	Orenstein & Koppel, Germany		
P	Peckett & Sons, Bristol	SS	Sharp, Stewart & Co
Penrhyn	Penrhyn Slate Quarries	T&G	Thwaites & Garbutt
PWG	Penmaenmawr Welsh Granite		Thwaites Bros
PyO	PenyrOrsedd Slate Quarries	TRCo	Talyllyn Railway Co
R&R	Ransomes & Rapier, Ipswich	Unilok	Unilok Road-Rail Tractors
RBL	R.B.Longridge, Bedlington	Unimog	Unimog Road-Rail Tractors
Redstone	Mr Redstone, Penmaenmawr	VF	Vulcan Foundry, Newton-le-Willows
RH	Hornsby Locomotives, Lincoln		
	Richard Hornsby		Charles Tayleur
	Ruston & Hornsby		Vulcan Foundry Co
Rhiwbach			(and see EE; EEV)
	Rhiwbach Slate Quarry	Votty	Votty & Bowydd Slate Quarry
RP	Ruston, Proctor & Co, Lincoln	W&M	Wilkins & Mitchell
RS	Robert Stephenson	WB	W.G.Bagnall, Stafford
RSH	Robert Stephenson & Hawthorns	WCI	Wigan Coal & Iron Co
		Wilson	J.H.Wilson, Liverpool
RSP	Regent Street Polytechnic	WJW	Wm.J.Williams, Blaenau Ffestiniog
S	Sentinel Locomotives, Shrewsbury		
		WkB	Walkers Pagefield Ironworks, Wigan
	Sentinel Waggon Works		
	Sentinel Shrewsbury		J.Scarisbrick Walker
	Rolls Royce Ltd		Walker Brothers
SB	Sharp Locomotives, Manchester	Wkm	Wickam & Co, Ware
	Sharp, Roberts & Co	WMCQ	Wrexham, Mold & Connahs Quay Rly
	Sharp Brothers		
Sdn	Swindon Locomotive Works	Worsdell	Thomas Worsdell, Birmingham
		WR	Wingrove & Rogers
		YE	Yorkshire Engine Co, Sheffield

ACKNOWLEDGEMENTS

During the years that this Handbook has been in production, very many people have assisted in various ways; such people include past and present individual members of the Industrial Railway Society, together with members of other kindred organisations such as the Industrial Locomotive Society, the Railway Correspondence & Travel Society, the Stephenson Locomotive Society, the Manchester Locomotive Society, and many more. Some of these people are not known individually, but their work has been available in various archives, in Society libraries, and in private collections. Considerable additional data has been provided, both directly and indirectly, by many of the locomotive builders and owners. Particular mention is due to the various Records Officers of the Industrial Railway Society, and to the Archivists and staff at the County Records Offices at Caernarfon, Denbigh, Dolgellau, Hawarden, and Llangefni, and at University College, Bangor. Specific mention is also due to Douglas Clayton, Michael Cook, Gordon Green and Eric Tonks in view of the extensive volume of input that they have individually provided, and to Philip Hindley who has not only drawn the index maps, but has accompanied me on innumerable site visits these past 30 years and more. Thank you - one and all.

SOURCES

Although it would be ideal to do so, it is impossible to indicate the source of every piece of information that appears in this Handbook, although all such sources are held on record and can be consulted should any data require further examination. As even a simple entry, such as a "locomotive origin footnote", can embody details from a number of sources, the referencing of each element is quite beyond the space available. Hence, individual sources are given only in cases where considerable problems are known to exist, or where argumentative data remains unresolved. Such sources are presented in a form of code, as explained below. Otherwise, data has been taken from the best primary sources available.

As regards the locomotive owners, principal sources include:
[Act]   - Parliamentary Acts of Incorporation
[CoHo]   - Companies House, Cardiff
[CRO]   - Caernarfon Record Office
[DRO]   - Denbigh Record Office, Ruthin
[DgRO]   - Dolgellau Record Office
[HRO]   - Hawarden Record Office
[LGaz]   - London Gazette
[LgRO]   - Llangefni Record office
[PRO]   - Public Records Office, Kew
[RegDC]   - Register of Defunct Companies
[SEY]   - Stock Exchange Yearbooks
[SEI]   - Stock Exchange Intelligentsia
[UCNW]   - University College of North Wales Archives, Bangor
the files of contemporary newspapers and journals
and occasionally from companies themselves.

For locomotives, the first prime source is ideally the locomotive manufacturers original "Engine Book" - not always a book in fact, and not necessarily thus titled - listing basic details of locos built, and (at least the original) customers. Fortunately, such records are now available for most of the major loco builders, in either original or photo-copy form, at certain depositories including, in many cases, York Museum Library. Printed copies (of variable accuracy) of some of these "Works Lists" have been published - whilst these may fill a accuracy) of some of these "Works Lists" have been published - whilst these may fill a general need, they have been disregarded here wherever the original has been accessible. Supplementing the "Engine Books" are other manufacturers records, including records of Spares Orders [SO], Workshop Repair Books [Rep], Paintshop Records [Paint], and any other available paperwork (such as Despatch Notes, Invoices, etc). Another primary source sometimes exists, though fragmentary, in the original papers of the locomotive owners - Minutes authorising loco purchases, Cash Books recording payments, etc. Fortunately large amounts of such records are now available for study in County Record Offices and elsewhere. Old photographs have also proved invaluable.

Secondary sources researched include associated Company paperwork such as Auction Catalogues, plus advertisements and articles in the contemporary press, together with the various editions of the larger-scale Ordnance Survey and other maps.

Tertiary sources studied consist mainly of modern writings in both the railway and technical press - magazines, journals, newspapers and books, including the Pocketbooks, Handbooks and Bulletins of the Industrial Railway Society; plus manuscript archives held by relevant societies and study groups. All such material has, however, been treated with an element of caution, and "proved again" from a primary source wherever this has been possible.

For "modern-day" matters, it has been possible to obtain considerable first-hand knowledge from a large number of people who have devoted their spare time to locomotive, railway and Company research and observation. To mention all such people by name is now impossible - over the twenty-odd years that this book has been in preparation, the number now exceeds several hundreds; but they know who they are, and that their efforts are greatly appreciated. Sadly, many are now deceased.

SPECIFIC SOURCES.

Where a Source Reference is given, it is placed in [ ] square brackets, and normally takes one of three forms:-
[MW], [HE], [SO] etc - Information from loco manufacturers records.
[J/code/issue/page] Information given in a Journal, Periodical, Newspaper or similar. For list of identity codes see below. Occasionally, the page number is followed by the column number for the item on that page, thus (eg) "6c4" [page 6 column 4]
[B/code/page] Information given in a book. For list of identity codes see 'Bibliography' below.
Sources not conforming to these patterns are given in a self-explanatory format.

JOURNAL IDENTITY CODES.

AC	Archaeologia Cambrensis
B&S	Biggs & Sons Contractors Record
BET	Building & Engineering Times
BLCILIS	B'ham Loco Club Industrial Loco Section
BO	Bangor Observer
Btn	Bulletins of BLCILIS & IRS
BWR	Builders Weekly Reporter
CC	Chester Chronicle
CDH	Caernarfon & Denbigh Herald
CG	Colliery Guardian
ChCy	Chronicl Cymru
CHS	Caernarfonshire Historical Society

CN	Cambrian News
ConChron	Contractors Chronicle
CRO	Caernarfon Record Office Bulletin
DHS	Denbighshire Historical Society
ENG	Engineering
FCC	Flint County Chronicle
FHS	Flintshire Historical Society
FRS	Ffestiniog Railway Society Magazine
GH	Glasgow Herald
HC	Herald Cymreig
ICTR	Iron & Coal Trades Review
IL	the Industrial Locomotive [ILS Magazine]
ILS	Industrial Loco Society Journal [pre 'IL']
ILSL	Industrial Loco Society archive ["Lists"]
IRON	Iron
IRR	Industrial Railway Record [IRS Magazine]
IRS	Industrial Railway Society archive
LI	Locomotives Illustrated
LM	Locomotive Magazine
LNRN	Loco News & Railway Notes
LRH	Llandudno Register & Herald
ME	Model Engineer Magazine
MJ	Mining Journal
MM	Machinery Market
MME	Mine & Minerals Engineering
MQE	Mine & Quarry Engineering
MRC	Model Railway Constructor
MRN	Model Railway News
MRS	Merioneth Historical & Record Society
MS	Mineral Statistics
MT	Modern Tramway
MW	Mechanical World
MYB	Mining Year Book
NG	Narrow Gauge [NGRS Magazine]
NGRS	Narrow Gauge Rly Society "Narrow Gauge News"
NGT	Narrow Gauge Times
NMRS	Northern Mine Research Society
NWC	North Wales Chronicle
NWE	North Wales Express
NWG	North Wales Guardian
NWO	North Wales Observer
NWOE	North Wales Observer & Express
NWP	North Wales Press
OAMM	Oswestry Advertiser & Montgomeryshire Mercury
PMR	Phillips Machinery Register
QMJ	Quarry Managers Journal
RCHS	Railway & Canal Historical Society
RMAG	Railway Magazine
RMOD	Railway Modeller
RO	Railway Observer
RPLR	Railway Pictorial & Locomotive Review
RT	Railway Times
RW	Railway World (also forerunner: "Railways")
SEY	Stock Exchange Yearbook

SLS	Stephenson Loco Society Journal	
SR	Steam Railway	
Surplus	Surplus Sales Catalogues [WW1]	
SW	Steam World	
TB	The Builder	
TE	The Engineer	
TI	Trains Illustrated (and "Steam Alive")	
TL	The Locomotive	
TRPS	Talyllyn News	
W&L	Llanfair Railway Journal (and "The Earl")	
WL	Wrexham Leader	
YG	Y Genedl Cymreig	

BIBLIOGRAPHY.

The following is a list of those books that have been found to contain some data of specific interest, or that contain general data which readers may find useful to supplement the statistical information given in this Handbook (as suggested in the '[Read:]' line of many Location entries). It is not a complete list of all publications which relate to the locos of North Wales; but many of the books listed here also contain their own references and bibliographies, which in turn may suggest further reading on specific topics.

Ref	Title	Author	Publisher	Year
B/101	Cambrian Railways Vol.I 1852-1888	Christianson & Miller	David & Charles	1967
B/102	Cambrian Railways Vol.2 1889-1968	Christianson & Miller	David & Charles nd	?c1968
B/103	Locomotives of the G.W.R.	[Parts A to N]	R.C.T.S.	various
B/104	Practical Stone Quarrying	Greenwell & Elsden	Crosby Lockwood	1914
B/105	Reflections on a Railway Career	Dunn J.M.	Ian Allan	1966
B/107	Collieries of Denbighshire	Lerry G.G.		1946
B/107A	Collieries of Denbighshire	Lerry G.G.	Willams Wrexham	1968
B/108	Industrial Revolution in North Wales	Dodd A.H.	Univ.Wales Press	1951
B/109	John Wilkinson & the Old Bersham Ironworks	Palmer A.N.	author	1899
B/110	History of Wrexham	Palmer A.N.		
B/111	Welsh & English in East Denbighshire	Dodd A.H.		1940
B/112	Practical Treatise on Coal Mining	Andre G.C.		1879
B/113	Industries of the Morda Valley	Thomas R.D.		
B/114	History of Ruabon	Palmer A.N.	mss Wrexham Library	
B/115	Private Siding Diagrams North Wales	L.N.W.Rly	LNWR	1915
B/116	Private Siding Diagrams (Wrexham/Minera)	LNWR/GWR joint	LNWR	1917
B/117	Industrialisation of Flintshire in 19th cent.	Williams C.R.	unpub.thesis NLW	1950
B/118	History of British Railways down to 1830	Dendy Marshall	Oxford U.P.	1938
B/119	Historical Geography of Rlys of British Isles	Carter E.F.	Cassell	1959
B/120	Dynasty of Ironfounders	Raistrick A	Longmans	1953
B/121	Two Centuries of Industrial Welfare	Raistrick A		1938
B/122	Lives of the Engineers Vol.2	Smiles S		1862
B/123	Chronicles of Boultons Siding	Bennett A R	David & Charles reprint	1971
B/124	Story of Telford	Gibbs A		1935

Ref	Title	Author	Publisher	Year
B/125	Great Central Railway Vol.1	Dow, George	Loco Pub Co	
B/126	Great Central Railway Vol.2	Dow, George	Loco Pub Co	1962
B/127	Great Central Railway Vol.3	Dow, George	Loco Pub Co	1965
B/128	Modern Traction for Industrial & Agricultural Rlys Hedley R		Loco Pub Co	nd
B/129	Liverpool Overhead Railway	Box C E	Rly World	1959
B/130	Stone Blocks & Iron Rails	Baxter B	David & Charles	1966
B/132	Cambrian Railways	Kidner R.W.	Oakwood	1965
B/133	North Wales Coal Industry	Dodd A H		
B/134	Longmoor Military Railway	Ronald & Carter	David & Charles	1974
B/135	British Internal Combustion Locomotive 1894-1940 Webb, Brian		David & Charles	1973
B/136	Railway Foundry, Leeds	Redman R N	Goose	1972
B/137	Fireless Locomotives	Baker & Civil	Oakwood	1976
B/138	Baguley Locomotives	Weaver C R	Ind.Rly.Socy	1975
B/139	Bagnalls of Stafford	Baker & Civil	Oakwood	1973
B/139A	Bagnalls of Stafford Works List	Baker & Civil	Ind.Loco.Socy	1984
B/140	Great British Tramway Networks	Bett & Gillham	L.R.T.L.	1962
B/141	Fairlie Locomotive	Abbott R A S	David & Charles	1970
B/142	Miniature Railways Vol.1 15inch	Clayton et al	Oakwood	nd c1970
B/143	Duffield Bank & Eaton Railways	Clayton H	Oakwood	1968
B/144	Light Railways of First World War	Davies W J K	David & Charles	1967
B/145	Little Wonder	Winton J	Fest.Rly.Co	1975
B/145A	Little Wonder [2nd Edn]	Winton J	Fest.Rly.Co	1986
B/146	Holyhead The Story of a Port	Hughes & Williams	authors	1967
B/147	Narrow Gauge Railways in North Wales Lee C E		Rly.Pub.Co	1945
B/148	Padarn & Penrhyn Railways	Turner S	David & Charles	1975
B/149	Slates to Velinheli	Carrington + Rushworth Maid Marian Loco Fund		1974
B/150	Penrhyn Railway [extract from B/147] Lee C E		WHLR(1964)Ltd	1972
B/151	Little Penrhyn Railway	Jones J K	Mei	1980
B/152A	Meet The Welsh Highland		WHLR(1964)Ltd	1969
B/152B	Meet The Welsh Highland		WHLR(1964)Ltd	1973
B/153	More About the Welsh Highland		WHLR(1964)Ltd	1966
B/154	Welsh Highland Railway [extract from B/147] Lee C E		WHLR(1964)Ltd	1970
B/155	Welsh Highland Rly Yearbook/Guide 1980/81		WHLR(1964)Ltd	1980
B/156	Welsh Highland Railway Yearbook 1979		WHLR(1964)Ltd	1979
B/157	Introducing Russell	Deegan P	Russell Fund	1969
B/158	Welsh Highland Rly: A Pictorial Guide		WHLR(1964)Ltd	c1980
B/159	Etude Technique sur les CdFer a Voie Etroite de'l Angleterre Vignes M E			1878
B/161	Llangollen Canal	Denton J H	R & C H Socy	1964
B/162	Canals of the West Midlands	Hadfield C	David & Charles	1966
B/163	Ellesmere & Llangollen Canal - Historical Background Wilson E A		Phillimore	1975
B/164	Shropshire Union Canal Guide		British Waterways	nd
B/166	Festiniog Railway Vol.1	Boyd J I C	Oakwood	1956
B/167	Festiniog Railway Vol.2	Boyd J.I.C.	Oakwood	1959
B/168	Festiniog Railway Vol.1	Boyd J.I.C.	Oakwood	1975
B/169	Festiniog Railway Vol.2	Boyd J.I.C.	Oakwood	1975
B/170	Narrow Gauge Rails to Portmadoc	Boyd J.I.C.	Oakwood	c1950

Ref	Title	Author	Publisher	Year
B/171	Narrow Gauge Railways in Mid Wales	Boyd J.I.C.	Oakwood	c1951
B/172	Narrow Gauge Railways in Mid Wales	Boyd J.I.C.	Oakwood	1965
B/173	Narrow Gauge Railways in Mid Wales	Boyd J.I.C.	Oakwood	1970
B/174	Narrow Gauge Railways in South Caernarvonshire [For later edition see B/450, B/451]	Boyd J.I.C.	Oakwood	1972
B/175	Narrow Gauge Railways in North Caernarvonshire Vol.1 - West	Boyd J.I.C.	Oakwood	1981
B/176	Narrow Gauge Railways in North Caernarvonshire Vol.2 - Penrhyn Rly	Boyd J.I.C.	Oakwood	1985
B/177	Narrow Gauge Railways in North Caernarvonshire Vol.3 - Dinorwic etc.	Boyd J.I.C.	Oakwood	1986
B/178	How Ffestiniog Got Its Railway	Lewis M J T	R & C H Socy	1965
B/179	Festiniog Railway Revival	Whitehouse P B	Ian Allan	1963
B/180	History of Caernarvonshire 1284-1900	Dodd A H	C'fon Hist.Socy	
B/181	Sentinel Patent Locomotives & Concrete Cases		Sentinel/E.P.Pub'g [publicity brochures]	1974 reprt
B/182	History of the North Wales Slate Industry	Lindsay J	David & Charles	1974
B/183	Historic Industrial Scenes - Iron & Steel	Gale W K V	Moorland	1977
B/184	Lilleshall Co Ltd 1764-1964	Gale/Nicholls	Moorland	1979
B/185	Historic Industrial Scenes - Wales	Rees, D.Morgan	Moorland	nd
B/187	Steam on the Narrow Gauge	Ind.Loco.Socy	David & Charles	1965
B/188	Hunslet Hundred	Rolt L T C	David & Charles	1964
B/189	Stephen Lewin & the Poole Foundry	Wear & Lees	IRS/ILS	1978
B/190	Ruston & Hornsby Locomotives	Tonks E S	Ind.Rly.Socy.	1974
B/191	Ruston Locomotives - Sales Works List	Ruston Hornsby	[private]	c1970
B/192	Locos of Ruston Proctor & Richard Hornsby	Codling C H	mss IRS Library	nd
B/199	Memoirs of the Geological Survey - Reports on the Mineral Resources of Great Britain IN PARTS AS FOLLOWS:			
199/07	Mineral Oil & Cannel Coals in England & Wales		HMSO	1920
199/09	Iron Ores, Sundry un-bedded ores...Wales		HMSO	1919
199/13	Iron Ores - Pre-carboniferous..Wales	Cantrill & Sherlock	HMSO	1920
199/19	Lead & Zinc Ores....North Wales	Smith	HMSO	1921
199/23	Lead & Zinc in Pre-carboniferous Rocks....N.Wales	Dewey & Smith	HMSO	1922
199/30	Copper Ores......Wales....	Dewey et al	HMSO	1925
B/201	Slates of Wales	North F J	Nat.Mus. of Wales	1946
B/202	Hanes Nant Nantlle	Ambrose W R	Penygroes	1872
B/203	Treatise on Slates & Slate Quarrying	Davies D C	London	1872
B/204	Penrhyn Quarry	Hobson W D	Bangor	1913
B/205	Hynafraethau Llandegai a Llanllechid	Hughes H D	Bethesda	1866
B/206	Wales - Volume 1	Jones, J Owen		1894
B/207	Slate Trade of North Wales	Kellow J	London	1868
B/208	Red Dragon - Volume 7	Owen Elias		1885

Ref	Title	Author	Publisher	Year
B/209	Llanberis, ei Hanes	Parry, G Tecwyn	Caernarfon	1908
B/210	Chwareli a Chwarelwyn Cymru	Parry W J	Caernarfon	1897
B/211	Lead Mining in Wales	Lewis W J	University of Wales	1967
B/212	Hanes Plwyf Ffestiniog	Williams G J	Wrexham	nd c1882
B/213	Mining for Metals in Wales	North F J	Nat.Mus. of Wales	1962
B/214	Mountains of Snowdonia - First Edn.	Carr & Lister		nd c1928
B/215	Description of Caernarvonshire 1809-1811		Hall E H	1952
B/216	Gossiping Guide to Wales			1913
B/217	Gadlys & Flintshire Leadmining	Evans, M Bevan	Flints.Hist.Socy.	
B/218	Historical Account...Railways...Great Britain	Priestley J	[Repeated in B/118]	1831
B/219	Thomas Telford	Rolt L T C		
B/220	Railway Adventure [2nd edition]	Rolt L T C		1961
B/221	Practical Treatise on Railroads	Tredgold T	[Repeated in B/118] 1825+1835	
B/222	Views of North Wales	Loftie W J		1875
B/223	Carnarvonshire [Cambridge County Geographies]	Lloyd J E	Cambridge	1911
B/224	Merionethshire [Cambridge County Geographies]	Morris A	Cambridge	1913
B/225	General Survey...Slate Industry	Richards W M	mss 10.591 NLoW	1933
B/226	Mineral Wealth of Wales....	Thomas, Trevor M	Oliver & Boyd	1961
B/227	Cry of the People	Parry W J		1906
B/228	Snowdonia	North F J et al		1949
B/229	Gold Mines of Merioneth	Hall G W	Griffin	nd c1973
B/230	Madocks & The Wonder of Wales	Beazley E	Faber & Faber	1967
B/231	Llanfyllin Railway	Cozens, Lewis	author	1959
B/232	Flintshire Railways	Dean R J	R & C H S	1968
B/233	Fletcher Jennings Works List	Cole D	Union	nd
B/234	Contractors Locos Part 1	Cole D	Union	1963
B/234A	Contractors Locos Part 1 [Revised]	Cole D	Union	1982
B/235	Contractors Locos Part 2	Cole D	Union	1965
B/236	Contractors Locos Part 3	Cole & Smith	Union	1967
B/237	Contractors Locos Part 4	Cole & Smith	Union	1970
B/238	Contractors Locos Part 5	Cole & Smith	Union	1976
B/239	Contractors Locos Part 6	Cole & Smith	Union	1982
B/243	Robert Stephenson Works List 1-1000	Cole D	Union	1986
B/244	Railways & Preservation	Latham J B	author	1975
B/245	Brookes Industrial Railways	Leleux S A	Oakwood	1972
B/246	Conway Valley Railway	Harman R G	Branch Line Handbooks	nd c1963
B/247	Wrexham, Mold & Connahs Quay Rly	Dunn J M	Oakwood	1957
B/248	Reservoir Railways Yorkshire Pennines	Bowtell H D	Oakwood	1979
B/249	Full Circle....Steelmaking on Deeside	BSC Shotton	BSC	1980
B/250	Railways in Gwynedd	Williams, G.Haulfryn	Gwynedd Archives	1979
B/251	Llandudno & Colwyn Bay Trams: Nostalgic Look Back	Martin B P	Llandudno Tramway Socy	nd c1980
B/252	History of Llandudno & Colwyn Bay Electric Rly	Anderson R C	Quail Map Co	1968
B/253	Snailbeach District Railways	Tonks E S	Tonks	1950
B/254	Snailbeach District Railways	Tonks E S	I.R.S.	1974
B/255	North Wales Tramways	Turner K	David & Charles	1979

Ref	Title	Author	Publisher	Year
B/256	Welshpool & Llanfair Light Rly	Cartwright & Russell	David & Charles	1972
B/257	Llandudno & Colwyn Bay Elect.Rly.in 1920s	L&CBER Socy	L&CBERS	nd (1987)
B/258	Trams Leave Here for Llandudno & Colwyn Bay		Deegan P	1983
B/261	Historical Review [Oakeley Qys 1755-1937]		Oakeley Slate Qys	1937
B/262	Slate Quarries of North Wales [B/376 Reprint is much better]	anon	C & D Herald	1873
B/263	Slate Quarries in Wales	Smith T C	Mining J'nal reprint	1860
B/264	Slate Industry of North Wales	Building Times rep't	Assoc.Slate Qys.	1936
B/265	Metalliferous Mines of Wales [offprint from Amgueddfa 12]	Rees, Morgan	Nat.Mus.of Wales	1972
B/266	Chwareli a Chwarelwyr	anon	Gwynedd Archives	1974
B/267	Llechi/Slate	Lewis M J T	Gwynedd Archives	1976
B/268	Quarry Tracks, Village Ways	anon	Talyllyn Rly	1977
B/269	Old Metal Mines Mid Wales - Part 5	Bick, David E	Pound House	1978
B/270	Metal Mines of North Wales	Williams C J	Charter Press	1980
B/271	Gold Mining in Western Merioneth	Morrison T A	Merioneth Record Socy	1975
B/272	Old Copper Mines of Snowdonia	Bick, David	Pound House	1982
B/273	Great Orme Copper Mines	Smith, Don	Creuddyn	1988
B/274	Copper Mountain [2nd Edition]	Rowlands, John	Anglesey Antiq.Socy.	1981
B/275	Greenfield Valley	Davies & Williams	Holywell Council	1977
B/276	Henry Robertson	Lerry G G	Woodalls	1949
B/277	Modest Millionaire [Vivian Hewitt]	Hywel, Wm.	Gwasg Gee	1973
B/278	Pioneers of Ffestiniog Slate	Lewis & Williams	Snowdonia Nat.Park	1987
B/279	Electric Traction as Applied to Quarries & Mines	Williams Ellis	ex QMJ	c1928
B/280	Age of Slate	Burn, Michael	Quarry Tours	nd
B/281	Llechwedd Its Slate & Its People	Wynne Jones, Ivor	Quarry Tours	nd
B/282	Llechwedd Slate Caverns	Wynne Jones, Ivor	Quarry Tours	1976
B/283	Llechwedd & Other Ffestiniog Railways	Jones & Hatherall	Quarry Tours	1977
B/285	Chwareli a Chloddfeydd yn y Pennant	Williams, Dewi	Gwynedd C.Council	1986
B/286	Slates from Abergynolwyn	Holmes A	Gwynedd Archives	1986
B/287	Narrow Gauge Railway Museum	Boyd J I C	Oakwood	1972
B/288	Industrial Railway Museum Penrhyn Castle		National Trust	nd c1970
B/289	North Wales Quarrying Museum	Ress, D.Morgan	HMSO	1975
B/290	Chwarel Foel & Chwarel Rhos	Plas Tanybwlch report	not published	1986
B/291	Moving Mountains	P & W G Co Ltd	PWGCoLtd	nd c1949
B/292	Rhosydd Slate Quarry	Lewis & Denton	Cottage Press	1974
B/293	Cwmorthin Slate Quarry	Isherwood G	Merioneth Field Study Press	1982
B/294	Beneath Snowdon - Britannia Mine	Colman & Laffeley	Peak District Mines Socy	1986
B/301	History of the GWR - Vol.1	McDermot	LPC	1927
B/301A	History of the GWR - Vol.1 (revised)	McDermot & Clinker	Ian Allan	1972
B/302A	History of the GWR - Vol.2 (revised)	McDermot & Clinker	Ian Allan	1972
B/303	Regional History of Rlys: Vol.11 - N & Mid Wales	Baughan P E	David & Charles	1980
B/304	Forgotten Rlys; N & Mid Wales	Christiansen R	David & Charles	1976
B/305	Snowdon Mountain Railway	Morris O J	Ian Allan	nd c1950
B/306	Snowdon Mountain Rly - 4th Edition	Wallis, P.Ransome	Ian Allan	1967
B/307	Snowdon Mountain Rly - Travelogue	Crew P	S.M.Rly	1971

Ref	Title	Author	Publisher	Year
B/308	Snowdon Mountain Railway	Turner K	David & Charles	1973
B/309	Glyn Valley Tramway	Davies D L	Oakwood	1962
B/310	Chester & Holyhead Rly	Dunn J M	Oakwood	1948
B/311	Great Orme Tramway - First 75 Years	Anderson R C	LRTL	nd c1979
B/312	Bala Lake Railway - Visitors Guide	Campbell & Jackson	BLRly	1980
B/313	Llanberis Lake Railway - Guidebook (2nd Ed)		LLRly	nd c1975
B/313A	Llanberis Lake Railway - Guidebook (1st Ed)		LLRly	nd c1973
B/315	Fairbourne Railway - Guidebook		Photoprecision	nd c1966
B/316	Centre for Alternative Technology - Guidebook			nd c1979
B/317	Gloddfa Ganol - Guidebook			nd c1977
B/318	Old Llanfair Quarry - Guidebook	Styles, Showell		1974
B/319	Into the Slate Mountain [Gloddfa Ganol]	Isherwood J G	Gloddfa Ganol	1979
B/320	Candles to Caplamps (2nd Ed)	Isherwood J G	Gloddfa Ganol	1980
B/321	Talyllyn Railway	Cozens, Lewis	Cozens	1948+
B/322	Corris Railway	Cozens, Lewis	Cozens	1949+
B/323	Mawddwy Railway	Cozens, Lewis	Cozens + Oakwood	1954+1972
B/324	Prestatyn & Dyserth Railway	Thompson, Trefor	North Clwyd Rly Assn	1978
B/325	Tanat Valley (The)	Wren, Wilfrid J	David & Charles	1968
B/326	Prestatyn & Dyserth Branch Line	Goodall	Oakwood	1986
B/328	Story of the Cambrian	Gasquoine C P	Woodall Minshall	1922
B/329	Mishaps on the Cambrian Railways	Jones, Elwyn V	Severn Press	1972
B/330	Brecon & Merthyr Railway	Barrie D S	Oakwood	1957
B/331	Chester & Holyhead Rly - Vol.1	Baughan P E	David & Charles	1972
B/333	Chester & Holyhead Rly; Historical Survey of	Anderson & Fox	OPC	1984
B/338	Llangollen Line	Rear & Jones	Foxline	1990
B/339	Conwy Valley Line	Rear W G	Foxline	1991
B/340	North Wales Branches (LMS Journal Vol.1)	Rear & Wakefield	Rear	nd c1974
B/341	LNWR Chronology 1900-1960	Clinker C R	David & Charles	1961
B/342	Gazetteer Railway Contractors.of Wales	Popplewell	Melledgen	1984
B/343	Chronology Construction Britains Rlys 1778-1855	James L	Ian Allan	1983
B/344	London & North Western Rly	Steel		
B/348	Glyn Valley Tramway	Milner W J	OPC	1984
B/349	The Ceiriog	Davies D Ll.	Author	1983
B/350	Mines, Mills & Furnaces	Rees, D Morgan	HMSO	1969
B/351	Industrial Archaeology of Wales	Rees, D.Morgan	David & Charles	1975
B/352	Minera	Davies, Glyn	author	1964
B/353	Flintshire Place Names	Davies, Ellis	Univ.of Wales	1959
D/354	Directory of Quarries - 1948 edition.		[J/QMJ]	1948
D/355	Quarrying at Trevor		P&WG Co Ltd	nd
D/358	Narrow Gauge Rlys - Wales & Western Front	Household H	Sutton	1988
B/359	Railways of the Manchester Ship Canal	Thorpe D	OPC	1984
B/360	Leighton Buzzard Light Railway	Leleux S A	Oakwood	1969
B/361	Railways of Port Sunlight	Lister M D	Oakwood	1980
B/362	North Devon Clay	Messenger M J	Twelveheads	1982

Ref	Title	Author	Publisher	Year
B/363	Ironstone Rlys....of the Midlands	Tonks E S	Loco.Pub.Co	1959
B/364	Bishops Castle Railway	Griffith E	author	1969
B/365	Shropshire & Montgomeryshire Rly	Tonks E S	IRS	1972
B/366	Welshpool & Llanfair Railway	Smith D J	Branch Line Handbooks	1966
B/367	Narrow Gauge Charm of Yesterday	Peters, Ivo	OPC	1976+1983
B/368	Shropshire & Montgomeryshire Lt Rly	Turner K & S	David & Charles	1982
B/370	British Steam Locomotive Builders	Lowe J W	Goose	1975
B/370A	[Supplement to B/370]	Lowe J W	TEE	1984
B/371	Vertical Boiler Locomotives	Abbott R A S	Oakwood	1989
B/372	Traction Engine Locomotives	Hutchinson I K	Road Loco.Socy.	1981
B/373	Cromford & High Peak Rly	Rimmer A	Oakwood	1985
B/374	Groby & Its Railways	Ramsey D A	T.E.E	1982
B/375	Sygun Copper Mines - Guidebook		Jarrold	1987
B/376	Slate Quarries of North Wales 1873 [ex B/262]	Lewis M J T (ed)	Snowdonia Nat.Park	1987
B/377	Return to Corris		Avon Anglia	1988
B/378	Slate from Blaenau Ffestiniog	Isherwood	A.B.Pub.	1988
B/379	Buckley & District	Cropper T		1923
B/380	Golden Age of Tramways	Klapper C	Routledge & KP	1962
B/381	Mines of Gwydyr Forest - 1. Llanrwst Mine	Bennett & Vernon	GMP	1989
B/385	Early Industry in Flintshire	Evans, M Bevan	Flints Rec.Office	1966
B/386	Memoirs of Samuel Holland		Merion.Hist.Socy.	1952
B/387	Keep Moving	Andrews J F	Williams, Barry	1976
B/388	Keep Moving - Supplement	Andrews J F	Andrews	1986
B/390	George & Robert Stephenson	Robbins M	OUP	1966
B/395	Great Western North of Wolverhampton	Beck K M	Ian Allan	1986
B/396	Greenwood & Batley Locomotives	Booth A J	IRS	1986
B/397	Story of the Steam Plough Works	Lane M R	Northgate	1980
B/398	Corris - A Narrow Gauge Portrait	J.S.Morgan	Irwell	1991
B/401	Cambrian Railways Album	Green C C	Ian Allan	1977
B/402	Cambrian Railways Album - 2	Green C C	Ian Allan	1981
B/404	London Midland Steam in North Wales	Rear W G	Bradford Barton	1979
B/405	North Wales Steam 1927-1968	Kneale E N	OPC	1980
B/406	North Wales Branch Line Album	Green C C	Ian Allan	1983
B/407	Yesterdays Golcondas	Bird R H	Moorland	1977
B/408	Welsh Narrow Gauge Railway	Prideaux J	David & Charles	1976
B/409	On the British Narrow Gauge	Harris M	Ian Allan	1980
B/410	On the Welsh Narrow Gauge	Boyd J I C	Bradford Barton	nd
B/411	Industrial Narrow Gauge Railways	Nicholson P	Bradford Barton	1975
B/412	Griffith Jones		Gwynedd Archives	1980
B/413	LMS Branch Lines in North Wales - Vol.1	Rear W G	Wild Swan	1986
B/414	North Wales Steam - Vol 2	Kneale E N	OPC	1986
B/415	Rails to Bala	Southern et al	Charter	1987
B/416	Cambrian Coast Railway	Rear & Williams	Foxline	1988
B/417	Welsh Railways in Heyday of Steam	Casserley H C	Bradford Barton	nd
B/418	North Wales Coalfield [pictorial]	Kelly, Ithel	Bridge, Wrexham	1990
B/419	Encyclopaedia of Narrow Gauge Rlys of GB & I	Middlemass T	Patrick Stephens	1991
B/420	Dolgarrog - Industrial History	Jones & Gwyn	Gwynedd Archives	1989

B/421	Courtaulds; An Economic & Social History: Vol 2			
		Coleman D C	Oxford	
B/422	History of Nobels Explosives Co Ltd		I.C.I.	1938
B/423	Manual of the Alkali Trade	Lomas J		1880
B/424	Chemical Industry 1900-1930	Haber L F	Oxford	1971
B/425	Chemical Industry during 19th Century			
		Haber L F	Oxford	1958
B/426	Chemical Foundations; Alkali trade to 1926			
		Warren K	Oxford	1980
B/427	Cement Industry 1796-1914	Francis A J	David & Charles	1977
B/450	N.G.Rails in South Caernarvonshire - Vol 1			
		Boyd J I C	Oakwood	1988
B/451	N.G.Rails in South Caernarvonshire - Vol.2			
		Boyd J I C	Oakwood	1989
B/800	British Locomotive Catalogue 1825-1923			
		Baxter B	Moorland	various
B/901	Works List - Bagnall	see B/139A		
B/902	Works List - Baguley	see B/138		
B/903	Works List - Black Hawthorn	Allan C.Baker	Ind.Loco.Socy.	1988
B/904	Works List - E.B.Wilson	Hardy C	Aleksandr	1982
B/905	Works List - Fletcher Jennings	see B/233		
B/906	Works List - Greenwood & Batley	see B/396		
B/907	Works List - Hudswell Clarke	Hardy C	Aleksandr	1982
B/908	Works List - Hudswell Clarke	see B/136		
B/909	Works List - Howard	J.M.Hutchings	private circ.	1986
B/910	Works List - John Fowler	see B/397		
B/911	Works List - John Fowler	F.Jux	Ind.Loco.Socy.	1985
B/912	Works List - Lewin	see B/189		
B/913	Works List - Lilleshall [incomplete]	see B/184		
B/914	Works List - Manning Wardle	Mabbot F W	Aleksandr	1982
B/915	Works List - McEwan Pratt	see B/138		
B/916	Works List - Peckett	F.Jux	Ind.Loco.Socy.	1987
B/917	Works List - Richard Hornsby	see B/192		
B/918	Works List - Robert Stephenson 1-1000		see B/243	
B/919	Works List - Ruston Hornsby	see B/191		
B/920	Works List - Ruston Proctor	see B/192		
B/930	Works Lists - various	see B/370, B/370A		
B/931	Works Lists - various	see B/371		
B/932	Works Lists - various	see B/372		

SOME CLUES FOR FURTHER RESEARCH

During the course of compiling this Handbook, various references to locomotives have arisen which it has not been possible to resolve. Readers may care to ponder on these, and hopefully provide further information - perhaps even more clues of a like nature.

1863: **BRYAN JOHNSON**, FLOOKERSBROOK FOUNDRY, CHESTER
was a regular advertiser in newspapers [eg. J/CDH/20.2.1864/1c4] as "Engineer, Millwright, Boiler Maker, Iron and Brass Founder"; he "designed and tendered" locos for the Ffestiniog Railway (PR/3) c10/1862. We have a copy of a drawing, dated 11 February 1863, of a 0-4-0T OC, apparently 4'8½" gauge, entitled "10 inch branch line locomotive" signed "Bryan Johnson. Engineer, Chester". Perhaps it is nothing more than an irrelevant sketch.

1863: **Mr COUSENS, HOLYHEAD:**
"Wanted, strong secondhand four-wheel coupled contractors tank loco narrow [ie, .4'8½" ?] gauge for ballasting, 10" to 12" cylinders - Harvey, 23 Holywell, Millbank [London], or Mr Cousens, Holyhead". [J/TE/4.9.1863].
Neither "Harvey", nor "Mr Cousens", have yet been traced; but it seems possible that this loco was needed for work for the LNWR in the Holyhead area, hence this item is repeated in PR/7 (Section 2).

1866: **RICHARD WILLIAMS, TREBAN:**
J/CDH/11.8.1866/1c6 then almost every week until J/CDH/23.3.1867/4 carried advertisement: "To Railway Proprietors and Contractors - On Sale - A Good Locomotive Engine, built under the superintendence of Mr Allen [sic], late Manager of Crewe Works, and at present Locomotive Superintendent of the Scottish Central Railway - apply to Richard Williams, Treban, near Holyhead." 'Treban' is a large house some distance from the railway, so there is nothing to confirm this loco was in Anglesey.
Almost certainly this would be "Engine No.63(a)" minuted by the LNWR as sold on 30/4/1866 for £190 to "Richard Williams, Treban". The identity of this loco is open to debate. LNWR 63 was a Grand Junction Railway 2-2-2 built in 1840 by George Forrester & Co, Vauxhall Foundry, Liverpool; it was replaced in 1855 by a second 63 which survived with the LNWR until 1887. If the Forrester 63 actually survived until 1857, when 'A' numbers were introduced, it could have become 63A - but the A number locos were renumbered into a 11xx series in 1862, and the 11xx series does not contain a loco formerly 63A.
Concurrently, LNWR Southern Division loco 63, an 0-6-0 by Stothert Slaughter, had become 663 in 1862 - it was, however, withdrawn 10/1865 being replaced by a new 663, so is perhaps another candidate for description as '63A'.
Why does Richard Williams (in 1866) mention Mr Allen (Allan ?). Alexander Allan had indeed been Works Manager at Forresters until 3/1840; he moved to the GJR at Edge Hill, then went to Crewe, where he resigned in 1853 on moving to Scotland.

1872: **A JOB AT RHYL:**
Per "Chronicles of Boulton's Siding" [B/123/65], one of Boulton's 2-4-0ST locos named PEVERIL (a rebuild of what could have been a St.Helens Railway 2-4-0) was hired (apparently to a contractor) to a job at Rhyl late 1871/early 1872. Neither hirer nor job have been identified.

1875: **"J.B.SEDDON**, contractor, Brymbo"
- 16" loco and tender "for sale, hire or exchange" [J/TE/5.11.1875 etc].

1878: **"J.B.SEDDON**, Royal Oak Hotel, Flint"
for sale, four-coupled six-wheel tender loco just had two new 16" cylinders, new brass tubes with slide blocks, suitable for contractor's ballast engine or for passenger running. [J/TE/11.1.1878 etc].

1879: **"E.& J.SEDDON**, BRYMBO"
for sale, 6 wheel loco 4 wheel-coupled, leading and driving wheels 5'0", trailing wheels 3'4", two new cylinders 24"x15.7/8", 157 tubes 2.", slide box motion, four wheel tender, to be seen at Canada Works, Liverpool. [J/CG/20.6.1879].
The above could all refer to the same loco, an 0-4-2; probably latterly (at least) at Thomas Brassey & Co, Canada Loco Works, Wallasey Pool, BIRKENHEAD. But who were the Seddons, and what were they doing at Brymbo and Flint ?

1878: **"W.GAMBLE, WREXHAM"**: for sale, tank loco 11" cylinders. [J/CG/16.8.1878]
"W.GAMBLE, MERCHANT, WREXHAM":
for sale, secondhand loco 12½"x16" outside cylinders, 76 tubes 2" diameter, 110 lbs working pressure, weight full 18 tons, round saddle tank. [J/CG/30.4.1880]
Unless the 11" dimension (1878) is wrong, these appear to be two different locos - the latter, from its weight, probably an 0-6-0ST although it is later [J/GC/1880/876] described as 4 wheels coupled "with under saddle tank" 12½ x 16 3'6". They may not, of course, have been at Wrexham; and no trace of any loco dealings involving a Mr Gamble have come to light.

1881: **W.H.HUGHES, PLASKYNASTON FOUNDRY, RUABON"**:
Wanted; secondhand tank loco, 10" to 12" 4wc about 3ft wheels. [J/TE/20.5.1881].
As the Foundry (GR:275427) had no 4'8½" gauge rail connexion, presumably this loco was intended for a customer.

1881: **BRADDOCK & MATTHEWS, CONTRACTORS,**
who often used locomotives, had a contract in 1881 for "Bridge & Roadworks, Elwy Estate, Rhyl". What this was we do not know, but very possibly the substantial road bridge with ramped approaches, which crosses PR/7 about quarter-mile west of Rhyl station; a job for which a shunting loco may have been required.

1885: **HOLME & KING, CONTRACTORS,**
obtained a Contract 3/1885 for "large reservoir [? Cilcain, ? GR:156642] and about 50 miles of pipeline" from Hawarden & District Water Works Co (who again advertised for tenders "by 8/3/1902" for a storage reservoir near Cilcain). Holme & King frequently used railway equipment, and may have done so on these works.

1896: **"E.WHELDON, near Mold"**:
Wanted - small loco for colliery siding. [J/MM/2.3.1986].
This advert is further discussed - inconclusively - under entry FFRITH/GLASCOED COLLIERIES in Section 3.

1899: **J.H.WILLIAMS & SON**,[dealers, Britannia Foundry] **PORTMADOC**.
For Sale: 23.1/4" gauge four-coupled loco, tank below, 6"x14" cylinders, 23" wheels, 4'0" wheelbase, copper firebox, 37 brass tubes 6'0" long. [J/MM/1.5.1899-1.7.1899].
Three apparent candidates for this loco are QUEENIE (Cilgwyn Quarry), GEORGE SHOLTO (Penrhyn Quarry Railway), and the Colwyn Bay Sea Wall Contract loco - though none match all the dimensions given. There is of course the possibility that Williams merely had details of a loco that was for sale somewhere in Britain, and thought the local quarries could be interested.

1902: **PECKETT AT LLANGOLLEN.**
An auction sale at Liverpool on 18/9/1902 included a Peckett saddle-tank loco "lying at Llangollen" [J/GH/8.9.1902].
(A possible explanation for this is suggested under Location PR/18 in Section 2 - but this guess may well be wrong.)

1905: **J.H.WILLIAMS & SON**, [dealers, Britannia Foundry] **PORTMADOC.**
Wanted, a 3 foot gauge tank loco. [J/MM/31.3.1905]. [? for Rhiw.]

1906: **CONWAY CORPORATION**
have ordered 1000 yards of portable track and six wagons from O.Wright & Sons, Leicester. [J/MM/7.12.1906]

1908: **CARNARVON CORPORATION**
placed an order 13/11/1908 with W.G.Bagnall Ltd, Stafford, for "Repair of locomotive fittings". [WGB records].
For the record: a study of the Corporation Minutes [CRO/XD1/812 page 336; XD1/441] confirmed that this was for repairs and renewals to the link motion of the "Ynys Mon", a ferry boat that plied between Caernarfon and Anglesey.

1912: **F.B.KINGDON, LONDON EC** "have supplied petrol locomotives to a quarry in North Wales" [J/MM/26.1.1912].
KINGDON & CO, LONDON advertising petrol locos from £160 [J/MM/6.12.1912].
The first reference seems to suggest delivery of two or more locos to one quarry in 1911, unless the announcement was premature. The earliest petrol locos in this Handbook are Deutz of 1912 at Votty & Bowydd Slate Quarry. Here, the name 'Kingdon' has not come to light.

1915: **NEWTOWN, FLINT:**
It is reputed that the Butterley Co Ltd, Hilts Quarry, Crich, Derbyshire, sold a 3'9" gauge 0-4-0VBT loco to "Newtown, Flint" in 1915. The very exhaustive 'Flintshire Place Names' (University of Wales Press 1959) does not list any Newtown (Newton, New Town, Tre Newydd, etc) - maybe a Mr Newtown in fact ?

1917: **"Bache, Trevor, Ruabon"**
offered For Sale, six wheel coupled saddle tank loco, 11" cylinders, 4'8½" gauge. [J/MM/17.8.1917].

1920: **Wm.ROWLANDS, BANGOR ROAD, CONWAY:**
For Sale, plant including two 2ft gauge 150 psi boiler pressure Bagnall saddle tank locos; and a 20" gauge complete portable railway 113 yards long with points, turntables, bogeys [sic; etc]. [J/MM/19.3.1920].
Maybe the locos lying at Maenofferen Slate Quarry, or those at Pantdreiniog Quarry, Bethesda ?

1922: **T.LLEWELYN DAVIES, RHOS, WREXHAM:**
For Sale, 0-6-0ST HC 15¾"x22" cylinders. [1/1922]

1923: **H.W.E.HUGHES, LLANRWST:**
For Sale, Fordson Muir Hill 24" gauge rail loco, fitted with cab, brake, four-wheel drive, £60.
[J/MM/26.5.1933].
This is mentioned, inconclusively, in DOLGARROG RAILWAYS entry in Section 3.

1923: **WALTER JONES & SONS LTD, CONTRACTORS**
(of 64 Victoria Street, London SW1) had spare parts for MR petrol loco delivered 6/12/1923 "to Cefnybedd" (brake blocks), and 20/12/1923 to "Llay Park" (piston rings, etc). [MR records/I.Jolly/D1182].
Walter Jones & Sons known on numerous housing, sewer and road building contracts in the 1920s [M.Cook], so presumably they were using a railway on a Contract in this area, but no details yet known. Concurrently, Walter Jones & Sons Ltd hired 4'8½" gauge steam locos from Thomas Wrigley & Sons via J.Wardell & Co; these were ANNIE (0-6-0ST IC MW 1481/1900) from 23/3/1923 to 10/1/1924, and NETHERTON (0-6-0ST IC MW 1603/1903) from 1/5/1923 to 5/10/1923. Where these were used is not yet known; certainly there is nothing to suggest that they were used in the Llay area.

1926: **G.BLAKEMORE, 180 PICCADILLY, LONDON**
had locos for sale in 1926 including a "3ft gauge Davenport [U.S.A.] lying in North Wales". [G.Alliez - source not quoted].

1930: **LEE, GWALIA FORGE, CAERGWRLE, WREXHAM:**
Wanted, second hand colliery locomotive, about 15" [cylinders] four-wheel or six-wheel saddletank. [J/MM/18.7.1930].

1931: **FOTHERGILL BROS LTD, MARKET HOTEL, LLANGEFNI, ANGLESEY**
ordered spare parts from MR 7/1931 to 4/1932, including "One Driving Chain Long", which would probably be for an old bow-frame 20hp or 40hp loco. [MR records/I.Jolly/D1181]. Presumably they had a rail-worked Contract in the area, but nothing discovered.
Fothergill are known to have tackled Sea Defence works (1915, Blue Anchor, Somerset), reservoirs (1923, Rowberrow, Bristol) and sewerage (1923-24, Llantrisant), [M.Cook]; a possible job near Llangefni could be the Cefni Reservoir.

1932: **Mr FREEMAN, ANGLESEY:**
1'11½" gauge 4wPM L 4472/1932 is recorded by Lister as delivered New 29/6/1932 to "Mr Freeman, Anglesey". No subsequent references to this loco have been found [L records].
A Mr H.Freeman was in business at Menai Bridge (by 1929, and to 1937 at least) trading in motor vehicle repairs and who, inter alia, is known to have repaired 3ft gauge petrol locos for Dinmor Park Quarry. The name "Freeman" crops up elsewhere - eg, Minera Limeworks Quarry, Gwynfynydd Gold Mine, etc.

1933: **CRICCIETH URBAN DISTRICT COUNCIL**
wished to purchase flat-bottom rails, and had a quote from Britannia Foundry, Porthmadog. [J/IRR/Vol.5/71 - CGDown].

1934: **T.B.GORST & SONS, COLWYN BAY:**
Wanted - to hire at Flint at end of February, track, skips and one 2ft gauge light loco and excavator, to remove spoil bank. [J/CG/10.1.1934].
In view of term "spoil bank", and that the advert was in CG, this could be the tidying up of one of the Flint Colliery sites ?

1957: **EAGRE CONSTRUCTION CO LTD:** For Sale, 3 miles of track lying North Wales. [J/CJ/11.4.1957].

1957: **DALESCROFT NURSERIES, GLADSTONE WAY, HAWARDEN:**
reputed to have had a locomotive for heating greenhouses. Ownership changed c1966, and in 1970 the current owner "had heard about it" but it was scrapped pre-1966. [J/ILS/Summer 1970/RHAppleton].

1985: **HORNSBY AKROYD LOCOMOTIVE**
There are repeated rumours that (half of a, or even a complete) Hornsby Akroyd WW1 bogie petrol loco (as used in Kent at Woolwich Arsenal, Chattenden & Upnor, etc) has survived "in a disused quarry on a farm in Wales, possibly North Wales". At least one Museum is very anxious to trace this item.

SECTION ONE

NON-STATIC LOCOMOTIVE FLEETS

This Section summarises the locomotives owned by dealers and contractors based in North Wales, but which were not used by their owners at these depots. Where such locomotives are known to have been used elsewhere within North Wales, they are also listed under the appropriate entries in Sections 2 and 3 of this book.

The locomotive owners listed in this Section are:

        Cudworth & Johnson, Wrexham
        R.S.Davies, Mold
        C.P.Hopley, Buckley
        H.Croom Johnson, Wrexham
        Ian Jolly, Mold
        T.E.Minshall, Wrexham
        Frank R.Powell, Broughton
        Ratcliffes of Hawarden
        Thomas Savin
        Whitley Brothers, Wrexham
        W.O.Williams, Harlech
        John Woolley, Wrexham

CUDWORTH & JOHNSON, WREXHAM

The origins of C&J have yet to be positively established, but a note in "Machinery Market" of 25/8/1904 tells us that the partnership of Mr Johnson and Mr Cudworth (senior) had recently been dissolved, Mr Cudworth then retiring "after 19½ years" with C&J.

This suggests that C&J was founded early in 1885. The earliest locomotive that we have evidence of is HC 213 (WARWICK/DIXON) - reputedly purchased by C&J late in 1886; and the earliest sale advertisement found so far is 2/1889. However, apart from locomotives, the Company operated the Eagle Foundry in Tuttle Street, Wrexham, and dealt in a wide range of engineering materials and equipment.

When Cudworth (senior) retired in 1904 his son, Arthur Cudworth, also left C&J to set up business on his own as an "iron, metal and machinery merchant" with "stores at Wrexham Central (WM&CQR) Station", though his address soon became "St.Marks Engineering Works". Here he constructed two 4'8½" gauge four-wheeled vertical boilered "locomotives"; machines rather akin to steam shunting cranes but without crane fittings, which he sold to the Langwith Junction (Derbyshire) Wagon Works of W.H.Davis & Sons. One of these machines was later transferred to the Neasden (North London) Works of the same Company, and both survived until 1959/1960. They were not used as locomotives in the usual manner, but remained permanently coupled to traverser cars at the entrances to the wagon repair workshops.

From 1904, the business of "Cudworth & Johnson" continued under the same title, but now under the sole control of the Johnson family. In 7/1920 it was registered as Cudworth & Johnson Ltd - capital £10,000; Engineers, Iron and Brass Founders, Boiler Makers - but continued to advertise as simply "Cudworth & Johnson". The Johnsons had other interests; Lerry [B/107A/126] tells us that "Mr William Johnson, of the firm of Cudworth & Johnson", was mechanical engineer at the Hope, or Gwern Alyn, Colliery, at Cefnybedd. He lived in Percy Road, Wrexham, where he named his house "Gwern Alyn".

C&J gradually built up a fleet of locomotives which they hired out throughout the area, particularly to operators (Wm.J.Lee; Rea Ltd; Joseph Perrin & Son) at the Birkenhead Docks - until 1966, when the last C&J loco was scrapped.

Locomotives associated with C&J fall into two groups: many were actually owned, to be cannibalised, hired-out, perhaps even sold, whilst others were "ghosts" - being never owned by C&J, but advertised for sale on behalf of their owners in the hope of earning commission on a sale. Such "ghosts" are difficult to identify from the scant details given in C&J advertisements. It is possible that there was a third group, being locos that never existed at all - just brief mentions of "desirable" machines put into adverts in the hope of catching the eye of would-be customers (as some motor-traders do to this day).

C&J carried out major rebuilds in a cramped shed (GR:330514) alongside the WM&CQJR (PR/28) line at Rhosddu, Wrexham - where the litter of discarded components and derelict locomotives was a familiar sight to passengers on passing trains for upwards of 80 years. Locos which emerged from this shed were usually fitted with large, distinctive, cast-aluminium "rebuild" plates, which are clearly visible in many photographs. Minor repairs, however, were usually executed at the hirers' premises, or use would sometimes be made of any convenient site available. Thus it was that AVON met its fate in an open field just south of Gresford Colliery, whilst DEPTFORD and others spent some time at Llay Hall. The facilities of the WM&CQ/LNER/BR loco depot at Rhosddu were used from time to time, under a local arrangement with the shedmaster there; and complete locos were sometimes stored at Wrexham Central (LNER) station, both in the goods yard or garaged under the arches.

NOTE: In the following list, the two right-hand data columns are the loco cylinder size (bore x stroke, in inches), and the wheel diameter (when new). These details are often useful when referring to C&J advertisements in trade journals.

Locomotives: Gauge 4'8½"

DIXON/WARWICK	0-4-0ST OC	BH	21	1867	12x20	3'3"
	rebuilt HC		213	1882	12x19	-

Per HC records, HC 213 was named DIXON; per "Gregory" [? of Little Mountain Colliery] it was named WARWICK. See entry "Little Mountain Colliery" in Section 3.

Reputedly owned by C&J, but not proven.
    wfw(tdx?): Little Mountain Colliery, Buckley - for sale there until 9/1886 at least.
Reputedly wlw(tdt?): PR/54 Hawarden Loop Line (1888-3/1890) Contract
    [? or is this a confusion with John Woolley loco MW 81 named WREXHAM ex WARWICK]; and may in some way be connected with a reputed WARWICK at Ffrwd Collieries, near Cefn-y-Bedd.

CYMRO	0-4-0ST OC				10x14	-

Confirmed with C&J.
    Some sources say assembled by C&J from assorted components c1892; but also suggested as obtained by C&J from Greens Foundry, Aberystwyth and reconditioned by C&J c1892.
wlw(tdt?): owned by Davies Bros, PR/57 Wrexham-Ellesmere Railway (1892-1895) Contract.

WINIFRED	[? 0-4-0ST	OC	N	3788	1888	12x20	3'0"]

C&J did own a loco named WINIFRED but details and identity not known.
    A possible identity is WINIFRED N 3788 which was for sale at Bebington, Wirral, 2/2/1905, ex Price & Reeves, Birkenhead-Ledsham railway widening Contract, (and wfw: Hockley Hall & Whateley Collieries, Warwickshire).
No further trace (of neither C&J WINIFRED nor of WINIFRED N 3788).

MERSEY	0-4-0ST OC	BH	1059	1892	12x19	3'3"
	rebuilt	HL		1902		
	rebuilt	C&J		1925		

wfw: Birmingham Corporation, Windsor Street Gasworks, and for sale there 4/1917.
    After 3/1919 by 3/1920 loco was with Lever Brothers, Port Sunlight, Wirral, named MERSEY. For sale (by Anon) 6/1920 [J/PMR/10 + 19/6/1920]. It is possible that this loco came to C&J after 4/1917 by 3/1919 (and then hired to Levers); or came to C&J after 6/1920 by 1925. Another source suggests that this loco passed through the hands of the Ratcliffes of Hawarden before reaching C&J. Note that C&J are not yet known to have ever used J/PMR as an advertising medium.
tdt(sold): North Devon Clay Co Ltd, Peters Marland, Devon, £745, 8/1925.

| - | 0-4-0ST | OC | P | 644 | 1896 | 10x14 | 2'6" |

wfw(tdx?): Earl of Bradford, Great Lever Colliery, Bolton
(which closed c1922 hence possibly to C&J then).
wlw(tdt?): owned by Low Beechburn Colliery, Crook, Co.Durham
(reputedly there from c1923; certainly by 1/1925 when the colliery closed).

| LORD WEASTE | 0-4-0ST | OC | P | 1079 | 1906 | 10x15 | 2'9" |

purchased by C&J after 4/1924 by 11/1926.
    wfw(tdx?): J.E.C.Lord, Weaste, Lancashire, until 26/4/1924 at least.
    tdt(sold): W.Vernon & Sons Ltd, Flour Mills, Seacombe, by 1/11/1926
    (on which date Vernons notified the Mersey Docks & Harbour Board that they were re-
    naming the loco MILLENNIUM).
    wlw: Joseph Perrin & Sons Ltd, Birkenhead; PREMIER.

| MILLENNIUM | 0-4-0ST | OC | AB | 820 | 1898 | 10x18 | 3'2" |

purchased by C&J by 11/1926.
    wfw(tdx?): W.Vernon & Sons Ltd, Seacombe; MILLENNIUM, until 7/4/1924 at least.
    (Vernons had difficulties with the Mersey Docks & Harbour Board as this loco was too
    heavy to cross certain bridges.) [It was probably part-exchanged with C&J for P 1079.]
    wlw(tdt?): owned by George Wooliscroft & Son Ltd, Canal Tileries, Etruria, Staffs;
    ETRUSCAN; reputedly by c1926.
    wlw: Joseph Perrin & Sons Ltd, Birkenhead; PERRIN.

| SHAKESPEARE | 0-4-0ST | OC | HL | 3072 | 1914 | 14x22 | 3'6" |

with C&J by 1/1926; reputedly obtained from a source [? dealer] in "the Stoke-on-Trent
area".
    wfw: Tilmanstone (Kent) Collieries Ltd.
    Hired to Hafod Colliery for six months [1926/27]; then from Hafod was tdt: Bersham
    Colliery, initially on hire but retained and purchased c1928 by Bersham.

| BRITISH No.1. | 0-4-0ST | OC | P | 976 | 1903 | 12x18 | 3'0" |

Arrived at C&J during [1927 ?].
wfw(tdx?): Wagon Repairs Ltd, Port Tennant, Glam.
    Hired to Llay Main Colliery [? c1928].
wlw(tdt?): owned by J.J.Bate & Son Ltd, Teapot Brick Works, St.Helens, [? c1929].

| 34 | 0-6-0T | OC | HL | 2879 | 1911 | 14x22 | 3'6" |

wfw(tdx?): Mersey Docks & Harbour Board, Liverpool, (number) 34.
    This loco was sold by MD&HB on 25/8/1927; what was apparently this loco was
    offered for sale by/from 9/1928 to 9/1930 (at least).
    wfw: Cannock Chase Military Railway (as 0-6-2T), WD 85 PYRAMUS; until 8/1921.
    wfw: Shropshire & Montgomeryshire Light Railway.
wlw(tdt?): owned by Nunnery Colliery, Yorkshire, after 9/1930 by 2/1931.

	0-6-0ST	OC	AE	1472	1904	14x20	3'3"
	rebuilt		C&J		1938		

tdx: Mersey Docks & Harbour Board, Liverpool, (number) 3; 25/8/1927.
    Probably hired out but no details known.
    C&J purchased numerous spare parts from 1/1933 at least.
tdt(sold): Eccles Slag Co Ltd, Scunthorpe, Lincs, after 1938 by 8/4/1939.

	0-6-0ST	OC	AE	1604	1912	14x20	3'3"

wfw: Mersey Docks & Harbour Board, (number) 15; sold at auction 25/8/1927; purchaser not known - may have been George Cohen, Sons & Co Ltd, dealer, or may have been C&J. Whatever, C&J purchased Spares for this loco on various dates from 9/1929 onwards - and possibly in 9/1928 also.
    Hired to Gresford Colliery in 1932; and returned.
    Hired to Black Park Colliery by 10/1937; and returned after 22/11/1937.
tdt(sold): G & T Earle Ltd, Hessle, Yorkshire, 21/1/1938; PELICAN.

DAISY	0-4-0ST	OC	P	581	1894	14x20	3'2"
	rebuilt		P		1904		
	rebuilt		P		1915		

wfw: Wynnstay Colliery, Ruabon; advertised for sale - apparently still lying at Wynnstay - by C.D.Phillips, dealer, Newport, Mon, from 4/1929 to 9/1929 (Phillips then being owner of the loco). Loco with C&J by 3/1932 - and very probably by 2/1930 when C&J advertised a 14" 4wc Peckett for sale.
tdt(sold): Amalgamated Anthracite Collieries Ltd, Glamorgan, after 3/1932 by 7/1933.

	0-4-0ST	OC	P	1297	1913	14x20	3'2½"

wfw(tdx?): Oughterside Coal Co (1928) Ltd, Bulgill, Cumberland.
    This colliery closed 3/1933 and Sales followed. Loco with C&J by 1936; (probably by 5/1935 when C&J advertised a 14" 4w Peckett for sale.)
    Hired to Gresford Colliery during 1936; and returned.
tdt(sold): Grovesend Steel & Tinplate Co Ltd, Gorseinon; after 9/1936 by 8/1937

PAT	0-4-0ST	OC	HC	276	1885	12x18	3'0"
	rebuilt		HC		1922		

With C&J by 10/1936.
    wfw(tdx?): Marford Sand & Gravel Quarry, Rossett.
    Hired to Gresford Colliery, by 2/10/1936.
    Reputed hired to Trevor (Garth) Silica Brick Works, near Acrefair.
tdt(sold): R.Briggs & Sons Ltd, Clitheroe, by 12/1937.

| | SIR JOSEPH | 0-6-0ST | OC | HC | 1196 | 1916 | 14x20 | 3'7" |

wfw(tdx?): Stancliffe Estates Co Ltd, Darley Dale.
    Purchased by C&J c1938, perhaps via Twigg, dealer, Matlock (who advertised what appear to be the two Stancliffe locos in J/MM/10.12.1937).
    Hired to Llay Main Colliery, in 1938.
    By 22/3/1940, this loco was at Llay Hall Colliery; though whether on hire to the colliery, or only under repair there by C&J, is not clear.
    Hired to Sir Lindsay Parkinson, contractor, Risley Royal Ordnance Factory Contract, Lancashire, in 1940.
    tdx: Risley, to Wrexham, 4/9/1940.
tdt(sold): Stanton Ironworks Co Ltd, Glendon East Ironstone Quarries, 10/1940.

| 4 | HENRY DAWSON | 0-6-0ST | OC | HC | 1305 | 1917 | 14x20 | 3'7" |

wfw(tdx?): Stancliffe Estates Co Ltd, Darley Dale.
    Purchased by C&J c1938, perhaps via Twigg, dealer, Matlock (who advertised what appear to be the two Stancliffe locos in J/MM/10.12.1937).
    By 26/2/1939, this loco was under repair by C&J men inside the repair shop at LNER Wrexham Locomotive Shed (Rhosddu). Still here, but re-assembled, 8/7/1939.
tdt(sold): New Hucknall Colliery Co Ltd, Huthwaite Colliery, Notts, after 8/7/1939 by 9/1941.

| | VULCAN | 0-4-0ST | OC | SS | 3419 | 1888 | 12x18 | 2'9" |

With C&J by 1938.
    wfw: Admiralty, Chatham Dockyard, Kent - reputedly sold by Chatham in 1934, but purchaser not yet known.
    Hired to Gresford Colliery - seen there 10/1938.
    Seen at C&J Rhosddu shed 26/2/1939 to 9/7/1939.
tdt(sold): Joseph Perrin & Son Ltd, Birkenhead; reputedly c1940, certainly by 20/7/1947.

| 26 | AVON | 0-6-0T | IC | MW | 1005 | 1887 | 13x18 | 2'11¼" |
| | | rebuilt | | C&J | | 1940 | | |

tdx: Nott, Brodie & Co Ltd, Otterspool Sea Wall Stabilisation and Improvement (c1931-c1935) Contracts, after 3/1937.
    The locos at Otterspool were offered for sale by various Agents; it is not known precisely who dealt with C&J.
    Possibly hired to Joseph Perrin & Son Ltd, Birkenhead, in 1937-1939 period.
    After rebuilding in 1940, hired out to (including):
    Unknown customer in North-East England (possibly Ashington Coal Co Ltd, Northumberland) - seen at North Blyth LNER Shed 29/3/1942 where used for shunting a coal stacking ground and stated to be on loan from "Ashington". Was possibly the loco AVON seen in a goods train at Darlington in 1942 [J/RO/9.1942/144].
    Per verbal information 6/1949, loco arrived at Joseph Perrin c1943, and seen here 3/1943, 1/1947, 3/1947 etc.
    Out of use at Perrin's by 5/1948; and scrapped c1951 after 30/9/1950.

29	DYNEVOR	0-6-0ST	IC	MW	1726	1908	13x18	3'0"
		rebuilt		VF		1925		
		rebuilt		C&J		1945		

tdx: Nott, Brodie & Co Ltd, Otterspool Sea Wall Stabilisation and Improvement (c1931-c1935) Contracts, after 3/1937.
　　The locos at Otterspool were offered for sale by various Agents; it is not known precisely who dealt with C&J.
　　Probably hired out during c1937 to 1945 period, but no details are known other than that spare parts were purchased by C&J from time to time. Noted under repair at Wrexham 22/8/1946, then:
tdt(sold): Park Colliery, Garswood, Lancashire; WASP.

	MONARCH	0-4-0ST	OC	P	503	1892	10x14	2'6"
		rebuilt		C&J		1940		

with C&J by 15/5/1938.
　　wfw(tdx?): Geo.& R.Dewhurst, Bamber Bridge, near Preston, Lancashire, (who closed down in 1934).
　　Hired to Currie Rowlands & Co Ltd, Seacombe, Cheshire, in 1941; seen at Wrexham under repair 4/4/1942; used for construction of new sidings at Royal Ordnance Factory, Dunham Hill, Cheshire (seen here 11/6/1942); hired again to Currie Rowlands in 1943; hired to Manchester Oxide Co, Salford [later Hardman & Holden Ltd] (seen here 23/6/1945).
　　Per unknown source, was at C&J Wrexham 4/1946.
tdt(sold): Scottish Agricultural Industries Ltd [or predecessors J & J Cunningham], Leith, Midlothian, [? 1946] after 6/1945 [or 4/1946].

	JESSIE	0-4-0ST	OC	P	1116	1907	14x20	3'2½"

With C&J by 1/1945.
　　wfw: Geo.Cohen Sons & Co Ltd, dealers (for sale by Cohen 1/1941).
　　wfw: Insoles Ltd, Cymmer Collieries, Porth, near Pontypridd, Glam.
　　Hired to Joseph Perrin & Sons Ltd, Birkenhead Docks, by 1/1945 to 6/1951 (at least). By 8/1951 on hire to Rea Ltd, Duke Street Wharf, Birkenhead until 6/2/1954 at least; by 15/4/1954 on hire to Wm.J.Lee, Seacombe, Cheshire; and scrapped at Seacombe in 1955.

	SWANSEA	0-4-0ST	OC	HE	648	1897	10x15	2'10"
		rebuilt		C&J		1943		

With C&J by 1942.
　　wfw(tdx?): W.Y.Craig & Sons Ltd, Ifton Colliery, Weston Rhyn, Salop; was still at Ifton Colliery 12/5/1940.
　　Possibly hired to Marford Sand & Gravel Pits, Rossett, c1941 (but not present at Marford 8/1942); on hire at Minera Lime Works in 1942. After rebuild in 1943:-
tdt(sold): Rowntree & Co Ltd, York, 9/1943.

B17C		0-4-0ST	OC	HL	2466	1900	14x20	3'6"

With C&J by 1942. [Possibly earlier, as loco was working at Shell Refining & Marketing Co Ltd, unknown location, in 1941. If this was Shell at Stanlow in Cheshire, loco could have been there on hire from C&J.]
wfw(tdx?): Butterley Co Ltd, Derbyshire.
On hire to Joseph Perrin & Sons Ltd, Birkenhead Docks by 3/1943 until 7/1944 at least.
On hire to Llay Main Colliery, after 7/1944 until 11/1944.
On hire to Perrin at Birkenhead from 11/1944 to early 1945.
On hire to Midland Tar Distillers Ltd, Oldbury, early 1945.
On hire to Wm.J.Lee, Seacombe Docks, by 7/1945 until 20/4/1948 at least; to Rea Ltd, Duke Street Wharf, Birkenhead, by 5/6/1948 until 6/1951 at least, but not at Birkenhead 12/1951.
On hire to Pilkington Bros. Ltd, Kirk Sandall, by early 1952 until 6/1952; then returned to Birkenhead Docks. Hired to Wm.J.Lee until 7/1953, then to Rea Ltd until early 1957. Lay disused at Duke Street from by 6/1957 until scrapped there after 17/11/1962 by 29/2/1964.

BOOTLE		0-4-0ST	OC	HC	812	1907	14x20	3'3½"

tdx: Wm.J.Lee, Shunting Contractor, Seacombe, Cheshire, after 23/3/1941 by 2/1943.
Stored in open at C&J Rhosddu depot by 2/1943; partially dismantled; never used again; scrapped after 18/5/1964 by 6/11/1965.

-		0-4-0ST	OC	AB	821	1899	10x18	3'0"

With C&J by 22/8/1944.
wfw: Mersey Docks & Harbour Board Engineers Department, Birkenhead Docks Maintenance Department, (numbers) 18 [Liverpool fleet number] and MDE 14 [Birkenhead local number]. Sold by MD&HB at auction, Birkenhead, 4/11/1942, buyer recorded as "Engineers (Ruabon) Ltd". Apparently re-purchased by C&J, perhaps at or very soon after this auction.
Stored in open at C&J Rhosddu depot by 22/8/1944; never used again; frame only remained by 18/5/1964, scrapped by 6/11/1965.

GORDON		0-4-0ST	OC	P	600	1895	14x20	3'2½"

tdx: Marford Sand & Gravel Pits, after 21/8/1942 by 4/1943.
Hired to Wm.J.Lee, Shunting Contractor, Seacombe Docks, by 4/1943 until 5/6/1948 at least. Stored disused at premises of Currie Rowlands & Co Ltd, Seacombe, by 7/7/1949; and broken up for scrap there between 6/1950 and 1951.

NETHERTON		0-6-0ST	IC	MW	1603	1903	12x17	3'0"

With C&J [very probably after 31/12/1942] by 8/1943
wfw(tdx?): Sir Lindsay Parkinson, contractor, Winwick Quay store, Warrington [very probably until after 31/12/1942].
One of several locos that had been used by SLP on Contracts at Chorley and Risley Royal Ordnance Factories.
Hired to Marford Sand & Gravel Pits (see Section 3), after 8/1943 by 28/5/1944.
Abandoned at Marford, and scrapped there 6/1952.

| WALTER SCOTT | 0-6-0ST | IC | MW | 1237 | 1892 | 12x17 | 3'1" |
| | rebuilt | | MW | | 1917 | | |

Source and dates as for NETHERTON above.
    Repaired at Rhosddu depot (seen 8/1943); may have been hired out but still at Rhosddu 8/1944 and 28/5/1945. Hired to Wm.J.Lee, Shunting Contractor, Seacombe Docks, by 8/1946; damaged in accident; stored in and near Shore Road Loco Shed [LNER/Perrin], Birkenhead, from by 2/3/1947 to 30/9/1950 and scrapped there early 1951. Some components taken to Rhosddu Depot for possible further use.

| DOLGARROG | 0-6-0ST | IC | MW | 1507 | 1901 | 12x17 | 3'0" |
| | rebuilt | | C&J | | 1932 | | |

    Owned by Dolgarrog Aluminium Works; sent to C&J at Wrexham for repair late 1931 by 1/1932; rebuilt 1932; returned to Dolgarrog.
tdx: Dolgarrog Aluminium Works after 30/4/1942 by 1945.
    Hired to Wm.J.Lee, Shunting Contractor, Seacombe Docks, by 3/1945 until 11/1948; hired to Joseph Perrin & Son Ltd, Birkenhead, 11/1948 "for a short time only"; dumped disused near Lee's shed by 3/1949 until scrapped there early 1951 after 30/9/1950.

| SIR THEODORE | 0-4-0ST | OC | AE | 1397 | 1899 | 14x20 | 3'3" |

wfw(tdx?): Gresford Colliery, after 3/10/1936 by 1/5/1942.
    Probably hired out but no reports until arrived C&J Rhosddu depot after 28/5/1945 by 28/4/1946; dismantled for repair; cab and saddletank remained at Rhosddu, boiler taken to Eagle Foundry. An AE loco chassis standing inside the Rhosddu workshop from by 1/1950 presumed to be from this loco. Loco never reassembled; chassis scrapped inside Rhosddu depot shed 11/1965.

| BARTON No.2 | 0-4-0ST | OC | MW | 1728 | 1908 | 14x18 | 3'0" |

wfw(tdx?): Barton Limestone Co Ltd. Locos were auctioned at Barton 25/9/1946 and arrived at C&J Wrexham (by) early 1947.
    With C&J at "Rhosddu Shed" [C&J, or LNER ?] by 20/4/1947.
tdt(sold): Bryant & May Ltd, Garston, Liverpool, after 15/6/1947 by 28/5/1948.

| MELSONBY No.3 | 0-4-0ST | OC | MW | 1681 | 1906 | 14x18 | 3'0" |

wfw(tdx?): Barton Limestone Co Ltd. Locos were auctioned at Barton 25/9/1946 and arrived at C&J Wrexham (by) early 1947.
    With C&J at Rhosddu 2/1947, 20/4/1947, 15/6/1947 then "Lost" until:
    Hired to Wm.J.Lee, Seacombe, Cheshire, after 9/1948 by 5/1949 until 6/1951.
    Hired to Rea Ltd, Duke Street Wharf, Birkenhead, 6/1951 to 10/5/1952 at least.
    Hired to Wm.J.Lee, 6/1952 until after 12/10/1953; dumped out of use in Dock Board Yard, Seacombe, c2/1954 by 8/5/1954 until scrapped there 10/1955
    NOTE: during the 1947/48 "Lost" period, reputed to have worked at Trevor Silica Brick Works, near Acrefair - but not proven.

| | CYCLOPS | 0-4-0ST | OC | HC | 451 | 1895 | 13x20 | 3'0" |

tdx: Currie Rowlands & Co Ltd, Seacombe, Cheshire; apparently purchased by C&J c4/1947 but not removed from Rowlands premises until 1948/49 (after 12/1947 certain).
Hired to Wm.J.Lee, Seacombe, by 9/6/1949 until 22/9/1961 at least.
Moved to Shore Road Loco Shed [BR(LNER)/Perrin] for repair by 1/1/1962.
Not repaired; dumped in Dock Board Yard, Seacombe, by 29/2/1964, and scrapped there after 25/4/1964 by 12/8/1964.

| | P L A 37 | 0-4-0ST | OC | P | 897 | 1901 | 14x20 | 3'2½" |

With C&J by 12/1946.
wfw(tdx?): Port of London Authority, (number) 37.
At Llay Hall Colliery by 14/12/1946 - loco derelict and said to be stored there by C&J. No further trace.

| | EASTWOOD | 0-4-0ST | OC | AB | 1304 | 1912 | 12x18 | 3'2" |
| | | | rebuilt | C&J | | 1949 | | |

tdx: Wallasey Gas Works, Cheshire, after 7/1937 by 12/1946; (painted name on tank:) W.EASTWOOD.
At Llay Hall Colliery by 14/12/1946; here also 31/8/1948 - premises being used by C&J to repair the loco.
Hired to Bersham Colliery in 1948/1949 period, then to Rhosddu depot for rebuilding. Nameplates EASTWOOD now fitted.
Hired to Rea Ltd, Duke Street Wharf, Birkenhead, by 10/1949 until 12/1949 at least; hired to Wm.J.Lee, Seacombe, by 14/5/1950 until 30/9/1950 at least; hired to British Enka Ltd, Aintree, Lancashire, by 1/1/1951; returned to C&J Rhosddu 1951.
tdt(sold): Tarmac Ltd, Rose Grove Opencast Coal Disposal Point, Burnley, Lancashire, between 1951 and 24/10/1953.

| | W.G.ELLERY | 0-4-0ST | OC | AB | 783 | 1897 | 11x16 | 2'9" |

tdx: Wallasey Gas Works, Cheshire, after 9/1943 by 1/1947.
Loco was worn-out and purchased "for spares" only; stored by C&J at premises of Currie Rowlands & Co Ltd, Seacombe, by 1/1947 until 1/6/1950 at least; scrapped there after 1/6/1950 by 6/1951.

| | GLANMOR | 0-4-0ST | OC | HL | 2034 | 1885 | 14x20 | 3'6" |
| | | | rebuilt | C&J | | 1949 | | |

tdx: South Wales, after 3/1948 by 1949.
Precise history is uncertain; loco wfw: Glanmor Foundry Co Ltd, Llanelli, but was seen under repair in workshop of Nevill's Dock & Railway Co Ltd, Llanelli, 27/3/1948. It was then understood to be the property of Nevill's Dock, but may in fact have been there only for repair prior to sale by Glanmor Foundry Co Ltd.
Hired to Rea Ltd, Duke Street Wharf, Birkenhead, by 10/1949 until 26/5/1958 at least; hired to Joseph Perrin & Son Ltd, Birkenhead, by 27/1/1960 "for 5 to 6 weeks"; hired to Rea Duke Street by 22/11/1960 but out of use there by 2/1/1961; remained thus until scrapped at Duke Street after 17/11/1962 by 29/2/1964.

| "MAYFLOWER" | 0-4-0WT OC Kit [rebuilt] Kit | [T109 1884] 1893 | 8x12 | 3'0" |

tdx: Liverpool Overhead Railway Co, after 10/1947 by 6/1949.
Some sources say taken to Wrexham [but no sightings there on record], other sources say taken directly to Birkenhead area; per one source it crossed the river Mersey on a tug boat. As yet, no reports of it being seen at Birkenhead prior to 6/1949; so actual transfer date from Liverpool [often quoted as 1/1948] remains in doubt.
The identity of this loco is open to doubt; it was plated "Kitson 1893" and has been identified in the past in some sources as Kitson T261 of 1892-93. From Kitson original archives, this is clearly wrong. Considering all known possibilities, this loco is almost certainly one of Kitson T109-T111, built 1884, New to West Lancashire Railway and all returned to Kitson in 1886 for resale. Two, identified as T110 and T111, were sold to the Corringham Light Railway (Essex) and to a contractor at Morecambe (though uncertain which was which). As the later fate of these can be traced with virtual certainty, then T109 must be the one sold [? after being re-plated "1893"] in 1894 to Richard White & Sons, dealers and contractors, Widnes; who MAY have re-sold to Liverpool Overhead Rly.
Hired to Rea Ltd, Monks Ferry Wharf, Birkenhead, by 6/1949 until scrapped there 15/9/1961.

| No.1 | 0-4-0F OC Hz | 4311 1925 | | |

tdx: British Enka Ltd, Aintree, Liverpool; for repair only; 12/1950.
Repaired by C&J inside the repair shop at BR(LNER) Wrexham Loco Shed (Rhosddu).
tdt: British Enka Ltd, Aintree, 1951 after 24/8/1951.

| SHAMROCK | 0-4-0ST OC HE rebuilt C&J | 411 1886 1954 | 13x18 | 3'1" |

tdx: Wm.J.Lee, Shunting Contractor, Seacombe, Cheshire, after 30/6/1951 by 12/1951.
Hired to Crawfords Ltd, Edge Lane, Liverpool, 1955 after 3/1/1955.
Hired to Wm.J.Lee, Seacombe, Cheshire, by 2/10/1955 until 1957.
Hired to Rea Ltd, Duke Street Wharf, Birkenhead, after 27/4/1957 by 11/8/1957; withdrawn from service at Rea Ltd by 1/1/1959; remained standing at Duke Street until scrapped there after 17/11/1962 by 29/2/1964.

| TYNESIDER | 0-4-0ST OC P rebuilt C&J | 458 1887 1951 | 14x20 | 3'2" |

tdx: Britannia Scrap Metal Co Ltd, Widnes, after 10/1950 by c2/1951.
wfw: Imperial Chemical Industries, Gaskell Marsh Works; PECKETT.
Apparently moved direct from Widnes to Birkenhead Docks, as seen there c2/1951, still named PECKETT, but perhaps not used; moved to C&J Wrexham Rhosddu depot; rebuilt; then:
Hired to Wm.J.Lee, Shunting Contractor, Seacombe, by 13/6/1951 until after 2/1/1956.
Hired to Rea Ltd, Duke Street Wharf, Birkenhead, by 2/2/1958; withdrawn from service at Rea Ltd by 12/2/1960; remained standing at Duke Street until scrapped there after 17/11/1962 by 29/2/1964.

| BRIAN | 0-4-0ST | OC | AE | 1796 | 1918 | 14x20 | 3'6" |

tdx: Lever Bros.(Port Sunlight) Ltd, Cheshire, 16204 LUX; moved from Levers to Wrexham 3/4/1952; re-named BRIAN.
Hired to Rea Ltd, Duke Street Wharf, Birkenhead, by 2/6/1952; withdrawn from service at Duke Street by 12/2/1960 until 1/9/1962 at least. Steamed again - in use 17/11/1962; possibly now on hire to Wm.J.Lee in fact. Withdrawn from use and stored in Dock Board Yard, Seacombe, by 29/2/1964, and scrapped there after 25/4/1964 by 12/8/1964.

DEPTFORD	0-4-0ST	OC	BH	1038	1891	12x19	3'2"
	rebuilt		CF		1901		
	rebuilt		YE		1925		
	rebuilt		YE		1933		

wfw(tdx?): Wm.Cory & Son Ltd, Purfleet, Essex, after 22/3/1952 by 8/1952 (was seen on lorry travelling west, north of London, early 7/1952).
Stored by C&J in sidings at Llay Hall Colliery - arrived there after 3/6/1952 by 8/1952. Hired to Tarmac Ltd, Rose Grove Opencast Coal Disposal Point, Burnley, Lancashire, from late-1953 [? c10/1953] until 6/1954; returned, Rose Grove to Llay Hall, 30/6/1954; stored unused at Llay Hall sidings until 7/7/1957 at least.
No further trace.

| - | 0-4-0ST | OC | AE | 1876 | 1921 | 12x18 | 2'11" |

wfw(tdx?): Crane Ltd, Ipswich, Suffolk, after 20/2/1952 by 5/6/1952.
May in fact have reached C&J via Thos.W.Ward Ltd, dealers, as loco carried a Wards' plate on arrival (also a small oval plate '528').
Loco stored under GWR main-line bridge on siding at Wrexham [Central] station by 5/6/1952 until 14/2/1954 at least.
No further trace.

| REMUS | 0-4-0ST | OC | HC | 1399 | 1920 | 14x20 | 3'3½" |

tdx: Robertson Thain Ltd, Ellesmere Port, Cheshire; moved directly from Ellesmere Port to Birkenhead Docks 18/4/1954.
Hired to Rea Ltd, Duke Street Wharf, Birkenhead, by 5/1954 until after 15/3/1959.
Hired to Wm.J.Lee, Shunting Contractor, Seacombe, Cheshire, by 2/1/1961 until c7/1965.
Hired to Joseph Perrin & Son Ltd, Birkenhead, c7/1965 by 8/8/1965 until 31/8/1965.
Returned to Wm.J.Lee shed 31/8/1965 and stored until scrapped there "by a Bootle firm" 4/1966.

| HOMEPRIDE | 0-4-0ST | OC | HL | 3589 | 1924 | 14x22 | 3'6" |

tdx: Paul Bros Ltd, Flour Mills, Seacombe Docks, 6/1958 (had been purchased by C&J 6/1957, but remained there for 12 months until moved directly to Wm.J.Lee).
Hired to Wm.J.Lee, Shunting Contractor, Seacombe, 6/1958 until 1964 after 2/1964.
Transferred to store at Birkenhead Shore Road Loco Shed [BR(LNER)/Perrin], and scrapped there late-1964 [c11/1964].

| KELVINSIDE | 0-4-0ST | OC | HC | 1798 | 1947 | 14x22 | 3'3½" |

tdx: Currie Rowlands & Co Ltd, Seacombe, Cheshire, 5/1962
Boiler failed test; loco not used from 5/1962. Stored in open in Dock Board Yard, Seacombe, by 29/2/1964; scrapped there after 25/4/1964 by 12/8/1964.

The following locomotives have been attributed to C&J by some sources, but no confirmatory evidence has yet been found. It is possible that they were advertised by C&J on behalf of other owners.

| WYNNSTAY | 0-6-0ST | IC | MW | 1646 | 1905 | 16x22 | 3'9" |

wfw: Wynnstay Colliery, Ruabon.
Loco was surplus there from 9/1927 and apparently was the loco offered for sale [J/MM/16.9.1927] by Marple & Gillott Ltd, dealers, Sheffield. However, Wynnstay Collieries Ltd purchased spares for this loco 12/1927 and 1/1928. Loco MAY then have passed to C&J, but no evidence found.
wlw: Perry & Co (Bow) Ltd, contractors, Bromborough Dock (1927-1931) Contract, Cheshire, after 1/1928 by 3/7/1928.
wlw: Garswood Hall Colliery, Wigan, Lancs, after 7/1929 by 2/5/1933

| - | 0-6-0ST | OC | AE | 1603 | 1912 | 14x20 | 3'3" |

wfw: Mersey Docks & Harbour Board, Liverpool, (number) 13.
Sold by MD&HB to Geo.Cohen, Sons & Co Ltd, dealers, in 1927; offered for sale by Cohen [eg: J/CJ/2.5.1928]; purchased by Avonside Engine Co Ltd but remained at MD&HB until 9/1928. Spares were supplied 9/1928 to C&J for EITHER AE 1603 OR 1604 (the Spares Order is not precise) and this may be the source of allegations of C&J ownership. And note: Cohen re-advertised this loco in J/CJ/6.2.1929 but presumably in error - because:
wlw: Hafod Colliery, Johnstown, by 10/1928; CHAMPION.

| TYNESIDER | 0-6-0ST | IC | BH | 1116 | 1896 | 12x18 | 3'0½" |

wfw: S.Pearson, contractor, Gretna Munitions Factory (1915-1917) Contract.
  wfw: John Scott, contractor, Vittoria Dock (c1908-1914) Contract, Birkenhead.
The Gretna locos were dispersed c1917; TYNESIDER is then "Lost" until c1935, when it was photographed working for Wm.J.Lee, Shunting Contractor, Seacombe Docks. In the 1960s a driver at Lee's recalled that it had been bought by Lee from C&J before WW2 - whilst this seems plausible, it is not proof. Lee had in fact obtained permission from MD&HB to use the loco for some weeks in 1911, apparently on hire from the Vittoria Dock job.
Withdrawn from service by Wm.J.Lee c1946; subsequently removed from Lee's shed and stored in open until scrapped 1951. It is possible that Lee had then sold it to C&J (? for spares or repair) but this is not proven.

R.S.DAVIES, MACHINERY MERCHANT, MOLD

by 1910 -	:	**R.S.Davies**, dealer, Hendre, Mold.
from c1916 -	:	**R.S.Davies**, Bromfield Colliery Yard, Mold.
4/1928 -	:	**R.S.Davies & Co Ltd** (reg.4/1928 £7K)
by 1967 -	:	**H.L.Hughes**, trading as **'R.S.Davies'**.

This company has always dealt principally in materials and equipment for quarries, being based since c1916 in the premises of the former Bromfield Colliery which closed 6/1916 (see Section 3).

The locomotives listed below are those thought to have actually visited Bromfield Yard. Advertisements noted in trade journals generally refer to locos "wanted" rather than for sale - eg: 2/1927 - Wanted, 25hp petrol loco. 11/1929 - Wanted, 2ft gauge 7x10 steam loco. 6/1931 - Wanted, a 9"/10" 4'8½" gauge steam loco.

Locomotives: Gauges as listed.

2'0"		0-4-0WT	OC	HC	1142	1915	(a)	(1)
1'11.5/8"		0-4-0ST	OC	WB	1916	1910	(b)	(2)
1'11½"		4wPM	6hp	L	3804	1931	(c)	(3)
2ft		4wPM	10hp	RP	51901	1917	(d)	(4)
600mm	PERTHEL KOLN 5	4wDM	20hp	HE	2036	1040	(e)	(5)
600mm		4wDM	20hp	HE	2975	1944	(f)	(5)
2'0"		4wDM	13hp	RH	264252	1952	(g)	(6)
2'0"		4wBE		LMM	1049	1950	(h)	(7)
2'0"		4wBE		LMM	1053	1950	(h)	(7)

(a) there is no proof that this loco was ever at Mold, but R.S.Davies did try to sell it to Flintshire County Council late in 1921, and the Council records suggest that they viewed it at Davies' yard.
However, this may not be the case, as:-
Loco New 5/1915 to Balfour Beatty & Co Ltd, contractors, Ripon Camp Contract; apparently for sale in auction at War Department Depot, Slough, Bucks, 27/4/1920. Perhaps then purchased by R.S.Davies.
However, it could have been the loco for sale 6/1921 by Trent Concrete Ltd, New Basford [J/MM/3.6.1921], (in which Davies may have perhaps hoped to act as intermediary). Flintshire C.C. did not purchase in fact.
Identical loco still for sale 8/1923 at Trent Concrete Ltd, Netherfield, Notts. [J/CJ/1.8.1923]. See footnote (1).
(b) wfw(tdx?): Glynceiriog Slate Quarries, after 2/1921 by 7/1924
(c) tdx: Lister, 5/1931
wfw: "Arnold & Sons Ltd" [? who. Shown thus in Lister records.]
(d) here by 9/1952
wfw: Oakeley Slate Quarry - to Davies per or via Williams, dealer, Harlech.
(e) here by 9/1952
wfw: Ministry of Supply, in Germany.
(f) here by 9/1952
(g) here by 9/1952
Had been despatched New 5/3/1952 to Allen Oil Equipment & Supply Co Ltd, London E2 [presume intended for export, but cancelled and re-sold to R.S.Davies].
(h) tdx: ?, c1964
wfw(tdx?): E.Nuttall, Sons & Co Ltd, contractors.

(1) was purchased by Oakeley Slate Quarries "at Nottingham" in 1924. No mention of Davies acting as or for seller - though he regularly sold items to Oakeley, hence may have been involved.
(2) tdt: Thos.Mosedale, c/o Flixton Station CLC [ie, Flixton Brickworks, Davyhulme], after 7/1924 by 5/1925
(3) disposal unknown; possibly to Lane End Brickworks (see Section 3).
(4) scrapped at Bromfield Yard after 9/1952 by 6/1953
(5) here 6/1953, gone by 6/1954; disposal not known.
(6) tdt: Votty & Bowydd Slate Quarry, after 9/1952 by 6/1953
(7) tdt: Trap Brickworks, Buckley, c1964

C.P.HOPLEY, CYNLAS, TABERNACLE STREET, BUCKLEY, CLWYD

Mr Hopley built an experimental 2ft gauge 0-2-2 gas-electric loco c1982; a gas driven generator powering an electric motor via experimental electronic controls. Stored at above address from 9/1989.

H.CROOM JOHNSON, CONTRACTOR, KING STREET, WREXHAM

CONTRACTS UNDERTAKEN:

c1887 -	1888	:	Kerry Tramway, Montgomery, 2ft gauge for C.J.Naylor
1887 -	1889	:	PR/42 Glyn Valley Tramway reconstruction.
1890...		:	PR/54 work on Connah's Quay branch.
12/1891 -	8/1892	:	PR/54 Aston Hall Railway connection.
12/1892 -	7/1893	:	PR/22 Lane End Colliery extension.
12/1892 -	7/1893	:	work for Wirral Railways Joint Committee.
2/1894...		:	Dee Embankment for ditto.

Locomotives: Gauge 4'8½"

STANLEY	0-6-0ST	IC	MW	818	1882	(a)	(1)
[? AMY]	0-6-0ST	IC	MW	1105	1889	(b)	(2)

(a) per MW records this loco was here and possibly in/by early 1890s.
  wfw: J.D.Nowell, contractor, [? LYR Manchester Victoria Station Extension (1881-1884) Contract] and [? LYR Halifax Station Enlargement (1885-1886) Contract] and [? Manchester Central Station (1889-1892) Contract].
(b) wfw: J.D.Nowell, contractor, Manchester Central Station (1889-1892) Contract; (named) AMY.

(1) wlw: Pethick Brothers, contractors, [? Vale of Glamorgan Railway (1894-1897) Contract, or ? Burrator Reservoir (1894-1898) Contract, Princetown, Devon.]
(2) tdt: Wrexham, Mold & Connah's Quay Junction Rly Co, number 14, 1895

NOTE: In 1/1895 H.C.Johnson was advertising three locos for sale; MW 12" and MW 14" - very likely MW 818 and 1105 above - and 2ft gauge WB 5". This latter could be WB 970, redundant on closure of Kerry Tramway, and perhaps being sold on behalf of C.J.Naylor at Kerry. The possibility remains, however, that Johnson may have used the 5" WB [? WB 970] on one of his Contracts.

IAN JOLLY, 1 LLEWELYN DRIVE, BRYN-Y-BAAL, MOLD

Mr Jolly has assembled a collection of locomotives and established a private railway. The locomotives have been stored at various (mostly private) locations; at the time of writing they are not all in one place, and therefore the collection is listed in Section One for convenience.

Locomotives: Gauge 4'8½"

ARMY 9036	3	2w-2PMr		Wkm	8196	1958	(a)	
DB 965051		2w-2PMr		Wkm	[?7574	1956]	(b)	Dsmt
TR27		2w-2PMr		Wkm	4132	1947	(c)	
TR6		2w-2PMr		Wkm	6901	1954	(d)	(1)
-		4wDM	40hp	MR	1944	1919	(e)	

Locomotives: Gauge 2ft (Ø : 2'8")

-		4wPM		L	30233	1946	(f)	
264		4wPM	20hp	MR	264	1916	(g)	
No.21		4wPM	20hp	MR		[c1920]	(h)	(5)
-		4wPM	12hp	MR	6013	1931	(i)	
-	(Ø)	4wPM	20hp	MR		1918	(j)	
-		4wPM	30hp	MR	5297	1931	(k)	(2)
-		4wPM	20hp	MR	20558	1955	(m)	
LBLR 9		4wDM	20hp	MR	9547	1950	(n)	
-		4wPM	20hp	MR	8723	1942	(o)	
-	A.H.WORTH	4wDM	20hp	MR	5852	1933	(p)	
41		4wDM	20hp	MR	5859	1934	(q)	(3)
-		4wDM	20hp	MR	7201	1937	(r)	Dsmt
-		4wPM	20hp	MR	4803	1934	(s)	
LR 2718		4wPM	20hp	MR	997	1918	(t)	
LR 2832		4wPM	20hp	MR	1111	1918	(u)	(4)
-		2w-2PMr		Wkm	3030	1943	(v)	
-		4wDM	20hp	MR	5025	1929	(w)	Dsmt
-		4wBE		WR	7661	1974	(x)	
LR 3041		4wDM	40hp	MR	1320	1918	(y)	

(a) tdx: K.Gardner, Milnthorpe, Cumbria, 23/12/1979
 wfw: Longtown Army Depot
(b) tdx: Llanrwst Transport Museum, 10/5/1980
(c) tdx: Mr R.P.Morris, private store [at Gloddfa Ganol], 10/5/1980
(d) tdx: British Railways, Llanbrynmair, 11/1981
(e) tdx: Alyn Works, Mold, 8/5/1986
(f) tdx: E.J.Godwin Ltd, Westhay, Somerset, 21/10/1977
(g) tdx: E.J.Godwin Ltd, Westhay, Somerset, 25/11/1977
(h) tdx: Joseph Arnold & Sons Ltd, Leighton Buzzard, Beds, 30/3/1978
(i) tdx: Strathclyde Regional Council, Cairngryffe, Lanarks, 2/6/1978
(j) tdx: P.Finnie, New Pitsligo, Aberdeenshire, 2/9/1978
(k) tdx: Great Bush Railway, Sussex, 21/10/1978
(m) tdx: Joseph Arnold & Sons Ltd, Leighton Buzzard, Beds, 8/12/1978
(n) tdx: Joseph Arnold & Sons Ltd, Leighton Buzzard, Beds, 15/1/1979
 tdt: Welsh Highland Railway (PR/44), Porthmadog, 31/5/1980
 tdx: Welsh Highland Railway (PR/44), Porthmadog, 5/5/1986

(o)	tdx:	Joseph Arnold & Sons Ltd, Leighton Buzzard, Beds, 2/6/1979
(p)	tdx:	George Garside (Sand) Ltd, Leighton Buzzard, Beds, 24/11/1979
(q)	tdx:	Joseph Arnold & Sons Ltd, Leighton Buzzard, Beds, 1/12/1979
(r)	tdx:	Runcorn Transport Museum, Cheshire, 31/8/1980
	wfw:	Cementation Co Ltd, contractors, Doncaster
	wfw:	Sir Lindsay Parkinson & Co Ltd, ROF Chorley Contract in 1937.
(s)	tdx:	Runcorn Transport Museum, Cheshire, 31/8/1980
	wfw:	Joseph Arnold & Sons Ltd, Leighton Buzzard, Beds.
(t)	tdx:	private collection at Bala Lake Railway (PR/66), 9/11/1980
(u)	tdx:	Mr P.N.Lowe, Leeds, 22/11/1980
(v)	tdx:	Bromyard & Linton Light Railway, Worcs, 19/4/1981
(w)	tdx:	Mr I.Sutcliffe, Surrey
	wfw:	Dyserth Limeworks & Quarry
(x)	tdx:	Hendre Spar Mine, Rhydymwyn, 1988 by 6/1988
(y)	tdx:	Chalk Pits Museum, Sussex, 31/10/1989
(1)	tdt:	Llangollen Railway (PR/68), 31/1/1982
(2)	tdt:	Mr P.Smith, Rustington, Sussex, 11/7/1980
(3)	tdt:	Mr P.N.Lowe, Leeds, 22/11/1980
(4)	tdt:	Old Kiln Light Railway, Sussex, 27/10/1989
(5)	tdt:	Grange Cavern Military Museum [see GRANGE QUARRIES; Section 3], 1984
	tdx:	Grange Cavern Military Museum, 1990
	tdt:	Alan Keef Ltd, Lea Line, Ross-on-Wye, 18/9/1990

T.E.MINSHALL, RAILWAY ENGINEER, QUEEN STREET CHAMBERS, WREXHAM

Mr Minshall held the post of Resident Engineer for the early 1860s construction of the Wrexham, Mold & Connah's Quay Junction Railway (PR/28), and in 1872 was busy with proposals for railways in the Oswestry area. He moved from Wrexham to Oswestry some years later.

Whilst at Wrexham, he also dealt in second-hand locomotives and other machinery, though there is no evidence that this was anything but speculative, and the locos may never have been anywhere near North Wales. However, the details as quoted in the advertisements are recorded here, in case something more positive is learned in the future.

J/CG/2.1869	- for sale, locomotive engines.
J/CG/17.9.1869/288	- for sale, tank loco 13½x24 cylinders, 4'0" leading and driving wheels coupled, 3'6" trailing wheels, 17 tons, £300.
J/MJ/19.3.1870	- "several excellent tank locos of different sizes".
J/TE/14.2.1873	- for sale, 3 tank locos by BP, second-hand, 16", 6w 4wc, two fitted with patent bogie. Also one 12" 6wc 3ft diameter; and 11" ditto. [sic]
J/TE/30.5.1873	- for sale, tank locos; two 16" BP 4wc 5ft diameter, one with patent bogie, the other with trailing wheels 3'6". 10" 4wc 3ft diameter by Hughes & Co, and other sizes. [sic]
J/CG/11.1873/713	- for sale, tank locos new and secondhand 8" to 15", and tender l locos up to 18".
J/GC/12.1873/760	- WANTED - Two tank locos 12" to 16" 4wc and one small loco 2'10" gauge
J/MJ/7.11.1874	- for sale, "tank locos 9" to 17" cylinders by leading builders"

The 16" locos of 2/1873 and 5/1873 could likely be three of North London Railway numbers 38 to 42, BP 186-190/1860, though these were recorded by the NLR as being sold with no reference to Minshall; except that for 4 of the 5 locos the NLR did pay commission to an un-named broker. 39 was sold 10/1872 and 41 9/1872, leaving 38, 40 and 42 for sale in 1873. Of these, 0-4-4ST 38 was sold to Mr Grice of Cwmbran Works, Newport, Mon. 40 was reported 6/1873 as sold to Hendry & Co, and 42 was sold 7/1873 to a Mr McConnochie. Minshall's description "6w 4wc" would seem to preclude 0-4-4 type locos, yet "patent bogie" would suggest 0-4-4 (or 4-4-0 etc). Thus maybe confirming Minshall had not actually seen the locos, but was relying on (erroneous ?) written details (from NLR ?).

FRANK R.POWELL, ENGINEERING & MACHINERY MERCHANT, BROUGHTON, CLWYD

Powell placed extensive advertisements in J/MM from 1/1896 to 4/1897 (only) and, from his telegram address ("Powell, Broughton Hall Station") it would appear that he was the new tenant of Ratcliffe's yard there. It would seem that Powell's business, in locomotives at least, was shortlived.

His advertisements included three locomotives "for sale":-

A: Geared drive four-wheeled contractors tank loco, 8"x20" cylinders, Lowmoor firebox and tubes, suit small colliery.

B: Manning Wardle saddle tank, 6 wheel coupled, 3ft wheels, 12" inside cylinders.

C: 4 wheel coupled loco, 10" outside cylinders, Lowmoor firebox.

Perhaps none of these were at Broughton; items B and C may be the locos of identical description offered in Cudworth & Johnson advertisements between 5/1896 and 2/1899.

THE RATCLIFFES OF HAWARDEN

Members of the Ratcliffe family were active as engineers, machinery merchants, dealers in locomotives, and allied activities, from 1846 to 1933 or later. Their activities are not fully known, and further research could be rewarding. Indeed, there were points in time when there was more than one business, different members of the family sometimes trading individually. Four separate premises are known, three of which were co-existent and in common ownership in the 1890s.

The address given in advertisements is usually "Hawarden" and sometimes "Hawarden Iron Works" with, it would appear, no meaningful significance as to which was chosen. In either case, the post-town 'Chester' would sometimes be added to the address, though they do not appear to have had premises in that city.

The term "Hawarden Iron Works" creates confusion. An advertisement in Railway Times 10/7/1847 offered this Works for sale, and explained there were two premises - one at Hawarden Village "established a great number of years", the other at Sandycroft "erected 1836". Would-be purchasers were to contact Robert Roberts, Slate Merchant of Chester. W.& J.Rigby are recorded as owners of Hawarden Ironworks - presumably the Village premises - as early as 1812, where a wide range of foundrywork, engineering fabrication and boiler repairs were undertaken, principally for the local lead mining industry. The Village Iron Works was then taken by Daniel Ratcliffe. Robert Roberts re-advertised "Sandycroft Works" in J/RT/2.7.1853 - for later history see SANDYCROFT FOUNDRY in Section 3. Confusion is compounded, however, by OS/25"/1871 which marks the Bagillt Engineering Works (GR:213761) as "Hawarden Iron Works"; whilst in J/MJ/2.12.1871 we read that "The Hawarden Works, close to the country residence of Mr Gladstone, are very active, the Messrs Ratcliffe having extensive orders in hand, including a large engine for the Carnarvonshire Slate Company and another for Mr Thompson, at the Tryddyn Vale Cannel Colliery, Leeswood....". [These would be stationary engines, no doubt.]

Daniel Ratcliffe was succeeded by his sons Edward and James, who traded as Ratcliffe & Sons - a title in use by 1867 [J/CDH/24.8.1867] to as late as 1917, and which by 1926 had become Ratcliffe & Sons (Hawarden) Ltd.

From c1872, however, "Edward Ratcliffe" also advertised in his own name only - he died 1897 and, by 6/1897, the "Exors of the late Edward Ratcliffe" were trading as such, and continued to advertise under this title until 1904. However, in 3/1904 Edward's sons, Arthur and Edgar, purchased their late father's business from the Executors, and henceforth traded under the old title of "Edward Ratcliffe" - though until 5/1904 advertisements continued to appear under both "Exors of Edward Ratcliffe" and "Edward Ratcliffe" titles.

Premises acquired by Edward Ratcliffe included the Broughton Engineering Works, adjacent to Broughton Hall - later Broughton & Bretton - station (on PR/9); the Providence Iron Works (previously Phoenix Wagon Works) at Ffrith (Padeswood) Junction (PR/9-10); and a yard at Hawarden station on the WM&CQJ Rly 'loop line' (PR/54) - which did not exist prior to 1889. The Broughton Works lease was reported to have expired in 1896, and there was an auction 12/8/1896 "by order of Edward Ratcliffe" to clear the site - this sale included at least one locomotive. However, advertisements in 10/1898 and for years thereafter still referred to stores at "Broughton Hall, Padeswood, and Hawarden MSL stations". The Ffrith Junction (Padeswood) site was in Edward Ratcliffe's possession by 2/1896, but had been vacated by 1915.

The last reference seen to the business is an advertisement placed by "F.J.Ratcliffe, Hawarden" in J/MM/20.1.1933.

With the exception of the Hawarden station site, the other premises each had sidings sufficient to justify the (perhaps occasional) use of shunting locos, but no evidence has been found as to such useage. As dealers, there may be locomotives featured in their advertisements which are merely 'ghosts' - locos owned and retained by others, offered for sale by Ratcliffes as speculative agents hopeful of commission. It is virtually impossible to identify such locomotives today.

Locomotives known to have passed through Ratcliffe hands are as follows:

Locomotives: Gauge 4'8½"

WEST YORKSHIRE	0-6-0ST	IC	MW	126	1864	(a)		(1)
ELLEN	0-4-0ST	OC	MW	444	1873	(b)		(2)
JUBILEE	0-4-0ST	OC	MW	991	1887	(c)		(3)

(a) wfw(tdx?): Manston Coal Co Ltd, near Leeds [c10/1882 ?]
(b) wfw(tdx?): Hindley Field Coal Co Ltd, Bickershaw, Lancs.
(c) wfw(tdx?): John Woolley, contractor (of Wrexham) [c1890 ?]

(1) wlw(tdt?): Ord & Maddison Ltd, Middleton in Teesdale.
(2) wlw(tdt?): Thos Bolton & Sons Ltd, Widnes, Lancs
    wlw: Mostyn Ironworks, by 1914.
(3) wlw(tdt?): Thos Bolton & Sons Ltd, Widnes, Lancs.

Also: In 7/1872 the North Hendre Lead Mining Co Ltd purchased a secondhand locomotive engine from "Ratcliffe & Sons of Hawarden" for £250, and used it as a stationary engine. [see HENDRE LEAD & LIMESTONE in Section 3.]

"Ratcliffe & Sons near Chester" ordered, on 1/8/1899 and 7/9/1899, two new AE locos. These locos, AE 1407 and AE 1408, were delivered direct to Ratcliffes' customers - MOSTYN IRONWORKS, and QUEENSFERRY CHEMICAL WORKS [see Section 3]. For another locomotive that may have passed through Ratcliffe hands, see CUDWORTH & JOHNSON, loco MERSEY BH 1059 (footnotes).

Sample advertisements seen which refer to locos ("ghosts" or "real"):-

6/1879:	3'6" gauge Chaplin loco for sale	(Ed.Ratcliffe, Hawarden).
8/1879:	4wc 11" BP £400	(Ed.Ratcliffe, Hawarden).
3/1884:	6wc tank MW	(Ed.Ratcliffe, Hawarden).
1888:	4wc 8" cyl loco for sale	(Ed.Ratcliffe, Hawarden).
4/1892:	3'0" gauge tank loco	(Ed.Ratcliffe, Hawarden).
4-12/1896:	Locos 8" to 11" (Ed.Ratcliffe, "Four [sic] works; Broughton Hall, Padeswood, Hawarden - no connection with any other firm".)	
4-11/1896:	Full page separate advert., no locos, but by "Ratcliffe & Sons Established 1846, Hawarden Iron Works, Chester -Hawarden Station".	
8/1896:	Auction Broughton Works including loco or locos [not clear], for Ed.Ratcliffe	
4/1904:	Two 10" locos for sale, in need of repair	(Ratcliffe & Sons).
9/1904:	3'0" gauge loco WANTED	(Ratcliffe & Sons).
8/1917:	10" 4w loco for sale	(Ratcliffe & Sons).
7/1926:	14" 4w ST by P 1917	(Ratcliffe & Sons (Hawarden) Ltd).
1/1933:	8" to 10" 4w loco WANTED	(F.J.Ratcliffe, Hawarden).

NOTE: The 3'0" gauge loco in 1892 is perhaps the same one advertised by Cooper & Tullis in 7/1892 - see PR/54 (Section 2).

THOMAS SAVIN, RAILWAY CONTRACTOR; 1856 to 1866

The history of public railways in mid-Wales dates from around October 1855, when David Davies ("Top Sawyer", of Llandinam), together with a partner named Parry, commenced his career as a railway contractor by starting construction of the Llanidloes & Newtown Railway. Parry soon withdrew, his place being taken by Thomas Savin. Davies and Savin took on other jobs, until the partnership was dissolved on 29/10/1860.

Thereafter, Davies continued at first alone, then in partnership with a Mr Roberts, building railways south into Cardigan; whilst Savin concerned himself with central- and north-Wales, occasionally working alone, sometimes joined by his brother John, but more usually it was his brother-in-law John Ward who assisted. The "company" was variously known as 'Savin & Ward', 'Savin & Co', or just simply 'Savin' - and this latter form is used within this Handbook.

Savin was not a simple contractor, but became deeply involved in everything he touched. He financed some of his own work, often accepted payment in the form of Shares, joined some Companies as a Director, and usually operated - initially at least - the railways he had built. He was thus in a position to expand "his" locomotive fleet at the expense of individual railway Companies - and he did not hesitate to transfer locomotives from railway to railway with no apparent regard as to their legal ownership.

Savin "failed" (ie, became insolvent, though actually never made a bankrupt) on 5/2/1866. He effectively then retired from railway contracting, and Companies were obliged to find others to complete their lines, or to take over their own operations. On the Cambrian Railways, for example, Henry Coneybeare (Engineer) played an active part until his dismissal in 11/1866; David Davies then re-emerged as a working director to supervise, together with Sir James Falshaw, the completion of construction.

Nevertheless, the Savin name survived; John Savin remaining as lessee operator of the Nantlle Railway (PR/2) and as Manager of the Carnarvonshire Railway (PR/29); Savin & Co - later Savin & Co Ltd - continued operating their coal mine and limestone quarries around Porthywaen and Oswestry. Just how much influence Thomas Savin exerted from the shadows seems unknown.

In 1863-1864 Savin numbered all "his" then-existing locomotives into one numerical series; after 5/2/1866 it took time for some of the locos to be traced and returned to their rightful owners. However, the majority belonged to Companies which had amalgamated as, or into, the Cambrian Railways ("Cam.Rys.") Company - formed 25/7/1864 - and thus the Savin fleet numbers became the basis of the Cam.Rys. locomotive number series (1 to 56, with gaps).

Of the railways dealt with in this book, Savin was involved in PR/2, PR/15, PR/20 (as Davies & Savin), PR/24, PR/29, PR/30, and PR/32 (as Savin). Locomotives known to have been used on these railways are dealt with in Section 2; but as further research will doubtless reveal other loco transfers, a composite listing of all the locos known to have been connected with Savin is given here for reference. However, a few of these, particularly those associated with the original Rumney Railway, must be considered very doubtful for north-Wales useage.

Locomotives: Gauge 4'8½"

1	ENTERPRISE	0-6-0T		EBW	[? 301	1852]		
		[? sold by EBW as 601 1857]					New 2/59	CR
	DOVE	2-2-2	IC	SB	55	1839	(a)	s/s by/1864
	SQUIRREL						(b)	s/s by/1864
3	MILFORD	0-4-2ST	IC	SS	1123	1859	New 3/59	CR
	LLEWELYN						(c)	s/s by/1864
	LLANIDLOES						(d)	s/s by/1864
	DART	tender loco					(e)	BM
	FAIRY	tender loco					(f)	BM
	LEON						(g)	(1)
	STAG							(2)
	ANTELOPE	0-6-0	IC	SG	[? 358]	1857	(h)	BM
	ELEPHANT	0-6-0	IC	SG	[? 359]	1858	(h)	BM
4	WYNNSTAY	0-4-2	IC	SS	1146	1859	New 10/59	BM
5	MONTGOMERY	0-4-2	IC	SS	1147	1859	New 10/59	CR
6	GLANSEVERN	0-4-2	IC	SS	1148	1859	New 11/59	BM
2	RUTHIN	0-4-0	OC	MW	19	1860	New 10/60	CR
7	LLANERCHYDOL	0-4-2	IC	SS	1224	1860	New 12/60	CR
8	LEIGHTON	0-4-2	IC	SS	1225	1860	New 12/60	CR
9	VOLUNTEER	0-4-2	IC	SS	1226	1860	New 12/60	CR
10	PIONEER	0-6-0ST	IC	MW	35	1861	New 12/61	BM
11	QUEEN	0-6-0	IC	SS	1301	1861	New 12/61	CR
12	PRINCE OF WALES	0-6-0	IC	SS	1302	1861	New 12/61	CR
13	GREEN DRAGON							
	(WHIXALL to c1863)	0-6-0ST	IC	MW	36	1862	New 1/62	CR
25	DWARF	0-4-0ST	OC	Worsdell		1862	New 3/62	(3)

No.		Name	Type	Cyl	Mkr	MkrNo	Year	Notes	Owner
14		NANTCLWYD	0-6-0ST	IC	MW	45	1862	New 4/62	CR
15		HEREFORD	0-6-0ST	IC	MW	49	1862	New 5/62	BM
16		DE WINTON	0-6-0	IC	MW	41	1862	New 6/62	BM
17		MERION	0-6-0ST	IC	MW	52	1862	New 8/62	(4) CR
18		CARDIGAN	0-6-0ST	IC	MW	55	1862	New 10/62	CR
19		HERCULES	0-6-0	IC	SS	1341	1862	New 11/62	CR
20		VULCAN	0-6-0	IC	SS	1342	1862	New 11/62	BM
21		LILLESHALL	0-4-0ST	OC	LIL		1862	(i)	CR
22	Ø	LITTLE USK (f. USK)	0-6-0ST	IC	MW	58	1862	New 12/62	BM
23		TINY	0-4-0ST	OC	MW	63	1862	New 12/62	(5)
24		BORTH	0-6-0ST	IC	MW	66	1863	New 1/63	(6)
26		TUBAL CAIN	0-6-0	IC	SS	1343	1863	New 2/63	CR
27		CAMBRIA	0-6-0	IC	SS	1344	1863	New 2/63	CR
28		MAZEPPA	2-4-0	IC	SS	1400	1863	New 3/63	CR
29		PEGASUS	2-4-0	IC	SS	1401	1863	New 3/63	CR
30		ALBION	2-4-0	IC	SS	1412	1863	New 3/63	CR
31		MINERVA	2-4-0	IC	SS	1413	1863	New 3/63	CR
1		ALEXANDRA	0-6-0	IC	SS	1408	1863	New 3/63	BM
2		BRECKNOCK	0-6-0	IC	SS	1409	1863	New 3/63	BM
34	*	CADER IDRIS (f. TALERDDIG)	0-6-0	IC	SS	1310	1861	(j)	CR
35	*	CASTELL DEUDRAETH (COUNTESS VANE to pre 5/1865)	0-6-0	IC	SS	1311	1861	(j)	CR
36		PLASFYNNON	0-4-0ST	IC	SS	1431	1863	New 6/.63	CR
37		MOUNTAINEER	0-4-0ST	IC	SS	1432	1863	New 6/63	(7) CR
38		PROMETHEUS	0-4-0ST	IC	SS	1433	1863	New 6/63	CR
39		SIR WATKIN	0-6-0	IC	SS	1445	1863	New 6/63	CR
40		CYFRONYDD	0-6-0	IC	SS	1446	1863	New 6/63	CR
41	*	COUNTESS VANE (f. CADER IDRIS)	2-4-0	IC	SS	1485	1864	New 3/64	CR
42		GLANDOVEY	2-4-0	IC	SS	1486	1864	New 3/64	CR
43		PLYNLIMON	2-4-0	IC	SS	1487	1864	New 3/64	CR
44		RHEIDOL	2-4-0	IC	SS	1488	1864	New 3/64	CR
45		RHIEWPORT	0-6-0	IC	SS	1530	1864	New 8/64	CR
46		TOWYN	0-6-0	IC	SS	1531	1864	New 8/64	CR
47		USK	2-4-0	IC	SS	1580	1865	New 4/65	BM
48		WYE	2-4-0	IC	SS	1579	1865	New 4/65	BM
4		CAERLEON	0-6-0	IC	SS	1587	1865	New 4/65	BM
5		CAERPHILLY	0-6-0	IC	SS	1588	1865	New 4/65	BM
51		SNOWDON	0-6-0	IC	SS	1590	1865	New 4/65	CR
52		HARLECH	0-6-0	IC	SS	1597	1865	New 5/65	CR
53		GLADSTONE	2-4-0	IC	SS	1633	1865	New 10/65	CR
54		PALMERSTON	2-4-0	IC	SS	1632	1865	New 10/65	CR
55		TREFLACH	2-4-0	IC	SS	1655	1865	New 12/65	CR
56		WHITTINGTON	2-4-0	IC	SS	1656	1865	New 12/65	CR
-			2-4-0		EBW		1856	(k)	(8)
-			2-4-0		Jones		[? 1853]	(m)	(8)

Ø Loco 22 USK probably renamed LITTLE USK about the time that loco 47 was delivered, ie c4/1865. C.D.Phillips, dealer of Newport, Mon, was advertising 3/1882 for sale a 6wc 12" [J/CG/1882/808] MW loco named LITTLE USK, which was probably MW 58.

*   The changes of names of locos 34, 35 and 41 are uncertain. 41 is reported as being renamed COUNTESS VANE by Cam.Rys. in 1867; from this one may presume that loco 34 was renamed at much the same date - hence neither alteration is applicable to this SAVIN list. However, a loco was definitely named CASTELL DEUDRAETH by 5/1865.

(a) reputed to have come from south-Wales to David Davies for the Llanidloes & Newtown Rly construction c1856; it was perhaps a one-time Birmingham & Derby Junction Rly loco.
(b) purchased by Davies & Savin in 1858; source unknown.
(c) with Davies & Savin on Llanidloes & Newtown Rly by 8/1859; source unknown.
(d) source unknown; with Davies & Savin on Llanidloes & Newtown Rly.
(e) source unknown; was with Savin on Brecon & Merthyr Rly 3/1865, and later on Aberystwyth to Machynlleth contract 10/1868.
(f) source unknown; with Savin on Brecon & Merthyr Rly in 1865.
(g) current information is as footnote (e).
(h) possibly Rumney Railway locos used by Savin on Brecon & Merthyr Rly; but also reputed to have been with David Davies on Newtown & Machynlleth Rly before passing to Savin in 1863.
(i) exhibited by Lilleshall Iron Co at the London Exhibition in 1862; sold to Savin "as new" 12/1862.
(j) tdx: David Davies, Newtown & Machynlleth Rly, 1/5/1863
(k) LNWR number 1141 sold by LNWR 12/1865 to Savin for Denbigh to Corwen Rly (see PR/20).
(m) LNWR number 1136 sold by LNWR 12/1865 to Savin for Denbigh to Corwen Rly (see PR/20).

CR - locos taken into Cam.Rys stock after 2/1866
BM - locos taken into Brecon & Merthyr Rly stock after 2/1866

(1) still lying at Savin's yard, Ysyslas, 10/1868; sold for £20 in 7/1870 by Cam.Rys. on behalf of Brecon & Merthyr Rly.
(2) the "remains" of this loco sold 1/1870.
(3) all sources seem agreed that this loco did not become Cam.Rys. property; it was however auctioned in "The Railway Yard, Oswestry" on 2/7/1867 along with other railway materials [J/CDH/22.6.1867/4] and purchased by I.W.Boulton, dealer, Ashton-under-Lyne [B/123/215].
(4) see also BRYNKINALLT COLLIERY (Section 3).
(5) nominally Brecon & Merthyr Rly property; in 2/1866 it was "lost" but found 10/1868 working at Savin & Co, Coed-y-Go Colliery, Porthywaen. Sold to Savin & Co by B&M Rly for £450, 11/1868.
(6) nominally a Cam.Rys. loco; sold by Cam.Rys. for £775 to Llynfi Coal & Iron Co, 12/1867
(7) nominally a Cam.Rys. loco, but loaned by Savin to Brecon & Merthyr Railway, who hired it to Dowlais Iron Co c1866; later retrieved by Cam.Rys.
(8) presumably delivered as intended to the Denbigh, Ruthin & Corwen Rly - certainly there in later years (see PR/20 - Section 2).

WHITLEY BROTHERS, CONTRACTORS, WREXHAM

Operated from various addresses, including Hirdar Lodge, Salisbury Park and Holt Road; general civil engineering contractors including roadworks; ceased trading in 1970s. They used narrow-gauge railways on some contracts, and the locos they are known to have owned are listed below. In 1953 a large number of 3ft gauge wagons were found stored at the Rhosesmor Sand Pits, near Mold - a few still remained 9/1967. Local advice was that these had been stored there by Whitley Bros since pre-WW2 and that there had been at least two steam locos stored with them. Other locos may have been stored at Wrexham between contracts.

Locomotives: Gauge 2'0"

		4wPM	20hp FH	1666	1930	New		A	s/s
		4wPM	10hp FH	1928	1935	New #	B	(1)
		4wPM	10hp FH	1929	1935	New #	B	(5)
		4wPM	10hp FH	1930	1935	New		B	s/s
		4wPM	8hp FH	1931	1935	New		B	(2)
		4wPM	8hp FH	1932	1935	New		B	s/s

\#   FH 1928 a rebuild of FH 1653;   FH 1929 a rebuild of FH 1596.

Locomotives: Gauge 3'0"

		BIDDY	4wTG	VB	S	6897	1927	(a)	C	s/s
		BARBY	4wTG	VB	S	6898	1927	(b)	C	s/s
No.4	STOCKS	0-4-0ST	OC	HE	1436	1922	(c)	C	(3)
12	HOLLINS	0-4-0ST	OC	HE	1437	1922	(d)	C	(4)
6	DIKE	0-4-0ST	OC	HC	1452	1921			
		rebuilt		HC		1933	(e)	C	(3)

A: delivered to Colwyn Bay 4/1930, for unknown contract.
B: delivered to Ince & Elton (presume for Helsby-Shotwick roadworks) 6/1935
C: used on construction of Helsby-Shotwick Arterial Road (A5117) in c1933-1936.
Whitley also had 1938-1939 contract, repairs to storm damage Aberystwyth Promenade, where a 2ft gauge railway is believed to have been used.

(a) arrived after 9/8/1932 by 1934.
      wfw(tdx?): County Borough of Derby Riverlands Scheme.
(b) arrived after 7/6/1933 by 1934 - also wfw(tdx?): Derby Riverlands.
(c) arrived c1934 after 2/3/1933 - also wfw(tdx?): Derby Riverlands.
(d) arrived after 12/6/1933 by 12/10/1934 - wfw(tdx?): Derby Riverlands.
(e) arrived by 5/1935.
      wfw(tdx?): Barnsley Corporation, Scout Dike & Royd Moor Reservoirs, for sale there 9/1934.

(1) loco scrapped on or by 10/9/1946.
(2) wlw: S.J.Seager, Aeroplane Sand & Gravel Pits, Woodley, Reading.
(3) wlw(tdt?): Stewarts & Lloyds Ltd, Islip Quarries, Northants, 1940
(4) s/s; [? wlw: Lehane, McKenzie & Shand Ltd, contractors]
(5) wlw: Maen Offeren Slate Quarry, by 4/1954

Note: the five 3ft gauge locos listed above were advertised for sale by Whitley Bros in 5/1936 [eg J/CJ/20.5.1936].

W.O.WILLIAMS, MACHINERY MERCHANT, HARLECH
(Gm/GR:582315)

Based at a depot in Nant Road, "Will Scraps" (as he was known throughout the area) dismantled many closed quarries - sometimes using locomotives in the process - and also dealt in locos and railway equipment.

Relevant details, where known, are shown under the appropriate quarry entries in this Handbook.

To date, only two locos have actually been reported as being observed at his premises; a plate-less Hudson Hunslet 20hp model seen in 1954, and R&R 93 seen in 1956 (both are included in the list below). Details of other sightings would be welcome.

Two 2ft gauge 16/20hp RH locos known to have been owned are listed; it is probably one of these that was advertised ["16/20hp diesel Ruston built 1941 2'0" gauge"] for sale by Williams in J/MM/25.8.1950.

Locomotives: Gauge 2ft

-		4wPM	10hp RP	51901	1917	(a)	(1)
	DIANA	0-4-0T	OC KS	1158	1917	(b)	(2)
No.14		4wPM	20hp MR	[? c1922]		(c)	(3)
242		4wDM	20hp RH	210955	1941	(d)	(4)
-		4wDM	20hp RH	203001	1941	(e)	(5)
		4wBE	BE			(f)	(6)
		4wBE	BE			(f)	(6)
		4wDM	20hp HE	c1940		(g)	(7)
		4wDM	R&R	93		(h)	s/s

(a) purchased from Oakeley Slate Quarry 1/2/1941; may have remained at Blaenau Ffestiniog until re-sold.
(b) purchased from Oakeley Slate Quarry 31/3/1942; may have remained at Blaenau Ffestiniog until re-sold.
(c) with Williams by 1948.
     wfw: Shanks & McEwan Ltd, contractors, Carnbroe Depot, Lanarkshire, to 8/7/1943 at least.
(d) here by 5/10/1949.
     wfw: Army, RASC Bottesford, Notts, until 9/1947 at least.
(e) tdx: Thos.W.Ward Ltd, dealers, Templeborough, Sheffield, 29/11/1948
     wfw: Ministry of Supply; purchased by Thos.W.Ward "lying at Derby" 25/10/1946; and hired out in Yorkshire prior to sale to Williams.
(f) on 3/2/1950 Thos.W.Ward Ltd, dealers (of Sheffield) bought two 2ft gauge Battery Electric locos from E.Smith & Son, Chester, and re-sold them the same day "as and where lying" to W.O.Williams.
(g) at Harlech by 4/1954 [? wfw: Ministry of Supply].
(h) tdx: Caernant (Croft) Granite Quarry, Llithfaen, after 7/1954 by 7/1956.

(1) wlw(tdt?): R.S.Davies, dealer, Mold, by 9/1952.
(2) wlw(tdt?): Penyrorsedd Slate Quarry, by 4/1946.
(3) Used by Williams on demolition contract, Croesor Junction to Porthmadog section of Welsh Highland Rly (see PR/44). Abandoned on site.
(4) used on Ffestiniog Railway (see PR/3) for demolition work at Moelwyn Granite Quarry 6/1952 to 1/1953.
    tdt: Caernant (Croft) Granite Quarry, Llithfaen, by 26/7/1954.
(5) tdt: Caernant (Croft) Granite Quarry, Llithfaen, by 26/7/1954.
(6) no further trace.
These were probably the "two Brush battery locos 2ft gauge without batteries" for sale by W.O.Williams in J/MM/16.2.1951.
(7) not at Harlech 6/1955; no further trace.

JOHN WOOLLEY, CONTRACTOR, WREXHAM

Contracts undertaken:

1/1887 -	10/1887	:	PR/52 Wrexham Exchange to Central construction.
1888 -	8/1888	:	PR/52 Wrexham Exchange to Central widening.
c1888 -	1889	:	PR/47 Gwersyllt (Stansty) to Brymbo upgrading.
2/1889 -	3/1890	:	PR/54 Buckley Junction to Shotton construction.

Locomotives: Gauge 4'8½"

Name	Type	Cyl	Builder	No.	Date		
JUBILEE	0-4-0ST	OC	MW	991	1887	New 3/87	(1)
WREXHAM	0-4-0ST	OC	MW	81	1863	(a)	(2)

(a) the only evidence that Woolley had this loco seems to be a scribbled entry "J.Woolley" amongst a much-altered list of owners beside this loco in the MW 'Engine Book'. It appears that the previous owner was Knight & Pilling, contractors (of Bolton) [and perhaps on their LNWR Moor Street Station (-1874) Contract].
This loco was previously named WARWICK [a name which arises at both FFRWD IRONWORKS and LITTLE MOUNTAIN COLLIERY - which both see].

(1) wlw: Thomas Bolton & Sons, Widnes, Lancashire;
per or via Edward Ratcliffe, dealer, Hawarden [c1891-94 ?]
(2) apparently wlw: J.T.Firbank, contractor [and perhaps on his Chesham to Rickmansworth Metropolitan Railway (1887-1889) Contract].

SECTION TWO

PUBLIC RAILWAYS
AND ASSOCIATED CONTRACTS

This Section summarises the Public Railways that have been constructed, or partly constructed, within North Wales. The basic details of each railway are set out in chronological order based on dates of first opening to traffic. A diagram index appears on the next few pages for quick reference; for more extended reference the index at the rear of this book should be consulted.

A principal purpose of this Section is that it provides a framework for the listing of details of the contractors' locomotives used for the construction, reconstruction and demolition of railways. This approach has the advantage that it is easier to find details concerning any particular line, even if the name of the contractor concerned is unknown. It also clearly reveals those locations where knowledge is currently lacking.

A secondary purpose of this Section is the listing of locomotives used for the actual operation of such railways. In the case of standard gauge railways, such locos were often of "industrial" character, and in many cases were in fact used as "industrial" locomotives elsewhere during their lives.

Standard-gauge locomotives within the fleet of a Major Railway Company are not listed. In this context, within this Section, Major Railway Companies are defined as British Railways, LMSR, LNWR, LNER, GCR, MS&LR, GWR, and Cambrian Railways (Cam.Rys.).

The ownership of each railway is listed beneath its title, but only so far as to a Major Railway Company; thereafter it is to be assumed that ownership took the normal national course of 1923 Grouping and 1948 Nationalisation where appropriate.

Each "railway" is referenced by a number in the 'PR/n' series, and such numbers are used for cross-reference purposes throughout this Handbook.

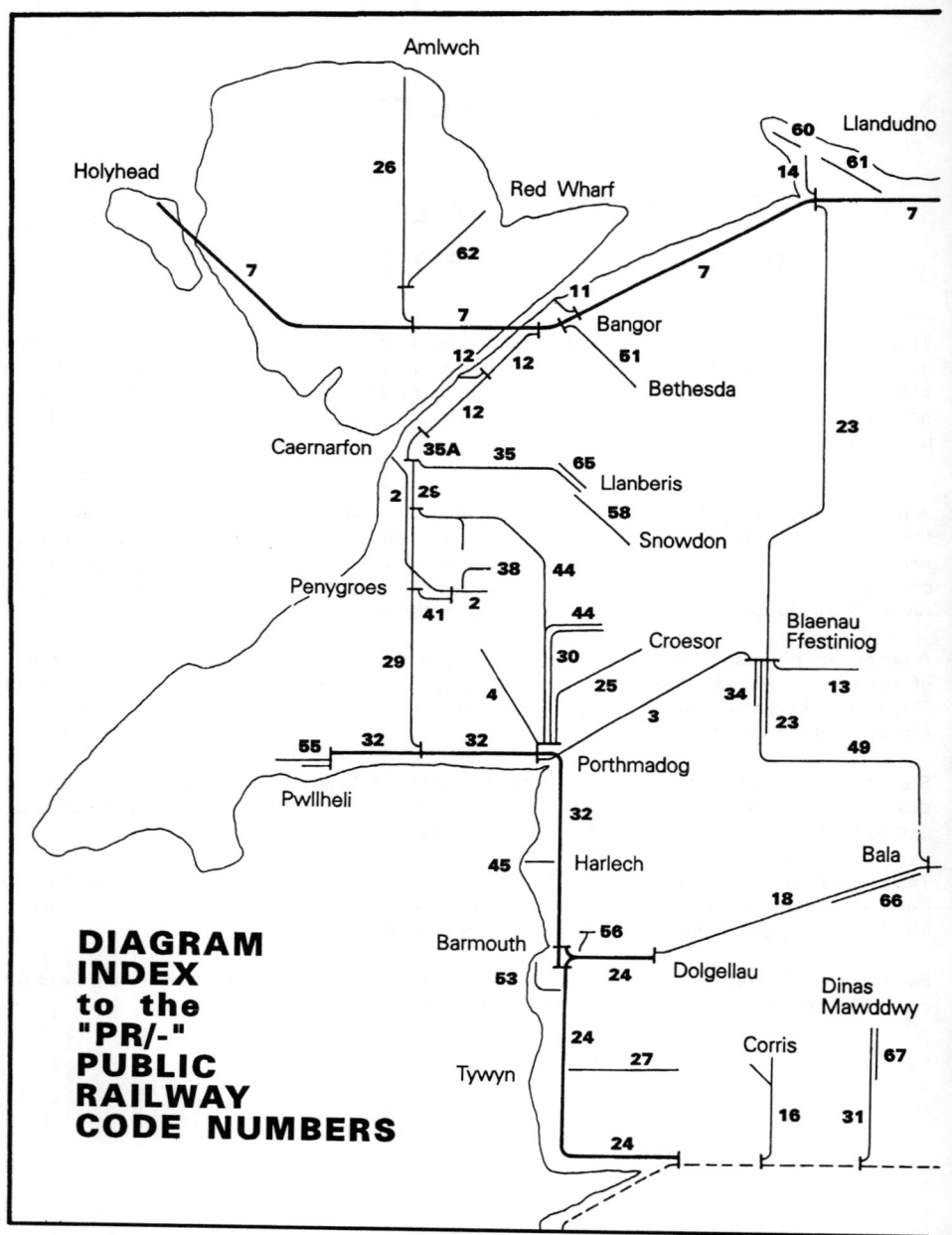

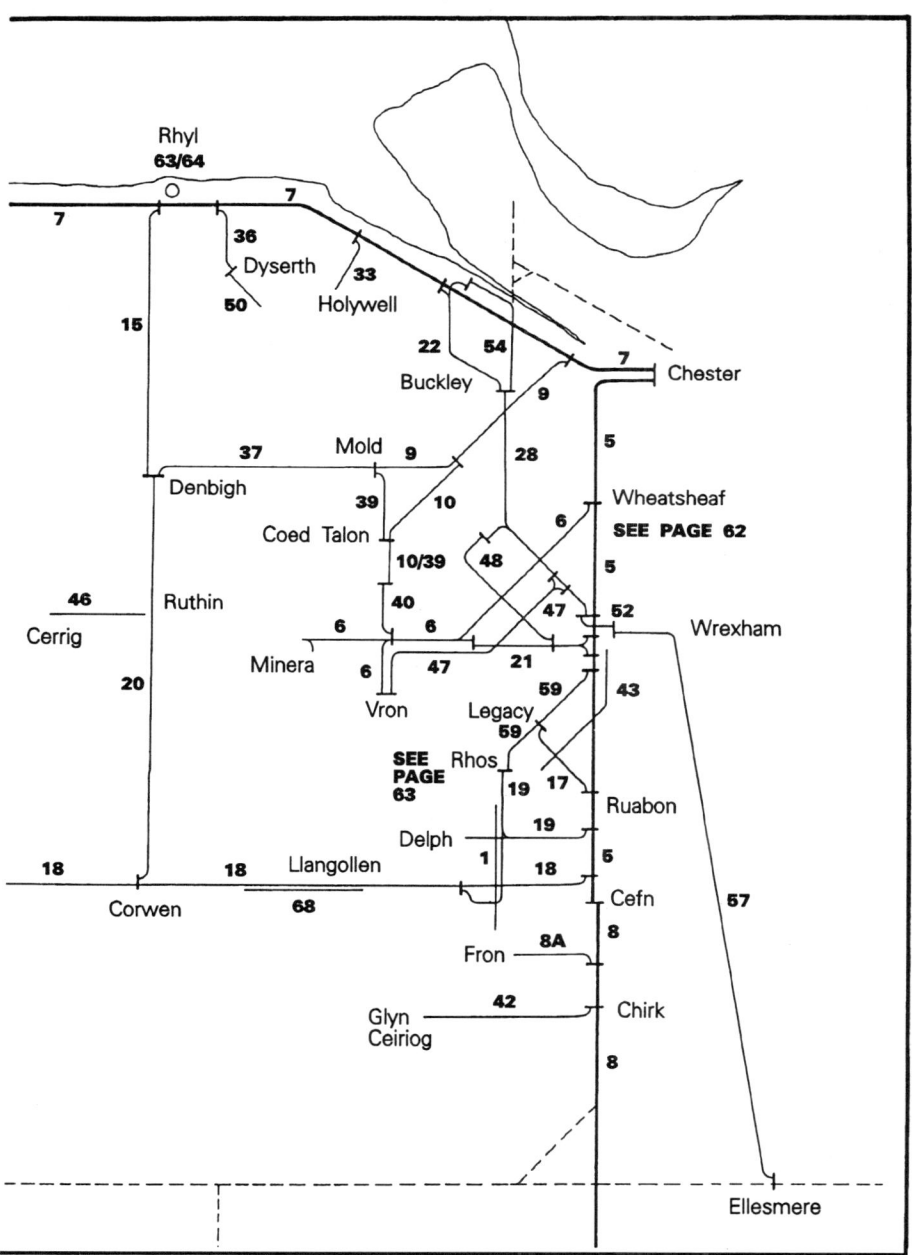

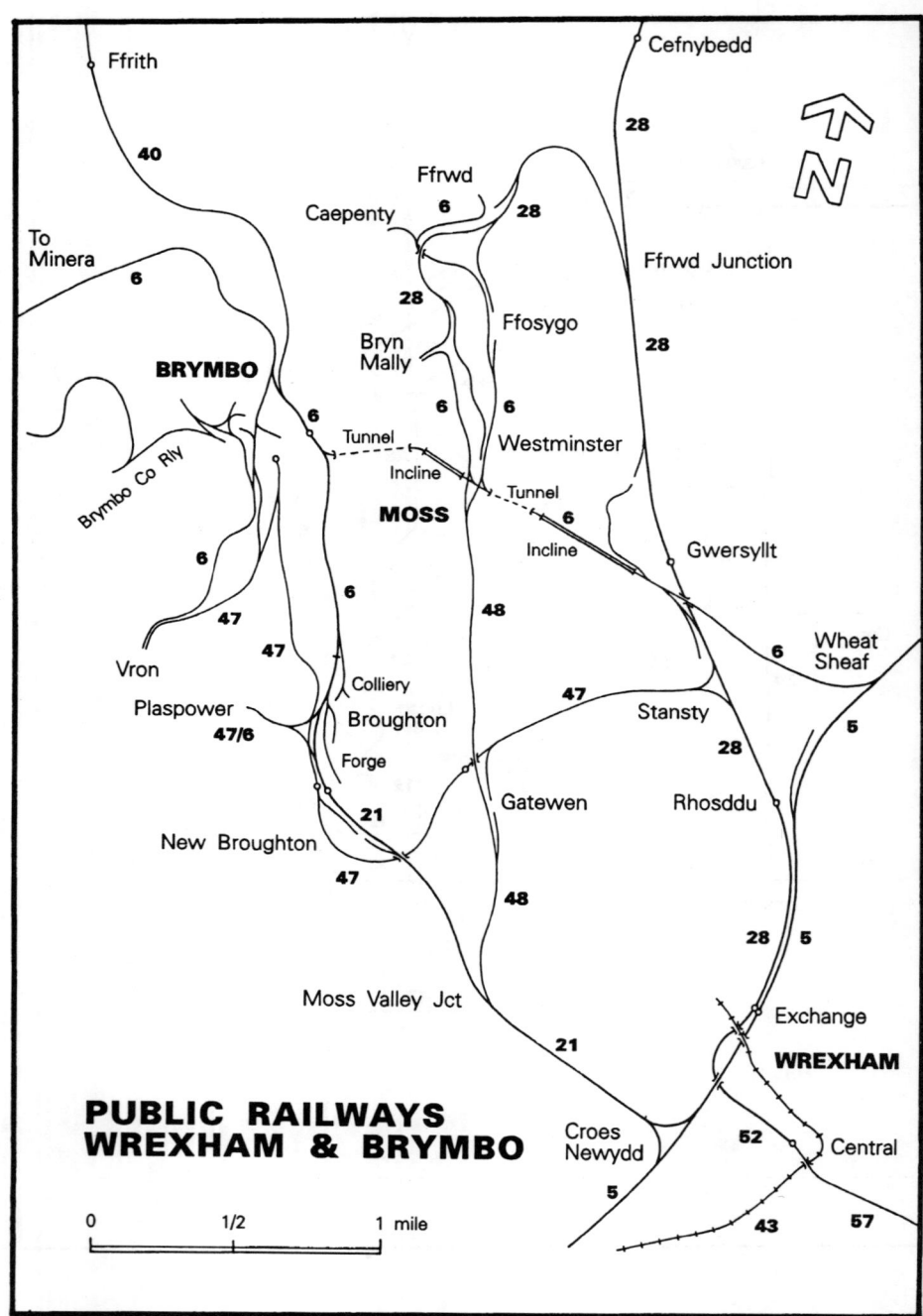

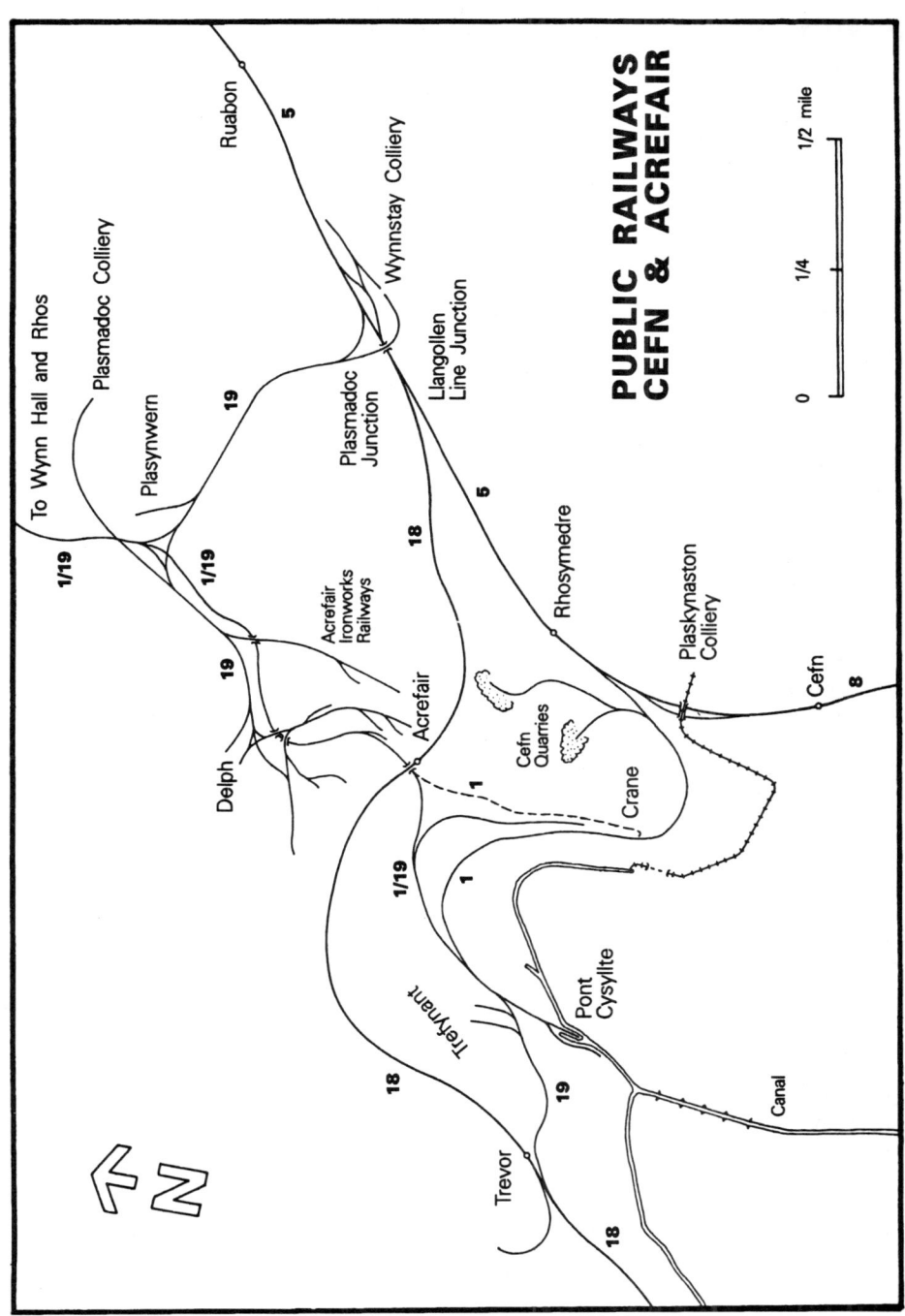

PONTCYSYLLTE to AFON EITHA (WYNN HALL) PR/1
"Ruabon Brook Tramroad" & "Cefn Tramway"

3¼ miles

Ellesmere Canal Company	: Act 29/6/1804
Ellesmere & Chester Canal Company	: from 1/7/1813
Birmingham & Liverpool Canal Co	: from 1845
Shropshire Union Railways & Canal Co	: from 1846
Leased to LNWRly (by Act 6/1847)	: from 1/7/1849

LMSR/BR as inheritors of the SUR&C Co lease - Wharf area.
GWR/BR as purchasers of most of the line - (see PR/19).

CONSTRUCTION

Gauge: narrow

Contractor	: **William Hazeldine** of Plas Kynaston, Cefn.
Work started	: 1804. First useage of Tramroad: 26/11/1805.
Work completed	: c1809.

Narrow-gauge tramroad from the canal wharf (GR:273424) at Pontcysyllte to Hazeldine's Plaskynaston Colliery (a number of small pits in the general vicinity of Plas Kynaston house (GR:282422); the Plaskynaston deep mine (Waterloo Pit) was not sunk until 1865). This Tramroad first used 26/11/1805. From a mid-point (GR:278423; subsequently known as The Crane) on this line, the Tramroad was extended northwards via Acrefair Ironworks and Collieries (serving, inter-alia, other Plaskynaston pits) to Plas-y-Waen (Plas-yn-Wern) and to the "Plas Madoc Colliery" (again, small pits, centred on GR:289442); line open to Plas Madoc 1808.   Extended further c1809 from Plas-y-Waen to Plas Bennion coal pits, to Ruabon Foundry (GR:293447), to various pits of Wynn Hall Colliery, the Wynn Hall Spelter Works (GR:287452) and to Afon Eitha (Ruabon Brook) Colliery (GR:285453).

The line was horse-worked and described as a "double rail way", a term then in vogue to describe track in which each "rail" consisted of two cast-iron plates (for strength), and not meaning "double track" in the modern sense of the phrase.

"The Crane" was used to trans-ship long rigid loads (e.g. girders) which could not negotiate the extremely sharp reverse-curvature of the Tramroad at this junction.

NOTES

A)   A branchline commenced near Plaskynaston Pottery (GR:277423) and ran southwards to Dolydd Colliery (GR:278421) then generally south-easterly to Wm.Lacon's Newbridge Forge on the River Dee. This branch, open by 1820, closed in 1823. The track was removed and used for repairing the remainder of the system.

B)   From c1810, a network of rudimentary plateways extended northwards from Afon Eitha to Pant and Rhos, thence along Market Street and Hall Street to GR:289468, thence northerly through open country to Llwyneinion Iron & Brick Works. From GR:289468 a branch (which had largely been built as an isolated line c1760) ran easterly via Mountain Street etc. to Ponkey Ironworks; and a second branch ran westerly to coal pits and brickworks around GR:286466.   These plateways were under various ownerships, but precise details are not yet known.   They had become fragmented, and mostly disused, by 1860.

C)   From GR:285443, north of Plas y Waen, a branch line ran north-westerly to the Christionydd Collieries (GR:282449).

[Read: J/DHS/1982, 1983; B/118/107; B/163; B/303]

RECONSTRUCTION - STAGE ONE   Gauge: 4'8½"

Contractor - no details known. Work started   : 11/1861
                                Completed   : 1/1867

In late 1861 the LNWR started to replace the Tramroad with a 4'8½" gauge locomotive railway, constructed at leisure on a route which incorporated sections of the Tramroad. This new line reached Afon Eitha c1865; was extended northward in 1866 to Llwyneinion (thus effectively replacing the privately owned tramroad 'B' above) and opened throughout in 1/1867. The 4'8½" gauge line was now 4¼ miles long.

The branch from Plas-y-Waen to Plas Madoc was not converted but remained tramroad until replaced by the private Plas Madoc Railway (see PR/19, and ACREFAIR IRONWORKS).

The new loco line followed a much shorter direct route between Trefynant and Acrefair, the Tramroad between Acrefair and The Crane being then closed and dismantled. This trackbed was sold 1/1867 and became King Street.

The original Tramroad from Pontcysyllte via The Crane to Plas Kynaston was sometime extended to serve two of the stone quarries at Cefn, and remained in use until 1882. As such, it was about 1¼ miles long and became known as the CEFN TRAMWAY. In 1882 it was truncated at both ends, the central portion being dismantled. At Pontcysyllte, a portion remained in use connecting the canal wharf to the Trefynant Brickworks and Pits, whilst at the Cefn end a portion remained in use connecting the stone quarries to exchange sidings on the GWR main line (PR/8) ¼ mile south of Rhosymedre Station.

[Note also that a new tramroad was built c1865, on a parallel but more southerly course to the above abandoned section, connecting Plaskynaston (Deep) Mine to the branch canal at Plaskynaston Pottery. This line closed c1897.]

OPERATION

Locomotives: Gauge 4'8½"

Initially the line was operated by locos from the Acrefair Ironworks (New British Iron Co).
From 1/1871 the SUR&C Co (i.e. the LNWR) worked the line, until 2/1896. "The other day, an engine which takes trucks to and from Messrs Bertrams' coal pit to the wharf at Ruabon, smashed a gate to pieces at the level crossing at Plasbennion" [J/CDH/27.4.1872/6c5]. (Bertram & Co operated Wynn Hall Colliery - J/CDH/26.10.1872/1c5.) "On the Shropshire Union Railway at Ruabon, a coal train came into collision with another train that was shunting. Mr Beddows, local manager of the Company....[was injured]." [J/CDH/31.1.1874/5c4]. This suggests more than one loco on the line, but so far only one has been identified.

      ACTON   0-4-0tank   SB   663   1850 (a)   (1)

(a)   tdx: LNWR, 1118 ACTON, 12/1870.
      wfw: Coed Talon Collieries.

(1)   a loco built by Sharps, named ACTON [thus perhaps this loco] was scrapped 3/1883 at
      LNWR Crewe Works.

RECONSTRUCTION - STAGE TWO   Gauge: 4'8½"

Traffic ceased between Afon Eitha and Llwyneinion in 1879, and the track was lifted. The 4'8½" gauge line, including the trackbed to Llwyneinion, but excluding the Pontcysyllte canal wharf sidings (which remained SURC/LNW/LMS/BR-LMR property) was purchased with effect from 12/2/1896 by the GWR. For later history see PR/19.

It is unlikely that the SURC/LNW/LMS retained a loco at Pontcysyllte Wharf but confirmation has not been found. The Wharf was virtually disused by 1945; the track was later removed, probably in 1953.

CAERNARFON (QUAYS) to PENYGROES to TALYSARN to NANTLLE PR/2
"Nantlle Railway"   9¼ miles

Nantlle Railway Company	: Act	20/5/1825
Leased by **Edward Preston**	: by	c7/1856
Owned by **Thomas Savin**	: from	1862
Carnarvonshire Railway Company	: from	25/7/1867
London & North Western Railway Co	: from	4/7/1870

CONSTRUCTION   Gauge: 3'4½"(clear); 3'6"(c/c)

Contractors   : **H.Owen & Co**, and **Edward Parry**.
First contract let 17/4/1827: Track laying started 1/1828.

OPERATION

Opened for full distance 12/7/1828 (for freight); 11/8/1856 (for passengers). All traffic horse-operated until c1960, when a farm tractor was also occasionally used. In recent times at least, and certainly since British Railways took over in 1948, actual operation of the line was contracted to local hauliers who provided their own horses.

RECONSTRUCTION & PARTIAL CLOSURE

The last official public passenger tram ran on 10/6/1865.
The line from Caernarfon (Pant) to Tyddyn Bengam (north-Penygroes) was converted to 4'8½" gauge and operated in conjunction with the Carnarvonshire Railway (PR/29) from 1866, until the two companies amalgamated 25/7/1867.
Section Caernarfon (Pant) to Caernarfon (Quays) closed 22/2/1872.
Section Tyddyn Bengam to Talysarn closed 1/8/1872 (replaced by PR/41).
The remaining section Talysarn to Nantlle was diverted at various locations over the years to suit adjacent quarrying activities.

CLOSURE & DEMOLITION (Talysarn-Nantlle)

Last freight tram ran 11/1963; line officially closed 2/12/1963.
Track lifting started 11/1965 in piecemeal fashion: in 4/1968 track still in-situ Talysarn Quarry to Dorothea Junction - this was lifted late in 1968.

Details of demolition contractors not known.

[Read: B/118, B/147, B/175]

PORTHMADOG HARBOUR to BLAENAU FFESTINIOG (DUFFWS)   PR/3
(and GLANYPWLL to DINAS (Rhiwbryfdir) : 1¼ miles)   13¼ miles

    Festiniog Railway Company   : Act 23/5/1832
    Assisted by Festiniog Railway Society Ltd (reg.24/12/1954) since 1954.

CONSTRUCTION   Gauge: 1'11½" (clear); 2'1" (c/c)

First Sod: 26/2/1833.
Contractor   : **James Smith** (of Caernarfon) until 4/1834
Festiniog Rly Co direct labour from 4/1834.
Track laid with rails at 2'1" centre gauge; when heavier rails were substituted this became 1'11½" clear-between-rails gauge.

OPERATION

Opened for freight 20/4/1836, horse and gravity operation.
Steam locomotives used from 23/10/1863 [J/NWC/31.10.1863/8].
6 coaches are "now at Portmadoc" - J/CDH/20.2.1864/5c1.
Opened to passengers 6/1/1865.
Also leased and operated the Welsh Highland Railway (see PR/44) from 19/7/1934 to 21/6/1937.

DEVIATIONS

Moelwyn tunnel cut from 12/1839 and opened 24/5/1842 to replace adjacent route via inclines. Other deviations, to avoid sharp curves, were made at Boston Lodge Cottages, Garnedd Tunnel, west of Tanygrisiau, and elsewhere. It is understood that no contractors' locomotives were involved in these works.
A contract was "open" 4/1898 for deviation of the route of the Dinas branch near Blaenau Ffestiniog; this work was done, but not known by whom.

CLOSURE & PARTIAL DEMOLITION

Dinas branch closed to passengers 1870. Entire railway closed to passengers 15/9/1939, and to freight 1/8/1946. From 7/10/1946 until 11/1963 a short section from Duffws to Blaenau Ffestiniog LMS Yard (PR/23) was leased and operated, for freight only, by the Maenofferen and Votty & Bowydd slate quarries. For details of locos used by these quarries see Section 3.
Track lifted on Dinas Branch 10-12/1955 by George Cohen, Sons & Co Ltd - no locos used.
Track lifted Tanygrisiau to Moelwyn Tunnel by Sir Alfred McAlpine & Sons Ltd in 1957 - no locos used.
Remaining tracks at Duffws lifted by FR Co, 10-11/1968.

REOPENING & RECONSTRUCTION

Reopened to passengers Porthmadog to Boston Lodge 23/7/1955, and onwards in stages, to Blaenau Ffestiniog opened 25/5/1982.
New route constructed by FR Co and FR Society between Dduallt and Tanygrisiau; work started 1965, section opened 25/6/1978. For details of locomotives used on this work see later.
The original route Dduallt-Moelwyn Tunnel was retained as a siding during these works, but subsequently abandoned, and track removed by FR Co.

[Read: B/147, B/166-170, B/178; J/FRS]

Locomotives: Gauge 1'11½"

To aid understanding of the extensive fleet, the locomotives are segregated here into three groups - firstly, those that are (or have been) fully equipped and used for train operation; secondly those used only for shunting, maintenance and construction works, and, thirdly, those not belonging to the FR but which have been long-term guests of the railway. All listings are, as far as possible, in chronological order of arrival on the railway. The Welsh Highland Railway locos, included in FR stock from 7/1934 to 6/1937, are not included here - see PR/44 for details.

Most of the "train operation" locos have been extensively rebuilt over the years - some, indeed, many times. Full details are not given here as extensive information is readily available (in, e.g. B/168 and B/169).

Only the current, or last-carried, identity numbers and name are listed. Changes known to have occurred are keyed to the asterisk (*) footnote.

Locomotives: Train Operation

		Name	Wheel	Cyl	Builder	Works No.	Date	Notes	Ref
	*	MOUNTAINEER	0-4-0Tt	OC	GE		1863	New 7/63	(1)
No.1	*	PRINCESS	0-4-0STt	OC	GE	[± 200] 1863		New 7/63	Ø
	*	PALMERSTON	0-4-0STt	OC	GE		1863	New [/64 ?]	Ø
No.2	*	PRINCE	0-4-0STt	OC	GE	[± 199] 1864		New /64	
No.5		WELSH PONY	0-4-0STt	OC	GE	234	1867	New /67	Ø
No.6		LITTLE GIANT	0-4-0STt	OC	GE	235	1867	New /67	(2)
"No.7"	*	LITTLE WONDER	0-4-4-0T	4OC	GE		1869	New (a)	(3)
No.8		JAMES SPOONER	0-4-4-0T	4OC	AE	+ +	1872	New /72	(4)
No.7	*	TALIESIN	0-4-4T	OC	VF	791	1876	New 8/76	(5)
No.10		MERDDIN EMRYS	0-4-4-0T	4OC	FRCo		1879	New 7/79	
No.3	*	LIVINGSTON THOMPSON	0-4-4-0T	4OC	FRCo		1885	New 6/86	(6)
		MARY ANN	4wDM		MR	[? 596] 1917		(b)	
(No.11)		MOELWYN	2-4-0DM		BLW	[?49604 1918]		(c)	
No.11		MOEL TRYFAN	0-6-4T	OC	VF	739	1875	(d)	(7)
		-	0-6-0ST	OC	P	2050	1944	(e)	(8)
		LINDA	2-4-0STt	OC	HE	590	1893	(f)	
		BLANCHE	2-4-0STt	OC	HE	589	1893	(g)	
K1			0-4-4-0gt	4OC	BP	5292	1909	(h)	(9)
		MOUNTAINEER	2-6-2T	OC	ALCo	57156	1917	(i)	
		UPNOR CASTLE	4wDM		FH	3687	1954	(j)	
	*	EARL OF MERIONETH	0-4-4-0T	4OC	FRCo		1979	New 6/79	
	*	CONWAY CASTLE	4wDM		FH	3831	1958	(k)	

± These numbers not confirmed, but were found stamped on parts of motion of these locos [J/FRS/No.100/28]. Logically, one may suspect that '199' on PRINCE was on parts inherited from MOUNTAINEER.

Ø These locos survive on FR but are not in the operational fleet:

PRINCESS: Wdn 8/1946; later on display at Blaenau Ffestiniog, and subsequently within museum at Porthmadog Harbour Station.

PALMERSTON: Loaned to Vale of Rheidol Railway, Aberystwyth, for part-summer seasons 1912, 1913, 1914, 1921 and 1922. Loaned to Sir Robert McAlpine & Sons Ltd, contractors on Welsh Highland Railway (see PR/44) 9/5/1923 to 6/1923. Wdn by 1940; used as stationary boiler at Boston Lodge. tdt: Mr A.Headech for preservation 20/7/1974; later returned to FR incomplete for restoration to continue at Boston Lodge.

WELSH PONY: Wdn by 1938; subsequently on static display outside Porthmadog Harbour Station (where for a period it displayed additional name MERLEN GYMRAEG).

+ + There are doubts re the AE works number/s of this locomotive. From the evidence in the few surviving AE building records, it appears that three numbers were used during construction - 914 (for the boiler) plus 929 and 930 for each power bogie unit. One photo exists showing a plate reading: Avonside Engine Co/late/Slaughter Gruning & Co/1872 No.930/Bristol.

*Renumbering, Renaming, Alternative names:
There are numerous published versions of the "running numbers" applied to the first four locos. From contemporary documents and newspaper reports, there is little doubt that MOUNTAINEER was the first to arrive, followed closely by THE PRINCESS. The first loco arrived in Porthmadog "on Saturday last" and "about two hours after its arrival in the town it was placed on the line of railway, and pushed across the embankment to the foundry....another engine is on its way to the Port...." [J/NWC/25.7.1863/2]. The second soon arrived - "THE PRINCESS... MOUNTAINEER...whilst LORD PALMERSTON has not reached here yet" [J/HC/1.8.1863/2c6]. There were still only two locos here when the line opened to steam [J/NWG/31.10.1863/8] but three had arrived by 2/1864 [J/CDH/20.2.1864/5c1]. Clearly THE PRINCE arrived last, and subsequently the four locos were referred to as if numbered in the arrival sequence. However, any evidence that the locos actually carried such numbers seems totally lacking. Early photographs show THE PRINCESS bearing No.1 - other early photographs of this group of locos reveal no numbers at all. In later years, No.2 was applied to PRINCE, and PALMERSTON carried No.4 on front bufferbeam in c1920's.

No.1 PRINCESS; ex No.1 THE PRINCESS (as 0-4-0Tt).
No.2 PRINCE; ex PRINCE; ex THE PRINCE (as 0-4-0Tt).
PALMERSTON; no evidence found to confirm name 'Lord Palmerston' carried; note that the quotation of this name above was in advance of its arrival.
LITTLE WONDER referred to as No.7 in archives, but no evidence found to confirm number ever actually carried.
No.7 TALIESIN; ex No.9 TALIESIN until 1885.
No.3 LIVINGSTON THOMPSON;
    ex No.3 EARL OF MERIONETH/IARLL MEIRIONYDD until 31/10/1971;
    ex No.3 TALIESIN until 22/4/1961;
    ex No.3 LIVINGSTON THOMPSON until 5/1932.
    Built New as "No.11" but apparently renumbered No.3 before entering service 6/1886.

EARL OF MERIONETH (1979) carries name IARLL MEIRIONYDD on other side.

CONWAY CASTLE carries name CASTELL CONWY on other side. A third nameplate reading CONWY CASTLE was used at the naming ceremony 5/7/1986 but was not carried by the loco in service.

Locomotives: Shunting & Engineering

	-	4wPM	20hp	MH		c1922	(sa)	(s1)
	-	4wPM	c20hp	AD			(sb)	Scr/1934
	-	6wDM	60hp	KS	4415	1928	(sc)	(s2)
	-	2w-2PMr	c2hp	?			(sd)	Scr
	"BUSTER"	2w-2PMr	c2hp	FRCo		1955	(se)	
	-	2w-2PM		Wkm	1543	1934	(sf)	
	TYKE	4wDM	20hp	HE	2290	1941	(sg)	(s3)
JGF1	SANDRA (f.JANE)	4wDM	20hp	MR	8565	1940	(sh)	#
	THE COLONEL	4wDM	20hp	MR	8788	1943	(si)	#
	ALISTAIR	4wDM	13hp	RH	201970	1940	(sj)	(s7)
	MOEL HEBOG	0-4-0DM		HE	4113	1955	(sk)	
5628	MONSTER	2w-2PM	10hp	FRSociety		1974	(sm)	(s4)
	ANDREW	4wDM	13hp	RH	193984	1939	(sn)	(s7)
JGF2	THE LADY DIANA (f.DIANA)	4wDM	20hp	MR	21579	1956	(so)	
	"THE GROGAN"	4wBE		WR	5537	1956	(sp)	(s5)
JGF4	"SLUDGE"	4wDM		L	41545	1955	(sq)	(s6)
JGF3	CORA (f."SANDRA")	4wDM	20hp	MR	22119	1961	(sr)	
	ASHOVER	4wDM	50hp	FH	3307	1948	(ss)	
	HARLECH CASTLE) CASTELL HARLECH)	0-6-0DH		Bg	3767	1983	(st)	

\# Locos originally privately owned by Col A.H.CAMPBELL and used on FR by special arrangement; later incorporated in FR stock. See footnotes for further details.

Locomotives: Guests of the Railway

NOTE: Short term visits of locos for repair etc., and non-essential "transfers for fun" (see Introduction), are not listed.

242		4wDM	20hp	RH	210955	1941	(ga)	(g1)
	KIDBROOKE	0-4-0ST	OC	WB	2043	1917	(gb)	(g2)
No.1	BRITOMART	0-4-0ST	OC	HE	707	1899	(gc)	
99.3462		0-8-0	OC	OK	12518	1934	(gd)	(g3)
		4wDM	6hp	L	29890	1946	(ge)	(g4)
		4wDM	6hp	L	34521	1949	(ge)	(g4)
		4wPM	20hp	MR	1895	1919		
		rebuilt		MR	3694	1924	(ge)	Dsmt/1975
		4wDM	20hp	MR	21615	1957	(ge)	Dsmt/1975
		2-6-0	OC	BLW	15511	1897	(gf)	OOU
	"SYBIL MARY"	0-4-0ST	OC	HE	921	1906	(gg)	(g5)

(a) This loco is sometimes credited to the Fairlie Engine & Steam Carriage Co Ltd, who took over the GE works in autumn 1869 (perhaps 9/1869). This loco, delivered by 24/8/1869, must have been built by GE, though perhaps invoiced by FE&SC Co Ltd.

(b) purchased 7/1923 from Kent Construction & Engineering Co Ltd, Ashford, Kent - a reconditioned 40hp Petrol Simplex loco. This loco has worksplates MR 507/1917, but per MR records, MR 507 was rebuilt by MR in 1926 as MR 3848, for another customer. Loco arrived on FR with petrol engine Dorman 4JO 6247, which was originally fitted to MR 596, hence suggested identity here - but this engine could have

been removed from MR 596, reconditioned, then fitted to this (FR) loco by KC, who handled many similar locos.
MR 596 was new to War Department, WDLR 2317.
Converted to diesel loco by FR. No name carried until 8/1971; it was referred to as number 101 pre 1939, but not known if this number was actually carried.

(c) In 3/1925 Col.Stephens contracted with Honeywill Bros, dealers, Ashford, Kent for the purchase (on hire-purchase terms arranged by E.W.Farrow & Sons, Engineers Merchants, Spalding, Lincs) of TWO "Baldwin Tractors" for the "Festiniog & Welsh Highland Railway" but only one such loco appears to have arrived in Wales.
Reconditioned 45hp 0-4-0Petrol loco ex French Artillery Railways.
Loco arrived on FR without BLW plates, and its suggested identity has been deduced from the serial number of its Pittsburgh Model Engine Co engine and BLW records.
If indeed BLW 49604, then:-
    wfw: French Artillery Railways No.1491.
        Re-engined diesel in 1956.
        Modified to 2-4-0 and nameplates fitted in 1957.

(d) tdx: Welsh Highland Railway (PR/44), 1937. (Loco actually VF 739 chassis, with VF 738 boiler, cab, tanks, name, etc.)

(e) tdx: North Eastern Gas Board, Harrogate Gas Works, Yorks.
     per W.Grace & Sons, dealers (of Oldham, Lancs) 20/8/1957

(f) tdx: Penrhyn Slate Quarries (as 0-4-0ST) 14/7/1962.
     Modified by FR to 2-4-0ST in 1970

(g) tdx: Penrhyn Slate Quarries (as 0-4-0ST) 17/12/1963.
     Modified by FR to 2-4-0ST in 1972

(h) tdx: BP, Gorton, Manchester, 23/3/1966.
    wfw: Tasmanian Government Railway, until 1947

(i) tdx: Mr P.J.G.Ransom, private store in London, 15/10/1967.
    wfw: Tramway de Pithiviers a Toury, France, 3.23. orig: WDLR 1265.

(j) tdx: Welshpool & Llanfair Light Railway (as 2'6" gauge), 13/2/1968.
    wfw: Admiralty, Lodge Hill & Upnor Rly, Kent, YARD No.44, to 2/1962

(k) tdx: Admiralty, Ernesettle, Devon, (as 2'6" gauge), 29/4/1981

(sa) tdx: Aluminium Corporation, Dolgarrog, 4/1924 [see DOLGARROG RAILWAYS in Section 3].

(sb) tdx: P.& W.Anderson Ltd, contractors, Torrington & Halwill Railway construction (1923-1925) Contract, Devon.
Per J.I.C.Boyd [B/169/330; B/174/334], loco purchased 7/1925.
However, the sale of the Anderson equipment at Marland 9/9/1925 included a 2ft gauge Austro-Daimler loco.

(sc) tdx: Welsh Highland Rly (PR/44) 3/1929; on trial, per KS.

(sd) this entry represents one or more very small self-propelled platelayers trolleys formerly used on both Welsh Highland Rly (PR/44) and FR, and which was/were later "dumped" at Boston Lodge Works. In 7/1952, one example was noted as "Sheffield Car No.17633" and it carried a plate "Supplied by George Cohen, Sons & Co Ltd".

(se) New: a reconstruction of one of the above.

(sf) tdx: British Railways (as 4'8½" gauge), 1962

(sg) tdx: Festiniog Railway Society, Leeds, 9/3/1964
    wfw: HE, Leeds, to 8/10/1962.
    wfw: WD, Long Marston, Warwicks.

(sh) tdx: St.Albans Sand & Gravel Co Ltd, Smallford, Herts; R4: 15/7/1966.
Property of Col.A.H.Campbell of Dduallt until transferred to FR stock 4/1971

(si)   tdx: St.Albans Sand & Gravel Co Ltd, Smallford, Herts; R14: 15/7/1966.
       Property of Col.A.H.Campbell of Dduallt.
       tdt: Llanberis Lake Railway (PR/65) 2/1977
       tdx: PR/65 to Col.Campbell, 8/6/1979; later transferred to FR stock.
(sj)   tdx: Bierrum & Partners Ltd, Smallford Depot, Herts, 27/2/1968
(sk)   tdx: HE, Leeds, 1968.
       wfw: NCB, Shaw Cross Colliery, Dewsbury, Yorkshire
(sm)   arrived New 5/1974; built by FR Society North Staffs Group, incorporating engine of Lister Road Truck No.5628 ex British Rail Engineering Ltd, Crewe.
(sn)   tdx: Smith & Son Ltd, Raunds Manor Brickworks, Northants, 7/4/1974
(so)   tdx: FR Society, North Staffs Group, 1974 by 20/7/1974
       wfw: Upper Tame Drainage Authority, Minworth, Warwicks, to 10/1972
(sp)   tdx: Alan Keef, dealer, Cote, Oxon, 27/9/1975
       wfw: Wheal Jane Ltd, Clemows Shaft, Cornwall.
(sq)   tdx: FR Society Midlands Group, 1/5/1976.
       Incorrect plate on loco reading L 41445.
       wfw: R.Taylor, Stoneleigh N.A.C., Warwicks.
       wfw: Coventry Corporation, Finham Sewage Works.
(sr)   tdx: Anglian Water Authority, Ely, Cambs, 24/6/1977
       per Track Supplies & Services Ltd, Wolverton, Bucks.
(ss)   tdx: East Anglian Transport Museum Society, Carlton Colville, Suffolk, 10/1981
       wfw: Ashover Light Railway, Derbyshire.
(st)   tdx: Bg, loan, 5/1985 - new loco built for I.N.A. (Instituto Nacional do Acucar), Mozambique, but order cancelled.
       tdt: Bg, off loan, c1987.
       wlw: Bredgar & Wormshill Light Rly, Kent
       tdx: Bredgar, 22/2/1989

(ga)   tdx: W.O.Williams, Harlech Plant Depot, 6/1952; used at Tanygrisiau for demolition of Moelwyn Granite Quarry.
(gb)   tdx: Oakeley Slate Quarry, Blaenau Ffestiniog, c11/1961;
       stored by owner Mr R.Hilton at Minffordd Yard.
(gc)   tdx: Penyrorsedd Slate Quarry, Nantlle; per Mr A.J.Hills, 6/1963
(gd)   tdx: Steamtown, Carnforth, 11/5/1972
       stored by owner Vale of Rheidol Equipment Ltd at Boston Lodge.
(ge)   from Cumberland Moss Litter Industries Ltd, Anthorn, Cumbria; per or via Mr E.N.Jones of Leeds, 11/1975; stored at Minffordd.
(gf)   tdx: Usina Santa Thereza de Goiana, Pemanbuco, Brasil, 5/1990
(gg)   tdx: Mr C.Pealling, c/o Lynton & Barnstaple Railway Association, Landkey, Devon, 1991 by 26/2/1991

(1)   Possibly this was the loco hired to Mr Bray in 1876 (see PR/44); Wdn/1879; Scrapped.
(2)   Wdn/1932; dismantled; most components scrapped 1955
(3)   Wdn/1879; Scrapped 1883
(4)   Wdn/1929; dismantled by 9/1933; most components later scrapped.
(5)   Wdn/1930; dismantled by 9/1933; most components scrapped 1935
(6)   Wdn 31/10/1971 (named EARL OF MERIONETH); stored pending restoration, firstly at Minffordd, then at Glanypwll; returned to Minffordd 30/12/1987.
       tdt: York Railway Museum, 10/1988
(7)   Not used since 1937; partly dismantled c1938; scrapped c10/1954
(8)   Never used on FR.
       tdt: Bredgar & Wormshill Light Rly, Kent, 23/2/1989
(9)   Never user on FR
       tdt: York Railway Museum, 25/6/1976

(s1) tdt: Aluminium Corporation Ltd, Dolgarrog, 8/1924
(s2) tdt: KS at Stoke on Trent, 8/1929;
       wlw: Sir Lindsay Parkinson, contractor, East Lancs Road construction, 21/8/1919
(s3) Wdn by 1975; chassis only:-
       tdt: Bicton Woodland Railway, Devon, 1985
(s4) tdt: Mr R.P.Morris, private store, 2/5/1976
       wlw: Gloddfa Ganol (see OAKELEY SLATE QUARRY).
(s5) tdt: private store near Mold for repairs, 1978
       wlw: Gwynfynydd Gold Mine, by 12/5/1982
(s6) tdt: Mr D.W.Best, Bredgar, Kent, 19/5/1983
(s7) tdt: Mr A.Gartell, Yenstone, Templecombe, after 3/4/1991 by 5/1991

(g1) tdt: W.O.Williams, Harlech Plant Depot, 1/1953
(g2) tdt: Mr R.Hilton, North Moreton, Didcot, Berks, 19/4/1970
(g3) tdt: Dampfkleinbahn Muhlenstroth, Gutersloh, W.Germany, 11/12/1978
(g4) tdt: Leeds City Museum, per Exors of Mr E.N.Jones, c5/1977
(g5) sold to Groudle Glen Railway, Isle of Man, 1991

PORTHMADOG to TREMADOG to BRAICHYBIB to GORSEDDAU   PR/4
BRAICHYBIB to BLAEN PENNANT   8 miles and 5 miles
"Gorsedda Railway"

Martin Williams Esq. (of Bryngwyn, Denbighs)	: by 1845 - 1857
Bangor & Portmadoc Slate & Slab Co Ltd	: 2/1857 - 1870
(reg.25/2/1857 £105K vol.liq.4/1870)	
Gorsedda Junction & Portmadoc Railways Co	: Act 25/7/1872

CONSTRUCTION   Gauge: 3ft

Contractors: no details discovered.

First section constructed was 3ft gauge horse-worked tramroad 1½ miles long from Porthmadog Harbour to Tremadog Ironstone Mines. The route of this "intended" line was open for lease 9/1840; the line was in use by 1845. Extension of 3ft gauge line from Tremadog to Gorseddau Slate Quarry (6½ miles); tenders for construction invited 4/1856, line opened 5/1857 [J/NWC/16.5.1857]. [Note: 'Gorseddau' is spelled 'Gorsedda' in almost all contemporary documentation. 'Gorseddau' is a more correct spelling in fact.]

RECONSTRUCTION & EXTENSION   Gauge: 2ft

Plans were made in 1869 for a 2ft gauge line, from Cwm Dwyfor (Blaen Pennant) via Prince of Wales then direct to Cricieth Harbour, to be constructed by the Tram-Railway Company of Great Britain Ltd (reg.1869, £500K) and operated by Patent Locomotives designed by Thomas Page [who built Westminster and Chelsea Thames bridges, etc] - [J/MJ/1869/668, 673, 815]. The New Prince of Wales Slate Co Ltd (reg.1868) was an interested party in this venture [J/MJ/1869/936]. The scheme was abandoned, and the GJ&P Rlys Co was formed in 1872 to take over the disused Gorsedda Tramroad and extend it to Blaen Pennant [J/MJ/1872/886, 893].

Extension from Braichybib to Blaen Pennant constructed from 1873 using 2ft gauge; existing line Braichybib to Porthmadog re-gauged to 2ft. It is unlikely that the disused Braichybib to Gorseddau section was re-gauged. On 24/6/1881 (another) Prince of Wales Slate Co Ltd was registered, with the intention of acquiring the Prince and Gorseddau Quarries, and the Railway [J/MJ/30.7.1881/922].

OPERATION

Porthmadog to Blaen Pennant opened for public freight traffic in early 6/1875 [J/MJ/12.6.1875/631].
Line not opened to passengers.
The locomotive listed was used during the latter part of the construction of the line, and initially for traffic, but apparently only horses were used as from 1878.

[Read: B/147; B/450; B/285]

Locomotive: Gauge 2ft

PERT	0-4-0VBT VC	DeW	1874 New 7/74	(1)

(1) stored 1878 to 1894 (at least); believed later to Owen, Isaac & Owen, dealers, Union Ironworks, Porthmadog. [and see COEDMADOC SLATE QUARRY - Section 3].

CLOSURE & DEMOLITION

Braichybib to Gorseddau probably not re-opened after the c1876 closure. Entire railway disused by 1892. Track later removed; not known when or who by.

SALTNEY JUNCTION (CHESTER) to RHOSYMEDRE (RUABON)   PR/5
14 miles

SALTNEY JUNCTION to WREXHAM (9 miles)
    North Wales Mineral Railway Company   : Act 6/8/1844

WREXHAM to RHOSYMEDRE (5 miles)
    North Wales Mineral Extension Railway   : Act 21/7/1845

SALTNEY JUNCTION TO RHOSYMEDRE (Complete line)
    Shrewsbury & Chester Railway Co   : From 23/8/1846 (Act 27/7/1846)
    Great Western Railway Co   : From 1/9/1854

CONSTRUCTION   Gauge: 4'8½"

Engineer   : Henry Robertson
Contractors: SALTNEY JUNCTION to WREXHAM:
    Contract let 17/12/1844 to **William Betts** [of Leicester];
    and became **Wm.Betts & Son.**
  : WREXHAM to RHOSYMEDRE:
    Contract let 9/1845 to **Thomas Brassey.**

Locomotives: Gauge 4'8½"

If any locomotives were used during construction, perhaps these would be those first purchased for the operation of the line.

OPERATION

All sources appear to claim that the line from Chester (running powers over PR/7) via Saltney Junction to Rhosymedre, PLUS the freight branch to Saltney Wharf, all opened on either 2/11/1846 or 4/11/1846. However, it does seem more likely that sections of the line would be open, to freight at least, prior to this date.

[Read: B/276; B/301; B/302; B/303; B/304; B/395]

Locomotives: Gauge 4'8½" (prior to GWR 1/9/1854)

No.	Name	Wheel	Cyl	Maker	No.	Date	Status	(Qty)
1		0-6-0	IC	RBL		1845	New	(1)
2		2-4-0	IC	RBL		1845	New	(2)
3		2-2-2	IC	RBL		1845	New	(1)
4		2-4-0	IC	RBL		1845	New	(2)
5		2-4-0	IC	RBL		1846	New	(1)
6		2-4-0	IC	RBL		1847	New 1/47	(1)
7		2-4-0	OC	Jones		1846	New	(1)
8		2-4-0	OC	Jones		1847	New	(1)
9		2-2-2	IC	SB	400	1847	New 2/47	(1)
10	PRINCE OF WALES	2-2-2	IC	SB	405	1847	New 3/47	(1)
11		2-2-2	IC	Bury		1847	New 8/47	(1)
12		2-2-2	IC	Bury		1847	New 9/47	(1)
13		2-2-2	IC	SB	441	1847	New 9/47	(1)
14		2-2-2	IC	SB	[? 521]	1848	New 7/48	(1)

15		0-4-0ST	IC	Bury		1847	New 11/47	(1)
16		0-4-0WT	IC	SB	580	1849	New 5/49	(1)
17		0-4-2	IC	Bury		1848	New 7/48	(1)
18		0-4-2	IC	Bury		1848	New 8/48	(1)
19		2-2-2	IC	Bury		1848	New 9/48	(1)
20		2-2-2	IC	Bury		1848	New 9/48	(1)
21	VICTORIA & ALBERT	2-2-2	IC	SB	[? 524]	1848	New 7/48	(1)
22		2-2-2	IC	SB	555	1848	New 11/48	(1)
23		2-2-2	IC	SB	[? 589]	1849	New 7/49	(1)
24		0-6-0	IC	Hick		1849	(a)	(3)
25		0-6-0	IC	RBL		1849	(b)	(1)
26		0-6-0	IC	Hick		1849	(c)	(3)
27		0-6-0	IC	Hick		1849	(d)	(3)
28		0-6-0	IC	RS	716	1849	(e)	(1)
29		0-6-0	IC	Hick		1849	(f)	(3)
32		2-2-2	IC	Jones		[?c1848]	(g)	(1)
33	WREKIN	0-4-2					(h)	(4)
34		0-4-0	IC	VF	316	1848	(i)	(1)
35		0-4-0	IC	VF	317	1848	(i)	(1)
30		0-4-2	IC	VF	342	1853	New 7/53	(1)
31		0-4-2	IC	VF	343	1853	New 8/53	(1)
24		0-4-2	IC	VF	344	1853	New 9/53	(1)
26		0-4-2	IC	VF	345	1853	New 9/53	(1)
27		2-2-2	IC	SS	744	1853	New 10/53	(1)
29		2-2-2	IC	SS	743	1853	New 10/53	(1)

(a) loan from Birkenhead Railway, No.11 BIRKENHEAD, 11/1851
(b) loan from Shrewsbury & Birmingham Rly, No.11, [? 10/1851]
(c) loan from Birkenhead Railway, No.12 CHESTER, 11/1851
(d) loan from Birkenhead Railway, No.13, 11/1851
(e) loan from Shrewsbury & Birmingham Rly, No.16, [? 10/1851]
(f) loan from Birkenhead Railway, No.14, 11/1851
(g) purchased 11/1852. [? wfw: Shrewsbury & Birmingham Rly, No.24]
(h) purchased 12/1852 - "second-hand", but source not traced.
(i) tdx: VF (the makers), 3/1853 [and see PR/8 Construction Locos].

(1) tdt: GWR, with railway, 1/9/1854
(2) tdt: Birkenhead Rly, loan, c11/1851
    tdx: Birkenhead Rly, off loan, c4/1853
    tdt: GWR, with railway, 1/9/1854
(3) tdt: Birkenhead Rly, off loan, c4/1853
(4) for sale 10/1853; no further trace.

NOTE: the locos referred to by footnotes (a)(c)(d)(f) may not have been renumbered (by the S&CR) in precisely the sequence assumed in the list above, the major source for which is B/103/C [RCTS Locos of GWR].

CLOSURE & DEMOLITION

The ¾ mile freight branch from SALTNEY DEE JUNCTION to SALTNEY QUAY became disused in 1970; the track was lifted c1972 but details are not known.

WHEATSHEAF JUNCTION to MOSS to BRYMBO to MINERA   PR/6
6½ miles

ALSO BRANCHES AS DETAILED BELOW

        North Wales Mineral Railway Company   : Act 21/7/1845
        Shrewsbury & Chester Railway Company   : From 23/8/1846
        Great Western Railway Company   : From 1/9/1854

CONSTRUCTION   Gauge: 4'8½"

Engineer   : Henry Robertson - Brymbo Mineral & Rly Co
Contractor   : **Thomas Brassey** (Contract Let 5/12/1845)

The line ran from Wheatsheaf Junction (on PR/5) to Gwersyllt (thence short branch to Gwersyllt Colliery); up Gwersyllt (rope-worked) Incline to enter 220 yard Summerhill Tunnel to reach Moss (branches here, see below); up Moss (rope-worked) Incline - "the brake" - and through 400 yard Brymbo Tunnel to Brymbo "junction" (branch - see below); to Brymbo "middle" (branch - see below); then via Caello and Coed Poeth to Minera Limeworks (and, later, by reversing junction at Minera, to New Brighton).

OPERATION

Opened to freight, Wheatsheaf Junction to Minera, 7/1847.
[Possibly opened in part, to Moss, to Brymbo, prior to this ?]

BRANCHES - all reputedly opened to freight 11/1847.

Moss to Brynmally Colliery (½ mile) Ø
Moss to Westminster to Ffosygo to Ffrwd (1½ miles) Ø
Brymbo "junction" to Broughton Forge (Southsea) (1¼ miles)
Brymbo "middle" to Ironworks to Vron Colliery (1 mile)

    Ø   Moss branches were authorised by the North Wales Mineral Railway Deviation & Branches Act of 27/7/1846.

[Read: as for PR/5; B/406]

Locomotives: Gauge 4'8½"

Wheatsheaf Junction to Gwersyllt worked by PR/5 locos.
At Moss (between the inclines, and on the branches) only horses were used until c1852. Traffic between Minera, Brymbo and Moss Brake was worked by gravity and horses until c1849, when a locomotive was introduced, named CHAROLETTE [in most sources, though occasionally CHARLOTTE]. On 2/7/1852 two men on this loco were killed when it was hit, at Brymbo Church, near West Crossing, by a wagon running by gravity from Minera. And on 30/7/1866 this loco was derailed between Brymbo and Caello when hauling empty wagons to Minera - the report states that the "first wagon was jammed to the tender of the engine". The identity of this loco is unknown, though it may be one of those listed under PR/5. The 1925 "Brymbo Works Magazine" states it was the "first railway locomotive to Brymbo" and "it did good work for the Company on the Brymbo and Moss branches for many years". But theoretically, by 7/1866, the line to Minera was both owned and operated by the GWR; not by Brymbo Works as "the Company" may infer.

RE-ARRANGEMENT & PARTIAL CLOSURES

Incline and Tunnel from Moss to Brymbo "junction" closed 22/5/1862 when superseded by (PR/21) Wrexham to Brymbo direct line. PR/21 utilised much of the Brymbo "junction" to Broughton Forge branch as part of its route.

Tunnel and Incline Moss to Gwersyllt was virtually superseded by the 1881-82 opening of the (PR/48) Wrexham to Moss ("Moss Valley") line, but was retained as a more direct route to Chester for some traffic until closing 10/1908. The land on which this incline was built was mostly sold to the Westminster Brymbo Coal & Coke Co Ltd 3/1917.

Ffosygo to Ffrwd closed 1904 (track lifted 1915).
Westminster to Ffosygo closed 1917.
Moss to Westminster closed 1925 (track lifted c1940 by 8/1943).
Moss to Brynmally closed 1935 (track lifted 1940).
Brymbo Ironworks to Vron closed c1936.

PASSENGER SERVICE

Introduced Wrexham to Brymbo (via PR/21) 24/5/1882; extended to Coed Poeth 15/11/1897, and to Berwig Halt (Minera) either 1/5/1905 or 6/1905 (sources vary). Closed to passengers Berwig Halt to Coed Poeth 1/1926; Coed Poeth to Wrexham on 31/12/1930.

MINERA to NEW BRIGHTON - (1¼ miles)

This line, built c1850 as a private railway to the Lead Mines (see MINERA in Section 3) was closed in 1914 and lifted.

In 1930, the GWR relaid the line to serve the Minera Silica Stone Quarries; it was then worked by GWR/BR locos until closed in 1957. Per Chester Division Appendix to Working Timetable 1/1/1935, the line was 1m 26ch long with sidings at 73ch up side (Graig Fawr Quarry), 79ch down side (concrete works), 95ch up side (Tir Celyn Quarry). Also, closer to Minera, a facing point (against traffic going up to New Brighton) led to the Minera Lime Company's Tip Siding - the Limeworks loco was Registered by the GWR to permit its use over this section of the branch. Per RCH Handbook of Stations 1956, the concrete works siding was then "Minera Mines Gravel & Concrete Co (Wynne's Siding)".

CLOSURE & DEMOLITION

Wheatsheaf Jct to Gwersyllt closed 1951; track lifted Gwersyllt to Wheatsheaf in 1951; 0m26ch Wheatsheaf to Wheatsheaf Junction (PR/5) retained as siding but lifted in 1952 by 6/1952.
Minera to New Brighton fell out of use in 1950s; track lifted 1962.
Minera to Brymbo (West Jct) closed 1/1/1972 (track lifted c1972).

Thus leaving only Brymbo (Steelworks) to Wrexham (Croes Newydd) open for freight from 1/1972 - for subsequent history see PR/21.

NOTE: Precise details of track lifting, and information re any Contractors or locomotives used for demolition presently not known.

CHESTER to HOLYHEAD   PR/7
                                                    84½ miles

    Chester & Holyhead Railway Company   : Act 4/7/1844
    London & North Western Railway Company : From 1/1/1859

CONSTRUCTION   Gauge: 4'8½"

First Sod 1/3/1845 at Conwy.
Principal Contracts were let between 3/1845 and 5/1846 as follows:

8 miles Chester-Shotton	: Edward Ladd Betts
22 miles Shotton-Rhyl	: William Mackenzie
9 miles Rhyl-Old Colwyn	: Mackenzie, Brassey & Stephenson
5¾ miles Old Colwyn-Lland.Jct(excl)	: Gregson
2 miles Lland.Jct-Conwy & bridge	: John Evans
1 mile Penmaenbach incl.tunnel	: John Harding & John Cropper
7¾ miles Penmaenbach-Llandegai	: Warton & Warden [Sale A below]
6¼ miles Llandegai-Menai	: Thomas Jackson [D]
½ mile Britannia Bridge	: Nowell, Hemmingway & Pearson [B]
22¼ miles Llanfairpwll-Holyhead	: Edward Ladd Betts

Locomotives: Gauge 4'8½"

It is very likely that some, at least, of the Contractors would have used locos (Brassey, for example, owned numerous locos by this time), but details are lacking.

    Sale A : at Penmaenmawr 6/11/1848 for Warton & Warden [J/RT/14.10.1848]; no locos listed.
        B : at Britannia Bridge 4/1850 [J/RT/27.4.1850] (for B.J.Nowell & Co) and 8-11/4/1851 [J/RT/22.3.1851] (for Nowell, Hemmingway & Pearson); no locos listed either sale.
        C : sale [J/RT/1.6.1850] for Peto & Betts included a "loco & tender".
        D : sale 11/1850 for Thomas Jackson included a 14" cylinder "2 coupled" loco. [B/331/188].

On 11/4/1848 the LNWR Minutes record that LNWR four-wheel coupled loco No.78 had been sent to the Holyhead line to be used "in the construction department under Mr Foster". Per B/331/188 this loco was for use by Thomas Jackson on the Bangor section. As LNWR No.78 (a 14" 0-4-0 goods loco built by Bury 1839) was back in LNWR stock 8/1949, and still in stock 6/1852, it is unlikely to be the loco in Sale 'D' above.

The LNWR supplied c2/1848 an unidentified loco to John Evans on the Conwy Bridge contract - this was probably a short-term loan.

A contractors special train conveyed members of the traffic committee over the Llanfairpwll-Holyhead section 31/3/1848. As no LNWR traffic locos were then in Anglesey, this could indicate that Betts had a loco on the island at that date.

A "tramway" was laid around the Britannia Bridge construction site.

OPERATION

Line opened Chester-Saltney 4/11/1846 (for PR/5 trains only).
Line opened Saltney-Bangor 1/5/1848; Llanfairpwll-Holyhead 1/8/1848; Bangor-Llanfairpwll 18/3/1850.
The line was operated from the outset by L&NWR Co under various agreements.

Locomotives: Gauge 4'8½" - railway operation

Although the Chester & Holyhead Rly Co had ordered 50 locos for their line, all of these that were built were apparently delivered direct into LNWR stock - and not necessarily used on PR/7.
Loco DIAMOND 0-4-0 tank SB 663/1850 is reputed to have been sold by Edward Oakeley of Coed Talon Colliery [see Section 3] to the Chester & Holyhead Rly in 3/1852; re-sold by C&H to Birkenhead Rly, No.27, 1/1854; becoming LNWR 356 MEMNON 1/1/1860 (and later used on PR/1 which see). This loco could possibly be connected with the phrase "Lord Penrhyn's locomotive" (see PR/11), but note that all published sources seem to claim that the C&H Rly never owned a loco.

EXTENSIONS AT HOLYHEAD

HA) "Tramway" from Holyhead Station to Admiralty Pier - 1¼ miles.
    George Giles, contractor; started work 12/1850.
    Line opened 20/5/1851; worked by horses.

HB) Main line extended to new Holyhead terminus - ½ mile.
    Contractor not known.
    Opened 14/9/1851 (and Tramway to Pier now shortened).

HC) Reconstruction of Pier Tramway as loco line.
    J.& C.Rigby, contractor - contract let 16/6/1858.
    Line opened c9/1859. (Closed to passengers 31/3/1925, to freight 25/3/1955; track removed.)
    [Note: J.& C.Rigby were busy around Holyhead from 1848 on various harbour contracts, mostly for the Admiralty. See "Holyhead" in Section 3.]

HD) Enlarging inner harbour; building east-shore quay with additional passenger platforms - all per LNWR Act 5/8/1873.
    Contract initially let to **Thomas Bugbird** 10/1874 [J/CDH/24.10.1874/5c1]; re-let 11/1874 to **John Scott (Wigan), John Price Edwards (Wigan)** and **Thomas Bugbird (Caernarfon).** Bugbird withdrew 19/3/1877; thereafter just Scott & Edwards.
    Opened 17/6/1880.

Locomotive: Gauge 4'8½" - Scott & Edwards

ANGLESEY	0-4-0ST	OC	MW	553	1875	New 8/75	(1)

(1) wlw: John Mackay, contractor, Woking-Weybridge widening (c1887) Contract.

The end-of-contract auction at Holyhead 7/7/1881 offered only a 12" 4w MW loco; MW 553 was a 10" loco. 12" could be an error, or it could refer to another loco. The only 12" MW known to be owned by Scott & Edwards at that period is MW 592, which is not recorded as having been used at Holyhead.

AND PERHAPS OF RELATED INTEREST ?

Advert J/TE/4.9.1863: "Wanted, strong secondhand 4 wheel coupled contractors tank loco narrow [ie 4'8½" ?] gauge for ballasting; 10" to 12" cylinders - Harvey, 23 Holywell, Millbank, London, or Mr Cousens, Holyhead".

ADDITIONS & RECONSTRUCTIONS

RA)   CONWY QUAY BRANCH from Llandudno Junction - ½ mile.
      Contractor not known. Opened (freight only) in 1852.

RB)   SEA DEFENCE BRANCHES - lengthy "freight only" branch lines connected to and
      running parallel with the main line, and used for sea-wall maintenance.

   RBa: GREENFIELD to MOSTYN - track removed in 1960s.

   RBb: KINMEL BAY (TOWYN) - built by **Thomas Bugbird**, contractor; track removed in
         1960s.

   RBc: LLANFAIRFECHAN   - track removed c1941 by 4/1942.

RC)   WIDENING MAIN LINE (two tracks to four.)
   a)   2 miles Prestatyn-Gronant   : opened 14/6/1896
   b)   4½ miles Gronant-Mostyn   : opened   7/1900
   c)   7 miles Saltney-Connah's Quay   : work in hand 1899-1900
   d)   3½ miles Rhyl-Prestatyn   : opened   6/1901
   e)   3¼ miles Mostyn-Holywell Jct   : opened 22/6/1902
   f)   4¼ miles Rhyl-Abergele   : work in hand 1901-7/1902
   g)   4 miles Colwyn Bay-Llandudno Jct   : opened 12/6/1904
   h)   1¾ miles Flint (Muspratts)-Bagillt : work in hand c1902-1904, + 1907
   i)   2¼ miles Bagillt-Holywell Jct   : work in hand 1907-5/1909
   j)   2 miles Abergele-Llandulas   : opened 22/6/1915

      Little seems to be known regarding the above contracts other than:-

GATES & THOMAS, CONTRACTORS (of Warrington):
Awarded contracts:-
14/12/1898 contract for enlarging Rhyl Station buildings and other works connected with widening.
15/11/1899 contract widening two bridges between Prestatyn & Rhyl.
23/1/1902 completed new bridge replacing level crossing at Holywell Junction.

Locomotive: Gauge 4'8½" - Gates & Thomas

LADYSMITH No.18	0-6-0ST	IC	HC	560	1900	New Ø		(w1)

Ø   delivered new to Gates & Thomas at Eyton Sidings, Mostyn, 3/1900

(w1) wlw: S.Pearson & Son Ltd, Admiralty Harbour (1898-1909) Contract, Dover, Kent.

C.J.WILLS, CONTRACTOR, "NORTH WALES LINE CONTRACT 1905-1908"

Locomotive: Gauge 4'8½" - C.J.Wills

LILIAN	0-4-0ST	OC	HC	657	1903	(wb)	(w2)

(wb) wfw: T.Wrigley, contractor, Horbury Jct, JEANIE

(w2) wlw: Stowmarket Explosives Factory, 1915.

LOUIS P.NOTT, CONTRACTOR, ABERGELE-LLANDULAS WIDENING
Contract let 15/10/1913 : widening part opened 7/3/1915, fully opened 27/6/1915

Locomotives: Gauge 4'8½" - L.P.Nott

	4wc	OC	HC				(w3)
TUXFORD	0-6-0ST	IC	HE	579	1893	(wc)	(w4)

(wc) here by 8/6/1914
      wfw: L.P.Nott elsewhere; perhaps was used at the Cardiff Corporation Llwynon Reservoir (1910-1914) Contract, Merthyr Tydfil.

(w3) identity unknown; 10"x16" cylinders; for sale here 8/12/1914
(w4) wlw: Cardiff Corporation Waterworks, Cwm Taff, Merthyr Tydfil, by 31/5/1919.

RD)   **RHYL LOCOMOTIVE SHED**

   Contract £1233 for construction let 19/5/1870 to **C.H.Chester** (of Prestatyn). No locos known.

RE)   **LLANDUDNO JUNCTION RECONSTRUCTION**

   Track layout extensively revised and new station built, c1896. Works included a new diversionary route, opened 1/10/1897, onto the Conwy Valley line - see PR/23 for details.

RF) BRITANNIA BRIDGE RECONSTRUCTION

Bridge extensively damaged by fire 23/5/1970.
Contract let 9/1970 for reconstruction.
Reopened for rail traffic (single line only) 30/1/1972.

CLEVELAND BRIDGE & ENGINEERING CO LTD, CONTRACTORS.

Locomotives: Gauge 4'8½"

185   DAVID PAYNE   0-4-0DM   80hp JF   4110006   1950   (wd)   (w5)

There were also two Landrover cars fitted with rail wheels in use on this contract in 1971. Another loco, JF 4110012 was reputedly sent to this job by C.C.Crump & Co (see Connah's Quay Wagon Works - Section 3) but apparently never noted at Britannia Bridge.

Locomotive: Gauge 2ft - track laid through one tube.

No.2   4wDM   20hp RH   235711   1945   (we)   (w6)

(wd)   arrived after 9/1971 by 5/1972;
      wfw: Leslie Sanderson Ltd, Birtley, Co.Durham
(we)   tdx: Penyrorsedd Slate Quarry, Nantlle, by 9/1971

(w5)   left the site after 8/1975 by 3/1976;
      [? tdt: the contractors' depot at Darlington]
(w6)   tdt: Llanberis Lake Railway (PR/65) for storage, 13/6/1974

RG) DEVIATION MOCHDRE to COLWYN BAY

Section diverted 1983-1984 onto adjacent alignment to enable former route to be occupied by new A55 "Expressway" road. No contractors' locomotives were involved in this work.

RH) MOLD JUNCTION LOCO SHED

This depot, opened 1/10/1890, closed on 17/4/1966, had a 2ft gauge railway, with hand-propelled tipper wagons, for removal of ash from fire-dropping point to tip. This line remained in use until 1966.
After closure, the shed and yard were occupied by P.Dobbins (Chester) Ltd, Scrap Merchants - who received loco P 2084 from Llangollen Railway (PR/68) in 10/1978. This loco was visible in the yard here until last noted 30/7/1986, it then being transferred to Steamtown, Carnforth, by 16/8/1986.

CLOSURE & DEMOLITION

All "widened" sections of main line were "narrowed" to two tracks during the 1970s. It is understood that British Railways did this work, and no contractors were involved.

RHOSYMEDRE (RUABON) to CHIRK VIADUCT (to Shrewsbury)   PR/8
5 miles

Within this book we are concerned only with the 5 mile northerly section, extending south from PR/5 to the Wales boundary, of the line to Shrewsbury which totals 25 miles in length.

    Shrewsbury, Oswestry & Chester Junction Rly Co : Act 30/6/1845
    Shrewsbury & Chester Rly Co (Act:27/7/1846)   : From 23/8/1846
    Great Western Railway Company   : From 1/9/1854

CONSTRUCTION   Gauge: 4'8½"

Engineer   : Henry Robertson
Contractor : **Brassey, Mackenzie & Stephenson**
Agent   : Meakin

Locomotives: Gauge 4'8½"

0-4-0	IC	VF	316	1848	New Ø	(1)
0-4-0	IC	VF	317	1848	New Ø	(1)

(Ø)   Locos reputed to have been used by contractor, but not proven.

(1)   reputedly returned to VF for overhaul then re-sold by VF to Shrewsbury & Chester Rly Co, 3/1853

OPERATION

Ceremonial opening of the line on 12/10/1848
Public trains operated from 14/10/1848 or 16/10/1848 (sources differ)

Locomotives: Gauge 4'8½" (until 1/9/1854)

See list of locomotives under entry PR/5

CEFN VIADUCT to FRONCYSYLLTE LIME KILNS   PR/8A
"The Fron Branch"   ¾ mile

Owned by the Great Western Railway in conjunction with the Chirk Castle Estate. No Act was obtained for its construction.

CONSTRUCTION   Gauge: 4'8½"

Contractor: no details known.

OPERATION

The Shrewsbury & Chester Railway Company, prior to it being formally incorporated by Act of 30/6/1845, entered into an Agreement on 4/3/1845 to work this line; and from 1/9/1854 the line was worked by the Great Western Railway Company. Only freight traffic was carried. This line, which was always worked by horses except for a short distance at the viaduct end, passed beneath the canal (at the mid-point of the branch) by means of two turntables, one each side of the canal, plus a short length of track connecting these under the canal bridge.

CLOSURE & DEMOLITION

Traffic ceased some time after 5/1940. Track lifted 10/1949; no details known.

[Read: B/304/128]

MOLD JUNCTION (SALTNEY FERRY) to MOLD   PR/9
                                                10 miles

Mold Railway Company	: Act 9/7/1847
Chester & Holyhead Railway Company	: by 12/1849
London & North Western Railway Company	: as from 1/1/1859

CONSTRUCTION   Gauge: 4'8½"

Contractor   : **Edward Ladd Betts; Peto & Betts** from 7/1848
              Work started   :4/1847 (prior to Act)
              Opened : 14/8/1849 or 14/9/1849 (sources differ)

Locomotives: Gauge 4'8½"

A tender locomotive was included in the sale of contractors' plant held on 25-28/6/1850 [J/RT/8.6.1850; MJ/15.6.1850].

OPERATION

Operated by the LNWR (initially, on behalf of the C&HR); by the LMSR, and BR.

RECONSTRUCTION

As originally built, the 2¾ mile section Ffrith Junction to Mold was single track. This was widened to double track sometime later, apparently by 7/1870. Further details unknown.

CLOSURE & DEMOLITION

Closed to passengers (last train ran on) 30/4/1962, except unadvertised workmen's trains from Broughton to Chester until 2/9/1863.
Mold Junction to Penyffordd Junction closed to freight 1/3/1965.
        Track lifted - details not known.
Penyffordd Junction to Mold closed to freight 12/1983.
        Track lifted - details not known.

[Read: B/303, B/304, J/RMag/6.1962/380]

FFRITH JUNCTION to LLANFYNYDD

PR/10
4 miles

    Mold Railway Company   : Act 9/7/1847
    Chester & Holyhead Railway Company   : by 12/1849
    London & North Western Railway Company : as from 1/1/1859

CONSTRUCTION

Gauge: 4'8½"

Contractor: Constructed within the PR/9 Contract, which see.

OPERATION

As for PR/9, but see COED TALON COLLIERIES and NERQUIS COLLIERY in Section 3.
Opened to freight 14/8/1849.
Sources vary as to the initial extent of this branch - to Coppa only [J/RMAG/5.1949/209]; to Coed Talon only [B/304/149]; or complete to Llanfynydd Limeworks.
It was certainly complete prior to the construction of PR/39.

RECONSTRUCTION

Ffrith Junction to Coppa (½ mile) was widened to double track in 1866.
Coed Talon to Llanfynydd was partially re-aligned 1868/1869 when it was incorporated in PR/39 - which see.

CLOSURE & DEMOLITION

Ffrith Junction to Coed Talon - last train ran on 29/7/1934.
Official closure date 26/5/1936; though track from 1m35ch to 1m72ch (from Ffrith Junction) was removed 5/1936 [reputedly consequent upon a derailment having occurred]; other track lifted later in 1936.
For section Coed Talon to Llanfynydd see PR/39.

[Read: B/303, B/304, J/RMag/6.1962/380]

PORT PENRHYN BRANCH

PR/11
1½ miles

Precise legal ownership not yet discovered. Constructed, without an Act, upon land entirely within the estate of Lord Penrhyn.

CONSTRUCTION

Gauge: 4'8½"

Constructed 1851 "by the Chester & Holyhead Railway Company" [B/126] - or "by Lord Penrhyn" [B/303]; in either case it is likely that a Contractor did the work, but no details yet known.

OPERATION

Opened 1/1852, for freight only; not used for passenger traffic. The freight traffic was almost entirely slate trans-shipped at Port Penrhyn from the narrow-gauge PENRHYN QUARRY RAILWAY (Section 3).
Branch worked by L&NW Rly (initially on behalf of C&H Rly), and later by LMSR and BR.
C&H Rly documents refer to the branch being worked "by Lord Penrhyn's locomotive" - which could refer to something yet unknown, or more likely to a loco specifically allocated to this duty.

CLOSURE & DEMOLITION

Last train ran on 2/3/1963. Branch officially closed 30/6/1965.
Track lifted 1965/1966 - details of this work not known.

[Read: B/176, B/303, J/RMag/10.1961]

MENAI BRIDGE to CAERNARFON   PR/12
                                                          7¼ miles

Bangor & Carnarvon Railway Company	: Act 20/5/1851
Chester & Holyhead Railway Company	: Lease from 1852
London & North Western Railway Company	: as from 1/1/1859

CONSTRUCTION   Gauge: 4'8½"

Contractor   : William McCormick & James Holme   1851-1852

OPERATION

London & North Western Rly Co (initially on behalf of Chester & Holyhead); LMSR, and BR.
   Opened: for freight Menai Bridge to Port Dinorwic   1/3/1852
            for passengers Menai Bridge to Caernarfon   1/7/1852
            for freight Port Dinorwic to Caernarfon   10/1852

ADDITIONAL CONSTRUCTION

Branch line PORT SIDING JUNCTION to PORT DINORWIC HARBOUR (1 mile) constructed by agreement over private (Vaynol Estate) land, with no formal Act.
Contractor for this work not known. Work "in hand" 3/1856.
Opened 1856; used only for freight traffic

RECONSTRUCTION

Contract let 23/9/1869 to "Mr Chester" [presumably Thomas W. Chester] for "alterations and additions to Carnarvon Station - £3050"; this probably included the new loco shed (built 1869, closed 1931). This station was further enlarged in 1911.
Line Menai Bridge-Caernarfon, built as single track, was widened to double track by Act of 1871.
Contractor: **Thomas W.Chester** - Contract let 20/4/1871, £25,726.
Double line opened throughout on 1/7/1874.

Locomotives: Gauge 4'8½"

No positive evidence has been found to confirm the use of ANY loco on the Menai Bridge-Caernarfon widening contract, but circumstantial facts suggest two possible Chaplins - one 8" loco (perhaps Chaplin No.153) from Southampton, later to Mountsorrel; one 7" loco source unknown, later to Ireland.
A sale advertisement [J/CDH/27.9.1873] of "railway plant and materials used on the Bangor & Carnarvon Railway - for T.Chester Esq" and held at Port Dinorwic on 29/9/1873 did not mention a loco. The catalogue of this sale has not yet been traced.

| | 0-4-0VBT VC | Ch | [? 153 c1860] (a) | (1) |
| | [? 0-4-0VBT VC | Ch | | (2)] |

(a) The Southampton Docks Co sold a Chaplin 0-4-0VBT loco in 1/1872 (by 17/1/1872) to T.W.Chester, Carnarvon, for £150 [although the writing in the SDCo Minutes at PRO Kew has led to misreadings of the 'T.W.' initials as 'J.M.', 'I.N.', 'I.W.' etc; only one Mr Chester has been traced at Caernarfon at this period]. The obvious inference, though no proof has been found, is that this loco was used on this PR/12 Contract. The Southampton Chaplin was apparently of 8" cylinder, 21hp type; and (from our incomplete knowledge of Chaplin locos) it was possibly Chaplin 153 built c1860 - though Southampton recorded the boiler of their loco as dated 1862.

(1) Late in 1872 [J/CG/27.9.1872/356], "T.W.Chester, Contractor, Carnarvon" was offering for sale "Chaplin loco, 4'8½" gauge, pair of 8" cylinders , 27hp [sic]". Chaplin 153 is reported to have passed (by 1874), from "a contractor", to the Mountsorrel Granite Co Ltd, Leicestershire [IRS/PBE/bulletins].

(2) Thomas W.Chester subsequently constructed the Island Bridge to Glasnevin railway in Ireland, c1874-1877; and a 7" cylinder Chaplin loco was advertised [J/GH/19.10.1877] for sale from that Contract 24/10/1877. [This loco may then have passed to C.M.Holland for his Maghera-Magherafelt Rly Contract, where a Chaplin loco was for sale in 1880.]

CLOSURE & DEMOLITION

PORT DINORWIC HARBOUR BRANCH last used 30/10/1961.
    Track lifted c1962 - no further details known.
MENAI BRIDGE to CAERNARFON reduced to single track 1966.
    Closed to freight 4/8/1969; to passengers 5/1/1970.
    Reopened to freight 15/6/1970, until 5/2/1972.
    Track lifted 1972 - no further details known.

[Read: J/RMag/9.1958/591; B/303; B/413]

RHIWBACH TRAMROAD
"Ffestiniog Extension Railway"

PR/13

3¼ miles

Festiniog Slate Quarry Co Ltd (reg.11/1859)	: no Act
Festiniog Slate Co Ltd (reg.24/4/1877)	: from 4/1877
Rhiwbach Slate Quarry owners [see Section 3]	
Maen Offeren Slate Quarry Co Ltd	: from 1928

CONSTRUCTION

Gauge: 1'11½"

Tenders for construction invited 14/3/1861 [J/MJ/16.3.1861/174].
Contractor : **Gethin Owen Jones** [of Penmachno]
Started c1861; completed c1863.

An extension of the Ffestiniog Railway (PR/3) from the terminus of the latter at Duffws to the Rhiwbach Quarry, serving other quarries en-route including Maenofferen, Cwtybugail, Blaen-y-Cwm, and Bwlch Slaters (New Manod).

OPERATION

Opened for freight traffic by 31/3/1863 [B/169/460]; not opened to passengers. The line climbed from Duffws by three long double-track inclines worked by gravity, with "level" sections c¼ mile long between these inclines. From the top of the third incline, a c2½ mile summit section across moorland at a ruling grade of 1in70 to the head of a single-track incline, down to Rhiwbach Quarry, worked (latterly at least) by a steam-haulage engine, though the original specification [J/MJ/16.3.1861/174] drawn up by the engineer, C.E.Spooner, called for a water-balanced incline.

[Read: B/168; B/169]

Locomotives: Gauge 2ft

Initially, the sections between inclines were worked by horses but in the 1920s the Rhiwbach Quarry, being owners and operators of the railway, obtained a Baguley and a Muir Hill locomotives, either or both of which were probably used on the summit-section of the railway. Maenofferen Quarry purchased Rhiwbach Quarry and the railway in 1928, and in 1933 ordered a special Planet Simplex loco (FH 1821) "capable of 10mph and able to haul 15 tons up 1in70 grades" - presumably for use on the summit section. By 8/1951 the Muir Hill loco was working the railway's traffic in the ex-GWR and LMS yards at Blaenau Ffestiniog, FH 1821 was working the first level section above Duffws, a choice of Maenofferen Quarry locos worked the second level section, and Maenofferen loco MR 1904 was working the summit section. By 8/1953, and until it closed, the summit section was worked by Cwtybugail Quarry using their loco RH 223687.

To avoid repetition, all these locomotives are listed under the respective quarries in Section 3.

CLOSURE & DEMOLITION

Rhiwbach to New Manod (Bwlch Slaters) Junction closed by 1953
Bwlch Slaters to Cwtybugail closed by 4/1954
Rhiwbach to Cwtybugail track lifted 1956.
Cwtybugail to Top No.3 Incline closed 1961; track removed by 6/1964
No.3 Incline, one track removed by 6/1964; second track retained as winch-powered line for reservoir repair work.
No.3 Incline closed c1965 and track removed.
From 1961, No.3 Incline Foot to Duffws used solely by Maenofferen Slate Quarry; see Section 3 for further details.

LLANDUDNO JUNCTION to LLANDUDNO   PR/14
                                         3 miles

St Georges Harbour & Railway Company   : Act 20/8/1853
London & North Western Railway Company : Leased by Act of 1/8/1861
The line was vested in the LNWR by Act of 28/7/1863

CONSTRUCTION   Gauge: 4'8½"

Contractor   : Samuel Morton Peto

OPERATION

Line opened 1/10/1858.
Operated by St Georges Harbour & Railway Co, using a locomotive hired from the LNWR, except during some winter months when horses were used.
Operated by LNWR (later LMSR and BR) from 1/8/1861.

RECONSTRUCTION

Built as a single track line; widened to double track in the late l870s - work was reported as having begun "in an unostentatious manner" 2/1875 [J/CDH/13.2.1875/5] but contractor not named.
On 17/11/1875 a contract was let to S.Parry of Llanrwst for alterations to Llandudno and Deganwy stations.

[Read: B/303; B/310]

FORYD JUNCTION (RHYL) to DENBIGH
FORYD JUNCTION to FORYD PIER
"Vale of Clwyd Railway"

PR/15

10 miles and 1¼ miles

Vale of Clwyd Railway Company : Act 23/6/1856
London & North Western Rly Co : Leased the line 1/7/1861
: Absorbed line by Act 15/7/1867

CONSTRUCTION

Gauge: 4'8½"

Contractor : **Davies & Savin**   First Sod cut 7/8/1856
Opened 5/10/1858

A temporary ballast siding was built from Foryd Junction to Foryd Beach, by permission of the landowner, Mr H.R.Hughes. By Act of 30/6/1862, this siding became the Foryd Pier Branch; it had in fact been in use as such by 8/1859.

Locomotives: Gauge 4'8½"

The Contractors probably used locos from "their" fleet (see SAVIN - Section 1) but no positive details have been found. An unidentified LNWR "Crewe Goods" 0-6-0 was hired in 1858 for ballasting work.

OPERATION

5/10/1858 -4/10/1859	: **Davies & Savin** for Vale of Clwyd Rly Co	
5/10/1859 -30/6/1861	: **Vale of Clwyd Rly Co**	
1/7/1861 - 1867	: LNWR as lessee	
(1/3/1862 -31/7/1865	: LNWR (VoC) also operated to Corwen PR/20)	
1867 - closure	: LNWR/LMS/BR	

Locomotives: Gauge 4'8½"   1858-1861 and possibly later

No.1	CLWYD	0-4-2ST	IC	SS	1079	1858	New (oa)	(o1)
No.2	ELWY	0-4-2ST	IC	SS	1080	1858	New (oa)	(o1)
No.3	GALLTFAENAN	0-4-2ST	IC	SS	1136	1859	New (oa)	(o1)

(oa) ordered by Davies & Savin for Vale of Clwyd Rly Co

(o1) to LNWR with railway 1867;
became LNWR 1686, 1687, 1688 respectively.

CLOSURE & DEMOLITION

Foryd Pier branch closed to freight from 6/4/1959.
Foryd Junction to Denbigh closed   to passengers from 19/9/1955
                                    to freight from 1/1/1968

No details known regarding contractor or locos used for demolition.

[Read: J/RMag/2.1957/75; B/303]

DERWENLAS (QUAY WARD) to RATGOED   PR/16
MAESPOETH to UPPER CORRIS (ABERCWMMEIDDAW) 9½ miles and 2 miles
"The Corris Railway"

Corris, Machynlleth & River Dovey Tramroad Co	: Act 12/7/1858
Corris Railway Company	: Act 25/7/1864
Subsidiary of Imperial Tramways Co Ltd	: From 1878
Great Western Railway Company purchase by	: Act 4/8/1930
British Railways	: From 1/1/1948
Corris Railway Co Ltd (part of route only)	: From 1977

CONSTRUCTION   Gauge: 2'3"

Contractor: no details known.
Built as horse-worked tramroad from Corris area quarries to the River Dovey at Derwenlas (Quay Ward).

OPERATION

Opened for freight 30/4/1859 - worked by horses.

RECONSTRUCTION   Gauge: 2'3"

By the 25/7/1864 Act, the section Derwenlas to Machynlleth was closed. Section Machynlleth to Corris to Aberllefeni was rebuilt c1877-1878 as a steam railway; opened to freight 2/1879, and opened officially for passengers (by Act of 18/6/1883) on 4/7/1883 to Corris, and on 25/8/1887 to Aberllefeni.
No details known of any contractors involved; the upgrading of the Corris to Aberllefeni section reputedly a "direct labour" job.
Aberllefeni to Ratgoed, and Maespoeth to Abercwmmeiddaw, remained as horse-operated freight-only lines.

Locomotives: Gauge 2'3"

1		0-4-0ST	OC	FE	HLT324	1878	New 11/78	
	rebuilt as: 0-4-2ST	OC	BE		1895		(o1)
2		0-4-0ST	OC	FE	HLT322	1878	New 11/78	
	rebuilt as: 0-4-2ST	OC	BE		1898		(o1)
3		0-4-0ST	OC	FE	HLT323	1878	New 11/78	
	rebuilt as: 0-4-2ST	OC	BE		1900		(o2)
4		0-4-2ST	OC	KS	4047	1921	New 6/21	(o2)

(o1) Wdn 6/1921; scrapped by Peter Vaughan & Son of Machynlleth in 1930.
(o2) Wdn 8/1948; tdt: Talyllyn Railway (PR/27), 3/1951.

CLOSURE & DEMOLITION

Maespoeth to Abercwmmeiddaw closed c1940; track in situ 2/1941 but lifted soon thereafter by George Cohen, Sons & Co Ltd.
Machynlleth to Aberllefeni last passenger train ran on 31/12/1930; last freight train ran on 20/8/1948. Track lifted by BR employees 16/11/1948 and into 1949; work abandoned; completed by W.O.Williams of Harlech in 1951.
Aberllefeni to Ratgoed closed by BR 1/7/1952; track removed by 7/1953.
It is understood that no locomotive was used during any of these demolition works.

RECONSTRUCTION

The Corris Society opened a Museum at Corris Station 30/3/1970; re-formed as Corris Railway Society mid-1970, and as Corris Railway Co Ltd c1977. A short length of track was laid beside the Museum in 1971. In 1981 the Company took possession of the locomotive shed at Maespoeth Junction, and by 1986 had laid track between Maespoeth and Corris.

Locomotives: Gauge 2'3"

No.5	ALAN MEADEN	4wDM	40hp MR	22258	1965	(ra)	
	CORRIS No.6	4wDH	48hp RH	518493	1966	(rb)	

(ra) tdx: Corris Railway Society store, Loughborough, Leics, c3/1978 by 12/4/1978
     wfw: Mr A.J.Wilson, private store, Notts
     wfw: Staveley Lime Products Ltd, Hindlow, Derbyshire (2'0" gauge).
(rb) tdx: a dealer, 22/5/1982
     wfw: BICC Metals Ltd, Prescot, Lancashire (2'6" gauge).

[Read: B/322; B/173; B/398; and J/NG/No.131/18 for Ratgoed branch]

RUABON (GARDDEN LODGE JUNCTION) to LEGACY   PR/17
"The Ponkey [Ponciau] Branch"   3 miles

Great Western Railway Company : No Act
built by Agreement with landowner Henry Dennis.
Confirmed by Acts of 21/7/1873 and 12/8/1889.

CONSTRUCTION   Gauge: 4'8½"

Contractor: no details discovered.

RECONSTRUCTION

The 1899 Act allowed for the diversion of the line, between Afongoch (Monk & Newell) Brickworks Junction (GR:303444) and Gardden Lodge Cokeovens Junction (GR:301453), onto a new more easterly parallel route. This diversion was built, but not known by whom.

OPERATION

Opened	: Gardden Lodge Junction to Aberderfyn	1/8/1861 for freight
	Aberderfyn to Bryn-yr-Owen Colliery	for freight
	Aberderfyn to Legacy	27/8/1876 for freight
	Ponciau Crossing to Legacy	5/6/1905 passengers

The RCH Handbook of Stations 1912 lists sidings at Aberderfyn as: Aston & Sons Works; Moreton Siding; Rhos Gas Works; and Ruabon Wagon Co Jenkins & Jones Siding.

CLOSURE & DEMOLITION

Aberderfyn to Bryn-yr-Owen Colliery "abandoned" 3/7/1893; track removed.
Ponciau Crossing to Legacy closed to passengers 22/3/1915.
Aberderfyn to Legacy closed to freight 18/1/1917; track removed 1917.
    A short length of track was later reinstated at the Legacy end of this section; this formed a siding from the Rhos branch (PR/59) to the Llwyneinion Electricity Works of the North Wales Power Co Ltd and remained in-situ until demolition of PR/59.
Gardden Lodge Works to Aberderfyn closed to freight 25/10/1954.
Gardden Lodge Junction to Works closed to freight 31/8/1964.

No details known regarding precise dates of tracklifting, or of any contractors or locomotives used for demolition.

[Read: B/302; B/303; B/304]

RUABON (LLANGOLLEN LINE JUNCTION) to DOLGELLAU   PR/18
                                                                                                                          45 miles

RUABON JUNCTION to LLANGOLLEN   5¼ miles
    Vale of Llangollen Railway Company   : Act 1/8/1859

LLANGOLLEN to CORWEN   9¾ miles
    Llangollen & Corwen Railway Company   : Act 6/8/1860

CORWEN to BALA [Lake Halt]   12½ miles
    Corwen & Bala Railway Company   : Act 30/6/1862

BALA [Lake Halt] to DOLGELLAU   17¼ miles
    Bala & Dolgelley Railway Company   : Act 30/6/1862

All four Companies were sponsored by the Great Western Railway Company, which absorbed the Bala & Dolgelley Rly Co 1/8/1877; the other three Companies were amalgamated into the GWR 1/7/1896 (all per a GWR Act of 1867).

[Read: J/RMag/3.1976/128; B/395/95; B/303; B/304; B/338; J/TI/3.1950/44]

CONSTRUCTION   Gauge: 4'8½"

Contractor	: **Thomas Brassey;** becoming **Thomas Brassey & Wm. Field;** traded as "**Brassey & Field**".
Engineer	: Henry Robertson (Ruabon-Bala) Edward Wilson (Bala-Dolgellau)
First Sod Cut	: 1/9/1859
Work Completed	: 8/1868

Locomotives: Gauge 4'8½"

No positive evidence has been found to confirm the use of any locos during the construction of these railways. The end-of-contract sales of "Brassey & Field" equipment were held (re: Corwen & Bala Rly) 11/9/1868 at Bala, 12/9/1868 at Llandrillo, and (re: Bala & Dolgelley Rly) 20/10/1868 at Llanuwchllyn, 21/10/1868 at Dolserau. None of the advertisements for these sales make any mention of locomotives. (There was a 6hp "portable steam engine" and waggons etc in the latter sale.)
However, purely circumstantial evidence suggests that the following locomotives MAY have been used:

```
        STONEYWAY       0-6-0ST  IC  MW   155  1865  (a)         s/s
                        4wWT     SC  AP   221  1866  (b)         s/s
                        4wWT     SC  AP   235  1866  (b)         s/s
```

(a)   wfw: Brassey & Ballard, Bedford-Elstree MR (1865-1867) Contract.
(b)   New to "W.Brassey & Lucas" at unknown location 9-10/1866.

OPERATION

Operated from opening by GWR (later BR) locomotives.
Opening dates: Ruabon Junction to Llangollen 1/12/1861 (freight), 2/6/1862 (passengers); to Corwen 1(or 8)/5/1865; to Llandrillo 16/7/1866; to Bala 1/4/1868; to Dolgellau 4/8/1868 (passengers), 1/10/1868 (freight).

RECONSTRUCTION

As built, the line was laid with single track. Ruabon Junction to Llangollen was widened to double track 1898-1900; opened c10/1900. Details of Contractor, or of any locos used, are not known.
However, a Peckett saddle-tank loco "lying at Llangollen", was auctioned at Liverpool 18/9/1902 [J/GH/8.9.1902] - perhaps it had been used for this work.

CLOSURE & DEMOLITION

Llangollen to Dolgellau closed to freight 2/11/1964.
Ruabon Junction to Dolgellau passenger trains, due for withdrawal on 18/1/1965, ceased 12/12/1964 due to extensive flood damage, as did the Trevor to Llangollen freight service.
Ruabon to Llangollen, and Bala to Dolgellau passenger services were reinstated 17/12/1964, then ceased as planned 18/1/1965.
Trevor to Llangollen reopened to freight 17/12/1964.
Ruabon Junction to Llangollen closed to freight 1/4/1968.

Track materials sold to Thos.W.Ward Ltd [of Sheffield]. Demolition started 25/6/1968 near Llandrillo and headed east, reaching Ruabon Junction 5/1969; also started 2/7/1968 at Llandderfel, headed west to Dolgellau - and continued to Barmouth Junction (PR/24) reached 26/2/1969.

Locomotives: Gauge 4'8½"

344		0-4-0DM 204hp AB		D394	1955	(da)	s/s.1969
SPRITE		0-4-0DE	BP	Ø 7859	1958	(db)	(d1)

Ø   loco built jointly by BP and BT : BT [BE] 102/1958

(da)   tdx: Stanley Davies Plant Hire Ltd, Castleford, Yorks, by 8/1968.
          wfw: Lever Brothers Ltd, Port Sunlight, Cheshire.
(db)   tdx: Brush Electrical Engineering Co Ltd, Loughborough, Leics, loan
          per: Stanley Davies Plant Hire Ltd, Castleford, Yorks, by 8/1968

(d1)   tdt: Brush Electrical Engineering Co Ltd, Loughborough, off loan, c5/1969.

RECONSTRUCTION

Route between Bala Lake Halt and Llanuwchllyn later used by Bala Lake Railway (see PR/66).
Route between Llangollen and Glyndyfrdwy later used by Llangollen Railway (see PR/68).

ACREFAIR FREIGHT LINES   PR/19

Great Western Railway Company.

To consolidate its position in the industrial zone around Acrefair, the GWR, with effect from 12/12/1896:

1. **"The Pontcysyllte Branch"**: purchased by Deed of 14/8/1896, from the London & North Western Railway Company, the railway from Pontcysyllte Canal Basin (exclusive) to Afon Eitha (Wynn Hall), plus the trackbed of the former extension of that line, from Wynn Hall to Llwyneinion. The purchase included wagons, but no locos. See PR/1 for previous history.

2. **"The Plasmadoc Branch"**: purchased, from the Wynnstay Colliery Co Ltd, the "Plasmadoc Railway", from Wynnstay Colliery (exclusive) to Delph via Plas-yn-Wern (where this line crossed the above ex-LNWR line on the level). See ACREFAIR IRONWORKS (Section 3) for previous history.

3. **"Edwards Private Siding"**: leased, from J.C.Edwards, their private branch line from Trevor Station to Trefynant Brickworks near Pontcysyllte, - thus obtaining access from PR/18 at Trevor to the ex-LNWR line above.

Apart from short connections at Trefynant and the "Plasmadoc Loop" (a north to east arc connection, between lines 1 and 2 above, at Plas-yn-Wern), no new construction was involved. However, the disused trackbed north of Wynn Hall was re-layed [rails shown on OS/25"/1900 as far as Llwyneinion]. The section from Rhos to Llwyneinion was soon incorporated into a new "Rhos Branch" (PR/59), which was the last link in providing a through route Trevor-Acrefair-Wynn-Pant-Rhos-Wrexham.

[Read: J/DHS/1983/42; B/162/176; B/304/124]

NEW CONSTRUCTION

A short branch was built, at a later (undiscovered) date, to serve Cefn Mawr (Monsanto) Chemical Works.
Nothing yet known re any Contractor for this work.

OPERATION

None of the lines south of Wynn Hall were ever used for public passenger trains. (For north of Wynn Hall see PR/59.)
The lines were worked by GWR (later BR) locomotives.
Per J/DHS/1983/47, Wynnstay Colliery locomotives continued to work on the Plasmadoc Railway to Delph until 1927; but other evidence of this is lacking.

CLOSURE & DEMOLITION

Wynnstay Colliery connection closed 7/1927.
Plas Madoc Junction (PR/5) to Delph closed 1953; lifted 1959.
Acrefair Ironworks [*] to Wynn Hall closed 1953; lifted 1959.
Acrefair Ironworks [*] to Monsanto Branch Junction closed 1960.

Pontcysyllte Canal Basin lines closed 1953.
Trevor to Monsanto, traffic ceased c6/1966; officially closed 1/1/1968.

[*] Acrefair Ironworks known latterly as Hughes & Lancaster's Siding.

Track lifted after closure in each case; precise dates not known.
Nothing yet known re Contractors or any locomotives used.

DENBIGH to RUTHIN to CORWEN PR/20
18¾ miles

Denbigh, Ruthin & Corwen Rly Co : Act 23/7/1860
London & North Western Rly Co : From 1/7/1879 (or 1/7/1878 ?)

CONSTRUCTION   Gauge: 4'8½"

Contractor   : **Savin & Co** First Sod: 4/9/1860
Open   : Denbigh-Ruthin   1/3/1862
                  Ruthin-Corwen DRC   6/10/1864
                  Corwen DRC-GWR   1/9/1865

Locomotives: Gauge 4'8½"

| 2 | RUTHIN | 0-4-0 | OC | MW | 19 | 1860 | (a) | | (1) |
| 14 | NANTCLWYD | 0-6-0ST | IC | MW | 45 | 1862 | New 4/62 | | (2) |

(a)   (tdx ?) Savin at Oswestry - see Section 1.

(1)   tdt: Savin (? at Oswestry) - see Section 1.
(2)   tdt: Savin (at Llanfyllin by 3/1863) - see Section 1.

OPERATION

1/3/1862 - 31/7/1865 : Vale of Clwyd Rly, using VoCR locos (PR/15)
1/8/1865 - 5/2/1866 : Savin & Co
6/2/1866 - 30/6/1869 : Denbigh, Ruthin & Corwen Rly Co
1/7/1879 -   closure : LNWR/LMSR/BR

Locomotives: Gauge 4'8½" (used 1/8/1865-30/6/1879)

7	LLANERCHYDOL	0-4-2	IC	SS	1224	1860	(oa)		(o1)
4		2-4-0		Jones	[?1853]		(ob)		(o2)
2		2-4-0		EBW		1856	(oc)		(o3)
3		0-6-0	IC	Kit	1251	1865	(od)		(o4)
1		0-6-0	IC	SS	2510	1875	New 9/75		(o5)

(oa)   tdx: Cambrian Railways, per Savin, hire.
(ob)   tdx: LNWR, 1136 CHANDOS, 12/1865; per Savin & Co.
(oc)   tdx: LNWR, 1141, 12/1865; per Savin & Co.
(od)   tdx: Mid Wales Rly Co, 7/1866

(o1)   tdt: Cambrian Railways, off loan
(o2)   tdt: LNWR (with railway), 1860, 1/7/1879
(o3)   tdt: LNWR (with railway), 2347, 1/7/1879
(o4)   tdt: LNWR (with railway), 2348, 1/7/1879
(o5)   tdt: LNWR (with railway), 2346, 1/7/1879

NOTE: In 1875, the DR&CR advertised [J/IRON/2.10.1875] for sale a second-hand loco and tender; loco 16x22 OC, 3'8" leading wheels, 5'6" trailing wheels coupled [ie, a 2-4-0 or 4-4-0 or similar]. This could be EBW loco number 2 but these dimensions do not exactly agree with the dimensions of LNWR 1141 quoted elsewhere.

CLOSURE & DEMOLITION

Ruthin-Corwen   : Closed to passengers   from 2/2/1953
                                to freight   from 30/4/1962
   Track removed - no information re any contractor or locos used.
Denbigh-Ruthin   : Closed to passengers   from 30/4/1962
                                to freight   from 1/3/1965
   Track lifted c2/1966-c10/1966 by unknown contractor, using locos:-

Locomotives: Gauge 4'8½"

0-4-0DM	40hp JF	22288	1938	(da)		(d1)
4wPM	40hp MR	3730	1925	(db)	s/s by 9/1966	

(da) tdx: J.Pugsley & Sons Ltd, Stoke Gifford, Glos, loan, by 2/3/1966
(db) tdx: Craig Lelo Granite Quarry, by 11/5/1966

(d1) tdt: J.Pugsley & Sons Ltd, Stoke Gifford, Glos, 5/1966

[Read: J/RMag/3.1957/193; B/303/68]

CROES NEWYDD to BROUGHTON FORGE JUNCTION (to Brymbo) PR/21
3¼ miles

   Wrexham & Minera Railway Company   :Act 17/5/1861
   Great Western Railway Company   :absorbed W&M Rly Co 31/7/1871

CONSTRUCTION
Gauge: 4'8½"

Contractor: not known. Line opened to freight 22/5/1862.

The line started from PR/5 just south of Wrexham, and connected into the Broughton Forge branch of PR/6, thus creating a through route to Brymbo, and permitting closure of the tunnel and incline Moss-Brymbo section of PR/6.

OPERATION
Operated from opening 22/5/1862 by GWR (later BR) locomotives.

RECONSTRUCTION

During 1881-1882 the line was upgraded for passenger traffic; this would include widening to double track over the PR/6 branch section from Broughton Forge Junction to Brymbo, if this had not been done previously.

Opened for passenger traffic (Wrexham-)Croes Newydd-Brymbo 4/1882; probably 24/4/1882 but sources vary.
An earlier passenger service, in 1866, was prepared for. If indeed it operated, it was short lived..

Contractor : **Davies Brothers** [of Wrexham].

Locomotives: Gauge 4'8½"

No specific locos identified on this work.
For further details of Davies Bros. see PR/57.

CLOSURE & DEMOLITION

Closed to passengers 1/1/1931
Closed to freight   1/10/1982
Some track was lifted by 9/1986; remainder disused until lifted from Brymbo to Moss Valley Junction in 1989. Understood that track was recovered by BR for use elsewhere.
Croes Newydd-Moss Valley Junction-Gatewen (PR/48) retained pending possible future use of Gatewen Coal Depot (see GATEWEN COLLIERY - Section 3).

[Read: J/RW/2.1987/90; B/304/119]

BUCKLEY to CONNAH'S QUAY   PR/22

5 miles

Buckley Railway Company   :   Act 14/6/1860
Wrexham, Mold & Connah's Quay Junction Rly Co
    worked the line as from 1866   : by Act 23/7/1866
    leased the line from 30/6/1873   : by Act 5/8/1873
Great Central Railway Company
    absorbed Buckley Railway Company from 1/1/1905: by Act 22/7/1904
LNER from 1/1/1923; BR from 1/1/1948.

CONSTRUCTION   Gauge: 4'8½"

Contractor: not known. Tenders were invited "by 15/11/1860"
    "Mr Climie" [? Daniel Climie of Shrewsbury] did some work.

From Connah's Quay to Northophall, this railway used some of the route of the Dublin Main Colliery horse-tramroad, which the Buckley Railway (inter-alia) replaced.

OPERATION

Opened for freight 7/6/1862. Never opened for passenger traffic though was used for some Wrexham-Rhyl excursion trains.

Locomotives: Gauge 4'8½"

WHEATLEY	0-6-0ST	IC	HC	2	1861	New 4/61	(1)
KENYON	0-6-0ST	IC	HC	3	1861	New 4/61	(1)
LORD RICHARD	0-6-0ST	IC	HC	63	1865	New 11/65	(1)
SIR STEPHEN	0-6-0ST	IC	HC	64	1865	New 12/65	(1)

(1) pooled with WM&CQJR (PR/28) locos from 1866

RECONSTRUCTION & EXTENSION

The facilities at Connah's Quay were extended in 1874-75; around 1890, further alterations were made at Connah's Quay, consequent on dock extensions, and the construction of the Shotton-Connah's Quay branch - see PR/54 for details.
In the period 12/1892 to 7/1893, the line was extended at Buckley from Knowle Lane to Lane End Colliery. Contractor for this work was H.CROOM JOHNSON - see his entry in Section 1.

CLOSURE & DEMOLITION

Lines to the south-west of Ashton's Branch Junction were abandoned upon closure of the Works served (Lane End Colliery 1903; Mountain Colliery 1929), but not removed for many years.
Connah's Quay to Castle Brickworks closed 1959.
Castle Brickworks to Ashton's Branch Junction (and thence via PR/28 to Buckley Junction) last used 3/5/1965; closed 5/7/1965.

Tracks lifted after closures, but no details known.

[Read: B/127/52; B/247; B/232; J/RMag/11.1937; B/304]

LLANDUDNO JUNCTION to BLAENAU FFESTINIOG   PR/23
"The Conwy Valley Line"   27½ miles

LLANDUDNO JUNCTION to LLANRWST   11¼ miles

Conway & Llanrwst Railway Company	: Act 23/7/1860
London & North Western Railway Company	
leased line from	: 28/7/1863
absorbed line	: 1867

CONSTRUCTION   Gauge: 4'8½"

Contractor   : Edward Preston & Edmund Sharpe   First Sod 25/8/1860
           [Sharpe was first Chairman of the Company]   Opened 17/6/1863

Locomotives: Gauge 4'8½"

A tender locomotive was for sale at Llansantffraid (ie, Glan Conwy) 21/7/1863, on behalf of Edward Preston [J/MJ/4.7.1863].
This could be the 0-4-0 tender loco, built by Bury in 1839 for the London & Birmingham Rly, which became LNWR 1191, and was sold to E.Preston, Contractor (at Rhyl ?) in 2/1863.

LLANRWST to BETTWS-Y-COED   3¾ miles

       London & North Western Railway Company   : Act 5/7/1865

CONSTRUCTION   Gauge: 4'8½"

Contractor   : Parry & Co (Parry &Collingwood)   Contract Let 17/5/1866
              [of Menai Bridge]   Opened freight 9/9/1867
                                                      Opened passengers 6/4/1868

Locomotives: Gauge 4'8½"

Parry & Collingwood advertised [J/TB/1.12.1866] "wanted" a loco not less than 10hp.
A sale of plant used on the construction of this railway was held 15/10/1867, and included a 20hp "contractors locomotive engine".
A further sale "on instructions of Contractors of the Bettws-y-Coed Railway" at Llanrwst 16/2/1869 included a "20hp locomotive engine suitable for a Railway Contractor or a Colliery Proprietor" [perhaps same loco, not sold previously ?].

BETTWS-Y-COED to BLAENAU FFESTINIOG   13 miles

       London & North Western Railway Company   : Act 18/7/1872

CONSTRUCTION   Gauge: 1'11½" & 4'8½"

Contractor   : Owain Gethin Jones [Penmachno]
Contract Let 6/1874; £120,000. [J/CDH/4.7.1874/4]
The original plans were for a 1'11½" gauge line, but soon altered to use 4'8½" gauge, with an amended route. This led to disputes with the Contractor [J/CDH/1.8.1874/4] - the LNWR Engineer Wm.Smith took direct control, and construction continued using many sub-contractors, Owen Morris & William Jones [of Caernarfon] taking on much of the work [J/CDH/24.10.1874/5, 21.11.1874/4], Gethin Jones retaining some portions including Ponty-Pant Viaduct ["Pont Gethin"], where a narrow (2ft ?) gauge rail system was used during construction according to contemporary photographs.
The Blaenau Tunnel (3860 yards) was started by Gethin Jones but completed by the LNWR.
For details of 3'0" gauge tramroad used for its construction see J/IRR/Vol.4/222.

Locomotives: Gauge 4'8½"

D		0-6-0ST OC	(Cromford	1859?)	(ca)	(c1)

(ca) This loco was photographed at Dolyddelen [Dolwyddelen] reputedly on construction work c1878. It had previously been a shunter at LNWR Crewe Works;
wfw: LNWR number 1943;
wfw: Cromford & High Peak Railway No.4 - which was reputedly "built" by the C&HPR using frame and other components of an older (unidentified) loco built by Bury. The LNWR Minutes of 14/3/1877 state that a "small locomotive" was then in use on the Blaenau Contract. Perhaps co-incidentally, LNWR 1943 was apparently renumbered 'D' in 3/1877 [B/373/68-71].

(c1) wlw(tdt ?): LNWR, Crewe Works (being withdrawn from service there in 5/1882.) This loco was not at Crewe 2/1879. On 3/7/1879 two men died when the "lorry" [trolley ?] on which they were riding through the Blaenau Tunnel collided with "the little engine that is employed at the tunnel" [J/CDH/5 + 12.7.1879] - perhaps this loco ?

OPERATION

Bettws-y-Coed to Dolyddelen [later Dolwyddelen] open "for traffic of the locality" by 19/2/1879 [LNWR Minutes]; first train passed through Tunnel 20/6/1879 [J/IRR/Vol.4/223] and line then opened for freight; opened passengers 22/7/1879 using temporary terminal at Dinas (Rhiwbryfdir). Opened through to permanent Blaenau Station 1/4/1881.

LNWR/LMSR/BR locomotives used.

RECONSTRUCTION

A   The line was relocated onto new alignment for ¼ mile at Llandudno Junction; the new route coming into use 1/10/1897.
This work was probably done by MONK & NEWELL, the contractors who were re-modelling the Junction Station at that time.

B   During 1962-1963, the line was extended at Blaenau Ffestiniog to connect it to the former GWR line (PR/34, PR/49) to create a new route through to Trawsfynydd Power Station. Although intended for freight only, this extension has occasionally carried passenger traffic.
This connection built by BRITISH RAILWAYS ENGINEERS DEPARTMENT.

Locomotives: Gauge 2ft

L1D		4wDM	40hp RH	186339	1937	(ra)	(r1)
THE FLORISTON FLYER		4wDM	30hp RH	375702	1954	(ra)	(r1)

(ra) tdx: BR, Newton Heath Plant Depot, Manchester, by 4/1963
            [RH 375702 was onetime used on construction of new curve Mossband to
            Longtown-Gretna branch, and worked a railway which crossed the river Esk to
            Floriston station; hence name on loco. - J/RO/3.1960]

(r1) tdt: BR, Newton Heath Plant Depot, Manchester, c12/1963

[Read: J/TI/1949/131;   J/RMag/12.1959/820;   J/IRR/Vol.4/222;   B/105/166;   B/303/117; B/339;]

DOVEY (GLANDOVEY) JUNCTION to DOLGELLAU   PR/24
                                                  27¾ miles

Aberystwith & Welsh Coast Railway Company   : Act 22/7/1861
Cambrian Railways Company from 5/8/1866 per : Act 5/7/1865

CONSTRUCTION   Gauge: 4'8½"

Contractors   : **Savin & Co** until 5/2/1866   First Sod   4/1862
                      Henry Coneybeare   Completion 1/8/1869

Initially an isolated line, opened Aberdovey Harbour to Llwyngwril (10 miles) for public traffic 9/1863 [J/CDH/26.9.1863/5c6]; official opening ceremony 10/1863 [? 24/10/1863 [B/101, B/304]].
Extended to Penmaenpool (9¾ miles) 3/7/1865 - work at this end then ceased. Work on section Aberdovey-Dovey Junction interrupted by Savin's "failure" 5/2/1866; later completed, and opened 14/8/1867.
Work restarted at Penmaenpool 9/1868; opened to Dolgelley temporary station 21/6/1869; opened to permanent station (shared with PR/18) on 1/8/1869.

Locomotives: Gauge 4'8½"

Apart from construction work, Savin also operated all the trains on behalf of the A&WCR until 5/2/1866; any locomotives in his "fleet" (see Section 1) are potential candidates for listing here.
Locos MEIRION, MILFORD and CARDIGAN have been positively identified as being used on this section prior to 2/1866.

OPERATION

Initially by Cam.Rys. (Savin) locos; then Cam.Rys./GWR/BR locos.

CLOSURE & DEMOLITION

Aberdovey (Junction) to Aberdovey Harbour branch closed passengers 14/8/1867, closed freight 4/5/1964. Track subsequently removed but no details known.
Barmouth Junction to Dolgellau closed to freight 14/12/1964; and to passengers 18/1/1965. Track lifted 1968-1969 together with PR/18 (which see).

[Read: B/101; B/303; B/416]

CROESOR VALLEY to PORTHMADOG HARBOUR
"Croesor Tramway"

PR/25
c7 miles

Built 1863-1864 "by" Hugh Beaver Roberts, no Act.
    From 1865 ownership became divided; the Lower Section (4 miles) from Porthmadog to Carreghylldrem becoming the property of the companies listed below, the Upper Section remaining with Roberts and later becoming the Parc [Park] & Croesor Estate.

LOWER SECTION:
    Croesor & Port Madoc Railway Company   : Act 5/7/1865
    Portmadoc, Croesor & Beddgelert Tram Railway Company   : Act 21/7/1879
    Portmadoc, Beddgelert & South Snowdon Rly   : as from 30/6/1901
        Purchase confirmed by PB&SS Rly Company Act 17/8/1901

See PR/44 for later details.

CONSTRUCTION
Gauge: 2ft

Contractor   : **Pritchard & Gregory** [of Bangor].
                    Work started by 4/1863 [J/MJ/11.4.1863/251]
                    "Near completion" 8/1863 [J/HC/1.8.1863/2c6]
                    Part opened for freight 2/1864; Fully opened for freight 1/8/1864

Track laid to 2ft gauge, using light bulb-tee section rail in cast-iron chairs on timber sleepers. The plans included a branch to Beddgelert and the lease anticipated the use of a locomotive [J/MJ/11.4.1863/251] but neither branch nor loco materialised in fact.

OPERATION

Trains were gravity-operated on the inclines, which connected the Upper and Lower Sections of the line, and by horse-haulage elsewhere; usually under contracts, with farmers and hauliers, arranged from time to time by H.B.Roberts, the Estate, and the Rhosydd, Parc and Croesor Quarries operators. Changes of ownership of the Lower Section did not materially alter these arrangements until 1923 when with the opening of the Welsh Highland Railway (see PR/44) the Lower Section traffic became part of the freight traffic of that Railway.
No suggestion has been found as to the use of any locomotive, other than (by the WHRly) on the Lower Section after 1923.

CLOSURE & DEMOLITION

Regular traffic ceased 1930 upon closure of the quarries served.
Casual traffic on the Upper Section, by farmers, continued through to the early 1950s.
Track on inclines removed late 1940s; from incline head to Croesor Village in Summer 1950 (by W.O.Williams of Harlech); remainder up valley mostly intact 6/1968 ; lifted c1970.
For demolition of Lower Section see PR/44.

[Read: B/147; B/174; B/292; B/303; B/450]

GAERWEN to AMLWCH PR/26
17¾ miles

Anglesea Central Railway Company : Act 13/7/1863
LNWR leased the line : Act 6/8/1866
LNWR purchased the line as from 1/7/1876 : Act 24/7/1876

CONSTRUCTION
Gauge: 4'8½"

Contractor : John Dickson & Russell   First Sod   11/9/1863
              [of Neath]   Work started   1864
    Later   John Dickson alone.   Work completed 6/1867
Engineer : R.Algeo

Locomotives: Gauge 4'8½"

ANGLESEA	0-6-0WT	OC	HoL	284	1862	(a)	(1)
DIRECTOR						(b)	s/s
MOUNTAINEER	0-4-4-0T	OC	Cross		1866	New	(2)
WELLINGTON						(c)	s/s

(a) believed brought by Dickson from the Neath & Brecon Rly c1864
(b) a locomotive named DIRECTOR pulled the "first train" [presumably a trial run] from Gaerwen to Llangefni 16/12/1864 [J/CDH/17.12.1864].
(c) a locomotive named WELLINGTON double-headed, with "ANGLESEY" [sic], the first passenger train into Amlwch 3/6/1867 [J/CDH/8.6.1867/5c4]

(1) tdt: Neath & Brecon Rly, c1868 (after 6/4/1868)
(2) tdt: Neath & Brecon Rly, late 1866/early 1867

MOUNTAINEER was a Fairlie Patent locomotive and apparently not very successful. It has often been confused with a similar loco, also built by Cross (in 1865), named PROGRESS, which was used by Dickson on the Neath & Brecon Rly. On 2/11/1868 an auction in Swansea offered PROGRESS for sale, plus a BP tank loco called NEATH, and a Neilson 10x16 cylinders 3'6"wheels tank loco named BULKELEY. Perhaps this sale was consequent upon the 1867 bankruptcy of Dickson - and the Anglesey Central Rly ran through much land owned by the Bulkeley Estate. Thus the Neilson loco may perhaps have worked on the ACR. Apparently purchased at the auction by T.B.Forwood, BULKELEY was hired back to the N&B Rly 1870-1871. [This loco is also mentioned under Padeswood & Nant Mawr Collieries - Section 3.]

OPERATION

Line opened: Gaerwen-Llangefni (4½ miles); ceremonial opening on 16/12/1864;
             open to public on 8(or 12)/3/1865.
    Llangefni-Llanerchymedd (6½ miles) 1/2/1866.
    Llanerchymedd-Amlwch (6¾ miles) mid-1866 (or 3/9/1866) for freight;
             3/6/1867 for passengers.

Until the LNWR lease took effect, the contractor John Dickson operated the completed sections on behalf of the ACR Co, whilst he also carried on the construction works. Dickson became bankrupt in 1867.

Locomotives: Gauge 4'8½"

Initially worked by Dickson locos included in list above, and a loco hired from LNWR as needed. Subsequently LNWR/LMSR/BR locos.

EXTENSION OF LINE

In 10/1952 the ¾ mile "Amlwch Light Railway" (LRO: SI 520/1951) was opened between Amlwch Station and Amlwch Chemical Factory (which see - Section 3). From c1970, Light Railway operated by BR as an end-on extension to PR/26, thus eliminating need for exchange sidings at the junction of the two railways.

CLOSURE

Closed to passengers; last train ran on 5/12/1964.
Closed to public freight 1/12/1964.
Line subsequently used only for Amlwch Chemical Factory traffic.

[Read: J/RMag/4.1960/225; B/303/82]

TYWYN to BRYNEGLWYS PR/27
"The Talyllyn Railway" 9 miles

```
       Aberdovey Slate Co Ltd        : 1864 - 1865
       Talyllyn Railway Company      : Act 5/7/1865
                 Aided by Talyllyn Railway Preservation Society from 1951.
```

CONSTRUCTION   Gauge: 2'3"

Contractor   : not known. Work started 1864
Engineer   : James Swinton Spooner

Built as freight railway from Tywyn (Cam.Rys. wharf) to Nant Gwernol (7½ miles), plus (1½ mile) extension (including three gravity operated inclines) to central area of the quarries; also a branchline (via an incline) to Abergynolwyn village.

OPERATION & PARTIAL CLOSURE

Opened to freight 7/1866.
Opened to passengers Tywyn Pendre to Abergynolwyn Station 1/10/1866
Opened to passengers Tywyn Pendre to Tywyn Wharf 1911.
Freight traffic virtually ceased when quarries closed in 1946.
Abergynolwyn village branch in use 1948; closed ?; track lifted in 1951.
Bryneglwys to Abergynolwyn (junction) track lifted 1952-1954.
No contractors were involved in track lifting.
RECONSTRUCTION

Abergynolwyn Station to Nant Gwernol section rebuilt as passenger railway during early 1970s by TRCo/TRPS.
Opened to passengers 22/5/1976.

Locomotives: Gauge 2'3" - Train Operation

No.	Name	Wheel				Year	Notes
No.1	TALYLLYN	0-4-0ST	OC	FJ	42	1864	New 9/64
	rebuilt as	0-4-2ST	OC	FJ		Jan 1867	
No.2 Ø	DOLGOCH	0-4-0WT	OC	FJ	63	1865	New /66
No.3	SIR HAYDN	0-4-2ST	OC	rebuilt BE		1900	(a)
No.4 Ø	EDWARD THOMAS	0-4-2ST	OC	KS	4047	1921	(b)
No.5	MIDLANDER	4wDM	44hp	RH	200792	1941	(c)
No.6	DOUGLAS	0-4-0WT	OC	AB	1431	1918	(d)
No.7 Ø	TOM ROLT	0-4-2WT	OC	TRCo		1991	New
	rebuild of	0-4-0WT	OC	AB	2263	1949	(e)
No.8	MERSEYSIDER	4wDH	48hp	RH	476108	1964	(f)
No.9	ALF	0-4-0DM	65hp	HE	4136	1950	(g)

Ø No.2 carried name PRETORIA during Boer War (early 1900s).
No.4 carried name PETER SAM temporarily, from 1988.
No.7 commonly referred to as "IRISH PETE" during 1969-1989 period.

Locomotives: Gauge 2'3" - Engineering Service Units

No.	Name	Type			Year	Notes	
No.5		4wPM	DCL		1952	New 10/52	(1)
No.7		4-2wPM	TRCo		1954	New	(2)
No.8	TOBY	2w-2PM	TRPS London		1954	New 12/54	
	rebuilt as	4wPM	TRCo		1985		

Locomotives: Gauge various - purchased as spare parts

Gauge	Type				Year	Note	Disposal
2'0" gauge	4wDM	44hp	RH	189968	1939	(h)	Dsmt/1964
3'0" gauge	4wDH	48hp	RH	476109	1964	(f)	Dsmt/1970
3'0" gauge	4wDM	*	HE	6292	1967	(f)	Dsmt/1969
2'3" gauge	0-4-0DM	65hp	HE	4135	1950	(g)	Dsmt
2'0" gauge	4wDM	44hp	RH	200800	1941	(i)	Dsmt/1980

* Loco received without engine.

(a) tdx: Machynlleth (PR/16), 3/1951, rebuild of 0-4-0ST FE/HLT 323/1878
(b) tdx: Machynlleth (PR/16), 3/1951
(c) tdx: Jees Hartshill Granite Quarries, Warwicks, 23/3/1957
(d) tdx: Hunt Bros (Oldbury) Ltd after overhaul there, 19/7/1954
    wfw: Abelson & Co (Engineers) Ltd, dealers, Birmingham;
    wfw: Air Ministry, Calshot Light Railway, Hants (2'0" gauge).
(e) tdx: Bord na Mona, Clonsast, Offaly, Ireland, 3/1969 (3'0" gauge)
(f) tdx: Park Gate Iron & Steel Co Ltd, Rotherham, Yorks, 6/1969 (3'0" gauge)
(g) tdx: O'Sullivan Bros Ltd, dealers, Manchester, 3/12/1970
    wfw: NCB, Huncoat Colliery, Lancs.
(h) tdx: Blockleys Ltd, Wellington, Salop, 26/9/1963
(i) tdx: Raynesway Plant Ltd, Derby, 6/12/1979
    wfw: Balfour Beatty Ltd, Dartford Tunnel Contract.

(1) Wdn 1954; dismantled; chassis used as a wagon [No.19].
(2) Wdn 1959; later scrapped.

WREXHAM (Exchange) to BUCKLEY
FFRWD JUNCTION to FFOSYGO/BRYNMALLY/MOSS

PR/28

12½ miles

Wrexham, Mold & Connah's Quay Junction Rly Co	: Act 7/8/1862
Manchester, Sheffield & Lincolnshire Rly Co	
controlled WM&CQ (through share holding)	: from 8/1890
MS&LR became **Great Central Railway Co**	: on 1/8/1897
Great Central absorbed WM&CQ as from 1/1/1905	: per Act 22/7/1904
LNER from 1/1/1923; **BR** from 1/1/1948	

CONSTRUCTION

Gauge: 4'8½"

Contractor   : **Savin & Co** (8/1862-2/1864; ittle or no work done)
          : **Benjamin Piercy** (1864-1866) - sublet part to R.S.France
First Sod cut 22/10/1862 by W.E.Gladstone (Chancellor of Exchequer)

Locomotives: Gauge 4'8½"

CHANCELLOR	0-6-0tdr	IC	[?Bury	1846] (ca)	(c1)
ANNA MARIA	0-4-0tk			(cb)	s/s

(ca) purchased by Piercy ex LNWR for £1250 in 1865 for ballasting work on WM&CQ.
   Was LNWR 1377; wfw: St.Helens Rly, No.11 TYNE.
(cb) here [per J/RMAG/1905/189] but no other details known. The name is unusual; a
   loco of this name is recorded as being sometime at Thos. Booker's Pentyrch Blast
   Furnaces, Taff Vale, South Wales, believed to be 0-4-0ST or 0-6-0ST of unknown build,
   rebuilt by Watkins & Phillips.

(c1) to WM&CQ operational stock, No.3.

OPERATION

Wrexham-Buckley opened to freight 1/1/1866.
Opened to passengers Wrexham-Gwersyllt 1/5/1866; and to Buckley a few days later.
Ffrwd Junction to Ffosygo & Brynmally believed opened to freight in 1866: extended Brynmally to Moss (Westminster Colliery) in 1883, opened 27/4/1884. These branches never used for passenger traffic.
  Operations on the Buckley & Connah's Quay line (PR/22) were amalgamated into WMCQ from 1866.

Locomotives: Gauge 4'8½"

No.	Name	Type				Date		Disposal
3	CHANCELLOR	0-6-0	IC	[?Bury		1846]	(a)	Scr/1876
1	WHEATLEY	0-6-0ST	IC	HC	2	1861	(b)	Scr 4/1906
2	KENYON	0-6-0ST	IC	HC	3	1861	(b)	Scr 5/1905
4	LORD RICHARD	0-6-0ST	IC	HC	63	1865	(b)	
	rebuilt as 0-4-0ST		IC			1884		
	rebuilt as 0-4-2T		IC			1889		Scr 2/1905

No.	Name	Type		Builder	Works No.	Date		Disposal
5	SIR STEPHEN	0-6-0ST	IC	HC	64	1865	(b)	
	rebuilt as	0-6-0T	IC	WMCQ		1884		
	rebuilt as	2-4-0T	IC	WMCQ		1893		
	rebuilt as	0-6-0T	IC			1898		Scr 2/1905
	HERCULES	0-6-0	IC	T&G		[? c1850]	(c)	
	rebuilt as	0-6-0ST	IC	IWB		1868		(1)
6	QUEEN	0-6-0ST	IC	[ex SB	348	1846]	(d)	
	rebuilt as	0-8-0ST	IC	WMCQ		1880		
	rebuilt as	0-6-2ST	IC	WMCQ		1888		
	rebuilt as	0-8-0ST	IC	WMCQ		1903		(2)
3	(7, until 1876)	0-6-0ST	IC	[?ex RS	774	1851]	(e)	
	rebuilt as	0-6-2ST	IC	WMCQ		1882		(3)
7	DUKE	0-4-0ST	OC	HC	189	1876	New	Scr 8/1909
8	PREMIER	0-6-0T	IC	SS	2932	1880	New	(4)
9	DEE	0-4-0ST	OC	HC	119	1872	(f)	Scr 8/1909
10	EMILY	0-6-0ST	IC	BP	2157	1882	(g)	(5)
11		0-4-0ST	OC	HC	278	1885	New	Scr 2/1907
12		0-6-2ST	IC	BP	2649	1885	New	(6)
13		0-6-2ST	IC	BP	2650	1886	New	(7)
14		0-4-2T	IC	[ex Dodds		1854]	(h)	(8)
15		0-6-2ST	IC	BP	2962	1888	New	(9)
16		0-6-2ST	IC	BP	2963	1888	New	(10)
14		0-6-0ST	IC	MW	1105	1889	(i)	Scr 3/1906
17		0-6-2T	IC	BP	3866	1896	New	(11)
18		0-6-2T	IC	BP	3867	1896	New	(12)
3		2-6-0T	IC	WMCQ		1901	New (j)	Scr 6/1907

Locomotives numbered 19 to 26 were MS&LR property, repainted in WMCQ livery to enable them to be used on trains to Seacombe; using running powers to which only the WM&CQ had rights. These locos are thus outside the scope of this book.

Additional locos were hired from time to time; from Cam.Rys., from LNWR (in 2/1872 and 9/1873), from LYR (9/1873), from Hughes of Loughborough (on trial only, 8/1867 - 9/1867). The identities of such hired locos have not been found, other than that one Cam.Rys. loco was 9 VOLUNTEER.

(a) tdx: B.Piercy, construction of this railway.
(b) Buckley Rly Co locos (see PR/22) pooled with WM&CQ from c7/1866
(c) tdx: I.W.Boulton, dealer, Ashton-under-Lyne, £900, 8/1867
    The 1868 rebuild apparently financed by "Parry & Co", of London, who then hired loco to WM&CQR.
(d) tdx: LNWR 1829, £900, 6/1872 as 0-6-0ST.
    Built new as 0-6-0 IC SB 348 in 1846 for Manchester & Birmingham Rly; rebuilt by LNWR 1858 and 3/1870

(e) hired 3/1874 from "Crowther" [? financier]; purchased (presumably from Crowther) for £1100 in 1876. [? Perhaps hire purchase over two years]
Generally presumed to have been built as 0-6-0 IC RS in 1851 for South Staffordshire Rly, No.12 PELSALL; becoming LNWR 909, 1188, 1806, and rebuilt by LNWR as 0-6-0ST in 1865.
SSR No.12 is given as RS 774 in some sources, RS 633 in others.
RS 633 is elsewhere quoted as one of the locos ordered by the Chester & Holyhead Rly Co but delivered to the LNWR in 1848-1849. There were 14 such C&HR RS 18" 0-6-0 locos, only 12 of which can be found in LNWR lists - hence two may have become SSR Nos.12,13. Surviving RS records, at London Science Museum, are inconclusive.
(f) tdx: HC, Leeds, £750, 10/1881
wfw: T.Butlin & Co Ltd, Irthlingborough, Northants.
(g) tdx: Gatewen Colliery (see Section 3), per E.D.Till [? financier], 1887
(h) arrived 1887.
wfw (tdx?): Bishops Castle Railway, Salop: wfw: GWR number 227.
Reputedly built as a tender loco, either 0-4-0 or 0-4-2, by Dodds in 1854, and rebuilt as 0-4-2 at Newport Works of the Newport, Abergavenny & Hereford Rly in 1860, and converted to 0-4-2T by the West Midland Railway c1861 (ie, prior to coming to WM&CQJR).
(i) tdx: H.Croom Johnson, contractor, Wrexham, £660, 1895.
(j) New loco, incorporating some parts of scrapped 0-6-2ST number 3.

(1) tdt: I.W.Boulton, dealer, Ashton-under-Lyne, c1871
wlw: Garswood Park Colliery, St.Helens, Lancs.
(2) tdt: GCR, 400, 1/1/1905 (and Scr 10/1923).
(3) Dismantled 1899; some parts used to built 2-6-0T number 3 in 1901.
(4) tdt: GCR, 401, 1/1/1905 (and Scr 9/1922).
(5) tdt: GCR, 402, 1/1/1905 (and Scr 3/1913).
(6) tdt: GCR, 403, 1/1/1905
(7) tdt: GCR, 404, 1/1/1905
(8) reputedly sold to Brynkinallt Colliery (see Section 3), 9/1895.
(9) tdt: GCR, 405, 1/1/1905 (and Scr/1922).
(10) tdt: GCR, 406, 1/1/1905 (and Scr/1922).
(11) tdt: GCR, 409, 1/1/1905.
(12) tdt: GCR, 410, 1/1/1905.

RECONSTRUCTION

Built as single track, the 'main line' was widened to double track by Act of 18/8/1882.
Caergwrle to Penyffordd completed 8/1884.
Wrexham Rhosddu to Caergwrle opened to passengers on 15/4/1885.

Penyffordd to Buckley Junction completed by 7/1885.
 Benjamin Piercy, the WMCQ Engineer, was nominally the contractor for this work, but it was apparently assigned to his associate F.G.Whitwham who submitted the only quotation.
Wrexham Rhosddu to Wrexham Exchange completed 1889.
 Piercy died 24/3/1888 and work in hand was then managed by his Trustees (one of whom was Whitwham).

Locomotives: Gauge 4'8½"

No definite information found; in view of Piercy's position as owner of the majority of WM&CQJR shares, it is likely that WM&CQJR locos would be used. However, these reconstruction works were partially integrated with the new works on the lines Buckley Jct to Connah's Quay (the "Hawarden Loop" - PR/54) and Wrexham Exchange to Central (PR/52). The latter was completed prior to the completion of the Rhosddu to Exchange doubling; hence the advertisement for "plant at Buckley Junction and Wrexham stations on WMCQR for sale, including two six-wheel locomotives by Robert Stephenson and Manning Wardle - apply Engineers Office, Old Vicarage, Wrexham" [in J/CJ/29-10-1890] could refer, in part or whole, to the doubling works. This RS loco could possibly be one of RS 2309 and 2310, which were vaguely mixed up with an earlier contract that Piercy handled in Sardinia - construction of Royal Sardinian Railways 1860s/1870s) - but there is no proof.

LLAY HALL JUNCTION to LLAY MAIN COLLIERY Branch Line   1 mile

Contractor   : Chas. Baker & Sons   Work started c5/1914
                                                          Completed   ?c7/1915

Locomotives: Gauge 4'8½"

TEES VALLEY	0-6-0ST	IC	MW	1594	1903	(ba)	(b1)
DANBY LODGE	0-6-0ST	IC	MW	1595	1903	(ba)	(b2)
CHARLES BAKER	0-6-0ST	IC	HE	1167	1914	New 8/14	(b3)

Other locos sometimes reputed to have worked on this Contract, but for which no definite evidence has yet been found, are:-

TYNE	0-6-0ST	IC	MW	1593	1902
MIDDLESBORO	0-6-0ST	IC	MW	1598	1903

and it should be noted that the name TYNE has been (incorrectly ?) associated with MW 1594 [TEES VALLEY] in some sources, whilst other sources have drawn in 0-6-0ST BH 467/1878, also named TYNE.

(ba) wfw: John Scott, contractor, Grassholme Reservoir (1900-1914) Contract; may have been one of the three MW for sale there 8/1914.

(b1) tdt: Llay Main Colliery, c1915
(b2) tdt: Chas Baker & Sons, Lockoford Lane Plant Depot, Chesterfield, by 1/1916
      wlw: Ministry of Munitions, National Filling Factory, Chilwell, Notts (for sale there 6/1919)
      wlw: L&NWRly, Engineers' Department.
(b3) wlw: Shap Granite Co, Shap, by 5/8/1915 - perhaps per/via HE.

It is of interest to note that Baker's delivery address for HE 1167 was "Rossett", and that during 1914-1915 Baker was advertising for navvies for the "Llay Main Colliery Railway, Gresford".

Perhaps Rossett and Gresford were postal addresses, but there was originally an intention to build a branchline from Llay Main to the GWR (PR/5) as well as to PR/28. The branch to PR/5 was not built.

For further details of the Llay Main Branch see LLAY MAIN in Section 3.

CLOSURE & DEMOLITION

BUCKLEY JUNCTION to BUCKLEY: closed to passengers 31/3/1890 (but re-used for workmen's trains 6/1893 to 2/1895); closed to freight (with PR/22) 5/7/1965 - last used 3/5/1965.
Track lifted soon after closure, but no details known.

FFRWD JUNCTION to MOSS etc: the Ffosygo sub-branch was cut-back to form a stub-siding prior to 1899. Other lines ceased traffic upon closure of the locations served (Westminster Colliery closed 2/1925; Brynmally Colliery closed 10/1935). The LNER surveyed the branch in 2/1936 with a view to closure, all traffic having ceased. The Ffosygo Sub-branch was lifted, and bridge 69 filled-in in 1937.
Main branch track lifted pre WW2, but no details known. The fan of sidings at Ffrwd Junction was lifted 12/1949.

[Read: B/126; B/127; B/247; J/RMag/1.1972/4; J/RW/4.1961/116]

CAERNARFON (PANT) to AFONWEN   PR/29
                                    17¼ miles

Carnarvonshire Railway Co (Registered 1/11/1856)	: Act 29/7/1862
absorbed the **Nantlle Railway Company** (PR/2) by	: Act 25/7/1867
London & North Western Rly Co absorbed CR Co	: Act 4/7/1870

CONSTRUCTION & OPERATION to 1/9/1867   Gauge: 4'8½"

Contractor	: **Savin & Co** to 5/2/1866	Work started 11/1864
	: **Carnarvonshire Rly Co** from 2/1866	Line opened by 8/1866
Engineer	: C.E.Spooner	

Savin owned and operated the Caernarfon-Nantlle Horse Tramroad from 1862 (see PR/2) and obtained an Act permitting conversion of much of his tramroad to 4'8½" gauge. Concurrently, the Carnarvonshire Rly planned to build its own 4'8½" gauge route Afonwen-Penygroes-Caernarfon, along a different, more coastal, route, north of Penygroes. The schemes amalgamated, the coastal route then being abandoned in favour of the tramroad route from Tyddyn Bengam (Penygroes) to Pant.

The CR Act included authority to construct a line from Afonwen to Porthmadog; this section was "adopted" by the A&WC Rly (see PR/32) as part of the route from Barmouth to Pwllheli. Savin constructed both lines concurrently, and used "his" Cam.Rys. locos throughout. After Thomas Savin's financial "failure" 5/2/1866, John Savin, as General Manager of the CR, arranged for the line to be worked by the Cam.Rys. until arrangements were made for the CR to work its own line using hired Cam.Rys. locos.

Line officially opened Pant-Afonwen 2/9/1867, but sections had been used prior to this for freight, and the first passenger train was an excursion from Pant to Penrhyndeudraeth 28/6/1866 [J/CDH/30.6.1866/8c6]; others ran Aberdovey to Caernarfon 23/7/1866 [J/CDH/28.7.1866/5c3] and Pant to Barmouth 17/8/1866. Another excursion train, hauled by loco CASTELL DEUDRAETH, crashed at Bryncir 6/9/1866 [J/CDH/15.9.1866/4c3]. It was so crowded that some passengers were riding in the loco tender !

Locomotives: Gauge 4'8½"

The following locomotives have been positively identified as having worked on the Carnarvonshire Railway; it is likely there were others (see SAVIN in Section 1).

1	ENTERPRISE	0-6-0T		EBW	[? 301	1852]	(ca)	(c1)
35	CASTELL DEUDRAETH	0-6-0	IC	SS	1311	1861	(cb)	(c2)
9	VOLUNTEER	0-4-2	IC	SS	1226	1860	(cc)	(c1)
10	PIONEER	0-6-0ST	IC	MW	35	1861	(cc)	(c3)
18	CARDIGAN	0-6-0ST	IC	MW	55	1862	(cd)	(c1)
7	LLANERCHYDOL	0-4-2	IC	SS	1224	1860	(ce)	(c4)
59	SEAHAM	2-4-0T	IC	SS	1683	1866	(cf)	(c5)

(ca)	on CR after 1863		(c1)	later on Cam.Rys.
(cb)	on CR from 5/1865		(c2)	to Cam.Rys. after 9/1866
(cc)	on CR by 2/1866		(c3)	to Cam.Rys. 7/1868
(cd)	on CR by 9/1866		(c4)	to Cam.Rys. c5/1868
(ce)	ex Cam.Rys., hire, 11/9/1867		(c5)	to Cam.Rys. c12/1868
(cf)	ex Cam.Rys., hire, 16/9/1867			

OPERATION from 2/9/1867

2/9/1867 - 3/7/1870 : Carnarvonshire Rly Co
4/7/1870 - closure : LNWR/LMSR/BR

Locomotives: Gauge 4'8½"

Initially locos on hire from Cam.Rys. by agreement dated 14/9/1867, included in list above. Own locos subsequently obtained as below, but hirings probably continued in addition to these.

1	GLYNLLYFNI	2-4-0	IC	SS	1757	[1867?]New	(o1)
2		2-4-0	IC	SS	1899	1868 New 12/68	(o2)

(o1) tdt: LNWR, 1790, 4/7/1870; into LNWR general stock 8/1871.
(o2) tdt: LNWR, 1791, 4/7/1870; into LNWR general stock 8/1871.

CLOSURE & DEMOLITION

Last passenger train ran on 5/12/1964.
Freight trains ceased earlier in 1964.
Track lifted Dinas Junction-Afonwen in 1968
    (lifting at Groeslon 8/1968, Bryncir 10/1968, Afonwen 11/1968).
BR locos used on demolition trains.
Dinas Junction-Caernarfon retained as siding until 1970, then track lifted. No information re any contractor or locos used.

[Read: J/RMag/9.1958/591; B/303; B/340]

PORTHMADOG to NANTGWYNANT   PR/30
9 miles

Beddgelert Railway Company   : Acts 5/7/1865, 16/7/1866

CONSTRUCTION   Gauge: 4'8½"

Contractor: **Savin & Co**
Engineers: R.M.Ordish, W.H.LeFeuvre

Work started 1865; 6 miles reported complete by 2/1866 [J/RN/17-3-1866] when Savin became insolvent. A Board of Trade report 5/3/1870 lists numerous incomplete earthworks with just a mile of track laid but not ballasted; surviving earthworks suggest only 4 miles at most had been attempted, none truly completed.

Locomotives: Gauge 4'8½"

No evidence found to confirm use of any locomotives; if any were used they would doubtless be from Savin's Fleet (see Section 1).

CLOSURE & DEMOLITION

No work done after 4/1866; project abandoned. The Beddgelert Railway Co was in Chancery 8/1870 [J/CDH/13-27.8.1870/1c1].

Materials removed other than a stub at Porthmadog, retained as ("the Beddgelert") siding. These sidings were lifted c1959, and their site was subsequently used by the (1964) Welsh Highland Railway - see PR/44.

[Read: B/303/124; J/Welsh Highland Rly Socy/No.76-No.79]

CEMMES ROAD to DINAS MAWDDWY
"The Mawddwy Railway"

PR/31
6½ miles

    Mowddwy Railway Company   : Act 5/7/1865
    Mawddwy [Light] Railway Company   : LRO 2/3/1910
        Absorbed by GWR   :   1/1/1923

CONSTRUCTION
Gauge: 4'8½"
Contractor   : **R.S.France** (possibly sub-let to **James Taylor**)
                  Work started 1866, completed 9/1867

Locomotives: Gauge 4'8½"

ALYN	0-6-0ST	IC	MW	140	1864	(ca)	(c1)

(ca) wfw: R.S.France on another contract. Per MW records, this loco was New in 1864 to "R.S.France, Llanymynech", but that may have been an "office address". Actual delivery to or use on France's PS&NW Rly contract is not proven. In view of the name ALYN it seems likely that this loco was previously used on the Alyn Valley Line (PR/37) Contract.

(c1) tdt: Mowddwy Railway Company, 9/1867

OPERATION

Mowddwy Railway Company from 1/10/1867
        Closed to passengers 17/4/1901; to freight 8/4/1908
Reopened 31/7/1911; worked by Cambrian Railways Co
GWR from 1/1/1923; BR from 1/1/1948

Locomotives: Gauge 4'8½" (until 1908)

MAWDDWY	0-6-0ST	IC	MW	140	1864	(oa)	(o1)
DISRAELI	0-6-0ST	IC	MW	268	1869	New 2/69	(o2)

(oa) tdx: R.S.France (or J.Taylor ?), constructor of the line, 9/1867

(o1) tdt: Cam.Rys. 2/3/1910; became Cam.Rys. 30, GWR 824, Wdn 9/1940
(o2) tdt: Cam.Rys. 2/3/1910; Scrapped at Oswestry 8/1912

RECONSTRUCTION

After 2/3/1910, the line was reconstructed by Cam.Rys. using their loco No.22. Line reopened 29/7/1911 and subsequently worked by Cam.Rys., GWR and BR locos.

CLOSURE & DEMOLITION

Closed to passengers 1/1/1931; to freight (last train ran on) 5/9/1950).
Track lifted by Rhodes of Sheffield from 26/1/1952 to 26/5/1952, using loco 2323 supplied by BR.

[Read: B/102/42; B/303/177; B/323; J/RW/11.1975/446]

BARMOUTH JUNCTION to PWLLHELI   PR/32
                                                 33¼ miles

      Aberystwith & Welsh Coast Railway Company   : Act 22/7/1861
      Cambrian Railways Company as from 5/8/1866   : Act 5/7/1865

CONSTRUCTION   Gauge: 4'8½"

Contractor   : **Savin & Co**   to 5/2/1866
              : **Henry Coneybeare**   Completed 10/1867

The section from Afonwen to Penrhyndeudraeth had been constructed by the Carnarvonshire Rly Co (PR/29) - by Savin & Co - and was now incorporated into the A&WCR.

Locomotives: Gauge 4'8½"

Many locomotives in the "Savin fleet" (see Section 1) are possible candidates for listing here, but specific identities are unknown other than that a loco PIONEER (presumably No.10, MW 35/1861) was reported as having been maliciously damaged at Pwllheli 11/2/1867 [J/CDH/2-3-1867].

OPERATION

A limited horse-drawn passenger service commenced 3/6/1867 over the viaduct from Barmouth Junction to Barmouth.
Afonwen-Penrhyndeudraeth opened by Carnarvonshire Rly on 2/9/1867; line opened throughout by Cam.Rys. on 11/10/1867 [J/CDH/12.10.1867/1].

EXTENSION & RECONSTRUCTION

PWLLHELI EXTENSION, from first terminus to new terminus (½ mile).
Extension opened 19/7/1907.
Details of contractor, etc., not known.

AFONWEN to PENYCHAIN line (1¼ miles) widened, from single to double track, 1946-1947
Details of contractor, etc., not known.
This section narrowed to single track after closure of PR/29.
Details of contractor (if any) not known.

PARTIAL CLOSURE

Line closed to freight 5/1963.

[Read: B/101; B/102; B/416; J/RW/4.1972/176]

GREENFIELD (HOLYWELL JUNCTION) to HOLYWELL   PR/33
1 ¾ miles

	Holywell Railway Company	: Acts 27/7/1864, 13/7/1868
	Holywell Lime Co Ltd	: leased incomplete line c1868-1878
	John T.Eachus	: leased incomplete line 1878-
1884		
	Holywell Lime & Cement Co Ltd	: leased incomplete line 1884-1895
	LNWR purchased line	: 1891; closed and dismantled 1895
	LNWR build new line on route	: Acts 20/7/1906, 26/7/1907

CONSTRUCTION   Gauges: 3'0" & 4'8½"

Contractor   : **Jardine & Son**   Work started c1868
                                                      Construction abandoned c1871

The early history of this railway is intimately entwined with the Crockford's Spelter Works Tramroad and the Grange Quarries Tramroad which preceded it - see GRANGE QUARRIES in Section 3. Briefly, the Crockford's line pre-dated the Chester & Holyhead Rly (PR/7); it was later incorporated into the 3ft gauge Grange Tramroad, which in turn was built-over by the 4'8½" gauge Holywell Rly; mixed-gauge track being laid over much of this railway. Upon abandonment, the incomplete railway was leased to, and operated by, the Limestone Companies, using their own locomotives. This activity ended c1895; the equipment was sold, and the track on the railway was removed.

Locomotives: Gauge 4'8½"

The advertisement for the 11/7/1871 auction sale, of Jardine & Son equipment, does not mention any locomotives.
Locomotives used by the Limestone Companies : listed in Section 3.

RECONSTRUCTION   Gauge: 4'8½"

Contractor   : Not known.   Work in hand c1910-1912.

Apart from relaying track (4'8½" gauge only) and the completion of the station site at Holywell, the principal work involved a revised junction arrangement at Greenfield to permit direct running into Holywell Junction station. This included a high-level bridge and substantial steeply-graded curved embankment.

OPERATION

Opened by LNWR 1/7/1912.Worked by LNWR/LMSR/BR locomotives.
Closed to all traffic 6/9/1954, except for ½ mile Holywell Junction to Crescent Mill Siding which remained open for freight only until 11/8/1957.

CLOSURE & DEMOLITION

A contract was let in 1957 (c6/1957) for the removal of the track but identity of contractor not known.
The work was completed by 27/7/1958, on which date the junction with PR/7 was removed.

[Read: B/232; B/275; B/303; J/RMag/11.1971/630]

LLAN FFESTINIOG to BLAENAU FFESTINIOG　　　　PR/34
3½ miles

Festiniog & Blaenau Railway Co Ltd　　　　　　　　: registered 7/8/1862
Vested jointly in GWR Co and Bala & Festiniog Rly Co　: 13/4/1883
Great Western Railway Company [alone]　　from　: 1/7/1910

CONSTRUCTION　　　　　　　　　　　　　　　　　　　Gauge: 1'11½"

Contractors　　: D.McKenzie, J.Stacey,　　　　Tenders invited 2/1867
　　　　　　　　　James Green, Isaac Williams.　Work started　1867
Engineer　: Charles.M.Holland　　　　　　　　　Work completed 5/1868
Sale of Contractors' Plant: 9/11/1867 [J/CDH/2.11.1867/1.c6]

OPERATION

Opened to passengers　　　　: 30/5/1868 (official ceremony)
　　　　　　　　　　　　　　　　: 1/6/1868 (public trains) [see J/FRS/130/408]

Locomotives: Gauge 1'11½"

Trains initially operated by Festiniog Railway Company (PR/3) using FR locos and stock, until F&B locos delivered. FR locos were later hired from time to time as necessary.

| No.1 | [SCORCHER ?] | 0-4-2ST | OC | MW | 259 | 1868 | New 8/1868 | (o1) |
| No.2 | [NIPPER　 ?] | 0-4-2ST | OC | MW | 260 | 1868 | New 9/1868 | (o1) |

These locos may have been named, or nick-named, either as shown, or in inverse sequence; or not named at all.　Sources differ on this point, and no proof has yet been found.

(o1)　there is considerable doubt as to the fate of these locos, made redundant by the 1883 conversion of the line to 4'8½" gauge (below).
　　　Wm.Dean (GWR, Swindon) was offering these locos and other F&B stock for sale (to, e.g., Penrhyn Quarries [see J/FRS/No.86/20; No.88/18]) in 11/1883; later the Bala & Festiniog Rly Co invited tenders [e.g. J/B&ET/21-6-1884] for the F&B locos etc "by 7/7/1884...may be seen at Festiniog Station GWR".
　　　Reputedly all the F&B stock was unsold, and taken to Swindon 8/1884 "where it was scrapped" [J/IRR/Vol.7/392].　However, [B/103/N.31] states that the GWR sold the locos to the Ruabon Coal & Coke Co - for further comment on this see HAFOD COLLIERY in Section 3 [and see J/FRS/No.130/408.]

RECONSTRUCTION　　　　　　　　　　　　　　　　　Gauge: 4'8½"

Contractor　　　　: J.P.Edwards

Contract for work to convert line to 4'8½" gauge signed 28/6/1882; work under way 4/1883 to 9/1883 - included some deviations to ease curves etc.　Converted first as dual gauge and some sections (at least) remained open for traffic as work progressed.
Line closed 5/9/1883 for final conversion; reopened 10/9/1883.

Locomotives: Gauge 4'8½"

[INFLEXIBLE ?]	0-4-0ST	OC	MW	575	1876 (ra)	(r1)

(ra) wfw: T.J.Waller, contractor, [Cheetham Hill & Radcliffe Rly (1876 - 1879; sale held 6/1882) Contract ?], named MANCHESTER.

(r1) wlw: Wm.Rigby & Co, near Stoke on Trent [? Bunkers Hill Colliery, Talke] [? by c1888], named INFLEXIBLE.

OPERATION

After reopening, the line was operated by the GWR, as an extension of the line from Bala (PR/49).
Closed to passengers - last train ran on 2/1/1960.
Closed to freight, last train ran on 27/1/1961.
Line disused until reopened 20/4/1964 for special freight traffic only, as an extension of the line from Llandudno Junction (see PR/23 for details). Occasional excursion and charter passenger trains have operated (from Blaenau Ffestiniog to Maentwrog Road) including the full length of the F&B Rly.

[Read: B/147; B/450; J/FRS/No.130/408; J/IRR/Vol.7/166, 392]

CAERNARFON (MORFA) to LLANBERIS   PR/35
                                                                                                                                                    8 miles

       Carnarvon & Llanberis Railway Company   : Act 14/7/1864
       C&LR & LNWR Joint Line (4 miles only at Llanberis end) from : c1867
       Vested entirely in **L&NWR** Company   by: Act 4/7/1870

CONSTRUCTION   Gauge: 4'8½"

Contractor   : **Dalrymple & Finlay** (1866 only)
                     : **S.C.Ridley & S.L.Seckham** (1867 only)
                (partnership dissolved 10/1867 [J/CDH/2.11.1867/1c1])
                     : **S.C.Ridley & Co** (1867-1869)

First Sod: 15/9/1864. Work started 1866; Track completed by 9/1868

Locomotives: Gauge 4'8½"

0-4-0ST	FE(HH)	1867	New(a)	(1)

(a) arrived Caernarfon 26/11/1867; thence by road to PR/35 at Cwmyglo, arriving 28/11/1867. Weight 12 tons. [J/NWC/30.11.1867]

(1) tdt: PR/35A contract (Caernarfon Town Line)

OPERATION

Opened to public traffic 1/7/1869. LNWR/LMSR/BR locos used.

CLOSURE & DEMOLITION

Closed to passengers 22/9/1930, except summer excursions to 1962.
Closed to freight 3/9/1964 (actual last use); 7/9/1964 (official).
Track lifted by George Cohen, Sons & Co Ltd, 1966.
BR locos used on demolition trains.

[Read: J/RMag/10.1958/715; B/303; B/340]

CAERNARFON TOWN LINE (LNWR to PANT & MORFA)   PR/35A
1½ miles

London & North Western Railway Company : Act 5/7/1865

CONSTRUCTION   Gauge: 4'8½"

Contractor   : **S.C.Ridley**   Work started   ?
                                           Tunnel collapsed 9/1869
                                           Work completed   6/1870

Locomotives: Gauge 4'8½"

0-4-0ST	FE(HH)	1867	(a)	(1)

(a)   tdx: PR/35 Contract

(1)   the 6+7/7/1870 end-of-contract sale of Ridley's equipment included a "powerful tank loco engine, nearly new" [presumably this loco].
      No further trace.

OPERATION

Official opening 5/7/1870.
Opened to freight 5/7/1870; to passengers 1/1871.
LNWR/LMSR/BR locos used.
Built as a double-track line, but from 1894 the junction at Pant (Morfa) was removed, and the route worked as two parallel single-line extensions of the branches, from Llanberis and Afonwen, into Caernarfon.
Thus later history is as for these lines - see PR/29 and PR/35.

PRESTATYN to DYSERTH

PR/36
2¾ miles

London & North Western Railway Company : Act 16/7/1866

CONSTRUCTION

Gauge: 4'8½"

Contractor : **Scott & Edwards** [of Wigan]   Work started 5/1868
Completed   8/1869

Nothing known re locomotives used, if any.

OPERATION

Opened to freight 1/9/1869; to passengers 28/8/1905
Operated by LNWR/LMSR/BR locos.

CLOSURE & DEMOLITION

Closed to passengers - last train ran on 20/9/1930
Closed to freight - last train ran on 8/9/1973
Track lifted during 1980 - no details known re any contractor or re locos used.

[Read: J/RMag/12.1978/582; B/324; B/326]

MOLD to DENBIGH JUNCTION   PR/37
                                                           15¾ miles

           Mold & Denbigh Junction Railway Company : Act 6/8/1861
           London, Midland & Scottish Railway Co   : from 1/1/1923

CONSTRUCTION   Gauge: 4'8½"

Contractor   : R.S.France   Work in hand 8/1864-7/1866
                                       Contract terminated 10/1868

                : Scott & Edwards   Work re-started 11/1868
                                       Work completed   9/1869

Locomotives: Gauge 4'8½"

No positive information found as to the use of locomotives by any contractor on this line. However, the railway follows the valley of the River Alyn, and in 11/1864 R.S.France took delivery of a new loco 0-6-0ST IC MW 140/1864, named ALYN. The "official" delivery address was Llanymynech, where R.S.France had an office, and a contract on the Potteries, Shrewsbury & North Wales Rly. Thus we have only the name of the loco, plus its date of delivery, to suggest actual (or intentional) use on PR/37. If here, then this loco was probably transferred to the PS&NWR in 1866, and later reached the Mawddwy Railway - see PR/31.

Although Scott & Edwards owned locos at this time [eg, 0-6-0ST IC MW 91/1863] no evidence has yet been found of any loco being used by them on PR/37. Advertisements for sales of contractor's plant held at Rhydymwyn and elsewhere 7-9/4/1869 do not mention any locomotives [though presumably ballasting was not then completed].

OPERATION

Line opened 2/9/1869 [poster in RRO, BD/A/480] [and J/MJ/4-9-1869 reports the line opened in the "preceeding week"]. However, many secondary sources quote 12/9/1869, whilst B/342/19 has 11/9/1869, and the Minutes at PRO/Kew record 6/9/1869. [Perhaps differences arise from various public and official openings, of all or parts of the line ?]
Worked by LNWR from opening; later by LMSR and BR.

CLOSURE & DEMOLITION

Closed to passengers (last train ran on) 30/4/1962
Closed to freight:
   Denbigh-Dolfechlas Crossing (Olwyn Goch Mine Siding) on 30/4/1962
        Dolfechlas Crossing-Mold (Alyn Works) traffic ceased 1/1/1968
        Mold (Alyn Works)-Mold plus PR/9 closed 12/1983

Track lifted Denbigh-Dolfechlas c1962; Dolfechlas-Alyn 1978-79 (and removed by BR loco). Remainder lifted with PR/9.
No details known of any contractors or other locos that may have been involved in demolition.

[Read: J/RMag/7.1962/466; B/303; B/232]

TALYSARN to VRON (CESAREA) PR/38
1½ miles

Vron & Talysarn Tramroad (John Robinson)
Permission to construct granted 1867 by Crown Agents (landowners)

CONSTRUCTION
Gauge: 3'4½" (clear); 3'6" (c/c)

Contractor : no details known - possibly a "direct labour" job.
Work started 12/1867; Completed 7/1870.

Route: From junction (near Talysarn) with Nantlle Tramroad (PR/2), along an abandoned former route of PR/2 to foot of three gravity inclines up to Cilgwyn, thence c1 mile 'level' to Fron (Vron & Old Braich) Slate Quarries, Cesarea. Connection later (by 1/1872) made via incline from Cesarea to New Braich Quarry which then used PR/38 also.

OPERATION
Tramroad on 'level' reputedly worked by horses only, though there is the possibility that a suitable 0-4-0VBT DeW loco was obtained for the line - for further comment see TALYSARN QUARRY in Section 3. Line originally intended to serve Old Braich Quarry only; it is recorded that, after New Braich Quarry started to use the line, the latter worked their traffic with their own horses.
The lower incline, plus approach to PR/2, was also used by Talysarn Quarry.

Locomotives: Gauge 3'4½"

Unconfirmed DeWinton loco - see notes above.

RECONSTRUCTION

The upper two inclines at Cilgwyn were replaced by a single incline having summit slightly to west of original, to permit expansion of Cilgwyn Quarry workings.

CLOSURE & DEMOLITION

The North Wales Narrow Gauge Railway (PR/44) reached Bryngwyn in 5/1877, and offered a better outlet to the Cesarea quarries. PR/38 closed late-1881; track lifted 1882 and rails used to build new 2ft gauge line Fron(Vron)-Bryngwyn. The lower incline, and connection to PR/2, at Talysarn, was retained as part of the Talysarn Quarry rail system.

MOLD (TRYDDYN Jct) to COED TALON to PANTYSTAIN (LLANFYNYDD)
PR/39
"Mold & Treiddyn Railway"
5½ miles

London & North Western Railway Company : Act 16/7/1866

A complicated length of railway. From Tryddyn Junction to Nerquis Hall (2 miles) was new construction; thence 2¼ miles to Coed Talon was reconstruction (with deviations) of route of Nerquis Colliery Railway (formally purchased by LNWR on 13/5/1868 - see NERQUIS, Section 3). From Coed Talon it was an upgrading of the existing LNWR line to Llanfynydd (PR/10) as far as Tryddyn Road (B 5101) Pantystain Crossing; beyond which the remaining ½ mile of PR/10, to Llanfynydd, was then sold to the (GWR/LNWR Joint) Wrexham & Minera Extension Railway Company - see PR/40.

CONSTRUCTION
Gauge: 4'8½"

Contractor : **James & George Nowell** [of Cefnybedd]

Contract let 1/1867; Nowells were made bankrupt 1/1869 but probably continued with this contract, as LNWR were making payments to them until 6/1870 at least.

No information found re use of any locomotives by the contractors.

OPERATION

Opened to freight: Tryddyn Junction to Oak Pits Colliery 16/3/1869,
  to Coed Talon 8/7/1870; thence by pre-existing (PR/10) service to Llanfynydd.
Opened to passengers Mold-Coed Talon 1/1/1892;
  Coed Talon-Brymbo via PR/39 + PR/40 15/11/1897 or 2/5/1898 [sources vary].
Operated by LNWR/LMSR/BR locomotives.

CLOSURE & DEMOLITION

Closed throughout to passengers on 27/3/1950.
Closed to freight: (Bwlchgwyn Sidings to) Pantystain to Coed Talon
  (Star Quarry Siding) 1/1/1951: Track lifted 4/1951.
  Coed Talon to Mold 22/7/1963: Track lifted 1964, final lifting at Tryddyn Junction 11/1964; BR locos used for this demolition.

No information found re any demolition contractors or locos used.

[Read: B/232; B/304; B/341; J/RW/11.1987/647]

BRYMBO (EAST JUNCTION) to LLANFYNYDD to PANTYSTAIN   PR/40
"Wrexham & Minera Extension Railway"
2¾ miles

Wrexham & Minera Extension Railway Company : Act 5/7/1865
Jointly owned by **LNWR** and **GWR** from 1866 : Act 11/6/1866

The W&MER Co remained nominally independent until 1/1/1948. Its somewhat misleading title reflected the fact that it was a branch line off the Wrexham to Minera railway (PR/21 + 6).

CONSTRUCTION
Gauge: 4'8½"

Contractor   : **Nathaniel B.Fogg & Co** [of Liverpool]

The line was new construction from Brymbo to Llanfynydd, then an upgrading of existing line (PR/10) for c½ mile to Pantystain.

No details found re use of locomotives by the contractors.

OPERATION

Opened: for freight 27/1/1872
        for passengers 15/11/1897 or 2/5/1898 - sources vary.
LNWR/LMSR/BR locos used.

CLOSURE & DEMOLITION

Closed to passengers on 27/3/1950
Closed to freight Bwlchgwyn Siding to Pantystain (to Coed Talon) 1/1/1951; track lifted 4/1951.
Closed to freight Brymbo to Bwlchgwyn 1/10/1963; track lifted.
Nothing discovered re any demolition contractors or locos used.

PENYGROES to TALYSARN (NANTLLE)   PR/41
1½ miles

London & North Western Railway Company : Act 4/7/1870

CONSTRUCTION
Gauge: 4'8½"

Contractor   : **S.C.Ridley**

Contract let to Ridley 18/8/1870; earthworks finished 15/6/1871; permanent-way laid throughout 18/1/1872; junction inspected 18/5/1872; line inspected for passenger use 9/9/1872.

This line was built to replace the Tyddyn Bengam-Talysarn (Village) section of the Nantlle (Horse) Railway (PR/2), following a new route generally adjacent to PR/2.

No references have been found to the use of locomotives by Ridley, though he had previously used a loco nearby, on PR/35+35A. The end of contract auction 1/10/1872 advertisements did not mention a loco [J/CDH/7-28.9.1872/1].

OPERATION

Opened for freight 21/5/1872; for passengers 1/10/1872.
LNWR/LMSR/BR locos used.

CLOSURE & DEMOLITION

Closed to passengers from 1/1/1917 to 5/5/1919: J/RMAG/10-1926 has a report that the line "has been reopened for passenger traffic"; this could be a late report, or perhaps refers to another period of closure. Finally closed to passengers as from 8/8/1932.
Closed to freight 4/11/1963 (actual); 2/12/1963 (official).
Track lifted 11/1965 to 2/1966.

No information found re any demolition contractor or locos used.

CHIRK to GLYNCEIRIOG to HENDRE — PR/42
"Glyn Valley Tramway" — 8 miles

Ellesmere & Glyn Valley Railway Company : Act 6/8/1866
renamed: **Glyn Valley Tramway Company** : Act 10/8/1870
reformed as: **Glyn Valley Tramway Co Ltd**: Reg 22/8/1935
for purposes of liquidating the Company.

CONSTRUCTION

Gauge: 2'4"/2'4¼"

Contractor : **Elias Griffith**   Contract Let: 5/1872

Built as 6 mile roadside horse-worked freight tramroad from Chirk Bank Wharf on Shropshire Union Canal to Glynceiriog, with incline extension to slate quarries. In contemporary documents, the gauge is quoted as 2'4", but given as 2'4¼" in later Board of Trade Returns.

OPERATION

Line opened to freight 4/1873; being worked by the Shropshire Union Railway & Canal Company. As this Company had been leased (in 1847) to the LNWR, the latter could be regarded as the true operator.
Operated by Ceiriog Granite Co Ltd from 1/7/1881 until 1889.
A horse-hauled passenger service operated 1/4/1874 until 31/3/1886.

Locomotives: Gauge 2'4"

TUNIS		0-4-0IST	OC	WB	358	1881 (ta)	(t1)

(ta) loaned by W.G.Bagnall for trial work on the horse-tramway; first trial trip 23/7/1881 [J/MJ/30.7.1881/943]; passenger trip (with Sir Theodore Martin et al, band playing, etc) 25/7/1881 [J/NWG/30.7.81]. Loco had previously been on display at Royal Agricultural Society Show, Derby, 7/1881. [Reporting this latter, J/ENG/15.7.1881/58 and J/CJ/27.7.1881 state loco was named THE TIMES, and J/MJ/30.7.1881 (above) repeats this name. However, "Staffordshire Advertiser" 16/7/1881 p.2 gives name as TUNIS, and this name is confirmed for this loco in WB records (though the latter make no mention of the GVT trial). [Perhaps handwritten "The Tunis" was misinterpreted by one typesetter, whose work was then copied by others.]

(t1) presume returned to WB, Stafford, late 7/1881 by 9/1881 (BoT report of 17/9/1881 states loco has been removed from GVT [B/348/24]).
Subsequently sold by WB to agents Figee Bros., Holland, 2/1882 as TUNIS; spares ordered by Luis Smulders & Co, for "TUNES", in 1896.

RECONSTRUCTION   Gauge: 2'4½"

By Act 31/7/1885, the GVT Co was authorised to construct new lines Pontfaen to Chirk GWR (1 mile); Glynceiriog to Hendre (1¾ miles); to abandon Pontfaen to Chirk Bank; and to upgrade, with deviations, the remaining section Pontfaen to Glynceiriog; all as a 2'4½" gauge steam operated tramway.

Contractor   : **H.Croom Johnson** [of Wrexham]

Work started 1887; mostly completed by 1889.
Freight traffic continued whilst this work was in progress.

Locomotives: Gauge 2'4"

FERNHILL	0-6-0ST	OC	[?Bs]	(**)	(ra)	(r1)
BELMONT	0-4-2ST	OC	FE(HH)	[1877?] (ra)		(r1)

(**) This loco was supplied to SDRlys by Lennox Lange & Co, dealers, (of Glasgow) and carried one of their plates. It had an "ogee" saddle tank, and was perhaps built by Bs (Barclays & Co, Kilmarnock).
There seems nothing to support a popular theory which connects this loco with a 2'6" gauge 0-6-0ST built by Lewin in 1875, which was advertised for sale at Waterford, Ireland, in 3/1879, and which is claimed by some references to have been also named FERNHILL.

(ra) these locos were borrowed from the Snailbeach District Railways Co, Salop, between early 1887 and c5/1889. From SDR traffic returns for the period it seems clear that only one loco was hired at any one time and it seems likely that FERNHILL came first, being later replaced by BELMONT. There are reports of derailments which are usually blamed on the small difference in gauge between the SDR and GVT - a more likely explanation is that FERNHILL was too heavy and rigid for contractors' use over the old GVT tramroad track.

(r1) both had been returned to Snailbeach District Railways by c5/1889

OPERATION

After reconstruction, the line was operated by the Glyn Valley Tramway Company until final closure; taking over operation of the freight traffic in 1889, and operating a passenger service between Chirk (GWR) and Glynceiriog (only) from 16/3/1891 (a partial service having started in 1890).

Locomotives: Gauge 2'4½"

	SIR THEODORE	0-4-2T	OC	BP	2969	1888	New 10/88	(o1)
	DENNIS	0-4-2T	OC	BP	2970	1889	New 4/89	(o2)
No.3	GLYN	0-4-2T	OC	BP	3500	1892	New 5/92	(o3)
-	-	4-6-0PT	OC	BLW	45221	1917		
		rebuilt by BP				1921	(oa)	(o4)

(oa) New to War Department, WDLR 1089; lying at Purfleet, Essex, and sold to GVT by Ministry of Munitions. Sent direct from Purfleet to BP 1/1921 for overhaul and alteration from 2ft gauge.
   tdx: BP, Manchester, c8/1921

(o1) tdt: Snailbeach District Railways, Salop, loan, 1905
     tdx: Snailbeach District Railways, off loan, 1905
     Scrapped c9/1936 at Chirk, by Davies Bros *
(o2) Scrapped c9/1936 at Chirk, by Davies Bros *
(o3) Scrapped 8/1936 at Chirk, by Davies Bros *
(o4) Scrapped   1937 at Chirk, by Davies Bros *

*Davies Bros; reputedly of Barmouth, though another source has them as "of Wrexham".

CLOSURE & DEMOLITION

Closed to passengers - last train ran on 6/4/1933
Closed to freight   - last train ran on 6/7/1935
Track removed by Davies Bros., using road vehicles.

RE-USE OF SITE AT CHIRK

The Tramway buildings and yard at Chirk (GWR) were later occupied by the Forestry Commission, and used for the storage of locomotives and other equipment. For details see CHIRK FORESTRY DEPOT in Section 3.

[Read: B/348; B/173; B/303; B/309]

WREXHAM to RHOSLLANERCHRUGOG STREET TRAMWAY   PR/43
4½ miles

Wrexham District Tramways Company	: Act	16/6/1873
Wrexham Tramways Ltd	: from	1879
Drake & Gorham Electric Power & Traction Co	: from	1900
British Electric Traction Co Ltd	: from 22/12/1900	
Wrexham & District Electric Traction Co Ltd	: Reg 26/8/1901	
Wrexham & District Transport Co Ltd	: from 9/3/1914	

CONSTRUCTION   Gauge: 3'0"

Contractor: no details known.
Built as horse-worked tramway - from Wrexham (Ruabon Road Cemetary) to Johnstown (New Inn) - 2¾ miles, single track.
Extended immediately from Cemetary to Ruthin Road Junction.

OPERATION

Opened for passenger and freight traffic 1/11/1876; the extension opened 12/1876. Operated by owning companies until c1880 leased to Frederick Llewelyn Jones (who purchased the trams and horses in 6/1884). [Operation may have reverted 1896 to Wrexham Tramways Ltd but sources are unclear on this point.]

Passenger Trams: Gauge 3'0"

No.1 - Fourwheel toast-rack singledeck built by Starbuck Car & Wagon Co Ltd, Birkenhead, 1876. Rebuilt as doubledeck c1878.
No.2 - Fourwheel open-top doubledeck also built Starbuck, in c1877.
No.3 - Fourwheel copy of No.2, built Fred.Ll.Jones, Wrexham.

CLOSURE

Last tram ran on 26/4/1901. Route incorporated into route of new electric tramway. Passenger trams listed above scrapped or sold.

RECONSTRUCTION   Gauge: 3'6"

Contractor   : Dick, Kerr & Co Ltd

New line 550v overhead-wire, from Wrexham (GWR station) to New Inn at Johnstown; extended immediately Johnstown to Rhos (Gardden Road/ Hill Street junction, Ponciau) and Wrexham(GWR) to Turf Hotel.

OPERATION

Opened for passengers: Wrexham (GWR) to Johnstown 4/4/1903; to Turf Hotel 26/5/1903; to Rhos (Ponciau) end of 1904.
Line now 4½ miles long, single track with passing loops.

Passenger Trams: Gauge 3'6"

Ten vehicles, numbered 1 to 10; all similar four-wheel doubledeck opentops built BE 1902-1905.

CLOSURE & DEMOLITION

Tramway closed - last tram ran on 31/3/1927. Trams all scrapped except for body of car 6 privately preserved.
No details known re any demolition contractor.
Track lifted or buried; except at Johnstown Depot, where tracks and building survived to 6/1989 (at least).

[Read: B/140; B/255; B/380]

DINAS JCT to TRYFAN JCT to BEDDGELERT to PORTHMADOG   PR/44
                                                                                27 miles
TRYFAN JUNCTION to BRYNGWYN   2¾ miles
BEDDGELERT to NANTGWYNANT (SOUTH SNOWDON)   3½ miles

North Wales Narrow Gauge Railways Company	: Act 6/8/1872
Portmadoc, Beddgelert & South Snowdon Rly Co	: Act 17/8/1901
Welsh Highland Railway (Light Railway) Company	: Reg 30/3/1922
Welsh Highland Light Railway (1964) Ltd	: Reg 30/1/1964

CONSTRUCTION: NWNGR   Gauge: 1'11½"

Contractor   : Hugh Unsworth McKie & George Lea - spring 1873-7/2/1876
                           : J.Boys   -   2/1876- 5/1881

Line built Dinas Junction-Tryfan Junction-Cwellyn (Quellyn); plus Tryfan Junction-Bryngwyn; all finished by 5/1877.
Extended Cwellyn-Rhyd Ddu; finished 5/1881. Total route: 12 miles.

Locomotives: Gauge 1'11½"

No positive information. In 1956 an "old man" recalled that a small 0-4-0T VB had been used. From 16/2/1876 the Festiniog Rly Co (PR/3) hired a "small locomotive" for six months to "Mr Bray, the contractor of NWNG lines" - perhaps "Bray" was an error for "Boys".

OPERATION: NWNGR

Dinas Junction to Cwellyn, and Tryfan Junction to Bryngwyn, opened to freight 21/5/1877; to passengers 15/8/1877.
Cwellyn to Snowdon Ranger opened 1/6/1878 and to Rhyd Ddu 14/5/1881.
Rhyd Ddu station was named "Snowdon" for many years.

Locomotives: Gauge 1'11¼"

Vignes [B/159] writing in 1878 refers to the two VF locos listed below, and also to a small four-coupled tank loco (having 7"x12" cylinders, 1'9" wheels, 4'0" wheelbase) reported as being on the NWNGR. It seems likely that he heard this from Mr Spooner, and in fact refers to VF 805 working at Bryngwyn (see ALEXANDRA QUARRIES in Section 3).
NOTE: On 3/12/1878 the NWNGR locos were sold to, and leased back from, the Moel Tryfan Rolling Stock Co Ltd.

MOEL TRYFAN	0-6-4T	OC	VF	738	1875	New	
	rebuilt by DM				1902		Scr/1917
MOEL TRYFAN	0-6-4T	OC	VF	739	1875	New	
(SNOWDON RANGER	rebuilt by DM				1903		
until 1917)	rebuilt by NWNGR				1917	(*)	(n1)
BEDDGELERT	0-6-4ST	OC	HE	206	1878	New 7/78	Scr/1906
RUSSELL	2-6-2T	OC	HE	901	1906	New 6/06	(n1)
GOWRIE	0-6-4T	OC	HE	979	1908	New 9/08	(n2)

(*) in 1917, the frame of VF 739 was fitted with boiler etc from VF 738 resulting in a single locomotive named MOEL TRYFAN.

(n1) tdt: Welsh Highland Railway stock in 1922.
(n2) tdt: Ministry of Munitions, c1916 after 7/1/1916 (possibly not until after completion of rebuild of loco VF 739 in 1917; some sources say in 1918, but MoM had largely ceased loco purchases of this nature by that date); destination unknown - may not have been used. Sent by MoM to J.F.Wake, dealer, Darlington, where it was "rebuilt" in 1918. Offered for sale by Wake from 1919 to 1927 during which time it bore the number 1516; demonstrated, to Festiniog Railway (PR/3) staff in 4/1923, in steam and working - possibly at Marske, near Redcar, Yorks (where Hughes, Bolckow & Co Ltd were developing a former aerodrome site and may have been using a 2ft gauge rail system). Apparently sold, with sundry other old locos, by Wake to Hughes Bolckow, (who were also in the scrap trade) in late 1927. Advertised for sale by Hughes Bolckow, Marske, 1/1928; no further trace. [No evidence has been found to support the idea that GOWRIE was employed on the 1918 Marske Aerodrome Extension Contract, on which a 2ft gauge rail system with locomotives was certainly used by contractors J.Gerrard & Son].

FURTHER CONSTRUCTION: NWNGR

Contractor: not known.

By Light Railway Order (LRO) [of 30/10/1900 or 3/11/1900 - sources vary] extension of railway authorised Rhyd Ddu to Beddgelert.
Some work was apparently done, but project soon abandoned; it was re-started in 1904 by the PBSSR (see below).

CLOSURE: NWNGR

Tryfan Junction to Bryngwyn closed to passengers 31/12/1913.
Dinas Junction to Rhyd Ddu closed to passengers 31/10.1916.
Not closed to freight but traffic declined to virtually nil.

ABNORMAL WARTIME USE OF NWNG RAILWAY

During 2/1917 some 4wPE locos were test-run over the NWNGR from Dinas Junction, by or for the War Department.
[For further details see B/144/158, B/451/62 and J/IRR/Vol.6/178.]

CONSTRUCTION: PBSSR

Apart from an 1843 scheme to build a primitive tramroad [B/182/131], the first positive proposal was for the "Snowdon & Portmadoc Railway"; surveyed c1858 and pegged out by Allen Searell as a means of conveying output from mines and quarries in Nant Gwynant. This line was to be "twe fut" gauge, was to carry passengers, and steam traction was envisaged [UCNW/Searell]. When Searell died in 1865, the railway proposal died too.

Around 1900 this scheme was re-born, the PB&SS Rly Co being promoted as an electric railway, again running between Porthmadog, Beddgelert and Nant Gwynant (for South Snowdon Slate Quarry), with a hydro-electric power station at Cwm Dyli in Nant Gwynant. In the Beddgelert area it was to remain on the eastern side of the Glaslyn river, with no connection to the NWNGR whose extension from Rhyd Ddu was planned to terminate on the west bank at a station behind the Royal Goat Hotel.

Much of this proposal was authorised by the Act of 1901; the route included the Portmadoc-Carreg Hylldrem portion of the Croesor line (PR/25 - purchased with effect from 30/6/1901), but no actual work was done on the ground.

The North Wales Power & Traction Co Ltd was registered in 1903 and, in effect, took over the PB&SSR - but was mainly concerned with the latter's rights to generate and distribute electricity. Nevertheless, the NWP&T did arrange for Bruce Peebles & Co Ltd, of Edinburgh, to supervise construction of the PBSSR, and manufacture locomotives for use on the line.

Work did start c1903, Peebles giving the actual engineering work to contractors A.Krauss & Son [of Bristol] (who had done work elsewhere for Peebles and, when Peebles collapsed in 1906, were one of the major creditors). Krauss constructed new formation from (Croesor Junction on) PR/25 to Aberglaslyn (long tunnel not completed); up Aberglaslyn pass on east bank and thence towards Nant Gwynant. Some track was laid, including Croesor Junction to Ynysferlas, and in the Gwynant Valley.

Concurrently, the PBSSR/NWP&T combine planned to take over the NWNGR and incorporate it in a through route, from their Aberglaslyn line, to Caernarfon. To this end, an Act was obtained 15/8/1904 for construction of a line from Dinas Junction to Caernarfon (this was never started in fact); by Agreement of 26/8/1904 confirmed by LRO of 24/10/1906 they took over the NWNGR powers (of LRO 30/10/1900) to complete the section Rhyd Ddu to Beddgelert; the 1906 LRO also permitted the construction of a short connection between Beddgelert (Royal Goat) station and the PBSSR line on the east bank of the river. Some work was done on this connection, including road bridge and part embankment, but it was never completed. Some work was also done on the line to Rhyd Ddu, Krauss obtaining permission in 1904, from the County Council, for a temporary level crossing at Pitts Head.

Locomotives: Gauge 1'11½" (A.Krauss & Co)

        PROGRESS   0-4-0ST OC WB   1731 1903 New 7/04   (k1)

(k1) in 5/1906, Krauss (Bristol office) advertised a 1'11½" gauge WB loco for sale - probably this loco.
    WB 1731 wlw: Jersey Granite Quarries Ltd, Ronez, Jersey, by 17/2/1909

Locomotives: Gauge 1'11¼" & 1'11" (for PBSSR operation)

PBSSR ordered steam loco RUSSELL, apparently for the Dinas-Caernarfon section, but on delivery it was taken into NWNGR stock as listed earlier.

In anticipation of a formal order from PBSSR, Bruce Peebles & Co Ltd arranged for construction of ten 0-4-0 electric locos, having twin trolley-poles for overhead-wire 550/600v AC 3-phase current.

Apparently Bruce Peebles were to build these locos within the terms of their license to manufacture articles covered by Patents held by Ganz & Co, of Budapest, Austria; but it is likely that frames, wheels and even bodywork were subcontracted - perhaps to Brush of Loughborough. Ganz were also probably involved in manufacture, if only of motors. At least 5, possibly 6, of these locos were completed at Edinburgh between 1905 and 1908 - when the PBSSR scheme was abandoned, the locos were left on Peebles hands and almost certainly none ever came to Wales. Bruce Peebles went into voluntary liquidation 2/1908, and in 8/1908 advertisements appeared [J/MM/28.8.1908] for the sale, by NWP&T Co Ltd, Llanberis, of 6 of these locos. They apparently remained unsold, and were scrapped at Edinburgh during WW1. [See J/NG/No.94/10; No.101/29; No.103/29; No.107/28; No.110/27; No.123/23; B/450/291 for extended details of these locomotives].

ABANDONMENT: PBSSR

Construction of the PBSSR was abandoned in 1908; the work having actually ceased early in 1906.

ABNORMAL WARTIME USE OF PBSS RAILWAY

During World War 1, the uncompleted sections between Rhyd Ddu and Beddgelert were used for temporary forestry railways. For details see RHYD DDU FORESTRY in Section 3.

CONSTRUCTION: WHR

In 4/1920, Aluminium Corporation Ltd purchased the bankrupt NWNGR [B/420/75] and, having purchased a controlling interest in NWP&T Co (of which the PBSSR was still a wholly-owned subsidiary) in 11/1918 [B/420/69], AC Ltd were now able to promote the Welsh Highland Rly Co to take over these lines.

The WHR scheme involved the refurbishment of the NWNGR "main line" Dinas Junction to Rhyd Ddu; the completion with deviations of section Rhyd Ddu to Beddgelert; construction of new route from Beddgelert (Royal Goat) to Aberglaslyn (Brynfelin); completion of PBSSR route through Pass (including finishing of tunnels) and on to Croesor Junction; refurbishment of (PR/25) thence to Portmadoc ("New"), and over level crossing with GWR (PR/32); thence part new route to join Ffestiniog Railway (PR/3) at Harbour Station. Total distance 27 miles.

The remaining incomplete sections of the PBSSR - Brynfelin to Nant Gwynant (South Snowdon Inclines), plus the original short but steep connection from this line to Beddgelert (Royal Goat), and the never-started section from Dinas to Caernarfon, were not within the WHR scheme. The track that had been laid in the Gwynant Valley was lifted sometime after 1928.

Contractor   : **Sir Robert McAlpine & Sons Ltd**   Work started   3/1922
                                                           Work completed 5/1923

Locomotives used: Gauge 2ft - McAlpine

Plant No.01884	0-4-0ST OC	WB	2080	1918	(ra)		(r1)
Plant No.1646	4wPM 20hp	MR	2179	1922	New	(rb)	(r2)
Plant No.1447	4wPM 20hp	MR	2192	1922	New	(rc)	(r3)
Plant No.1637	4wPM 20hp	MR	2193	1922	New	(rd)	(r4)
Plant No. [1667 or 1677]	4wPM 20hp	MR	2197	1923	New	(re)	(r5)
Plant No.1666	4wPM 20hp	MR	2199	1923	New	(rf)	(r6)
PALMERSTON	0-4-0STt OC	GE		1863	(rg)		(r7)

(ra) tdx: Great Stanney Plant Depot, Cheshire, c3/1922 (by 8/6/1922)
      wfw: McAlpine at Dolgarrog - see DOLGARROG RAILWAYS in Section 3.
(rb) delivered to Dinas Junction 6/1922; despatched from Bedford 31/5/22
(rc) delivered as "New" to Porthmadog Station Cam.Rys., 9/1922; but in fact a rebuild of loco MR 1739/1918, repurchased by MR from French Disposals Board per Wm.Jones, dealer, 1/4/1922.
(rd) delivered as "New" to Porthmadog Station, 10/1922; but in fact a rebuild of loco MR 1684/1918, repurchased by MR from French Disposals Board per Wm.Jones, dealer, 1/4/1922.
(re) delivered as "New" to Porthmadog Station, c1/1923; but in fact a rebuild of an earlier MR loco, identity unknown, repurchased by MR from French Disposals Board per Wm.Jones, dealer, 1/4/1922.
(rf) delivered as "New" to Porthmadog Station c2-3/1923 (despatched from Bedford on 28/2/1923); but in fact a rebuild of loco MR 992/1918, repurchased by MR from French Disposals Board per Wm.Jones, dealer, 1/4/1922.
(rg) tdx: Ffestiniog Railway (PR/3), loan, 9/5/1923

(r1) tdt: ?, after 8/6/1922
      wlw(tdt ?): McAlpine at Dolgarrog (again), by 22/6/1923
(r2) tdt: ? (remained with McAlpine until sold to "Hall, Middlesboro" in 1927).
(r3) tdt: ? (later used by McAlpine at New Southgate Bridge Contract, London, in 1931; and still in McAlpine stock in 1942).
(r4) tdt: ? (later used by McAlpine at Dalbeattie in 1941 - no further trace).
(r5) tdt: ? (probably remained in McAlpine stock for some years).
(r6) tdt: ? (later used by McAlpine at Tilbury, Essex, in 1927; renumbered Plant No.2953 in 1932; used by McAlpine at Scunthorpe in 1938 and at Burghfield in 1941; no further trace).
(r7) tdt: Ffestiniog Railway (PR/3), off loan, 6/1923

NOTE: The McAlpine petrol locos listed above are known to have been on this Contract because delivery details survive in MR archives. However, when the WHR work started, McAlpine already had 34 similar locos in stock, not all of which can be accounted for elsewhere. As only one New MR was sent to Dinas Junction, it seems likely that one or more ex-stock locos could have been used at that end of the Contract. All the petrol locos probably left the WHR c5/1923 as work was completed, and probably initially went to the Great Stanney Plant Depot, Cheshire; though positive records are lacking.

OPERATION: WHR

Line opened to all traffic Dinas Junction to Rhyd Ddu 31/7/1922; Rhyd Ddu to Porthmadog New 1/6/1923; Porthmadog New to Harbour 8/6/1923. From 15/12/1924 the line was closed to passengers except during summer months. Tryfan Junction to Bryngwyn remained open for freight continuously from NWNGR days, but was not reopened for passengers (ie, since 31/12/1913).
Rhyd Ddu Station, which had been re-named "Snowdon" by the NWNGR, was re-named "South Snowdon" by the WHR; thus causing considerable confusion as it was not, of course, the "SS" as in "PB&SS" Railway.
From 19/7/1934 the WHR was leased to the Festiniog Railway Company, and the FR and WHR were then worked (in theory) as one system. In fact, even when independent, both lines were controlled from the same office.

Locomotives: Gauge 1'11½" - WHR

No.11	MOEL TRYFAN	0-6-4T	OC	VF	739	1875		
			rebuilt	DM		1903		
			rebuilt	NWNGR		1917	(wa)	(w1)
No.12	RUSSELL	2-6-2T	OC	HE	901	1906	(wa)	(w2)
590		4-6-0PT	OC	BLW	45172	1917		
			rebuilt	WB	March	1919	(wb)	Scr 6/1942
-		6wDM	60hp	KS	4415	1928	(wc)	(w3)

Also Ffestiniog Railway locos hired as required, and regularly from "amalgamation" in 7/1934.

(wa) tdx: NWNGR (with railway), 1922
(wb) [tdx ?]: E.W.Farrow & Sons, dealers, Spalding, Lincs, 4/7/1923
    wfw: War Office, WDLR 1040, Purfleet Disposal Depot, Essex, 4/1919
(wc) tdx: KS, New loco on trial/loan, c7/1928 (by 8/1928)

(w1) tdt: Ffestiniog Railway (PR/3) stock, 1937
(w2) stored at Dinas Junction from 1937 until:
    tdt: Brymbo Steelworks for overhaul, per Ministry of Supply, 5/1942
    wlw: Hook Norton Ironstone Mines, Oxon (and see WHR(1964) below).
(w3) tdt: Ffestiniog Railway (PR/3), loan per KS, 3/1929

Maintenance Railcars: Gauge 1'11½" - WHR

One or more 2w-2PMr or 4wPMr were in use for track maintainance by 1933, but details are not known. One at least of these units was reputedly later used by the Ffestiniog Railway (PR/3) but, with no accurate records apparently available, precise ownership (WHR or FR) during the "amalgamated" period is now difficult to define.

CLOSURE & DEMOLITION: WHR

Closed to passengers (last train ran on) 26/9/1936.
Closed to freight (last train ran 1/6/1937) officially 21/6/1937.
Closure to freight included the branch Tryfan Junction to Bryngwyn.
Track subsequently lifted in three stages:

DA) DINAS JUNCTION to PITTS HEAD, HAFOD RUFFYDD to CROESOR JUNCTION
Contractor   : **George Cohen, Sons & Co Ltd**
Work started at Rhyd Ddu 8/1941 (by 13/8/1941); completed to Dinas Junction by 2/5/1942; to Croesor Junction by 6/1942.

Locomotives: Gauge 2ft - (Cohen)

Two or more 4wPM/DM. One, a 40hp MR ex WDLR (built c1917) type [and which was possibly a FH "Planet-Simplex" rebuild] was at Dinas Junction 18/6/1942 but had left the area 20/6/1942.

[Possible identities of these locos include FH 1677/c1931, FH 1678/c1931 and FH 1779/1931 - all were supplied New by FH to J.C.Oliver, dealer, Leeds, who re-sold to a contractor building the Colchester By-Pass Road (1930-1934) Contract, Essex. One is illustrated in J/NG/No.132/4. Two of these (at least) passed to George Cohen, Sons & Co Ltd, dealers, who advertised them for sale at their Stanningley, Leeds, Depot in 1941.]

DB) PITTS HEAD to HAFOD RUFFYDD
Contractor   : [W.O.Williams of Harlech ?]
Track left in-situ 1941 and used by Army for gunnery practice; wagons carrying targets being run by gravity down this section. Most rails removed in 1948; remainder salvaged by Ffestiniog Railway for re-use, 11/1958.

DC) CROESOR JUNCTION to PORTHMADOG (PR/25 section of WHR)
Contractor   : **W.O.Williams of Harlech**
Track left in-situ 1942 pending possible reopening of Cwm Croesor slate quarries; lifted between 8/1948 and 8/1949.

Locomotive: Gauge 2ft - (Williams)

| No.14 | | 4wPM | 20hp MR | [? c1922] | (dca) | (dc1) |

(dca) wfw: Shanks & McEwan Ltd, contractors, Carnbroe Depot, Lanarks., (there 8/7/1943)

(dc1) abandoned on site by "GWR" crossing 8/1949; scrapped on site 1955

DINAS RIVER AUTHORITY DEPOT, DINAS JUNCTION

The vacant station and yard at Dinas Junction were later occupied by various organisations, including the River Authority which stored railway equipment on the site. For details see DINAS RIVER AUTHORITY DEPOT in Section 3.

RECONSTRUCTION: WHR(1964)

Plans to reopen at least part of the WHR as a tourist railway have resulted in the formation of the "1964 Company" and the laying of track from Porthmadog (adjacent to BR station) to Penymount - about ½ mile - though this line is on the trackbed of PR/30, and not on the former WHR PR/25. Proposed extensions beyond Penymount will be on PR/25, however, therefore this Company is listed here under this heading.
Construction started in 1973 - "direct labour", no Contractor - and opened for passengers to Penymount 2/8/1980.

Locomotives: Gauge 1'11½"

		Name	Type			Works No.	Date		
		"CILGWYN"	4wDM	20hp	RH	175414	1936	(a)	(1)
		PEDEMOURA	0-6-0WT	OC	OK	10808	1924	(b)	(3)
(2)		KINNERLEY	4wDM	40hp	RH	354068	1953	(c)	
No.7		KAREN	0-4-2T	OC	P	2024	1942	(d)	
No.1		RUSSELL	2-6-2T	OC	HE	901	1906	(e)	
		NANTMOR **	0-6-0WT	OC	OK	9239	1921	(f)	OOU
No.1		GLASLYN	4wDM	40hp	RH	297030	1952	(g)	
No.9			4wDM	20hp	MR	9547	1950	(h)	(2)
(No.5)			4wDM	40hp	HE	6285	1968	(i)	
36		CNICHT	4wDM	20hp	MR	8703	1941	(j)	
8, 13		(f. 4)	4wDM	60hp	MR	60s333	1966	(k)	
9		KATHERINE	4wDM	60hp	MR	60s363	1968	(k)	
6		JONATHAN	4wDM	60hp	MR	11102	1959	(k)	
No.3			0-4-2T	OC	WB	3023	1953	(m)	
No.5		GELERT	0-4-2T	OC	WB	3050	1953	(m)	
No.10			4wDM	30hp	RH	191658	1938	(n)	(3)
-			4wDM	30hp	RH	237914	1946	(n)	(3)
-			4wDM	48hp	RH	370555	1953	(o)	
482			4wDH		HE	7535	1977	(p)	
1			4wDM	48hp	RH	481552	1962	(q)	
16			4wDM		HE	*8518	1977	(r)	

```
     **   named FOJO until 8/1980.
      *   loco has dual identity - is also AB 632.
```

(a) tdx: Moel Tryfan Slate Quarry, 5/1974
(b) tdx: Pleasurerail Ltd, Knebworth Park, Herts, 15/6/1975
(c) tdx: WHR(1964)Ltd store, Kinnerley, Salop, c7/1975
 wfw: Blockleys Ltd, Hadley Lodge Brickworks, Salop, until 5/1963
(d) tdx: Flying Scotsman Enterprises, Market Overton, Rutland, 6/3/1976
(e) tdx: Hills & Bailey Ltd, Llanberis (see PR/65), 29/8/1977
(f) tdx: private store at Tremadoc, 1/6/1980
 wfw: Crockway Farm, Nr.Maiden Newton, Dorset, until 3/11/1979
(g) tdx: Llanberis Lake Railway (PR/65), 1/6/1980
(h) tdx: Mr Ian Jolly (see Section 1), loan, 31/5/1980
(i) tdx: Sanders & Forster Ltd, Stratford, London, 14/2/1981
(j) tdx: private store, 27/2/1981
 wfw: Yorkshire Water Authority, Riccall, North Yorks, to 13/12/1980
(k) tdx: Wm.Ainscough & Sons Ltd, dealers, Wigan, Lancs, 14/12/1981
 wfw: Pilkington Bros Ltd, Rainford, Merseyside
(m) tdx: Rustenberg Platinum Mines, South Africa, 4/1982
(n) tdx: D.S.F.Refractories Ltd, Friden Brickworks, Derbys, 6/1982

(o)	tdx:	Mr M.Jacob, Long Eaton, Notts, 7/1987
	wfw:	Hoveringham Gravels Ltd, Holme Pierrepont, Notts
(p)	tdx:	British Coal, Holditch, Staffs
(q)	tdx:	Amalgamated Construction Co Ltd, Barnsley, 9/1990
	wfw:	Gresford Colliery, Wrexham
(r)	tdx:	Maerdy Colliery, South Wales, 1/1991
(1)	tdt:	Alan Keef, dealer, Cote, Oxon, c12/1974
	wlw:	Vale of Teifi Railway, Dyfed, by 2/1985
(2)	tdt:	Mr Ian Jolly (see Section 1), 5/5/1986
(3)	tdt:	Mr J Quentin, private store, Hereford, after 23/8/1991 by 28/8/1991

NOTE   During 1977-78 two 4'8½" gauge Wkm motorised platelayers trolleys were stored on this site, prior to removal to Llanrwst Transport Museum (which see - Section 3).

[Read: B/450; B/451; B/147; J/RW/6.1983/298; B/152-158]

HARLECH BEACH TRAMWAY/S   PR/45
c ¾ mile

There is considerable confusion regarding this line or lines.
References and surviving earthworks confirm that there was a tramroad of some sort, commencing at or very near an occupation crossing on the Cambrian Railways (PR/32) near to Quarry Cottage, and running to (or towards) the beach. Per J/MRS/1977/7 this was perhaps originally a short line used in connection with the quarries nearby. It may have been repaired, and possibly extended, at a later date for carrying passengers
J/MRS/1977/7 suggests there was another tramway, commencing near to Harlech station, and running down what is now Beach Road to the shore.
The existence of two lines, at different dates, could explain the conflicting descriptive details, and operation dates, given in various sources.
A tramway for passengers was definitely built in 1878 as detailed below: all evidence points to it being one that ran from the crossing near Quarry Cottage, to the beach, and it is shown thus on OS/6"/1887-1891. Details of construction and ownership of the other line, if indeed there was one, have not been ascertained.

Owner	: Samuel Holland	First Sod: 19/4/1878
Contractor	: **Godfrey Morton** [of Tremadoc]	
Engineer	: Thomas Roberts [of Porthmadog]	

CONSTRUCTION   Gauge: 2ft ?
Single track horse-worked line, reported as completed 6/1878 "and handed over to the proprietor" [J/CDH/29-6-1878] - thus line built in some 10 weeks - indicating perhaps that it was not all new work.

OPERATION

Reputedly only one passenger tramcar, built by Rees Evans, Harlech.
Line reported in 1890 "Gossiping Guide" as having not worked every summer; and it apparently closed soon after that date - though per J/NG/No.86/28 a lady born in 1887 could personally remember a tram [? this tram] working at Harlech.

DEMOLITION

Track reputedly lifted by 1899.

[Read: J/NG/No.84/20]

RUTHIN to CERRIGYDRUDION   PR/46
16½ miles

Ruthin & Cerrigydruidion Railway Company   : Act 27/6/1876

CONSTRUCTION   Gauge: 2ft

Contractor   : **James B.Fryer** [of London]   Contract let: 2/1879
Engineers   : C.E.Spooner; Henry Robertson; George Smith

Work started 5/1879; c5½ miles of earthworks built at Ruthin end of route, but little or no track laid. There is little likelihood of any locomotives being used for this work, but the line is worthy of inclusion as work was done here.

ABANDONMENT

Work on project ceased 11/1879; a further Act was obtained 3/6/1881 granting an extension of time for construction, but a formal Act of Abandonment was obtained 23/6/1884.

[Read: J/RCHS/10.1972 , J/DHS/1979/183]

GWERSYLLT (STANSTY) to BRYMBO to VRON   PR/47
c3½ miles

Wrexham, Mold & Connah's Quay Junction Railway Co   : Act 18/8/1882
Later ownership as PR/28

CONSTRUCTION   Gauge: 4'8½"

Contractor   : **Meakin & Dean**

Construction of the line was arranged by the Broughton & Plas Power Coal Co Ltd, and financed by Henry Robertson and Benjamin Piercy.
Opened for freight Stansty to Gatewen Colliery (¾ mile) 8/1882; to Plas Power 28/6/1884; to Brymbo 12/1887.
The WM&CQJ Rly Co informed the B&PPC Co Ltd that it was "taking over" the line from Stansty to Brymbo on 1/7/1888.
For extended details of this early period, and locomotives used, see GATEWEN COLLIERY in Section 3.

RECONSTRUCTION & EXTENSION

Contractor : **John Woolley** [of Wrexham - see Section 1]

Line Gwersyllt to Brymbo upgraded 1888-1889 for passenger traffic.
Board of Trade inspection of line to Brymbo took place on 13/7/1889
A "zig-zag" extension from Brymbo [Passenger Station] to Vron Colliery and [reverse] to Brymbo Ironworks - known as both the "Vron Mineral Branch" and "Fishponds Branch" - was constructed by Piercy & Robertson privately, without Parliamentary Powers. It remained Brymbo property, but was worked by the WM&CQ/GC/LNE Companies who paid a tonnage rate to Brymbo Co for the privilege.

OPERATION

Opened to freight in sections; to Brymbo 12/1887 as recited above.
Brymbo to Vron opened to freight 8/10/1888.
Opened to passengers Gwersyllt to Brymbo 1/8/1889.

Locomotives: Gauge 4'8½"

For early locos see GATEWEN COLLIERY in Section 3.
For later locos see WM&CQJRly list in entry PR/28.

CLOSURE & PARTIAL DEMOLITION

Closed to passengers 1/3/1917, and to freight in 1954.

In 1954, a short connection was made at Plas Power to the Wrexham-Brymbo line (PR/21) at Broughton Forge Junction; the PR/47 route Plas Power to Brymbo Steelworks via Fishponds Branch was then reopened to freight on 30/11/1954.

Track between Plas Power and Gatewen lifted 1958; details of any contractor or locomotives used not known.
Stansty to Gatewen reopened for freight 1958.
Plas Power to Brymbo closed to freight 19/6/1958; but later reopened again for freight 1/3/1965.

FINAL CLOSURE & DEMOLITION

Gatewen to Stansty closed to freight 14/3/1960.
Plas Power to Brymbo Steelworks closed to freight 5/10/1970.
Tracks lifted after these closures, but no details known re any contractors or locos used for this work.

[Read: J/RMag/11.1937/362; J/RMag/1.1972/7; B/127; B/247; B/304; J/RW/2.1987/89]

MOSS VALLEY JUNCTION to MOSS   PR/48

1¾ miles

Great Western Railway Company   : Act 21/7/1873

CONSTRUCTION
Gauge: 4'8½"

Contractor: not known

Construction was delayed for reasons unknown; but apparently work started in 1880, and reported "practically completed" in 12/1881.

OPERATION

Opened to freight (to Moss) 20/3/1882 or 11/5/1882 [sources vary].
Opened to passengers (Wrexham to Moss Crossing Halt) 1/5/1905.

The line was worked by GWR/BR locomotives.

At Moss, this line connected with the network of freight branches (to Ffrwd, Ffosygo, Westminster and Brynmally) of PR/6 and thus the GWR was able to close the section of PR/6 from Moss to Gwersyllt via Summerhill Tunnel and incline.

CLOSURE, DEMOLITION & PARTIAL RECONSTRUCTION

Closed to passengers 1/1/1931.
Closed to freight: Ffosygo to Ffrwd 1904 (track lifted 1915).
                Westminster to Ffosygo 1917
                Moss to Westminster 1925

The last freight from the branches at Moss ceased with the closure of Brynmally Colliery in 1935, and the line to Moss Valley Junction became disused. Track was lifted on the branch from Pentre Broughton Halt to Moss, together with the extensions to Brynmally and Westminster (etc) Collieries, in 1940. The 1m 66ch section Moss Valley Junction-Gatewen-Pentre Broughton was retained as sidings until track lifted 1952; nothing known re any contractor or locomotives used for this work.

In 1957 the site of Gatewen Colliery was reopened as an Opencast Coal Disposal Point, and the ½ mile section Moss Valley Junction to Gatewen was reinstated. By 1958, however, it was disused and part lifted to make way for the use of the trackbed by lorries (the railway Gatewen to Stansty - PR/47 - being used in lieu). In 1960 the line to Moss Valley Junction was reopened (and PR/47 to Stansty closed).

This section was in intermittent use until 1984; was then closed; track still in situ 1991 but heavily overgrown.

[Read: B/303; B/304]

BALA JUNCTION to LLAN FFESTINIOG PR/49
22 miles

    Bala & Festiniog Railway Company : Act 28/7/1873
    Great Western Railway Company   : from 1/7/1910

CONSTRUCTION
Gauge: 4'8½"

Contractor   : **Meakin & Dean**   Tenders invited 6/1878
                    (Agent: T.W.Davies)
Nothing known re any locomotives used by contractor.

OPERATION
Great Western Railway Company worked the line from opening day.
Opened to all traffic 1/11/1882.
Service through to Blaenau Ffestiniog (via PR/34) from 1883
GWR/BR locomotives used.

CLOSURE & DEMOLITION
Bala Town to Llan Ffestiniog (and to Blaenau Ffestiniog via PR/34):
Last passenger train ran on 2/1/1960; last freight ran 27/1/1961.
Track lifting commenced at Tyddyn Bridge 28/1/1961.
Track lifted to Bala Town by 31/2/1961.
Track lifted Tyddyn Bridge to Trawsfynydd Power Station (on dates unknown).
No details known re any contractors or locos used for demolition.

Bala Town to Bala Junction: closed to freight 2/11/1964
                       closed to passengers 18/1/1965
Track lifted 8/1968 with track of PR/18, which see for details.

PARTIAL REOPENING
Section from Trawsfynydd Power Station to Llan Ffestiniog (and on to Blaenau Ffestiniog via PR/34) reopened for freight traffic only, on 20/4/1964; all as an extension of the line from Llandudno Junction (see PR/23 for details and further comment).

[Read: J/RMag/4.1961/270; B/303]

DYSERTH to TRELAWNYD (NEWMARKET)

PR/50
¾ mile

Mr H.D.Pochin, Golden Grove Estate, Newmarket   : No Act

CONSTRUCTION

Gauge: 4'8½"

Contractor: not known

In 1883-1884 approximately ¾ mile of earthworks and bridges were completed, from end-on junction with PR/36 at Dyserth, to Marian Mill. The project was then abandoned.

Not known if any track was laid, or if a loco was used.

NOTE: the LNWR subsequently obtained a Light Railway Order 17/1/1908, and another LRO in 1915, permitting completion of this project, but in fact no further work was done.

OF RELATED INTEREST ?

In 1885, H.D.Pochin & Co, Manchester, advertised "wanted" a tank loco, 3'0" gauge, 6" cylinders [J/MM/2.2.1885].
And in 1879 "H.D.Pochin" purchased the Higher Gothers Clay Works, St.Denis, Cornwall, and built a 3'0" gauge line from this works to the GWR. This Pochin later became a constituent of English Clays, Lovering Pochin & Co Ltd.

[Read: B/324; B/326]

BETHESDA JUNCTION to BETHESDA

PR/51
4¼ miles

London & North Western Railway Company   : Act 6/8/1880

CONSTRUCTION

Gauge: 4'8½"

Contractor   : Thomas Nelson & Co [of York]

Work started 3/9/1881; completed c6/1884. Single track line.

Locomotives: Gauge 4'8½" - Thomas Nelson & Co

0-6-0ST	IC	MW	171	1865 (a)	s/s

(a)   tdx: ?
       wfw: Hopper, Radcliffe & Co, Britannia Ironworks, Fencehouses, Co.Durham (and could be the MW loco auctioned there "for J.G.Blumer" on 14/9/1876).

OPERATION

Opened to passengers 1/7/1884; for freight 1/9/1884.
Worked by LNWR/LMSR/BR locomotives.

CLOSURE & DEMOLITION

Closed to passengers (last train ran on) 1/12/1951.
Closed to freight from 7/10/1963.
Track lifted 1964; completed 6/1964; junction removed 8/11/1964.

No information re any contractors used for demolition.
Demolition trains were hauled by BR locomotives.

[Read: J/RMag/10.1961]

WREXHAM (EXCHANGE) to WREXHAM (CENTRAL)   PR/52
½ mile

Wrexham, Mold & Connah's Quay Junction Rly Co   : Act 18/8/1882
Subsequent ownership as PR/28.

CONSTRUCTION   Gauge: 4'8½"

Contractor   : **John Woolley** [of Wrexham]

Tunnelling under GWR (PR/5) commenced 18/5/1885; main construction started 14/1/1887; completed first as single line 7/10/1887.
Immediately widened to double track - completed 8/1888.

Locomotives: Gauge 4'8½"

No definite information; but a photograph of the works in progress shows a 0-4-0ST of MW appearance.
For details of locos owned by Woolley see Section 1.

OPERATION

Opened for traffic as an extension of PR/28 on 1/11/1887.
For locomotives used, and subsequent history, see PR/28.

FAIRBOURNE STATION to FAIRBOURNE FERRY   PR/53
1 ½ miles

McDougall (Fairbourne Estate)	: No Act	
Narrow Gauge Railways Ltd	: from	1916
Barmouth Motor Boat & Ferry Company	: lease	1921 - 1923
Fairbourne Estate & Development Co	: from	1924; (closed 1940)
Fairbourne Miniature Railway Co	: from	1946; (opened 1947)
Fairbourne Railway Ltd	: from	1958
North Wales Narrow Gauge Railway Ltd	: from	1/1984

CONSTRUCTION & OPERATION   Gauge: 2ft

Originally built 1890 by McDougall "direct labour" to carry freight from Cam.Rys. siding and small brickworks to building construction; extended c1900 to a ferry terminal near Penrhyn Point, and opened to passengers using two (at least) single-deck toastrack-type horse drawn tramcars (builder not known). Line closed c1915.

RECONSTRUCTION & OPERATION   Gauge: 1'3"

Tramway relayed as narrow-gauge railway in 1916; opened in summer of that year. Later deviated and extended at Ferry end, to Penrhyn Point. From 1928 to c1934 a section of the line, from Fairbourne to Golf Club, was laid dual gauge (1'3" + 1'6"). Line damaged during WW2 closure; reconstructed 1946 on virtually same route, and reopened 4/1947. Line closed on 15/9/1985; converted to 12¼" gauge miniature railway (which is outside the scope of this book).

Locomotives: Gauge 1'3" [and 1'6" **]

	PRINCE EDWARD								
	OF WALES	4-4-2	OC	BL	22	1915	New		(1)
	KATIE (*)	0-4-0T	OC	DB	4	1896	(a)		(2)
	COUNT LOUIS	4-4-2	OC	BL	32	1924	(b)		(3)
No.1	(**)	4-2-2	OC	RSP		1898	(c)		(4)
(5)	WHIPPIT QUICK	4wPM	9hp	L	6502	1935	New 5/35		
	rebuilt as	0-4w-4PM				1955			
	rebuilt as	0-4w-4PM				1962			(5)
	GWRIL	4wPM	6hp	L	20886	1943	(d)		(6)
	DINGO	4w+4wPM		W&M		1951	New		(7)
5751	PRINCE CHARLES	4-6-0	OC	Guest	9	1946	(e)		(8)
(57512)	ERNEST W.TWINING	4-6-2	OC	Guest	10	1949	(f)		(9)
	SYLVIA	4w+4wPH		Guest	14	1961	New 8/61		(10)
8	RACHEL	0-6-0PM		Guest	15	1959	New /61		
	rebuilt as	0-6-0DM				1974			(11)
	SIAN	2-4-2	OC	Guest	18	1963	New		(12)
	SHON (KATIE) (#)	2-4-2	OC	Guest	#13	1954	(g)		(11)
	TRACY JO	2-6-2PH		Guest	20	1964	(h)		(13)

The following were major rebuilds of two locos included above:

362	SYDNEY	2-4-2	OC	Fairbourne	1984	(ex SIAN)	(14)
6	LILIAN WALTER	4w+4wDH		Fairbourne	1985	(ex SYLVIA)	(15)

(*) : KATIE name may not have been actually carried on loco here.
(**): This loco 1'6" gauge.
(#): Ran named KATIE until 1984, when renamed SHON. This loco ran many years without a builders' plate (the number 13 being considered unlucky by some). When a plate was fitted, it bore the incorrect number '14'.

(a)   tdx: Llewelyn's Miniature Railway, Southport, Lancs, 1923
(b)   arrived here 4/1925. Built for (and perhaps delivered to) Count Louis Zborowski, Higham's Railway, Bridge, near Canterbury, Kent; but loco with BL for re-sale after 10/1924 death of Zborowski.
(c)   tdx: Exors of E.F.S.Notter, London, c1927 after 9/1927
(d)   tdx: Wilkins & Mitchell Ltd, Darlaston, Staffs, 1947
(e)   tdx: H.T.Guest, loan, 1960 by 8/1960
      wfw: Dudley Zoo Miniature Railway
(f)   tdx: H.T.Guest, loan, 1961
      wfw: Dudley Zoo Miniature Railway
      tdt: H.T.Guest, 1964 by 31/10/1964; rebuilt; '57512' removed;
      tdx: H.T.Guest, 1968
(g)   tdx: Exors Capt.V.Hewitt, Cemlyn, Anglesey (private store), 1965
      wfw: Dudley Zoo Miniature Railway
(h)   tdx: H.T.Guest, loan for trials, 26/9/1964

(1)   tdt: Llewelyn's Miniature Railway, Southport, Lancs, 1923
(2)   dismantled 1926; frame used as coach and/or wagon;
      tdt: Tywyn Museum 12/1970 (frame only)
(3)   retained on site as static exhibit from 1984;
      tdt: Birmingham Railway Museum, Tyseley, 7/1987
(4)   tdt: R.H.Morse, dealer, 1935 (after 4/1935)
      wlw: Jaywick Miniature Railway, Clacton, Essex, 1935
(5)   tdt: R.P.Morris (private store), 31/8/1975
      wlw: Gloddfa Ganol (see OAKELEY QUARRIES in Section 3)
(6)   tdt: Talycafn Transport Museum, Gwynedd, 12/1985
(7)   disused by 1970; dismantled by 8/1974; frame scrapped 5/1975
(8)   tdt: H.T.Guest, 1962 (and rebuilt as 4-6-2; auctioned 5/1969)
      wlw: Steamtown Museum, Carnforth, by 1986
(9)   tdt: Milner Engineering Ltd, Chester, 1984;
      wlw: Birmingham Railway Museum, Tyseley, by 8/1986;
      wlw: exported to Japan.
(10) rebuilt as LILIAN WALTER - see final entries in loco list above.
(11) tdt: Haigh Hall Country Park Miniature Rly, Lancs, winter/1984
(12) rebuilt as SYDNEY - see final entries in loco list above.
(13) tdt: H.T.Guest, after 9/7/1966 by 25/9/1966.
(14) tdt: Littlecote House Miniature Rly, Hungerford, Berks, 2/12/1985
(15) converted to 12¼" gauge in 1985 and retained at Fairbourne.

[Read: B/142; B/173; J/RW/4.1972/170]

BUCKLEY JUNCTION to SHOTTON (HAWARDEN BRIDGE JCT)   PR/54
HAWARDEN BRIDGE JUNCTION to CONNAH'S QUAY   4½ miles and 1 mile

Wrexham, Mold & Connah's Quay Junction Railway Co   : Act 29/6/1883
For subsequent ownership see PR/28.

CONSTRUCTION   Gauge: 4'8½"

BUCKLEY JUNCTION TO SHOTTON
Contractor   : **Exors of Benjamin Piercy** (who died 24/3/1888); work was started by Piercy on 6/9/1887 but suspended by 1/1889:
Assigned to Contractor **John Woolley**, who had been Agent for Piercy.
                                    Work restarted 2/1889.

SHOTTON to CONNAH'S QUAY
Contractor   : not known
H.Croom Johnson [of Wrexham] was awarded a contract or contracts on this section, though the earliest date noted for an accepted tender is 30/8/1890; hence Johnson's work may have been associated tasks on riverside embankments, and/or Connah's Quay Docks, with perhaps alterations to PR/22 in that area.

ASTON HALL COLLIERY JUNCTION
Contractor   : **H.Croom Johnson**
PR/54 passed over the private ASTON HALL RAILWAY; a connection was made to that line between 12/1891 and 8/1892. (For further details see ASTON HALL in Section 3.)

John W.Dean is also reported as having taken on some of the PR/54 works - presumably he was the 'Dean' of Meakin & Dean, contractors, known to have been active in this area. For further comment on this partnership see entry GATEWEN COLLIERY in Section 3.

Locomotives: Gauge 4'8½"

No specific locomotives have been identified as used by contractors on these works, though an unconfirmed report suggests loco WARWICK was hired for use here from Cudworth & Johnson (see Section 1), and a loco PIERCY, owned by Woolley, reported on the line 9/1888 [J/Wrexham Advertiser/8.9.1888].
For locomotives owned by Woolley and by Croom Johnson, see their entries in Section 1.

Locomotives: Gauge 3'0"

Cooper & Tullis, contractors, of Preston, Lancs, advertised 7/1892 "3ft gauge four-coupled 10" loco, 2'5" wheels, 10 tons for sale - can be seen working at Hawarden station". This may, or may not, be related to PR/54 works.

OPERATION
Buckley Junction to Shotton "Loop Line" opened 31/3/1890; Shotton to Connah's Quay (freight only) connection was "not quite ready" in 1891 but apparently opened later in that year.

Locomotives: Gauge 4'8½"

See listing under PR/28.

CLOSURE & DEMOLITION

SHOTTON to CONNAH'S QUAY regular freight traffic ceased from 1/4/1967; officially closed 4/9/1967.
Track subsequently lifted, but no details known re any contractors or locomotives used for this work.

PASSENGER TRAMWAYS AT PWLLHELI   PR/55

PWLLHELI (West End) to CARREG-Y-DEFAID to LLANBEDROG   3 miles
    Solomon Andrews & Son [of Cardiff].

CONSTRUCTION   Gauge: 3'0"
Line built by owners 1893-1894 on the shore, as a 2 mile tramway to carry stone from quarry at Carreg-y-Defaid to their building developments at West End. Opened to passengers 3/8/1894. Tramway extensively damaged by storm 10/1896.

RECONSTRUCTION
Original line temporarily repaired while new line built on parallel route through sandhills above tide level; this line opened 12/1896; extended to Llanbedrog, opened by 7/1897.

OPERATION
All traffic worked by horses. There were 14 open and 4 covered single-deck four-wheel tramcars (this fleet being shared with the Cardiff Road Tramway - below).

CLOSURE & DEMOLITION
Line severely damaged by storm 28-29/10/1927; tramway abandoned and track subsequently removed. Tramcars scrapped, other than for the body of a Falcon-built covered car now [1989] preserved in Pwllheli.

PWLLHELI (West End) via CARDIFF ROAD to PWLLHELI (Post Office)   ¾ mile
    Solomon Andrews & Son [of Cardiff].

CONSTRUCTION   Gauge: 3'0"
Line built by owners 1895-1896; street tramway; single track.

OPERATION
Opened late-summer 1896. All traffic worked by horses. The trams used were from the fleet shared with the Llanbedrog line (above).

RECONSTRUCTION
More than half the route was converted to double track c1906.

CLOSURE & DEMOLITION
Line closed 1928 (c9/1928); track removed 1928-1929.

PWLLHELI (Station) via EMBANKMENT ROAD to PWLLHELI (South Beach)   ½ mile

Pwllheli Corporation/Pwllheli Borough Council.

CONSTRUCTION   Gauge: 2'6"

Built 1888-1889, possibly by a Contractor, but no details known; single-track street tramway.

OPERATION

Opened to passengers 24/7/1899; all traffic horse-worked. Two open and one covered four-wheel trams (at least); two built by Midland Railway Carriage & Wagon Co Ltd, Shrewsbury 1899, with a third from same builder in 1901.

CLOSURE & DEMOLITION

Closed c9/1919; track removed 1920-1922.
Trams sold to Solomon Andrews & Son in 1921 [? 7/1921].

[Read: B/387; B/175]

BARMOUTH JUNCTION to ARTHOG TRAMWAY   PR/56
c1½ miles

Solomon Andrews & Son [of Cardiff]

CONSTRUCTION   Gauge: 2'0"

Mineral tramroads existed in this area serving Tyddyn Sieffre Quarry prior to land being purchased for residential development by Solomon Andrews & Son in 1894. Some parts of these tramroads were incorporated into a passenger tramway system built c1895.

OPERATION

One covered four-wheel horse-drawn tramcar.
The principal route was from Barmouth Junction Station to The Crescent to Barmouth Bridge (for footpath over bridge to Barmouth).

CLOSURE & DEMOLITION

Scheme to develop the area was abandoned c1900; tramway closed and track removed. Tramcar transferred to Pwllheli, altered to 3'0" gauge and added to Llanbedrog Tramway (PR/55) fleet.

[Read: B/387]

WREXHAM (Central) to ELLESMERE PR/57
12¾ miles

Wrexham & Ellesmere Railway Company : Act 31/7/1885
Great Western Railway Company : From 1/1/1923

CONSTRUCTION   Gauge: 4'8½"

Contractor   : **Davies Brothers** [of Wrexham]   First Sod: 11/6/1892

Locomotives: Gauge 4'8½"

PENWYLLT	0-6-0(T?) FW	(? 29)			(a)		(1)
BANTAM	0-4-0tank						(2)
WEEDON	0-6-0ST IC	MW	976	1886	(b)		(3)
DOROTHY	0-4-0ST OC	MW	977	1886	(b)		(4)
CYMRO	0-4-0ST OC				(c)		(5)

(a)   A loco named PENWYLLT was used c1872 on a contract for the Swansea Vale and Neath & Brecon Railways, lines with which John Dickson had had connections; Penwyllt is a station on the N&B Rly.
A 0-6-0ST named PENWYLLT was used in 1873 by John Dickson, contractor, on Whitby-Loftus construction for North Eastern Rly; this loco carried a plate 'FW 29 of 1873' - almost certainly spurious, as FW numbers had reached 170 by 1873; perhaps it indicated FW 29 rebuilt [? by FW] in 1873. This loco passed to C.Morrison [? dealer], London, who repaired it and then resold it as PENWYLLT.
It is possible that we are here considering just one locomotive.
(b)   wfw: Naylor Brothers, contractors, LNW Weedon-Daventry (c1886-1888) Contract.
(c)   for discussion re origin of this loco see Cudworth & Johnson entry in Section 1.

An auction was held 1/6/1897 by G.N.Dixon for Davies Bros "on completion of Wrexham & Ellesmere Rly" and advertised in various journals as under:

(1)   auction 1/6/1897 - 13½" 6wc FW PENWYLLT: no further trace.
However, a loco PENWYLLT 0-6-0ST OC FW is reputed to have worked for Monk & Newell, contractors, on LNWR Atherstone-Tamworth Widening (c1901-1904) Contract.
(2)   auction 1/6/1897 - 4wc tank BANTAM [description in J/CG/14-5-1897 as 6wc 12" MW is apparently a confusion with MW 976 not otherwise listed in that journal]: no further trace.
However, auction was held "at yard adjoining Abenbury Brick Works" and these Works belonged to Davies Bros. Perhaps BANTAM was retained here, as an unknown 4wc tank loco was for sale in 7/1909. See ABENBURY BRICKWORKS in Section 3.
(3)   auction 1/6/1897 - 12" 6wc MW: per MW records was subsequently with Wynnstay Colliery, then A.Kellett, contractor. Per ILS lists, was with Kellett at Birmingham Corporation Water Works, Frankley Reservoir Construction (1897-1903) Contract, which indicates only a short stay at Wynnstay - perhaps, in fact, a hire from Davies Bros between completion of PR/57 (11/1895) and the auction (6/1897).
(4)   not shown in auction list hence perhaps sold prior to 6/1897.
wlw(tdt ?): Pethick Bros, contractors, Vale of Glamorgan Railway (1894-1897) Contract.
(5)   auction 1/6/1897 - 10" 4wc tank CYMRO: reputed to have departed south under its own steam to either Littlehampton or Shoreham; no further trace.

OPERATION

Line opened 2/11/1895, worked by Cam.Rys.
Worked by GWR from 25/3/1922.
Cam.Rys., GWR and BR locos used.

CLOSURE & DEMOLITION

Closed to passengers 10/6/1940 to 6/5/1946 because of heavy wartime traffic over line, including workmens' trains from Wrexham to the Ordnance Factory at Marchweil.
Closed to passengers (last train ran on) 8/9/1962.
Closed to freight: Ellesmere-Pickhill Creamery 8/9/1962
                     Pickhill-Abenbury Brickworks summer 1973
                     Abenbury-Wrexham Exchange (later).

Track lifted on each section after closure, but no details known re any contractors or locomotives used.

[Read: B/102; J/RW/6.1965/204]

LLANBERIS to SUMMIT OF SNOWDON MOUNTAIN   PR/58
4¾ miles

Snowdon Mountain Tramroad & Hotels Co Ltd   : Reg 16/11/1894
Snowdon Mountain Railway Ltd   : from 15/5/1928
Snowdon Mountain Railway PLC   : from   c1982

CONSTRUCTION   Gauge: 2'7½"

Contractor   : **A.H.Holme & C.W.King** [of Liverpool]
                    First Sod: 15/12/1894. Viaducts at Llanberis built first.
                    Tracklaying started after 5/1895; completed 6/1/1896.

800mm gauge Abt-rack railway; contract for supply of track let to Richard White & Sons (of Widnes), who subcontracted supply of items to Charles Cammell & Co Ltd (rack bar blanks), Yorkshire Engine Co Ltd (rack bar teeth cutting and track assembly); Cammmell's plant at Workington made the fishplates and probably also the rails; Ebbw Vale Steel, Iron & Coal Co provided the pressed steel sleepers.

Locomotives: Photographs show that SMT&H Co Ltd locos were used during the construction period.

OPERATION

Opened 6/4/1896; closed same day due to accident.
Reopened 19/4/1897; trains operating spring to autumn only.

Locomotives: Gauge 2'7½"

The steam locos appear as 0-4-2T but in fact rack-drive only on the two coupled axles, all wheels being free-turning carrying wheels.

1	L.A.D.A.S.	0-4-2T	OC	SLM	923	1895	New	(1)
2	ENID	0-4-2T	OC	SLM	924	1895	New	
		rebuilt	HE		58833	1958		
3	WYDDFA	0-4-2T	OC	SLM	925	1895	New	
		rebuilt	HE		58948	1960		
4	SNOWDON	0-4-2T	OC	SLM	988	1896	New	
	disused from 1938; rebuilt	HE		59092	1963			
		rebuilt	HE			1978		
5	MOEL SIABOD	0-4-2T	OC	SLM	989	1896	New	
		rebuilt	HE		58889	1959		
6	PADARN *	0-4-2T	OC	SLM	2838	1922	New	
7	RALPH **	0-4-2T	OC	SLM	2869	1923	New	
8	ERYRI	0-4-2T	OC	SLM	2870	1923	New	
9	NINIAN	0-4-0DH	320hp	HE	9249	1986	New 4/86	
10	YETI	0-4-0DH	320hp	HE	9250	1986	New 4/86	
11		0-4-0DH	320hp	AB #	775	1991	New 4/91	

*   PADARN; named SIR HARMOOD until 1924.
** RALPH; named RALPH SADLER to 2/5/1987; AYLWIN to 4/10/1978.
\#   AB 775; dual identity loco - is also HE 9305/1991

(1) destroyed in accident 6/4/1896; boiler salvaged and sold for £190, 2-3/1898, [reputedly to Dinorwic Slate Quarry for stationary use].

Locomotive: Gauge 2'10½" - (not used).

4wDM RH 283869/1949 arrived on 27/8/1971, from Llanddulas Limestone Quarry (see Section 3) per Colwyn Model Railway Club, with the intention that it be rebuilt as a yard shunter. The idea was not persued, and loco transferred 24/10/1977 "as received" to Llanberis Lake Railway (PR/65) - which see.

[Read: B/305-308; B/175]

WREXHAM (Rhos Junction) to RHOS to WYNN HALL   PR/59
4½ miles

Great Western Railway Company   : Acts 20/7/1896 and 6/8/1897

CONSTRUCTION   Gauge: 4'8½"

RHOS JUNCTION to RHOS: "Rhos Branch"   3¼ miles

Contractor   : **Walter & Herbert Chambers**   ; work in hand by 10/1899

Line on new formation Rhos Junction to Llwyneinion, thence upgrading the existing Pontcysyllte Branch (see PR/19) to Rhosllanerchrugog ("Rhos") Station (3 miles) and on to a point 3m 19ch from Rhos Junction, a few yards short of Rhos (Brook Street) Goods Depot.

Locomotives: Gauge 4'8½"

[THORNHILL ?]   0-6-0ST   IC   MW   101   1864   (a)   (1)

(a) neither this loco, nor any loco, is yet confirmed on this Contract; but W.& H.Chambers apparently obtained MW 101/1864, from Llay Hall Colliery, around the time of their PR/59 Contract

(1) no further trace. An auction of plant and machinery belonging to W.& H.Chambers was held, at Legacy Station on PR/59, on 27/7/1910; presumably not directly from the PR/59 Contract at this late date.

RHOS to WYNN HALL: "Pontcysyllte Branch (part of)"   1¼ miles

This section of line was operated as an extension of the Rhos Branch from 1905 for passenger trains (to Wynn Hall) and for freight after the 1953 closure of PR/19 south of Wynn Hall. Wynn is often spelled Wynne.

OPERATION

Opened Rhos Junction-Rhos 3/10/1901 (passengers and freight).
     Rhos-Wynn Hall   1/5/1905 (passengers) (freight earlier)
GWR/BR locomotives used.

CLOSURE & DEMOLITION

Closed to passengers   : Wynn Hall-Rhos   22/3/1915
                                        Rhos-Wrexham   1/1/1931 (except football specials until 1953)
Closed to freight   : Wynn Hall-Pant   by 4/1959 (? 1953)
                                      Pant-Rhos Junction as from 14/10/1963

Track lifted Wynn Hall-Pant 1959, remainder 1969-1970.
No details known re any contractors or locomotives used.

LLANDUDNO to SUMMIT OF GREAT ORME　　　　　　　PR/60
　　　　　　　　　　　　　　　　　　　　　　　　　　1 mile

        Great Orme Tramways Company　　　: Act 23/5/1898
　　　　　　　　became **Great Orme Tramways Co Ltd** : for liquidation only, in 1934
        Great Orme Railway Ltd　　　　　　: Reg 25/3/1935
        Llandudno Urban District Council　: From 1/1/1949
        Aberconwy Borough Council　　　: From 1/1/1974

CONSTRUCTION　　　　　　　　　　　　　　　　　　　Gauge: 3'6"

Contractor　　　　: **Thomas & John Owen** [of Llandudno]
　　　　　　　　　　Richard White & Sons [of Widnes]
Engineer　: H.Enfield Taylor [of Chester]

Cable-haulage tramway, operated as two separate lines, Llandudno to Halfway, and Halfway to Summit.
Construction started 4/1901, finished 5/1903. No locomotives used.

OPERATION

Opened (lower section) 31/7/1902; (upper section) 8/7/1903.
Closed due to accident on 23/8/1932; reopened 17/5/1934.

Tramcars: Gauge 3'6"

Cars 1, 2 and 3, variously described as "vans" or "20 seat coaches" were four-wheel vehicles built by Hurst Nelson & Co Ltd, Motherwell in 1902. They were scrapped (at unknown date) by 1960.
Cars 4, 5, 6 and 7 are eight-wheel bogie passenger coaches, built by Hurst Nelson in 1902 (4 & 5) and 1903 (6 & 7). In 1991 these cars were named ST. TUDNO (4); ST. SILIO (5); ST. SEIRIOL (6); ST. TRILLO (7).

[Read: B/255; B/311]

LLANDUDNO to COLWYN BAY to OLD COLWYN　　　　PR/61
　　　　　　　　　　　　　　　　　　　　　　　　　　8¼ miles

        Llandudno & Colwyn Bay Electric Traction Co Ltd　　: by　3/1904
        Carnarvonshire Electric Traction Syndicate Ltd　　:　　1906
        Llandudno & District Electric Tramway Construction Co Ltd : Reg 25/7/1906
        Llandudno & Colwyn Bay Electric Railway Ltd　　　: Reg 21/4/1909

CONSTRUCTION　　　　　　　　　　　　　　　　　　　Gauge: 3'6"

Contractor　　　　: **Hewitt & Rhodes** - at work by 3/1904 until c1906
　　　　　　　　　　Bruce Peebles & Co Ltd - at work from 1907

Various Companies proposed various schemes from the mid-1890s, but the only effective work done was by those listed above.

Locomotives: Gauge 3'6"

Two photographs exist - the poorer having been reproduced in B.258 and J/NG/No.131/30 - of a very primitive 0-4-0 tank loco, fitted with small diameter wheels running outside the frames, a large diameter unlagged industrial-type horizontal boiler, what appear to be very low "side-tanks", and, apparently, having inside cylinders. In both views, it is standing at a passing-loop on the newly-constructed tramway. The design and detail of the loco is such that it is unlikely to have been built by any established locomotive builder.
Advert in J/CJ/10-1-1906: Wanted, 3'6" gauge loco, for contractor work on tramway line - A.E.Morrish [? who], Colwyn Bay.
Two four-wheel 26 seat single-deck trams built BE 1904 were brought from Canvey Island Tramways, in 1/1907, for testing the line; these were returned to BE in 1907.

OPERATION

Opened as electric (overhead-wire) passenger tramway Llandudno to Rhos 19/10/1907; Rhos to Colwyn Bay 7/6/1908.
For list of tramcars used see below.

RECONSTRUCTION and EXTENSION

Contractor: not known. [Bruce Peebles & Co Ltd ?]
Existing line widened to double track in 1911.
Extension Colwyn Bay-Old Colwyn built 1914-1915; opened 26/3/1915.

CLOSURE & DEMOLITION

Closed to all traffic : Colwyn Bay-Old Colwyn 22/9/1930
                         Llandudno West Parade-West Shore 1917
                         Remainder of line (6½ miles) last car ran on 24/3/1956
Surviving equipment dismantled 1956 by Walter & Co, of Conwy, other than much track buried by road resurfacing.

The Company operated a replacement bus service until 27/5/1961.
The Company was liquidated 14/11/1961.

Tramcars: Gauge 3'6"

No.		Type	Builder	Year		Disposal
1		8w/SD	MRCW	1907	New	Wdn/1932-33; Scr
2		8w/SD	MRCW	1907	New	Wdn/1932-33; Scr
3		8w/SD	MRCW	1907	New	Wdn/1932-33; Scr
4		8w/SD	MRCW	1907	New	Wdn/1932-33; Scr
16	(6 until 1936)	8w/SD	MRCW	1907	New	Scr/1944 due to a fire
7		8w/SD	MRCW	1907	New	Wdn/1936; Scr
8		8w/SD	MRCW	1907	New	Wdn/1936; Scr
9		8w/SD	MRCW	1907	New	Wdn/1936; Scr
19	(10 until 1936)	8w/SD	MRCW	1907	New	Wdn/1937; Scr
18	(11 until 1936)	8w/SD	MRCW	1907	New	Wdn/1956; Scr
12		8w/SD	MRCW	1907	New	Wdn/1936; Scr
13		8w/SD	MRCW	1907	New	Wdn/1936; Scr

17	(14 until 1936)	8w/SD	MRCW	1907	New	Wdn/1956; Scr
15		4w/SD	UECP	1909	New	Wdn/1936; (1)
16		4w/SD	UECP	1909	New	Wdn/1936; (1)
17		4w/SD	UECP	1909	New	Wdn/1936; (1)
18		4w/SD	UECP	1909	New	Wdn/1936; (1)
19	(23 in 1936+1937)	8w/TRO	EEP	1920	New	Wdn/1955; Scr/1956
20		8w/TRO	EEP	1920	New	Wdn/1955; Scr/1956
21		8w/TRO	EEP	1920	New	Wdn/1955; Scr/1956
22		8w/TRO	EEP	1920	New	Wdn/1955; Scr/1956
23A	(23 until c1947)	4w/SV	GFM	1901	(a)	Scr
1		8w/SD	BE	c1921	(b)	Wdn/1956; Scr
2		8w/SD	BE	c1921	(b)	Wdn/1956; Scr
3		8w/SD	BE	c1921	(b)	Wdn/1956; Scr
4		8w/SD	BE	c1921	(b)	Wdn/1956; Scr
5		8w/SD	BE	c1921	(b)	Wdn/1956; Scr
6		8w/DDO	UECP	1914	(c)	(2)
7		8w/DDO	BE	c1925	(c)	Wdn/1956; Scr
8		8w/DDO	BE	c1925	(c)	Wdn/1956; Scr
9		8w/DDO	BE	1921	(c)	Wdn/1956; Scr
10		8w/DDO	BE	1921	(c)	Wdn/1956; Scr
11		8w/DDO	BE	1921	(c)	Wdn/1956; Scr
12		8w/DDO	BE	c1925	(c)	Wdn/1956; Scr
13		8w/DDO	BE	1921	(c)	Wdn/1956; Scr
14		8w/DDO	BE	c1925	(c)	Wdn/1956; Scr
15		8w/DDO	BE	c1925	(c)	Wdn/1956; Scr
23		8w/DD	EEP	c1936	(d)	Wdn/1954; Scr/1957
24		8w/DD	EEP	c1936	(d)	Wdn/1954; Scr/1957
-		4w/SV	BE	1901	(e)	Wdn/1936; Scr

(a) tdx: Bournemouth Tramways, 55, 1936
(b) tdx: Accrington Corporation, 1932-1933
(c) tdx: Bournemouth Tramways, 1936 : (L&CB 6 = BT 85, 7 = 115, 8 = 116, 9 = 108, 10 = 103, 11 = 95, 12 = 128, 13 = 112, 14 = 121, 15 = 114)
(d) tdx: Darwen Tramways, Lancashire, 8/1946
(e) tdx: Leamington & Warwick Tramways, 11, 1930

(1) Scrapped in 1941; trucks sent to Leeds, two bodies to Kinmel Camp.
(2) Preserved; Clapham Museum in 1956; Bournemouth Transport Museum by 1983.

ABBREVIATIONS USED IN LIST ABOVE:
Car Types: 4w = Four Wheel,   8w = Eight Wheel bogie car.
             SD = Single Deck, DD = Double Deck, O = Open top
             TRO = single deck Toast Rack Open top
             SV = Service Van workscar

Car Builders:
BE   : Brush Electrical Engineering Ltd, Loughborough
EEP   : English Electric Co Ltd, Preston
GFM   : G.F.Milnes, Birkenhead
MRCW   : Midland Railway Carriage & Wagon Co Ltd, Shrewsbury
UECP   : United Electric Car Co Ltd, Preston

[Read: B/140; B/251; B/252; B/255; B/257; B/258; J/NG/No.102/1]

HOLLAND ARMS to RED WHARF BAY

PR/62

6¾ miles

London & North Western Railway Company : Acts 1/8/1899, 6/8/1900

CONSTRUCTION

Gauge: 4'8½"

Contractor : **John Strachan** [of Cardiff]
Work started 6/1907 (possibly 4/1907); Strachan died 2/4/1909.
Work completed 5/1909 by Exors of John Strachan.

Locomotives: Gauge 4'8½"

J.STRACHAN No.3	0-4-0ST	OC	HE	365	1885		
		rebuilt	MW		1904	(a)	(1)
J.STRACHAN No.7	0-6-0ST	IC	MW	1576	1903	(b)	(2)
J.STRACHAN No.10	0-6-0ST	IC	MW	1617	1903	(a)	(2)

NOTE: The above locomotives are the only ones positively identified as having worked on this Contract, but the Sales at Red Wharf, which commenced 28/7/1909, included 5 locos, two of which may have been brought from elsewhere for sale here, because of the business being wound up following the death of Strachan.
These additional locomotives appear to be:-

4'8½"gauge   J.STRACHAN No.5   0-6-0ST IC MW [373 1871?]   (c)   (1)
2'6" gauge   J.STRACHAN No.9   0-4-0ST OC WB 1655 1901   (d)   (2)

NOTE: There seems to be no evidence to support the suggestion that loco J.STRACHAN No.6 (MW 1605) was also at Red Wharf. Earlier used by Strachan on his Tanat Valley Rly contract, it was next known with Naylor Bros, contractors, on their LNWR Wilmslow-Levenshulme job (1903-1909), and is likely to have been the 6wc MW 12" loco in the sale there 7/1909.

The locos offered by auction at Red Wharf 28/7/1909 were described as "Three nearly new 6wc tank locos 4'8½" 12x18 MW, two 4wc tank locos by WB and HE" [J/RSC/15-7-1909], which, if literally true, would have to include MW 1605, though Nos.7 & 10 were both 12x17 per MW records. However, all were apparently not sold, but later more fully described in Phillips Register [J/PMR/1-12-1910] as [Nos.3,7,9,10 as above] plus:

"No.5 6wc 12x17 IC 11'0"wb 3'0"dw MW" - Nos.7 & 10 were similarly described except for "12x18, New 1903/04". There is of course a possibility that the No.5 in J/PMR was a typographical error for 6.

(a)   wfw: Strachan, LNWR Sudbury-Wembley (1903-1906) Widening Contract.
(b)   wfw: Strachan, Tanat Valley Railway (1901-1904) Contract.
(c)   assuming this No.5 is same loco as the previously known No.5, which was MW 373, then:- wfw: Strachan, Tanat Valley Railway (1901-1904) Contract.
(d)   wfw: Strachan, LNWR Welham Marshalling Yard Contract, by 9/1903 to 5/1908 at least.
        wfw: Strachan, Welshpool & Llanfair Railway Contract, to 6/1903 at least.

(1) offered in various sales at Red Wharf Bay including on 6/5/1913; no further trace.
(2) sold between 12/1910 and 4/1911
wlw(tdt ?): E.Nuttall & Co, contractors, Walker-on-Tyne RN Shipyard (1910-   ) Contract.
(3) sold 6/5/1913 and tdt: WB, Stafford, for re-tyring to 2'6½" gauge;
tdt: Jees Hartshill Granite & Brick Co Ltd, Nuneaton, by 11/1913 and named BUTCHER

OPERATION

Line opened, Holland Arms-Pentraeth   1/7/1908
              Pentraeth-Red Wharf Bay 24/5/1909
Worked by LNWR/LMSR/BR locomotives.

CLOSURE & DEMOLITION

Closed to passengers on 22/9/1930; to freight "on and from" 3/4/1950 [J/RO/6.1950/133].
Track lifted by James N.Connell Ltd, contractors [of Coatbridge].
Lifting started 9/4/1953; completed on 16/10/1953.
Demolition trains were hauled by BR locomotives.

[Read: J/SLS/1.1954/10; B/303; B/304]

RHYL MINIATURE RAILWAY - MARINE LAKE PARK   PR/63

1 mile

Narrow Gauge Railways Ltd	: 1910-1912
Rhyl Amusements Ltd	: 1912-1970
Fortes Ltd)	
Trust House Forte Leisure Ltd)	line closed : 1970-1977
Entam Leisure Ltd)	
Rhuddlan Borough Council	: 1978-
leased to : Keef Railways Ltd	: 1978-1979
: Leslie Leisure Ltd	: 1980-1985
	line closed : 1986
: Mr Ken Dove	: 1987-

CONSTRUCTION   Gauge: 1'3"

Site work started 12/1910; tracklaying started 3/1911.
Line opened 4/5/1911; closed 30/9/1969.
Track removed by 31/7/1970; relaid generally on same route 1978.
Line reopened 8/7/1978; closed 29/9/1985.
Line reopened 5/7/1987.

The railway has operated only during "summer" periods in any year.

Locomotives: Gauge 1'3"

GENERAL NOTES

From 1911 to 1920 the railway used two (at least) Bassett-Lowke locomotives. The General Manager was Mr Albert Barnes who also ran a business known as A.Barnes & Co, Albion Works, Rhyl; though this was actually a subsidiary of Rhyl Amusements Ltd (itself a subsidiary of Butlers Structural Engineering of Stanningley, Leeds). The railway built its own bogie coaches in 1912-1913 (and more later); perhaps these were early products of the Albion Works which, in 1919, began construction of new locos for the railway. All sources seem to agree that there were six locos built by Barnes, and this is presumed correct, though no official records of Albion Works products seem to have been found. However, there is much confusion as to the identities and histories of these six locos - "lists" have appeared in various publications and all differ from each other to a greater or lesser degree. No useful purpose can be served by simply publishing yet another list in this Handbook, without first discussing the locomotives both generally and in detail.

During the "first life" (1911-1970) of the railway, it is generally thought that four of the locos remained permanently at Rhyl, the other two spending all their days elsewhere, though perhaps returning to Barnes for occasional winter overhauls. As with any group of theoretically identical locos maintained at one depot over a period of around 50 years, it is very likely that some interchange of components has taken place, and that boilers and other parts have been renewed to not-necessarily the same precise pattern. Likewise, there can be no certainty that some apparent identities have not been exchanged over the years. If two locos were to concurrently "fail" during a summer - which surely happened more than once in 40 years - it is reasonable to presume that Barnes would remount the 'best boiler' onto the 'best chassis' in order to get a loco back into traffic with the minimum of delay. But, would he re-fit the cab (hence the numberplate) appropriate to the boiler (to suit the pipework), or the cab appropriate to the chassis (to suit the fixing bolts)? Would the loco emerge with the name related to the boiler, or to the chassis? Indeed, would Mr Barnes even think such trivia at all important, when his main aim was to operate a viable railway service? It certainly would not have occurred to him that, oneday, historians would worry about such things. Proof of an identity exchange in recent times is now available, enhancing the belief that it may also have occurred on earlier occasions.

The Barnes locos were designed by Henry Greenly; his general arrangement drawing, dated 1920 and indicating a loco with worksplates Albion Works 101 and nameplate JOAN, was published in magazines in 1921. Two obvious features of this drawing are the "two piece cab" (ie, the upper half could be removed to facilitate maintenance) and that the tender has a raised coal-collar extending fully to and around the rear end. Both coupling (wheel to wheel) rods, and connecting (wheel to piston) rods are it seems, plain (not fluted).

Apparently only one tender was built to this pattern, and photographs show it used with different locos over the years. The other tenders had symmetrical collars not extending to the rear of the body. It is likely that tender bodies would be renewed from time to time due to corrosion (particularly in the water space), and therefore any identification based on tenders must be regarded with extreme caution.

Although (apparently) specifically designed for use at Rhyl (to replace the underpowered Basset Lowke locos), what is believed to be the second loco built was soon sold; an action difficult to understand. Another loco, built later, was also sold. Neat, oval, brass works plates reading: ALBERT BARNES & CO/101/ MAKERS/ALBION WORKS, RHYL were carried by the first loco built and, as they feature in Greenly's 1920 drawing, it may be assumed they were fitted, to the loco, when new. Similar plates having identical wording but number 99 were fitted to Bassett Lowke loco GEORGE THE FIFTH; which begs certain questions regarding the application of other Barnes numbers prior to 101. Perhaps coaches account for some of these. No Barnes worksplate known carries a date, hence building dates for his second and subsequent locos can be deduced only from observations.

The only worksplates, known to have been observed, (apart from 99) are 101, 103 and 105. Previously published references to numbers 102, 104 and 106 seem based entirely on a presumed sequence of construction of the six known locos. Also, plate 103 is not known to have been seen prior to 1928; and it does seem strange that neither of the locos apparently built for other customers were (or so it seems) fitted with plates. An old employee has stated that Barnes fitted plates retrospectively to some locos; it therefore is possible that, in 1928, having then three locos at Rhyl, plates were made and fitted to the other two (ie, apart from 101) to produce a uniform appearance in the fleet. There is, however, reason to suspect that the loco given number 105 was not the fifth loco built; and, if the number 103 was chosen retrospectively, this could also be an incorrect choice for the loco to which it was fitted. Particularly so if, as has been claimed, the second and third locos were assembled almost concurrently.

The arbitrary allocation of number 106 to the sixth known loco is especially dangerous, implying that the Albion Works produced nothing else considered worthy of a number between 1928 and 1933 (at least), and in the absence of evidence to the contrary this number must be discounted.

We now examine the individual locos, allocating to each an identity letter (A to E) - not necessarily indicative of, though thought to comply with, the sequence of construction.

LOCOMOTIVE 'A'

Construction commenced 1919 [per Greenly articles]; loco put to work at Rhyl 8/1920 [Everyday Science 4/1921]. Nameplates JOAN and worksplates 101 consistently observed at Rhyl (and Belle Vue) 1923 to 1985. This loco, and loco 'D' below, differ from Greenly's drawing by (apparently always) having a one-piece cab (no horizontal joint level with foot of side window). In recent years at least, this loco has had prominent drain-cock linkage on the front footplate, a feature apparently shared only with loco 'B'. Also, in recent years at least, has had fluted coupling but plain connecting rods. In the 1980s it ran without front buffers.

LOCOMOTIVE 'B'

Built sometime 1920-1923 and may have worked at Rhyl (if only on trials) but no observation or contemporary report has been found. Some sources say it was first named BILLY or BILLIE but no definite evidence of this has come to our notice. This loco was working on the Woodland Park Miniature Railway at Upnor, Kent, in 9/1923, where it had Barnes-pattern nameplates MICHAEL and no worksplates. Incidentally, per "Worlds Fair" of 7/6/1924, Barnes was also manager of "the Woodlands Pleasure Park, Upnor". What is thought to be the same loco worked at the Saracen's Head Miniature Railway, Heatley Warburton, near Lymm, Cheshire, in 1927. The Barnes loco here had Barnes-pattern nameplates GEORGE V JNR and (apparently) no worksplates. The loco from Saracen's Head is known to have moved to Belle Vue Miniature Railway, Manchester, and first put to work there 28/5/1928 [Manchester Evening News 28/5/1928]. It is therefore presumed to be the Barnes loco which was at Belle Vue for many years, named RAILWAY QUEEN (though often running nameless in fact). RAILWAY QUEEN was reboilered in winter 1948 and thereafter carried a noticeably taller dome; at sometime prior to 1976 the smokebox door was altered to hinge on the opposite side compared to all other Barnes locos. Both MICHAEL at Upnor, and RAILWAY QUEEN at Belle Vue, had fluted coupling rods; but no photo is yet known of GEORGE V JNR at Saracen's Head. The front buffers of RAILWAY QUEEN, like those of BILLIE at Margate (loco 'D'), were oval (the other locos having circular buffers). RAILWAY QUEEN had draincock linkage on the front footplate, as did loco 'A'; but this was not fitted to MICHAEL at Upnor.

Mr Gordon Limb, the driver of GEORGE V JNR at Saracen's Head, studied both RAILWAY QUEEN (at Rhyl) and JOHN (at Alton Towers) in 1982 and, based on his recollection of variable details, he formed a positive opinion that the RAILWAY QUEEN of 1982 was not the loco he once drove, but that JOHN could well have been. This tends to support the suggestion that the identities of these two locos were exchanged at some time, perhaps by Barnes in 1928, and could perhaps explain the very many published references which connect the number 102 to the name JOHN. But, of course, the differences he noticed could have their origin in periodic overhauls, and more particularly perhaps in 1948 when RAILWAY QUEEN received her new boiler.

After returning to Rhyl, RAILWAY QUEEN was significantly altered in winter 1982-1983 by having individual splashers fitted over each driving wheel; she then ran at Rhyl, known as "LOUISE", and numbered 1 - though the number had been removed by 8/1985, and no name was actually carried. The 4/1986 auction catalogue described this loco as "103 BILLIE built 1924"; undoubtedly erroneously.

In 1988 this loco was again modified by being fitted with the splashers and nameplates of MICHAEL - thus perhaps (and perhaps by accident) reverting to its original (Upnor) name.

LOCOMOTIVE 'C'

Everyday Science, issue 4/1921, reported the third Barnes loco as "now being ready for service" though the first reported sighting is in 1923, named JOHN, and no worksplates seen. First reported observation of JOHN carrying '103' worksplates is 9/1928; and since then frequently observed at Rhyl as JOHN 103. In recent years at least, running with plain connecting rods. Stored at Rhyl from 1970 until sold to Alton Towers in 1978, and resold in 1985 to Mr Raymond Dunn of Bishop Auckland for the Whorlton Lido Railway; used at Whorlton Lido still carrying plates 103 and JOHN.

LOCOMOTIVE 'D'

Although perhaps first used at Rhyl, the earliest definite observation found is at Dreamland Miniature Railway, Margate, Kent, in 1928; then named BILLIE and not, apparently, carrying a Barnes worksplate. Like loco 'A', BILLIE had a one-piece cab; it ran at Margate for many years with smoke-deflectors each side of the smokebox. By 1951 the washout-plugs over the firebox had been replaced by a manhole fitting, and during a winter rebuild 1974-1975 by D.C.Pether the injector feed clacks were moved to prominent positions on the sides of the boiler just to the rear of the smokebox, and the (running) number 104 was fixed on the side of the cab.

This loco returned from Margate in 1980 to Rhyl and was then sent to Mr A.J.Cork at Mold for repair; it went to Dudley Zoo in 1982 but after a short period of use was returned to Rhyl in 1984, still painted green and carrying running number 104. The 4/1986 auction catalogue described this loco as "104 BILLIE built 1928", though positive evidence for this 1928 date seems lacking. "Worlds Fair" 7/6/1924 reports on the Dreamland Railway stating "its two beautiful engines [are] well worth going to see" which may indicate that BILLIE was built and delivered by 6/1924.

LOCOMOTIVE 'E'

First noted at Rhyl 9/1928, named MICHAEL and with worksplates 105, and frequent observations thus until 1986. However, there is a possibility that the loco MICHAEL seen 9/1928 was in fact the loco from Upnor (loco 'B') which had been refurbished and put to work at Rhyl as a re-newed loco being given 105 plates - in which case, the true "loco E" would have been despatched new to Saracen's Head, named GEORGE V JNR.

Incidentally, two origins have been suggested for this choice of name: either a Barnes choice based on his previous operation of an older GEORGE THE FIFTH (Bassett Lowke) loco, or the choice of the owner at Saracen's Head - George V.Tonner - in honour of his son perhaps. Whatever the origin, the plates were of standard Barnes pattern, thus perhaps suggesting the loco left Rhyl thus named.

In recent years, MICHAEL 105 at Rhyl carried plain connecting rods, and fluted coupling rods.

LOCOMOTIVE 'F'
Reputedly built c1933-1936, named BILLY; has worked only at Rhyl and has never carried genuine Barnes worksplates. By 1979 was running with the "full-collared" tender originally running with loco 'A' and, in recent years at least, had fluted connecting rods. Stored at Rhyl from 1970, it was auctioned in London 10/1978 and there purchased by Rhyl Town Council. It subsequently saw further use on the Rhyl Miniature Railway, but in 1986 was installed as a static exhibit in the booking hall at Rhyl (BR) station, fitted with "artificial" worksplates reading Barnes 106.

SUMMARY LIST OF BARNES LOCOS
A summary list of the six (presumed) locos, built by A.Barnes & Co, would now read as follows:

A:	101 of	1920	- JOAN Rhyl/Belle Vue/ Carnforth/ Rhyl
B:		c 1921	- MICHAEL Upnor/GEORGE V JNR Saracens/ RAILWAY QUEEN Belle Vue/RAILWAY QUEEN - 1 "LOUISE" - MICHAEL Rhyl
		OR:	MICHAEL Upnor/MICHAEL 105 Rhyl/Dudley Zoo/Rhyl
C:	103 of	1921	- JOHN Rhyl/Alton Towers/Whorlton Lido
D:		c 1927	- 104 BILLIE Margate/104 Dudley Zoo/104 Rhyl
E:		c 1928	- MICHAEL 105 Rhyl/Dudley Zoo/Rhyl
		OR:	GEORGE V JNR Saracens/RAILWAY QUEEN Belle Vue/RAILWAY QUEEN - 1 "LOUISE" - MICHAEL Rhyl
F:		c 1934	- BILLY Rhyl.

Bearing in mind the foregoing paragraphs, and disregarding any test running or similar trials, the listing of the Rhyl Miniature Railway locos is:-

Locomotives: Gauge 1'3" - First Life (1911-1970)

No.15	PRINCE EDWARD OF WALES	4-4-2	OC BL	15	1909	(Fa)	(F1)
	GEORGE THE FIFTH	4-4-2	OC BL	[?18	1911]	(Fb)	
			rebuilt Barnes	99			(F2)
	JOAN	4-4-2	OC Barnes	101	1920	New	(F3)
	JOHN	4-4-2	OC Barnes	103	1921	New	(F4)
	MICHAEL	4-4-2	OC Barnes	105	[1928?]	(Fc)	(F5)
	BILLY	4-4-2	OC Barnes		[1934?]	New	(F6)

Locomotives: Gauge 1'3" - Second Life (1978-1985)

	MICHAEL		4-4-2	OC Barnes	105	[1928?](Sa)	(S2)
	CLARA		0-4-2DM	Guest		1961 (Sb)	(S2)
	BILLY		4-4-2	OC Barnes		[1934?](Sc)	(S1)
104			4-4-2	OC Barnes		[1927?](Sd)	(S2)
	RAILWAY QUEEN		4-4wPH			(Se)	(S2)
	JOAN		4-4-2	OC Barnes	101	1920 (Sf)	(S2)
1	"LOUISE"	(*)	4-4-2	OC Barnes		[1921?](Sg)	(S2)

(*) Carried name RAILWAY QUEEN during 1982 only.

Locomotives: Gauge 1'3" - Third Life (1987-   )

Since 1987, the railway has been operated each season by locos brought to the line in April/May each year, and returned to off-site stores in September. Theoretically, the six locos listed above as disposal footnote '(S2)' have been available, though in fact not all are serviceable or required. As actual transfer dates to/from store pass unrecorded, and footnotes could go on forever, it is better to summarise the position as follows:

1987 season locos: CLARA diesel, plus JOAN.
1988 season locos: CLARA diesel, plus "LOUISE" with MICHAEL nameplates.
1989 season locos: CLARA diesel, plus "LOUISE" with MICHAEL nameplates.
1990 season locos: CLARA diesel, plus JOAN.
1991 season locos: CLARA diesel, plus JOAN.

(Fa) tdx: BL, 1911; wfw: White City Exhibition Rly, London, RED DRAGON
(Fb) arrived 1913; if BL 18 then wfw: Southport Miniature Rly.
     An article published 8/1913 stated "named KING GEORGE and is of the same type as PRINCE EDWARD [sic] but has a brass dome and a higher boiler pressure.
(Fc) Perhaps built c1928 and New to Rhyl; perhaps built c1921 and came to Rhyl after working at Upnor - see notes on Locos 'B' & 'E' above

(Sa) tdx: Alan Keef, Cote, Oxon, 24/6/1978;
     tdt: Dudley Zoo, loan, 7/1981;
     tdx: Dudley Zoo, off loan, 9/1984
(Sb) tdx: Alan Keef, Cote, Oxon, 24/6/1978; wfw:Dudley Zoo.
          Altered 0-4-2PM to 0-4-2DM in 1979.
     tdt: Dudley Zoo, loan, 7/1981;
     tdx: Dudley Zoo, off loan, (and put directly into store), 9/1984
(Sc) tdx: Rhyl Town Council, loan, 5/1979
(Sd) tdx: Margate Miniature Railway, c6/1980
     tdt: Mr A.J.Cork, Mold, for repairs, 8/1980
     wlw: Dudley Zoo, loan, by 4/1982
     tdx: Dudley Zoo, off loan, 9/1984
(Se) tdx: Margate Miniature Railway, c6/1980
(Sf) tdx: off-site store, c6/1981
     wfw: Steamtown, Carnforth, until 1979 move to off-site store.
(Sg) tdx: off-site store, 1982 (by 6/1982)
     wfw: Belle Vue Miniature Railway, Manchester, RAILWAY QUEEN

(F1) tdt: Dreamland Railway, Margate, 1920 [J/ME/16.9.1920]
(F2) tdt: Skegness Pleasureland Railway, 1922
     wlw: Southend Miniature Rly;
     wlw: Belle Vue, Manchester (still named GEORGE THE FIFTH and with Barnes 99 plate).
(F3) tdt: Belle Vue, Manchester, 1970
     wlw: Steamtown, Carnforth, by 11/1978
(F4) tdt: off-site store, 1970
     wlw: Alton Towers, Staffs, c4/1978
     wlw: Whorlton Lido Rly, Barnard Castle, Co.Durham, (tdx:Alton Towers 5/3/1985).

(F5) tdt: off-site store, 1970
    wlw: Alan Keef, Cote, Oxon, 1978
(F6) tdt: off-site store, 1970
    sold at auction 6/10/1978 to Rhyl Town Council then stored at the Old Town Hall, Rhyl. (Footnote 'Sc' then applies).

(S1) tdt: Rhyl Town Council, 1982
    wlw: Mr D.Gratton, Derby, for repairs, 12/1984; returned to Rhyl Town Council 8/1985 fitted with identity plate "Barnes 106"
    wlw: placed on static display in booking hall at Rhyl (PR/7) station, 1986.
(S2) offered for sale at auction at Saltney 30/4/1986 but not sold; remained in store at Rhyl.

NOTE: in all footnotes, the phrase "off-site store" refers to private premises not located at the Miniature Railway Marine Lake site.

[Read: B/142; J/RW/9.1987]

RHYL (VORYD PARK) ELECTRIC TRAMWAY   PR/64
¼ mile

    Mr C.W.Lane (Lancaster Electrical Co, Barnet, Herts)   : 1952-1953
    Modern Electric Tramways Ltd   : 1953-1954
    Twigdons   : 1955-1957

CONSTRUCTION   Gauge: 1'3"

Track laid during winter 1951-1952. 60vdc overhead-wire passenger tramway from West Parade Promenade to Wellington Road Coach Park; within the Voryd Park fairground area and on the route of 11" gauge steam operated model railway which had ceased operating c1951.

OPERATION

The line operated during "summer months" only, 1952-1957.

Tramcars: Gauge 1'3"

23	[model of Darwen car]	8wDD	Lane	1948	(a)	(3)
225	[model of Blackpool car]	8wSDo	Lane	1950	(a)	(1)
3	[Freelance design]	4wDDo	Lane	1952	New	(1)
6	[Toastrack car]	8wSDo	Lane	1953	New	(2)

NOTE: 4w = four-wheel car   8w = eight-wheel bogie car
    SD = Single Deck   DD = Double Deck   o = opentop

(a) arrived 1952; had been used elsewhere on temporary lines, latterly at St.Leonards, Sussex.

(1) tdt: Eastbourne Tramway, Sussex, 1953
(2) tdt: Barnet Works, Herts, 1954, and rebuilt there.
    wlw: Eastbourne Tramway, Sussex.
(3) tdt: Barnet Works, Herts, 11/1957
    wlw: Merseyside Tramway Preservation Society, Princes Dock, Liverpool, by 1985.

CLOSURE & DEMOLITION

Tramway closed 9/1957; dismantled 11/1957.
All equipment transferred to Eastbourne, Sussex, for further use.

[Read: B/140; B/255; J/NG/No.123/9]

LLANBERIS (PADARN) to CEI LLYDAN to PENLLYN   PR/65
"Llanberis Lake Railway"   2 miles

Cymdeithas Rheilffordd Llyn Llanberis : incorp. 6/1969 : No Act.
Rheilffordd Llyn Padarn Cyf (Ltd)   : from 1/6/1977

CONSTRUCTION   Gauge: 1'11½"

Passenger railway built over part of route of 4'0" gauge Padarn Rly (see Dinorwic Slate Quarries - Section 3). "Direct labour" job, no Contractor. Tracklaying started 20/11/1970 completed 4/1972.

OPERATION

Opened to Cei Llydan 19/7/1971; to Penllyn 31/3/1972.
Passenger trains operate during "summer months" only; Freight trains run as required during winter months from 1975 to serve the private sidings, of the Dinorwic Power Station, which are connected to the railway.

Locomotives: Gauge 1'11½"

No.	Name	Type	Cyl	Mfr	Works	Year	Note		
No.1	ELIDIR	0-4-0ST	OC	HE	493	1889	(a)		
No.2	THOMAS BACH *	0-4-0ST	OC	HE	849	1904	(a)		
No.3	DOLBADARN	0-4-0ST	OC	HE	1430	1922	(a)		
No.14	(No.4 to 3/1975)	4wDM	30hp	RH	277265	1949	(a)		(1)
15	(5 to 3/1975)	4wDM	20hp	MR	5861	1934	(b)	±	(11)
No.16	(No.6 to 3/1975)								
	W.K.WILLIAMS	4wDM	20hp	MR	21513	1955	(b)		(2)
No.17	GARRET (No.7 to 3/75)	4wDM	32hp	MR	7902	1939	(c)		(3)
No.18	BRAICH (No.8 to 3/75)	4wDM	32hp	MR	7927	1941	(c)		(4)
	MAID MARIAN	0-4-0ST	OC	HE	Ø		(d)		(5)
No.6	GINETTE MARIE	0-4-0WT	OC	Jung	7509	1937	(e)		(6)
No.19	LLANELLI	4wDM	48hp	RH	451901	1961	(f)		
No.11	CERNYW	4wDM	40hp	RH	200748	1940	(g)		(7)

No.12	MOR LEIDR	4wDM	40hp RH	375316	1954	(g)	(8)
No.5	HELEN KATHRYN	0-4-0WT	OC Hen	28035	1948	(h)	(12)
No.9	DOLGARROG	4wDM	28hp MR	22154	1962	(i)	
No.14	RHYDYCHEN	4wDM	50hp MR	11177	1961	(j)	(9)
No.10	YR ENFYS	4wDM	40hp RH	297030	1952	(k)	(10)
No.8	TWLL COED	4wDM	48hp RH	268878	1956	(m)	
No.7		4wDM	48hp RH	441427	1961	(n)	
No.10	BRAICH	4wDM	48hp RH	203031	1942	(o)	
No.11	GARRET	4wDM	48hp RH	198286	1940	(o)	

* : named WILD ASTER until 9/1988
± : used as passenger train brake van 1971-1980; Wdn 9/1980.
Ø : identity unknown - plated HE 822/1903 in error; but neither the chassis nor the boiler appropriate to that number.

(a) tdx: Dinorwic Slate Quarries, Llanberis, 13/12/1969
(b) tdx: Birmingham Corporation Water Dept, Frankley Works, 23/12/1970
(c) tdx: Murex Ltd, Rainham, Essex, 28/4/1971
(d) tdx: Bressingham Gardens, Diss, Norfolk, 24/10/1971
    wfg: Dinorwic Slate Quarries, Llanberis.
(e) tdx: Eiserfelder Steinwerken, Kauser Steimel, Germany, 23/12/1971
(f) tdx: Thyssen (Great Britain) Ltd, Llanelli Depot, 5/12/1974
(g) tdx: A.R.C.Ltd, Penlee Quarries, Newlyn, Cornwall, 5/2/1975
(h) tdx: Bala Lake Railway (PR/66), 12/3/1975
(i) tdx: Llyn Cowlyd Tramway [see Dolgarrog Railways], 11/9/1975
(j) tdx: A.Keef, dealer, Cote, Oxon, 8/10/1975
(k) tdx: Welsh Highland Rly, Kinnerley Store Depot, Salop, 22/8/1976
(m) tdx: J.G.Ashurst, dealer, Newton-le-Willows, Lancs, 1/11/1976
(n) tdx: NCB, Bestwood Training Centre, Notts, No.3, 15/7/1977
(o) tdx: MoPB&W, RAF Depot, Fauld, Staffs, 27/3/1981

(1) tdt: A.Keef, dealer, Cote, Oxon, 9/10/1975
(2) tdt: A.Keef, dealer, Cote, Oxon, 6/7/1979
(3) tdt: Brecon Mountain Railway Ltd, Pant, Mid.Glam., 29/6/1983
(4) OOU from 3/1975; dismantled 1976; chassis converted to ballast plough.
(5) tdt: Bala Lake Railway (PR/66), 24/3/1975
(6) tdt: Mr W.S.Key, Strumpshaw Old Hall, Norwich, 22/2/1980
(7) tdt: Bala Lake Railway premises (PR/66), 4/4/1980
(8) tdt: CEGB, Stabla Cable-laying Contract, loan, 20/1/1978
    tdx: Stabla Contract, off loan, 10/8/1979
    tdt: Mr Mann, c/o Knebworth Park Railway, Herts, 29/3/1982
(9) tdt: Brecon Mountain Railway Ltd, Pant, Mid.Glam., 4/1981
(10) tdt: CEGB, Stabla Cable-laying Contract, loan, 20/1/1978
     tdx: Stabla Contract, off loan, 10/8/1979
     tdt: Welsh Highland Railway, Porthmadog (PR/44), 1/6/1980
(11) tdt: Alan Keef Ltd, dealer, Ross on Wye, 18/9/1990
(12) tdt: South Tynedale Railway, Alston, Cumbria, 2/4/1991

Locomotives purchased for scrapping: Gauge various.

The railway has obtained some locomotives, solely to provide spare parts for the operational fleet.
Components, including some chassis, survived for some time.

2'0" gauge	4wDM	40hp RH	287664	1952	(sa)	Scr 3/1978
2'0" gauge	4wDM	48hp RH	425796	1958	(sb)	Dsmt/1978
2'10½" gauge	4wDM	48hp RH	283869	1949	(sc)	Scr 3/1978

(sa) tdx: A.R.C.Ltd, Penlee Quarries, Newlyn, Cornwall, 5/2/1975
(sb) tdx: National Coal Board, Gedling Colliery, Notts, 15/7/1977
(sc) tdx: Snowdon Mountain Railway (PR/58), 24/10/1977

Other locomotives on the premises.

Apart from brief "Transfers for Fun", other locomotives which may be, or may have been seen on this railway are as follows:

WELSH SLATE CENTRE STOCK

Locomotives belonging to the Centre are both used and demonstrated on the Railway from time to time. For details of these locos see Welsh Slate Centre entry in Section 3.

STORED ON BEHALF OF OTHER OWNERS

1'11½" gauge	2-2-0PMr		W.J.Williams		(xa)	(x1)
2'0" gauge	4wDM	20hp RH	235711	1945	(xb)	(x2)
2'0" gauge	4wDM	20hp RH	213834	1942	(xc)	(x2)
1'11½" gauge	4wDM	20hp MR	8788	1943	(xd)	(x3)

(xa) tdx: Mr W.J.Williams, Tai Gloddfa Ganol, Oakeley Slate Quarry, Blaenau Ffestiniog [a "private store"], 15/10/1970
(xb) tdx: Britannia Bridge Reconstruction Contract (PR/7), 13/6/1974
(xc) tdx: Dinas River Authority Depot, Nr.Caernarfon, 3/7/1975
(xd) tdx: Col.Campbell, c/o Ffestiniog Railway (PR/3), 2/1977

(x1) tdt: Mr D.Woods, private store at Dinorwig, 10/1/1975;
    wlw: Welsh Slate Centre, Llanberis.
(x2) tdt: Private Store elsewhere, 4/9/1976
    wlw: Gloddfa Ganol [see Oakeley Slate Quarry - Section 3].
(x3) tdt: Ffestiniog Railway (PR/3), 8/6/1979.

HILLS & BAILEY LTD, & Mr.A.J.HILLS, LLANBERIS DEPOT

Locomotives stored and repaired (primarily, though not exclusively) for the then future Brecon Mountain Railway, in premises and sidings connected to PR/65 at Gilfachddu, Llanberis. Locos were sometimes both tested and used on PR/65.
Depot opened 1970, closed 12/1977.

Locomotives: Gauge 2ft

	SYBIL	0-4-0ST	OC	HE	827	1903	(ha)	(h1)
	-	4wDM	48hp	RH	444207	1961	(hb)	(h2)
	UNA	0-4-0ST	OC	HE	873	1905	(hc)	(h3)
	DIANA	0-4-0T	OC	KS	1158	1917	(hc)	(h4)
	EIGIAU	0-4-0WT	OC	OK	5668	1913	(hd)	(h5)
	MESOZOIC	0-6-0ST	OC	P	1327	1913	(he)	(h6)
	-	0-4-0WT	OC	OK	12722	1936	(hf)	(h7)
	"PENDYFFRYN"	0-4-0VBT	VC	DeW		1894	(hg)	(h8)
	"REDSTONE"	0-4-0VBT	VC	Redstone		1905	(hh)	(h9)
99-3353		0-6-2WTt	OC	Jung	1261	1908	(hi)	(h8)
	DOROTHEA	0-4-0ST	OC	HE	763	1901	(hj)	(h10)
	-	4-6-2	OC	BLW	61269	1930	(hk)	(h11)
	"RUSSELL"	2-6-2T	OC	HE	901	1906	(hm)	(h12)

(ha) tdx: home of Mr A.J.Hills, Knowle, Warwicks, 25/8/1970
  wfw: Penyrorsedd Slate Quarry, Nantlle
(hb) tdx: home of Mr A.J.Hills, Knowle, Warwicks, 12/9/1970
  wfw: British Gypsum Ltd, Tutbury, Staffs
(hc) tdx: home of Mr G.J.Mullis, Salwarpe, Worcs, 24/10/1970
  wfw: Penyrorsedd Slate Quarry, Nantlle
(hd) tdx: home of Mr G.J.Mullis, Salwarpe, Worcs,, 24/10/1970
  wfw: Penrhyn Slate Quarries, Bethesda
(he) tdx: home of Mr G.J.Mullis, Salwarpe, Worcs, 24/10/1970
  wfw: Rugby Portland Cement Works, Southam, Warwicks
(hf) tdx: Bressingham Gardens, Diss, Norfolk, 10/1/1972
(hg) tdx: home of Mr A.J.Hills, Knowle, Warwicks, 12/8/1972
  wfw: Penyrorsedd Slate Quarry, Nantlle
(hh) tdx: Plas-yr-Eifl, Trefor, 3/9/1972 [see Trefor Granite Quarry]
(hi) tdx: Deutsche Reichbahn, Mecklenburg, East Germany, 26/10/1972
(hj) tdx: home of Mr D.L.Walker, Sutton Coldfield, Warwicks, c1/1973
  wfw: Dorothea Slate Quarry, Nantlle
(hk) tdx: Eastern Province Cement Co, Port Elizabeth, South Africa, 6/7/1974
(hm) tdx: Steamtown Ltd, Carnforth, Lancashire, 20/7/1974

(h1) tdt: Welsh Slate Centre, Llanberis, loan, 13/6/1974
(h2) tdt: Brecon Mountain Railway, 2/9/1976
(h3) tdt: Welsh Slate Centre, Llanberis, 15/12/1977
(h4) tdt: Brecon Mountain Railway, 2/9/1976
(h5) tdt: Bressingham Gardens, Diss, Norfolk, 11/1/1972
(h6) tdt: Mr D.Compton, Bromyard, Worcs, 9/12/1977
(h7) tdt: Betws-y-Coed Railway Museum, 9/10/1975
(h8) tdt: Brecon Mountain Railway, 16/12/1977

(h9) tdt: Brecon Mountain Railway, 28/10/1977
(h10) tdt: home of Mr D.L.Walker, Minsterley, Salop, c12/1975
  wlw: Launceston Steam Railway, Cornwall, from 6/1989
(h11) tdt: Brecon Mountain Railway, 31/8/1976
(h12) tdt: Welsh Highland Railway, Porthmadog (PR/44), 29/8/1977

[Read: B/177/219; J/RMag/8.1971/418; J/IRR/Vol.5/205]

BALA (Llyn Tegid Station) to LLANUWCHLLYN   PR/66
"Bala Lake Railway"   4¼ miles

Rheilffordd Llyn Tegid Ltd (Bala Lake Railway) : Reg. 1971

CONSTRUCTION   Gauge: 1'11½"

Constructed over part of route of ex-GWR 4'8½" gauge PR/18.
Direct Labour job - no contractor.
Tracklaying started 29/5/1972; completed 3/1976.

OPERATION

Opened Llanuwchllyn to Pentrepiod 14/8/1972, to Glanllyn 8/1972, to Llangower 15/9/1972; extended to Pant-yr-Hen-Felin 20/5/1975 and to Bala (Llyn Tegid) [ex Bala Lake Halt GWR] 27/3/1976.
Trains normally operated during "summer months" only.

Locomotives: Gauge 1'11½"

No.	Name	Type		Builder	Works No.	Date	Notes	
No.1		4wDM	30hp	RH	432652	1959	(a)	(1)
2		4wDM	20hp	RH	182137	1936	(b)	(1)
No.3	HELEN KATHRYN	0-4-0WT	OC	Hen	28035	1948	(c)	(2)
D1087	MEIRIONNYDD	4w+4wDH	100hp	SL	22	1973	New	
	TRIXIE	0-4-0ST	OC	Barber		1974	New	(3)
No.4	MAID MARIAN	0-4-0ST	OC	HE	(*)		(d)	
No.3	HOLY WAR	0-4-0ST	OC	HE	779	1902	(e)	
	CHILMARK	4wDM	40hp	RH	194771	1939	(f)	
No.10	JONATHAN	0-4-0ST	OC	HE	678	1898	(g)	(4)
	ASHOVER	0-4-0ST	OC	KS	3114	1918	(h)	(5)

(*) identity unknown - plated HE 822/1903 in error; but neither the chassis nor the boiler are appropriate to this number.

(a) tdx: Oakeley Slate Quarry, 1971 OR 6/6/1972 (sources vary).
(b) tdx: Private Store at Halkyn, Clwyd, between 1/1973 and 5/1973
  wfw: Glynceiriog Private Railway
  wfw: Oakeley Slate Quarry

(c) tdx: Private Store at Kelsall, Cheshire, loan, 20/3/1973
    wfw: location in West Germany.
(d) tdx: Llanberis Lake Railway (PR/65), 24/3/1975
(e) tdx: Mr J.M.Hutchings, Quainton Railway Centre, Bucks, 14/12/1975
    wfw: Dinorwic Slate Quarries
(f) tdx: Track Supplies & Services Ltd, Wolverton, Bucks, 23/11/1976
    wfw: Air Ministry, Chilmark, Wilts, AMW No.160 [arrived Bala carrying plate AMW No.161 apparently in error.]
(g) tdx: Lytham Motive Power Museum, Lytham, Lancs, loan, 10/1/1980
    wfw: Dinorwic Slate Quarries, Llanberis, BERNSTEIN.
(h) tdx: Gloddfa Ganol [see Oakeley Slate Quarry], loan, 5/9/1980

(1) tdt: Track Supplies & Services Ltd, Wolverton, Bucks, 23/11/1976
(2) tdt: Llanberis Lake Railway (PR/65), 14/3/1975
(3) tdt: Llwyngwern Quarry (Alternative Technology Centre), c30/10/1974
(4) tdt: West Lancashire Light Rly, Hesketh Bank, Lancs, 6/10/1986
(5) tdt: Gloddfa Ganol, off loan, 8/1985

PRIVATE COLLECTION OF LOCOMOTIVES STORED AT LLANUWCHLLYN

A number of locomotives owned by various enthusiasts, stored here by arrangement with the Railway Company.
Whilst not part of the operational fleet, some have "run for fun" upon the railway from time to time.

Locomotives: Gauge 2ft

	ALICE	0-4-0ST	OC HE	780	1902	(pa)	(p4)
	INDIAN RUNNER	4wDM	40hp RH	200744	1940	(pb)	
2	ALISTER	4wDM	12hp L	44052	1958	(pb)	(p1)
(727/69)		4wDM	HU	38384	1930	(pb)	
	-	4wDM	20hp MR	5821	1934	(pb)	
	-	4wDM	20hp FH	2544	1942	(pb)	
	-	4wDM	20hp HE	1974	1939	(pc)	
	(WD LR2718)	4wPM	20hp MR	997	1918	(pc)	(p2)
	-	4wDM	13hp RH	189972	1938	(pc)	
	(U 190, T.R.A.15)	4wDM	30hp RH	283512	1949	(pd)	
No.11	CERNYW	4wDM	40hp RH	200748	1940	(pe)	
	-	4wDM	L	34025	1949	(pf)	
	-	4wDM	13hp RH	209430	1942	(ph)	

Locomotive: Gauge 2'6"

-	4wDM	48hp RH	235729	1944	(pg)	(p3)

(pa) tdx: West Lancashire Light Rly, Hesketh Bank, Lancs, 5/2/1977
     wfw: Dinorwic Slate Quarries, Llanberis
(pb) tdx: Narrotrack Ltd, Long Eaton, Derbyshire, 6/7/1977
(pc) tdx: Narrotrack Ltd, c/o A.Keef, dealer, Cote, Oxon, 13/10/1977

(pd) tdx: Mill Lane Commercials, dealer, Sandiacre, Derbys, 19/2/1979
wfw: Severn Trent Water Authority.
(pe) tdx: Llanberis Lake Railway (PR/65), 4/4/1980
(pf) tdx: Private Store, 8/11/1980
wfw: British Steel, Prothero Works, Wednesbury, West Midlands.
(pg) tdx: Private Store, 23/7/1982
wfw: Ministry of Defence, Navy Department '
(ph) tdx: ? (source uncertain)
wfw: Narrotrack Ltd, Long Eaton, Derby

(p1) tdt: Kew Bridge Steam Museum, Brentford, Middlesex, 4/6/1987
(p2) tdt: Mr I.Jolly [see Section 1], 9/11/1980
(p3) tdt: Gloddfa Ganol [see Oakeley Slate Quarry], 8/1985
(p4) tdt: Mr E.Scott, private store, Llandderfel, 1991 by 1/3/1991

[Read: J/RMag/4.1979/174; J/NGT/No.4/2; J/NG/No.70/1; B/312]

DINAS MAWDDWY to MAESCAMLAN   PR/67
½ mile

Meirion Mill Ltd

CONSTRUCTION   Gauge: 2'0"

Tourist railway built on part of route of PR/31.
Direct Labour job - no contractor. Work started c3/1975.

OPERATION

Opened to passengers 19/4/1975.
Operated during "summer months" only.

Locomotives: Gauge 2'0"

	TRIXIE		0-4-0ST	OC	Barber		1974	(a)		(1)
	-		4wDM	20hp	MR	21282	1959	(b)		(2)

(a) tdx: Llwyngwern Quarry (Alternative Technology Centre), after 12/1974 by 2/1975
(b) tdx: A.Keef, dealer, Cote, Oxon, 6/1975
wfw: Eastwoods Brickworks

(1) tdt: A.Keef, dealer, Cote, Oxon, c1976 by 7/1976
wlw: Rail Rebecq Rognon, Belgium, PAULA, 4/1977
(2) tdt: Cumberland Moss Litter Industries Ltd, Kirkbride, 10/1977

CLOSURE & DEMOLITION

The railway was little used in 1977, and by 7/1977 the track and equipment were advertised for sale. Track lifted soon afterwards.

LLANGOLLEN to CARROG
"Llangollen Steam Railway"

PR/68
7¼ miles

Flint & Deeside Railway Preservation Society : c1974-c4/1977
Llangollen Railway Society Ltd : c4/1977-

CONSTRUCTION
Gauge: 4'8½"
Line built over part of former PR/18 route: "Direct Labour" job.
Tracklaying started at Llangollen 1975 [still in progress 1991].

OPERATION
Opened to passengers Llangollen to Fford (½ mile) 26/7/1981; extended to Berwyn 19/10/1985 or 14/12/1985 [sources differ]; to Deeside Loop 9/12/1989; to Glyndyfrdwy 17/4/1992.

Locomotives: Gauge 4'8½"
Most of the locomotives at Llangollen are the property of private individuals or groups; few (if any) actually belonging to the railway. To aid understanding of the fleet, the locomotives are segregated here into four groups.

Firstly there are locos which are normally based at Llangollen and are (or have been) used for regular train operation or shunting duties. The second group comprises operational locos not normally based at Llangollen, but which have been "hired" and used on the line. Thirdly there are locos which have never been used, and can best be described as "long term restoration projects" (though work on some of these makes constant and praiseworthy progress); whilst lastly there are locos which have been mainly stored here pending ultimate removal elsewhere (though a very few of these did see very limited use in the early years for tracklaying, etc).

OPERATIONAL LOCOS - HOME BASED

No.5459	AUSTIN No.1 (*)	0-6-0ST IC	Kit	5459	1932	(oa)	
7298		0-6-0T IC	HE	1463	1924	(ob)	
51618		4w+4wDHr	Derby		1959	(oc)	
	PILKINGTON	0-4-0DE 200hp	YE	2782	1960	(od)	
7822	FOXCOTE MANOR	4-6-0 OC	Sdn		1950	(oe)	
D3265	MARK (f.08195)	0-6-0DE 350hp	Derby		1956	(of)	
D9502		0-6-0DH 650hp	Sdn		1964	(og)	OOU
D7629	(f.25279)	4w+4wDE	BP	8039	1965	(oh)	
25313	(f.D7663)	4w+4wDE 1250hp	Derby		1966	(oi)	OOU
	DARFIELD No.1	0-6-0ST IC	HE	3783	1953	(oj)	
D2162	(f.03162)	0-6-0DM 204hp	Sdn		1960	(ok)	
	RICHARD BORRETT	0-6-0DE 400hp	YE	2669	1958	(om)	
		0-4-0DE 220hp	YE	2854	1958	(on)	

(*) Named BURTONWOOD BREWER c1980 - c12/1991

OPERATIONAL LOCOS - VISITORS

193		0-6-0ST	IC	HE	3793	1953	(va)	(v1)
1466		0-4-2T	IC	Sdn		1936	(vb)	(v2)
7715		0-6-0PT	IC	KS	4450	1930	(vc)	(v3)
5572		2-6-2T	OC	Sdn		1929	(vd)	(v4)
7760		0-6-0PT	IC	NB	24048	1930	(ve)	(v5)
7828	ODNEY MANOR	4-6-0	OC	Sdn		1950	(vf)	(v6)
46443		2-6-0	OC	Cwe		1950	(vg)	
4566		2-6-2T	OC	Sdn		1924	(vh)	

NON-OPERATIONAL LOCOS FOR RESTORATION

7754		0-6-0PT	IC	NB	24042	1930	(ra)	Dsmt
5538		2-6-2T	OC	Sdn		1928	(rb)	(r1)
2859		2-8-0	OC	Sdn		1918	(rc)	OOU
5199		2-6-2T	OC	Sdn		1934	(rd)	(r2)
5532		2-6-2T	OC	Sdn		1928	(re)	OOU
7821	DITCHEAT MANOR	4-6-0	OC	Sdn		1950	(rf)	Dsmt
5952	COGAN HALL	4-6-0	OC	Sdn		1935	(rf)	OOU

NON-OPERATIONAL LOCOS STORED ON SITE

D2	ELISEG Ø	0-4-0DM	40hp	JF	22753	1939	(sa)	OOU
3		0-4-0ST	OC	P	2084	1948	(sb)	(s1)
(1243	RICHBORO)	0-6-0T	OC	HC	1243	1917	(sc)	OOU
(D3)	(12032)	0-4-0DM	60hp	JF	40000007	1947	(sd)	(s6)
D4	(No.14 CADBURY)	0-4-0DM	107hp	HC	D1012	1956	(se)	(s5)
	(ACKTON HALL)	0-6-0ST	IC	P	1567	1920	(sf)	OOU
D1		0-4-0DH	225hp	NB	27734	1958	(sg)	OOU
TR6		2w-2PMr		Wkm	6901	1954	(sh)	(s2)
	WINNINGTON	0-4-0DE	165hp	RH	416213	1957	(si)	(s6)
	-	0-4-0DE	165hp	RH	416207	1957	(sj)	(s6)
D9500	No.1 9312/92	0-6-0DH	650hp	Sdn		1964	(og)	(s3)
	-	4wDM		FH	3953	1960	(sk)	(s4)

Ø   named ELISIG until 9/1975.

(oa) tdx: private store [at Prestatyn] 11/9/1975
     wfw: British Leyland, Longbridge, Birmingham, AUSTIN 1; (arrived Prestatyn ex Longbridge 16/11/1973)
(ob) tdx: Steamport Ltd, Southport, Lancs, 31/5/1983 OR 5/6/1983
     tdt: East Lancashire Railway, 9/4/1988
     tdx: D.Foster, private store, Liverpool, 28/6/1991
(oc) tdx: British Railways, 9/3/1984
(od) tdx: Pilkingtons Ltd, St.Helens, Lancs, c3/1985
(oe) tdx: Cambrian Railways Society, Oswestry, Salop, 2/11/1985
(of) tdx: British Railways, Swindon, Wilts, 25/3/1986
(og) tdx: Ashington Colliery, Northumberland, 26/9/1987
(oh) tdx: British Railways, 19/3/1988
(oi) tdx: Vic Berry Scrapyard, Leicester, 2/6/1988

(oj) tdx: Yorkshire Dales Railway, 10/6/1988
(ok) tdx: British Railways, Chester, 1990; per owners Wirral Borough Council.
(om) tdx: ICI Ltd, Runcorn, Cheshire, 10/1989
(on) tdx: Padeswood Cement Works, 18/10/1991

(va) tdx: Peak Rail Ltd, Buxton, Derbyshire, 17/5/1985
(vb) tdx: GWR Society Ltd, Didcot, Berks, 3/7/1986
(vc) tdx: Quainton Railway Centre, Bucks, 14/7/1987
(vd) tdx: GWR Society Ltd, Didcot, Berks, 18/6/1988
(ve) tdx: Birmingham Railway Museum, Tyseley, 16/3/1989
(vf) tdx: Gwili Railway, Carmarthen, 30/3/1989
(vg) tdx: Severn Valley Railway, Bridgnorth, 1991 by 24/5/1991
(vh) tdx: Severn Valley Railway, Bridgnorth, 8/10/1991

(ra) tdx: Mountain Ash Colliery, Mid Glamorgan, 6/9/1980
(rb) tdx: Woodham Brothers, Barry Scrapyard, 1/2/1987
(rc) tdx: Woodham Brothers, Barry Scrapyard, 2/11/1987
(rd) tdx: Gloucester Warwickshire Railway, Toddington, 26/11/1988
(re) tdx: Forest of Dean Railway, Lydney, 29/1/1989; on arrival allocated boiler from loco
           5538, and MAY be rebuilt as a loco bearing number 5538.
(rf) tdx: Gloucester Warwickshire Railway, Toddington, 5/6/1989

(sa) tdx: Cambrian Railways Society store at Oswestry, Salop, 6/9/1975
      wfw: Broughton Aircraft Factory.
(sb) tdx: Greenfield (Courtaulds) Factory, Holywell Junct., c18/10/1975
(sc) tdx: Gresford Colliery, c7/2/1976
(sd) tdx: Burmah-Castrol Ltd, Ellesmere Port, Cheshire, 13/2/1976
(se) tdx: Cadbury Schweppes Foods Ltd, Moreton, Wirral, 5/1977
(sf) tdx: Keighley & Worth Valley Rly, Yorkshire, 10/1979
(sg) tdx: Shell UK Oil Ltd, Stanlow, Cheshire, 23/2/1980
(sh) tdx: Mr I.Jolly [see Section 1], 31/1/1982
      wfw: British Railways until 11/1981
(si) tdx: ICI Ltd, Winnington, Northwich, Cheshire, 6/1986
(sj) tdx: ICI Ltd, Winnington, Northwich, Cheshire, 8/1986
(sk) tdx: T.A.C.Construction Materials Ltd, Widnes, POILITE II, 26/7/1989

(v1) tdt: Peak Rail Ltd, Buxton, Derbyshire, 16/3/1989
(v2) tdt: GWR Society Ltd, Didcot, Berks, 1986
(v3) tdt: Quainton Railway Centre, Bucks, 24/9/1987
(v4) tdt: GWR Society Ltd, Didcot, Berks, 3/1989
(v5) tdt: Birmingham Railway Museum, Tyseley, 11/1/1990
(v6) tdt: East Lancashire Railway, Bury, 20/3/1991

(r1) loco frame only tdt: Dean Forest Railway, Lydney, 1989
(r2) chassis tdt: Long Marston Army Depot, Warwicks, for repair, 10/12/1990

(s1) tdt: Mold Junction Loco Shed Scrap Metal Depot [see PR/7], 10/1978
(s2) tdt: Peak Rail Ltd, Buxton, Derbyshire, c4/1983
(s3) tdt: Swindon Railway Workshops, Wiltshire, c3/1988
      wlw: West Somerset Railway, from 11/1989
(s4) tdt: Cambrian Railways Society Depot, Oswestry, Salop, 6/10/1990
(s5) tdt: Premier Brands Ltd, Moreton, Wirral (for display), 19/1/1991
(s6) tdt: Nostalgia World, Myddlewood, near Baschurch, Salop, c12/1990.

SECTION THREE

LOCOMOTIVE OPERATED INDUSTRIAL and CONTRACT RAILWAYS

This Section lists all locations where locomotives are known - or believed - to have been used (other than those included in Section 2).

Entries are sorted alphabetically by the name of the location, with no regard to the County in which the location falls. For the purposes of this Section, the Counties of Gwynedd and Clwyd are amalgamated into one "North Wales" area.

Each Location is identifed by a National Grid reference number by which it may be located on the more recent editions of Ordnance Survey (etc.) maps. In this Handbook, these reference numbers are shown with a prefix which indicates both the present and former Counties in which the Location falls, as follows:

Cd	: Clwyd ex Denbighshire/Sir Ddinbych
Cf	: Clwyd ex Flintshire/Sir Fflint
Cfd	: Clwyd ex Flintshire Detatched/Fflint a Maelor
Cm	: Clwyd ex Merioneth/Sir Feirionnydd
Ga	: Gwynedd ex Anglesey/Ynys Mon
Gc	: Gwynedd ex Caernarfonshire/Sir Gaernarfon
Gm	: Gwynedd ex Merioneth/Sir Feirionnydd

Each Location has been given a reference code in the form "Xn", where 'X' is the alphabetical initial of the Location, and 'n' a serial number within that alphabetical group. These reference codes are used for cross-reference purposes elsewhere within this Handbook, and on the Index Maps. As published here, only "even" numbers are used for these codes, leaving "odd" numbers for allocation to any further Locations that may be discovered.

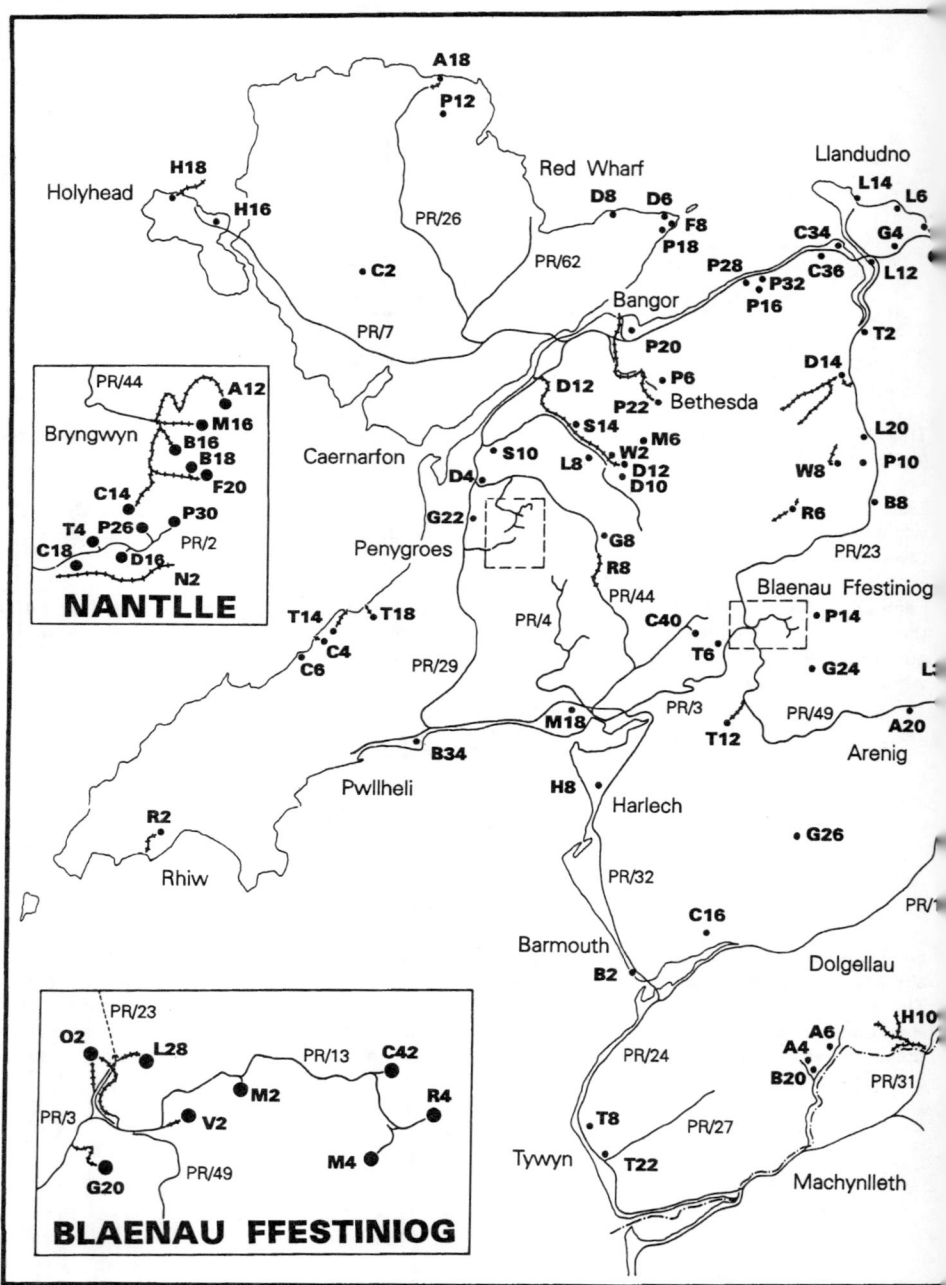

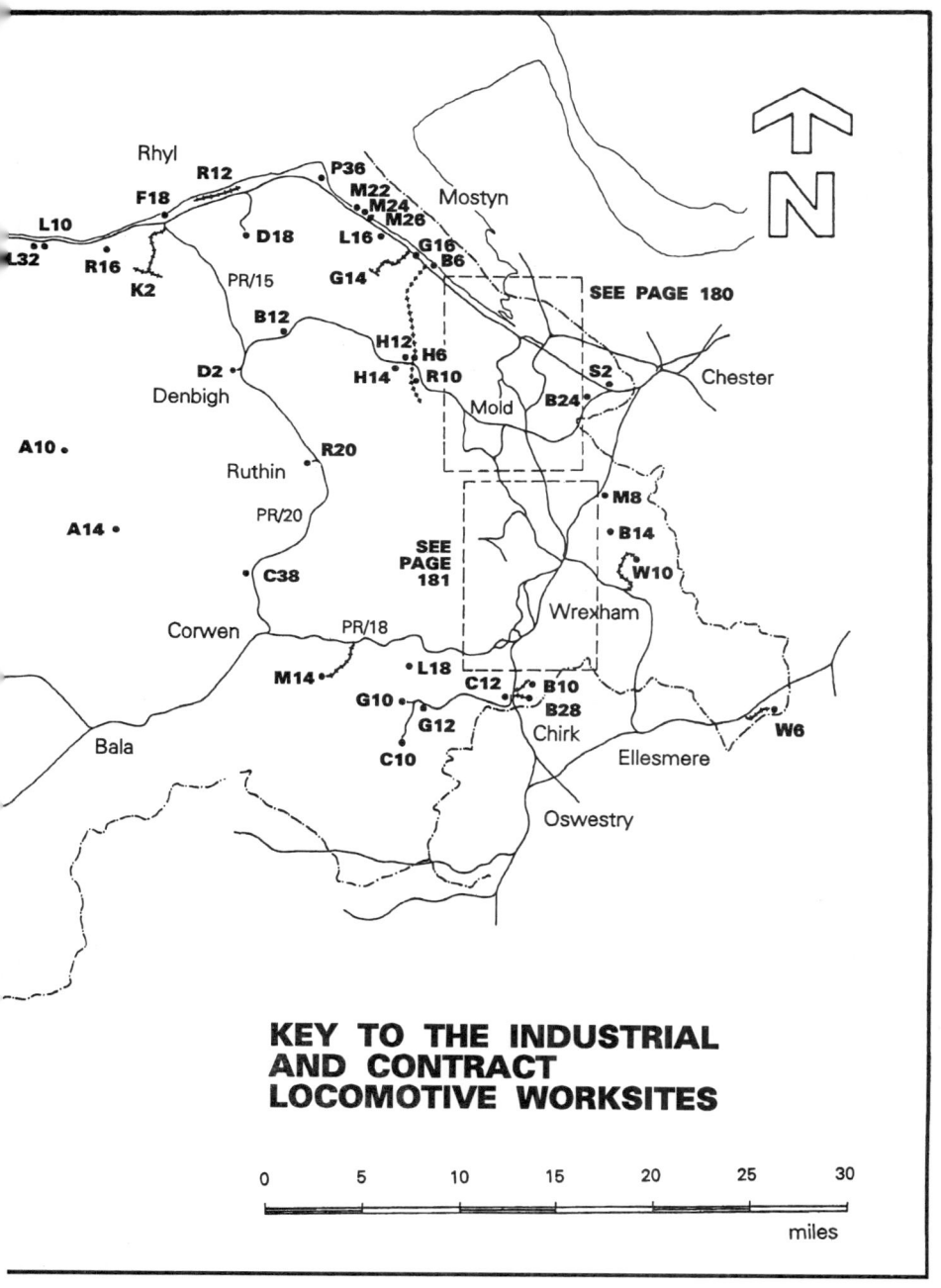

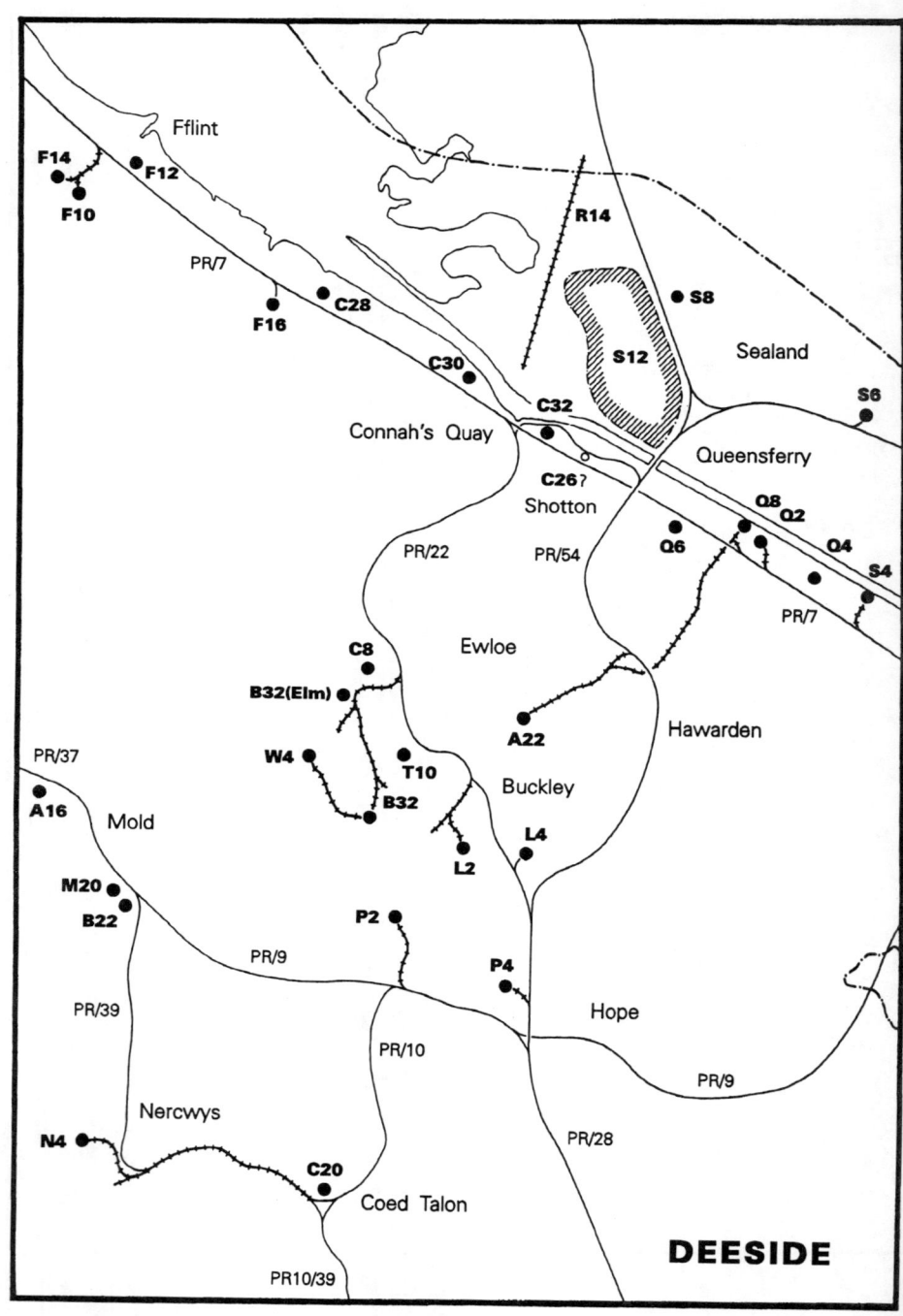

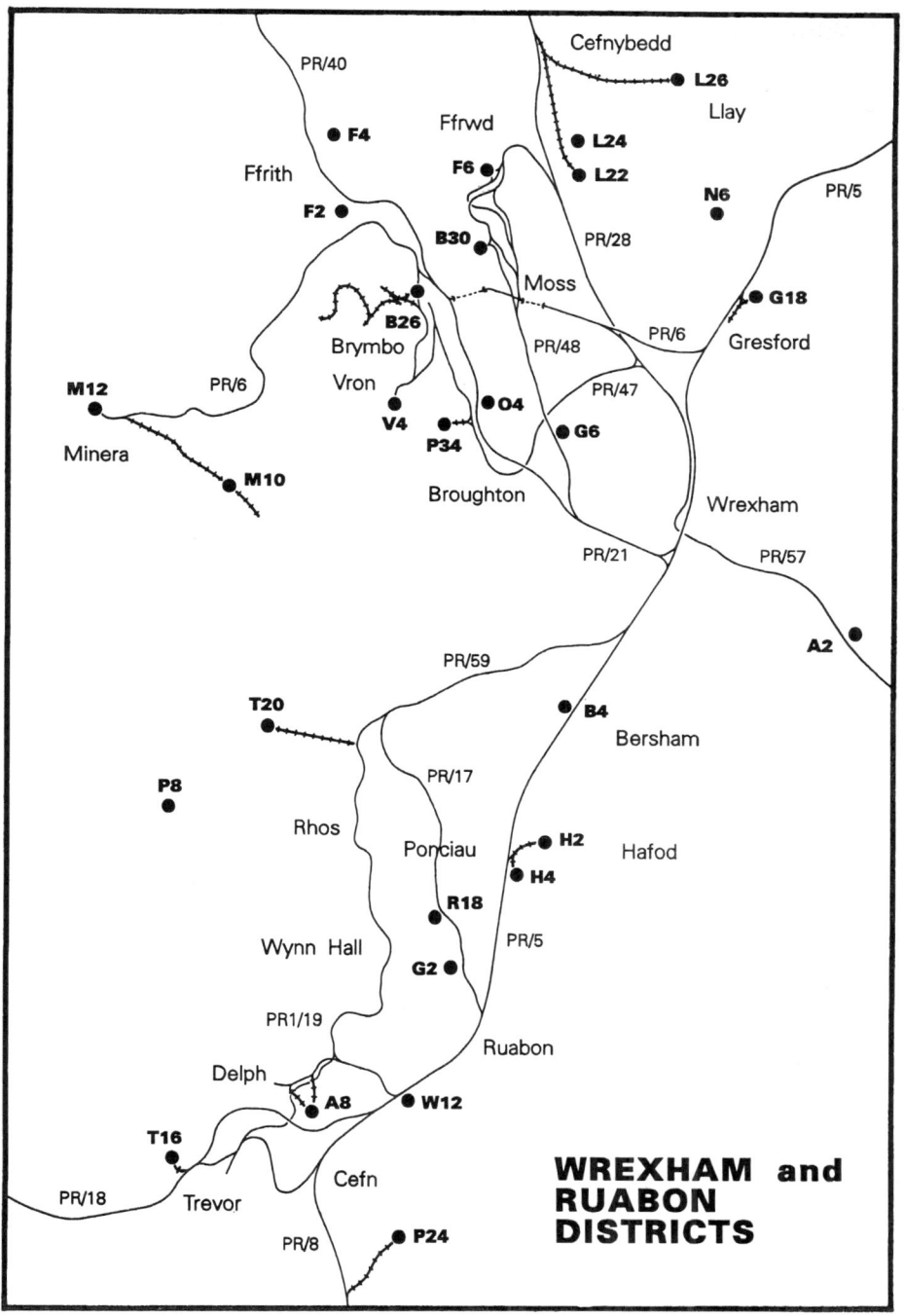

ABENBURY BRICKWORKS, KINGSMILLS, WREXHAM   A2
(Cd/GR:349491)

    1895   : opened
    1895 -   : **Davies Bros.** [the contractors, of Wrexham]
    by 1909   : in hands of **E.Noel Humphreys** (Trustee)
    by 1924   : **Oughtibridge Silica Firebrick Co Ltd** [of Sheffield]

This, the southerly of two adjacent works (the other being Kings Mills Brickworks), had a narrow-gauge line connecting the Works to the nearby claypit, and a short 4'8½" gauge siding off the adjacent PR/57 railway. Siding still in use 5/1969 but subsequently removed.
[Read: J/DHS/Vol.20/244]

Locomotives: Gauge 4'8½"

    [?   BANTAM   0-4-0tank   (a)   (1)]

(a)   if indeed BANTAM, then:
        tdx: Davies Bros, PR/57 Wrexham-Ellesmere Rly Contract [c6/1897 ?]

(1)   the plant of Abenbury Brickworks, including a 4wc tank loco, was for sale here by unreserved auction 14/7/1909 [J/MM/9.7.1909].
        No further trace.

A steam crane, which possibly also shunted the siding, was for sale here 1/1930 [J/MM/10.1.1930].

ABERCWMEIDDAW SLATE QUARRY, UPPER CORRIS   A4
(Gm/GR:745093)

    1876   : opened
    1876 -   1905   : **Abercwmeiddaw Slate Quarry Co Ltd**
                                          (reg.15/5/1876   liq.6/3/1905-23/1/1907)
               21/3/1906   : dispersal auction
                                 : re-opened [by ?]
    after 1922   : closed and dismantled

Extensive open quarry connected to the Upper Corris branch of the Corris Railway (PR/16) by railways and inclines. This site is of particular interest for the clearly visible remains of circular tunnels cut by a large diameter boring machine, though much of the area was extensively disturbed by a land reclamation scheme in 1990.

Locomotive: Gauge 2'3"

                         0-4-0VBT   Ellis   (see below)

This quarry was offered for sale as a going concern on 24/7/1893; the sale catalogue [DRO/Z/DCA/30] listing (inter alia) 51 iron rubbish wagons plus 14 "wooden slate trams with powerful brakes for carrying slates &c to Machynlleth, 2 iron trams with side doors hinged for dropping down....to carry coals". Within the quarry was a "Horizontal winding steam engine" with 24"x12" cylinders "by H.& J.Ellis, Salford", and "One small Locomotive Engine of 2ft 6in Cylinder and 1 Multitubular Boiler, with Water Tanks and Coal Bunkers, by H.&.J.Ellis, Salford". If the quarry was then sold, the name of the owning Company was not changed.

The 21/3/1906 liquidation sale advertisement [J/CJ/28.2.1906] again included "one small loco engine of 2'6" cylinder". Maden & McKee, of Liverpool, then advertised [J/NWWN/30.3.1906] that they had purchased the plant, for re-sale, including "locomotive with vertical multi-tubular boiler, 2'6" cylinders, 4 wheels coupled, 2'3" gauge, by H.& J.Ellis, Salford". Perhaps 'two 6 inch cylinders' was the proper description ?

Little seems to be known of Ellis, though in 1878 "H.& J. Ellis, Irwell Works, Salford" were advertising [J/TE/1878, etc] as "manufacturers of steam engines, boilers, railway plant [etc]", and seem to be successors of S.Ellis & Co, Irwell Works, Salford, who advertised [J/RT/24.7.1858] in 1858 as "manufacturers of railway plant, cranes [etc]".
From [J/MM] 7/1892 to 12/1893 Thomas Greenwood, dealer, Bailey Hall Ironworks, Halifax, was offering for sale a new 4wc 6x10 IC loco "by H.J.Ellis, Manchester - boiler 8'6" long, 2'10" diameter, with dome, injector, water tank [etc]". This could in fact be the "small new 6 inch loco" Greenwood had advertised since 1888. And, from 11/1893 to 11/1894 George Bush, Engineer & Railway Plant Merchant, The Old Foundry, Dalton-in-Furness, advertised [J/MM] various locomotives in such a way that identification is difficult; however, his early adverts include "4 wheel 3'8½" gauge horizontal multi-tubular boiler by Ellis & Co", whilst his later adverts include "Vertical type loco, 2'8½" gauge, 6 inch cylinders". It is possible that neither Bush nor Greenwood actually had the locos, hence perhaps the apparent confusion through the series of adverts. Little doubt, it would seem, that Ellis did build a number of locos; but of no apparent assistance in settling the source or fate of the Abercwmeiddaw loco. No positive evidence has been found in the Upper Corris area, except that the loco has been recalled as being somewhat like a DeWinton. As it had a vertical boiler, this is not surprising !

An Engineer's Report and valuation of plant of 1/11/1922 records that the quarry tramways and wagons were then intact, but makes no mention of a locomotive.

ABERLLEFENNI SLATE QUARRIES, near CORRIS   A6
(Gm/GR:769103)

c1500	: primitive workings at this site
1873	: recorded as an organised, active, unit
by 1948	: **Aberllefeni Slate & Slab Quarries Co**
by 5/1963	: **Aberllefeni Slate Quarries Ltd** - a company associated with **Bow Slate & Enamel Co Ltd** and which subsequently traded as : **Wincilate Ltd**

Extensive workings both on the surface and underground; originally opened up as individual quarries including CEUNANT DU, FOEL GROCHAN, and HEN CHWAREL. Extensive system of railways and inclines connected to the Corris Railway (PR/16). Locomotives were first used at the quarry in 1963, principally underground. The railway from the quarry to the Mill near Aberllefenni Station was worked by horses and farm tractor - this line closed in 1982 and its track was removed in 1983.

Locomotives: Gauge 2'3"

4wBE	5hp	Votty *	c1939	(a)	(1)
4wBE	10hp	BE	c1917	(b) #	(2)
4wBE		LMM		(c)	(3)
4wBE		CE	B0457 1974	New	

\# : fitted with electric motor 7036
* : built at Votty Quarry using the frame of steam loco TAFFY, and recognizable by its inside-framed chassis

(a) tdx: Votty & Bowydd Slate Quarry, Blaenau Ffestiniog, 8/1963.
(b) tdx: Votty & Bowydd Slate Quarry, Blaenau Ffestiniog, 8/1963. (Axleboxes fitted outside the wheels)
(c) tdx: Braich Goch Slate Quarry, Upper Corris; after 10/1971 by 7/1972

(1) fell into flooded underground workings 7/1971, and abandoned
(2) tdt: Welsh Slate Museum, Llanberis, 19/4/1983
(3) tdt: private store (at Caernarfon) c4/1983
    wlw: Groeslon (Tudor) Slate Works (which see)

ACREFAIR (RUABON NEW) IRONWORKS and PLASMADOC RAILWAYS
A8
(Cd/GR:below)

by 1/1790	-	1820	: **E.Ll.Rowland & Co**
1820	-	1822	: **Ruabon Iron Co** (E.Ll.Rowland & Geo.Homfray)
1825	-	11/1843	: **British Iron Co** (reg.28/4/1825 - Small, Shears & Taylor)
11/1843	-	11/1883	: **New British Iron Co** (reg.2/11/1843)
11/1883	-	11/1887	: **New British Iron Co Ltd** (reg.28/11/1883 £600K)
11/1887	-	1891	: closed. (NBICoLtd liq.11/1887)
1891	-	1950s	: **Hughes & Lancaster Engineering Co Ltd**
1950s	-		: **Air Products Ltd**

Edward Lloyd Rowlands was interested in many enterprises, the principal being the (Old) Ruabon Ironworks at Brandie, and some coal pits at Acrefair. On this latter site (GR:281431) he built (c1817) the (New) Ruabon Ironworks, and laid a system of tramroads to connect this works with various collieries and brickworks in the area. These included early workings at Delph, Plasynwern, Cristionydd, Newbridge, Plas Bennion, Plas Madoc and Wynnstay.

The original tramroads were replaced by a system of 4'8½" gauge locomotive railways which, after 1887, were taken over by the GWR where required. The line from Wynnstay to Plasynwern became the GWR Plasmadoc Branch (see PR/19); other lines (eg, to Delph Brickworks) becoming GWR sidings from that line.

After 1887 the Acrefair site declined in importance, some sections being taken over by Hughes & Lancaster with only limited rail sidings off PR/19 and rail traffic had completely ceased before Air Products moved in.

Excellent articles describing Acrefair Ironworks etc. appeared in J/DHS of 1982 & 1983.

Locomotives: Gauge 4'8½"

No local information has been found regarding locomotives used here. In 1886 an article [J/TE/12.11.1886/381] describing the Works stated there were then four locos here, but gave details of just two of them - one, a 0-4-0VBT VCG built at Acrefair, the other described only as "old locomotive, built no-one knows where, with 11" by 20" outside cylinders"; no loco listed below fits the dimensions given.

	0-4-0	IC	Fbn		1839	(a)	(1)
	0-4-2	OC	VF	[? 319]	1848	(b)	s/s
	0-4-0VBT	VCG	NBI Co		New		s/s
WELD BLUNDELL	0-4-0ST	OC	MW	802	1882	(c)	(2)

OTHER POSSIBLE LOCOMOTIVES:

	"TAFFY"	0-6-0ST	IC	SS	1859	1868	(d)	?
		[0-4-0]ST	IC	BP	68	1857	(e)	?

(a) tdx: Lancashire & Yorkshire Railway Co, No.124 (ex No.188), 4/1854.
     This loco is specifically recorded as sold to NBI Co, Ruabon, £650.
(b) if indeed here [see below], then:
     tdx: Lancashire & Yorkshire Railway Co, No.223, £1000. 10/1854.
     wfw: Liverpool, Crosby & Southport Railway [? No.2].
     This loco is recorded in L&Y Rly Co Minutes as sold to NBI Co but destination not stated, thus it may have been Acrefair, or perhaps one of the NBI Co locations (eg, Abersychan) in South Wales. The same Minutes record that NBI Co had this loco (223) in preference to loco "222/306" which NBI Co had earlier agreed to purchase for £1050.
(c) per MW records, this loco apparently with NBI Co by 1886.
     wfw: J.P.Edwards, contractor, "Ainsdale" - [presume means Aintree to Southport CLC (1882-1885) Contract, and thus possibly one of the three locos 10" to 13" by MW and SS for sale there 5/1885].
(d) A loco named, or nicknamed, TAFFY, possibly 0-4-0ST, recalled at NBI Co, Corngreave Furnaces, Staffs. A possible identity for TAFFY is 4'8½" gauge 0-6-0ST IC SS 1859/1868, New to New British Iron Co at unknown site. The name TAFFY suggests the loco moved to Corngreaves from Wales, but perhaps from Abersychan (etc) rather than from Acrefair. However, SS 1859 has also been associated (or confused) with the 15" loco for sale [J/TE/18.10.1895] by the North British Maleable Ironworks, Coatbridge, Scotland. Indeed, some copies of the "SS Works List" do show SS 1859 as New to NORTH British Iron Co, at unknown site.
(e) [0-4-0?]ST IC BP 68/1857 4'8½" gauge was supplied New to New British Iron Co at unknown site. 1857 is too early for Corngreaves (where 4'8½" gauge tracks were not laid in until 1863), hence BP 68 was either at Acrefair or in South Wales. Mr Peacock was promoting sales of BP locos in North Wales at that time, through his connections at Brymbo, so Acrefair does seem a distinct possibility.
     BP 68 is said to have been rebuilt as 0-4-2ST in 1865. However, per BP records, BP 68 was built to the same design as BP 27, 28, 42, 43, 50, 51, 52 but, per B/103/F5-6, BP27, 50, 51 (GWR 342, 91, 92) were 0-4-2ST IC when new.

(1)   this loco had 12"x18" cylinders. A 12" 4wc loco was included in the 7-10/10/1890 dispersal sale at Acrefair. No further trace.
(2)   wlw: Wynnstay Colliery (which see).   Indeed, this loco may have always been at Wynnstay, initially under NBI Co ownership.

ALED RESERVOIRS CONSTRUCTION, DENBIGH MOORS   A10
(Cd/GR:below)

c1932   -   1939   : **Rhyl Urban District Council** (direct labour).

c1932-1934: A low dam was built at the outflow (GR:917579) of Llyn Aled (a natural lake) to increase its capacity as a reservoir. The work included a diversion of the mountain road on the shore of the lake. A 2ft gauge railway was laid along the new road from GR:923574 to the dam, and carried materials for road and dam construction. The V-Skip wagons were pulled by horses.

1934-1939: A large dam was built downstream at GR:915599 to create Aled Isaf reservoir. Stone, obtained from a quarry opened up immediately below this dam, was hauled up a 2ft gauge incline to a crusher, then cast into large concrete blocks which were used to build the dam wall. Traces of this incline can be seen today [1990]. Another 2ft gauge railway was laid southwards from the dam to a clay-pit at GR:913588; this line was used for construction of the new road beside the reservoir, and for carrying clay infilling for the dam. Whilst initially horse-worked, a locomotive was used on this line from c8/1935.
The railway equipment - loco, wagons and track - was later taken by lorry to Cornwall for re-use.

Locomotive: Gauge 2'0"

```
                        4wPM     20hp MR     5072    1930  (a)                  (1)
```

(a)   tdx: M.A.Boswell, contractor (of Wolverhampton), by 8/1935
              [possibly direct from "Penyclip Roadworks Contract" - which see]

(1)   tdt: Falmouth Corporation, Argal Dam Construction, Cornwall, after 4/1938 by 4/1939

ALEXANDRA (CORS-Y-BRYNIAU) SLATE QUARRY, MOEL TRYFAN   A12
(Gc/GR:519562)

```
        1861                 :  opened
     3/1861    -     1863    :  B.Lloyd & Wm.Griffith
    10/1863    -    c1869    :  Alexandra Slate Co Ltd
                                [Bateson, Bateson, McConnell] (liq.1/7/1869)
by    1874    -    7/1914    :  Alexandra Slate Co Ltd   (liq.2/1918)
    7/1914    -    7/1918    :  closed - leased 10/10/1917 to:
    7/1918    -   11/1930    :  Amalgamated Slate Association Ltd
    4/1932    -     1934     :  Carnarvonshire Crown Slate Quarries Co Ltd
        1934                 :  closed; dismantled. In later years the pit was worked as an
                                extension of Moel Tryfan Quarry.
```

The quarry was extensively developed from 1874 [J/CDH/19.9.1874/5c2]. Locomotives were put to work in the quarry in early 1876. Tenders were invited [J/CDH/28.8.1876] for construction of c2 miles railway from quarry to Bryngwyn Incline Drumhead (PR/44) - this rather spectacular steeply-graded line with horse-shoe curves was being built by 12/1876 and opened c6/1877 [Crown Land Records]. The construction contractor was very likely Spooner & Co. OS Maps mark a second "Alexandra Quarry" (GR:517567) beside its route, though in fact only waste-dumps exist here; it may have been the site of a Mill, with possibly adit access to a lower level within the quarry. All rail tracks were removed c1939.

[Read: B/450/183-184,205-206]

Locomotives: Gauge 2ft

		ADDA	0-4-0VBT	VC	DeW		1876	New (*)	(1)
		EVA	0-4-0VBT	VC	DeW		1877	New (*)	(2)
[?		FLORINDA	0-4-0VBT	VC	DeW		1877	New (a)	s/s]
		KATHLEEN	0-4-0T	OC	VF	805	1877	(b)	(3)

(*) A report of 23/12/1876 [Crown Land Records] has one loco at work "for last twelve months" and "two more have been ordered for delivery in next 2-3 months". This may be read as confirming the third DeWinton (see footnote 'a'), assuming KATHLEEN (ex works 5/1877) was then the property of Spooner (& Co). EVA may have been spelled EFA.

(a) There have been vague references for many years to a DeWinton loco here named FLORINDER/FLORINDA. In 1879 there was a lady "The Hon Florinda Bateson - Widow" [CRO/XM/6703/15]; presumably related to one of the Batesons who formerly owned this quarry. If there were three DeWinton locos here, then this third seems confirmed as listed. Alternatively, FLORINDA (if indeed it did exist) could be either ADDA or EVA renamed.

(b) supplied by Spooner & Co, perhaps consequent upon construction of railway from Quarry to Bryngwyn Incline.

(1) disused by 1914 - possibly scrapped by then - not here in 1920 and no further trace.
(2) disused by 1914; possibly later used again; disused here in 1920 and scrapped c1930 by 1932 certain.
(3) after 1917 the locos of the Amalgamated quarries (Alexandra, Braich, Moel Tryfan and Cilgwyn) were transferred between duties as required. KATHLEEN reputedly repaired at some time using parts of KELSO obtained from Penyrorsedd. Dismantled after 1932, and remains sold as scrap in 1940.

ALWEN RESERVOIR CONSTRUCTION, near CERRIG-Y-DRUDION   A14
(Cd/GR:954528)

Birkenhead Corporation.   Started 1911, completed 1917.
Sir Robert McAlpine & Sons , contractor.

Photographs of work in progress indicate that a number of locomotives were used here, but none seen so far are clear enough to confirm the identity of the locos, or the numbers/names that they carried, and no other local records have yet come to our notice. The following listing, therefore, requires some confirmation. As explained in entry "Dolgarrog Railways", the history of early McAlpine locomotives is rather confused, and the surviving Plant Registers post-date the Alwen Contract.

Locomotives: Gauge 3'0"

[No.6	?]	0-4-0ST	OC	HE	404	1886	(a)	(1)
[No.8	HANNAH ?]	0-4-0ST	OC	BH	1125	1895	(b)	(2)
No.22	COOLMORE	0-4-0ST	OC	HE	832	1903	(c)	(3)
No.28		0-4-0ST	OC	HC	998	1912	New (d)	(4)
No.29		0-4-0ST	OC	HC	999	1912	New (d)	(5)
[?	OGDEN	0-4-0T	OC	WB	1761	1905	(e)	(6)]

(a) "Plant No.6, No.25, purchased 1906" in McAlpine Register of 1917; hence perhaps 'No.25' rather than 'No.6'. Vendor not stated.
   Spare parts consigned to Alwen for 404 by HE in 5/1913.
   wfw: McAlpine, Metropolitan Water Board Island Barn Reservoir (1908-1911) Contract, East Molesey, until 3/5/1911 at least.
(b) "Plant No.8, purchased 1907" in Register, and thought to be BH 1125.
   wfw: P.Drake & Sons, Ogden Reservoir Contract, Haslingden, HANNAH; locos were for sale at Haslingden from 12/1907.
(c) Register entry "Plant No.22, purchased 1906" is presumed to refer to HE 832.
   wfw: McAlpine at Letterkenny & Strabane Railway (1906-1908) Contract, Ireland, named COOLMORE.
   Spare parts consigned to Alwen for 832 by HE in 1/1912, 7/1913, 7/1914.
(d) both locos delivered New 6/1912 to Corwen [nearest railhead for Alwen] but there remains some doubt as to running numbers carried.
   From 1917 they were "Plant No.28/29" - but see notes re HC 1037 in entry "Trawsfynydd Reservoir".
(e) not confirmed here, but:
   wfw: McAlpine, Metropolitan Water Board Island Barn Reservoir (1908-1911) Contract, East Molesey, until 3/5/1911 at least, then spares purchased by McAlpine 5/1912.
   wfw: Phineas Drake & Sons, Ogden Reservoir, Haslingden (where locos were for sale from 12/1907).

(1) tdt: Great Stanney Depot, Ellesmere Port, Cheshire [c1917 ?].
   Renumbered "Plant No.315 Loco No.25" in 1921, and sold as scrap in 1929.
(2) tdt: Great Stanney Depot, Ellesmere Port, Cheshire, by 1917
   wlw: Cowlyd Reservoir (etc) Contract - see "Dolgarrog Railways".
(3) wlw: McAlpine, "Corby near Grantham" - presumed Corby Glen, on McAlpine GNR Little Bytham to Stoke widening Contract - after 1/1912 by 6/1912, until 28/10/1912 at least.
   Returned to Alwen Reservoir by 29/3/1913; here to 15/7/1914 at least.
   tdt: Great Stanney Depot, Ellesmere Port, Cheshire, by 1917
   wlw: Burnley Corporation, Hurstwood Reservoir, by 3/1924, named COOLMORE
   wlw: Lehane, McKenzie & Shand, Brownhill Reservoir (1924-1931) Contract, by 12/1924, named BROWNHILL.

(4) tdt: Great Stanney Depot, Ellesmere Port, Cheshire, by 1917
    wlw: McAlpine [Ministry of Munitions] National Spelter Avonmouth Contract from 1918 to 28/10/1919
    wlw: Great Stanney Depot, Ellesmere Port, Cheshire
        (re-registered there 31/10/1921 as "Plant No.53 No.28")
    wlw: Trawsfynydd Reservoir (which see).
(5) tdt: Great Stanney Depot, Ellesmere Port, Cheshire, by 1917
    wlw: McAlpine [Ministry of Munitions] National Spelter Avonmouth Contract from 1918 to 1/11/1921. Re-registered as "Plant No.52" and sold as scrap in 1937.
(6) wlw: Fylde Water Board, Grizedale Lea Reservoir, by 1914; was probably the loco for which Fylde Water Board paid £340 to dealer T.H.Walker in 6/1914.

ALYN WORKS, MOLD   A16
                                            (Cf/GR:233650)

```
    1792 -     c1866  : a cotton mill
    1874 -      1876  : Mold Tinplate Co
    1878 -      1896  : Alyn Tin Plate Co
    1896 -    4/1939  : Alyn Steel Tinplate Co Ltd
                             subsid.of Richard Thomas & Co Ltd from 7/1936
  4/1939 -      1939  : Richard Thomas & Co Ltd
    1939 -   10/1943  : closed
 10/1943 -     c1945  : Ministry of Supply (store depot)
  3/1946 -            :  tinplate mills dismantled
    1947 -            : Synthite Ltd - chemical works (opened 3/1950).
```

Served by sidings beside PR/37 by 1878 at least. Rail traffic ceased in 12/1983 (and PR/37 then completely closed). Track lifted 1984.

[Read : Chronology of the Tinplate Works of Great Britain - E.H.Brooke 1944]

Locomotives: Gauge 4'8½"

	ALYNVA		0-4-0ST	OC	AB	1761	1922	New 2/22	(1)
3		Ø	4wPM	40hp	MR	2033	1920	(a)	Scr/1965
-			4wDM	40hp	MR	1944	1919	(b)	(2)

Ø MR 2033 re-engined Diesel in 1959.

(a) arrived after 1947 by 1950
    wfw(tdx?): R.Robinson & Co (Contractors) Ltd, of 42 Parliament Street, London SW1 - was in use on their Contract at Southern Railway, Ravensbourne Station, in 3/1941
    wfw: Barnstone Cement Co Ltd, Barnstone, Nottinghamshire
    wfw: Lancashire & Yorkshire Railway, number 3.
(b) tdx: Flint Paper Mill, Oakenholt, 8/1965

(1) scrapped 1/1951; major components survived here until after 6/1953
(2) tdt: Mr Ian Jolly, 8/5/1986 (see Section 1).

AMLWCH (OCTEL) CHEMICAL FACTORY
A18
(Ga/GR:446935)

1951 -   : Associated Ethyl Co Ltd
         : Associated Octel Co Ltd

Factory constructed 1950-51; connected to Amlwch station (PR/26) by ¾ mile long 'Amlwch Light Railway' [LRO: SI 520/1951] which was built by Marples, Ridgeway & Partners Ltd, contractors. Light Railway first used c12/1952 and worked by locos listed below. Since c1972 the line has been worked by British Railways, the industrial locos then being confined to shunting within the factory area.

Locomotives: Gauge 4'8½"

1	4wDM 88hp	RH	321727	1952	New 4/52	
2	0-4-0DM 165hp	RH	313394	1952	New 8/52	(1)
4	0-4-0DM 165hp	RH	319284	1952	(a)	(2)
-	0-4-0DH	HE	7460	1977	New	

(a)   tdx: Associated Octel Ltd, Ellesmere Port, Cheshire, 10/1976

(1)   tdt: Associated Octel Ltd, Ellesmere Port, Cheshire, 7/11/1977
      tdx: Associated Octel Ltd, Ellesmere Port, Cheshire, 2/1979
      tdt: Associated Octel Ltd, Ellesmere Port, Cheshire, 10/1979
(2)   tdt: Associated Octel Ltd, Ellesmere Port, Cheshire, 7/11/1977

ARENIG GRANITE QUARRIES, CWM CELYN
A20
(Gm/GR:830391)

c1903   : opened
by 7/1904 : Arenig Granite Co
by 5/1914 : Arenig Granite Co Ltd
             (in later years a subsidiary of
             Amalgamated Roadstone Corporation Ltd)
c1980   : closed; dismantled.

Principal quarry located adjacent to Arenig Station (PR/49) but on the opposite side of the road. Screens (served by a private siding; agreement of 15/7/1904) at the Station were connected to the quarry by a bridge carrying a 2ft gauge railway (later replaced by a conveyor belt). From the quarry, a 2ft gauge railway was built some ¾ mile westwards to a second, smaller, quarry; the locomotive was reputedly obtained to work this railway. The second quarry did not develop as expected, and the track was removed from the railway by 1954 (and in fact probably early in WW2), though hand-worked tramming was retained in both quarries for some years later.

Locomotive: Gauge 2'0"

    MINERALS *   0-4-0ST   OC   WB   1668   1903 (a)   (1)

*   WB recorded loco as having brass plates MINERAL when new, but this may be an error, as subsequent owners Hills and BPCM both referred to loco as MINERALS when ordering spare parts. Spelling of name at Arenig has yet to be confirmed.

(a) originally despatched new 30/4/1903 to Canada Dock, Liverpool, for shipment to unknown destination, per Richard White & Son, dealers, Widnes. The contact at Canada Dock was a Mr Crooke (or Crooks). Loco was fitted with "Richard White" plates, not "Bagnall" plates. Apparently returned to Whites who were advertising a loco of this type "practically new, used only a few weeks" from 6/1905 to 4/1906. By 1/5/1906 until 9/1907 at least, loco was with W. (Wm.) Hill & Co, contractors [who had a number of jobs going at this time particularly around Portland Dockyard; at Elderslie (Clyde Navigation); and at Garston Dock, Liverpool]. By 2/1913 loco was with British Portland Cement Manufacturers Ltd, Premier Works, Irthlingborough, Northants; and by 5/1914 loco was at Arenig.

(1) still here 1939 but not in use; gone by 1946; probably scrapped.

ASTON HALL & QUEENSFERRY COLLIERIES & RAILWAY   A22
                                                                                            (Cf/GR:below)

```
by   1864  -    1865     : Aston Hall Coal Co
     1866  -             : Aston Hall Coal Co Ltd
by   1871  -    1878     : Aston Hall Colliery Co Ltd
     6/1878 -            : Aston Hall Coal & Brick Co Ltd (reg.6/6/1878)
     1883              : sale of assets; Company survived or revived:-
            -   6/1913   : Aston Hall Coal & Brick Co Ltd
                6/1913   : closed
            24/7/1913    : dispersal auction
```

The history of the various Aston Hall and Queensferry collieries is very complicated; originally many small pits existed, served by the narrow-gauge horse-worked 'Dundas Tramroad' which operated between Buckley and Queensferry. Here, however, we are concerned with the two major sites that came to be connected, to the LNWR (PR/7) and to a wharf on the (canalised) river Dee, by the 4'8½" gauge Aston Hall Colliery Railway. Tenders for the construction of this c3 mile long line were invited in 1871 [J/TE/7.7.1871], the successful tenderer being **Jardine & Son, contractors**; the first sod being cut 11/1871 [J/MJ/2.12.1871/1]. It was reported as under construction early 1872 [J/CG/23.2.1872], and was apparently opened for traffic later the same year.

From the River Dee wharf (GR:323686) it followed the route of the tramroad to (the second) Queensferry (or 'Lower Aston') Colliery at GR:317677; a new route then led to GR:305666 where the tramroad was rejoined to reach Aston Hall (deep) Colliery, and the adjacent Aston Hall Brickworks (GR:293658).

Operators of the (first) Queensferry Colliery are recorded as:
```
1856  ,1857          : Haworth & Thompson
1858                 : John Thompson
1859  -      1865    : Isaac Thompson
1866  -      1868    : Exors of Isaac Thompson
1869  -      1871    : Queen's Ferry Coal Co
1871  -      1876    : Fred Thompson - plan of abandoned mine deposited 1876.
1878                 : Alex Ward sells colliery to Aston Hall Coal & Brick Co Ltd
                       New pit sunk adjacent to the old colliery.
```

Apart from Queensferry Colliery, Alex Ward also sold to the new Company the Aston Hall Colliery & Brickworks, and the Pentrobin Hall Colliery. Pentrobin is near Dob's Hill, and now served by the Aston Hall Railway, yet the 1883 sale book lists the three 4'8½" gauge locos as being then at the Carpenter's Shop, Smithy & Store House at Pentrobin, Buckley.

The Aston Hall Railway must have soon reopened after 1883; when the Wrexham, Mold & Connah's Quay Junction Railway 'loop line' (PR/54) was built in 1889, it bridged over the Aston Hall Railway at GR:309666 and a steeply graded curving connection was made between the two railways by contractor H.Croom Johnson (see PR/54 for details). After closure of the collieries and railway in 1913 the tracks were removed [the GCR sidings at the "Croom Johnson" junction were lifted in 1917, and the bridge (No.38) was replaced by embankment in 1971]; but much can still be traced [1991] despite opencast coal extraction and major road works in the area in recent years. OS/6"/1914 shows the railway, whilst OS/6"/1870 shows the previous tramroad.

Locomotives: Gauge 4'8½"

```
     [   GLYNNE  ? ]        0-6-0ST   OC   FW     167    1872  New         (1)
         ?                  ?              FW     ?      ?                 (2)
     [   DOCTOR  ? ]        [ ? 0-6-0ST IC] WkB   [? 890 1875  New ]       (2)
         STALYBRIDGE        0-6-0T    IC   SS     3475   1888  (a)         (3)
```

(a)   wfw(tdx?): Exors of T.A.Walker, contractor, Manchester Ship Canal Construction Contract, c1894

(1)   s/s - no further trace.
      This was possibly the 13x20 3'6" wheel 6wc FW advertised for sale by Cudworth & Johnson, dealers, Wrexham, 2/1889
(2)   the 1883 sale list has three locos - two by FW and one by WkB. The identity of this second FW is a mystery. The identity of the WkB loco can only be surmised, on the basis of the incomplete records available of WkB products.

NOTE: presumably one (at least) of the above locos was retained here after the 1883 sale, to work the railway prior to arrival of SS 3475

(3)   reputedly - tdt : Lane End Colliery, Buckley [c1902 ?]
                  tdx : Lane End Colliery [c1903 ?]
      The final auction 24/7/1913 included just one loco - 13" 6wc SS - presumably SS 3475. No further trace.

BARMOUTH SEA DEFENCES   B2
(Gm/GR:below)

6/1930 - 1932 : **Barmouth Urban District Council**

The sea wall and promenade along Marine Road (GR:603172 north to 610158 south, approximately), built in 1887 [contract details not known], was severely damaged by storm in 1923, and deterioratated thereafter. BUDC obtained an Act to raise finance for reconstruction and let the Contract 6/1930, for (inter alia) new sea wall 7200 ft long and 46 timber groynes. Work was completed in 1932 but some equipment remained on site for some years afterwards.

DEMOLITION & CONSTRUCTION CO LTD, contractors.

Locomotives: Gauge 4'8½"

-		0-4-0ST OC	MW	1106	1888	(a)	(1)

Locomotives: Gauge 2'0"

	4wPM 20hp	FH	1708	1930	New	(2)
	4wPM 20hp	FH	1725 [c1930]	New		(3)

(a) here by 5/1931
wfw: G.Shellabear & Son Ltd, contractors, Southend Corporation Maldon Reservoir (1926-   ) Contract; then to Shellabear Plant Depot, Coronation Road, Park Royal, London, where a sale of plant 9/4/1931 included a 14" 4w MW loco - presumably MW 1106.

(1) left lying on site when work was completed; still here 7/6/1935, but later s/s - no further trace.
(2) returned to FH [? in 1932] who re-sold loco to:
    The Stuart (Tharnesmouth) Sand & Shingle Co, Mucking Hall Gravel Pit, near Stanford-le-Hope, Essex, 21/10/1932
(3) disposal not known [? also returned to FH for re-sale].

BERSHAM COLLIERY, BERSHAM, near WREXHAM   B4
(Cd/GR:315482)

1864		: sinking, on site of old brickyard
1864 -	2/1869	: **Bersham Coal Co (Barnes & Co)** - sinking proved difficult; first coal not sold until 7/1874.
1879		: sinking finished - 420 yards.
2/1869 -	1936	: **Bersham Colliery Co Ltd**
		from 1/1912 a subsidiary of (absorbed 1936 by):
1936 -	12/1946	: **Broughton & Plas Power Coal Co Ltd**
		from 1936 a subsidiary of:
		Lancashire Steel Corporation Ltd
1/1947 -	4/1986	: **National Coal Board**
4/1986 -		: **British Coal Corporation**
18/12/1986		: coal winding ceased; colliery dismantled.

Located directly beside PR/5, with small fan of sidings connected-up to PR/5 in 8/1869. Due to tight curvature, only short-wheelbase locos could be used, until the yard was remodelled in 1981 to suit "merry-go-round" wagons. Underground locos were not used at this colliery.

[Read: J/CG/30.3.1899. B/107]

Locomotives: Gauge 4'8½"

	SARAH	0-4-0ST	OC	[?BP	91	1857]	(a)	(1)
	SNOWDON	0-4-0ST	OC	BP	811	1868	(b)	(2)
63.000.403	SHAKESPEARE	0-4-0ST	OC	HL	3072	1914	(c)	Scr 11/1980
	NEPTUNE	0-4-0ST	OC	MW	1922	1916	(d)	(3)
	(JAMES HALL)	0-4-0ST	OC	AB	1831	1924	(e)	(4)
	(EASTWOOD)	0-4-0ST	OC	AB	1304	1912	(f)	(5)
	SPIDER	0-4-0ST	OC	HL	2623	1905	(g)	(6)
	PIRAEUS	0-4-0ST	OC	AB	643	1889	(h)	(7)
47006		0-4-0ST	OC	Hor		1953	(i)	(8)
63.000.404	HORNET	0-4-0ST	OC	P	1935	1937	(j)	(9)
63.000.328		0-6-0DM 325hp		HE	6664	1969	(k)	(10)
63.000.427		4wDM 88hp		RH	326068	1953	(m)	(11)
63.000.329		0-6-0DM 325hp		HE	6663	1969	(n)	(12)
63.000.314		0-6-0DM 400hp		HE	7018	1971	(o)	(13)

Locomotive: Gauge 1'10½" - Surface Stockyard.

63.000.405	4wDM	48hp	RH	497547	1963	(p)	(14)

(a) a loco SARAH recalled here but not identified; probably BP 91 hence possibly tdx: Old Broughton Colliery [? c1878].
(b) tdx: Brymbo Steelworks, 5/1919
(c) hired from Cudworth & Johnson, dealers, Wrexham, c1928; retained and purchased from C&J. Reputedly came direct to Bersham from Hafod Colliery, where it had previously been on hire.
  tdt: Llay Workshops, after 6/1958 by 8/1958
  tdx: Llay Workshops, after 9/1958 by 7/1959
(d) tdx: Liverpool Corporation, City Engineers' Department, Otterspool, Embankment contract, c1935, after 6/1931 by 7/1935. [? per or via Rapid Electric Arc Welding & Metals Co Ltd, dealers/repairers, Liverpool]
(e) arrived after 5/1940 by 8/1948
  wfw: Gatewen or Plas Power collieries.
(f) tdx: Cudworth & Johnson, hire, c1948
(g) tdx: Black Park Colliery, 1949
  tdt: Llay Main Workshops, after 6/1952 by 5/1953
  tdx: Ifton Colliery, Salop, 2/1964
(h) tdx: Ifton Colliery, Salop, after 9/1949 by 5/1953
(i) tdx: British Railways, loan, 8/1958
(j) tdx: Ifton Colliery, Salop, 21/11/1968
(k) tdx: Walkden Workshops, Lancs, 10/1/1980
  wfw: Granville Colliery, Salop.
(m) tdx: Point of Ayr Colliery, 3/1980 by 15/3/1980
(n) tdx: Walkden Workshops, Lancs, 19/6/1980
  wfw: Granville Colliery, Salop.

(o) tdx: Walkden Workshops, Lancs, 6/4/1982
     wfw: Hem Heath Colliery, Staffs.
(p) tdx: Walkden Workshops, Lancs, 11/1974
     wfw: Gresford Colliery
     tdt: Walkden Workshops, Lancs, 2/1981
     tdx: Walkden Workshops, Lancs, 4/6/1981

(1) gone away by 5/1940 - no further trace.
(2) gone away by 5/1940 - no further trace.
(3) tdt: Lancashire Steel Corporation Ltd, Irlam, Lancs, 1943
(4) not here 9/1949
     wlw(tdt?): Llay Main Workshops, by 10/1950
     scrapped at Llay Workshops, 1952
(5) tdt: Cudworth & Johnson, off hire, c1949
(6) tdt: Ifton Colliery, Salop, 10/1964
(7) tdt: Hafod Colliery, after 7/6/1954 and 6/8/1954
(8) tdt: British Railways, off loan, 1958 after 8/11/1958
(9) tdt: Steamport Ltd, Southport, Lancs, 1/1984
(10) tdt: Point of Ayr Colliery, 4/3/1980
(11) still here 15/7/1984, gone by 30/4/1986 - believed scrapped.
(12) tdt: Holditch Colliery, Staffs, 1987 by 4/7/1987
(13) tdt: Holditch Colliery, Staffs, c1987
(14) tdt: Point of Ayr Colliery, after 2/1984 by 4/1986

BETTISFIELD COLLIERY, BAGILLT   B6
(Cf/GR:217760)

1868	-	1874	: sinking; 280 yards. [J/CDH/14.2.1874]
1873	-		: **Bettisfield Colliery Co Ltd**
25/3/1897			: for sale as a going concern
1902			: **S.W.Higginbottom**
1904	-	c1911	: **Bagillt Coal Co Ltd** (reg.27/12/1904 £75K liq.12/10/1911)
			: [closed ?]
by 1913			: **Mold Collieries Ltd**, who formed:
10/1915	-	1/1934	: **Bettisfield Colliery Ltd**
			(reg.2/10/1915 liq.12/2/1934-16/7/1940)
c12/1933			: closed; later dismantled except for some buildings (later occupied by Allsopp's Plant Hire & C.Griffiths Scrap Metals depots).

The original shafts GR:215758 were on the south side of the LNWR (PR/7), being served by a siding which passed under bridge 58 of PR/7. Later a deeper mine was sunk on the north side of this bridge, served [? from 1879] by more extensive sidings. In the 1980s, a number of diesel locos from Shotton Steelworks were stored, and later scrapped, by Allsopp's.

[Read: J/CG/17.2.1893/311]

Locomotives: Gauge 4'8½"

		0-4-0ST	OC	AB	176	1876	New (a)	(1)
LADY STEVENSON No.7		0-6-0ST	IC	MW	1570	1903	(b)	
		rebuilt		HL	4267	1925		(2)
ACTIVE		0-6-0ST	IC	MW	510	1874	(c)	(2)
		0-4-0ST	OC	P	1649	1924	(d)	(3)

(a) supplied per J.H.Riddel & Co, dealers, Glasgow, 10/1876
(b) perhaps arrived Bagillt late 1905, as Bagillt Coal Co Ltd were advertising for a loco of this type at that time [J/CG/6.10.1905].
  wfw (tdx?): Henry Jackson & Co, contractors, Mid Suffolk Light Railway (1902-1904) Contract.
(c) wfw (tdx?): Jas.B.Watson & Sons, dealers, Leeds.
  wfw: A.M.Mundy, Coppice Collieries, Ilkeston, Derbyshire; subsequently Shipley Coal Co, and was probably the MW 13x18 IC 6wc 2'10"dw 11'6½"wb for sale there 1/12/1899 [J/CG/1.12.1899]. MW records list owner at Bagillt as Bettisfield Colliery Ltd [only], suggesting loco arrived Bagillt after 10/1915 - though perhaps MW did not learn of the transfer to Bagillt for some years after it had taken place.
(d) tdx: Thos.W.Ward Ltd, dealers, Sheffield, 10/1933; on hire arranged by R.& W. Hawthorn Leslie & Co, Newcastle on Tyne.

(1) the 25/3/1897 sale included one tank loco 12x19 cylinders, 3'6" wheels [perhaps AB 176 - 12x20 and probably 3'7" new] - no further trace.
(2) MW 1570 confirmed here in 1926, and one loco such as these observed (from passing train) standing derelict 28/1/1934.
  Otherwise, the fate of both locos is yet unknown.
(3) tdt: Queensferry Tar Works, 11/4/1934, per Thos.W.Ward Ltd.

BETWS-Y-COED RAILWAY MUSEUM B8
(Gc/GR:796565)

opened 1974 : Mr Alan Pratt
by 1986 - : Conwy Valley Railway Museum Ltd

The museum contains many exhibits and relics of both standard and narrow gauge railways, and has operating miniature railways including a 7¼ inch gauge circuit. This has steam and internal combustion locos, but they do not qualify for listing in this Handbook.

Locomotives: Gauge 2ft - Static display.

-	0-4-0WT	OC	OK	12722	1936	(a)		(1)
SYBIL	0-4-0ST	OC	HE	827	1903	(b)		(2)
SGT.MURPHY	0-6-0T	OC	KS	3117	1918			(3)
	rebuilt		Bethesda		1932	(c)		

Locomotive: Gauge 1'3" - Miniature railway.

70000   BRITANNIA   4-6-2   OC   *   1987 (d)

*built jointly by T.M.A.Engineering Ltd (number 8753) and by L.Engineering (number 1968).

Tramcar: Gauge 1'3" - Miniature railway.

In 1989 a passenger carrying electric tramway was built at the Museum, with a tram having bodywork built at the Museum on a chassis built by T.M.A.Engineering Ltd.

(a)   tdx: Hills & Bailey Ltd, Llanberis (see PR/65), 9/10/1975
(b)   tdx: Welsh Slate Museum, Llanberis; per owners Hills & Bailey Ltd, 13/2/1976
(c)   tdx: Cadeby Rectory, per owner Mr C.Pealling, 17/1/1977
      wfw: Penrhyn Slate Quarries, Bethesda.
(d)   tdx: Mr C.Cartwright [private store, West Midlands], c1989

(1)   tdt: Brecon Mountain Railway, 5/12/1977
(2)   tdt: Brecon Mountain Railway, c4/1979
(3)   tdt: private store (Winson Engineering) for overhaul, 15/12/1991 [then destined to move to Ffestiniog Railway (PR/3)]

BLACK PARK COLLIERY, CHIRK   B10
(Cd/GR:301393)

```
     by   1653   -              : early workings recorded on this site
          1805   -    1856      : T.E.Ward
      8/3/1832                  : first sod ceremony, Green Lane Pits
          1857   -    1861      : John Dickin
          1862   -    1877      : Black Park Colliery Co [John Stott-Milne & Co]
          1877   - 12/1946      : Black Park Colliery Co Ltd  (reg.27/1/1877 #50K)
       1/1947    -              : National Coal Board
      20/1/1951                 : coal winding ceased - colliery closed.
```

The 17th Century workings expanded to become six shafts around High Barracks (GR:298403), two at Low Barracks (GR:296396), two at Top Park Wood (GR:298395) and two in Chirk Green Wood (GR:294391). A 1½ mile horse-worked narrow-gauge tramroad ran through these workings, from High Barracks to a landsale yard known as Top Wharf (GR:291390) and later to Bottom Wharf beside the canal basin (opened 1805).
The tramroad was replaced by a 4'8½" gauge railway, constructed c1847 by the Shrewsbury & Chester Rly Co as a condition of their being permitted to build PR/8 through Chirk Castle Estate property. This railway followed the tramroad route from PR/8 and Bottom Wharf to Low Barracks, then diverted south-east to the new centre of mining at Green Lane. The tramroad north from Low Barracks was abandoned; stone sleeper blocks could still be found on this section in the 1970s.
After closure 1/1951, Black Park shaft was filled and capped, but from 1966 was re-opened and used to ventilate Ifton Colliery (Salop) until that pit closed 11/1968. The railway track was lifted in 1951. Top Wharf, including the loco shed, became a potato crisp factory, but was demolished 2/1970.
In 1986 the NCB commenced extensive opencast coal extraction at Black Park.

[Read: B/107; B/349; B/163/65-67]

Locomotives: Gauge 4'8½"

The earliest known loco dates from 1863. The railway may have been horse-worked prior to this date, or perhaps a loco was supplied by PR/8.

No.1		0-6-0ST	IC	MW	93	1863	New 10/63	(1)
	THE FLY	0-6-0ST	IC	MW	1111	1889	New (a) Scr/c1938	
	SPIDER	0-4-0ST	OC	HL	2623	1905	New	(2)
	HORNET	0-4-0ST	OC	P	1935	1937	New 11/37	(3)
	-	0-6-0ST	OC	AE	1604	1912	(b)	(4)

OTHER POSSIBLE LOCOMOTIVES:

	0-4-0ST	IC	WkB	1017	c1876	(c)	s/s
	?	?	?	?	?	(d)	s/s
LILLESHALL	0-4-0ST	OC	LIL		1862	(e)	s/s
ARIADNE	0-6-0ST	IC	IWB		1874	(f)	s/s
ANT	?	?	?	?	?	(g)	s/s
BEE	?	?	?	?	?	(g)	s/s

(a) tdt: Penybont Brickworks [J.C.Edwards], loan, c1910
    tdf: Penybont Brickworks, off loan, c1910
(b) here 10/1937 on loan from Cudworth & Johnson, dealers, Wrexham.
(c) reputed tdf: J.Scarisbrick Walker, Wigan - but not proven.
(d) B/103/K.56 states that this colliery had an ex-Cambrian Railways loco, but no proof yet found of this; and there is a possibility of confusion with the adjacent Brynkinallt Colliery railway, which did have a Cam.Rys. loco (MW 52) from 1875.
(e) An unconfirmed report suggests that LILLESHALL (see Savin list, loco 21, in Section 1) may have come here after it was sold (to an unrecorded purchaser) by Cam.Rys. for £850 in 1/1868.
(f) Some sources have credited this loco to this colliery, but recent research has established that Boulton sold this loco to Poynton Collieries, Cheshire, in 1891 - and one of the Poynton pits was known as "Black Park". A case of mistaken location, perhaps, though positive exclusion from Chirk is still lacking.
(g) In 1940, an old employee at Black Park stated that early locos here had included two called ANT and BEE. Whilst numerous locos are known that have carried such names, none can yet be associated with Chirk.

(1) wlw: Collins Green Colliery Co Ltd, Lancashire [by 4/1883 ?]
    wlw: Wm.Beattie & Sons, contractors, Edinburgh.
(2) tdt: Bersham Colliery, 1949
(3) tdt: Ifton Colliery, Salop, c3/1951
    wlw: Bersham Colliery.
(4) tdt: Cudworth & Johnson, off loan, after 22/11/1937 by 21/1/1938

BODFARI CASTING-SAND PITS B12
(Cf/GR:095701)

```
1924  -  7/1930  : Partington Iron & Steel Co Ltd (reg.15/8/1910)
8/1930 -          : Lancashire Steel Corporation Ltd (reg.1/8/1930)
c1934             : closed (after 4/1933 by 8/1934)
```

Sidings laid beside the LMS (PR/37) immediately east of Bodfari station to serve a loading facility for sand, destined for Irlam Steelworks, brought by road vehicles from nearby pits. Installation dismantled c1939, but sidings reputedly remained until 3/1943 at least.

Locomotives: Gauge 4'8½"

```
         ARKAYAR      0-4-0ST   OC   HC    303   1888   (a)           (1)
```

(a) tdx: Irlan Steelworks, Lancashire, c1924

(1) left on site after closure; last seen 13/3/1938; Scr/c1939

BORRAS AIRFIELD, RHOSNESNI, WREXHAM B14
(Cd/GR:365525)

```
1940  -  1947  : Air Ministry - "R.A.F. Wrexham"
                : Sir Alfred McAlpine & Sons Ltd (private use)
```

Airfield construction commenced 16/12/1940; opened June 1941; used during WW2 and later for training flights and, from 6/1945, as RAF Workshops. Closed 1947; one runway retained and used for private flying.

SIR ALFRED McALPINE & SONS LTD, contractors.
Railway and locomotives used during construction work.

Locomotives: Gauge 2'0"

```
                    4wDM  20hp   MR    8603   1941   New 1/41    (1)
                    4wDM  20hp   MR    8604   1941   New 1/41    (1)
```

(1) presumably tdt: McAlpine elsewhere, as both locos were noted in open store at McAlpine Ellesmere Port Depot 5/1954, 1/1955, 10/1955 by which time they were numbered R14 (MR 8603) and R15 (MR 8604).
No further trace.

BRAICH/NEW BRAICH SLATE QUARRY, MOEL TRYFAN   B16
(Gc/GR:510552)

This site apparently dates from 1830, when the Braichrhydd Land was leased to Cilgwyn Quarry. In 1868 the Land was divided into New and Old Braich leases - for the latter see the next location entry.

BRAICHRHYDD:

-	7/1845	: as listed for Cilgwyn Slate Quarry
4/1848 -	1852	: **Robert Williams & Owen Griffith**
7/1852 -	1853	: **Henry Richardson**
12/1853 -		: **William Carpenter**
by 1861		: closed
by 1864		: **Charles Curling & Hugh Beaver Roberts**

NEW BRAICH:

10/1868 -	: [? **Griffith Jones**]
in 1875	: **Hugh Beaver Roberts**
3/1880 -	: **Braich Slate Co** [John Pearson]
by 1886 -	: **Braich & Coed Madoc Slate Co** [John Pearson]
1887 -	: **Braich & Coed Madoc Slate Co** [George Pearson]
10/1890 -	: **Owners of Talysarn Slate Quarry**
11/1908 -	: **Bangor Slate Quarry Ltd** (reg.10/1908)
by 1910 -	: **New Braich Slate Quarries Ltd** (reg.2/11/1908 liq.10/10/1915)
4/1911	: closed
10/1917 -	: **Amalgamated Slate Association Ltd** little or no work done; closed; dismantled.

The quarry, which by 1870 consisted of a single large pit with three floors, plus a Mill close to the lip of the pit, was connected to the John Robinson Tramroad (PR/38) by a 3½ft gauge self-acting incline falling south-west to join PR/38 at Fron crossroads. The route of the incline is clearly visible today [1990]. Subsequently, between 1877 and 1881, this outlet was abandoned in favour of a new 2ft gauge outlet down a new incline to the north-west, thence by short connecting railway to the head of the Bryngwyn Incline of PR/44.

Locomotives: Gauge 2ft

0-4-0VBT SVC DeW	(1)

(1)   reputedly scrapped c1914.
An inventory [in Crown Estate Papers] of New Braich Quarry 8/8/1908 does not list any loco, though this is not conclusive [? perhaps temporarily at Talysarn Quarry on that date].

BRAICH/OLD BRAICH SLATE QUARRY, MOEL TRYFAN   B18
(Gc/GR:513549)

Until 1868 this site was part of the Braichrhydd Lease held by the Cilgwyn Quarry and Others - for details see previous site "Braich/New Braich". After 1868 the Lease was held by the Lessees of the Vron Quarries (adjacent to the east); for details see entry "Fron Slate Quarry, Moel Tryfan".

Old Braich was not an extensive working; the output from the small Mill was probably carted away by road until, sometime after 1868, a 2ft gauge line was laid from Old Braich Mill to Fron Quarry.

Locomotives: Gauge 2ft

A Vulcan Foundry loco named KELSO has been attributed to "Braich Quarry", but this seems extremely unlikely as neither Old Braich nor New Braich had any apparent need for such a locomotive - Old Braich particularly so. An inventory of the New Braich quarry 8/8/1908 does not list any locomotive - nor do lists of equipment at the combined "Vron & Old Braich" quarries dated 29/7/1893 and 25/9/1901.

Bearing in mind, however, that Spooner apparently supplied a Vulcan Foundry loco KATHLEEN to Alexandra Quarry, it seems possible that he could have arranged for a similar loco to work at, or be tried out at, Old Braich & Fron. As such, this loco could also have been tried on the rather short connection between the Bryngwyn Incline (PR/44) and the foot of the New Braich (new) incline.

For further comments, see entry "Fron Slate Quarry".

BRAICH GOCH SLATE QUARRY, UPPER CORRIS   B20
(Gm/GR:748078)

Early workings on this site date from the 1830s, but organised commercial exploitation commenced in the 1870s.

from c1870 -	: Braichgoch Slate Quarry Co Ltd
by 1970	: Braich Goch Slate & Slab Quarries Ltd
	: subsidiary of the Wincilate Group
1971	: closed; work transferred to Aberllefenni Qys.
	rail tracks and other equipment removed.

During WW2 some underground chambers were used by the Ministry of Supply as an explosives store. After closure, site cleared under a Derelict Land Reclamation Scheme; main road re-routed through, and a 'craft village' erected on, the site of the workshops and Mills. Since 4/1983 a narrow-gauge diesel locomotive from the Gloddfa Ganol collection (see OAKELEY SLATE QUARRIES) has been a static exhibit at the craft village.

Locomotives: Gauge 2'3"

-	4wDM 20hp	MR	8786	1942	(a)	Scr/1970
-	4wBE	LMM			(b)	(1)

(a) Ministry of Supply loco; New from MR 9/1942 for explosives store duties. Loco became quarry property after MoS departed.
(b) arrived 2/1967 - [? tdx: Coleford];
purchased from Alan R.Davies Ltd [alternatively: Llewelyn Davies] of Cator Road, Bristol; who in turn obtained it from Fred Watkins (Engineering) Ltd, dealers, Coleford, Glos.
Identity and former user unknown.

(1) tdt: Aberllefenni Quarries, after 10/1971 by 7/1972

BROMFIELD COLLIERY, MOLD   B22
(Cf/GR:243633)

1854			: Rev.B.Crompton
1854	-	1860	: E.Walkinshaw
1861	-	1868	: Bromfield Coal Co Ltd
1869	-	1871	: Wm.Southall
21/12/1870			: sale of assets; Closed. Pit flooded.
2/1873			: purchased by **Oak Pits Colly Co**
1906			: sinking Deep Pit
			:[Pontybodkin Colliery Co Ltd, reg.1903, became:-]
1905	-	1915	: **Mold Collieries Ltd** (reg.21/10/1905) [of Newcastle-on-Tyne]
1915	-	1916	: **Mold Collieries (1915) Ltd**
6/1916			: closed. Subsequently occupied by R.S.Davies, Machinery Merchant (see Section 1.)

The colliery was for sale in 1848 [J/CDH/26.8.1848/1], the lease then having six years to run. In 1863, the "Bromfield Colliery Co" was given permission to lay a tramway across Gas Lane Road; the 12/1870 Sale referred to 3 shafts with a "double line of rails to the Chester & Mold Railway" (PR/9), but made no mention of locomotives. From 1906 the colliery was served by a fan of sidings (off PR/9/39) which looped around beneath the screens then rejoined at the entry point; a peculiar arrangement for this very small site. After 1916, these sidings were removed

Locomotives: Gauge 4'8½"

BROMFIELD	0-4-0ST	OC	HL	2646	1906	New	(1)

(1) for sale here 7/1916 and 11/1918.
wlw(tdt?): Tees Side Bridge & Engineering Works Ltd, Cargo Fleet, Yorkshire NR

BROUGHTON AIRCRAFT FACTORY   B24
(Cf/GR:350644)

	1939	: opened
	1939 -	: **Vickers-Armstrongs Ltd**
by	1952 -	: **DeHaviland Aircraft Co Ltd**
		: **Hawker Siddeley Aviation Ltd**

Factory served by sidings off PR/9, west of that line just north of Broughton station. Sidings disused by 7/1969; junction to PR/9 removed by 10/1971.

Locomotives: Gauge 4'8½" - Factory Construction.

Factory built by **Sir Wm.Arrol & Co Ltd**, contractors; reputed to have used a steam loco here in 1939, but no further details known.

Locomotives: Gauge 4'8½" - Factory Operation.

	0-4-0DM	40hp	JF	22753	1939	New 10/39	(1)
	0-4-0DM	40hp	JF	21999	1937	(a)	(2)

(a) tdx: JF, Leeds, c1945
     wfw: Royal Ordnance Factory, Rotherwas, Hereford.

(1) tdt: Flint & Deeside Railway Preservation Society (store at Oswestry, Salop), 4/1975
     wlw: Llangollen Railway (PR/68)
(2) tdt: Barrow Steel Co Ltd, Lancashire, 1948.

BRYMBO COLLIERY, IRONWORKS & STEELWORKS   B26
(Cd)

1620			: COLLIERY ACTIVE: "Brymbo (Harwd) Pits"
in 1793	-	7/1808	: **John Wilkinson**
c1795			: IRON FIRST MADE
7/1808	-	10/1818	: **Trustees of the late John Wilkinson**
10/1818	-	1837	: **John & James Thompson**
1837	-	1840	: **Reid, Campbell & McDougall**
1841	-	1842	: **Robert Roy**; who then, with Henry Robertson, Wm.Betts and A.M.Ross formed:-
10/1842	-	1846	: **Brymbo Mineral & Railway Co Ltd** (reg.20/9/1842); ["Railway" in the title referred to promotion of North Wales Mineral Rly Co - See PR/5, PR/6]
1846	-	1884	: **Brymbo Company** [Robertson & Darby]
1/1885			: STEEL FIRST MADE
1884	-	6/1931	: **Brymbo Steel Co Ltd** (reg.4/6/1884 liq.6/1931-6/1936) Controlled by Baldwins Ltd from 1919
6/1931	-	1934	: Closed
1934	-	2/1948	: **Brymbo Steel (Successors) Co Ltd** (reg.1933) Controlled by Thomas Firth & John Brown Ltd from 1940
2/1948	-	2/1951	: **Wrexham Steel Works Ltd**; very soon re-titled:- **Brymbo Steel Works Ltd** - both being subsidiary of GKN Steel Co Ltd

```
2/1951  -   1955     : British Steel Corporation
   1955  -  7/1967   : GKN Steel Co Ltd
 7/1967  -           : British Steel Corporation (Holdings) Ltd
         -  3/1986   : Guest Keen & Nettlefolds Ltd, trading as:-
                       Brymbo Steelworks Ltd
 4/1986  -           : United Engineering Steels Ltd [of Rotherham]
11/1990              : closed
```

NOTE: Up to around 1900, the Companies casually used various titles, such as "Brymbo Coal & Iron Co", "Brymbo Coal Co", in official returns and other sources. Possibly some such were genuine subsidiaries of the main-stream Company.

The term "Brymbo Colliery" was used to describe 96 (at least) shafts and adits (drifts) scattered across the Brymbo Estate, in a triangular area of some 540 acres roughly bounded by the present-day B5101 road on the north-east, the Glascoed valley on the north-west, and an imaginary line from Bwlchgwyn to Tanyfron and Southsea at its base. The study of this "colliery" is a matter for the specialist; further details are available in B/107A and "Brymbo Works Magazine" 1928-1930. Of specific interest are the more modern pits which took on the appearance of individual collieries, and were served by tramroads and railways.

From the early 1840s to the mid-1870s, the higher ground to the west of the ironworks was served by a system of narrow-gauge plateways or tramroads connecting various pits to the Mount Pleasant (GR:290536) area, whence two consecutive inclines (opened 8/1843) ran down into the ironworks at a point adjacent to the BLAST [COLLIERY] PITS (1842-1914; GR:294535). From the head of the lower incline, branch tramroads ran south to the WONDER PIT (sunk in 1835, GR:290534, later buried by the slag bank) and north to Pits at MOUNT SEION (GR:289539). From the head of the upper (shorter) incline a branch tramroad ran south beside the road to PENRHOS ISSA (known as "I.M.G.") PIT (1832-1875; GR:288531). Slightly further on, the main tramroad reached Mount Pleasant and the TOP POOL PITS (1856-1867; GR:287536) where another branch ran south-west to PENRHOS (UCHA) COLLIERY (1852-7/1885; GR:284532); the main tramroad continued north-westerly to Shaft No.3 of SMELT COLLIERY (GR:284538), and possibly also served the adjacent SMELT LEAD WORKS (GR:284539).

In 1875-1876, PENRHOS COLLIERY (GR:284532) was reconstructed, and a new 4'8½" gauge line built from the Ironworks, via two reversal points and a horse-shoe shaped route, to supersede the tramroads and inclines. This line, however, closed with Penrhos Colliery in 7/1885. The lower section of this line, including the two reversal points, was then (or later) used for carrying slag to the Ironworks Tip, which eventually buried the WONDER PIT and other minor shafts. Thereafter, BRYMBO COLLIERY consisted of two small shafts near the Ironworks, known as the FURNACE or BLAST PITS, plus a shaft at the former WONDER PIT retained for ventilation. Despite some modernisation works in the late 1890s, BRYMBO COLLIERY finally closed 7/1914.

Today [1990] it is possible to find the capped shafts of many of the Pits, and to trace most of the tramroads and railways that served them. Some of the plateway rails, of about 2ft gauge, are preserved at the BERSHAM IRONWORKS Industrial Heritage Centre.

The Mount Pleasant area was drained, by a deep adit dug in John Wilkinson's time and known as LEVEL FAWR [the "big" - as in chief -"level"], into a short valley near Ffrith - sometimes, though somewhat incorrectly, referred to as "Glascoed". Nearly two miles long, LEVEL FAWR contained a narrow-gauge tramroad. For further reference to this see entry FFRITH COLLIERIES. Adits at SMELT COLLIERY were worked for clay, and coal when found, until the late 1960s - the clay was taken by 1'8" gauge horse-worked tramroad to CAELLO BRICKWORKS (GR:287543) until superseded by a lorry in 1963. Mining for clay ceased c1970, the adits being sealed.

Brymbo Ironworks was established on the western side of the Brymbo to Vron branch of PR/6, the later Steelworks being on the opposite side of this branch. This resulted in the GWR/BR railway being intimately entangled with the Works railways, with level rail-crossings. After closure of the BR line (PR/21) from Wrexham 1/10/1982, the Steelworks railway continued in use for internal traffic only. Works closed for production 11/1990, and rail traffic ceased 1/1991.

[Read: B/107; B/109; B/120; B/276; Brymbo Works Magazine]

Locomotives: Gauge 4'8½"

It is likely that locomotives would be in use here very soon after the arrival of the (PR/6) railway in 1847, though maybe that railway's locos were used initially. Indeed, as the Brymbo Mineral & Railway Co were promoters of the North Wales Mineral Rly (PR/6), some sharing of locos would seem very likely. See PR/6 for further details.

By the 1870s, Brymbo was sending scrap locos to I.W.Boulton for reconstruction, and in 1876-1877 the Brymbo Company advertised - For Sale a loco: 4 wheel, 13x18, 3'6" wheels, 5'10" wheelbase, about 19 tons, with "tank on boiler" (a saddle tank ?). No loco listed below fits this description.

	ROBERTSON	0-4-0T	OC	BP	92	1858	New		s/s
	PYTHON	0-4-2ST	IC	Kirtley		1841	(a)		(1)
	SNOWDON	0-4-0ST	OC	BP	811	1868	New		(2)
	BRYMBO	0-4-0ST	IC	IWB		c1875	(b)		Scr
	BASIC	0-4-0CT	OC	Dub	2064	1884	New		
		rebuilt Brymbo				1937		Scr c3/1958	
	WREKIN	0-6-0ST	OC	FW	291	1876	New 2/76		
		rebuilt Brymbo				1935		Scr c3/1958	
	GWYNEDD	0-6-0ST	OC	BH	1014	1890	New		(3)
	BOBS	0-6-0ST	IC	HE	449	1888	(c)		(4)
	ANZAC	0-6-0ST	OC	HL	3214	1916	New	Scr c2/1965	
	ARENIG	0-6-0ST	OC	AE	1770	1917	(d)	Scr c3/1958	
	SIR HENRY	0-6-0ST	OC	RSH	7026	1940	New 7/41		(5)
	BERWYN	0-6-0ST	OC	P	2115	1950	New 10/50		(6)
	(ESMOND)	0-6-0DE 260hp	YE		2604	1955	(e)	Scr 1/1983	
	HOPE	0-6-0DE 200hp	YE		2632	1957	New	Scr 1/1983	
	JOHN	0-6-0DE 200hp	YE		2658	1957	New	Scr 4/1984	
	SPENCER	0-6-0DE 200hp	YE		2659	1957	New	Scr 5/1991	
	WILLIAM	0-6-0DE 440hp	YE		2800	1962	New		(12)
	EMRYS	0-6-0DE 440hp	YE		2867	1962	New		(12)
	WINSTON	0-6-0DE 220hp	YE		2942	1965	New		(9)
	CHARLES	0-4-0DE 220hp	YE		2870	1962	(f)		(7)
	NEVILLE	0-4-0DE 220hp	YE		2853	1961	(g)	Scr/c1981	
	AUSTIN	0-4-0DE 220hp	YE		2855	1961	(g)		(8)
	CHARLES	0-4-0DE 220hp	YE		2858	1961	(g)		(8)
(No.8)	NEVILLE	0-6-0DE 440hp	YE		2884	1962	(h)		(11)
(No.38)	ESMOND	0-6-0DE 440hp	YE		2792	1961	(i)		(11)
(No.32)		0-4-0DE 400hp	YE		2752	1959	(j)		(10)
(No.29)		0-6-0DE 400hp	YE		2722	1958	(k)		(10)
9111/85		0-4-0DE	YE		2623	1956	(m)		(11)
-		0-4-0DE	S		10254	1967	(n)		(12)
		0-6-0DE	YE		*		(o)		(9)
		0-6-0DE	YE		*		(o)		(9)

*two of YE 2720/1958, 2721/1958, 2751/1959

NOTES:

A) Loco MINERVA HC 1241/1917 was hired for use at Brymbo from Shotton Steelworks "at some time".
B) Locomotives were also repaired at Brymbo for other locations, eg:
RUSSELL (ex PR/44) in 1942 for Hook Norton Ironstone Mines.
BETTY (ex Trefor Granite Quarries) 1940-1942 also for Hook Norton.
FW 318 in 1927 for Holditch Colliery.

(a) arrived Brymbo c1860;
wfw: a contractor in Spain
wfw: Sheffield, Ashton-under-Lyne & Manchester Railway Co, where it was a 0-4-2 tender loco.
(b) 'New'; assembled by Boulton using scrap supplied by Brymbo.
(c) purchased £904-17-0, 7/1900, from unknown vendor;
wfw: John Strachan, contractor, until 11/1897 at least.
(d) tdx: Ministry of Munitions, Banbury, Oxon, 3/1919
tdt: Gresford Colliery, loan, 1938
tdx: Gresford Colliery, off loan, c1938
(e) tdx: YE, on trial, 31/10/1955
tdt: Mostyn Steelworks, 4/11/1955
tdx: YE, purchased, 17/1/1956
(f) tdx: AEI Ltd, Trafford Park, Manchester, c1968 by 13/7/1969
(g) tdx: Port of London Authority, 15/12/1971
(h) tdx: British Steel, Normanby Park Works, Humberside, 1/5/1981
(i) tdx: British Steel, Normanby Park Works, Humberside, 2/5/1981
(j) tdx: Stocksbridge Works, Sheffield, 30/10/1987
(k) tdx: Stocksbridge Works, Sheffield, 11/2/1988
(m) tdx: Rotherham Engineering Steel Ltd, Wolverhampton Works, 1988
(n) tdx: G.E.C. Turbine Generators Ltd, Trafford Park, Manchester, 23/3/1989
(o) tdx: Stocksbridge Works, Sheffield, after 16/5/1988 by 21/3/1991

(1) dumped 'in a siding at Chester' by 1865;
purchased by I.W.Boulton, dealer, Ashton-under-Lyne, #160, 6/1865
later scrapped by Boulton.
(2) tdt: Bersham Colliery, 5/1919
(3) officially scrapped 3/1957;
seen virtually intact 13/4/1957 - presume subsequently scrapped.
(4) spare parts for this loco ordered 3/1920 by Baldwins Ltd, Pearson's Furnaces, Netherton, Staffs; hence perhaps loco on loan to Netherton at that time. If so, returned to Brymbo and:
tdt: Pentresaeson Foundry, near Coed Poeth, for scrap, 1926
(5) tdt: Foxfield Colliery Co Ltd, Staffs, loan, c10/1946
tdx: Foxfield, off loan, c10/1947
scrapped 1965.
(6) tdt: Gatewen Opencast Coal Disposal Point, loan, 12/1965
tdx: Gatewen, off loan, 1/1966
scrapped c2/1966
(7) scrapped, after 28/5/1972 by 8/1972
(8) tdt: Allen Rowland & Co Ltd, Tyseley, Birmingham, 6/3/1991
(9) tdt: ?, after 10/11/1990 by 26/8/1991
(10) tdt: Booth Roe Metals Ltd, Rotherham, 14 + 15/11/1991
(11) tdt: Booth Roe Metals Ltd, Rotherham, after 15/11/1991 by 11/1/1992
(12) tdt: Booth Roe Metals Ltd, Rotherham, 1992 after 11/1/1992

BRYNKINALT COLLIERY, CHIRK GREEN, CHIRK B28
(Cd/GR:296382)

1857		:	first sinking
1857 -	1861	:	**Walter Eddy & Co**
1862 -	10/1873	:	**Brynkinalt Coal Co** (dissolved 31/10/1873)
1873 -		:	**Brynkinallt Colliery Ltd**
1876		:	second sinking "by a Mr Blakewell".
1883 -	1893	:	**Brynkinalt Collieries Ltd** (reg.29/10/1883 £25K)
1893 -	1913+	:	**W.Y.Craig & Sons**
by 1923 -		:	**W.Y.Craig & Sons Ltd**
c1928		:	coal winding ceased.

Colliery connected to GWR (PR/8) by railway almost one mile long, on which the locomotives listed below were used. This line was being planned 2/1862 [NLW/Longueville] and believed built shortly thereafter. In late 1920s production was concentrated at the nearby Ifton Colliery (Shropshire), Brynkinalt shaft being retained as a pumping shaft to ventilate Ifton seams and, as such, it remained in use until Ifton closed 11/1968. Brynkinalt Colliery railway closed, and track lifted, c1928; most of the route has since been obliterated.

[Read: B/107]

Locomotives: Gauge 4'8½"

		0-6-0ST	IC	MW	52	1862	(a)	s/s
		0-4-2T	IC	(f.Dodds		1854)	(b)	s/s
	PIRAEUS	0-4-0ST	OC	AB	643	1889	(c)	(1)
[?	SWANSEA	0-4-0ST	OC	HE	648	1897	(d)	(2)]

(a) tdx: Cambrian Railways, number 17, 1875
(b) not positively confirmed here, but reputed:
   tdx: Wrexham, Mold & Connah's Quay Railway (PR/28), 9/1895
(c) here by 2/1894; probably tdx: previous known owner - Eckersley, Godfrey & Liddelow, contractors (of London), who [judging by its name] may have obtained loco for their Piraeus & Larissa (Greece) Railway Contract, but apparently it was sent New 5/1889 to their GNR Oakleigh Park - New Southgate Widening (1889-1890) Contract.
   [And note: E.G.& L. had a subsequent Canada Branch Dock (1890-c1894) Contract, Liverpool - thus possibly bringing the loco closer to North Wales to reach Brynkinalt "by 2/1894".]
(d) owned by "W.Y.Craig & Sons, Brynkinalt" by 25/4/1918 [HE spares order] - but 'Brynkinalt' could be just the office address, as loco recalled at Ifton Colliery 2/1919.
   wfw: David Evans, Llangennech Park, Carmarthenshire, until 11/1906 at least

(1) tdt: Ifton Colliery, Salop, [c1928 ?]
(2) In 3/1922 W.Y.Craig & Sons were offering for sale a "small 10 inch outside cylinder Hunslet loco, can be seen at Chirk." [J/CJ/1.3.22]. Perhaps this was SWANSEA (10x15 loco) - if so, was not sold, at that time, being photographed at Weston Rhyn yard [ie, Ifton] 5/1932 and 5/1940.
   wlw: Cudworth & Johnson, dealers, Wrexham - see Section 1.

BRYNMALLY COLLIERY, MOSS

B30
(Cd/GR:304542)

by	1764	-	c1775	: Charles Roe & James Venables
	c1775	-	c1815	: Richard Kirk
	10/1849	-	1896	: Thomas Clayton "Bryn Malley Colliery Co"
by	1902	-	1907	: Brynmally Colliery Co Ltd
	1907	-	1935	: New Brynmally Colliery Co Ltd (reg.22/6/1907 £20K)
				(subsidiary of Dutton Massey & Co (Liverpool) Ltd
	10/1935			: production ceased; abandoned 11/1935.
	(1936	-	12/1936	: prospected by J.P.Davies, 9 Pleasant View, Moss)

Colliery connected to the GWR, originally to PR/6 and later to the Moss Valley line (PR/48), by a branch line roughly 1/4-mile long southerly along Pendwll Road. Later a second connection was laid northerly to join the GCR Westminster Colliery Branch (of PR/28).

[Read: J/CG/10.3.1893/437; B/107]

Locomotives: Gauge 4'8½"

According to B/418/photo:54 caption - "...the locomotive JUMBO operated from Brynmally Colliery, bringing coal down to the GWR branch in the Moss Valley. On one occasion, this engine went out of control and crashed through the Moss Well [level crossing at Moss Crossing Halt] gates."

The locomotive "Jumbo" has not been identified; it MAY have been a colliery locomotive, or it MAY have been a familiar name for a GWR shunting loco. It is on record that the GWR did shunt for the adjacent, and much more important, Westminster colliery until that closed in 1925.

Per J/RO/8.1936/194, GWR 0-4-0ST Nos.45 and 92 were seen "on a recent date" out of service at Croes Newydd [Wrexham] Sheds; "The colliery for which these engines performed shunting and transfer work is now closed.". Unfortunately the RO does not name the colliery. Brynmally, however, is the only apparent candidate.

BUCKLEY COLLIERIES RAILWAY B32
(Cf/GR:below)

From an end-on connection to the sidings off PR/22 which served the Parry Brickworks (GR:278664), this 4'8½" gauge Private Railway, built in 1871 [J/MJ/2.12.1871/1] ran first westward to Elm Colliery, then southward (bridge over main road) to junction (short branch to Ash Colliery) and on to Oak, Willow and South Buckley collieries. By 1913 the line had been cut back to Ash Colliery; in 1914 it served only Elm Colliery. The last remnant, which from c1936 served only a landsale yard for coal from elsewhere, closed c1946.

[Read: J/CG/10.2.1893/253]

ELM COLLIERY (GR:272662)

Deep pit sunk from 1872, replacing shallow pits on the site.

1872 -	1/1920	: **George Watkinson & Sons Ltd** (reg.14/5/1872)
1/1920 -		: **Buckley Colliery Co Ltd** (reg.3/1920 £100K)
from 1920 -		: subsidiary of John Summers & Sons Ltd
4/1937		: Electric winding engines sold per Thos.W.Ward Ltd to Lofthouse Colliery, Wakefield - hence presume Elm closed for winding c1936. Site continued in use as landsale yard.
c1946		: closed (after 4/1944 by 8/1948); dismantled.

ASH (GREAT ASH/NEW ASH) COLLIERY (GR:271656)

1856 -	1860	: **Great Ash Coal Co**
1861 -	1867	: **Buckley Coal Co**
1872		: abandoned.
by 1894 -	11/1913	: **George Watkinson & Sons Ltd** "New Ash Colliery".
11/1913		: closed; dismantled.

OAK (GREAT OAK) COLLIERY (GR:276657)

A 2ft gauge railway ran from the pithead, via level crossing across Pinfold Lane, and through field to loading bay on BCR.

1860 -	1868	: **Buckley Coal Co**
1869 -	1871	: **Buckley Colliery Co**
1872		: closed.
5/1872 -		: **George Watkinson & Sons Ltd**
by 1913		: closed; dismantled.

WILLOW COLLIERY (GR:277648)

Served by siding direct off BCR.

by 1873 -	1878	: **George Watkinson & Sons Ltd**
1878		: closed.

SOUTH BUCKLEY COLLIERY & BRICKWORKS   (GR:274644)

Served by sidings at terminal of BCR. For a time, there was also a narrow-gauge railway from this site to West Buckley Colliery - which see.

	1866	-	1868	: South Buckley Coal Co
	1869	-	1875+	: South Buckley Coal & Fire-Brick Co Ltd
by	1886	-	6/1889	: North & South Buckley Colliery, Brick & Tile Co Ltd
	6/1889	-		: South Buckley Coal & Brick Co Ltd (reg.27/6/1889 £15K)
	by 1913			: closed; dismantled.

Locomotives: Gauge 4'8½"

NOTE: Mountain Colliery (c1880-1929; GR:282642), Buckley, though not connected to the BCR, was under the same ownership. There were a number of sidings at Mountain Colliery which could perhaps have utilised one or more of the locos listed below - but no confirmation has yet been discovered.

In 1944, an old employee at Elm Colliery Yard recalled two previous locos as having been named CHARLIE and SYMONDS [? spelling]. These, if indeed they did exist, have not yet been identified. SYMONDS may be SIEMENS in fact.

		WATKINSON	0-4-0ST	OC	HC	133	1873	New (a)	(1)
		WATKINSON No.2	0-4-0ST	OC	HC	179	1876	New 9/76	s/s
3	[	GRAHAM ?]	0-4-0ST	IC	WkB	412	c1873	(b)	s/s
	[	SIEMENS	0-4-0ST	OC	HC	627	1902	(c)	(2) ?]
		SEALAND	0-4-0ST	OC	HC	563	1900	(d)	(3)

(a)   Kitson 1773/1871 was one of twelve locos (Kit 1773-1782, 1838, 1839) built for S.S.Polyakov, contractor, Koslov-Rostov Railway (1871-1876) Contract, Russia. Ten of these locos, numbers uncertain, were later recorded on this and an associated railway. The two missing locos are thought to have been in the cargo of the ship INO which sank near Sweden. Salvaged locos from this ship were auctioned near Gothenburg 2-3/10/1872. Subsequently, two Kitson locos were rebuilt by HC as HC 132 and HC 133 - the latter being noted by HC as Kitson number 1773.

(b)   tdx: Thomas Mitchell & Sons Ltd, dealers, Bolton, Lancs, 2/1908
      wfw: Earl of Ellesmere's Bridgwater Collieries, Lancashire; purchased 10/1907 by Mitchell as "lying at Little Hulton" [perhaps Wharton Hall Colliery ?] named GRAHAM.

(c)   After John Summers & Sons Ltd   took over the Buckley Colliery Co Ltd in 1920, locomotives were supplied "on loan" from Shotton Steelworks from time to time. SIEMENS is reputed to be one such loco, but no date for any loan has been ascertained.

(d)   tdx: Shotton Steelworks, loan, by 4/1943 when it was noted working at Elm Landsale Yard.

(1)   tdt: HC c1877 - who "rebuilt" it - again - and renumbered it HC 198.
      wlw: Sutton Lodge Chemical Co Ltd, St.Helens, Lancashire.
(2)   if loco was here, then tdt: Shotton Steelworks.
(3)   tdt: Shotton Steelworks, after 4/1944 by 8/1948

BUTLINS HOLIDAY CENTRE, PEN-YCHAIN, near PWLLHELI B34
(Gc/GR:434363)

Locomotives: Gauge 4'8½" - Static Display.

32640		0-6-0T	IC	Bton		1878 (a)	(1)
6203	PRINCESS MARGARET ROSE	4-6-2	4C	Cwe	253193	5 (b)	(2)

Locomotives: Gauge 1'9" - Miniature Railway, opened 1950, closed 1977.

6203	PRINCESS MARGARET ROSE						
	[also] QUEEN ELIZABETH	4-6-2DM	32hp	HC	D612	1938 (c)	(3)
	PRINCESS ELIZABETH	4-6-2DM	32hp	HC	D611	1938 (d)	(4)
	OLD SPARKY	4wDM	48hp	RH	487963	1963 (e)	(5)

Locomotives: Gauge 2'0" - Miniature Railway, opened 1978.

		4wDM	20hp	MR	8729	1941 (f)	(6)
157	C.P.HUNTINGTON	4w-2-4wPM		Chance *	157	1978 New	
31	C.P.HUNTINGTON	4w-2-4wPM		Chance *	31	1964 (g)	(7)

* Chance locos appear as 4-2-4 tender locos, but in fact the drive is to the leading and trailing bogies. They have multi-element serial numbers (eg, 78-50157 24) comprising: Year built [1978]/Model type [50]/Works number [157]/Track gauge [24"].

(a) tdx: British Railways, 9/1960
(b) tdx: British Railways, 5/1963
(c) tdx: Butlins Clacton Camp, Essex, 1950
(d) tdx: Butlins Minehead Camp, Somerset, 1951
(e) tdx: John H.Rundle Ltd, New Bolingbroke, Boston, Lincs, 1971
(f) tdx: Alan Keef Ltd, Cote, Oxon, 1977 - here for use only by Alan Keef Ltd on contract for gauge conversion of railway.
   wfw: Skegness Brick & Tile Co.
(g) tdx: Butlins Minehead Camp, Somerset, by 8/1985

(1) tdt: Wight Locomotive Society, Isle of Wight, 1/1973
(2) tdt: British Railways, Derby, 11/5/1975
   wlw: Midland Railway Co (1973) Ltd, Ripley, Derbyshire.
(3) tdt: John H.Rundle Ltd, New Bolingbroke, Boston, Lincs, 1971
(4) tdt: John H.Rundle Ltd, New Bolingbroke, Boston, 1972 by 6/1972
(5) tdt: Alan Keef Ltd, Cote, Oxon, 1978 by 3/1978
(6) tdt: Alan Keef Ltd, Cote, Oxon, 1978
(7) tdt: Butlins Minehead Camp, after 8/1985 by 4/9/1986

CAERGLAW GRANITE QUARRY, GWALCHMAI C2
(Ga/GR:382770)

by	1936	-	1944+	: North Wales Construction Co Ltd
		-	1965	: Penmaenmawr & Welsh Granite Co Ltd
	1965	-	12/1985	: Kingston Minerals Ltd
	1/1986	-		: A.R.C.Western (later Northern) Ltd

Roadstone quarry beside the A5 road, c ½ mile west of Gwalchmai village.

Locomotives: Gauge narrow

From 9/1/1936 to 30/4/1944, regularly ordered spare parts from MR for a petrol loco fitted with a cone clutch [hence possibly an early bow-frame model]. On 22/9/1947 ordered from MR a waterproof apron for a loco - perhaps the same loco. No further details.

CAERNANT (RIVALS) GRANITE QUARRY, NANT GWRTHERYN C4
near LLITHFAEN
(Gc/GR:353452)

1875			: Vaynol lease to **Edmund Spargo**, assigned to:
8/1875	-	3/1877	: **John Menzies & Robert Newton**, assigned to:
3/1877	-	5/1882	: **Cambrian Granite Co Ltd**
			(reg.10/3/1877 vol.liq.5/1882-5/1886)
5/1882	-		: assigned to **Masson & Henry Barde**, who:
1/1888	-		: mortgaged to Mr E.H.Ledward who arranged:
			auction of quarry 30/6/1888 and 6/9/1890
9/1890	-		: Owen Roberts (Porthmadog) who stripped railways
			and machinery from the premises.
c1891	-	1892	: **H.J.Wright**
1902	-	1910	: **Rival Granite Quarries Ltd**
			(reg.21/11/1902 : in 8/1920 changed name to
			Granite, Lime & Clinker Ltd [active elsewhere])
1910	-	1922	: [? closed]
1922	-	1963	: **Croft Granite, Brick & Concrete Co Ltd**
1963			: closed and dismantled.

This quarry, which had virtually no road access, despatched all output by sea. The railway system within the quarry was connected to the pier by a ¾ mile incline built in 1877 and used until 1963. The locomotives were used within the quarry; this railway was replaced by road vehicles c1955.

[Read: B/175/254-255]

Locomotives: Gauge 2'0"

-	4wPM		MH	5	1926	New	(1)
-	4wDM		R&R	93		(a)	(2)
-	4wDM	20hp	RH	203001	1941	(b)	(3)
7	4wDM	20hp	RH	210955	1941	(c)	(3)

(a) wfw: Fitzpatrick & Sons, Cork
(b) tdx: W.O.Williams, dealer, Harlech, after 29/11/1948 by 26/7/1954
    wfw: Thos.W.Ward Ltd, dealer, Templeborough, Sheffield
    wfw: Ministry of Supply, Derby, until 25/10/1946
(c) tdx: W.O.Williams, dealer, Harlech, after 1/1/1953 by 26/7/1954
    wfw: Ministry of Supply, RASC 'Bottisford', Notts, in 9/1947

(1) wlw(tdt?): Croft Works, Leicestershire, by 7/1954
(2) tdt: W.O.Williams, dealer, Harlech, for scrap, after 7/1954 by 7/1956
(3) tdt: Croft Works, Leicestershire, c1955 after 26/7/1954

CARREG-Y-LLAM (WEST NANT) GRANITE QUARRIES   C6
near LLITHFAEN   (Gc/GR:338438)

1877		: Vaynol lease to **E.Spargo & Sir Ll.Turner**
in 1879		: open [J/MJ/2-1879/169]
in 1886		: **West Nant Granite Co**
1913 -	1918	: **H.J.Wright** (Spanish & General Corporation Ltd)
11/1920 -	6/1935	: **Carreg-y-Llam Quarries Ltd**
		(reg.2/11/1920; liq.1935 but reformed under same title but as a subsidiary of:-)
6/1935 -	9/1963	: **Amalgamated Roadstone Corporation Ltd**
9/1963		: closed; site taken over by Penmaenmawr & Welsh Granite Co Ltd, but not worked.

There was a simple rail system and pier on this site prior to 1920; as the quarry expanded the pier was renewed slightly to the east, and inclines installed from pier to first bank, and from first to second bank. This latter bank, at least, used 2'6" gauge track - the locos worked here. Rail system replaced by road transport and conveyors c1951. The incline from the crushing Mill at pier level up to a lorry loading point at first bank was retained (or possibly later re-laid) in 2'0" gauge, to enable crushed stone to leave by road. This incline remained in use until 1963.

[Read: J/IRR/Vol.2/269]

Locomotives: Gauge 2'6"

LM8		4wPM	20hp	FH	1838	1933	New (a) Scr/1949
LM38		4wDM	20hp	FH	2401	1949	New (b) (1)

(a) supplied as a new loco 10/1933, but FH records suggest it was in fact a rebuild of an earlier bow-frame Simplex-type loco.
(b) supplied as a new loco 10/1949; in fact, originally supplied to the War Office as 600mm gauge, later returned to FH, re-gauged and re-engined. FH number 2401 is appropriate to c1941.

(1) tdt: Penlee Quarries, Cornwall, 7/1951. (Altered to 2'0" gauge by FH "on site; new wheels and axles fitted").

CASTLE BRICKWORKS, EWLOE GREEN, near BUCKLEY   C8
(Cf/GR:below)

founded 1865			: G.H.Alletson
1865	-	7/1875	: Castle Fire Brick Co [G.H.Alletson et al]
7/1875	-	8/1889	: Castle Firebrick & Coal Co
8/1889	-	1917	: Castle Firebrick Co Ltd (reg.3/8/1889 - by Alletson et al)
1917	-	c1970	: subsidiary of John Summers & Sons Ltd
c1970			: closed, later demolished.

The original Works of 1865 was located at GR:276668; it had a short siding off the adjacent Buckley Railway (PR/22), and a short narrow-gauge incline into the claypit immediately south of the Works. A new and larger Works, known as Elm Works, was built nearby (GR:273664) in 1925, adjacent to Elm Colliery. Both Works, "Old" and "Elm", continued in operation until c1970, when production was transferred to Trap Works, Buckley (which see).
Elm Works was connected to the same claypit by 2ft gauge railway, which was later extended across the main road, following the first part of the route of the Buckley Colliery Railway to gather material from the tips of the former Ash Colliery (GR:271656), and to a lorry tipping dock at GR:276663. Locomotives were introduced to operate this extended system which closed c1950 (after 24/4/1949) in favour of road transport; three locos remained disused on site for many years.
The 4'8½" gauge sidings at Old Works remained in use until 5/1965, shunting being performed originally by horses and later by road vehicles, including a Fordson farm tractor fitted with dumb buffers. A nearby, but separate, siding off PR/22 to the Elm Colliery was loco worked - for details see entry "Buckley Colliery Railway".
New Works, after closure, was completely demolished; much of Old Works survived as a road haulage depot.

Locomotives: Gauge 2'0"

The KS locos were 'canibalised' during WW2, the best of the components being from time to time assembled into a working loco. The following list is correct as regards chassis identity.

3		0-4-0ST	OC	KS	2473	1916	(a)	Scr 9/1958	
No.1		0-4-0ST	OC	KS	4005	1918	(b)		(1)
2		0-4-0ST	OC	KS	2460	1915	(c)		(2)
		4wDM		OK	5675				(3)
		4wDM		OK	7733	c1938			(3)
No.6		0-4-0ST	OC	WB	2037	1915	(d)	Scr 9/1958	
No.7		0-4-0ST	OC	WB	2075	1918	(d)	Scr 9/1958	
		4wDM	48hp	RH	244487	1946	New 10/46		(3)

(a)   first loco here; arrived early 1930s.
       wfw (tdx?): Aubrey Watson & Co Ltd, contractors, until 7/1930 at least. Believed to have been used on their Benson By-pass Road (1931-1932) Contract, Oxon, then stored at their Henley-on-Thames plant depot.
(b)   tdx: ? by 5/1935. In 4/1933 this loco was for sale by Frank Young & Son Ltd, dealers, Windsor Works, Liverpool - loco was lying at Cartford Bridge, Little Eccleston, near Blackpool, Lancs.
       wfw: Thos.W.Ward Ltd, dealers, Grays, Essex, [? ref.TW 148] c1927.
       [? wfw: Muirhead, MacDonald, Wilson & Co Ltd, Southend Arterial Road (1921-1924) Contract, Essex - see J/IL/No.60/7, No.61/32]

(c)   tdx: ? by 2/1936.
      wfw: Thos.W.Ward Ltd, dealers, Grays, Essex, [? ref.TW 152] 5/1935.
      wfw: Sheffield Corporation Water Works, Ewden Valley, in 6/1932
      [? wfw: Muirhead, MacDonald, Wilson & Co, contractors; possibly used on Southend
      Arterial Road (1921-1924) Contract, Essex [J/IL/No.60/7, No.61/32]]
(d)   arrived after 2/1935 by 7/1970.
      wfw: Liverpool United Gas Light Co, Linacre Gas Works, Bootle, Lancs. Possibly came
      direct to Castle from Bootle, but WB 2037 carried WB pattern 'No.3' plates at Bootle,
      yet similar pattern 'No.6' and 'No.7' were carried at Castle - did Castle order new
      plates from WB, or did the locos travel via WB for overhaul ?

(1)   dismantled c1940; boiler reconditioned and fitted to KS 2460 by 4/1943. Coupling
      rods and some other chassis components later fitted to KS 2373. Chassis etc.
      scrapped during 1952.
(2)   in steam 4/1943 with boiler from KS 4005. Own boiler then reconditioned, and later
      fitted to KS 2473.
      Dismantled by 8/1948; chassis scrapped 1950.
(3)   tdt: Buttington Brickworks, near Welshpool, 1950 (c10/1950)

CEIRIOG GRANITE QUARRY, HENDRE, near GLYNCEIRIOG   C10
                                                      (Cd/GR:193349)

```
   1875                 : opened
   1875    -   1881     : Glyn Ceiriog Granite Co
 8/1881    -            : Glyn Ceiriog Granite Co Ltd (reg.23/8/1881 £30K)
           -  2/1929    : Ceiriog Granite Co Ltd
 2/1929`   -            : British Quarrying Co Ltd (reg.4/2/1929 £700K)
   1950                 . closed; dismantled.
```

The quarry floor was connected to a crushing plant by a level railway of 2'4" gauge, with inclines to upper galleries within the quarry. From beneath the crusher, rails of the Glyn Valley Tramway Mineral Extension (PR/42) ran northward via other quarries to Glynceiriog, and thence to Chirk. Prior to construction of the GVT Mineral Extension (Act of 31/7/1885) the Ceiriog Granite Co Ltd operated the GVT, from Glynceiriog to Chirk Bank Wharf, from 1/7/1881 to 1889. The quarry ceased using the GVT c1930; internal rail operation at the quarry continued for some years. During the early 1900s, the quarry loco worked for a short distance down the Mineral Extension hauling crushed stone to a tarmac plant installed at the Lower Pandy Quarry.

[Read: B/348; B/173; B/309]

Locomotive: Gauge 2'4"

            -           0-4-0T   OC   [? LIL   1869] (a)   Scr 11/1944

(a) This loco carried a plate
"Lilleshall Company/Engineers/1880/Shropshire"
which is generally presumed to be a 'builders plate', though this remains to be proved. Suggested in some sources as being the loco by "Lilleshall Iron Co, 2'8" gauge, new copper box, perfect condition, £180" for sale anonymously in J/PMR/5-6.1900 (material offered is PMR was not necessarily in Phillip's hands). Possible origins of such a loco include the six 4w and 6w 2'7½" gauge locos for sale at Main Colliery Co, Neath Abbey, 11/1899; or maybe [see J/IL/No.38/43] a loco from the tramroad that ran from New Priestfield Ironworks, Willenhall to the LNWR at Willenhall; this was a narrow-gauge line opened c1880, and which had locos (of some sort) which were redundant in the late 1890s.
Also, J/PMR/6-10/1900 contained an anonymous "wanted" advertisement for "loco, 2'4½" gauge, or one that can easily be altered to that gauge".
Other sources suggested have included "steelworks at Wolverhampton" [? Willenhall], and "Criggion Quarries". However, the late W.K."Bill" Williams was of the opinion that this loco was built in 1869, and came to Ceiriog via Lilleshall (as dealers ?) in 1880.
According to the personal records maintained by a Mr Hoggins, who worked for the Lilleshall Company from c1885 and became Engineers' Accountant there, The Lilleshall Company constructed two 0-4-0T 2'4" gauge locos in 10/1869 for the Lilleshall Companies Lodge Furnaces, Oakengates, Salop; and that one was sold c1881 - the other being sold c1885/ 1886 when Lodge Furnaces closed down.
All things being considered, at present it seems most likely that the Ceiriog Quarry loco was built by LIL 1869, reconditioned (and re-plated) for sale 1880, and came to Ceiriog either then or (if the J/PMR/6-1900 advert is relevant - and who else indeed could require a loco of that gauge ?) later.

CHIRK FORESTRY PLANT DEPOT   C12
(Cd/GR:283380)

: Forestry Commission

During and after WW2 the former Glyn Valley Tramway (PR/42) yard at Chirk was used as a store yard and plant depot, being a base for operations in many areas of North Wales. Railways were used for timber recovery at various locations but details are sparse. See, for example, "Hendre-ddu" and "Llangollen Area Forestry" entries.
The following locomotives have been noted at Chirk Depot.

Locomotives: Gauge 2'0"

4wPM	20hp	MR	7097	1941	(a)	(1)
4wDM	20hp	MR			(b)	(2)

(a) tdx: Hendre-ddu Forestry Railway, c1949 by 8/1950
(b) tdx: Hendre-ddu Forestry Railway, 6/1965

(1) s/s, by 5/6/1954
(2) sold by auction, c1960 - no further trace.

CILGWYN SLATE QUARRIES, CILGWYN   C14
(Gc/GR:500540 etc)

The history of Cilgwyn Quarry is complex, and dates from the 12th Century - probably the oldest organised slate quarry in North Wales. Being on Crown land, as indeed were all the quarries in the 'Moel Tryfan' group, we are fortunate that extensive historical records survive, though these are difficult to summarise. The earliest known reference to railways at Cilgwyn is to a "waste tip railroad" of 1810 [CRO/PyAur/27375], so 1800 seems a reasonable starting date for the purpose of this Handbook.
By 1849 the site contained three quarry pits - Old Kilgwyn, Veingoch, and Muskett's - each with its own history. Later, but prior to 1870, two more pits were created - Cloddfa-Dwr and Cloddfa-Clytiau. Different renderings of all names occur from source to source. After 1870, the individual pits became less distinct, as extensive working spread across the site.

OLD KILGWYN: from 5/4/1800 - John Evans et al, who formed the Cilgwyn & Cefndu Slate Co [Cefndu being a quarry in the 'Llanberis West' group].
VEINGOCH: to 3/1805   - in lease to Captain Robert Evans
                from 3/1905 - worked with Old Kilgwyn
COMBINED QUARRIES:

3/1805	-	1827	: **Cilgwyn & Cefndu Slate Co** (liq.1830)
1827			: quarry auctioned
4/1835	-		: **George Morris**
12/1835	-		: **George Muskett** [who started the third pit]
by 1844			: closed
1844	-	c1846	: small scale working by local men
c1846	-	1849	: **Cilgwyn Slate Co** [John Hayward & Co]
1849	-	1884	: **Cilgwyn Slate Co** [William Hayward & Co]
2/1884			: for sale, due to death of Haywards
by 1888	-	4/1897	: **Cilgwyn Slate Co** [Mr Blaikie]
4/1897	-	4/1918	: **Cilgwyn Slate Co Ltd** [lease renewed 10/10/1897]
			(reg.18/11/1896 £40K liq.1918)
4/1918	-	10/1929	: **Amalgamated Slate Association Ltd**
			(reg.1918 £50K vol.liq.1/1931-12/1933)
11/1929	-	1932	: closed
1932	-	1956	: **Carnarvonshire Crown Slate Quarries Co Ltd**
1956			: closed; dismantled.

         In 1980s became a major refuse tip.

As mentioned above, railways existed here by 1810 and continued in use to 1956. These were mostly 2ft gauge. About 1830 a 3½ft gauge incline was constructed down to the Nantlle Railway (PR/2), slate then being sent to Caernarfon by that route. Space for tipping waste was very limited at Cilgwyn, which resulted in the 1887 construction of a spectacular railway which gained height by horse-shoe curves to a new tip at GR:500549. Loco QUEENIE was obtained specifically to work this line but proved to be too small; it was replaced by LILLA. A second lengthy railway was built c6/1895 westwards to further tipping space at GR:499550; worked by JUBILEE 1897, this line is now [1990] largely incorporated into the route of the refuse-tip access road.

Following the 1918 takeover by Amalgamated Slate, the incline to PR/2 was abandoned in favour of a new 2ft gauge line running north-eastwards to connect into the railway from Fron/Old Braich to Bryngwyn Incline, output then being rerouted via PR/44. This connection opened 9/1919, closed 10/1929; road transport being used from 1932. As discussed under heading "Braich/Old Braich Quarry", the existence of this private railway system connecting the various Amalgamated Slate quarries doubtless resulted in locomotives appearing at different quarries from time to time.

Locomotives: Gauge 1'11½"

LIZZIE	0-4-0VBT VC	DeW		[? 1876 New]	(a)	(1)
GERTRUDE *	0-4-0VBT VC	DeW		1877 New	(a)	(1)
MADGE	0-4-0VBT VC	DeW		[? 1880 New]		(1)
QUEENIE	0-4-0 IT OC	WB	930	1887 New	(b)	(2)
LILLA	0-4-0ST OC	HE	554	1891 New 11/91		(3)
JUBILEE 1897	0-4-0ST OC	MW	1382	1897 New 7/97		(3)
	4wPM	**		New		(4)
	4wDM 10hp	RH	166031	1933	(c)	(5)
	4wDM 20hp	RH	175414	1936 New 2/36		(6)

* named by Gertrude Carter at quarry ceremony 7/11/1877 [J/CDH/10.11.1877/5]
** built at Cilgwyn Quarry; engine and gearbox ex Morris (or Austin) car.

(a) there was one loco here [? early in] 1877 [UCNW/Nantlle/1] and, if this pre-dates arrival (c11/1877 ?) of GERTRUDE, it does suggest a loco [? LIZZIE] was indeed New c1876.
(b) arrived 10/1887; ordered via Coalbrookdale Co acting as dealers.
(c) came here from RH on demonstration only; had previously been on demonstration or tests at Longside Sand & Gravel Co Ltd, Thorpe, Surrey, until 18/4/1934. Hence loco probably at Cilgwyn c5/1934 to c8/1934, and may have been tried out at other Crown quarries also, but records are imprecise.

(1) Per J/CDH/2.2.1884, the quarry had three (unidentified) locos at the time of the 2/1884 sale - presumably these locos. Disposal of these locos is uncertain; reputedly worn out and scrapped c1900 - but GERTRUDE (or components of it) may have gone to Coedmadoc Slate Quarry.
(2) no longer here c1903; may have been scrapped.
In J/MM/1.5.1899, J.H.Williams & Son, dealers, Porthmadog, were advertising for sale a 23¼" gauge loco 4wc "tank below", 23" wheels, 6x14 cylinders, 4ft wheelbase loco, having 37 brass tubes 6ft long. Maybe it was QUEENIE, though not all the dimensions fit.
(3) tdt: Penrhyn Slate Quarry, Bethesda, 5/1928 - despatched on own wheels via Bryngwyn, WHR (PR/44) to Dinas, thence on LMSR freight train to Port Penrhyn; unloaded there 21/5/1928.
(4) disposal not known; could perhaps be the mystery loco seen 12/1941 at Fron Quarry (which see).
(5) returned to RH after trials; subsequently despatched by RH to Shawell Sand & Gravel Co Ltd, Clifton, Rugby, on 5/9/1934.
(6) probably used elsewhere within the local Carnarvonshire Crown slate quarries from time to time, but spare parts were supplied to Cilgwyn Quarry up to 3/1938, and to Moel Tryfan Quarry from 11/1940.
For later history see "Moel Tryfan Quarry" entry.

CLOGAU St.DAVID'S GOLD MINE, BONTDDU   C16
(Gm/GR:below)

The mountains to the north of Bontddu are a virtual rabbit-warren of gold (and other metals) mines; the various shafts, adits and underground areas are comprehensively described in (eg) B/229, B/271, J/MRS/1974/155; J/NMRS/No.6/22.

Workings developed over the years into three major holdings - the Clogau, Vigra, and St.Davids mines - which were separately and/or jointly worked by a large number of Companies, most of which remained active for less than ten years. Doubtless there is plenty of gold there, but it is both difficult and costly to find and extract. The principal surface railways that were created, and can still [1990] be traced, consist of a 500 yard incline built 1865 from Vigra Mill (GR:668191) up to a drumhouse (GR:673195); a 'level' railway, completed 21/3/1866, which contoured north-easterly from this drumhouse to Clogau No.2 Adit (GR:675201), and on to St.David's No.1 Adit (GR:676204). Another rail track emerged at Tyn-y-Cornel Adit (Level Fawr - GR:672201) to feed a self-acting 1100 yard 11-pylon ropeway (in use c1898-c1905) down to Vigra Mill; yet another railway emerged at the Llechfraith (Deep) Adit (GR:668195) direct to the nearby West Clogau Mill. The Llechfraith and Tyn-y-Cornel Adits have been the centre of recent activities; a 1980s proposal to open Llechfraith as a tourist attraction did not receive Planning Permission.

Commercial exploitation ceased in 1939 when Hillside Mining Co Ltd gave up; from then until 1983 little was done other than prospecting, then:

      1/1983 - c1986 : **Carnarvon Mining Co Ltd**
      c1986 - c1987 : **Clogau St.David's Gold Mines Ltd** [Wm.Roberts etc]
      c1987 - 1990 : not commercially worked
      1/1990 - : **Mrs & Mr Bob Gunn** - mining by license.

Locomotives: Gauge 2'0"

                     0-4-0BE   WR   L1009   1979 (a)
                     4wBE   WR   10114   1984 (b)

(a)   tdx: Wheal Concorde Ltd, Blackwater, Cornwall, c2/1983
(b)   tdx: WR, c9/1984. Loco is a rebuild of WR 7556/1972.

COEDMADOC (CLODDFA'R GLAI) SLATE QUARRY, TALYSARN   C18
(Gc/GR:492531)

    pre 1820   : started
        1822 - 1828 : **George Bettis**
    in 1859   : **Hafodlas & Coedmadog Welsh Slate Co** [J/HC/5.3.1859]
        1864 - 1877 : **Coedmadoc Slate Co Ltd** (liq.1877)
        1877 -   : **Coedmadoc Slate Co**
    by 1888 -   : **Braich & Coed Madoc Slate Co** [Pearson et al]
      10/1896 - 12/1908 : **Coedmadoc Slate Co Ltd** [Pearsons et al]
                               (inc.9/10/1896 vol.liq.12/1908-3/1910)
      12/1908   : closed; breakup sale 31/3/1909

2ft gauge railways in and around quarry plus direct line to Talysarn station - this latter converted to 4'8½" gauge 4/1881, and has been recalled locally as a mixed-gauge line, on which 2ft gauge locos hauled standard-gauge wagons - though this is not proven. Coedmadoc quarry was adjacent to, but to the south of, Cloddfa'r Coed quarry; by 1902 they were separated only by a narrow dyke which, after closure of Coedmadoc, was quarried away by Cloddfa'r Coed - who continued to use the 4'8½" line mentioned above - the track not being removed until 1927. As far as is known, Cloddfa'r Coed never used locomotives of any gauge.
The derelict site was virtually obliterated by a 1970s land reclamation project.

Locomotives: Gauge 2ft

An old Blacksmith (now deceased) at Dorothea Quarry recalled seeing a photograph of a loco at Coedmadoc, which had a vertical boiler, but a chassis quite different to the DeWinton type. Perhaps this was loco VIOLET illustrated in B/419 ? [This book is quite wrong in attributing the loco illustrated to the Penrhyn Railway, of course.]   And see note under TALYSARN QUARRY.

	MOELEILIA	0-4-0VBT VC	DeW		1880 [New ?]		s/s
		0-4-0VBT VC	DeW	[? c1874]	(a)		s/s
[?	GERTRUDE]	0-4-0VBT VC	DeW	[? 1877]	(b)		s/s

(a) origin uncertain; could possibly be the Gorsedda Railway (PR/4) loco named PERT, which was available for purchase c1895, though name PERT was not recalled by old Coedmadoc employees interviewed in 1950s.
(b) two DeW locos of the MOELEILIA type appear to have worked at Coedmadoc; this one could perhaps be GERTRUDE from Cilgwyn Quarry, though name GERTRUDE not recalled by old employees. If loco did come from Cilgwyn, then it came c1900.

COED TALON COLLIERIES   C20
(Cf/GR:268594)

There have been a large number of small collieries in the Coed Talon and Leeswood district, active on a commercial basis from the early 1800s to the mid-1930s, with isolated instances of "private mine" working up to the present day [1991]. The OS 6" and 25" maps of 1914 and earlier mark a multitude of "tramways" and sidings serving not only collieries, but also oil-works which produced a form of paraffin - from which candles could be made - from the local cannel ["candle"] coal; iron-works, brickworks and quarries. A complete study of this area would be a fascinating topic, regretfully beyond the capacity of this Handbook.

By the 1850s, much of the coal mining was controlled by the Oakeley family (often incorrectly given as 'Oakley'), of Oakeley House (formerly Leeswood New Hall), Queen Street, Leeswood. Edward Oakeley traded both under his own name, and as Coed Talon Colliery Company (with variations of that title).

The first 4'8½" gauge railway into the area was the LNWR line (PR/10) from Ffrith Junction, reputedly opened some-time late 1849.   Sources vary and are imprecise, but it seems that Oakeley initially worked that line using his own locomotive. From Coed Talon, a private railway was built from the end of PR/10 to Nerquis Colliery (which see). In 1868, much of the Nerquis Railway was incorporated in the second LNWR route to Coed Talon, being the line from Mold (PR/39).

With the coming of the LNWR outlet c1850, it appears that Oakeley built a central coal-screening and loading facility (GR:268594) on what later became the northern line of the "Coed Talon triangle"; this facility became both the hub of, and known as, "Coed Talon Colliery". A hybrid locomotive was later assembled at Coed Talon as a shunter for these screens. In fact, the coals originated from many small local pits and drifts; for example, when "Edward Oakley Esq." exhibited the "biggest lump of coal in the World" at the 1851 Crystal Palace Exhibition, it was stated to have come from the "Lamp Mawr Push-on Pit of Coed Talon Colliery".

by 1851 -	1860	: Edward Oakeley / & Co
1861 -	1872	: Coed Talon Coal Co Ltd
1873 -	1896	: Coed Talon Colliery Co Ltd
18/9/1896		: sale by auction - Coed Talon Colliery
27/7/1897		: sale by auction - Black Diamond Colliery
-	1907	: Coed Talon Colliery Co (S.Howl)
2/1907 -	1916	: Coed Talon Colliery Ltd (reg.19/2/1907 £12K)
1916 -	1926	: Coed Talon Collieries Ltd (Higginbottom & Co)
by 1923		: per W.D.Haswell, Receiver
7/1926		: closed; abandoned 1927.

[Read: J/CG/3.3.1893/395; 10.3.1893/441; B/199/7/64 - also "History of the Coed Talon Coalfield" by Thomas Jones; Leeswood; 1918]

Locomotives: Gauge 4'8½"

DIAMOND	0-4-0tank	SB	663	1850	New	(1)
EXPRESS	0-2-2T	SCG	CoedTalon	1874	New (a)	
	rebuilt as 0-2-2VBT	SCG	CoedTalon	c1900		(2)

(a) per J/RMAG/11.1904/403, and J/Great Central Railway Journal/3.1912: built at Coed Talon Collieries, designed by Wm.Lea [? Engineer; was listed as Manager in J/MS/1894 but not 1888 or 1889]. Consisted of frame and wheels of old coal wagon with old portable engine fitted on; drive by cog wheel to front axle. Single 9"x12" cylinder. Replacement vertical boiler fitted c1900, redundant horizontal boiler left in situ.

(1) "sold to Chester & Holyhead Railway, at cost price, 3/1852" per RCTS B/103/C.17. Exactly what this infers is unclear, as the C&H Rly is generally said to have never owned its own locomotives, being worked from the outset by the LNWR. However, the railway from Ffrith Junction to Coed Talon (PR/10) was legally the property of the C&H until absorbed by the LNWR in 1859; hence perhaps the "sale" was compensation to Oakeley when he no longer needed the loco because, as appears, the LNWR took over the operation of the line.
wlw: Birkenhead Railway, No.27, 1/1854
wlw: LNWR, No.356 MEMNON, 1860; renamed ACTON in 1869.
wlw: Shropshire Union Railways & Canal Co - see PR/1.

(2) listed in 18/9/1896 auction catalogue as having 9"x18" cylinder; apparently remained in use at Coed Talon as per J/Great Central Railway Journal/3.1912/250 it had "just recently ceased running". No further trace.

COLWYN BAY & RHOS-ON-SEA SEA WALL & PROMENADE   C22
(Cd/GR:below)

A combined sea defence wall and promenade extends westwards from Old Colwyn (GR:871787) to Penrhyn Bay (GR:825816). The creation of this 'wall' is the result of various Contracts, one of which certainly used railway equipment and a steam locomotive.

5/1876: Tenders invited....extensive sea wall, Promenade, Carriage Drive along the sea from of the Pwllycrochan Estate: for COLWYN BAY & PWLLYCROCHAN ESTATE CO LTD.

7/1896: Jacob Biggs of Birmingham had £11787 Contract from COLWYN BAY DISTRICT COUNCIL for New Promenade at Colwyn Bay. Work was nearing completion 7/1897 - final cost £15000.

7/1903: William Underwood & Brother (of Dukinfield, Cheshire) awarded Contracts for Promenade (£34351) and Sewerage Works with 6¾ miles of Sewer (£55876) by COLWYN BAY & COLWYN U.D.COUNCIL. The works were authorised by Act of 31/7/1902. Contract signed 3/7/1903. Work started 23/7/1903, completed 1907.

4/1913: William Underwood & Brother awarded another Contract, Promenade extension work at Rhos for COLWYN BAY & COLWYN U.D.COUNCIL.

Locomotives: Gauge Narrow - 1903-1907 Contract. - WM. UNDERWOOD & BRO.

A photograph taken of these works shows, not very clearly, a small locomotive, apparently 0-4-0WT OC. It bears some resemblance to a 'mystery' contractors loco illustrated in J/TL/15.10.21 and in J/IRR/No.88/274 - there described as 2ft gauge, 6½x14 cylinders, 2ft wheels, 4ft wheelbase, weight 5 tons empty, 6½ tons in working order. And note, there is possible similarity with the loco advertised for sale in 1899 by J.H.Williams, Porthmadog [see "Clues for Further Research"].

COLWYN BAY STATION "PLATFORM THREE" RAILWAY MUSEUM   C24
(Cd/GR:851791)

              1988   : new premises in disused platform area at station.
   1988 -   : Mr R.Ireland
   1991 -   : Mr John Perkins

Locomotive: Gauge 4'8½" - On Static Display.

(1   FIREFLY)   0-6-0T   OC   HC   1864   1952 (a)   OOU

(a)   tdx: Steamtown Railway Centre, Carnforth, Lancs, 5/10/1988
      wfw: National Coal Board, Whitwood Colliery, Yorkshire.

CONNAH'S QUAY ALKALI WORKS   C26
                                                         (Cf/GR:below)

active 1/1883   : Connah's Quay Alkali Co
                       : closed and demolished.

Information available at present is rather vague - there are two possible sites for this Company:

WEPRE CHEMICAL WORKS, near SHOTTON   (GR:302694)

PENTRE FFWRNDAN ALKALI WORKS, OAKENHOLT, near FLINT   (GR:260723)

Both of these works are now demolished. The "Connah's Quay Chemical Works" employed 150 men and boys in 1/1874...."Mr Flowers, one of the proprietors of the Company...." [J/CDH/24.1.1874/5, 8]

Locomotives: Gauge [? 2' 6"]

It is reputed that the Connah's Quay Alkali Co operated two narrow-gauge locomotives, named GLADSTONE and ASTON - names which are very appropriate to the Connah's Quay area. The builder of GLADSTONE may have been WkB (Walker Bros of Wigan) but the builder of ASTON has not been suggested.

Coincidentally, two locomotives named GLADSTONE and ASTON, of c30" gauge, did work at one of the Salt Union Ltd (later Imperial Chemical Industries Ltd) factories at Winsford, Cheshire; the Works was officially "National Works" though often referred to in the Winsford area as "Stubbs Works" after the original owners Stubbs Brothers. This rail system was abandoned shortly after WW1 and the locos were transferred to Meadow Works, Winsford, for storage. By 10/1946, the Winsford GLADSTONE was lying in the Warrington scrap yard of Joseph Brierley & Son, where it survived until broken up c1953. What became of Winsford ASTON seems unknown.

The inference of course - though it is certainly not proven - is that the locos at Winsford originated at Connah's Quay.

Of related interest, what was apparently a third loco, named SAMSON built WB 272 in 1879 to 2'7" gauge, was supplied New to Stubbs Brothers, Winsford. SAMSON seems to have become confused with Brierleys' loco GLADSTONE by some researchers.

CONNAH'S QUAY MARSH DRAINAGE CONTRACT   C28
                                                         (Cf/GR:267715)

        1964   : unknown customer or contractor.

Contract for laying concrete drain pipes in trenches in the salt marsh to the west of Connah's Quay Power Station. Information elusive, but an unconfirmed report suggested work was to prepare ground for tipping of Power Station ash.

Locomotives: Gauge 2ft

A photograph, taken from a passing train 19/5/1964, shows "portable" track laid parallel to PR/7, with a train loaded with large pipes, hauled by a 4wDM MR locomotive [of type 22xxx or similar].

CONNAH'S QUAY POWER STATION   C30
                                                     (Cf/GR:288706)

	1952	:	new station
1952 -	3/1955	:	British Electricity Authority
4/1955 -	12/1957	:	Central Electricity Authority
1/1958 -		:	Central Electricity Generating Board
	5/1983	:	closed - held intact on reserve.

Coal-fired plant served by sidings off PR/7. Rail traffic ceased 1982 in favour of deliveries b
road. Rail tracks lifted 1/1987.

Locomotives: Gauge 4'8½"

-		0-4-0DM 150hp JF	22992	1942	(a)	(1)
No.1		0-4-0DM 150hp JF	4210077	1952	New	Scr 1/1986
No.2		0-4-0DM 150hp JF	4210090	1954	New	Scr 2/1986
3		0-4-0DM 150hp JF	4210069	1952	(b)	Scr 1/1986
10	D.ARTIS	0-4-0DM 150hp JF	4210001	1949		
		rebuilt as 0-4-0DH 203hp JF		1966	(c)	(2)

(a)	tdx:	Clarence Dock Power Station, Liverpool, 4/1952
(b)	tdx:	Whitbirk Power Station, Blackburn, Lancashire, 29/9/1976
(c)	tdx:	Skelton Grange Power Station, Yorkshire, 3/1981

| (1) | tdt: | Bromborough Power Station, Cheshire, 1953 by 6/1963 |
| (2) | tdt: | Kearsley Power Station, Lancashire, 10/1984 |

CONNAH'S QUAY (DENTITH'S SIDINGS) WAGON WORKS   C32
                                                     (Cf/GR:297697)

| by 3/1911 | : R.Williams & Sons |
| by 1/1965 | : C.C.Crump & Co |

Prior to 1966 the sidings were shunted by the Connah's Quay Dock loco provided by
PR/22/54; after closure of these lines, the Wagon Works used only the direct connection to
PR/7. Apart from wagon repairs, Crumps have scrapped locomotives at this site, including
some British Railways steam locos, and 0-6-0F OC AB 2232/1948 from Shell, Stanlow,
Cheshire, scrapped 3/1970.

Locomotives: Gauge 4'8½"

NELLIE		4wDM 50hp FH	2346	1940	(a)		(1)
-		4wDM Bg	3003	1937	(b)	Scr c3/1969	
-		0-4-0DM 80hp JF	4110012	1951	(c)		(2)
MARIE		0-4-0DM 150hp JF	22882	1939			
	rebuilt as	0-4-0DH 203hp JF	1651608	1963	(d)		
AMW No.170		0-4-0DM 150hp JF	22879	1939	(e)	Scr c5/1973	
M.O.P.No.7		0-4-0DM 150hp JF	4210144	1958	(f)		
AMW No.223		0-4-0DM 150hp JF	22970	1942	(g)	Scr 10/1973	
AMW No.245		0-4-0DM 150hp JF	23002	1943	(g)	Scr 10/1973	
-		0-4-0DE 200hp YE	2732	1959	(h)		

a) tdx: Mostyn Wagon Works, after 12/2/1966 by 27/9/1967 [? on 14/8/67]
b) tdx: Shell-Mex & B.P. Ltd, Benzole Works, Stanlow, Cheshire, c4/1966
c) tdx: Trevor Silica Brickworks, near Acrefair, 7/1967
d) tdx: Shell Oil Refinery, Stanlow, Cheshire, c1970 by 8/1970
e) tdx: Sealand Air Force Depot, after 10/1970 by 10/1971
f) tdx: Ministry of Power, Bramhall, Cheshire, 12/2/1972
g) tdx: Sealand Air Force Depot, 13/1/1973
h) tdx: Rea Bulk Handling Ltd, Bidston Dock, Birkenhead, 26/4/1990

1) s/s after 12/7/1969 by 10/1970
2) s/s 1970 after 10/1970
[reputed tdt: Britannia Bridge Reconstruction Contract (PR/7) but not confirmed there]

CONWY GAS WORKS later SCRAPYARD, CONWY MORFA   C34
(Gc/GR:766783)

The Gasworks was served by a short private siding off PR/7 one mile west of Conwy station. The LMSR entered into agreements regarding this siding with Conway Corporation 3/5/1929, and with Conway Gas Co Ltd 30/11/1937. The Gasworks site subsequently became a scrapyard operated by Shone Hughes, dealer and metal merchant.

Locomotives: Gauge 4'8½"

From other sources, we have details of two locomotives sold and later despatched to "Conway for scrap" - we do not know the identity of the purchaser, but this is a convenient place to mention them. Likewise, note that RH 171902, recovered from Rhos Slate Quarry and later at Votty & Bowydd Quarry, is reported by one source as being handled by "a dealer at Conwy Wharf". Perhaps "wharf" was a misunderstanding of "morfa"?

70201	DILLICHIP	0-4-0ST	OC	HE	304	1883	(a)	Scr
70202	TARTAR	0-4-0ST	OC	AE	1407	1899	(b)	Scr

a) at War Department depot, Dillichip, Dunbartonshire; where it was sold as scrap c9/1947. Sent first to LMSR St.Rollox depot (here 10/1947) then despatched south on own wheels in freight train 22/10/1947.
b) as (a) but arrived St.Rollox 10/10/1947; despatched 10/1947.
[For this loco see also "Queensferry Government Factory" entry.]

CONWY (PENMAENBACH) STONE QUARRIES, CONWY MORFA C36
(Gc/GR:757782)

	pre 1874	: open
1874 -	1878	: **Penmaenbach Stone Quarries Co** (Owen & Henshaw) [J/CDH/28.2.1874/6c3; 20.6.1874/6c7]
1878 -	pre 1887	: **Isaac Anwell** [? Anwyl]
1899 -		: reopened
1902		: leased to "Gardner"
11/1906 -		: **Carder's Stone-Lino Ltd**
by 1909 -		: **Conway Stone Quarries Ltd**
by 1913 -		: **North Wales Granite Co** (sub.of Brookes Ltd)
by 3/1922 -		: **North Wales Granite Co Ltd** (sub.of Brookes Ltd)
by 7/1948	closed;	dismantled 9-10/1952; most buildings demolished 1965.

Prior to 1874 stone was loaded into boats on the beach at low tide. A pier was constructed by Fisher & Henshaw, completed in 1877, but caused dispute with the Board of Trade and Crown Commissioners. The quarry was at that time served by a single incline, from the foot of which stone was taken to the pier by road. At a sale in Liverpool on 28/2/1878 the quarry, "held on lease from 6/9/1874" was offered complete with "pier, tramway, rails, wagons...." [J/CDH/16.2.1878/4c5]. Use of road carts was superseded by a peculiar arrangement, whereby trucks off the incline were mounted onto a transporter trolley which ran [? on rails] alongside PR/7, turned to cross PR/7 on the level, then returned along the northern side of PR/7 to reach the pier. It is unclear as to whether the crossing of PR/7 was made on rails, or by using the roadway at the crossing.

The LNWR provided a siding on the north side of PR/7 in 1881; subsequently the quarry tramroad crossed the main road and the LNWR (PR/7) by a bridge, and the pier became disused and was removed. By 1887 all track had been removed.

The incline was relaid 1899 by Conway Corporation (the landowners) and the quarry then leased to tenants. Further inclines were later provided to serve the eventual total of five quarry levels. The track gauge was 3'0". New 4'8½" gauge sidings were provided on the south side of PR/7 in 5-6/1907. The quarry workings were to the west of the PR/7 sidings; two inclines were built in 1907 to develop the easterly direction, but were disused and partly removed by 1911. Alongside the road, beneath these inclines, the Corporation had a second smaller, quarry which became known as the KLEENEEZI QUARRY (GR:761782), as during its short life it was leased to Kleeneezi Ltd (of Mold) in 9/1906. The Kleeneezi Co soon pulled out, and the assets, including a 5 ton steam crane, rails and sleepers, were sold 3/5/1907. Conway Corporation workman was killed here 24/5/1907, having been hit by a rock dislodged by other men then constructing the easterly inclines above. This quarry has since been filled in and obliterated.

The date of final closure of Conway Quarry is uncertain; in 1936 there were discussions between Brookes and the Penmaenmawr Granite Quarries, intended to lead to the closure of Conway Quarries after which Brookes were to be supplied with stone from Penmaenmawr. But, as the equipment within Conway Quarries survived WW2 scrap collections, it would seem possible that closure was in fact deferred.

[Read: B/177/194, B/245/33]

Locomotives: Gauge 3'0"

MORFA	0-4-2T	OC	DK	(a)	(1)

Locomotives: Gauge 4'8½"

CONWAY	4-4-0T	OC	BP	1878	1879	(b)	(2)
-	0-4-0ST	OC	Hor	1105	1910	(c)	Scr

(a) Purchased by Brookes Ltd from MW, and leased by Brookes to North Wales Granite Co from 31/5/1915.
wfw: Shap Granite Co, 2'6" gauge, named POPSY
Gauge altered to 3'0" by MW in 1915.
(b) wfw(tdx ?): Bradford Corporation, Nidd Valley Light Railway, Yorks WR; per/via Brookes Ltd, Lightcliffe, Yorks, 1/1914.
wfw: Metropolitan Railway, London, number 34.
(c) tdx: R.Fraser & Sons Ltd, dealers, /c1934.
wfw: LMSRly, number 11251, until 4/1933.

(1) still here 31/3/1920; gone by 1926; no further trace.
(2) tdt: Brookes Ltd, Lightcliffe, Yorks, between 1/1919 and 6/1926;
[returned to Conwy by mid-1929 per one unverified source]
(sold to Thos.W.Ward Ltd in 1930, probably as scrap).

CRAIG LELO GRANITE QUARRIES, GWYDDELWERN   C38
(Cm/GR:066492)

by 1923 - 1966+ : Craig-Lelo Quarry Co Ltd

Small fan of sidings laid in 1924 off the LMS Ruthin-Corwen line (PR/20), 1¾ miles north of Gwyddelwern station. Rail traffic ceased 6/1954 and loco disused until sold.

Locomotive: Gauge 4'8½"

	4wPM 40hp	MR	3730	1925	New 3/25	(1)

(1) sold after 2/3/1966 by 11/5/1966 to the unknown contractor who was then lifting the track of PR/20.

CROESOR SLATE MINE, CWM CROESOR   C40
(Gm/GR:657456)

c1833   : small scale workings.
              by 9/1860 : Croesor Slate Quarry Co
9/1864 - 8/1866   : Croesor Fawr Slate Quarry Co Ltd (£80K)

(**Upper Croesor Slate Quarry Co Ltd** reg.9/1865 £60K to prospect around GR:662458. The two companies amalgamated:-)

8/1866	-	9/1875	: **Croesor United Slate Co Ltd** (reg.8/1866 £160K) sales 15/9/1974 and 2/1875
1/1876	-	6/1883	: **Croesor New Slate Co Ltd** (£45K) No work done. sale 29/6/1883
7/1883	-	1895	: Samuel Pope QC [of 74 Ashley Gardens, Victoria, London, and Hafodybryn, Llanbedr] who formed:
8/1895	-	12/1930	: **Park & Croesor Slate Quarries Co Ltd** (reg.21/8/1895 £100K liq.8/2/1931)
		24/5/1932	: break-up sale
1931	-	1942	: closed
1942	-	1949	: **Ministry of Supply Explosives Store**
1949	-	1971	: **Cooke's Explosives Ltd** - ICI Nobel Division
		1971	: closed
		1979	: dismantled by Ffestiniog Slate Quarry Co Ltd

Underground workings reached from the Mill by a half-mile tunnel along which the locos were used. From the Mill an incline descended to join the Croesor Tramway (PR/25). In 1866 there was a 12hp steam engine at the top of the main air shaft, working cables down the shaft to drive an underground incline. The sale list of 6/1883 includes two steam engines. A report of 1873 refers to the cracked bed of a steam engine. The sale lists of 9/1874 and 2/1875 include "two 12hp Locomotive Steam Engines put up for temporary purposes". In 1897 the Company was prosecuted for allowing "the smoke of an underground engine" to fill the workings. All these, and similar references, refer to stationary engines, and to road locomotives ("traction engines") used as stationary engines. Despite what has been written elsewhere, no evidence of there being steam railway locomotives here has yet been found.

[Read: J/MRS/1972/391]

Locomotives: Gauge 2ft

	4wWE	30hp	Kellow *	c1904 New	(1)
	4wDM	40hp	RH 198297	1939 (a)	(2)
	4wDM	20hp	RH 211625	1941 (b)	(3)
5	4wDM	40hp	RH 189962	1939 (c)	Scr/c1966

* designed, and built under the superintendance of, Moses Kellow - the General Manager at this Quarry.

(a) here by 2/1944; probably arrived 1942.
    wfw: Charles Brand & Son Ltd, contractor, Royal Edward Dock Extension (1939-1940) Contract, Avonmouth
(b) here by 8/1953
    wfw: Board of Trade, Powder Ham Saw Mill, Kenton, near Exeter, Devon, in 8/1947
(c) here by 4/1953
    wfw: Standard Brick & Sand Co Ltd, Redhill, Surrey, until 6/1951 at least. Loco not used at Croesor as unsuitable for underground work - was probably obtained as a source of spare parts.

(1) "Powerful electric loco" included in sale here 24/5/1932
    No further trace - probably scrapped.
(2) tdt: Gloddfa Ganol (see OAKELEY SLATE QUARRY) 19/11/1979
(3) last reported here 8/1955 - no further trace.

CWT-Y-BUGAIL SLATE QUARRY, RHIWBACH, FFESTINIOG   C42
(Gc/GR:733470)

		1835	:	opened by Mr Gregory
1863	-	5/1875	:	Cwt y Bugail Slate Co Ltd (reg.4/1863 £50K liq.1/1875)
		10/5/1875	:	sale: no locos mentioned. [J/CDH/8.5.1875/1]
1875	-	7/1891	:	Bugail Slate Co Ltd (reg.4/1875 £71K liq.7/1891)
8/1893	-	6/1909	:	Bugail Slate Quarry Co Ltd (reg.8/1893 £4K liq.6/1909)
1911	-	1913	:	New Welsh Slate Co Ltd (reg.1911)
1913	-	1921	:	closed
1921	-	1923	:	working.
1923	-	1961	:	Cwt-y-Bugail Slate Quarries Ltd (reg.22/11/1923 £10K)

Closed 1939-1947; from 1961-c1966 occasionally worked by individuals by license from the Company; from c1971 to date [1992] occasionally worked by the Company, by now a subsidiary of Ffestiniog Slate Co Ltd and mainly concerned with working the nearby Manod (Bwlch Slaters) Quarry.

A remote quarry until construction c1856 of the Rhiwbach Railway (PR/13), which provided a direct rail outlet to Blaenau Ffestiniog. After closure of Rhiwbach Quarry, Cwt-y-Bugail became sole user and operator of PR/13.

[Read: B/182; B/169]

Locomotives: Gauge 2ft

-		4wPM	10hp FH		c1925		(1)
-		4wDM	20hp RH	223687	1944	(a)	(2)
-		4wPM	6hp L	3742	1931	(b)	(3)
9		4wDM	20hp HE	2024	1940	(c)	(4)

(a) here by 12/1949
    wfw: Ministry of Supply.
(b) a gearbox from, apparently, L 3742 was discovered 4/1970 in use as part of a winch within the Cwt-y-Bugail workings. There is no other evidence that L 3742 was ever a loco here. A possible explanation for this is further discussed in entry "Groes-y-Ddwy-Afon Quarry".
(c) arrived c1962
    wfw(tdx?): Trefor Granite Quarry.
    Never used at Cwt-y-Bugail as too large to enter the adit.

(1) disused by 1953; sold as scrap in 1960.
(2) disused by 6/1964; sold as scrap after 4/1974 by 9/1977.
(3) gearbox sold to Mr P.Vallins, Reigate, Surrey, 4/1970
(4) purchased for preservation by Mr M.A.G.Jacob - removed to Manod Quarry 4/1974; to PenyrOrsedd Quarry 1/9/1976; and:
    wlw: Gloddfa Ganol (see OAKELEY SLATE QUARRY) 20/5/1978.

DENBIGH (GRAIG) LIMESTONE QUARRY   D2
(Cd/GR:054667)

```
                -       1873    : Robert Foulkes
        1873    -       c1927   : Denbigh Lime & Stone Co Ltd (reg.1873  £10K)
    by  1923                    : a subsidiary of Buxton Lime Firms Co Ltd
    by  3/1930                  : Ruthin & Denbigh Lime & Limestone Co
    by  1948                    : Ruthin & Denbigh Tar Macadam Co Ltd (and Cheshire
                                  & North Wales Tarred Macadam Co Ltd here also).
                -       c1967   : Denbigh Quarries Ltd - which became:
    by  7/1967  -       c1973   : Gwynedd Quarries Ltd
        c1973   -               : Tarmac Roadstone (Northern) Ltd;  Tarmac Ltd.
```

A private siding to this quarry from PR/15 existed by 1873; was disused by 6/1954 but track not lifted until 1970s. A narrow gauge line, which also existed by 1873 [J/CDH/1.2.1873/5c2, 4c4] operated from the quarry face to the kilns, and to a rail (later lorry) loading point; it was replaced by road vehicles after 6/1954 by 7/1960, and track removed.

Locomotives: Gauge 4'8½"

It has been said that a locomotive GLADSTONE 0-4-0ST was here in 1941, but no evidence has been found to confirm this.

```
                        0-4-0ST   OC   AE    1913   1923  New 4/23          (1)
LLOYD GEORGE            0-4-0ST   OC   HC     676   1905  (a)               (2)
```

Locomotive: Gauge 2'0"

```
                        4wDM   20hp   RH   192844   1938  (b)               (3)
```

(a) here by 6/1928. Was earlier for sale 6/1924 to 12/1924 (at least) by Maden & McKee, dealers, Liverpool.
     wfw: Ministry of Munitions, St.Helens, Lancs, in 1/1917 - variously referred to as
          CSD 1201 Sutton (Glassworks) Bond Works, and as CSD 34 Pocket Nook Works.
     This loco may have been the 4wc ST HC included in a 12/10/1920 sale of equipment at "Trafford Park and CSD 1201 St.Helens" [J/Surplus/1.10.1920].
(b) tdx: ?
     wfw: Baldry, Yerburgh & Hutchinson Ltd, contractors, Admiralty (c1938) Contract, Lyness, Hoy, Orkneys.

(1) wlw(tdt?): The Buxton Lime Firms Co Ltd, Tunstead, Derbyshire.
             (arrived Tunstead after 4/1925 by 7/1928)
(2) disused here 9/1936; not here 6/1954 - no further trace.
(3) here 6/1954; gone by 4/1964 - no further trace.

DINAS LLANWNDA RIVER AUTHORITY DEPOT, near CAERNARFON   D4
(Gc/GR:476585)

10/1950	-	10/1953	: North West Wales River Authority
10/1953	-	9/1964	: Gwynedd River Board
10/1964	-	3/1974	: Gwynedd River Authority
4/1974	-		: Welsh National Water Development Authority

A plant depot established at the former northern terminus of the Welsh Highland Railway (PR/44) using some of the WHR buildings. 2ft gauge railway equipment was used on various jobs throughout Gwynedd, usually river-bank protection works, and this equipment included the following locomotive which was stored at Dinas between jobs. The only job it is known to have been used on was "Towyn Riverworks c1963" - presumably a contract near Tywyn (Merioneth).

Locomotive: Gauge 2'0"

    -                        4wDM   20hp   RH   213834   1942   (a)   (1)

(a)   wfw(tdx?): Cardigan Agricultural Executive Committee, Ynyslas Yard, Borth, until 8/1949 at least.

(1)   sold to Mr M.A.G.Jacob for preservation and:
      tdt: Llanberis Lake Railway (PR/65), for storage only, 3/7/1975
      wlw: Gloddfa Ganol (see OAKELEY SLATE QUARRY).

DINMOR PARK LIMESTONE QUARRY, PENMON   D6
(Ga/GR:633815)

1/1910	-	c7/1925	: Dinmor Park Quarries Syndicate Ltd
			(reg.22/10/1903 liq.1926)
c7/1925	-	c4/1937	: Minerals Concentration Co Ltd
			(reg.7/10/1920 liq.1937-1958)
c4/1937	-		: Dinmor Quarries Ltd (in the Cawood Wharton Group by 1946)
		21/12/1984	: closed.

A small quarry on this site was closed by 1901. Re-started by DPQS who commenced paying wages 5/2/1910; quarry considerably enlarged to supply fluxing-stone to Glasgow steelworks. MCCL installed new railway system from 1926, initially horse-worked. Replaced by road vehicles 1966.
In 1968 part of quarry leased to JOHN HOWARD & CO (NORTHERN) LTD, who installed a new railway to obtain stone for construction of Seaforth Container Terminal, Liverpool Docks. This was short-lived, and all railtrack was removed in early 1970s.
By 1982 the quarry was owned by Steetley Construction Materials Ltd, using road vehicles only.

Locomotives: Gauge 3'0"

-		4wTG	VB	S	8085	1929	New 12/29	(1)
-		4wPM	20hp	FH	1799	1932	(a)	(2)
-		4wTG		FH	1847	1934	(b)	(3)
-	*	4wPM	20hp	MR	5342	1931	(c)	(4)
3	*	4wPM	20hp	MR	5236	1930	(d)	(4)
-		4wPM	20hp	MR	5461	1937	New (e)	(4)
-		4wDM	20hp	MR	9215	1946	New 6/46	(4)
-		4wDM	40hp	JF	3900011	1947	New 3/47	(5)

* later converted to diesel using engines purchased from G.W.Bungey, dealer, Hayes, Middlesex, 4/1946 and 6/1947.

Locomotives: Gauge 3'6" - JOHN HOWARD & CO (NORTHERN) LTD.

N860	HOWARD	0-6-0DE 165hp RH	384143	1955	(f)	(6)
	HOWARD	0-6-0DM 165hp RH	390775	1956	(f)	(6)

(a) arrived 19/8/1932 ex FH as 'New', but actually a rebuild by FH of an older MR (number unknown) loco.
(b) believed to be the only steam loco built by FH; consisted of a new chassis with secondhand boiler, cylinders etc from Foden No.11320, which was a 6-ton 3-way tipping road wagon supplied New 31/3/1924 to Hamilton Estates Ltd, Birkenhead, registration No. CM5323.
  [The registered office of MCCL was 8 Hamilton Square, Birkenhead]
  Loco delivered ex FH works to Dinmor 8/2/1934.
(c) tdx: purchased from Petrol Loco Hirers Ltd, Bedford, 1/1936
         (converted by PLH from 2'0" gauge for Dinmor)
(d) tdx: purchased from Petrol Loco Hirers Ltd, Bedford, 10/1936
    wfw: Thrapston Washed Sand & Ballast Co, Thrapston, Northants, 2ft gauge, until
         4/1936. (Converted to 3'0" gauge by PLH).
(e) arrived 4/1937; per MR records a "reconstructed" loco, but original serial number not known.
(f) tdx: Howards' Depot at Slough, Bucks, by 8/1968
         These locos had originally worked for Parkinson-Howard Ltd at Tema Harbour Contract, Ghana. After return to UK they were overhauled at Slough, using some components from RH 375719 (also ex Tema Harbour) and from RH 323606 (ex NCB Ellistown Colliery, Leicestershire).

(1) received extensive repairs at Dinmor 3/1946 but little used there-after; reputedly sold for scrap c1950 to "Lock of Menai".
(2) tdt: Flagstaff Quarry, after 11/1937 by 12/1947
(3) spare parts ordered up to 7/1939 then s/s; no further trace.
(4) tdt: Cattybrook Brick Co Ltd, Almondsbury, Glos, 12/1970
         per Madoc Jones, dealer, Denbigh.
(5) tdt: Alan Keef, dealer, Cote, Oxford, 20/9/1972
         per Madoc Jones, dealer, Denbigh.
    wlw: Cotswold Light Railway, South Cerney, Gloucestershire.
(6) not used after 7/1969 storm damaged the railway.
    Scrapped on site by merchant Murphy after 3/1971 by 10/1971

DINORBEN (TAN DINAS) LIMESTONE QUARRY, LLANDDONNA   D8
(Ga/GR:583820)

Prior to 1907		:	A small, insignificant, working
6/1907	- 7/1911	:	**Mersey Docks & Harbour Board**
by 5/1928	- 12/1928	:	**Dinorben Quarries Ltd**
by 3/1931	- 1956	:	**Tan Dinas Quarries Ltd**
from 1956		:	closed

Fitted out in 1907 with a new pier and 4'8½" gauge rail system, to obtain dump stone, but was not successful. Pier destroyed by a storm in 1915. By 1928 a new pier and 2ft gauge rail system was in existence (the sale 4/12/1928 included 900yds of track, 30 sets of points, 90 side tipping wagons) and this rail system survived until after final closure. Most of track removed in 1966.

Locomotives: Gauge 4'8½"

MDE 14	0-4-0ST	OC	AB	821	1899	(a)	(1)

(a)   purchased, by Mersey Docks & Harbour Board 1909, from T.H.Walker & Co, [? dealer, Liverpool] - presumably delivered direct to Dinorben.
    wfw: "J.Henderson" [? possibly Sharp, Henderson; dealers and loco repairers, Airdrie, Scotland] in 9/1906.
    wfw: A.H.Boyle, contractor, Larkhall, Scotland, until 2/1904 at least, and perhaps until his retirement sale 29/8/1907, which included plant lying at Sharp, Hendersons' yard.

(1)   tdt: Mersey Docks & Harbour Board, Liverpool, No.18, after 5/1911 by 7/1911.
    wlw: Cudworth & Johnson, dealers, Wrexham.

DINORWIC POWER STATION, LLANBERIS RIVER TUNNEL CONTRACT
D10
(Gc/GR:below)

    Contractor   : **"MBZ"** (McAlpine/Brand/Zschokke consortium)

To enable Llyn Peris (a natural lake) to be used as the lower reservoir of the CEGB Dinorwic Pumped Storage Hydro-Electric Generating Station (built within the disused Dinorwic Slate Quarry), a by-pass tunnel was built (GR:601584 to GR:586600) to contain the river which had hitherto flowed through the lake. A rail system was used within this tunnel during its construction 1976 to 3/1978. Excavated material was brought out at Central Adit (GR:593592), where the locomotives were stabled.

For other locomotives used in connection with the Power Station, see entries MARCHLYN MAWR RESERVOIR and STABLA CABLE CONTRACT.

Locomotives: Gauge 750mm

286	4wBE	SIG	706716	1976 New	(1)
287	4wBE	SIG	706717	1976 New	(1)
-	4wBE	[? GB]		(a)	(2)

(a)   tdx: ?, by 9/1977.
       wfw(?tdx): Bill Malcolm (Equipment) Ltd [a Company within the Edmund Nuttall group].

(1)   tdt: Edmund Nuttall Ltd, contractor, Meegate Water Scheme, Peebles, Scotland, 4/4/1978
(2)   tdt: ?, by 4/1978 [? also to Meegate].

DINORWIC SLATE QUARRIES, LLANBERIS   D12
                                                                                                                 (Gc)

c1750	-	1787	: various local men
1787	-	1809	: Dinorwic Slate Company
1809	-		: Dinorwic Quarry Company
	-	7/1969	: Dinorwic Slate Quarry Co Ltd
11/7/1969			: closed; dismantled.

THE QUARRIES developed, from initial separate small diggings near Dinorwig Village, on Elidir Mountain, into a single main unit comprising a number of adjacent quarries, plus a few separate quarries near-by. Initially the slates were lowered down the mountainside on sledges then carried on horseback to Caernarfon for shipment. The first iron rails were introduced in the quarries in 1811 [CRO/Porthyraur/30435].

PORT DINORWIC was a purpose-built shipment port first used in 1793; in 7/1824 work started on a tramroad to connect the Quarries to the Port. It came into use 10/1825, was 2ft gauge, horse-worked, and had rope-worked inclines within its route. This tramroad was replaced by the 4ft gauge Padarn Railway in 1843, being finally closed 7/1843. Many parts of its route can still be seen, particularly the inclines.

An extensive 2ft gauge railway system was established at Port Dinorwic; it is not known when the first locomotive was introduced here, but from 1898 orders were placed for locos specifically for Port duties, and thereafter the Port retained its own locomotive allocation unchanged for long periods. From 1898 to 1922 - HE 678 & 679; 1922 to 1936 - HE 1430; 1922 to 1963 - HE 1429; 1935 to 1945 - diesel A2; 1942 to 1961 - diesel A1; 1948 to 1962 - AB 1995. The latter loco never went to the Quarry, though all the others were sent there when no longer required at the Port.

The bulk of the 2ft gauge loco fleet was used within the quarries; from c1910 all engineering maintenance was done at the quarry workshops, Gilfachddu, Llanberis; and all boiler repairs (including the manufacture of replacement boilers) were done at the Port Dinorwic workshops.

The Padarn Railway closed 27/10/1961, slates then being despatched by road vehicles from Llanberis and the Port became largely disused. After final closure in 1969, the Quarry Workshops became a Museum (see WELSH SLATE CENTRE); a Power Station was built within the main quarry (see DINORWIC POWER STATION), and a portion of the Padarn Railway route became the Llanberis Lake Railway (see PR/65 - Section 2).

[Read: B/147; B/177; B/148; B/149; J/FRS/No.15/14; etc etc]

PADARN RAILWAY : 1843-1961
Llanberis Gilfachddu to Y Felinheli (Port Dinorwic)   - 6½ miles.

Locomotives: Gauge 4'0"

FIRE QUEEN	0-4-0	OC	AH		1848	New (*)	(p1)
JENNY LIND	0-4-0	OC	AH		1848	New (*) Scr/1886	
DINORWIC	0-6-0T	OC	HE	302	1882	New 12/82	(p2)
AMALTHAEA (f.PANDORA *)	0-6-0T	OC	HE	410	1886	New 11/86	(p2)
VELINHELI	0-6-0T	OC	HE	631	1895	New 7/95	(p3)
-	4wPM 55hp	HRM		954	1925	New	(p4)

(*) loco PANDORA renamed AMALTHAEA 5/1909.
     loco FIRE QUEEN delivered by sea to Caernarfon; landed there 16/8/1848 then by road to Llanberis.
     loco JENNY LIND was noted at Caernarfon harbour 25/9/1848.

(p1) Wdn/1882; stored at Gilfachddu until
     tdt: Penrhyn Castle Museum, Bangor, 17/12/1969.
(p2) Scr 8/1963 at Gilfachddu by Pittrail Ltd.
(p3) Dismantled for repairs 11/1953; never reassembled; most components Scr 4/1963 at Gilfachddu by Pittrail Ltd.
(p4) Scr 4/1963 at Gilfachddu by Pittrail Ltd.

LLANBERIS QUARRIES and PORT DINORWIC

Locomotives: Gauge 1'10¾"

CHARLIE f.DINORWIC	0-4-0ST	OC	HE		51	1870	New 10/70	(1)
HARRIET	0-4-0VBT					c1874	(a)	(2)
PERIS	0-4-0VBT	VC	[?HH]			c1875	(b)	(3)
VICTORIA						c1876	(c)	(3)
WELLINGTON	0-4-0VBT	VC	DeW			1877	New	(4)
GEORGE	0-4-0ST	OC	HE		184	1877	New 4/77	(5)
LOUISA	0-4-0ST	OC	HE		195	1877	New 11/77	(6)
VELINHELI	0-4-0ST	OC	HE	±	409	1886	New 10/86	(7)
KING OF THE SCARLETS f.ALICE	0-4-0ST	OC	HE	±	492	1889	New 11/89	(8)
RED DAMSEL f.ENID	0-4-0ST	OC	HE		493	1889	New 11/89	(9)
ROUGH PUP f.No.1	0-4-0ST	OC	HE		541	1891	New 6/91	(10)
CLOISTER f.No.2	0-4-0ST	OC	HE		542	1891	New 8/91	(11)

JERRY M f.VAENOL	0-4-0ST	OC	HE	638	1895	New 9/95		(12)
CACKLER f.PORT DINORWIC	0-4-0ST	OC	HE	671	1898	New 5/98		(13)
BERNSTEIN f.THE FIRST	0-4-0ST	OC	HE	678	1898	New 8/98		(14)
GEORGE B f.WELLINGTON	0-4-0ST	OC	HE	680	1898	New 10/98		(15)
COVERTCOAT f.THE SECOND	0-4-0ST	OC	HE	679	1898	New 11/98		(16)
HOLY WAR f.No.3	0-4-0ST	OC	HE	779	1902	New 6/02		(17)
ALICE f.No.4	0-4-0ST	OC	HE	780	1902	New 6/02		(18)
MAID MARIAN f.No.5	0-4-0ST	OC	HE	± 822	1903	New 10/03		(19)
IRISH MAIL f.No.6	0-4-0ST	OC	HE	823	1903	New 11/03		(20)
WILD ASTER f.No.7	0-4-0ST	OC	HE	849	1904	New 6/04		(21)
SYBIL	0-4-0ST	OC	WB	1760	1906	New 5/06		(22)
LADY MADCAP f.ELIDIR	0-4-0ST	OC	HE	652	1896	(d)		(23)
No.1 f.LADY JOAN f.No.1	0-4-0ST	OC	HE	1429	1922	New 8/22		(24)
DOLBADARN f.No.2	0-4-0ST	OC	HE	1430	1922	New 8/22		(25)
MICHAEL	0-4-0ST	OC	HE	1709	1932	New 9/32		(8)
A2	4wDM	30hp	RH	175987	1935	New 10/35		(26)
A1	4wDM	30hp	RH	181807	1936	New 12/36		(27)
-	4wPM	10hp	L	28068	1946	New 1/46		(28)
C1 No.1	4wDM	20hp	FH	2782	1944	New 5/46*		(29)
C2 No.2	4wDM	20hp	FH	2792	1944	New 5/46*		(29)
C3 No.3	4wDM	20hp	FH	2791	1944	New 5/46*		(29)
B2	4wDM	30hp	RH	246809	1947	New 3/47		(30)
B1	4wDM	30hp	RH	252799	1947	New 4/47		(31)
E1	4wDM	20hp	RH	211598	1941	(e)		(32)
E2	4wDM	20hp	RH	211620	1941	(f)		(33)
-	0-4-0WT	OC	AB	1995	1931	(g)		(34)
ELIDIR	0-4-0T	OC	AE	2071	1933	(h)		(35)
D1	4wDM	30hp	RH	277265	1949	New 4/49		(36)
D2	4wDM	30hp	RH	273854	1949	New 7/49		(30)
D3	4wDM	30hp	RH	277269	1949	New 7/49		(37)
E3	4wDM	20hp	RH	186322	1937	(i)		(30)
E4	4wDM	20hp	RH	186342	1937	(j)		(37)
E5	4wDM	20hp	RH	191645	1938	(k)		(33)
E6	4wDM	20hp	RH	191661	1938	(m)		(37)
E7	4wDM	20hp	RH	221605	1943	(n)		(37)
E8	4wDM	20hp	RH	203009	1941	(o)		(30)
E9	4wDM	20hp	RH	235704	1945	(p)		(37)
E10	4wDM	20hp	RH	202979	1940	(q)		(37)
E11 74	4wDM	20hp	RH	222081	1943	(r)		(30)

NOTES: Re-named locos : HE 51 DINORWIC renamed CHARLIE after 1/1877 by 9/1892. Other HE locos renamed at various dates in 1920s, except HE 1429 renamed LADY JOAN in 1930s and reverted to No.1 (when this lady fell from grace) after 10/1947 by 10/1953; and HE 1430 was renamed DOLBADARN on 23/11/1946.
In latter years, certain diesel locos carried incorrect numbers due to components being exchanged during overhauls.

±HE locos 409, 492, 493, 541, 542, 680, 779 to 849 were of similar design, known at Dinorwic as the "Alice Class". Of these, 409 to 542 had 'old type' frames which can be recognised by the taper-shaped cut-out beneath the cab; the remainder had 'new type' frames in which this cut-out was of parallel form.   HE 822 (later MAID MARIAN) was originally delivered with a central dome on the boiler (the other Alice Class locos lacking this feature) for duty on the steeply graded tramroad between Steam Mills and Allt Ddu. In later years MAID MARIAN inherited 'old type' frames and later a dome-less boiler. HE 492 (KING OF THE SCARLETS) was latterly running on 'new type' frames; but it cannot, however, be safely assumed that a 'straight swop' took place between HE 492 and 822, as former quarry staff have recalled many such exchanges of identities, of which no records seem to have survived. The boiler with dome, from HE 822, was later (and [1990] is still) fitted to HE 409 (VELINHELI). The quarry had more boilers than locos; these were numbered in a separate series for insurance purposes; locos developing a boiler fault received another boiler from the stock. In 1952, HE 1430 (DOLBADARN) was altered to enable it also to use boilers from this pool, and its appearance was considerably changed. With the general interchange of all components that is readily evidenced by the assortment of stamped numbers that could be found on these locos in later years, the true identity of any loco is now somewhat hypothetical. The listing above, therefore, is based on the false presumption that all locos are 'genuine'.

HE 51, 184, 542 and 638 were larger locos designed for trip-working between the incline foot at Hafod Owen and the Padarn Railway terminal at Gilfach Ddu. HE 195 was a small loco intended for use on light rails but found to be underpowered. HE 652 was purchased second-hand; it also had a dome, and was therefore suitable for use on the Allt Ddu tramroad, where it remained for most of its life.

The remaining Hunslets - 678, 679, 1429, 1430, and 1709 were "Port Class" locos, fitted with full-depth buffer beams ideal for use at Port Dinorwic, but unsuitable for passing the change of grade at the foot of quarry inclines. 1709 was, however, ordered for the quarry, the wrong type of chassis being specified by mistake.

Enclosed cabs were unsuitable for use in many parts of the quarries, due to restricted headroom in tunnels. All 'Alice Class' locos were supplied New without cabs except HE 823; but the upper half of this cab, and the upper halves of the cabs of 'Port Class' locos when they were transferred to quarry duties, were removed and stored at Gilfach Ddu workshops.

*C1, C2, C3 were Hibberd 'Planet Simplex' locos delivered 5/1946 as "new", but had in fact been supplied 1-2/1944 to the Ministry of Supply, repurchased by FH 5/1946 and reconditioned for resale.
Although of 'Motor Rail Simplex Bow-frame type', they were built New by FH in 1943, rather than being renewals of earlier MR locos.

(a) probably New; cost £350; boiler tubes 2'10" long.
(b) probably New; cost £360. John Beatson, dealer, of Derby supplied an 'engine' to 'Llanberis' in 1875, and this loco is a possible candidate. Beatson was a regular supplier of goods to Dinorwic from as early as 1870 [CRO/DQ/1715 etc].
(c) probably New; cost £220 hence maybe a small, single-cylinder loco.
(d) tdx: HE, Leeds, 5/10/1910; "Rebuilt HE 1910", which included alteration of gauge from 2'0".
wfw: Groby Granite Co Ltd, Leicestershire, named SEXTUS.
(e) tdx: ?, 12/1947.
wfw: Ministry of Supply.
(f) tdx: ?, 12/1947
wfw: Ministry of Supply (used at New Haden Colliery, Staffs.)
(g) tdx: Raisby Quarries Ltd, Co.Durham, No.70, /1948 by 7/1948
(h) tdx: Blythe & Sons (Birtley) Ltd, Co.Durham
per or via R.R.Dunn, dealer, Bishop Auckland.
Arrived Port Dinorwic 7/1948; gauge altered from 2'0" and sent to Dinorwic Quarry 7/1949; into service there 13/10/1949 but name ELIDIR not fitted until after 7/1950.

(i) from (tdx?): G.W.Bungey Ltd, dealer, Hayes, Middlesex, 21/7/1950
 wfw: A.M.Coke, Sleaford, Lincs, to 1/1949 at least.
 wfw: Durham County Council, Middleton St.George Slag Works.
(j) from (tdx?): G.W.Bungey Ltd, dealer, Hayes, Middlesex, 17/8/1950
 wfw: Durham County Council, Middleton St.George Slag Works.
(k) tdx: G.W.Bungey Ltd, dealer, Hayes, Middlesex, 16/11/1950
 wfw: Ministry of War Transport, by 3/1943 until 5/1948 at least.
 wfw: Chas.Brand & Sons Ltd, contractor, ROF 36 Bridgwater, by 9/1940 to 5/1942 at least.
(m) tdx: G.W.Bungey Ltd, dealer, Hayes, Middlesex, 16/11/1950
 wfw: Ministry of War Transport - at Feltwell Fen, Norfolk, 10/1942
 wfw: Chas.Brand & Sons Ltd, contractor, ROF 36 Bridgwater, by 10/1940 to 6/1942 at least.
(n) from (tdx?): George Cohen, Sons & Co Ltd, dealer, 4/4/1952
 wfw: Ministry of Supply (stock loco, never used).
(o) from (tdx?): George Cohen, Sons & Co Ltd, dealer, 4/4/1952
 wfw: Ministry of Supply (stock loco, probably never used).
(p) tdx: Minera Lime Works, 20/6/1956
(q) tdx: Minera Lime Works, 22/6/1956
(r) from (tdx?): G.W.Bungey Ltd, dealer, Hounslow, Middlesex, 11/6/1957
 wfw: Ministry of Supply - probably never used but carried number '74' on arrival
 [? auction lot number].

NOTE: locos shown above as "from" were purchased from the supplier shown, but may have come direct from (ie, "tdx") another owners' premises.

(1) advertised for sale by S.Fletcher, dealer, Haley Hill, Halifax, 9/1919 to 12/1923 at least, but remained at Llanberis unsold until 8/1935 (at least); Scrapped [c1936 ?].
(2) s/s after 10/1892 by 6/1899
(3) s/s by 6/1899
(4) tdt: Glynrhonwy Slate Quarry [see LLANBERIS WEST] after 1895 by 19/3/1898
(5) advertised for sale by S.Fletcher, dealer, Haley Hill, Halifax, 9/1919
 wlw: Cothercott Mining Co, Pulverbatch, Salop, by 7/1920
  [where it was named MINSTREL PARK and scrapped c1942]
(6) tdt: Glynrhonwy Slate Quarry [see LLANBERIS WEST] after 1895 by 6/1899
(7) OOU 9/1962;
 tdt: Mr J.A.Evans 7/1/1969 (private store at Exeter, Devon, later at Launceston, Cornwall)
(8) OOU 1/1962;
 tdt: Mr Charles Matthews, Thornhill, Toronto, Canada, via Liverpool, 6/1965
(9) OOU 9/1957; auctioned 13/12/1969 and:
 tdt: Llanberis Lake Railway (PR/65); No.1 ELIDIR.
(10) OOU by 1960;
 tdt: Tywyn Museum 15/6/1968
(11) OOU 4/1959;
 tdt: Mr N.C.U.Corbett, Hampshire Narrow Gauge Railway Society, Durley, Hants, 4/8/1962
(12) tdt: Mr J.M.Baldock, Hollycombe House, Liphook, Sussex, 20/4/1967
(13) OOU 8/1959;
 tdt: Mr D.C.Potter, Yaxham, Norfolk, 30/3/1966
 wlw: Mr G.T.Cushing, Thursford, Norfolk, by 8/1978

(14) OOU by 9/1966;
    tdt: Mr J.M.Morris, Lytham, Lancs, 7/1967
    wlw: Bala Lake Railway (PR/66).
(15) tdt: Mr A.C.White, Dowty Railway Society, Ashchurch, Glos, 10/1965
(16) OOU 10/1959;
    tdt: Mr J.L.Butler, Ripley, Surrey, 11/12/1964
    wlw: Launceston Steam Railway, Cornwall.
(17) OOU 11/1967;
    tdt: Mr J.M.Hutchings, Quainton Road, Bucks, 20/3/1970
    wlw: Bala Lake Railway (PR/66).
(18) OOU 2/1961;
    tdt: West Lancashire Light Railway, Hesketh Bank, Lancs, 22/11/1972
    wlw: Bala Lake Railway (PR/66) (chassis only).
(19) OOU by 9/1966; purchased by Maid Marian Locomotive Fund and:
    tdt: Bressingham Gardens, Diss, Norfolk, 3/5/1968
    wlw: Llanberis Lake Railway (PR/65) and Bala Lake Railway (PR/66).
(20) OOU 9/1954; Dismantled 7/1959; chassis auctioned 13/12/1969 and:
    tdt: West Lancashire Light Railway, Hesketh Bank, Lancs, 18/12/1969
    (and later fitted with boiler etc. of ALICE HE 780).
(21) OOU by 1962; Dismantled 2/1962; components auctioned 13/12/1969 and:
    tdt: Llanberis Lake Railway (PR/65)
(22) OOU by 1961;
    tdt: Mr J.A.Evans 7/1/1969 (private store at Exeter, Devon; later Launceston, Cornwall).
(23) OOU 24/3/1952; Dismantled; chassis cut up 1968 and removed 7/1969.
(24) sold to Mr T.L.Barber;
    tdt: Gower's of Bedford 2/2/1968 for overhaul
    then used in 1968 at Woburn Abbey Railway, Bedfordshire.
(25) OOU 26/5/1967; auctioned 13/12/1969 and:
    tdt: Llanberis Lake Railway (PR/65)
(26) OOU after 8/1965 by 7/1967; sold as scrap 3/1968
(27) OOU 31/1/1964; sold as scrap 3/1968
(28) used only on light rails at Allt Ddu Quarry Mills; OOU 4/1954 when work there ceased.
    Stored at Gilfach Ddu until sold as scrap 3/1968
(29) sold as scrap 3/1968
(30) auctioned 13/12/1969 and sold to R.N.Bradbury, dealer, New Haden Works, Draycott, Staffs;
    tdt: New Haden Works c20/12/1969 and later scrapped there.
(31) dismantled 6/1964; chassis sold as scrap [? c4/1970].
(32) dismantled by 1967; chassis sold as scrap 3/1968.
(33) auctioned 13/12/1969 as and where lying on Harriet Gallery (A4B);
    purchased by R.N.Bradbury, dealer, but not collected.
    Remained derelict at Harriet until scrapped there c10/1977.
(34) from Port Dinorwic tdt: Mr N.C.U.Corbett, c/o Hampshire Narrow Gauge Railway Society, 4/8/1962.
    wlw: Mr J.M.Baldock, Hollycombe House, Liphook, Sussex, from c5/1967
    named No.1 CALEDONIA.
(35) OOU 20/4/1959; despatched 20/7/1966 to Bootle for shipment to:
    York Locomotive Society, York Road Depot, Bolton, Toronto, Canada.
(36) auctioned 13/12/1969;
    tdt: Llanberis Lake Railway (PR/65).
(37) as footnote (30) but moved to New Haden on 16/12/1969.

DOLGARROG ALUMINIUM WORKS and ASSOCIATED RAILWAYS   D14
(Gc/GR:below)

The first significant industrial railway in the Dolgarrog area was built 1852-1853 to connect the ARDDA IRON-SULPHIDE MINE (GR:760659) to a roadside yard (GR:774663) near the Newborough Arms. This narrow-gauge line, built by/for the Ardda Sulphur Mine Co (Messrs Brodie & Hunt) was horse-worked from the mine to the head of two consecutive inclines which descended to the valley floor. It was short-lived, the materials being dismantled and sold by auction 3/1864. Much of the route can be traced today [1991]. [CRO/Glynllifon/514 etc; UCNW/Tynygongl/585 etc; J/CDH/12.3.1864]

Concurrently, the CWM EIGIAU (GR:702635) and CEDRYN (GR:718636) SLATE QUARRIES were being developed in the mountains, close to Llyn Eigiau and some miles west of the Ardda mine. In 8/1861, the Mostyn Estate Office invited tenders for the construction of a 5 miles long tramroad, "for H.E.Sullivan" (the then lessee of the Cwm Eigiau Quarry), from the Cwm Eigiau Quarry to the river Conwy at Dolgarrog. The line was to include a 600 yard incline down into the valley, with a bridge under the turnpike road [J/CDH/17.8.1861]. The line was not built at this time, except perhaps for the 1 ¼ miles or so from Cwm Eigiau quarry to a point near Cedryn quarry.

In 3/1863, W.A.Darbishire (lessee at Cedryn) invited tenders for the construction of much the same tramroad, but only from Cedryn to Dolgarrog [J/CDH/14.3.1863/4]; this time the line was proceeded with. When the Caedryn Slate Quarry Co Ltd issued its prospectus in 1864 it stated that the tramroad, 4¾ miles long, was complete [J/MJ/1864/457]; later that year, the British Slate Co Ltd (having taken over Cwm Eigiau quarry) stated that the agreement for connecting that quarry to the tramroad was imminent [J/MJ/3.9.1864/623] and, by 1/1865, having taken over Cedryn Quarry also, British Slate now issued a new prospectus advising that the tramroad was nearly 7 miles long and recently built at a cost of £8000, connecting both quarries to the river [J/MJ/21.1.1865/40]; though at a shareholders meeting 1/9/1865 the directors admitted that the tramroad from Cedryn to Cwm Eigiau had just "been re-laid" and that the line was now in working order [J/MJ/2.9.1865/577]. When the Caerhun Slate Co Ltd was floated in 12/1865, to lease and work part of the Cwm Eigiau quarry (as sub-lessees of British Slate), its prospectus [J/MJ/1865/771] included the statement that the company would be able to use the "tramroad already completed" to "the shipping port". Clearly both the length of the tramroad, and its precise opening date/s, are matters of question; however, the single incline down into Dolgarrog had in fact been built as three consecutive inlines, a fourth incline was included at Pwlldu part way along the route, and the turnpike road was crossed on the level rather than bridged. Archives refer to horse operation of the tramroad, and it is very unlikely that any locomotives were used.

When Cedryn Quarry was sold ("under powers of distress") 2/3/1881, the advertisement [J/CDH/26.2.1881/1] listed "About Eight Miles of Single Tram Railway of Bridge and Trails [sic - ? T-rails] 16lbs to the yard, 2 feet 3 inch guage [sic] with iron chairs....incline drums, rollers....43 Iron Box Waggons....". The gauge is certainly wrong; all other references quote 2ft, and sleepers found in 1961 confirm this. Presumably the tramroad survived, as an 1889 sale catalogue of the Cwm Eigiau quarry refers to it as then still existing; probably it was dismantled after this sale, as the tracks had gone by 1907.

In the early 1890s, the Conway & Colwyn Bay Joint Water Board planned to convert Llyn Cowlyd into a drinking water reservoir, the work being done by contractor Thomas Bugbird 1893-1896. To raise materials up from the valley, Bugbird built a water-balanced railway incline on the route of the former Ardda Mine tramroad inclines, but used sledges and other land vehicles from the incline head to the lake. When his equipment was sold at Llanrwst 23/2/1897 the advertisement did not mention any locomotives [J/CDH/12.2.1897]. Incidentally, a point (GR:774662) very close to the lower terminus of the Ardda/Bugbird incline was later to be the base of another, much shorter, incline - which climbed south-westerly for c200 yards to reach a Chlorination House of the Conway & Colwyn Bay Joint Water Supply Board. Built in 1940, this 2ft gauge rope-worked line was disused by 4/1967 and dismantled by 1979.

A consequential contract arising from the "Bugbird" Cowlyd job was the laying of 8½ miles of water main along the east bank of the Conwy, from Dolgarrog to Sarn Mynach (near Llandudno Junction). This work was done 11/1907-3/1909 by contractor Wm.Underwood & Brother (of Dukinfield, Cheshire). Underwoods handled many such jobs, and often used 2ft gauge locomotive operated temporary railways; though no evidence has yet been found to confirm that they used rail transport on this pipeline.

Construction of the Dolgarrog Aluminium Works commenced in 1907, and included a hydro-electric power station for which a reservoir was built at Llyn Eigiau. For this work, a single-track incline was built up from Dolgarrog generally on the route of the Eigiau/Cedryn Tramroad inclines, from the summit of which a 4'8½" gauge temporary railway was laid 3½ miles to Llyn Eigiau generally, though not entirely, on the old tramroad route. At the reservoir, some 2ft and 1'3" gauge rope-hauled railways were also used. On eventual completion of the ¾ mile long Eigiau Dam, all these railways were dismantled, with the exception of the Dolgarrog incline - retained by Aluminium Corporation Ltd for future maintenance works. The route from incline-head to Llyn Eigiau became a rough road.

The Aluminium Works was originally connected to a quay on the river Conwy by a 2ft gauge railway, built in 9/1910, on which the trucks were hauled by an endless rope. This line was duplicated (but not replaced) by a parallel canal c1913. It connected with a hand-worked system, laid out within the Factory, which remained in use until the 1930s, with some tracks still visible in the 1950s [B/420/136].

To increase the supply of water to Llyn Eigiau, a tunnel was built from its most northerly point to reach the river Dulyn in the next valley to the north. The tunnel itself is c1200 yards long, but, apart from the facts that it was started in 1914, completed in 1916, and that a narrow gauge railway was used through it during construction, little else is yet known about it [B/420/66].

In 5/1907 A.C.Ltd applied for permission to build a 4'8½" gauge "Abbey, Dolgarrog & Trefriw Light Railway", to run from the LNWR (PR/23) (junction at the site of the later Dolgarrog Station), across the river and so to the Works, then southwards to the town of Trefriw [PRO/Kew/MT /54/507, /513]. In 11/1907 the application was revised; the line was now to be a 2ft gauge electric railway [possibly to use surplus locomotives ordered by the Portmadoc, Beddgelert & South Snowdon Rly (PR/44) which A.C.Ltd currently owned]. Permission to build this line was granted in 1908, but no work was done. The Board of Trade confirmed permission by "The Dolgarrog Light Railway Order 1910"; still nothing was done. Some of the delay was caused by a stillborn "Conway Valley Light Railway" scheme, promoted in 1911 as a 4'8½" gauge line to run west of the river, from Conwy to Llanrwst. Eventually, in 1916, revised powers were applied for by A.C.Ltd [J/CJ/19.7.1916] and a 4'8½" gauge line was built from PR/23, via a new river bridge, to the Works. Opened 17/12/1916, it was 1¼ miles long, and traffic included workmens' passenger trains until c1932. Freight traffic ceased c1960; the track was lifted in 1963 and the rails went to the Welsh Highland Railway (PR/44) for re-use. The remainder of the original scheme, for a line to Trefriw from the Works, was never built.

As recited above, the Dolgarrog incline was retained, and in 1917 A.C.Ltd built a new 2ft gauge railway from incline-top to Llyn Cowlyd, where Bugbird's reservoir was now to be enlarged and thus provide a further supply for the power station. This work was initially tackled by A.C.Ltd direct labour without much progress; in 2/1919 the Contract was given to McAlpine. Stone for enlarging the dam was obtained from a quarry above the dam, and lowered down a 2ft gauge incline the site of which can still [1990] be seen. Apart from making use of the 2ft gauge access railway, McAlpine used 3ft gauge equipment at the reservoir, and made use of the 4'8½" gauge Factory Railway - thus having locomotives of three different gauges on the Contract. After completion in 12/1921, the Cowlyd Railway was retained for maintenance purposes until 8/1968.

After Cowlyd, McAlpines were soon to return to Dolgarrog; firstly to do work in the valley clearing land for housing and improving the main road (using 3ft gauge locomotives on temporary railways), and secondly to construct the Coedty Reservoir (close to the head of the incline) plus associated leats (where they used 2ft gauge locos, again on temporary railways. The southbound (Afon Ddu) leat included a 400 yard tunnel between incline-top and Ardda which was probably the site where the first two McAlpine battery locos were originally employed.

On 2/11/1925 the Eigiau Dam burst, washing rocks and silt down into the valley, destroying much of the northern end of Dolgarrog community and inundating the power station and the aluminium works. A further contract was quickly arranged with McAlpine, who laid temporary extensions to the Works railway and provided locomotives to carry the debris to tipping grounds near the river bridge. It was decided not to repair the dam, but to build a tunnel through the intervening mountain from Eigiau to Cowlyd, thus adding the Eigiau watershed to the Cowlyd sources. Again McAlpine got the job, using 2ft gauge locomotives during tunnel construction.

At some date prior to this, A.C.Ltd had opened a quarry at Porth Llwyd (GR:c778677) to obtain stone for their housing sites and similar works. Stone left the quarry by narrow-gauge railway, to reach a substantial roadside staith [photo: B/420/114] for transfer to road vehicles. No references have been found as to the possible use of locomotives on this line. The quarry and much of its railway was destroyed by the flood.

In 1936, the open watercourses which conveyed outflow from Cowlyd to near incline-head were replaced by a pressure pipeline. For this work, the contractors J.L.Eve made extensive use of the Cowlyd Railway, with their own fleet of locos brought in for the job. In subsequent years, other contractors attending to this pipeline made some use of the railway.

In 1955-1957, contractors John Laing built a c3 mile extension to a short leat which entered Coedty reservoir from the north-east. The temporary railway that they used along the route of the leat during this work was worked by locomotives.

After the lifting of the 4'8½" gauge line from PR/23 to the Factory in 1963, only the 2ft gauge Cowlyd Railway remained. Following a serious derailment 8/1968, the CEGB decided it was too worn out for further use. Alternative access was obtained by mountain road from Trefriw; the railway lay moribund until track removal was completed in 8/1984.

There are now no railways at Dolgarrog.

[Read: J/NG/No.86; B/177; B/420]

CWM EIGIAU SLATE QUARRY (Gc/GR:702635)

			: Bulkeley Estate
1827	-		: **James Rigby** [Hawarden] et al
by 1853	-	11/1856	: **Cwm Eigia Quarry Slate & Slab Co** [E.Pearson et al]
11/1856	-	8/1858	: **Cwm Eigia Quarry Slate & Slab Co Ltd**
			(reg.3/11/1856 liq.8/1858-10/1859)
by 8/1861	-		: H.E.Sullivan - **Cwm Eigiau Slate Co** [lease 6/9/61]
4/1864	-		: **British Slate Co Ltd** [lease signed 1/7/1865]
			(reg.18/9/1860 £75K-£25K liq.5/1874-1/1876)
c1/1866	-		: Part subleased to **Caerhun Slate Co Ltd**
			(reg.c12/1865 £30K liq.)
by 1870			: quarry is disused
7/1874	-		: 50 ex-Dinorwic men start work here [for ??]
			[J/CDH/18.7.1874/8c4]

```
    c4/1875   -                  : Caedryn & Cwm Eigiau Slate Co Ltd
                                   (reg.29/4/1875 liq.by BoT 17/7/1885)
                  1889          : dispersal auction; dismantled.
```

CEDRYN (CAEDRYN) SLATE QUARRY   (Gc/GR:718636)
```
                                : Newborough Estate
    c1827     -   c1832         : Samuel Holland Jnr.
    c1832     -                 : Mr ?? [of Ruthin]
                  6/1845        : for sale
    9/1862    -   12/1862       : W.A.Darbishire, Rch.Griffiths et al who formed:
    1/1863    -   12/1864       : Caedryn Slate Quarry Co Ltd
                                   (reg.31/1/1863 to buy lease dated 31/12/1862  £50K vol.liq.1865-68)
    12/1864   -   pre 1870      : British Slate Co Ltd [see Cwm Eigiau above]
    c4/1875   -   pre 1881      : Caedryn & Cwm Eigiau Slate Co Ltd
                                   (reg.29/4/1875 liq.by BoT 17/7/1885)
                  2/1881        : dispersal auction; dismantled.
```

ALUMINIUM WORKS   (Gc/GR:772675)
```
    4/1907    -   12/1908       : Aluminium Corporation Ltd
                                   (reg.10/4/1907 £500K liq.12/1908)
    12/1909   -                 : Aluminium Corporation Ltd
                                   (reg.14/12/1909 £500K)
```

POWER STATION   (Gc/GR:770675)
```
    4/1907    -   6/1929        : Aluminium Corporations, as above.
```
In 1918 ACLtd purchased a controlling interest in North Wales Power & Traction Co Ltd (reg.30/7/1903) which became North Wales Power Co Ltd 6/1922.
Dolgarrog Power Station was sold by ACLtd to:-
```
    7/1929    -   3/1948        : North Wales Power Co Ltd
    4/1948    -   3/1955        : British Electricity Authority
    4/1955    -   12/1957       : Central Electricity Authority
    1/1958    -                 : Central Electricity Generating Board
```

EIGIAU RESERVOIR CONSTRUCTION CONTRACT (6/1907-10/1908; 1910-1911)

Bott & Stennett Ltd (reg.4/1906), contractors.

J/Electrical Review/6.11.1908 refers to five locomotives having been hauled up the Dolgarrog Incline for use on this job. If true, one loco is missing from the list below - possibly two in fact, as UXBRIDGE is seemingly accounted for at Cleobury Mortimer during this initial period.

Whilst the HC archives are unclear, their loco LILY 0-6-0ST IC 12x18 HC 621/1902 was despatched New to Bott & Stennett at Harrow, Middlesex, for use on the Harrow-Uxbridge Metropolitan Railway Contract, but loco was intended for "New Pandora Mining Syndicate Ltd": this can hardly be strictly true, as NPMS Ltd was not registered until 10/12/1908, though perhaps the Syndicate did use the title informally prior to registration. NPMS Ltd was interested in the Willoughby Lead Mine (which see) just a few miles from Dolgarrog and, perhaps significantly, a G.N.Dixon auction of 3/1912 embraced both plant of NPMS Ltd lying at Trefriw and plant including locos of Bott & Stennett lying at Dolgarrog. Incidentally, LILY is also recorded as having worked on the Cleobury Mortimer (1/1907-6/1908) Contract, and was lying there for sale 4/1911 to 3/1912 at least. Also, MW archives note 0-4-0ST OC MW 634 1877 as sometime with "Bott & Stennett, Talycafn", but loco apparently accounted for elsewhere so a clerical error for MW 684 is suspected here.

The Eigiau Contract was interrupted by the failure of the first Aluminium Corporation, from 10/1908 to 1910. Work was at a standstill, and it has been claimed that some of the Bott Stennett railway was removed from the site during the interlude. Perhaps, therefore, a loco or locos were also removed for use at Cleobury Mortimer - and later returned ?

Locomotives: Gauge 4'8½" - Bott & Stennett Ltd

INCE	0-4-0ST	OC	HE	425	1887		
		rebuilt	HE		1901	(a)	(1)
LUCERO	0-6-0T	IC	MW	1098	1888	(b)	(2)
GORDON	0-6-0ST	IC	MW Ø	684	1878		
		rebuilt	MW		1894	(b)	(3)
UXBRIDGE	0-6-0ST	IC	HE	761	1902	(c)	(4)

Ø   identity '684/1878' not definitely confirmed, but very likely.

(a)   wfw: Bott & Stennett, Harrow-Uxbridge (1901-1904) Metropolitan Railway Contract.
       wfw: HE, who sold loco [to B&S ?] 5/1901, after rebuild
       wfw: H.M.Nowell, contractor, who sold loco to HE in 1900.
(b)   wfw: Bott & Stennett, Harrow-Uxbridge (1901-1904) Metropolitan Railway Contract.
(c)   wfw: Bott & Stennett, Harrow-Uxbridge (1901-1904) Metropolitan Railway Contract;
       and was used by Bott & Stennett on the Cleobury Mortimer-Ditton Priors Light Rly (1/1907-6/1908) Contract either prior to, or during, its use at Llyn Eigiau.

(1)   tdt: Thomas Mitchell & Sons Ltd, dealer, Bolton, Lancs, 2/1912
         Used then as hire loco (including to Electrolytic Alkali Co, Middlewich, Cheshire 11/1912-c2/1913) until sold to Director of War Materials, The War Office, 2/1918;
         wlw: G.Trollope & Sons & Colls & Sons Ltd, Oldham Aircraft Factory Contract, by 7/1918
(2)   for sale at Dolgarrog 27/6/1911; 8/1911; 27/3/1912;
         for sale by Thos.W.Ward Ltd, dealer, Sheffield, by 5/1916
         wlw: Blackwell Colliery Co Ltd, Alfreton, Derbyshire, c1920 (by 10/1927 certain).
(3)   for sale at Dolgarrog 17/6/1911; 8/1911; 27/3/1912
         [?wlw: Eskett Lime Co, Cumberland ?
(4)   for sale at Dolgarrog 17/6/1911; 8/1911 - perhaps then sold, as "hire of road wheels" invoiced by HE to Bott & Stennett Ltd, Ditton Priors office, 9/1911, and loco:
         wlw: Holme & King Ltd, Stone Yard Depot, Lower Ince, Wigan, by 4/10/1911 (and repaired/overhauled here).
         wlw: Holme & King Ltd, Coventry Loop Line (1911-1914) Contract, by 30/4/1912 (hire of road wheels at Coventry on this date).
         Holme & King bankrupt c1913 and Loop Line job taken by John Wilson & Sons of Birmingham.
         wlw: John Wilson & Sons, Loop Line Contract [spares orders 9/10/1913, 29/11/1913]. loco "property of LNWR" in end-of-contract sale 23/6/1914 [J/MM/19.6.1914 etc]
         wlw: Geo.Trollope & Sons & Colls & Sons Ltd, Brocton Camp (1915-1917) Contract, Staffs, by 7/1915 to 11/1915 at least.
         wlw: John Wilson & Sons [spares ordered by their office, 79 Soho Road, Birmingham, 22/12/1916 - delivery address not known]
         wlw: Aluminium Corporation, Dolgarrog, after 12/1916 by 28/9/1917 [see next list below].

ALUMINIUM WORKS RAILWAY (1916-c1960) -   1¼ miles.

Locomotives: Gauge 4'8½" - Aluminium Corporation Ltd

	DOLGARROG	0-6-0ST	IC	MW	1507	1901	(ra)	
			rebuilt C&J			1932		(r1)
	UXBRIDGE	0-6-0ST	IC	HE	761	1902	(rb)Scr/1952 by 7/52	
(	DOLGARROG No.1)	0-6-0ST	OC	RSH	7074	1943	New	Scr/1962

(ra) probably arrived in 1916 - certainly here 8/1928
   wfw: Wilson Lovatt & Sons Ltd, contractors   [? at Queensferry Government Works
       (1915-1916) Contract - which see]
   wfw: Isle of Axholme Railway Co, named HAXEY.

(rb) arrived here after 12/1916 by 28/9/1917 - purchase of loco was approved by
   Aluminium Corporation board meeting 8/1917
   wfw(tdx?): John Wilson & Sons, contractors, Birmingham, in 12/1916
   wfw: Bott & Stennett at Dolgarrog - see previous list above.

(r1) tdt: Cudworth & Johnson, dealer, Wrexham, c1943 (after 30/4/1942).

COWLYD RESERVOIR RAILWAY (1916-1968)   - 3 miles.

Ownership as for 'Dolgarrog Power Station' above.

Locomotives: Gauge 2'0"

	EIGIAU	0-4-0WT	OC	OK	5668	1913	(ca)	± (c1)
		another steam loco						± s/s
		4wPM	20hp	MH	Ø	c1922	New	(c2)
		4wPM	20hp	FH	1988	1936	(cb)	(c3)
		4wDM	28hp	MR	22154	1962	New 6/62	(c4)

± On 4/9/1917 A.C.Ltd resolved to purchase a second 2ft gauge loco for £500, and in
   1922/23 offered to sell TWO narrow gauge steam locos to the Ffestiniog Railway
   (PR/3) - presumably EIGIAU and Another.
   Apparently both locos were being offered for disposal via Joseph Buggins & Co, dealer,
   Birmingham.

Ø In the early 1920s, Muir Hill (Engineers) Ltd were selling rail chassis with, and without,
   a Muir Hill Fordson farm tractor engine and gearbox installed. These units pre-dated the
   purpose-made Muir Hill locomotives to which works-numbers were allocated.
   A disadvantage of this early type was that, whilst having three forward speeds, there
   was only a single reverse ratio.   Turntables were installed at each end of the Cowlyd
   Railway to overcome this.

(ca) arrived c1916 by 9/1917
   wfw: Charles L.Warren, contractor, Seacombe, Cheshire - had been used by Warren on
       Port Sunlight Village (1905-1914) Contract.
(cb) tdx: J.L.Eve Construction Co Ltd, Cowlyd Pipeline Contract, c1938

(c1) for sale 1922
   tdt: Penrhyn Slate Quarries 7/1929
(c2) tdt: Ffestiniog Railway (PR/3), on loan 4/1924; returned 8/1924
   tdt: ? , by 1936. [A loco of this type, gauge not stated, was for sale b
   H.W.E.Hughes (? dealer), Llanrwst, 5/1933. However, the Cowlyd loco may perhaps b
   the loco of this type which was at Rhiwbach Slate Quarry - which see.]
(c3) stored out of use from 1962
   tdt: Oldham Bros, Liverpool 7, for scrap, 3/1967
(c4) stored out of use from 1968
   tdt: Llanberis Lake Railway (PR/65), 11/9/1975

COWLYD RESERVOIR CONSTRUCTION CONTRACT (3/1919-12/1921)

Sir Robert McAlpine & Sons Ltd, contractors.

The early history of McAlpine locomotives is extremely confused, and we are indebted to Th
Hon.W.H.McAlpine for permission to inspect Company records. Surviving Plant Register
(which do not fully describe the Plant listed) commence 11/1917 - and unfortunately the
show only one loco arriving at, but three departing from, Dolgarrog Cowlyd Contract. T
confuse us further, Plant Numbers were altered during and after Contracts - and entries ar
not cross-referenced. Additionally, McAlpine steam locos carried loco running numbers, bu
these are rarely used in early records. The relevant entries are as follows:-

Arrive: Plant No.51 - 12" cylinder loco - to Dolgarrog 1919; was at National Spelter Contrac
   until 1918.

Depart: Plant No.0201 - 12" cylinder loco -left Dolgarrog 28/2/1921 and to Hayes UDC
   Contract 1921 (this is almost certainly the loco which left Hayes Contract 1/11/192
   as "Plant No.X615 No.15 12" loco" - here '15' seems to be a clerical error for '51'
   its former identity number).

   Plant No.0208 - 9" cylinder loco - Dolgarrog to Great Stanney 19/2/1921; with
   McAlpine until sold to ?, 1934.

   Plant No.1009 - 9" cylinder loco - Dolgarrog to Great Stanney Depot 11/8/1921; to
   Watling Street Contract 1922.

The Registers also list two (and only two) other locos transferred to an un-named Contract in
1920:-

Arrive ? Plant No.237 - 9" cylinder loco - located at Anglo Persian Oil Contract, Skewen, to
   31/5/1918; to ? Contract in 1920.

   Plant No.1780 - 9" cylinder loco - at Slough WD Contract until 5/7/1919; to ?
   Contract in 1920.

The second prime data source are the annual returns of plant on site, which quote only Plant
Numbers, those for locos being:-

1919: 51.   1920: 0201, 237, 01009, 1776.   1921: Loco No.5.

Of these numbers, '1776' cannot be traced to any loco in the Plant Registers - possibly it was the Ruston Proctor steam excavator used at Cowlyd for loading the Hudson 4 cub.yd. 3ft gauge tipping wagons.

Based on the above data, presumed identities of the "Departs" are:
0208 was ex 237
0201 was ex 51
1009 was ex 1780 - and was McAlpine Loco No.5.

The following lists of 3ft and 4'8½" locos are therefore based on the above presumptions.

Locomotives: Gauge 2ft - McALPINE

"Plant No.1461"	0-4-0ST OC	WB	2080	1918	(ma)	(m1)
"Plant No.1945"	4wPM	"Simplex"			(mb)	(m2)
	[? 4wPM	"Simplex"			(mb)	s/s]

Also used loco EIGIAU 'on loan' from Aluminium Corporation Ltd.

Locomotives: Gauge 3'0" - McALPINE

"P237/0208"	No.8 (HANNAH)	0-4-0ST OC	BH	1125	1895	(mc)	(m3)

Locomotives: Gauge 4'8½" - McALPINE

"P1780/1009"	No.5 (JACOBITE)	0-4-0ST OC	HC	521	1899	(md)	(m4)
"P51/0201"	No.32	0-6-0ST IC	HC	1028	1913	(mc)	(m5)

(ma) purchased from "Pritchard" 4/6/1919, and apparently delivered direct to Dolgarrog. Loco in New condition - one of a batch ordered by E.Thornton & Co, dealer, for delivery to Swansea for the War Office. In J/CJ/2.7.1919 "Pritchard, London EC" was advertising for sale un-used locos of this type for £700. McAlpines paid £680 for WB 2080.

(mb) McAlpine Registers confirm loco here, but give no details as to its arrival or source. Local information suggests a loco of this type was possibly tdx: J.C.Waddington, contractor, c7/1921, and that there were two such locos at Cowlyd - we cannot confirm the second.

(mc) arrived here 1920
wfw: McAlpine Anglo Persian Oil Contract, Skewen, until 31/5/1918

(md) arrived 1920 [19/5/1920 per Handbook J/115]
wfw: McAlpine Slough War Department Contract until 5/7/1919

(me) arrived 1919 [? from McAlpine Great Stanney Plant Depot]
wfw: McAlpine National Spelter Works Contract until 1918

(m1) tdt: Great Stanney Depot, 1921 (by 31/10/1921)
wlw: Welsh Highland Railway (PR/44) Contract
wlw: Coedty Reservoir Contract (see below)

(m2) tdt: Great Stanney Depot 24/10/1921 (becoming Plant No.2924)
(m3) tdt: Great Stanney Depot 19/2/1921 (becoming Plant No.X1120)
(m4) tdt: Great Stanney Depot 11/8/1921
 wlw: McAlpine Watling Street Contract, 1922
(m5) departed 28/2/1921: wlw(tdt?) Hayes UDC Contract, 1921

COEDTY RESERVOIR CONSTRUCTION (1923-1925) (Gc/GR:755666)
AFONDDU, LLUGWY, COEDTY etc LEATS CONSTRUCTION (1923-1926)
EIGIAU to COWLYD TUNNEL CONSTRUCTION (1925-1928)

    Sir Robert McAlpine & Sons Ltd, contractors.

Locomotives: Gauge 2'0" - McALPINE

It has been confirmed locally that battery locos were used in the Eigiau-Cowlyd tunnel; th Afonddu Leat also included a short tunnel. McAlpine Plant Registers list four (and only four battery locos as obtained in 1920s, but no Contract locations are given. It is presumed tha they were obtained for these tunnels. Petrol loco HC P252 is positively confirmed her 10/1926 by another source.

"Plant No.01884"	0-4-0ST OC	WB	2080	1918	(ta)		(t1)
	4wPM	MR			(tb)		(t2)
"Plant No.2148"	4wBE	BEV	603	1925	New	5/25	(t3)
"Plant No.2157"	4wBE	BEV	604	1925	New	6/25	(t3)
Plant No.2941	4wPM 25hp	HC	P252	1926	New	3/26	(t4)
"Plant No.2535"	4wBE	WR	667	1926	New	11/26	(t3)
"Plant No.2542"	4wBE	WR	668	1926	New	12/26	(t3)

(ta) arrived after 11/1922 by 6/1923
 wfw: Welsh Highland Rly (PR/44) Contract (& Cowlyd Contract above).
(tb) MR supplied spare parts to this site 9/1923 - McAlpine had many such locos by this time; there was very possibly more than one MR here.

(t1) tdt: Great Stanney Depot c1925 and sold there by auction 1/10/1929 probably direct to Lehane, McKenzie & Shand, contractors, who had this loco on their Vyrnwy Aquaduct (Colebrook-Norton Section) Contract, Delamere, Cheshire, by 18/10/1929.
(t2) disposal unknown - probably tdt: Great Stanney Plant Pool.
(t3) remained in McAlpine ownership until 1934, then s/s
(t4) remained in McAlpine ownership until sold as scrap in 1939

DOLGARROG VILLAGE DEVELOPMENT CONTRACT (12/1922-late 1924)

Sir Robert McAlpine & Sons Ltd, contractors.

Widening and straightening main road; Cowlyd Incline level crossing replaced by a bridge. Site preparation for 100 houses (Tayler Avenue; Graham, Gwydir & Bibby Roads) - GR:779673 south to GR:781667. 3'0" gauge temporary railway used, also temporary extension to 4'8½" gauge Works Railway. The houses, of a semi-prefabricated design, were subsequently supplied and erected by the Abdon Clee Stone Quarry Co Ltd [B/420/98].

Locomotives: Gauge 3'0" - McALPINE

There were certainly two, and local memory claims four, locos used on the 3ft system here. It is also locally claimed that use was made of the Aluminium Works loco DOLGARROG - which could explain vague references in other sources which suggest this was a McAlpine loco at some time. It does not appear in McAlpine Plant Registers. Only one 3ft gauge loco has so far been identified here.

No.50   0-4-0ST   OC   HC   1535   1924 New 7/24   (h1)

(h1) tdt: Trawsfynydd Reservoir Contract, Maentwrog, 1925

DAM DISASTER DEBRIS REMOVAL (11/1925-1926)

Sir Robert McAlpine & Sons Ltd, contractors.

It has been recalled that two McAlpine locos, plus Aluminium Works loco, worked continually on this task. Only one McAlpine loco has so far been identified.

Locomotives: Gauge 4'8½" - McALPINE

No.40   0-6-0ST   IC   HC   1525   1924 (da)   (d1)

(da) here 1925; wfw: McAlpine Wolverhampton New Road Contract.

(d1) tdt: Great Stanney Depot, 1926

COWLYD PIPELINE CONSTRUCTION (1936-1938)

J.L.Eve Construction Co Ltd, contractor.

Operated own trains over Cowlyd Reservoir Railway and reputed to have used a total of four locomotives.

Locomotives: Gauge 2'0" - J.L.EVE

4wPM	20hp	FH	1988	1936	New 6/36	(e1)
4wPM	20hp	MR	3831	1926	(ea)	(e2)
4wPM	20hp	MR	5061	1930	(eb)	(e3)
4wPM	20hp	MR			(ec)	(e2)

(ea) tdx: MR, despatched from Bedford 31/7/1936
 wfw: Petrol Loco Hirers Ltd, Bedford
 wfw: Carmichael, contractor, from 19/4/1926
 wfw: War Department, France, identity MR 985/1918
(eb) tdx: Greenham Plant Hire Ltd, c1936 - on hire only; Greenham ordered spares from MR 12/1936 and 1/1937 to be sent to J.L.Eve.
 wfw: Patterson & Dickinson, West Middlesex Sewerage Contract, Southall (on hire from Greenham).
(ec) a replacement 20hp petrol engine ordered 29/10/1936 by J.L.Eve from MR would presumably be for this fourth loco of unknown origin

(e1) tdt: Cowlyd Reservoir Railway permanent stock, 1938
(e2) presume one or both of these locos taken away by J.L.Eve, as they continued to purchase MR spare parts until 5/1941
(e3) tdt: Greenham Plant Hire Ltd, off hire, c1938
 wlw: G.Wimpey, contractor, by 1/1939 (altered to 3ft gauge).

COEDTY ADDITIONAL LEATS CONSTRUCTION (1955-1957)

John Laing & Sons Ltd, contractor.

Locomotives: Gauge 2'0" - LAING

1		4wBE		LMM			s/s
6		4wDM	20hp	RH	375362	1955	New 2/55	(q1)
9		4wDM	30hp	RH	387819	1955	New 6/55	(q2)
10		4wDM	30hp	RH	387820	1955	New 6/55	s/s
12		4wDM	30hp	RH	392102	1955	(qa)	(q2)

(qa) tdx: Trawsfynydd Reservoir Contract, c1956 (after 6/1956)

(q1) wlw: Rickmansworth Gravel Co Ltd, Herts, by 1965
(q2) wlw: Wanlip Sewage Works Contract, Leicester, by 4/1960

COWLYD PIPELINE MAINTENANCE CONTRACTS

Contractors operating own trains on Cowlyd Railway.

1965 CONTRACT - Wm.Latimer & Co Ltd, Stockport.

Locomotive: Gauge 2'0" - LATIMER

        4wDM 20hp RH 226292 1944 (ra)   (r1)

1967 CONTRACT - unknown contractor.

Locomotive: Gauge 2'0"

        4wDM 20hp RH 235652 1945 (rb)   (r2)

(ra) tdx: Parc Mine, Llanrwst, loan, 4/1965
(rb) tdx: Fred Watkins Ltd, dealer, Coleford, Glos., after 18/3/1967 by 18/4/1967
   wfw: Sir Alfred McAlpine & Sons Ltd, Deanhead Reservoir, Yorkshire (noted there 18/3/1967)
   wfw: English Clays, Lovering Pochin & Co Ltd, Wheal Remfry, Cornwall

(r1) tdt: Parc Mine, Llanrwst, off loan, c7/1965 after 24/6/1965
(r2) tdt: Fred Watkins Ltd, Coleford, Glos., c6/1967

DOROTHEA (CLODDFA TURNER) SLATE QUARRY, NANTLLE D16
                        (Gc/GR:499532)

        c1829 : opened
   c1829 - 1847 : Turner [of Parkia] & Morgan [of Old Braich]
        1848 : to be Let [J/CDH/26.8.1848/1]
   1848 - 1853 : **Dorothea Quarry Co** [local men]
   9/1853 - 1892 : **Dorothea Slate Quarry Co** [John Williams & Co]
   1892 - 1895 : **Dorothea Slate Quarry Co** [John Williams & Co Ltd]
   1895 - 1970 : **Dorothea Slate Quarry Co Ltd**
        2/1970 : closed. Sale 23/9/1970. Dismantled.

Slate was despatched via the Nantlle Railway (PR/2) from c1829 to c1959 (ceased by 8/1960). A siding ran direct from PR/2 to the Dorothea Mill. For internal movements - in pit, at Mill level, and on tips - 2ft gauge lines were used. Wagons originally raised from pit by inclined chainways, but Blondin ropeways were later used. Steam locos were used at Mill and tips, with petrol locos at Mill and in pit; but horses were generally preferred and remained in use until 1964, when replaced by a farm tractor running astride the tracks. Road vehicles were introduced in 1967, and rail traffic ceased in 1968. An interesting feature of this site was the Cornish beam pumping engine used for draining the pit; this still [1990] survives but its future is uncertain, as schemes to turn the derelict quarry into a tourist facility have not come to fruition.

Locomotives: Gauge 2ft

Early records are imprecise but three DeWinton locos are certain, all apparently stored out of use c1890 - one at least of these had geared transmission.

		0-4-0VBT	SVCG	DeW		c1870	(a)	Scr by 1914	
		0-4-0VBT	VC	DeW		1873	(b)	Scr by 1914	
	GLYN *	0-4-0VBT	VC	DeW		1874	New Ø	Scr by 1914	
	DOROTHEA	0-4-0ST	OC	HE	763	1901	New 10/01		(1)
	WENDY	0-4-0ST	OC	WB	2091	1919	(c)		(2)
	-	4wPM	20hp	Dtz	68179		(d)	s/s by 1953	
B/5		4wPM	6hp	L	33527	1949	New 4/49		(3)
No.95		4wPM	6hp	L	3916	1931	(e)		(4)
No.96		4wPM	6hp	L	3950	1931	(e)		(3)

Ø   Paid £291-10-0 on 28/5/1874 for new double-cylinder loco ex DeWinton.
*   reputedly named after Ivor Hedd Glynne Williams and, if so, actual name on loco may have been GLYNNE.

(a)   most probably New; was noted here 8/4/1873 [J/CDH/12.4.1873]
(b)   New; delivered to Dorothea on or by 14/7/1873 on which date it was first tested [J/HC/18.7.1873]
(c)   tdx: Votty & Bowydd Slate Quarry, Blaenau Ffestiniog. Was transferred c5/1930; invoiced £775 on 31/5/1930
(d)   tdx: Votty & Bowydd Slate Quarry, Blaenau Ffestiniog, c1936
(e)   here by 8/1953;
       wfw(tdx?): Tarmac Ltd, contractors, Wolverhampton.
       Locos were Tarmac Plant Nos. 95 and 96, and may have been obtained late-1951 when Tarmac Ltd were advertising 2ft gauge locos for sale. [J/CJ/5.9.1951]

(1)   disused from c1942 (working in 12/1941); eventually removed 1/3/1970 by Mr D.L.Walker for preservation - stored various locations including Hills & Bailey Ltd, Llanberis (see PR/65) and, by 1987, at home of Mr Walker at Minsterley, Shropshire.
       wlw: Launceston Steam Railway, Cornwall.
(2)   disused by late 1940s (working in 12/1941, 8/1942).
       tdt: Hampshire Narrow Gauge Railway Society, Hants, 1961
(3)   sold as scrap to "Hunt of Llanbradach" after 6/1964 by 1965
(4)   sold 23/9/1970 to Mr R.P.Morris & Mr P.D.Nicholson for preservation.
       Departed from Dorothea 1/10/1970 to Brockham Museum, Surrey;
       wlw: Gloddfa Ganol (see OAKELEY SLATE QUARRY).

DYSERTH LIMEWORKS & QUARRY   D18
                                                              (Cf/GR:062793)

		10/1878	: first lease from Lord Mostyn
1878	-	1884	: Rhyl Lime & Quarrying Co
1884	-		: Law & Ward
	-	c1959	: W.L.Hobbs (Dyserth) Ltd
c1959	-	c3/1973	: Limestone Products Ltd
c3/1973	-		: Tilcon (Tilling Construction Services Ltd)
		4/9/1981	: closed

4'8½" gauge private siding opened 1884 from kilns to LNWR (PR/36) at Dyserth. Shunting performed by horses until 1939, after which a farm tractor was used. Siding last used 8/9/1973 and track removed 1975.

The kilns were fed by a 2'7" gauge line which crossed the adjacent road by a bridge to reach the quarry at GR:063790. Originally the line was hand-worked and ran to the quarry face. In 1954 dumpers were introduced between the face and a new crushing plant built in the quarry. The narrow-gauge wagons were then loaded at the crushing plant hoppers, and locomotive haulage introduced thence to the kilns. Soon after Tilcon took over, the kilns were closed, and use of the railway ceased at that time. Track lifted 1974, remaining locos abandoned in quarry.

Locomotives: Gauge 2'7"

		4wDM 20hp	FH	(*)	1935	(a)	s/s c1962
		4wDM 10hp	RH	174529	1935	(b)	Scr c1965
3	D-L5	4wDM 20hp	MR	7221	1938	(c)	Scr c10/1965
4		4wDM 20hp	MR	5025	1929	(c)	(1)
R6		4wDM 20hp	RH	296091	1949	(d)	(2)

Locomotives: Gauge 2'0" (Not used; obtained for spare parts only)

-	4wDM 20hp	RH	193971	1938	(e)	(3)
-	4wDM 20hp	RH	235663	1947	(f)	(4)

(*) Loco probably either FH 1913 or FH 1914 (both 2'11" gauge locos of this type) and not FH 1911 (a 2½-ton bow-frame 1'10½" gauge loco) as has been suggested elsewhere.

(a) 4-ton plate-frame loco.
    tdx: Thomas Mitchell & Sons Ltd, dealer, Bolton, Lancashire, 3/1954. Loco purchased by Hobbs ex Mitchell 10/1953, then overhauled and altered from 2'11" gauge by Mitchell (job No.26523) prior to delivery.
    wfw: London Brick Co Ltd, Bedford.
(b) tdx: St.George Limeworks (see KINMEL PARK), c12/1958
(c) tdx: Trefor (yr Eifl) Granite Quarry, between 9/1963 and 3/1964
(d) tdx: Settle Limes Ltd, Threshfield Quarry, Yorkshire WR, between 4/1964 and 9/1965
(e) arrived 1963.
    wfw: General Plant Reconstruction Co Ltd, contractors, Cardiff (to 5/1942 at least), after use at ROF Glascoed in 1940.

(f)   arrived c1972 by 6/1972.
      wfw(tdx ?): Robert Teal Ltd, Lincolnshire.
      wfw: Royal Welsh Show, Abergele, in 7/1950.

(1)   little used; lay dumped in quarry virtually as received until:
      tdt: Mr I.Sutcliffe, private store, Surrey, 18/1/1984
      wlw: Mr I.Jolly (see Section 1)
(2)   tdt: Mr I.Sutcliffe, private store, Surrey, 18/1/1984
(3)   Chassis scrapped c1965. Other components had been used to repair RH 174529, which subsequently carried RH 193971 identity plate.
(4)   Many components used to repair RH 296091 which subsequently carried RH 235663 identity plate. Chassis later scrapped.

FFRITH/GLASCOED COLLIERIES/FIRECLAY MINES, FFRITH　　　F2
(Cd/GR:287546)

```
    6/1872  -  10/1874  : G.W.Charlwood;  Ffrith Colliery
                  1875  : Burr;  Ffrith Colliery
       1875  -   1876  : Glascoed Colliery Co Ltd;  Glascoed Colliery
                  1889  : Henry Lomax, Rhosddu;  Ffrith Colliery
               by 1902  : Chas Wheldon, Rock Ferry;  Ffrith Colliery
                  1902  : Ffrith Coal & Fireclay Co;  Ffrith Colliery
               by 1912  :   closed, dismantled, all track removed.
                        : Dutton Massey & Co;  Glascoed Colliery
                  1913  :   new sidings laid in for Dutton Massey
                  1913  : Glascoed Colliery Co Ltd;  Glascoed Colliery
       1914  -  12/1922  : Brynmally Colliery Co
    by 1928  -   1935  : Ffrith Fireclay Co;  Glascoed Colliery
       1936  -   197x  : Ffrith Fireclay Co Ltd;  Glascoed (No.2) Colliery
                  197x  :   closed and dismantled.
```

ALSO: in the mid-1930s, D.Morris & E.Williams of Penycraig, Brymbo, were undertaking small-scale activity at "Glascoed Adit [Colliery]", which perhaps was a part of this site.

The Deep Drainage Level ("Level Fawr") of Brymbo Colliery has its portal in a small valley a little way south of Ffrith Hall. Shafts, known at first as Ffrith Colliery, were sunk on the western slope of this valley, and were served by short sidings off PR/40 west of the viaduct by which that line crossed the valley. These sidings were removed by 1900.

"Ffrith Colliery, Brymbo" was auctioned "re Dimsdale" 5/3/1878 including pit-head, winding engines, 35 tons of rail and "about 2000 tons of fireclay" - but no locos are mentioned [J/CDH/2.3.1878].

Immediately adjacent, but on the eastern side of the stream, adits were driven easterly - to beneath Pencoed Farm - and served by narrow-gauge tramroads including tracks on the surface to a loading dock at PR/40 east of the viaduct. By 1912 these too had gone, and the valley abandoned.

In 1913, sidings were relaid off PR/40 into the western side, initially to serve the revived Ffrith - now Glascoed - Colliery; from c1928 these sidings were used by Ffrith Fireclay Co. One siding remained in situ for many years after the demolition of PR/40.

By 1928 the eastern side adits had reopened, primarily as a fireclay mine though coal was worked when it was found. These adits were now served by 1'9" gauge tramways, using rope-haulage both on the surface and underground. Known locally as "Ffrith Fireclay Mine", it was (in 1969) officially "Glascoed No.2 Mine". In 4/1969 three adits were in use; by 6/1970 this had increased to four. However, the site was abandoned in the 1970s and all equipment was removed.

Locomotives: Gauge 4'8½"

There is no positive evidence of, and the sidings hardly justified, any locos being used here; but two advertisements in contemporary journals are of interest:

J/TE/27.10.1871 - "Wanted on hire, standard gauge loco - Ffrith Colliery, Wrexham".
As PR/40 was not opened until 27/1/1872, could this indicate possible private use of a part of the uncompleted PR/40 ?

J/MM/2.3.1896 - "Wanted, small loco for colliery siding - E.Wheldon, near Mold".
Per J/MS, Chas.Wheldon was, in 1902, the registered owner of "Ffrith Colliery, Wrexham" (listed therein under 'Flintshire', despite both Wrexham, and the Ffrith Colliery (just), being located in Denbighshire. Mold, of course, was in Flintshire. Perhaps the "E.Wheldon" of the advertisement was connected with Chas.Wheldon. However, in the 1870s a Mr Edward Wheldon was sub-manager at Bedford Colliery, Mold, [J/CDH/20.6.1874], and this advertisement could well refer to a location other than Ffrith.

FFRITH LIMEWORKS later (TRIMLEY HALL) ROADSTONE QUARRY   F4

(Cf/GR:below)

		: [? Ffrith Lime Co]
by 11/1912	- 9/1931	: Ffrith Roadstone Quarries Ltd
10/1931	-	: now a subsidiary of Tarmac Ltd
after 12/1938		: closed; later dismantled.

The original works consisted of a large limekiln (GR:282556) [1986: still standing] served by sidings off the adjacent GWR/LNWR line (PR/40). Traces remain [1986] of an old narrow-gauge system feeding the top of these kilns from adjacent diggings, and of another system to other diggings immediately south-west of the kilns. The principal quarry, however, was developed on the opposite (eastern) side of the valley (around GR:285556). The internal narrow-gauge railway system here was connected by an aerial ropeway feeding direct to the crusher and tarmacadam plant built immediately south of the old kiln, and adjacent to PR/40.

Locomotives: Gauge 2'0"

Between 9/1921 and 12/1938 spare parts were ordered from time to time for both 20hp and 40hp types of MR locos - but the surviving records do not reveal their works numbers.

	4wPM 20hp	MR	1073	1918	(a)	(1)

(a) here by 13/7/1921.
    wfw: War Department, France, WDLR 2794

(1) wlw(tdt?): Midland Macadams Ltd, Oldbury, Worcs, by "late 1920s".

FFRWD COLLIERIES, IRONWORKS & BRICKWORKS   F6
near CEFN-Y-BEDD
(Cd/GR:305552)

by 1796	-	1815	: Richard Kyrke [collieries]
		1821	: collieries and unfinished ironworks for sale.
1824	-	c1854	: John Thompson
		1854	: Johnson Edwards "Frood Colliery & Frood Iron Co"
1855	-	1857	: W.Sparrow, Pearson & Co
1857	-	1858	: James Sparrow
1859	-		: James Sparrow & Co/Sparrow & Poole
by 1886	-	1904	: James Sparrow & Son/s
		7/8/1893	: serious fire destroyed most of colliery.
		9/1/1904	: closed. Dispersal auction 5-7/7/1904.

A large complex served by the GWR (PR/6 branch) and WM&CQR (PR/28 branch) with internal narrow-gauge system from pit-heads etc.
All demolished after closure; site still derelict land [1988].
[Read: B/107]

Locomotives: Gauge 4'8½"

There were at least three locomotives here over the years; one old employee recalled them as "STAFFORD, SCOTIA and WARWICK".
The dispersal auction included two locos, with 12x20 cylinders.
The name 'WARWICK' has been associated with HC 213 (DIXON) at Little Mountain Colliery, Buckley. We do not know why.
However, apparently HC 213 was available at Cudworth & Johnson, dealers, Wrexham, in 1886 - and it was a 12" cylinder loco.

Three colliers were charged before Wrexham Magistrates 11/1874 for "wilfully throwing sand upon the works of a locomotive engine employed at Frood Colliery" [J/CDH/28.11.1874/5c6]. This item, together with footnote (a) below, seems to confirm there were at least two locos here prior to AB 659.

0-4-0ST	OC					(1)
[? 0-4-0ST	OC]			(a)		(2)
0-4-0ST	OC	AB	659	1890	New 3/90	(3)

(a) "Sparrow Poole, Ffrwd Ironworks" were advertising Wanted a four-wheel-coupled tank loco not less than 12" cylinders, in 11/1875.

(1) an [as yet] unconfirmed report states that Sparrow advertised a loco 10x20 cylinders, 3'0" wheels, for sale 9/1882. Also, J/PMR has an (anonymous) advertisement from 9/1892 to 9/1893 "saddle tank loco 10x20 4wc 3'0" diameter, iron firebox and iron tubes (new), in splendid order, thoroughly overhauled, 4'8½" gauge, by Sparrow & Son, £260". Also, Cudworth & Johnson, dealers, Wrexham, were advertising 12/1891 to 11/1892 a similar loco "4wc tank loco 10x20 Low Moor Iron firebox, brass tubes, thoroughly overhauled, £250".
Both, either, or neither, may be this loco.

(2) 12x20 cylinders loco for sale 7/1904 - no further trace.

(3) 13x20 cylinders but perhaps the second "12x20" loco for sale 7/1904
wlw(tdt?): Distington Ironworks, Cumberland, by /1910

FLAGSTAFF LIMESTONE QUARRY, PENMON   F8
near BEAUMARIS
(Ga/GR:635806)

```
1/1888  -  1/1893   : William Baird & Co
2/1893  -  c6/1937  : William Baird & Co Ltd (reg.1/2/1893)
c6/1937 -  12/1947  : Dinmor Quarries Ltd
             1948   : closed; dismantled for scrap 1963.
```

There was a small quarry on this site, with pier and limekiln but no railway, by 6/1874. During the 1890s Bairds developed the quarry to obtain fluxing stone for their Glasgow steelworks. An extensive 3'0" gauge railway system was installed, which was entirely horse- and hand-worked. After 11/1928 production was minimal until 1937 when DQLtd commenced limited operations, principally the manufacture of kiln-burnt lime for agriculture. This working ceased in 1948. [LgRO/WDAH]
[J/IRR/Vol.6/48 contains a drawing of a wagon at this quarry.]

Locomotives: Gauge 3'0"

```
                    4wPM  20hp    FH     1799   1932   (a)         Scr/1963
```

(a)   tdx: Dinmor Park Quarry, Penmon, after 11/1937 by 12/1947

FLINT ABER WORKS   F10
(Cf/GR:238731)

```
             1909   : new factory
1909  -      1916   : British Glanzstoff Manufacturing Co Ltd
                         (reg.1909 liq.1916 - a subsidiary of:-
                         Vereinigte Glanzstoff-Fabriken AG)
1/1917  -  12/1957  : Courtaulds Ltd
           12/1957  : closed; rail track later removed.
             1980s  : Factory demolished and site redeveloped.
```

Factory construction Contracts:
2/1909   : Site excavation and levelling:-
            Lawrence Marr, contractor (of Liverpool).
5/1909   : Buildings erection:-
            Wm.Brown & Sons (of Salford); became insolvent.
            Renshaw & Sons (of Liverpool) completed the works.

Locomotives: Gauge 4'8½"

This factory made use of much of the former private railway from the LNWR (PR/7) to Flint (New Flint) Colliery - which see. It is likely that a loco would have been used from c1908, but no details have come to light re locos prior to Courtaulds' takeover in 1917.
It is not possible to present a true list of Courtaulds' locos here as they were exchanged from time to time with locos at Castle Works. During the 1950s, the locos stabled at Aber Works were P1810 and P2087, the latter having been ordered specifically for Aber Works.

Locomotive: Gauge 2'0"

4wPM	20hp	[MR	1552	(a)]	s/s

(a) spare parts for MR loco 1552 were ordered by Courtaulds (Coventry Head Office); fc Aber Works, Flint, 4/11/1924; and for same loco at unspecified location 15/6/1925 3/9/1925 and 5/1/1939. However, MR did not build a loco number 1552. Thu '1552' could perhaps be an engine number, a plant number, or another loco builders number.
Nothing has yet been discovered re the use of any such loco at Aber Works.

FLINT CASTLE WORKS and DEESIDE MILL   F12
(Cf/GR:244734 etc)

1755	-	1810	: Lead smelting works.
1812	-	1852	: **George Roskell & Co**
1852	-	6/1886	: **Muspratt Bros. & Huntley**
6/1886	-	10/1890	: **Muspratt Bros. & Huntley Ltd** (reg.22/6/1886)
11/1890	-	1926	: **United Alkali Co Ltd** (reg.1/11/1890)
1920	-	c1985	: **Courtaulds Ltd**
		1963	: rail traffic ceased.
		c1985	: Castle Works closed; site later redeveloped.
c1985	-	c1987	: **Courtaulds Fibre Ltd** [Deeside Mill only]
		c1987	: Deeside Mill closed.

The history of these sites commences 1755 with the establishment of a lead smelting works the by-products (particularly sulphur) of which led to the manufacture of chemicals Consequent upon a United Alkali scheme of rationalisation, Castle Works closed by 1919; the disused site being taken over by Courtaulds for their new rayon factory, which came into production 5/1922. A small section of the property, the "Mercerising Works", was retained by United Alkali until 1926; this became Courtaulds "Deeside Mill" in 1927. This latter property was on the opposite, inland side of the LNWR (PR/7), being reached by a siding from Castle Works via a low bridge, under PR/7. The bridge was built in 1845 when it was decided to raise the proposed level of PR/7 rather than cross on the level the "existing railway at Eytons Foundry and Shipbuilding Yards", so perhaps the Mercerising Works was built on the site of this Foundry. The early locos ordered for use here by MB&H were built to a maximum height of 9'0", to pass beneath this bridge.
[Read: J/FHS/1967/77; B/421; B/423]

Locomotives: Gauge 4'8½" - Factory Construction 1918-1920.
J.WILSON & SONS LTD (of Birmingham), contractors.

COURTAULDS LTD	0-4-0ST	OC	MW	1984	1919	New 5/19	(1)
-	0-4-0ST	OC	P	1044	1905	(a)	(1)

Locomotives: Gauge 4'8½" - Factory (including Flint Aber Works) Shunting.

		Ø 2-2-0TG	SC	JF	923	1868	New 1/68	s/s
	MABEL	± 0-4-0ST	OC	MW	264	1868	New 9/68	(2)
	LINCOLN	± 0-4-0ST	OC	MW	351	1871	New (b)	(3)
	SIR MAX (f.MAX)	± 0-4-0ST	OC	MW	502	1874	New 8/74	(4)
	ROLAND	± 0-4-0ST	OC	MW	778	1881	New 1/81	(5)
	MAX	0-4-0ST	OC	P	502	1890	(c)	(6)
	COURTAULDS LTD	0-4-0ST	OC	MW	1984	1919	(d)	(7)
	-	0-4-0ST	OC	P	1044	1905	(d)	Scr/c1950
No.1		*0-4-0DM		JF	17305	1927	(e)	(8)
	-	0-4-0ST	OC	P	1810	1930	New	Scr/c9/1963
	-	0-4-0PM	35hp	Bg	1442	1925	(f)	(9)
	-	0-4-0ST	OC	P	2085	1948	New 2/48	(10)
	DAFYDD	0-4-0ST	OC	P	2087	1948	New 6/48	(11)
	-	4wTG	VB	S	9596	1955	New	(12)

Ø   Convertible road/rail loco; may have been used here as road vehicle only.
±   Built to a maximum height of 9'0" to pass under LNWR (PR/7).
*   Built New with 40hp petrol engine; replaced by a diesel engine at Courtaulds Wolverhampton Works prior to coming to Flint.

(a) tdx: Constable Hart & Co Ltd, Cawdor Quarries, Matlock, Derbyshire, c4/1920
(b) wlw: United Alkali, Preesall Works, Fleetwood, Lancs, by 1916 (when it was 'rebuilt' there).
    arrived back at Flint [? ex Preesall] by 2/1929.
    departed from Flint again [to ?] after 12/1931
    tdx: Ribbleton Works, Lancashire, 4/1937
(c) here by 1906.
    wfw: Andrew Knowles & Sons Ltd, Clifton Hall Colliery, Manchester
(d) tdx: J.Wilson & Sons Ltd, contractors (this site), c1920
(e) tdx: Courtaulds Wolverhampton Works, Staffordshire, 3/8/1929
(f) tdx: Courtaulds Foleshill Works, Coventry, Warwicks, c1943

(1) tdt: Coutaulds Ltd (on this site), c1920
(2) still here in 1912, subsequently no further trace.
(3) scrapped at Castle Works, c1950
(4) wlw(?tdt): Fleetwood Salt Works, Lancashire.
(5) wlw(?tdt): United Alkali Tennant's Works, Glasgow, by c1905
(6) wlw(?tdt): York Gas Company, Layerthorpe, York.
(7) scrapped at Flint by J.& H.B.Jackson Ltd (of Coventry) c1956 (after 7/1955)
(8) scrapped at Flint by J.& H.B.Jackson Ltd, 6/1960
(9) scrapped at Flint by J.& H.B.Jackson Ltd, 6/1958
(10) tdt: Courtaulds Coventry Works, Warwickshire, 6/1964
(11) tdt: Courtaulds Dunstall Hall Works, Wolverhampton, 12/1957
(12) tdt: Courtaulds Coventry Works, Warwickshire, 6/1958

FLINT COLLIERIES

F14
(Cf/GR:below)

FLINT MARSH COLLIERY (GR: ?)
1854	-	1860	: Flint Marsh Colliery Co
		c1860	: Hugh Beaver Roberts & John Ormiston, who formed:-
1861	-	1871+	: Flint Marsh Coal Co
by 1873	-	1876+	: Flint Marsh Colliery Co Ltd
			: closed

GWAITH-Y-COED COLLIERY (GR:227730)
1854	-	1860	: Flint Marsh Colliery Co
		? 1861	: closed

FLINT (NEW FLINT) COLLIERY (GR:234733)
		1828	: [eleven miners killed at "Flint Colliery"]
1854	-	1856	: Eyton Brothers
1857	-		: Parry & Co
1857	-	1864	: Thomas Houghton
		1865	: closed
1866	-		: Edward Bowers
		9/1882	: colliery auctioned but no sale made
5/1883	-	9/1883	: Flint Coal & Cannel Co Ltd (reg.29/5/1883 £10K)
			(for sale 12/1887, including a loco; apparently no sale made)
9/1889	-	3/1899	: New Flint Coal & Cannel Co Ltd [Huntley, Muspratt and others]
3/1899	-	2/1902	: New Flint Colliery Co Ltd [not Huntley, Muspratt]
		10/2/1902	: sale by order of Sheriff [including a HE loco]
c1902	-	6/1907	: Deeside Colliery Co Ltd
		26/6/1907	: dispersal auction of plant and machinery.

Location of Flint Marsh Colliery not known - it has been suggested it was same place as Gwaith-y-coed but perhaps confused by the common ownership. Flint Marsh Colliery is reputed to have had a locomotive at some time. Both Gwaith-y-coed and Flint (New Flint) collieries are clearly marked on OS maps and it is easy to postulate an early tramroad between them and the River Dee. When the Chester & Holyhead Railway (PR/7) was built here c1845, its level was raised "west of the town" to bridge over "the tramways at Flint, in constant use".

Eyton & Co, who operated the Mostyn collieries, also had interests in Flint in 1844, and perhaps they were earlier operators of some or all of the Flint collieries, besides their foundry and ship-building work (see entry "Flint Castle Works").

At some time, maybe c1883, a 4'8½" gauge line was laid from PR/7 to Flint Colliery. In 1909 much of this line, and some land, was leased to the Flint Aber Works [Glanzstoff] by the Deeside Colliery Co Ltd.

[Read: J/CG/24.2.1893/359]

Locomotives: Gauge 4'8½" - Flint/New Flint Colliery.

0-4-0ST	OC	MW	62	1862	(a)	(1)
0-4-0ST	OC	HE	42	1870	(b)	(2)

a) here by 9/1889.
 wfw: John Mackay, contractor, Newport, Monmouth [? Alexandra Dock Contract] until c1885
 wfw: Denby Iron Co, Derbyshire, until 1873 at least.
b) here by 22/4/1899 [but perhaps after 28/2/1899 when some spare parts were ordered by "C.J.Mitchell" (? who) - BUT the colliery was advertsied for sale in J/CG/1898/1044 and then included two locos, hence EITHER "C.J.Mitchell" was associated with this colliery OR there was a third loco of which we yet know nothing].
 wfw: Babbington Coal Co, Nottinghamshire, named NORTHERN BELLE.

(1) left here after 3/1899 by 2/1902.
 wlw(tdt ?): Newton Chambers & Co Ltd, Chapeltown, Yorks [Scr/1934]
  A reference in the MW "Engine Book" suggests that this loco was at one time owned by Muspratt Brothers & Huntley, Flint; maybe this arises from repairs having been done at MB&H workshops on behalf of the colliery, in which Muspratt and Huntley had an interest.
(2) presumably this was the HE loco in sale 10/2/1902; no further trace.

FLINT PAPER MILL, OAKENHOLT, FLINT   F16
(Cf/GR:263716)

| by 1875 | : North Wales Paper Co Ltd |
| by 1986 | : J.J.Makin Ltd |

Sidings off PR/7, installed by 4/1875, controlled by ground-frame, with level crossing over main road to enter works yard. Rail traffic ceased c1964; track removed by 6/1965.

Locomotive: Gauge 4'8½"

  4wPM 40hp MR 1944 1919 New 12/19
  re-engined Dorman 4DWD Diesel 1959   (1)

(1) tdt: Alyn Works [Synthite Ltd], Mold, 8/1965

FORYD RIVER CHANNEL DIVERSION CONTRACT, RHYL   F18
(Cd/GR:997810 etc)

 c1936 - c1939 : **Sir Lindsay Parkinson & Co Ltd**, contractors.

A new outflow channel for the River Clwyd was cut through the beach to low-water mark, a distance of over half a mile, the intention being to eliminate the deposit of river silt onto Rhyl sands. The railway carried excavated material "out to sea" and could only be fully worked at low tide.

Locomotives: Gauge 2'0" - SIR LINDSAY PARKINSON

Reputed to have used a total of four internal combustion locos here, including an old bow frame petrol Simplex; but additional locos to those listed cannot yet be identified or confirmed. A former workman at Foryd recalled that all the locos later moved to Chorley.

No.3	305	0-6-0WT	OC	HC	1641	1929	(a)	(1)
No.4	303	0-6-0WT	OC	HC	1642	1929	(a)	(1)
		4wDM	20hp	MR	7140	1936	(b)	(2)
		4wDM	20hp	MR	7135	1936	(c)	(2)

(a) here by 30/9/1936; owned by SLP since New in 1929 and last recorded at Grimsb New Fish Dock (1930-1934) Contract.
(b) tdx: Diesel Loco Hirers Ltd, Bedford, 5/1937 (c10/5/1937)
(c) tdx: Diesel Loco Hirers Ltd, Bedford, 6/7/1937

(1) wlw(tdt?): Royal Ordnance Factory Construction (1937-1939) Contract, Chorley Lancashire, by 20/3/1938
(2) reputedly tdt: Royal Ordnance Factory Construction (1937-1939) Contract, Chorley Lancashire

FRON SLATE QUARRY, MOEL TRYFAN   F20
(Gc/GR:514549)

The original operations, started c1815 at GR:517547, were later referred to as OLD FRON after work was concentrated at a new pit at GR:514549. From 11/1868 the lease of OLD BRAICH (see entry "Braich/Old Braich Slate Quarry") was combined with the FRON lease, after which FRON & OLD BRAICH worked as a single unit.

FRON QUARRY
                    c1815   : John Evans
                    1837   : lessees of Moel Tryfan Slate Quarry
                    1851   : John Jones (Glan Ceunant) et al
        10/1857 -   : John Lloyd Jones
        by 6/1864 -   : British Slate Co Ltd (reg.18/9/1860 £30K)

FRON & OLD BRAICH QUARRIES
        11/1868 -   : British Slate Co Ltd (liq.1874)
        5/1869 -   : Carnarvon & Bangor Slate Co Ltd [of Talysarn Qy]
        6/1876 -   : Vron Welsh Slate Co [Williams, Pugh, Davies]
        6/1882 -   : Vron & Old Braich Welsh Slate Quarries Co Ltd
                                  (reg.1881)
                    by 10/1891 : both quarries have been closed.
        1893   : Exors of V.& O.B.W.S.Q.Co.Ltd.
                    29/7/1893   : auction of assets - wagons but no locos listed.
        7/1896 -   : W.H.Forshaw [of Gallt-y-Fedw Slate Quarry Ltd]
        c6/1897 -   : Vron & Old Braich Slate Quarries Ltd
                    9/1901   : most machinery transferred to Cloddfa'r Coed Slate Quarry, Nantlle.

8/1902 -		: Vron Welsh Slate Quarries Ltd [Wm.Williams et al]					
		(reg.24/7/1902 £5K liq.1914)					
	by 5/1909	: closed.					
10/1911 -	c1920	: J.R.Roberts & E.J.Davies [directors of VWSQ Ltd]					
	thereafter	: spasmodic small scale working from time to time until early 1950s. By 1987 the quarries were derelict with all machinery removed, apart from a few rails in a roadway near Old Braich Mill.					

The quarries had internal 2ft gauge railways and, from 1868, a link line between Fron and Old Braich Mill. In 10/1866, John Robinson obtained permission to build a 3'4½" (3'6" centre-to-centre) gauge tramroad from Fron Quarry to Nantlle (see PR/38), and output used that route from 1870 to 1881. On 5/4/1882 a lease was granted to permit [maybe after the event in fact] construction of a new 2ft gauge line from the quarry to the Bryngwyn Incline of the NWNGR (PR/44); output first used that route 9-10/1882, and PR/38 closed.

[Read: B/182; B/174; B/175]

Locomotives: Gauge 2ft

VRON	0-4-0VBT	VC	DeW		c1878	(a)	(1)
[? KELSO]	0-4-0T	OC	VF	810	1878	(b)	(2)
[? KELSO]	0-4-0T	OC	VF	832	1878	(b)	(2)
	4wPM					(c)	s/s

(a) This loco may have been here, New from DeW c1878, but proof not yet found. Information from the Talysarn area suggests it may have been 3'4½" gauge intended for use on PR/38.
(b) Either, or neither, of these locos may have been here; records concerning them are very confused. Per VF, both were sold New to Spooner & Co, Braich Quarry - yet there is no record of any financial connection between Spooner and Braich, though proof exists that Spooner did correspond with Braich Quarry [empty envelope in Ffestiniog Railway Archives]. However, no Braich quarry had any obvious need for even one such loco. One of these locos was in fact named KELSO, and was owned by Penyrorsedd Quarry - whose records show that they purchased it New from VF. But as yet the VF number of the Penyrorsedd loco has not been ascertained. The other loco MAY perhaps have been demonstrated by Spooner at Braich.
(c) observed by a visitor "in a shed at Fron Quarry", 12/1941

(1) ? wlw: Talysarn Quarry - which see for comment.
(2) One loco actually at Penyrorsedd Quarry from new and named KELSO -(see footnote (b)), the other wlw: Votty & Bowydd Slate Quarries, (which see), named TAFFY.

GARDDEN LODGE (NEW) COLLIERY later BRICKWORKS (JENKS), G2
RUABON
(Cd/GR:301448)

There have been numerous small coal pits in the grounds of Gardden Hall since the 1700s (perhaps even earlier), of which three made significant use of rail transport at sites to the south of Brandie (Ruabon Old) Pits. Unfortunately, all three have loosely used the name

"Gardden Colliery" at some time, hence there are confusions as to ownerships. We are here concerned with the "New" colliery, the other sites being "Gardden Hall (Moreton) Pits" (GR:301455) and "Gardden (Garden Lodge Old) Colliery" (GR:294451).

```
              1860   : sinking "by Messrs Wright".
  1861 -     1875   : Gardden Lodge Colliery Co
  1875 -     1876   : Gardden Lodge Colliery Co Ltd
  1876 -     1880   : Gardden Lodge Coal, Coke & Firebrick Co Ltd
  1880 -     c1885  : Gardden Lodge Coal Co Ltd (reg.19/10/1880 £40K)
              c1885  : closed; converted to brickworks.
  1888 -     1960   : Ruabon Brick & Terra-Cotta Co Ltd
  1960 -     c1976  : Dennis Ruabon Ltd
              c1976  : closed; demolished; now Gardden Industrial Est.
```

Colliery and Brickworks served by sidings off PR/17 (which closed 8/1964). Clay for the brickworks, obtained from a quarry immediately to the south (GR:302447), was brought to the works "by an endless chain tram way" [1892]. A diesel loco was later used in the quarry, but the "tram way" was replaced by road vehicles around the end of WW2.

[Read: B/107; J/DHS/Vol.20/246]

Locomotives: Gauge ?

In 7/1861, "Gardden Lodge Colliery" was offering for sale "a small tank locomotive, in excellent condition, weight about 7 tons".
The gauge is not stated, but 7 tons is very small for 4'8½" gauge. Perhaps it was used in connection with the colliery sinking.

Locomotive: Gauge 2'0"

    4wDM 21hp   RH   175127   1935 New 5/35   (1)

(1)   tdt: Maenofferen Slate Quarry, Blaenau Ffestiniog, after 7/1939 by 2/1946

GARTH SHALE QUARRY, MOCHDRE, COLWYN BAY   G4
(Gc/GR:820787)

```
              c1911   : opened
  c1911  -   9/1912  : Stanlow Works Estates Ltd
  9/1912 -   8/1929  : Ship Canal Portland Cement Manufacturers Ltd
  8/1929 -  12/1931  : Allied Portland Cement Manufacturers Ltd
 12/1931 -           : Associated Portland Cement Manufacturers Ltd
                     : closed [ ? c1931-32 ].
```

Sidings were provided by the LNWR (PR/7), by Agreement 2/4/1913 with the SCPCM Ltd. A short aerial ropeway linked these sidings to the quarry. 2ft gauge railway on the quarry floor supplied this ropeway, but date of opening of this railway is uncertain. The product was taken to the cement factory at Stanlow, Cheshire.

Locomotives: Gauge 2'0"

BABY		0-4-0T	OC	KS	639	1898	(a)	(1)
BABY SENIOR		0-4-2ST	OC	KS	1265	1914	(a)	(2)

(a)   The sequence of arrival of these locos at Mochdre is uncertain, but probably in the order listed. KS 639 was previously at the Stanlow Works. KS 1265 is recorded as having been delivered New to SCPC Ltd at Ellesmere Port (ie, Stanlow) in 12/1914 and name BABY SENIOR was painted on before delivery. It was at Garth by 1917 [J/TL/1917/186]

(1)   remained derelict at Garth Quarry until cut up for scrap c3/1942, reputedly by "Ward of Rhyl".
(2)   wlw(tdt?): Holborough Cement Works, Holborough, Kent [by c1928 ?].

GATEWEN COLLIERY & OPENCAST COAL DISPOSAL POINT   G6
(Cd/GR:314517)

	5/1875	:	sinking commenced; First Winning 26/10/1877
1875 -	12/1880	:	**Broughton Coal Co** (Robertson & Darby)
1/1881 -	1932	:	**Broughton & Plas Power Coal Co Ltd**
			(reg.1/1/1881 £200K)
	30/7/1932	:	closed.
	1957	:	site reopened as Opencast Coal Disposal Point.
1957 -	c4/1966	:	**Sir Alfred McAlpine & Sons Ltd** - for NCBOE
c4/1966 -	c1972	:	site idle.
c1972 -	c1/1980	:	**Lindley Plant Ltd** - for NCBOE
c1/1980 -	1984	:	site idle.
1984 -	1985	:	BR shunts for coal stocking on site for I.C.I.Ltd
1985 -		:	site idle.

This colliery initially operated as a landsale pit with no rail outlet; in 11/1881 the Directors were still complaining about the delay in completion of the GWR (PR/48) Moss Valley line connection, which was then "expected to be open for traffic in a few weeks"

The first Directors of the 1881 B&PPC CoLtd, apart from Henry Robertson and W.H.Darby (of Brymbo Works, etc), included Richard Peacock (of Beyer, Peacock), George Meakin and John William Dean (of Meakin & Dean, contractors). Desiring an outlet to the WM&CQ Railway (PR/28) Robertson, with Piercy (of the WM&CQR), financed the construction of a branch from that railway (Stansty Junction) to Gatewen Colliery. This branch, constructed by Meakin & Dean, opened in 8/1882, and in the same month the WM&CQ obtained an Act authorising the building of a line from Stansty via Gatewen and Plas Power to Brymbo ["GC Station"], to incorporate (in fact) the line just opened. Unable to proceed due to lack of capital, the WM&CQ arranged for Robertson and Piercy to continue to build the line as a private B&PPC Co Ltd railway - which suited the latter, as they wanted this line to reach their colliery at Plas Power as soon as possible. Construction was continued on to Brymbo, reached 12/1887. From Brymbo ["GC"], the line reversed up a "zig-zag" to Vron Colliery, (reverse) to Brymbo Ironworks. This section of line remained in the ownership of Robertson & Piercy but was worked by WM&CQ/GCR/LNER locos - see PR/47 for details.

In 4/1888, the B&PPC Co Ltd agreed to allow the WM&CQ to use "our sidings and engine" after the opening of the WM&CQ Goods Shed at Plas Power; but matters seem to have come to a head and the WM&CQ informed the B&PPC Co Ltd that they were "taking over" the line as from 1/7/1888. The WM&CQ duly paid the B&PPC Co Ltd the cost of building the line but it was not until 7/1902 that the representatives of Robertson and Piercy received benefit from this payment. For subsequent history see PR/47.

Locomotive: Gauge 4'8½" - MEAKIN & DEAN, contractors. Work started 9/1881

[COLWALL ?]	0-6-0ST	IC	MW	83	1863	(ma)	(m1)

(ma) wfw: Midland Wagon Co, Birmingham (c1873)

(m1) wlw(tdt?): Manning Wardle, Leeds, by 5/1885; used by MW as a hire loco.
 [? wlw: H.Arnold & Son, contractors]

The B&PPC Co Ltd purchased loco BP 2157 to work their trains along this new railway; it was later transferred to WM&CQ stock under a "hire-purchase" agreement arranged through loco dealer E.D.Till (of 26 Lombard Street, London). Payments extended from 9/1882 to 1887, and it seems that the loco remained on the Stansty-Plas Power services until paid for.

Because the B&PPC Co Ltd were frequently the sole, and always the major, users of this line, locomotives could be readily transferred between the Gatewen, Plas Power and Vron collieries. No records of such transfers have been found in the Company papers [HRO], hence only one combined listing can be presently produced. [For further details of Plas Power Colliery see entry under that title.]

The site of Gatewen colliery re-opened in 1957 as an Opencast Coal Disposal Point, where coal brought in by road from digging sites was loaded onto rail. Initially rail access was from the Moss Valley line (PR/48), but by 1958 access altered to the Stansty route (PR/47 + 28). This latter was closed in 1960 and access reverted to PR/48, and still [1990] remains thus, though disused from 1985.

[Read: B/107]

Locomotives: Gauge 4'8½" - Gatewen & Plas Power Collieries.

EMILY	0-6-0ST	IC	BP	2157	1882	New 5/82	(1)
COLLIER	0-4-0ST	OC	AB	179	1876	(a)	(2)
KNUTSFORD	0-6-0T	IC	SS	3471	1888	(b)	(3)
JAMES HALL	0-4-0ST	OC	AB	1831	1924	New 11/24	(4)

Locomotives: Gauge 4'8½" - Opencast Coal Disposal Point.

-	0-6-0ST	IC	RSH	7162	1944	(c)	(5)
BERWYN	0-6-0ST	OC	P	2115	1950	(d)	(6)
-	4wDM		Unilok	2005	1972	New	(7)
(D2148)	0-6-0DM	204hp	Sdn		1960	(e)	(8)
(D2182)	0-6-0DM	204hp	Sdn		1962	(f)	(9)

Also BR locos hired as required: eg, 0-6-0PT 7414 here in 1961, 1628 here 9/1963.

(a) tdx: Old Broughton Colliery, by 2/1891
(b) wfw: Griff Colliery Co Ltd, Nuneaton, Warwicks.
(c) tdx: Pemberton Opencast CDP, Lancashire, 1958
(d) tdx: Brymbo Steelworks, loan, 12/1965 (and not used).
(e) tdx: Bowers Row Opencast CDP, West Yorkshire, 8/1973
(f) tdx: A.R.Adams Ltd, dealer, Newport, Mon, 9/1973
    wfw: Glyn Neath Opencast CDP, Glamorgan.

(1) tdt: Wrexham, Mold & Connah's Quay Rly Co, per E.D.Till, 1887
(2) s/s after 8/1900 - no further trace.
(3) was photographed working at Gatewen Colliery [c1930 ? - B/107A] for sale at Plas Power Colliery 12/1938 - no further trace.
(4) wlw(tdt?): Bersham Colliery
(5) tdt: ? , after 22/9/1967 by 23/11/1967 - no further trace.
(6) tdt: Brymbo Steelworks, off loan, 1/1966
(7) tdt: Seymour Opencast CDP, Berbyshire, after 2/9/1975 by 6/1976
(8) **tdt:** Bowers Row Opencast CDP, West Yorkshire, 12/1973
(9) tdt: Bennerley Opencast CDP, Notts, c10/1981
    wlw: Victoria Park Childrens' Playground, Leamington Spa, Warwicks.

GLANRAFON SLATE QUARRY, near RHYD-DDU   G8
(Gc/GR:581540)

		: Vaynol Estate
	1878	: an incline, etc, existed by this date
1878	-	: lease to **E.H.Owen** (Vulcan Foundry, Caernarfon) et al, who formed:-
	2/1904	: **Glanrafon Slate Quarry Co**
2/1904	c1914	: **Glanrafon Slate Quarry Co Ltd** (reg.25/2/1904 £50K liq.12/1916-11/1919)
	c1914	: closed. Lease surrendered 1916. Dismantled.

Workings connected to PR/44 by two inclines, with other inclines and a tunnel within the quarry area. Site used as weapons testing area in WW2, for which an aerial ropeway was erected into the quarry.

Locomotives: Gauge 2ft

Considerable doubts exist regarding the loco fleet here, though SILURIAN is positively confirmed, and there seems little doubt that there was a DeWinton named MURIEL which was later used on the Rhyd-ddu Forestry work. Old men have recalled scraps of information concerning a third, and possibly a fourth, loco here, including memories of "vertical boiler", "also named MURIEL" [at some time; possibly name transferred to loco above ?] and "an ordinary loco with a big polished dome" [SILURIAN had no dome.] It seems very likely, in fact, that the TALYSARN QUARRY loco which fell off Pont Fawr, Nantlle in 1/1879, was subsequently repaired by E.H.Owen for further use (after 1894) at Glanrafon. However, the type and identity of that loco is not known. If indeed it was a VB loco, then the "ordinary loco" could be a fourth at Glanrafon. If, however, the Pont Fawr loco was an "ordinary loco" then perhaps Glanrafon had only three. It is all very vague, and documentary evidence seems totally lacking.

MURIEL	0-4-0VBT	VC	DeW		[c1879 New ?]	(1)
SILURIAN	0-4-0ST	OC	HE	601	1894 New 2/94	(2)

(1) tdt: Rhyd-ddu Forestry Railway, c1914
(2) still here 17/2/1913
wlw: Albert Sheet Iron Co Ltd, West Bromwich, Staffs, by 12/3/1917

In J/MM/7-7-1916, R.White & Sons, dealers, Widnes, were offering for sale "one 2ft gauge loco by Hunslet 6"x8" cylinders 4-wheel coupled, also 2ft gauge coffeepot loco". HE 601 was 6"x8" and such locos were uncommon; thus these locos could be SILURIAN and the mystery third loco here.
But, as luck would have it, the advert could equally apply to locos just then sold at Glynrhonwy Quarry - see LLANBERIS WEST.

GLYNCEIRIOG (CAMBRIAN & WYNNE) SLATE QUARRIES   G10
(Cd/GR:below)

CAMBRIAN SLATE QUARRY   (Cd/GR:189378)
   by 1854 -   : Cambrian Slate Co (reg.3/8/1854)
      1856 -   : Cambrian Slate Co Ltd (reg.23/10/1856 liq.1869)
      1872 -   1875   : New Cambrian Slate Co Ltd (reg.8/6/1872 : which became:-)
      1875 -   1892   : New Cambrian Slate Co Ltd (reg.19/4/1875 liq.1892)
      1892 -   1910   : Glyn Slate Co Ltd (reg.30/12/1892 vol.liq.16/7/1910)
      1910 -   1948   : Glyn Quarries Ltd (reg.14/5/1910 £20K vol.liq.12/9/1947)
                 1947   :   closed. Dispersal auction 14/7/1948.

WYNNE SLATE QUARRY   (Cd/GR:199379)
     c1750 -   c1881 : Edward Wynne
      1884 -   1892   : Pant Glas Slate & Slab Quarry Co Ltd
                            (reg.1883   vol.liq.15/1/1892)
      1892 -   1927   :   worked with Cambrian Quarry (but closed 1909-24)
      1927 -   c1980 :   closed
     c1980 -   c1982 : Brian James, Glyn Quarry Museum.
     c1982 -   : Glyn Quarry Enterprises Ltd

Originally two separate quarries working the same vein by open pits to the west of Glynceiriog village. Both became mines reached by level adit tunnels, the Wynne tunnel growing to ¾ mile long, the Cambrian more than 1 mile long. Under common ownership the mines amalgamated, with surface activities concentrated at the Cambrian premises. Both sites had incline connections to the Glyn Valley Tramway (PR/42) at Glyn, the Cambrian Quarry being the original promoters and users of that line.
Following closure, the Cambrian area has been somewhat lost in forestry plantation, but in the 1980s the Wynne Quarry was re-opened as a tourist amenity.

[Read: B/182; B/309; B/348; B/349; J/DHS/1985/115]

Locomotives: Gauge 2'0" - Cambrian Slate Quarry.

It is reputed that the quarry had a 0-4-0WT loco possibly of German origin, but no evidence yet found to confirm this.

-	0-4-0ST	OC	WB	1916	1910	New 10/10	(1)
	4wPM	20hp	MR	2102	1921	New 3/21	(2)
	4wPM	11hp	FH	1617	1929	New 6/29	(3)

Locomotives: Gauge 2'0" - Wynne Quarry Tourist Centre.

	BEAR		4wDM	30hp	RH	339209	1952	(a)
26			4wDM	20hp	MR	8720	1941	(b)

(a) tdx: Alan Keef Ltd, dealer, Cote, Oxon, 4/1980
    wfw: Bell Rock Gypsum Ltd, Notts.
(b) tdx: Cheshire Transport Collection,, Runcorn, 31/8/1980
    wfw: Joseph Arnold & Sons Ltd, Leighton Buzzard, Bedfordshire.

(1) loco still in use here 2/1921
    wlw(tdt?): R.S.Davies, dealer, Mold (see Section 1), by 7/1924
(2) tdt: Penmachno Slate Quarry, after sale in auction here 14/7/1948
(3) for sale in auction here 14/7/1948; no further trace.

GLYNCEIRIOG PRIVATE RAILWAY G12
(Cd/GR:206378)

1969 -   1971 : Mr Melvin Phillips
          1971 : closed; dismantled.

Situated in a riverside field adjacent to the route of the Glyn Valley Tramway (PR/42), construction of this railway commenced in 1969. It was intended for public use, and occasional trains ran over a short length, but Planning Permission was denied hence the line was never completed.

Locomotives: Gauge 2'0"

| - | 4wDM | 32hp | RH | 177598 | 1935 | (a) | Scr 10/1969 |
| - | 4wDM | 20hp | RH | 182137 | 1936 | (b) | (1) |

(a) tdx: Oakeley Slate Quarry, after 6/1968 by 7/1969
(b) tdx: Oakeley Slate Quarry, after 13/8/1969 by 26/10/1969

(1) tdt: Mr I.Hose, private store at Halkyn, Clwyd, after 10/1969 by 6/1972
    wlw: Bala Lake Railway (PR/66).

GRANGE QUARRIES & TRAMWAY, HOLYWELL & GREENFIELD   G14
(Cf/GR:below)

by 1848			: Holywell Limestone Co
from c1849			: Holywell Railway & Limestone Co
			[Evan Evans & Partners]
from c1866	-	1878	: Holywell Lime Co Ltd [Evan Evans et al]
1878	-	1884	: John T.Eachus
1884	-	1895	: Holywell Lime & Cement Co Ltd
		1895	: closed
WW2			: Ministry of Supply Explosives Store
c1980	-	10/1989	: Grange Cavern Military Museum
		10/1989	: closed

A short railway, of unknown gauge, was constructed to connect William Crockford's Spelter Works (built 1842) at Greenfield to a small harbour on the River Dee. It existed before the Chester & Holyhead Railway (PR/7) which, when built, crossed it on the level by an agreement dated 2/11/1847. In 5/1857, this Spelter Works railway was leased to the Holywell Railway & Limestone Co, who by that date had built a 3'0" gauge tramroad from a point near the Spelter Works, up the Greenfield Valley, to their limestone workings on the hill above Holywell. The principal workings were underground on the north side of the hill but the tramroad extended up and over the hill to serve open quarries to the east and west. The tramroad included nine inclines in its route.

By an Act of 1864, the Holywell Railway Co (see PR/33) was authorised to build a 4'8½" gauge railway to Holywell, generally following the tramroad route up the Greenfield Valley as far as St.Winefride's; but construction was not commenced until c1868/69. In the meantime, the right for the tramroad to cross PR/7 on the level was surrendered - by an agreement dated 11/8/1865 - and a timber bridge was built to carry the tramroad over PR/7 in 1867. However, this arrangement was soon replaced by an adjacent bridge over PR/7 built for the Holywell Railway Company line; this line then made a connection with PR/7 by a reversing junction on its north side. The new Holywell Railway route was graded such that it replaced three tramroad inclines between Greenfield and St.Winefride's, and this section was laid with three rails providing mixed 4'8½" and 3'0" gauges. This enabled tramroad wagons to travel through from the quarries to the harbour. There was a short branch near Greenfield to a crushing plant erected c1860 at the premises which were formerly a smelting works of the Parys Mine Company [of Anglesey].

The Holywell Railway Company line was never opened as a public railway; it was therefore operated by the Lime Company, for its own traffic, and locomotives were introduced. The Holywell Lime Co Ltd closed in 1878 on the death of Evan Evans; the business was advertised for sale by the Official Liquidator, including "locomotive and stationary engines, railway and tramway plant and waggons". A 3/1879 Prospectus of the Holywell Hydraulic Lime, Whitestone & Cement Quarries Ltd refers to the line as having been worked by two locomotives. This 1879 Company does not appear to have traded.

The final liquidation sale on 30/10/1895 included two locomotives, 48 main line wagons and 93 quarry wagons. All track on the Holywell Railway and tramroad was then removed. For subsequent history see PR/33.

During WW2 the underground quarry workings were used as a munition store and, in the 1980s, were opened to the public as the "Grange Cavern Military Museum"; which closed 10/1989. Close to St.Winefride's there was a Cement Factory in what had been John Smalley's "Yellow" Cotton Mill, built 1877 and the first of many in the Valley. Also close to St.Winefride's, and beside the tramroad, was the entrance to the "boat level" of the Holway Lead Mine. This was an adit used by small barges but, by 1830, dried out and fitted with a tramroad. It has been recorded that the Holywell Limestone Company and successors obtained limestone from the mine workings by means of this access.

The entire Greenfield Valley was occupied by a wide range of industries for over 200 years, including (for example) a Tinplate Works 1868-1874, operated by Thomas Boundy & Co and Holywell Tinplate Co. Readers seeking further general information should consult B/275. In the 1980s the Valley was opened to the public as an Industrial Heritage Park. [Read: B/275; B/232]

Locomotives: Gauge 4'8½" - Limestone Railway.

-	0-4-0ST	OC	FW	253	1874	New 10/74	(1)
	[? 0-4-0ST	OC]	FE(HH)			(a)	(1)

Locomotive: Gauge 2ft - Military Museum Static Display.

(No.21)	4wPM	20hp	MR	[c1920] (b)	(2)

(a) a spare injector was supplied by FW, and recorded as probably for the "Hughes loco the Co have". No further details known.
(b) tdx: Mr Ian Jolly (see Section 1), loan, 1984

(1) two locos - presume these two locos - in 30/10/1895 liquidation sale but no further trace.
(2) tdt: Mr Ian Jolly, off loan, 1990

GREENFIELD (COURTAULDS) FACTORY, HOLYWELL JUNCTION   G16

(Cf/GR:below)

	1934	:	new factory
1934 -	5/1985	:	**Courtaulds Ltd**
	5/1985	:	closed;
1986 -	1990	:	demolished; redeveloped for light industry

The factory consisted by two units, separated by the LMSR (PR/7) main line. On the south (inland) side, a Viscose Plant, opened in 1934; on the north (seaward) side, the Fibro Chemical Plant, opened 1936. Viscose Plant closed 7/1979; Chemical Plant closed 5/1985. Locomotives were kept in separate sheds within each Plant. There was a low-headroom railway tunnel passing beneath PR/7, for which the special reduced-height loco P.1900 was obtained. After 1954 this tunnel was little used except by road vehicles.

Locomotives: Gauge 2'0" - MELVILLE, DUNDAS & WHITSUN LTD, contractors (of Glasgow). Construction work at Fibro Chemical Plant, 1936.

No.2	4wDM	20hp	FH	1961[? 1936] New	s/s
No.3	4wDM	20hp	FH	1962[? 1936] New	s/s

Locomotives: Gauge 2'0" - Chemical Plant operation.   (GR:204773)

		4wPM	L	35588	1950	New 6/50	(1)
		4wPM	L	35589	1950	New 6/50	(1)

Locomotives: Gauge 4'8½" - Shunting both Plants.   (GR:201775;202775)

1		0-4-0ST	OC	P	1892	1935	New 7/35	(2)
2		0-4-0T	OC	P	1900	1936	New 1/36	(3)
2	(formerly: 3)	0-4-0ST	OC	P	1947	1938	New 8/38	(4)
3	(formerly: 4)	0-4-0ST	OC	P	2084	1948	New 4/48	(5)
4	(formerly: 5)	0-4-0ST	OC	WB	2963	1950	New 10/50	(6)
5		0-4-0ST	OC	RSH	7335	1946	(a)	(7)
-		4wDH 255hp		S	10231	1965	(b)	(8)
-		4wDH 255hp		S	10251	1966	New	(9)
-		4wDH 255hp		S	10252	1966	New	(10)

(*)   built 1935; ex works Bristol 31/12/1935; plate dated 1936

(a)   tdx: G.A.Harvey & Co (London) Ltd, Angerstein Wharf, London, WILLIAM BAILEY,
      arrived 1/1955 [en route since 10/1954 !]
(b)   here, on demonstration trials, by 4/7/1965

(1)   scrapped on site by J.& H.B.Jackson Ltd, after 20/8/1965 by 1967
(2)   scrapped here by J.& H.B.Jackson Ltd (of Coventry), 9/1967
(3)   advertised as for sale here 3/1955, but re-allocated to Courtaulds Great Coates Works
      Grimsby. Was at Pecketts Bristol Works for repairs in 1956 and may have gone direc
      to Bristol from Greenfield.
      wlw: Quainton Railway Centre, Buckinghamshire (preserved).
(4)   scrapped here by J.& H.B.Jackson Ltd (of Coventry), 1967
(5)   disused by 1967; tdt: Llangollen Railway (PR/68) c18/10/1975
(6)   scrapped here by J.& H.B.Jackson Ltd (of Coventry), 1966
(7)   scrapped here by J.& H.B.Jackson Ltd (of Coventry), 6/1969
(8)   departed from here after 4/7/1965, on completion of trials.
(9)   tdt: Courtaulds Ltd, Spondon Power Station, Derbyshire, 11/1987
(10) tdt: Courtaulds Ltd, Grimsby Works, Humber, 4/11/1987

GRESFORD (ACTON GRANGE) COLLIERY   G18
                                                              (Cd/GR:338537)

	6/11/1907	:	First Sod ceremony.
3/1908	- 6/1911	:	sinking - 2263ft deep.
1907	- 12/1947	:	**United Westminster & Wrexham Collieries Ltd**
			(reg.14/7/1905 £200K later £400K)
1/1948	-		: **National Coal Board**
	10/11/1973	:	closed
1974	- 1977	:	dismantled by Metallic Salvage & Supply Co Ltd

from sidings beside the GWR main line (PR/5) a short private railway climbed steeply into the colliery yard, where the loco shed was situated. After closure, the site of this colliery was virtually obliterated.

The owning Company was an amalgamation of Westminster Colliery (Moss) and Wrexham [Wrexham & Acton] [Rhos Dee] Colliery (Rhosddu, Wrexham). Both closed in 1925, men being transferred to Gresford. Both Westminster and Wrexham [Acton] collieries had extensive railway sidings, but as far as is yet known they did not use industrial locomotives.
[Read: B/107]

Locomotives: Gauge 4'8½"

		0-4-0ST	OC	MW	380	1871	(a)	s/s c1915	
KINROSS		0-4-0ST	OC	AB	1232	1912	New 12/12		(1)
SIR THEODORE		0-4-0ST	OC	AE	1397	1899	(b)		(2)
-		0-6-0ST	OC	AE	1604	1912	(c)		(3)
-		0-4-0ST	OC	P	1297	1913	(d)		(4)
PAT		0-4-0ST	OC	HC	276	1885			
		rebuilt	HC			1922	(e)		(5)
ARENIG		0-6-0ST	OC	AE	1770	1917	(f)		(6)
VULCAN		0-4-0ST	OC	SS	3419	1888	(g)		(7)
LEIGH		0-6-0ST	IC	HE	1439	1923	(h)		(8)
BERYL		0-6-0ST	IC	RSH	7088	1943	(i)	Scr/1964	
THE WELSHMAN		0-6-0ST	IC	MW	1207	1890			
		rebuilt	MW			1908	(j)		(9)
-		0-6-0ST	IC	HE	3206	1945	(k)	Scr 8/1977	
(GWYNETH)		0-6-0ST	IC	RSH	7135	1944	(m)		(10)
RICHBORO		0-6-0T	OC	HC	1243	1917	(n)		(11)
ALISON		0-6-0ST	IC	HE	3163	1944			
		rebuilt	HE		3885	1964	(o)		(12)

Locomotives: Gauge 2'0" - Surface Tubway System.

-	4wDM	31hp	RH	375700	1954	New 7/54	(13)
-	4wDM	31hp	RH	375701	1954	(p)	(14)

These locos were rather light for the work; hence the surface lines were normally operated by a 48hp loco from the underground fleet.

Locomotives: Gauge 2'0" - Underground.

2	(BERWYN)	4wDM	48hp	RH	481552	1962	New 9/62	(15)
3	(BALA)	4wDM	48hp	RH	481553	1962	New 10/62	(16)
3	(formerly: 4)	4wDM	48hp	RH	497547	1963	New 3/63	(17)
8		4wDM	48hp	RH	497761	1963	(q)	(18)
12		4wDM	48hp	RH	506494	1964	(r)	(19)
13		4wDM	48hp	RH	506495	1964	(s)	(20)
9		4wDM	48hp	RH	497762	1963	(t)	(21)
11		4wDM	48hp	RH	504628	1963	(u)	(22)
5		4wDM	48hp	RH	497549	1963	(v)	(23)
14		4wDM	48hp	RH	506496	1964	(w)	(24)
10		4wDM	48hp	RH	497763	1963	(x)	(25)

NOTE: The DIRECT RETURN TRANSFER of any loco to AND from Area Workshops, being common occurrence for routine overhauls, is not recorded in this list. Visits to Area Workshops are only noted when a transfer of the loco to/from another colliery concurrently occurred.

(a) here by 15/5/1911
     wfw(tdx?): Admiralty, Portsmouth Dockyard, Hampshire.
(b) tdx: Minera Lead Mines, c1914 after sale there 25/11/1914
     tdt: Hafod Colliery, loan, after 23/9/1915 by 5/2/1917
     tdx: Hafod Colliery, off loan, after 5/2/1917 by 4/1917
(c) hired from: Cudworth & Johnson, dealers, Wrexham, 1932
(d) hired from: Cudworth & Johnson, during 1936
(e) hired from: Cudworth & Johnson, c1936 by 2/10/1936
(f) tdx: Brymbo Steelworks, loan, 1938
(g) hired from: Cudworth & Johnson, 1938 by 10/1938
(h) tdx: Hough & Sons, dealers, Wigan, Lancashire, c1942
     wfw: West Leigh Colliery Co Ltd, Lancashire.
(i) tdx: War Department, Calais, France, WD 75052; arrived 7/1947 after 15/7/1947
(j) tdx: Llay Main Colliery, after 4/1953 by 5/1953
     tdt: Llay Main Colliery, after 8/1954 by 3/1955
     tdx: Hafod Colliery, after 3/1965 by 9/7/1965
(k) tdx: Llay Main Workshops 1962
     wfw: Hafod Opencast Coal Disposal Point.
(m) tdx: Llay Main Workshops 12/4/1966
     wfw: Llay Main Colliery
(n) tdx: Ifton Colliery, Salop, 12/1969 (and not used at Gresford).
(o) tdx: Walkden Workshops, Lancashire, 20/11/1970
(p) tdx: Walkden Workshops, Lancashire, 1966
     wfw: Llay Main Colliery
(q) tdx: Llay Main Workshops (New loco) 26/10/1963
(r) tdx: Llay Main Workshops (New loco) 5/1964
(s) tdx: Llay Main Workshops (New loco) 22/5/1964
(t) tdx: Llay Main Workshops 28/5/1965
     wfw: Point of Ayr Colliery
(u) tdx: Llay Main Workshops 12/3/1966
     wfw: Point of Ayr Colliery
(v) tdx: Point of Ayr Colliery 30/4/1966
(w) tdx: Walkden Workshops, Lancashire, 16/8/1966
     wfw: Llay Main Colliery
(x) tdx: Llay Main Workshops by 9/1966 (no previous location known).

(1) scrapped 9/1966 at Gresford by George Cohen, Sons & Co Ltd.
(2) tdt: Cudworth & Johnson, dealers, Wrexham, after 10/1936 by 5/1942
(3) returned to Cudworth & Johnson, off loan, 1932
(4) returned to Cudworth & Johnson, off loan, [? late 1936/early 1937]
(5) returned to Cudworth & Johnson, off loan, [? late 1936/early 1937]
(6) tdt: Brymbo Steelworks, off loan, c1938
(7) returned to Cudworth & Johnson, off loan, after 10/1938 by 26/2/1939
(8) scrapped 9/1966 at Gresford by George Cohen, Sons & Co Ltd.
(9) tdt: Lound Hall Mining Museum, Bevercotes, Notts, 7/1971
     wlw: Chatterley Whitfield Mining Museum, Staffs

(10) tdt: Walkden Workshops, Lancashire, 4/1974
    wlw: Bickershaw Colliery, Lancashire.
        In 1984 the boiler, cylinders and motion of this loco were used by Resco Railways Ltd in construction of 7'0" gauge loco IRON DUKE.
(11) tdt: Llangollen Railway (PR/68), 2/1976 (c7/2/1976)
(12) tdt: Bold Colliery, Lancashire, 4/1974
(13) tdt: Llay Main Colliery, 6/11/1964
(14) departed after 13/7/1969 by 27/6/1970, [? to Walkden Workshops].
    wlw: Amalgamated Construction Ltd, contractors, at Thorne Colliery.
    wlw: Mr John Waller, private store, Lincoln, by 12/1981
    wlw: Mr D.Billmore, Dorrington, Lincs (preserved).
(15) tdt: Point of Ayr Colliery, after 11/1967 by 1973
    tdx: Walkden Workshops, Lancashire, 7/1973
    tdt: Walkden Workshops, c1974
    wlw: Amalgamated Construction Ltd, contractors, at Thorne Colliery.
    wlw: Welsh Highland Railway (see PR/44)
(16) tdt: Walkden Workshops, Lancashire, 15/8/1966
    wlw: Point of Ayr Colliery
(17) tdt: Walkden Workshops, Lancashire, c1974
    wlw: Bersham Colliery
(18) tdt: Llay Main Workshops, 1/6/1964
    wlw: Point of Ayr Colliery
(19) tdt: Walkden Workshops, Lancashire, c1972; Scrapped there c1975
(20) tdt: Llay Main Workshops, 12/5/1965
    wlw: Point of Ayr Colliery
(21) tdt: Walkden Workshops, Lancashire, c1969 by 3/1969
    wlw: Point of Ayr Colliery
(22) tdt: Walkden Workshops, Lancashire, 10/1971; Scrapped there c1975
(23) tdt: Walkden Workshops, Lancashire, c1975 and Scrapped there.
(24) tdt: Point of Ayr Colliery [? c1973](25) s/s by 7/1978 - no further trace.

GROBY GRANITE QUARRY, BLAENAU FFESTINIOG   G20
(Gm/GR:693452)

```
           1901  : opened
                 : Festiniog Granite Co
        -  1927  : Festiniog Granite Quarries Ltd
 1927   -  1937  : Groby Granite Co Ltd
           1937  : closed; dismantled.
```

A short railway ran from the quarry face to an incline near Cefn Bychan; from foot of incline a sinuous branch line connected to the Ffestiniog Railway (PR/3). This branch, which was opened c1908, was worked by Ffestiniog Railway locos until c1930, when quarry locos were put onto this duty. Use of the branch line apparently ceased prior to closure of the quarry. The original quarry product was setts, but in later years a crushing plant was built near Cefn Bychan. Stone then passed through the crushers, rather than down the nearby incline.

[Read: B/374/59; B/169/480]

Locomotives: Gauge 2ft

Unknown quantity of 4wP locos, maker not known. All s/s c1937.

GROESLON (TUDOR) SLATE WORKS, near PENYGROES G22
(Gc/GR:471551)

1891   : William Owen
            : Jones & Ingham
            : Inigo Jones & Co Ltd

Slate processing factory served by short siding off PR/2/29, with a simple 2ft gauge hand operated rail system (disused by 12/1941) around the yard - track subsequently removed. By 1988 the works was open to visitors, with a small display of railway vehicles including the locomotive listed below.

Locomotive: Gauge 2'3" - Static Display.

                        4wBE   LMM   (a)   OOU

(a)   tdx: private store at Caernarfon 12/1987
       wfw: Aberllefenni Slate Quarries, near Corris.

GROES-Y-DDWY-AFON SLATE QUARRY   G24
PONT-YR-AFON-GAM, near LLAN FFESTINIOG
(Gm/GR:750424)

                   1861   : opened
     1920 -   1932   : L.M. & D.M. Colman
        -         1953   : Groesddwyafon Slate Quarries Co Ltd
     1953   1987   : closed (sale of equipment 4/1953)
     1987 -   : reopened: **M.Jones & P.Luck** (using road vehicles)
                                   : **Nationwide Slate Products Ltd**

A remote and comparatively small quarry, which had a railway from Mill to tips and, via a tunnel, from Mill to workings (some of which were underground).

Locomotives: Gauge 2ft

                        4wPM   L   [? 3742   1931]   (1)

(1)   at the 4/1953 auction this loco consisted of a chassis and front engine casing only. Cleared from site after 18/4/1953, probably as scrap.
       It is possible - though there is no real evidence - that it was Lister 3742/1931, the engine and gearbox of which were later found at Cwt-y-Bugail Quarry (which see).

GWYNFYNYDD GOLD MINE, MAWDDACH FALLS, near GANLLWYD G26
(Gm/GR:737281)

1968	-	: Geochemical Remining Ltd
c1976	-	: M.F.Freeman [of Minera]
1984	-	: M.Winberg
		: Gwynfynydd & Beddcoedwr Gold Mines Ltd
	1989	: closed.

One of very many gold mines in the area, also worked for copper and lead, with a typically long history of spasmodic activity under constantly changing ownerships dating back from the early 1800s [see eg B/229, B/271]. Situated beside the infant river Mawddach, in a wooded valley some distance from a public road, in close proximity to three other mines (Beddcoedwr/Marina, Cwmheisian West, and East Cwmheisian); the separating boundaries being indistinct - other than that the surface installations of the Cwmheisians have - latterly - been on the opposite bank of the river. This group of mines has, from time to time, been interworked and interowned, though never - it would seem - have all four been worked as one unit. All have had extensive surface railways, connecting shafts and adits to crushing-stamps and smelters; Gwynfynydd also had three separate incline systems ranging northerly up the hillside to other workings at higher altitudes. Much is now [1990] difficult to view due to forestry, but lengthy rail-routes can be traced on both sides of the river from the 1893 Gwynfynydd Mill site (GR:735274) to the Vaughan Shaft (GR:742282) area. The mine was abandoned in 1939 and the accessible equipment was salvaged; exploration restarted in 1968, eventually resulting in some commercial mining in the latter-1980s. On the surface, this was visible at the main riverside adit, into which a locomotive operated railway was installed, with loco shed outside adit entrance. Track in situ 9/1990.

[Read: J/MRS/1973; B/229; B/271; B/199/23/55

Locomotives: Gauge 2'0"

-	4wBE	WR	5537	1956	(a)	(1)
-	4wBE	WR	1277	1938	(b)	(1)
-	4wBE	CE	5370	1967	(c)	(2)
-	4wBE	CE	5885	1971	(c)	(2)

(a) wfw: Ffestiniog Railway (PR/3); taken to Mold area for repairs then brought to Gwynfynydd after 4/1981 by 12/5/1982
(b) tdx: Wheal Concorde Mine, Cornwall, c1/1985
(c) arrived c4/1985; purchased from South Western Mining & Tunnelling Co store in the Midlands.
wfw: Laporte Industries Ltd, Ladywash Mine, Derbyshire.
(1'6" gauge locos; converted to 2'0" gauge for use at Gwynfynydd.)

(1) taken by lorry to unknown destination/s after 17/5/1990 by 14/9/1990.
(2) footnote (1) applies to one of these locos; the other was:-
tdt: Parys Mountain Copper Mine, Anglesey, after 17/5/1990 by 14/9/1990

HAFOD (PRINCE OF WALES/HAFODYBWCH/RUABON NEW) H2
COLLIERY near JOHNSTOWN, RUABON (Cd/GR:313465)

		1862	: sinking commenced - First Sod ceremony 10/3/1863
		8/1867	: first winning
1862	-	c1872	: **Ruabon Coal Co**
c1872	-	7/1880	: **Ruabon Coal Co Ltd**
7/1880	-	12/1946	: **Ruabon Coal & Coke Co Ltd** (reg.14/7/1880 £30K)
from 8/1933			: controlled by Carlton Main Colliery Co Ltd
1/1947	-	1968	: **National Coal Board**
		8/3/1968	: closed; dismantled and shafts filled.

From 1856 the Ruabon Coal Co, then working the Ruabon Brandie Colliery, was controlled by Sir Daniel Gooch of the Great Western Railway Company. From 1867, the Coal Co transferred operations to deeper seams at Hafod Colliery; the sidings to this colliery also served the Hafod Tile Works which were under colliery ownership until 1934.

Per J/CG/30.7.1880 The Ruabon Coal & Coke Co Ltd was registered 14/7/1880 to acquire and work the undertakings of the Ruabon Coal Co Ltd. However, J/CC/7.6.1879 includes an advertisement for an auction 26/6/1879 of the Hafod-y-Bwch Colliery & Brickworks "re Ruabon Coal & Coke Co Ltd in liquidation". It is difficult to reconcile these conflicting items.

A fan of sidings adjacent to Johnstown station (PR/5) was used as a landsale depot, except from WW2 to 1962 when it was occupied by the Hafod Opencast Coal Disposal Point (which see). Opencast Depot locos were initially stabled and repaired at the colliery, resulting in confused reports as to their ownership. From mid-1967 output at Hafod was taken by road vehicles, the only railway duty then remaining being occasional shunts for the Tile Works; these terminated by 4/1968.

[Read: B/107; B/301; B/303; B/276]

Locomotives: Gauge 1'11½"

It is stated [B/103/N31] that locos MW 259 and 260 of the Ffestiniog & Blaenau Railway (PR/34) were sold by the GWR to the Ruabon Coal & Coke Co [c1884]. There has been no recollection of them at Ruabon. If they were here, a possible use may have been in connection with the 64 Beehive Coke Ovens at Hafod [Rylands Directory 1924] as elsewhere (in for example Co.Durham and South Yorkshire) such Ovens have been charged by loco-worked narrow gauge railways. Alternatively, the locos could have become stationary boilers. [See J/FRS/No.130/408]

Locomotives: Gauge 2'6"

The tubway gauge at Hafod Colliery was 1'9½"; a third rail was laid in the main underground roadway in 1957 to enable flameproof locos to be used. Loco hauled rail system replaced by conveyors c1965; locos then stored in surface stock-yard.

-	0-4-0DM	68hp HC	DM1082	1957	New	Scr 8/1970
-	0-4-0DM	68hp HC	DM1083	1957	New *	Scr 8/1970
-	0-4-0DM	68hp HC	DM1227	1960	New	Scr 8/1970

* ordered in error as "for Bersham Colliery"; delivered New to Hafod.

Locomotives: Gauge 4'8½"

It is likely that shunting was originally performed by the GWR, and indeed the use of GWR/BR locos was common throughout the life of the colliery. In recent times such locos included (all 0-6-0PT):-
28 (1950-51); 8734 (12/1960); 8727 (1961); 1619 (4/1963); 1663 (9/1963, 10/1963).

Apart from the locos listed below, there have been persistent tales of the colliery having had SPIDER 0-6-0ST IC MW, and YORK (YORKE ?) 0-4-0ST MW on loan from Cudworth & Johnson. Neither of these have been traced but, assuming memory to be not strictly accurate, the nearest possible known locos are : SPIDER 0-4-0ST OC MW 1229/1892 which was with Marple & Gillott, contractors, in 6/1908 and then "lost" - and YORK 0-6-0ST IC MW 1295/1895 which was with Ribble Navigation, Preston Docks, by 1947, and later scrapped there. All this, of course, is entirely hypothetical and probably irrelevant. There is a well-known 'SPIDER' at Bersham Colliery, but it was not built by MW.

	Name	Type	Cyl	Mfr	No.	Date	Note	Disposal	Ref
	HAFOD	0-6-0ST	IC	P	775	1899	New 3/99		(1)
	CHAMPION	0-6-0ST	OC	FW	287	1875	(a)	Scr/c1928	(2)
	SIR THEODORE	0-4-0ST	OC	AE	1397	1899	(b)		(2)
	SHAKESPEARE	0-4-0ST	OC	HL	3072	1914	(c)		(3)
	CHAMPION	0-6-0ST	OC	AE	1603	1912	(d)		(4)
(16379)	LMS	0-6-0T	OC	NB	21521	1917	(e)		(5)
	KINROSS	0-4-0ST	OC	AB	1232	1912	(f)		(6)
	FRANCES VALERIE	0-6-0ST	IC	HE	3700	1950	(g)	Scr 11/1968	
	PIRAEUS	0-4-0ST	OC	AB	643	1889	(h)	Scr 8/1955	
	THE WELSHMAN	0-6-0ST	IC	MW	1207	1890			
		rebuilt MW				1908	(i)		(7)
No.82		0-6-0ST	IC	RSH	7103	1943	(j)		(8)
	LINDSAY	0-6-0ST	IC	WCI		1887	(k)		(9)

(a) New 11/1875 to "C.Tottenham, Liverpool" - one of at least ten locos delivered to Liverpool 1874-75 for probable use by John Dickson, John Dickson Junior, & C.Tottenham, contractors, for docks building and associated works. Many of these locos were apparently amongst those advertised for sale [in, eg, J/MM] from 3/1879 to 1884.
FW 287 subsequently with Kirk & Randall, contractors [who, in 1885, had a contract for Workhouse Infirmary, Champion Hill, Dulwich, etc; note this possible source of name for loco]; loco was repaired by Pecketts in 1908 and despatched to Hafod Colliery 4/2/1908.
(b) tdx: Gresford Colliery, loan, after 23/9/1915 by 5/2/1917
(c) tdx: Cudworth & Johnson, dealers, Wrexham, loan, c1926-27
(d) arrived after 9/1928 by 10/1928
wfw: Mersey Docks & Harbour Board, Liverpool.
This loco was sold by MDHB to George Cohen, Sons & Co Ltd, dealers. Cohen was advertising it for sale in 5/1928 AND 6/1929, but by 9/1928 it had in fact been purchased by Avonside Engine Co, and spare parts were sent to Hafod Colliery 10/1928, 2/1929, 2/1930, etc.
(e) tdx: LMS Railway, (No.)16379, 4/1934 after 21/4/1934
wfw: Glasgow & South Western Railway, (No.)324.
(f) tdx: Gresford Colliery, loan, 1938 (c7/1938)
(g) tdx: Llay Main Colliery, 2/1951
(h) tdx: Bersham Colliery, after 5/1953 by 7/6/1954 (and not used).
(i) tdx: Llay Main Colliery, after 11/1959 by 1/1960

(j)   tdx: Port of London Authority, 11/1960 (plated RSH 7113 in error).
(k)   tdx: Chisnall Hall Colliery, Lancs, 8/1967 (and not used).

(1)   tdt: Llay Main Colliery, 8/1933
(2)   tdt: Gresford Colliery, off loan, after 5/2/1917 by 4/1917
(3)   returned to Cudworth & Johnson, off loan, c19287
            (reputedly tdt: Bersham Colliery (who later purchased this loco)).
(4)   s/s after 9/1959 by 11/1959; no further trace (presume scrapped).
(5)   tdt: BR, Oswestry Works, Salop, 26/11/1962
            wlw: Coplawhill Transport Museum, Glasgow.
(6)   tdt: Gresford Colliery, off loan, c7/1939
(7)   tdt: Gresford Colliery, after 3/1965 by 9/7/1965
(8)   scrapped at Hafod 6/1967 by Karalius Bros (of Widnes, Lancashire).
(9)   departed 5/1968 per or via Thos.W.Ward Ltd, Salford, Lancs, to
       Maudland Metals Ltd, Preston; and wlw: Steamtown Ltd, Carnforth.

HAFOD OPENCAST COAL DISPOSAL POINT, JOHNSTOWN   H4
(Cd/GR:307462)

```
           -      3/1952   : Ministry of Fuel & Power
       4/1952  -  2/1962   : National Coal Board Opencast Executive
                             operated under contract by Tarmac Ltd
                  2/1962   : closed; track removed.
                             site used as landsale yard by Hafod Colliery.
```

A fan of sidings beside Johnstown station where coal from various sites was loaded onto rail. Prior to c10/1955, when a loco shed was built here, the locos were stabled at the Hafod Colliery shed; some records suggest that these 'opencast' locos may have been maintained by, and even been used by, the operators of Hafod Colliery.

Opencast mining in the area has included sites at Coed Talon, Vron (Southsea), Lodge (Brymbo), Black Lane (Brymbo), Plas Power Park, Bryn-yr-Owen (Ponciau), Ty Gwyn (Vinegar Hill, Rhos), Black Park, High Barracks (Black Park), Windy Hill, Pentre Vron (Plas Mostyn, Coedpoeth), Wynn Hall (Christionydd) and Gardden Lodge (Ruabon). All are areas of interest to the railway archaeologist where disturbance has destroyed the remains of many early railways. [B/107A/81]

Locomotives: Gauge 4'8½"

75147	0-6-0ST	IC	HE	3187	1944	(a)	(1)
75060	0-6-0ST	IC	RSH	7096	1943	(b)	(2)
71442	0-6-0ST	IC	HE	3206	1945	(c)	(3)

(a)   here by 8/1946 - a War Department U.K.Coal Production Pool loco.
      wfw: Garswood Hall Collieries Co Ltd, Wigan, 9/1944-11/1944
      became WD 75147 in 11/1944 after repossession by Ministry of Supply.

b) tdx: Pemberton Opencast CDP, Lancashire, 9/1948
    tdt: Skiers Spring Opencast CDP, Yorkshire WR, 8/1950
    tdx: Pemberton Opencast CDP, Lancashire, 7/1951
c) tdx: West Tinsley Opencast CDP, Yorkshire WR, 9/12/1954

1) tdt: British Railways, Crewe Works, for repairs, 10/1949
    wlw: Backworth Opencast CDP, Northumberland, 3/1950
2) tdt: NCB, Walkden Workshops, Lancashire, 4/1955 (arrived 30/4/1955)
    wlw: Raglan Opencast CDP, Glamorgan, by 1/1956
3) tdt: NCB Llay Main Workshops, Llay, 12/2/1962
    wlw: Gresford Colliery

HALKYN DISTRICT MINES DRAINAGE TUNNELS   H6
(Cf/GR:below)

11/1818 -   1822 : Duke of Westminster
1838 -   : Absalom Francis
1878 -   : Halkyn District Mines Drainage Co (Act:1875)

The lead mines of the area had long been troubled by drainage problems, hence in 1818 construction commenced at Nant-y-Flint of the HALKYN TUNNEL (portal GR:229711) at around 200ft above sea level. Intended to drain several mines, the tunnel eventually reached the South Llyn-y-Pandy Mine (GR:194655) near Mold, a total length of about 5 miles. Doubtless a railway was used in the tunnel during construction, but we understand nothing of it now remains. This tunnel was of limited benefit due to its altitude, and was superceded by:-

THE MILWR (SEA LEVEL) TUNNEL
     1896 -   : Holywell-Halkyn Mining Co
   in 1902   : Holywell Halkyn Drainage Co Ltd
                -    1908 : Holywell-Halkyn Mining & Tunnel Co Ltd
     c1915 -   c1918 : Halkyn & District Drainage Co
     1928 -   1968 : Halkyn District United Mines Ltd (reg.31/3/1928 £250K)
[from 1962 -   1986 : wholly owned by Courtaulds Ltd]
     1968 -   1986 : Holywell Halkyn Mining & Tunnel Co Ltd
                   1986 : abandoned

When HDUM was formed in 1928, it took over the dormant H-HM&T and HDMD companies and (for reasons which do not concern us) these companies were kept 'alive' and certain actions conducted in their names; after 1968 the H-HM&T title was used for most purposes. The Llanarmon District Mines Drainage Co (Act of 1892 - no work done) was also incorporated into HDUM, the principal mining constituents of which were: Bryn Gwiog Mines Ltd; East Halkyn Mining Co Ltd; Halkyn Mining Co Ltd; Llynypandy Mining Co Ltd; Mount Halkyn Mining Co Ltd; New North Halkyn Mines Ltd; North Hendre Lead Mining Co Ltd; Pantymwyn Mining Co Ltd; and South Halkyn & Rhydymwyn Mining Co Ltd.

From a sea-level portal (GR:213760) near Bagillt, tunnel driven south-easterly c3½ miles to just south of Herward Mine, where work ceased in 1908. A short extension to Caeau Mine was made during WW1. Also during WW1, the Ministry of Munitions arranged erection of an electric pumping station at North Hendre to draw water from the mines - this was abandoned 2/1919. [The water was required by the Queensferry Factory.] By the 1920s virtually all the mines south of Caeau - as far as Gwernymynydd - had ceased work due to flooding, so the surviving companies (in effect) amalgamated to form HDUM, to extend and maintain the tunnel, and to exploit the veins thus de-watered. Both lead (with a little silver) and super purity limestone were subsequently won, but the most valuable product proved to be water pumped by Courtaulds Ltd from Bagillt portal to their factories at Greenfield. Mining had virtually ceased by 1970, and entire system abandoned when Greenfield factories closed in 1985.

A 1'10½" gauge railway was laid through the (10ft wide, 8ft high) tunnel during construction, and retained for subsequent maintenance and mining. The 'main line' from Bagillt to Gwernymynydd (GR:209628) was 8 miles long and there were branches to various shafts and veins. Three existing mine shafts were deepened to tunnel level; at Penybryn Shaft (GR:203707) a crushing plant was erected 1932, demolished 1962 and shaft sealed, at Pantymwyn Mine (GR:208652) reopened 1938 for tunnel access only, and later closed; at Olwyn Goch (GR:202678) which remained in use until 1985. During and after WW2 some sections of the old workings were used to store explosives by the Ministry of Supply, who operated trains over sections of the Milwr Tunnel railway - for further details see entry "Rhydymwyn Government Depot".

[Read: B/199/19/23(etc); B/211; B/407]

Locomotives: Gauge 1'10½"

744	4wBE	WR	744	1929	New	Wdn/1976	*
773	4wBE	WR	773	1930	New	Wdn/1976	*
	0-4-4-0DM 24hp	WB	2498	1934	New	Scr/c1939	
898	4wBE	WR	898	1935	New	7/35	*
899	4wBE	WR	899	1935	New	7/35	(1)
	4wDM 20hp	RH	182138	1936	New	11/36	*
	4wDM 20hp	RH	183727	1937	New	3/37	*
	0-4-0BE	WR	1080	1937	New	9/37	(1)
	4wDM 20hp	RH	331250	1952	New	10/52	*
	4wDM 20hp	RH	354029	1953	New	10/53	*
	0-4-0BE	WR	5311	1955	New	9/55	(1)

WR Locos : 898 and 899 originally worked as tandem pair.
   744 and 773 had centre cab; remainder had end cab.

* : It is reputed that most locomotives were abandoned below ground when the mine closed, some being too large to recover via Olwyn Goch shaft (having originally been lowered down the larger Penybryn shaft) and there being no operable rail access at the Bagillt portal. However, two locos arrived at Dolaucothi [see footnote (1)] so perhaps some others also were not lost.

Locomotives: Gauge 600mm - purchased for spare parts only.

4wDM 20hp	RH	226309	1944	(a)	Dsmt/1960
4wDM 20hp	RH	221593	1943	(b)	Dsmt/1966

a) tdx: George Cohen, Sons & Co Ltd, dealers, 13/8/1957
   wfw: for sale at WD, Liphook, Hampshire, 3/1957
b) tdx: ? : purchased per/via Madoc Jones, dealer, St.Asaph, 20/7/1966
   wfw: British Plaster Board Ltd, Kingston-on-Soar, Notts.

1) two locos (one of WR 1080 or 5311, plus WR 899) arrived 26/6/1987 at National Trust, Dolaucothi Gold Mine [Museum], Pumpsaint, Dyfed.
   [Thus note '*' presumed to apply to the other of WR 1080 or 5311.]

HARLECH MILITARY RAILWAY   H8
                                                            (Gm/GR:below)

1941 -   1946 : War Department (Royal Artillery Gun Ranges)
          1946 : depot closed
          1948 : railway dismantled.

Line from junction (GR:583317) with GWR (PR/32) north of Harlech station, turning north-west to ungated level crossings over minor and main roads to junction at GR:576324. Here line reversed through an arc swinging south-west to north-west, to first terminal located at GR:572323 (just beyond site of Harlech Cefn Mine). From this arc, a reversing junction to line running south to workshop and loco shed at GR:574318. The depot served a Gunnery Range in connection with the army camp at Trawsfynydd.

It has been suggested that John Mowlem & Co Ltd, contractors, built this railway using loco YEOVIL HC 1529, but proof is lacking. For further reference to Mowlem and YEOVIL see entry "Llanberis West".

[Read: J/RO/11.1947/198, 6.1948/111]

Locomotives: Gauge 4'8½"

A British Railways Movement Order of 10/2/1949 covered the transit of a loco "70225 0-6-0D" from Kinnerley (Salop) to Hunslet Engine Co, Leeds. The loco was stated as being "ex Harlech". However 70225 was an ex-LMSR 0-6-0D., a type not otherwise recorded at Harlech, and is therefore omitted from this list pending further information. The BR Movement Orders were not renowned for accuracy of detail.

	4wDM	48hp	RH	218049	1943	New 3/43	(1)
70226 (f. 226)	0-4-0DM	40hp	HE	1858	1937	(a)	(2)
A14620 THE HARLECH EXPRESS	4wPM	Guy lorry				(b)	(3)
WD No.2	0-4-0DM	60hp	JF	22500	1938	(c)	(4)
WD 28	0-4-0DM	150hp	JF	22889	1939	(d)	(5)
75191	0-6-0ST	IC	RSH	7141	1944	(e)	(6)

(a) here by 12/1943.
    wfw: WD, Chilwell, Nottinghamshire.
    Spares were ordered by REME, Park Hall Camp, Oswestry, Salop 3/1944 and 6/1944, but probably for loco located at Harlech.
(b) road vehicle fitted with rail wheels.

(c) doubt exists as to the true identity of this loco. 60hp JF 22500 was New to WD Hilsea, Portsmouth, 'No.2' - some souces claim that it later moved to Longmoor, and on to Harlech. They could, however, be confusing this 'No.2' with 150hp JF 22889 which was WD Corsham 'No.2', did move to Longmoor, became No.28, and did move to Harlech. Because, when a JF fitter visited Harlech to view JF 22889, he reported (20/8/1946) that he found two 150hp (JF) locos on site (and a HE with 40hp JF engine in it - doubtless HE 1858). Perhaps this fitter made an error, and the second loco was 60hp - an unlikely mistake, as the designs were quite different. If we assume he was correct, then JF 22500 should not be listed here, but replaced by a (unidentified) 150hp 0-4-0DM JF.
       If JF 22500, then - tdx: Longmoor Military Rly, Hants, 1943
(d) given as "WD28; arrived recently" in Harlech report of 5/6/1943.
    wfw: WD, Longmoor, Hants, in 6/1940
(e) tdx: WD, Kinnerley, Salop, after 10/5/1947 by 6/1948 (for track removal and demolition work only).

(1) departed by 8/1946.
    wlw: Mirrlees Watson Co Ltd, Hazel Grove, Cheshire.
(2) still here but disused, 24/6/1947
    wlw: WD, Sinfin Lane Depot, Derby (and later became WD 811).
(3) tdt: WD, Kinnerley, Salop, after 24/6/1947 by 9/1947
(4) departed after 20/8/1946 by 6/1948 - whatever it was.
(5) wlw(tdt?): WD, Bicester, Oxon, after 20/8/1946 by 5/1947
    wlw: Queensferry Government Depot.
(6) tdt: WD, Kinnerley, Salop, after 1/9/1948

HENDRE-DDU SLATE QUARRY and FORESTRY RAILWAYS, ABERANGELL   H10

(Gm/GR: below)

Radiating westwards from Aberangell station on the Mawddwy branch (PR/31) the Hendre-Ddu rail system has a complicated history with a multiplicity of owners, users and operators in need of further research. The original "main-line" from Aberangell via Abermynach, Cefn Gwyn, and Gartheiniog to Hendre-Ddu Quarry (3½ miles) was opened c1867 by Sir Edmund Buckley, to provide an outlet for his Hendre-Ddu Quarry. As well as minor spurs, two significant branch lines were added - from Abermynach south-west 1¼ miles to Coed-y-Chwarel Quarry, and from Gartheiniog northerly to Tal-y-mieryn Quarry and on to Maes-y-gamfa Quarry (1 mile). The branch to Coed-y-Chwarel was closed and track removed c1900.

During WW1, and perhaps for a few years thereafter, the Board of Trade obtained timber from the area, and used some (maybe all) sections of the system for timber haulage. The Coed-y-Chwarel branch was re-laid, and a new branch built from Cefn Gwyn, south-westerly for 1½ miles to Coed-Cwm-Caws. These two branches were removed when timber activities ceased.

Most, if not all, of the quarries had closed by 1939, when the remaining rail tracks were removed and the routes were converted into rough roads. The Hendre-Ddu quarry was used as an explosives store during WW2, and forestry work re-started; for this, the 1 mile extremity of the Coed-Cwm-Caws branch was reinstated, and small sections of track were used at Gartheiniog Junction (slate mill used as a saw mill) and at Aberangell (PR/31 wharf). After the War, occasional slate production occurred at Maes-y-gamfa and Hendre-Ddu quarries, but with only limited internal rail traffic. The forestry railway to Coed-Cwm-Caws was dismantled in 1954, the tracks at Gartheiniog saw mill were for sale in 1977; the disused rails on the Aberangell wharf were the last to survive.

Read: B/173, B/323]

HENDRE-DDU QUARRY (GR:798125)
	-	1872	: Hendre Ddu Slate & Slab Quarry Co Ltd (vol.liq.5/7/1872)
c1872	-	5/1876	: Hendreddu Slab & Slate Co (Sir Edmund Buckley)
in 1905			: Jacob Bradwell
1920	-	1921	: National Welsh Slate Quarries Ltd (reg.1920 vol.liq.20/10/1921)
1921	-	1933	: [? - perhaps the Melton Mowbray company below; as spares for loco MR 2059 were ordered by engineering companies of Leicester in 1920s]
1933	-	1939	: T.Glyn Williams & Co
in 1948			: Hendre-ddu Slate Quarries Ltd [of Melton Mowbray]

GARTHEINIOG (HENDRE MEREDYDD) QUARRY   (GR: 822114 quarry, 822112 mill)
	-	1881	: John Jenkins & James Williams
1881	-		: Gartheiniog Slate Co Ltd (reg.27/9/1881 £30K)
in 1893 and 1910			: Gartheiniog Slate & Slab Co (Owens & Mallory)
			: Gartheiniog Slate Quarries Ltd (reg.23/1/1926)
in 1948			: Bowley's Quarries Ltd [of London SW11]

MAES-Y-GAMFA QUARRY (GR:816125)
c1892   : opened. Major Walton.
         in 1914 : closed [but some later working noted].

TAL-Y-MIERYN QUARRY (GR:827119)
         by 1900 : closed

COED-Y-CHWAREL QUARRY (GR:828094)
         c1900 : closed

Details of operation of the original system are unclear, other than that horses pulled the wagons - though whether individual quarries worked their own traffic, or whether Hendre-Ddu quarry alone worked the "main line" (at least) seems unknown. The Board of Trade were the first to use a locomotive; the quarries soon copied that example. But the actual ownerships of the "home-made" machines are mysteries. The track gauge of the original line is always quoted as 1'11" and MR 2059 was ordered for that gauge - the Board of Trade loco was 2'0" gauge, and to what extent it was able to work over original track is not known.

Locomotives: Gauge 2'0" - TIMBER TRAFFIC Board of Trade

                    0-4-0PM 20hp Bg   [? 774   1919   New](a)   (1)

Locomotives: Gauge 1"11" - SLATE TRAFFIC

                    4wPM 20hp   MR   2059   1920   New 1/21   (2)
                    PM   *   c1930 New   (3)

Locomotives: Gauge 2'0" - TIMBER TRAFFIC Forestry Commission

        4wPM 20hp   MR   7097   1941 (b)   (4)
        4wDM 20hp   MR   (c)   (5)

*   "Home-made" loco, either 2-2-OPM or 4wPM, incorporating a six-cylinder engine from an 'Overland' lorry. Possibly there were a number of similar 'locos' here over the years - [B/173/282 - Boyd] refers to "old Ford engines mounted on wagons" and "a Hudson wagon with a petrol engine" in addition to the 'Overland'.

(a) whilst there seems adequate evidence that the BoT did use a loco at Hendre-Ddu, its identity has yet to be confirmed. Bg 774 is as yet the most obvious candidate consigned New to "Board of Trade, Home Grown Timber Supplies Department Machynlleth".
At that period, freight for various destinations (including the Dinas Mawddwy branch) in the area, was consigned "to Machynlleth" by Cam.Rys. However, a similar BoT Timber Dept. loco was bought by the Oakeley Quarries from Pennal (a few miles west of Machynlleth) where there may have been another BoT railway - which could have been the true destination of Bg 774.
(b) supplied New to Ministry of Supply Timber Control at unrecorded site (but very possibly Hendre-Ddu) 2/1941; was certainly here later.
(c) arrived c1949, from unknown source.

(1) Bg 774 was repurchased [? from where] by Bg in 1923, reconditioned, then exhibited at the Motor Transport Show 11/1923, and at British Empire Exhibition, Wembley 1924; later sold per J.C.Oliver & Co, dealer, Leeds, to Oakeley Slate Quarry.
(2) wlw(tdt?): Gillingham Pottery, Brick & Tile Co Ltd, Dorset, c1939
(3) withdrawn after accident c1935; engine, frame and gearbox later used as a winch in the Hendre-Ddu quarry.
(4) tdt: Chirk Forestry Depot, c1949
(5) tdt: Chirk Forestry Depot, 6/1955

HENDRE LEAD & LIMESTONE WORKINGS, RHYDYMWYN   H12
(Cf/GR:195679 etc)

Lead was mined in three veins, a high-purity limestone was also obtained underground, and limestone was quarried on land above the Coed Hendre vein. The mines, flooded out in 1908, were later drained and partially re-worked by the Halkyn District Mines Drainage Tunnel (which see), the Olwyn Goch shaft on the Coed Hendre vein becoming a base for these later operations.
[Read: B/199/19; J/NMRS/No.11]

NORTH HENDRE VEIN   (south GR:c193676 to north GR:c192692)
Three principal shafts: Bromleys (GR:191681), Lady Mary Engine (GR: 193682), No.2 (GR:192679); and adit to Hendre valley (GR:193676).

        -       1870   : **North Hendre Lead Mining Co**
  9/1870 -   1894   : **North Hendre Lead Mining Co Ltd**
                          (reg.28/9/1870 £30K)
              1894   : abandoned.

COED HENDRE VEIN and SOUTH LODE (west GR:c192679 to east GR:c208678)
Six shafts, west to east: Fron, Victoria GR:196678, Mostyn Engine, Engine, Olwyn Goch GR:202678, Taylors 1906 GR:205678.

```
            -          1894  : Cobden & Bright
         1894 -        1908  : North Hendre Lead Mining Co Ltd
                       1908  : drowned out.
```

HENDRE LIMESTONE QUARRY & KILNS   (GR:195679)
```
              by 11/1873  : Hendre Lime Co Ltd - auctioned 19/12/1878
         1894 -           : North Hendre Lead Mining Co Ltd (Limeworks Section
                            - which became:- )
         by 1913 -  c1956 : Halkyn & Hendre Lime Co Ltd
                    c1956 :  closed: dismantled and track lifted c1/1959
          1/1967 -        : United Gravel Co Ltd (road vehicles only used)
          by 1986 -       : Tilcon Ltd
```

Sidings off PR/37 served Olwyn Goch shaft by 1898, but no 4'8½" gauge locos discovered here. Other sidings served the adjacent Hendre workings by 1873, where locomotives were used. A narrow-gauge system within the quarry was worked by donkeys and gravity inclines until 1956.

Locomotives: Gauge 4'8½" - Hendre Quarry Sidings.

In 7/1872, NHLM Co Ltd purchased a second-hand "locomotive engine" from Ratcliffe & Sons, Hawarden (see Section 1) for £250, to be used for winding and pumping. In 3/1882 the "locomotive winding and pumping engine" was transferred from Lady Mary shaft to No.2 shaft, but by 12/1883 the No.2 shaft had a proper winding engine.

```
                   0-4-0ST   OC   MW    577   1875   (a)            (1)
         GWEN      0-4-0ST   OC   AB    875   1900   (b)      Scr c1/1959
```

(a) reputed to be here c1884.
     wfw(tdx?): Braddock & Matthews, contractors [? Bolton-Kenyon Widening (1882-
     1884) Contract]. [Named BEATRICE when New.]
(b) tdx: Boyd & Forrest, contractors, Kilmarnock, Scotland, No.5, £350, after 11/1908 by
     31/12/1908

(1) tdt: Thomas Mitchell & Sons Ltd, dealers, Bolton, Lancs, £30, 5/1909

HENDRE SPAR MINE, EFAIL PARCY, near RHYDYMWYN   **H14**
                                                              (Cf/GR:186676)
```
                  1929    : opened
         1929 -           : Cilcen Limespar Co
         after 1948 -     : Lloyd's Spar Quarries (Mold) Ltd
                26/2/1982 : working suspended
```

Extensive underground workings with incline drift up to screens at Efail Parcy, the main product being calcite (crystalised limestone) chippings ("pebbledash") for buildings. Rope haulage on inclines; hand tramming and, later, loco haulage, underground.

Locomotives: Gauge 2'0"

0-4-0BE	WR	7661	1974	New 8/74	(1)

(1) stored at surface screens from 2/1982
   tdt: Mr I.Jolly (see Section 1), 1988

HOLYHEAD ALUMINIUM SMELTING WORKS, PENRHOS   H16
(Ga/GR:264807)

: Anglesey Aluminium Co
: Anglesey Aluminium Metal Ltd

New factory constructed 1969-1971, with sidings off PR/7. Construction included a two mile tunnel to Holyhead Harbour; this tunnel was built using the 2'0" gauge locos listed below.

Locomotives: Gauge 2'0" - TAYLOR WOODROW CONSTRUCTION LTD, contractors.

No.3		4wDM 60hp	MR	10130	1949	(a)		(1)
-		4wBE	CE	* 5667	1969	New 8/69		(2)
-		4wBE	CE	* 5667	1969	New 8/69		(2)
-		4wBE	CE	* 5667	1969	New 8/69		(2)

* three identical locos all with same serial number.

Locomotives: Gauge 4'8½" - siding shunting.

56.007 (f. 52.060 *)		0-4-0DH 252hp HE		7183	1970	New 1/72		
D4		0-6-0DM 204hp HC		D1189	1960			
		rebuilt HE		8901	1977	(b)		(3)

* HE 7183 plate is dated 1970 but loco built 1971, delivered 1972.
  Loco renumbered from 52.060 to 56.007 after 10/1983 by 3/1984.

(a) here by 11/7/1969. wfw(tdx?): Murex Ltd, Rainham, Essex.
(b) tdx: HE, Leeds, loan, c6/1977
    wfw: Manchester Ship Canal Co.

(1) tdt: Taylor Woodrow private store at Wylfa Power Station, Anglesey, after 1/4/1970 by 3/8/1970
    wlw: Taylor Woodrow plant depot, Greenford, Middlesex, by 2/1973
(2) tdt: Taylor Woodrow plant depot, Greenford, Middlesex, after 1/4/1970 by 10/8/1970
    wlw: Alan Keef Ltd, dealer, Cote, Oxon, 8/1978
(3) tdt: HE, Leeds, off loan, 10/1977

HOLYHEAD HARBOUR WORKS, BREAKWATER, QUARRY & BRICKWORKS   H18
(Ga/GR:)

1810	-	12/1862	: Admiralty
1/1863	-	c1934	: Board of Trade
c1934	-	3/1948	: Ministry of Transport
4/1948	-	1980	: British Railways

The first substantial harbour at Holyhead was created by the construction of Admiralty Pier and South Pier; work started 8/1810 under supervision of John Rennie, and was completed 1821. Tenders for the supply of over 1000 yards of "double railway with plate rails" were invited in 1811 - [J/NWG/30.1.1811]. This original "Old Harbour" was increased in capacity by construction 1865-66 of the "Inner Harbour" by the Board of Trade (see below), further improved 1873-1881 by LNWR (for details see PR/7 entry).

A major "New Harbour" was created from 1847 by the construction of the "Great Breakwater", for which a quarry was opened on Holyhead Mountain to obtain stone. The quarrying revealed other materials, suitable for brick manufacture; a brickworks was later established at the quarry.

Read: J/CDH/23.8.1873/6; B/146; B/331; J/NWC/8.12.1911/12; J/RT/No.18/23]

CONSTRUCTION OF GREAT BREAKWATER: J.& C.Rigby, contractors.

Contract Let 24/12/1847, work started 1/1848. Quarry opened; 7'0" gauge railway built thence to Soldiers Point (start of Great Breakwater), to Mackenzie Landing (start of Packet Pier), to Salt Island (start of East Breakwater). Subsequently the two latter items were cancelled, the Great Breakwater being extended in lieu. Work was completed 30/6/1873. Official opening 19/8/1873 by Prince of Wales, who rode in a train hauled by loco PRINCE ALBERT.

Concurrently, J.& C.Rigby did improvement works at the Old Harbour in 1858, and constructed the Inner Harbour 1865-66. The 7'0" gauge railway was extended from Salt Island to these works.

Locomotives: Gauge 7'0" - J. & C. RIGBY

Per "Illustrated London News" 8/1853, there were then 8 locos in use; J/TB/1.4.1854 refers to "a dozen steam loco engines" but subsequently (2.6.1855, 31.1.1857) states there were eight.
In 11/1856, a 7ft gauge loco belonging to J&C Rigby fouled an overbridge between Crewe and Chester whilst en-route to Holyhead. This could be one of the locos listed [? returning from repairs] or it could be a further loco. A Parliamentary Report of 1868-69 states there were 6 locos here during 1868 but only one by 3/1869. Perhaps it refers only to locos in use - as at least four locos survived to be auctioned here 17 + 18/12/1872.
All RBL locos here are reputed to have had 10¼" diameter cylinders, and it is stated [B/123/183] that I.W.Boulton bought four of them. Boulton later [J/TE/10.1.1873] advertised for sale "three broad gauge tank locos 9", 10" and 12" as used at Holyhead Breakwater". N697 and N978 were 12" cylinder locos - did Boulton buy these also ?

PRINCE ALBERT *	0-4-0WT	IC	RBL	309	1852	New	(r1
LONDON	0-4-0WT	IC	RBL	c1852	New	(r2)	
HOLYHEAD	0-4-0WT	IC	RBL	c1852	New	(r2)	
CAMBRIA	0-4-0WT	IC	RBL	c1852	New	(r2)	
[QUEEN ?]	0-4-0WT	IC	RBL	c1852	New	(r2)	
-	0-4-0WT	IC	RBL	Ø	New	(r2)	
-	tank	IC	N	697	1862	New	s/
-	0-4-0ST	OC	N	978	1863	New	s/

* [? given this name in 1873 for opening ceremony perhaps. If so, it could previous have had another name - maybe QUEEN perhaps.]

Ø Carries a plate "J & C RIGBY, HOLYHEAD HARBOUR WORKS, 1861"; the f significance of this is unknown - RBL had ceased building locos in 1853.

(r1) retained in 1873 at this site by Board of Trade (below).
(r2) tdt: I.W.Boulton, dealer, Ashton-under-Lyne, 12/1872; converted to stationary engines.
(r3) found in 1961 at Ponta Delgada Harbour, Sao Miguel, Azores; may have been the since c1872 but no confirmation.

BREAKWATER MAINTENANCE: Board of Trade

The 7'0" gauge railway, from the quarry to Soldiers Point and along the Great Breakwate together with locomotive PRINCE ALBERT, was retained for subsequent maintenance but littl or no work was done.

QUARRY & BRICKWORKS: William Wild & Sons Ltd (reg.11/1924 £110K)

From a date between 1878 and 1902 the quarry was leased to Wilds [presumably a pre decessor of the 1924 Ltd Co], who erected a brickworks at the quarry to utilise material other than stone. The then disused railway was probably leased by Wilds for brickwork traffic. 2ft gauge manually operated railways were installed from brickworks to quarry face these 2ft lines survived until after the (by 7/1967) closure of the brickworks.

Locomotive: Gauge 7'0" - WILLIAM WILD

PRINCE ALBERT	0-4-0WT	IC	RBL	309	1852	(ba)	
				rebuilt	1902		Scr/1945

(ba) tdx: Board of Trade, 1901 (but not used after 1913).

RECONSTRUCTION OF BREAKWATER: S.Pearson & Son Ltd, contractors.

By 1910 the Great Breakwater was in need of considerable repair. Work started 8/1911, first by installing a new 4'8½" gauge railway along the Breakwater, and beside the remaining 7'0" gauge line from Soldiers Point to the Quarry. Some 150,000 tons of stone were used during 1912; work completed c1/1913

Locomotives: Gauge 4'8½" - S. PEARSON & SON LTD.

In 2/1913 Pearsons advertised plant for sale including locos 12x18 HC and 10x16 MW - location not stated - but very likely Holyhead, as MW 1384 was 10x16. A possible candidate for the HC is 0-6-0ST IC HC 833/1910 obtained by Pearsons after 9/1911 by 12/1911 from J.Wardell & Co and not sold, being later used by Pearsons on their King George V Dock (1912-   ) Contract, London.

CROWHURST	0-4-0ST	OC	MW	1384	1898	(pa)	(p1)
[?	0-6-0ST	IC	HC	833	1910	see above]	

(pa)   wfw: Pearsons [? King George V Dock (1906-1914) Contract, Hull].

(p1)   retained in 1913 at this site by Board of Trade.

SUBSEQUENT EVENTS

Apparently Wilds continued to use the 7'0" gauge during Pearsons' work - the Pearson Collection of contract photographs includes a view of PRINCE ALBERT in steam; negative dated 5 March 1912 - which may suggest that Pearsons made use of this loco also. The Board of Trade retained the new 4'8½" gauge line with a loco and railcar for future maintenance and inspection work. Wilds probably came to some arrangement to use this line, and the 7'0" gauge became disused.

1934 MODERNISATION

Much of the railway was re-laid with new rail in 1934, and probably any surviving 7'0" gauge track was then removed. Wilds entered into a contract to supply stone to the Breakwater as needed; the Ministry of Transport purchased a new steam loco (P 1873) "for W.Wild & Sons Ltd", a new railcar (DC 1818), and a new electric crane (ex William Arroll, Glasgow) which could travel the full length of the Breakwater on its own railtracks. From 1/4/1948, the Ministry of Transport passed on responsibility for the Breakwater to British Railways, who later supplied diesel locos to Wilds, which were used for Breakwater and brickworks traffic.

BREAKWATER & LIGHTHOUSE INSPECTION & ACCESS 1913-1980

Board of Trade/Ministry of Transport/British Railways

Railcars: Gauge 4'8½"

-		4wPMr	Bg	553	1914	(ma)	(m1)
-		4wPMr	DC	1818	1935	New	(m2)
TR33		4wPMr	Wkm	7692	1957		Scr 4/1975
TR23	B52M PWM4313	4wPMr	Wkm	7516	1956	(mb)	(m3)

(ma)   ordered by Pearsons for BoT use on completion of Contract.

(mb)   tdx: British Railways, Bangor, 4/1975

(m1) scrapped here; frame used to support oil tank in loco shed.
(m2) tdt: British Railways, Bangor, 3/1958
(m3) tdt: British Railways, Bangor, 30/10/1980

OPERATION OF RAILWAY 1913-1980

Board of Trade/Ministry of Transport/William Wild & Sons Ltd.
British Railways own labour from 1976.

Locomotives: Gauge 4'8½"

	CROWHURST	0-4-0ST	OC	MW	1384	1898	(oa)	Scr/c1938
	-	0-4-0ST	OC	P	1873	1934	New 6/34	(o2)
	STAFFORD VERNON	0-4-0ST	OC	AB	1584	1917	(ob)	(o1)
ED6		0-4-0DM	150hp	JF	4200045	1949	(oc)	(o3)
01.001 (f.D2954 to 6/74)		0-4-0DM	153hp	AB	396	1956	(od)	Scr 2/1982
01.002 (f.D2955 to 6/74)		0-4-0DM	153hp	AB	397	1956	(od)	Scr 2/1982

(oa) retained in 1913 from Pearsons' Contract.
(ob) wfw(tdx?): W.Vernon & Sons Ltd, Seacombe, Cheshire, c1938
(oc) (arrived Holyhead main-line depot 7/4/1966 ex Ditton Sleeper Depot) transferred to Breakwater Railway 23/6/1966 (into service 30/6/1966 with BR driver handed over to Wild's driver 15/9/1966)
(od) tdx: British Railways 9/6/1967 - AB 396 not used after 1971.

(o1) unfit for use by 1951; scrapped 1959 by W.J.Davies & Co, Holyhead.
(o2) unfit for use from 31/3/1966; scrapped 8/1967
(o3) last used 19/1/1967; tdt: sidings at Valley Station 9/6/1967; stored until scrapped there 12/1968 by Mona Fuel & Trading Co Ltd.

CLOSURE & DEMOLITION OF RAIL SYSTEM

The railway was last used between 5/1979 and 7/1980, by which time stone was being brought to Soldiers Point by road from elsewhere. Tracks removed from 10/1980 by Mona Fuel & Trading Co Ltd (of Mona, Anglesey) using road vehicles. Site of railway on Breakwater converted into lorry roadway.

KINMEL PARK MILITARY CAMP K2
& ST.GEORGE LIMEWORKS RAILWAY
(Cd/GR: below)

c1914	-	8/1916	: Construction contractors:- Baldry, Yerburgh & Hutchinson Ltd (who probably built the railway) W.Alban Richards & Co (who are believed to have built the camp)
8/1916	-	c1922	: War Department (Military Camp Railway)
c1920	-	c1975	: Government Store Depot - initially CSD 444.
1923	-	c1932	: London, Midland & Scottish Railway Co
1923	-	2/1965	: Limestone Products Ltd: subsidiary of Lime Firms Ltd, of Llandebie, Carmarthenshire

For the construction of a Military Camp (GR:995755 etc) within the grounds of Kinmel Park, contractors laid a railway some three miles long from Foryd station (GR:983800) on PR/7 to the Park. This railway was opened 2/1915, and extended 10/1915 from Kinmel to the adjoining Bodelwyddan Park. On completion of the majority of the construction contract, the railway was taken over by the War Department 7/8/1916 and, after some upgrading and repair, was opened as a Military Railway 1/11/1916. A diversion was then built at the northern end of the railway, to make connection with the LNWR on PR/15 (the Denbigh branch) rather than onto PR/7. The new connection, at Foryd Junction (GR:995798), was joined up 4/1917; the original route to Foryd station then closed, and the track was lifted. From 14/6/1917 WD locomotives operated a passenger train service between the Camp and Rhyl LNWR station. Most of the Camp closed, and War Department operation of the railway ceased, in 1922; though a portion of the site remained in use until the 1970s as a Store Depot, initially known as Central Stores Department 444.

Parc-y-Meirch (St.George) Limestone Quarry opened in 1923, and a railway was laid in to connect the Quarry to the former Military Railway. This latter was then operated for some years by the LMSR; the new line to the Quarry being worked by the Quarry locomotive. At some time during the 1930s the Quarry took over the working of the whole line to Foryd Junction, using their own locomotive. The Quarry ceased to use rail transport 2/1965, and the track from the Quarry through to Foryd Junction was removed 4-6/1965.

[Read: J/IRR/No.102/309]

MILITARY CONSTRUCTION CONTRACTS

Locomotives: Gauge 4'8½" - BALDRY, YERBURGH & HUTCHINSON LTD.

No details known. BY&H advertised in "Labour News" 8/5/1915 for "2 loco drivers wanted for Cannock Chase and Kinmel Park Camps"; and 1-8/4/1916 for "Loco engine driver wanted, Kinmel Park Military Camp".

Locomotives: Gauge 4'8½" - W.ALBAN RICHARDS & CO

MAESTEG		0-6-0ST	IC	HE	627	1895	(ca)	(c1)

Also believed to have had two other locomotives, one at least being a Manning Wardle, and one had a name sounding like 'Locher'.
A possible (but quite unproven) identity is:-

LOUGHOR		0-6-0ST	IC	MW	1744	1909	(cb)	(c2)

Locomotives: Gauge 2'0" - W.ALBAN RICHARDS & CO

	0-4-0WT	OC	HC	1129	1915	New 5/15	(c3)
HAMPSTEAD	0-4-0ST	OC	WB	1728	1903	(cc)	(c4)

Four 0-4-0 locos for sale here 11/10/1916, described as 6" and 5" cylinders by Bagnall an Koppel. Per J/IRR/Vol.5/114, four 5" HC locos were used here - though their identities (other than HC 1129) have not been traced.
Alban Richards were advertising two unidentified 24" gauge steam locos for sale 5/191 from their London address; perhaps they had originated on this Contract.

(ca) here by 2/1916.
   wfw: Manning Wardle, Leeds, in 12/1913;
   wfw: S.Pearson & Son Ltd, contractor, King George V Dock (1906-1914) Contract, Hull, in 5/1913.
(cb) MW 1744 wfw: Walter Scott & Middleton Ltd, contractors, Morriston for GW Swansea District Lines No.2 (1908-1914) Contract.
(cc) wfw(tdx?): West Buckley Colliery. Loco sent by W.Alban Richards to WB Stafford for alteration from 1'9" to 2'0" gauge 7/1915;
   tdx: WB, Stafford, 10/9/1915 to Alban Richards [presumably direct to Kinmel though not proven]; was certainly at Kinmel by 2/1916.

(c1) for sale at Abergele 11/10/1916
   spares to H.Lanceley & Co, repairers, Brook St, Chester, 2/1917
   wlw: Ministry of Munitions, Bradley, Huddersfield, by 6/1917
(c2) MW 1744 wlw: Disposal & Liquidation Committee, Ministry of Munitions Rainhill, Lancs;
   wlw: Buxton Lime Firms Ltd, Derbyshire, by 1922.
(c3) no further trace.
   [May possibly have been the loco of this type used late 1916 by Henry Boot contractor, Calshot Refinery Contract, Hants - but this is not proven].
(c4) still here 2/1916; [and included in locos for sale 10/1916 ?]
   wlw: J.Gerrard & Sons Ltd, contractors (at their New Salvage Depot Contract Alexandra Dock, Newport, Mon, by 5/1917) [and is probably the loco HAMPSTEAD used (by Gerrards ?) at Alexandra Park WW1 Aerodrome Construction Contract, Fallowfield, Manchester].
   wlw: Gerrards, Marske-on-Sea Aerodrome Contract, near Redcar by 7/1918; [and doubtless other Gerrard Contracts until:]
   wlw: Gerrards, Royal Naval College Construction (1930) Contract, Holbrook, Suffolk.
   After 1930, wlw: George Turner, dealer, Ipswich; Barnards Ltd, Mousehold (c1935) Chessington Zoo (1938, loco now named BURNT STUB); Barnards again; finally to King's of Ipswich for scrap c1950.

Locomotives: Gauge 4'8½" - Military Railway Operation
CSD 444 Government Store Depot

During WW1 the Government gathered together a large number of locomotives, mostly second-hand, for use throughout Britain by, for example, the Ministry of Munitions (MoM), the War Department (WD), Military Camp Railways (MCR), Inland Waterways & Docks (IWD), etc. No comprehensive official records seem to have survived, and historians rely on fragmented details from a multitude of sources. The picture which has emerged reveals considerable, but understandable, confusion; though clearly attempts were made to introduce comprehensive numbering systems for locos.. Available evidence tends to confirm that many of the locos were "pooled", and transferred between depots quite frequently; perhaps due in part to the Agreement whereby MCR locos were maintained at "Main Line" Workshops (eg, Crewe) - they were probably sent where most needed after repairs. This is certainly true at Kinmel MCR, and we have no reason to believe that the following list is complete. It does, however, include all locos recalled locally, or to which references have been found.

The following list is not presumed to be in chronological sequence.

	SIR JOHN FRENCH	0-6-2T	OC	HL	3088	1914	(wa)	(w1)
	NORTHUMBRIA	0-6-0T	OC	HL	3027	1913	(wb)	(w2)
84	[THISBE ?]	0-6-2T	OC	HL	2878	1911	(wc)	(w3)
85	[PYRAMUS ?]	0-6-2T	OC	HL	2879	1911	(wc)	(w4)
51		4-4-0T	OC	HC	224	1880	(wd)	(w5)
52		4-4-0T	OC	HC	232	1881	(wd)	(w5)
88		0-6-0ST	IC	HC	539	1899	(we)	(w6)
?108]	EVE	2-4-0T	IC	SS	[?4056	1895]	(wf)	(w7)
	RYE	2-4-0T	[?	BP	2465	1884]	(wg)	(w8)

wa) wfw(tdx?): Woolmer Military Railway, Longmoor, Hants.
      This loco worked at WD Bisley, Hants, c1918 - though whether this was before or after its visit to Kinmel is not known.

wb) reputedly wfw [?tdx] WD, Porton, Wilts.
      wfw: Sir John Jackson, contractor [and probably used by Jackson on various WD Camp Contracts around Salisbury, Wilts - including, perhaps, Porton Camp].

wc) arrived Kinmel 1916. Built originally for the Shropshire & Montgomeryshire Light Railway as HL 2878 named [apparently] PYRAMUS and HL 2879 named [apparently] THISBE; the nameplates were removed by the S&MR before that railway sold the locos (reputedly in 1914). An unconfirmed report states that both locos were overhauled at GWR Swindon Works in 1915. Advertisement [J/MM/11.2.1916] for sale "Two modern 0-6-2T sg OC 14x20 3'6" wheels, vacuum & steam brake" (apply Box No.) probably refers to these locos and, as the Government first requisitioned locos for MCRs in 1916, this is probably when they passed into Government service. One or both possibly first went to the Woolmer Military Railway before coming to Kinmel. There is no positive evidence that either loco was named at Kinmel; indeed, a contemporary observer recorded "W84D" (no name noted) at Crewe Works 5/1917.

wd) The Government obtained four locos of this type from the Midland & Great Northern Railway Co in 5/1917 which almost certainly were:-
      MGN 8, HC 209/1878 - [becoming, or allocated, WD number 54 ?]
      MGN 10, HC 224/1880 - which became WD 51
      MGN 19, HC 232/1881 - which became WD 52
      MGN 40, HC 210/1879 - [becoming, or allocated, WD number 53 ?]
      Various sources have contained confusing references which, collectively, record all four of these locos as at Kinmel at some time. This seems unlikely to be true, but in the absence of official records one cannot be certain. However, some of the references seem to be based on incorrect presumptions as to the relationship of the WD, HC and MGN numbers of each loco. Local memory, and the more positive references found, seem to agree that just two of these locos were at Kinmel, and that these were 51 and 52.
      Of particular note are:- J/SLS/7.1942 - two M&GN 4-4-0T were seen in 1917 "leaving Melton Constable painted black with large painted numerals 51 and 52....later saw both....separately, at Rhyl [but no dates given]". It seems they did not come directly to Kinmel in 5/1917 - though they were at Kinmel 5/1919 - as 51 was seen at WD

Pirbright, Hants, in 1918 [J/IL/No.47/243]; though 52 is not yet reported elsewhere in this period.
"Two M&GN 4-4-0T may be seen in service with a train of North London Railway coaches between Rhyl and Kinmel Park Camp" [per J/TL/3.1919] - and, "tank 51 works the branch to Kinmel Park Camp" [J/LNRN/25.9.1919].
 [Positive evidence regarding WD53 and WD54 seems lacking, though these two locos are often presumed to be locos "8" and "40" (ie, carrying M&GN numbers) used at Ministry of Munitions, Houston Factory, Georgetown, Renfrewshire.]

(we) here by 1918. Spare parts were supplied to H.Lanceley, Son & Co, locomotive (etc) repairers, Providence Foundry, Brook Street, Chester, in 1917 [presumably they were repairing the loco for the Government, perhaps even for or at Kinmel].
wfw: Balfour Beatty & Co Ltd, contractors [? Ripon Camp Contract] in 1915
wfw: Sir Robert McAlpine & Sons, contractors.

(wf) if SS 4056, wfw: Metropolitan Railway, London, (number) 72 - a loco which the Met.Rly. did sell to the Government for £1450 in 1916.
The only common factors, however, are that both EVE and Met.R. 72 were 2-4-0T by SS with 17x24 cylinders [and no alternative history for Met.R. 72 is yet known].

(wg) first reported at Kinmel 6/1923   -   [presumably by this date at CSD 444 and not the MCR]. Recalled locally as painted red, with a brass number plate, and of Midland Railway origin.
 [A possible identity is BP 2465 which was Midland & South Western Junction Railway No.29, which was for sale by J.F.Wake, dealer, from 1/1918 to early 1920 and thus available for Government purchase, though no proof has been found.]

(w1) [possibly wlw: WD Pirbright - see footnote (wa)].
wlw: Woolmer Military Railway, Longmoor, Hants, by 8/1922.
(w2) wlw: Ebbw Vale Steelworks, South Wales [by c1919 ?].
(w3) "W84D" (no name) repaired at LNWR, Crewe Works, 5/1917.
J/LNRN/25.8.1922 records 84 HL 2878 (no name) as being at Longmoor Military Railway, Hants - ie, in 1922. By 7/1931 this loco had been fitted with new nameplates THISBE. Reputedly scrapped at Longmoor in 1932, but in fact is probably the 0-6-2T 14x22 sg by HL advertised for sale [J/MM] 10/1931 to 4/1934 by James/Jas Clements & Co Ltd of Southampton & Cardiff (later just Cardiff).
No further trace.
(w4) Per the Government sale list [J/Surplus], a loco "85 PYRAMUS 0-6-2T 14x22 HL" was for sale at Cannock Chase Military Railway 4/1921 to 8/1921. It was apparently sold to Frank Edmunds, dealer, Stoke, in 8/1921, as Edmunds sold HL 2879 to the Mersey Docks & Harbour Board c7/1922.
 [Thus all the evidence indicates that names were re-fitted to both these locos, but very probably exchanged vis-a-vis the situation that originally existed on the S&M Rly.]
HL 2879 wlw: Cudworth & Johnson, Wrexham - see Section 1.
(w5) J/LNRN/10.6.1919 reports 52 at Eastleigh LSWR Works for repairs; J/LNRN/10.9.1920 states that both 51 and 52 have [at some unquoted period] worked at WD Longmoor; J/LNRN/25.8.1922 states 51 is at Longmoor. "Surplus" 2.8.1920-1.9.1920 lists 52 as for sale at RE Yard, Catterick Bridge - though this is probably a typographical error (not unusual in "Surplus") corrected in "Surplus" 15.11.1920-1.3.1921 which have 52 for sale at Fovant; though 52 apparently saw later Government service in the Ripon area [J/IL/No.43/158].
 Ultimate disposal of the four M&GN locos appears to be:
 51 remained at Longmoor until scrapped 10/1952.
 52 possibly to Edinburgh Collieries Ltd, Smeaton, via the Cohen- Armstrong Disposal Board, and scrapped 8/1938 [J/SLS/7.1942].
 53 to National Oil Refineries Ltd, Llandarcy, South Wales, and scrapped in 1934.

54 to Edinburgh Collieries Ltd, Ormiston Colliery, Links [J/RO/1.1931/12; 12.1935/238] [? and later Fleets Colliery] and scrapped 1/1935.

w6) observed near Grantham in 1921 [J/LNRN/10.8.1921]; and perhaps this was the HC loco for sale at WD Belton Park Military Railway, Peascliffe Sidings, Grantham, in 6/1921 [J/Surplus/1.6-15.9.1921]. Apparently then moved to Barnbow [Barnborough], Yorks, for sale, by 10/1921; no further trace.

w7) for sale at Kinmel Camp 4/1922 ("108 EVE"); and for sale at CSD 444 Kinmel 6/1922 ("103 EVE condition incomplete"), CSD 444 10/1922 ("103 EVE"). [Whether this loco was WD 108 or WD 103 remains unclear.] No further trace.

w8) no further trace.

Locomotives: Gauge 4'8½" - Limestone Products Ltd

MARGARET	0-6-0ST	OC	AE	1923	1923	New 6/23	(q1)
"ELEANOR"	0-6-0ST	OC	AE	1432	1902		
	rebuilt AE				1923	(qa)	(q2)
MARGARET	0-4-0DM	128hp HC		D1031	1956	(qb)	(q3)

Locomotives: Gauge 2'0" - Limestone Products Ltd

Railway from quarry face to kilns horseworked from 1923 to 1936; replaced by road vehicles 1958 and track removed.
A short length of track was retained at the kilns, the wagons being moved by hand.

-	4wDM	10hp	RH	174529	1935	New 1/36	(q4)

(qa) tdx: Llandebie Limeworks, Carmarthenshire, after 10/1947 by 4/1950.
(qb) tdx: B.P.Refinery (Kent) Ltd, Grain, Kent, c5/1960.

(q1) tdt: AE for repair c4/1934; returned 6/1934.
   tdt: Llandebie Limeworks c1948 (after 4/1945 by 4/1950)
   tdx: Llandebie Limeworks 2/1954
   Scrapped at St.George c7/1961 after 12/10/1960.
(q2) tdt: Llandebie Limeworks, 2/1954
(q3) tdt: W.J.,Lee, Seacombe, Cheshire; per Thomas Mitchell & Sons Ltd, dealer, Bolton, Lancs, after 7/7/1968 by 3/9/1968.
(q4) tdt: Dyserth Limeworks, c12/1958 (by 30/12/1958).

LANE END COLLIERY [and BRICKWORKS], BUCKLEY   L2
(Cf/GR:285644)

```
            1889    : sinking
1889    -   1902    : Lane End Colliery Co
1902    -   2/1903  : Aston Hall Coal & Brick Co Ltd
            28/2/1903 : closed
```

This was a small colliery, originally connected to the Buckley Horse Tramroads; between 12/1892 and 7/1893 a short (c¼ mile) 4'8½" gauge line was built from the Knowl Lane Siding of PR/22 to the colliery by contractor H.Croom Johnson (See Section 1).

[The colliery site was later quarried away by Hancocks' Lane End Brickworks - Wm.Hancock & Co (Hawarden) Ltd; later Castle Firebrick, British Steel, and Butterley Brick - and for a possible locomotive at this site see R.S.DAVIES (Section 1) loco L.3804. In the mid-1920s Hancocks filed returns for "Hancocks Lane End Colliery" stating men were employed underground. Presumably this was a drift mine on this site.]

Locomotives: Gauge 4'8½"

```
        PROGRESS        0-4-0ST [? OC  WkB    861   1874] (a)           s/s
        STALYBRIDGE     0-6-0T     IC  SS    3475   1888  (b)           (1)
```

(a) if WkB 861 then - wfw(tdx?): Brinsop Hall Colliery, Aspul, Wigan, Lancashire [which closed 10/1896].
(b) reputedly tdx: Aston Hall Colliery Railway - ? c1902

(1) reputedly tdt: Aston Hall Colliery Railway - ? 1903.

LITTLE MOUNTAIN COLLIERY, BUCKLEY   L4
(Cf/GR:296641)

```
by 1750  -              : Sir John Glynne & Mr George Berks
   1777  -     1790     : Stubbs, Berks & Co
   1790  -     1800     : Thomas Botfield
   1801  -              : Rigby & Hancock
   1864  -     1871+    : Thomas Rose et al
by 1873  -     1876+    : Little Mountain Coal, Iron & Clay Co Ltd
by 1882  -     1886     : Hawarden Collieries Co Ltd
               1886     : closed; later dismantled.
```

This colliery eventually grew to consist of eight shafts grouped around GR:296641. Soon after 1801 it was provided with a rail outlet to the River Dee via the Buckley Horse Tramroads. When PR/66 (Wrexham-Buckley railway) was built - opened 1866 - it bisected the colliery; a short branch was built from PR/66 to the screens at No.3 Pit.

[Read: J/FHS/1967/86]

Locomotives: Gauge 4'8½"

| DIXON | * | 0-4-0ST | OC | HC | 213 | 1882 | (a) | | (1) |

* Some sources quote name of this loco as WARWICK; we do not know why. Documentary evidence for name DIXON seems to be conclusive. See also FFRWD IRONWORKS for further note on name WARWICK.

(a) arrived here "New" 9/1882; but loco actually built BH 21/1867 and rebuilt HC 213/1882

(1) 12" 4wc tank loco for sale here "on expiration of lease" from 2/1886 to 9/1886 (at least) "apply Mr J.B.Gregory, Hawarden Collieries, Buckley". Loco reputedly wlw(tdt?): Cudworth & Johnson, dealers, Wrexham, c10/1886 [and possibly used on the Hawarden Loop Line (PR/54) Contract]. Note: J/CG/8.1887 still advertised the colliery for sale, but a loco was no longer mentioned.

LITTLE ORME LIMESTONE QUARRY, PENRHYN BAY   L6
(Gc/GR:819823)

	-	7/1889	: E.Fiddler
7/1889	-	c1911	: Little Orme's Head Limestone Co Ltd
			(reg.20/7/1889 £10K liq.6/1913-1914)
c1911	-	9/1912	: Stanlow Works Estates Ltd
			(reg.31/1/1911; which became:-)
9/1912	-	8/1929	: Ship Canal Portland Cement Manufacturers Ltd
			(reg.5/9/1912; which became:-)
8/1929	-	12/1931	: Allied Cement Manufacturers Ltd
			(reg.2/8/1929 liq.1931-1938)
		1931	: closed
12/1931			: Associated Portland Cement Manufacturers Ltd
			(quarry remained closed)

An auction 19/6/1862 of the "Rhos Limestone Quarry, on the Beach, one mile from Colwyn railway station and near Conway....on Mostyn Estate" included 5500 yards of tram rails, 40 tipping wagons, "5 feet break drum", incline rope, etc. [J/CDH/24.5.1862/8c3]. If this was Little Orme Quarry, then it is the earliest reference so far discovered.

The rail system was entirely internal, the product being despatched by sea from the premises. Quarry eventually worked on three levels - Main, Upper and Lower. The loco shed was on the Main level; this level fed direct into the crushing mill, the output going straight into hoppers from which ships were loaded directly - there being no pier as such. The small Upper level was connected by rope-worked incline; the Lower level being reached by a steep loco-worked line. After closure, some items remained in the quarry for many years, several wagons remaining into the 1950s. The mill hoppers were demolished in 1987.

[Read: B/177/197]

Locomotives: Gauge 3'0"

	[MONA ?]	0-4-0VBT	[? HVF; Ch		1685	1874]	(a)	(5)
	LITTLE ORME	0-4-0ST	OC	MW	478	1873	(b)	(1)
	ELLESMERE	0-4-2ST	OC	KS	1255	1912	New 5/12	(2)
	GARTH	0-4-2ST	OC	KS	1257	1914	New 6/14	s/s
	PENRHYN	0-4-2ST	OC	KS	3092	1918	New 6/18	(3)
1		4wVBT	VCG	S	6256	1927	New	(4)
2		4wVBT	VCG	S	6255	1927	New	(4)
3		4wVBT	VCG	S	6257	1927	New	(4)

(a) There is doubt as to the origins of this loco. Reputedly built by Owen Hughes, Valley Foundry, near Holyhead, and reputedly tdx: DeWinton & Co, Caernarfon, c1878, after modification and repair. If indeed from DeWinton, then probably wfw: Penmaenmawr Granite Quarries. However, "c1878" may be too early for Little Orme.
Per J/LM/15.9.1917/185, MW 478 was preceded by a Chaplin 0-4-0VBT. If true, it possibly was the 3'0" gauge Chaplin with 7x11 cylinders, named FIREFLY, for sale 29/11/1878 by F.Ellison, of Manley, Frodsham, Cheshire. Ellison's loco could possibly have been Chaplin 1685 of 1874 [J/IL/No.53/113].
(b) loco was new to Leeds Corporation, Swinsty Reservoir Construction (1871-1877) Contract, named WASHBURN. Probably later used by Leeds Corporation at Eccup Reservoir Enlargement (1879-1884) Contract; two locos used at Eccup were for sale 1884.
MW 478 is reported as reboilered by Hough & Sons, Newtown Boiler Works, Wigan in 1899 [J/LM/15.9.1917/185].

(1) still here 1914 - recalled as having been scrapped here.
(2) still here 7/1924 - no further trace.
(3) still here, derelict, 4/1940; gone by 4/1942 - reputedly to "Ward of Rhyl" for scrap.
(4) tdt: APCM Ltd, Harbury Cement Works, Warwickshire, c1931.
(5) "carefully taken to pieces, packed in cases, and forwarded to some new and distant field of usefulness" after arrival of MW 478 [J/LM/15.9.1917].

LLANBERIS WEST group of SLATE QUARRIES   L8
(Gc/GR:below)

A number of individual slate quarries, some consisting of more than one pit (sinc), were established on the eastern slope of Cefn Ddu Mountain, west of Llyn Padarn, to the north of Llanberis village. They all at some time shared some rail facilities, and for our purposes it is somewhat beneficial to deal with these quarries as a single group. Many came into the "Llanberis Slate Co" group, who could perhaps have used their loco on various of these sites from time to time.
To avoid confusion, it should be noted that (another) Llanberis Slate Co Ltd was registered c1864 and opened a quarry in this area; by 12/1865 they were building their third incline [J/MJ/30.12.1865/844] but, despite introducing a Cooke & Hunter 7-foot diameter tunnel cutting machine in 1868, the Company was in voluntary liquidation 5/1873 [J/MJ/4.1.1868/4; LGaz]. Precisely which quarry this Company worked seems uncertain.

[Read: B/182; B/175]

BRYNMAWR QUARRY (GR:555596)

1838	-	1854	: J.D.Barry
1855	-	1858	: Pullen & Crane
1858	-	c1867	: Brewer, Gordon & Liddell
1867	-	1871	: Donenlas Slate Co Ltd
1872	-	1875	: closed
1875	-	1879	:
1879	-	1883	: Brynmawr Slate Co [Newton et al]
1886	-	c1888	: Llanberis Slate Co Ltd [Newton, Menzies et al]
		c1888	: closed; dismantled.
		3/7/1930	: vacant quarry auctioned with Cefn Du Quarry etc.

Internal rail tracks here by 1855, connected to Chwarel Fawr system by 1861. No locos known.

BWLCH-Y-GROES QUARRY (GR:560600)

1838	-	1855	: J.D.Barry
1855	-		: Brewer & Alleyn
1855	-	1858	: Pullen & Crane
1858	-	1867	: Brewer, Gordon & Liddell
1867	-		: Bwlch-y-Groes Slate Co Ltd
1886	-	1904	: Llanberis Slate Co Ltd
		1904	: closed; dismantled.

Internal rail tracks connected by short level branch line to outlet railway inclines by 1861. No locos known.

CAERMEINCIAU QUARRY (GR:563601)

		by 1878	: working
1882	-	1897	: J.T.Campbell
1895	-	c1910	: Llanberis Slate Co Ltd
		c1910	: closed; dismantled.

This small quarry had, apparently, no internal railways; output was carted to the LNWR (PR/35) sidings. After 1895 it was worked as part of the adjacent Bwlch-y-Groes quarry.

CAMBRIAN (FFRIDD GLYN) QUARRIES (GR:567605 etc)

		by 1864	: working
1866	-	1878	: Cambrian Slate Quarries Co Ltd
1/1879	-	1930	: Llanberis Slate Co Ltd (reg.30/12/1878)
		by 1930	: closed; the site (including a few rails but little else remained) auctioned 3/7/1930

A quarry, apparently this quarry, was for sale in J/CDH/12.10.1833, and it then had a railway. Output from Ffridd Glyn quarry was originally routed via Glynrhonwy Quarry railway system; by 5/1873 the Cambrian Company had completed its own outlet - the "Ffridd Incline" - direct to a siding on PR/35 for which Agreement was reached with the LNWR in 1874. On 16/7/1879 the Llanberis Slate Co Ltd extended the Agreement to additionally cover its output from Goodman's and Cefn Du Quarries.

Ffridd Incline - later 'Incline No.4' - was 1000 yards long and single track; whilst wagons could decend by gravity the empties had to be hauled up, for which DeWinton & Co supplied a 14hp 14" cylinder steam winder which, known as Ffridd Engine, remained in use until 1930. From the summit of this No.4 Incline, three consecutive double-track gravity inclines lifted the railway to Penybwlch. At the head of Incline No.3 (265 yards long) were junctions to Twll Goch and Cook & Ddol; Incline No.2 (300 yards) served lines to Cefn Du and Bwlch-y-Groes; Incline No.1 (260 yards) led direct into the overland railway to Brynmawr and (the upper levels of) Chwarel Fawr.

CEFN DU QUARRY (GR:555604)

```
           after 1846   : opened
    1864     -    1875  : Pritchard & Stephens
    1875     -  12/1878 : Cefndu Slate Quarry Co [W.B.Jeffrey]
  1/1879     -    1930  : Llanberis Slate Co Ltd (reg.30/12/1878 liq.1930-1931)
              3/7/1930  : auction. Dismantled by Hibbert & Son Ltd [of Ettingshall,
                          Wolverhampton]
   c1945     -   c1948  : small scale working by local men.
```

The Mill at Cefn Du became the focal point of Llanberis Slate Co Ltd activity. Constructed (unusually) of greenstone, the shell of the building survives today [1991]. The Cefn Du Quarry ceased to be worked c1883, when a route was made through it tunnelling westward into Chwarel Fawr, which henceforth was the principal quarry of the Company. Whilst the driving of this tunnel very much reduced use of No.1 Incline, it and the overland route to Chwarel Fawr was still retained for access to the upper galleries. After the 1930 auction, equipment at Cefn Du, Chwarel Fawr and Cambrian (Ffridd Glyn) Quarries, plus the railway and four inclines of the through route to the LMSR (PR/35), was all dismantled. After WW2 some rails found on site were relaid by local men, but have since disappeared.

Fish-bellied rails can still [1991] be found in local fences, and possibly date from the early 1800s when the first "Cefn Du" quarry (see under "Chwarel Fawr" below) was jointly worked with Cilgwyn Quarry, Nantlle.

Locomotives: Gauge 2ft

Apart from the loco listed, a local farmer has recalled a shed, on the overland line to Chwarel Fawr, containing a loco "with portholes in the cab". This would be in the late 1920s. Perhaps it was a loco on loan from (Premier) Glynrhonwy ?
There were no locomotives included in the 3/7/1930 auction of all the Llanberis Slate Co Ltd quarries.
It is reputed - though not proven - that a "home-made" petrol loco was built and used by the "local men" in the post-WW2 era.

```
        CARNARVON CASTLE    0-4-0VBT VC    DeW        1876  New (a)              (1)
```

(a) here by 6/1876. Cost £315-10-0.

(1) still here 31/12/1912 "one old locomotive, value £5".
     Believed scrapped during WW1.

CHWAREL FAWR ["The Big Quarry"] (GR:552599)
The original Cefn Du Mountain Quarry

5/1800	-	1812	: Cilgwyn & Cefndu Slate Co [John Evans et al]
1812	-		: Thomas Bulgin & Partners
by 1819	-	1827	: Samuel Holland [auctioned 1827]
by 1840	-		: Cooper & Croft
7/1867	-	1874	: Chwarel Fawr Slate Co Ltd (reg.31/10/1867 liq.10/1874-1875)
1874	-	10/1883	: Northern Welsh Slate Co Ltd
10/1883	-	1930	: worked by Cefn Du Quarry, which see.

COOK & DDOL QUARRY (GR:560606)

by 1812	-		: Cilgwyn & Cefndu Slate Co [John Evans et al]
1812	-	1823	: Thomas Bulgin & Partners
10/1864	-		: George Strutton
by 1873	-	1880s	: Trew. Jegon
10/1892	-	1904	: J.O. & G.J.Hughes et al; who formed:- Cook & Ddol Slate Quarries Co Ltd who leased to Cambrian Slate Quarries Ltd (reg.5/2/1902)
1905	-	1909	: National Co-operative Quarries Ltd
1909	-	1913	: British Steel Smelters, Mill, Iron & Kindred Trades Association [the "Smelters Union"]
		1911	: for sale
		1913	: closed; dismantled.

Internal rail system at quarries connected to head of No.3 Incline; no locos known at these quarries.

TWLL GOCH QUARRY (GR:561602)
A small quarry; no record of operators found. It may have been worked with Cook & Ddol to which it had a direct rail connection.

GOODMAN'S QUARRY (CHWAREL Y PARSON) (GR:572606)

by 1873			: open
1/1879	-	1890	: Llanberis Slate Co Ltd (reg.30/12/1878)
		1890	: closed; dismantled.

A small quarry, having its own siding at PR/35, and reputedly its own tramway to this siding. No locomotives known, but Mr DeWinton advised Lord Newborough 31/10/1877 that Menzies "was seeking permission to use a small locomotive in place of horses on his railway line which crosses the road at Goodman's Quarry". [However, this could equally refer to a proposed use of a loco from the LNWR to the foot of Ffridd Incline.]

Between c1909 and 1913 the 'Goodmans Siding' was used by Alfred Hickman Ltd (of Wolverhampton) as the trans-shipment terminal of an aerial ropeway installed to carry iron ore, across Cefn Du mountain, from the Garreg Fawr Mine at Betws Garmon.

GLYNRHONWY (later UPPER GLYNRHONWY) QUARRY (GR:566609 etc)
and GLYN CANOL MILL

by 1825		: open (Newborough Estate)
1834 -	1873	: **J.W.Greaves & E.Shelton**
in 1846		: was the only quarry currently at work in the "Llanberis West" group.
? 1873 -	6/1890	: **Upper Glynrhonwy Slate Co**
6/1890 -	1/1920	: **Upper Glynrhonwy Slate Co Ltd** (reg.24/6/1890 £25K liq.1920-1922)
1/1920 -	1/1930	: **Premier Glynrhonwy Slate Quarry Ltd** (reg.24/10/1919 liq.6/5/1931)
	25/1/1930	: closed. Sold to Thos.W.Ward Ltd, dealers, who dismantled for scrap in 1931.

Railways were first laid down in 1825 [CRO/Glynllifon/2046] at this the first Glynrhonwy Quarry (GR:563607), which was located above the Clegir road, but by 1877 had expanded considerably, with a new Mill (Glyn Canol - Middle Glyn, GR:568608) below that road adjacent to but above the Middle Glynrhonwy Quarry. This Mill was exited from via a turnout approximately half-way down the Ffridd Incline. In 4/1922 the Premier company abandoned this outlet, a new incline having been built into the then disused Lower Glynrhonwy Quarry thus enabling the original connection, from that quarry, to PR/35, to be used. Some re-working of the Lower and Middle quarries by the Upper (Premier) Company then took place.

During the period 1883-1904 the Llanberis Slate Co Ltd had an interest in part (at least) of the Upper Glynrhonwy site (in 10/1894 L.S.Co.Ltd. demanded rent from U.G.S.Co.Ltd.).

Locomotives: Gauge 2ft.

[? CATHERINE FANNY]	0-4-0VBTG	SVC	DeW		(a)		s/s
EMILY	0-4-0VBT	VC	DeW	[? c1895	New]	(b)	(1)
	0-4-0ST	OC	KS	2419	1915	(c)	(1)
	0-4-0WT	OC	HC	1109	1914	(d)	(1)

(a) possibly New here, or possibly tdx: Lower Glynrhonwy Quarry (below).
(b) if indeed built c1895, may not have arrived here until 1897.
It could be the "new" loco advertised 21/1/1897 for sale by DeW.
(c) here by 4/1929.
wfw: Harper Bros. & Co, agents for the War Department at Catterick Camp, Yorks NR.
(Perhaps via Wm.Jones Ltd similar to footnote (d).)
(d) tdx: Wm.Jones Ltd, dealers, Banning Street, Greenwich, London, between 3/1925 and 4/1926.
wfw: War Department, Catterick Bridge, Yorkshire NR.

(1) an inventory taken at closure in 1930 lists existing locos as: 0-4-0 by R.Hudson in Lower Quarry shed; 0-4-0 by KS plus "one old locomotive for repairs" in Upper Quarry shed. Presumed to be the three locos listed (HC 1109 was built to the Order of Robert Hudson & Co Ltd, dealers, who normally arranged for their own plates to be fitted, rather than HC plates), and presumed purchased, with rest of machinery here, by Thos.W.Ward Ltd in 1931 - and scrapped ?

LOWER and MIDDLE GLYNRHONWY QUARRIES   (GR: below)

		c1855	: opened
c1855	-	1860	: Captain J.H.Taylor
1860	-	4/1884	: Glynrhonwy Slate Co Ltd (reg.1860)
4/1884	-	1915	: Glynrhonwy Slate Quarry Co Ltd (reg.10/4/1884)
		1915	: closed. Dispersal auction 25/4/1916.
1922	-	1930	: partially re-worked by Upper Glynrhonwy Quarry.
1940	-	1961	: Air Ministry (Munitions Store).

The Lower Quarry (GR:570610) could not easily be developed due to flooding, and most work was done at Middle Quarry (GR:566608). Slate Mill was near Padarn Lake, into which rubbish was tipped. Lower & Middle Glynrhonwy had own siding off PR/35; in 1922 the Upper (Premier) Company built their own connection to this to avoid paying tolls to Llanberis Slate Co Ltd for their use of the Ffridd Incline. In 1940 the Lower, Middle & Upper Glynrhonwy Quarries, and some surrounding land, were taken over by the Ministry of Supply for bomb storage. Part of the Lower Quarry was roofed over and disguised as a waste tip, with a 2ft gauge railway laid from within this store to new sidings installed at PR/35. These and subsequent activities virtually obliterated many traces of slate railways, including the lower length of the Ffridd Incline below the Clegir road. After 1961 the area was used by light industry, and in the 1970s by the Central Electricity Generating Board for temporary offices and stores. In the 1980s the Arfon Borough Council prepared plans for a massive derelict land reclamation scheme to affect all the "Llanberis West" quarries, but as yet [1991] little has been done other than in the vicinity of PR/35.

Locomotives: Gauge 2ft (Quarries)

Per J/TE/10.6.1955/798, two single-cylinder DeWinton locos with direct drive and double-flanged wheels were, at one time, used to supply steam to rock-drills at "Glyn-Rhonwy Slate Quarries". We cannot confirm this, nor presume which quarry (Lower or Upper) the item refers to. However, J/CDH/31.5.1873 states "a couple of locomotive steam engines are employed" at Lower Glynrhonwy. Available evidence is that both were single cylinder locos with geared drive.

	0-4-0VBTG	SVC	DeW		c1869	New	(1)
	0-4-0VBTG	SVC	DeW		by 1873	New	(2)
PADARN	0-4-0VBT	SVC	DeW			(a)	(3)
BALADEULYN	0-4-0VBT	SVC	DeW			(b)	(3)
WELLINGTON	0-4-0VBT	VC	DeW		1877	(c)	(3)
LOUISA	0-4-0ST	OC	HE	195	1877	(c)	(2)

(a) possibly New here; or was possibly loco "STARSTON" tdx: PenyrOrsedd Slate Quarry c1894. If PADARN was New, and if "STARSTON did come here, then the latter is as yet omitted from this list.

(b) tdx: PenyrOrsedd Slate Quarry, Nantlle, £55, 10/1893

(c) tdx: Dinorwic Slate Quarry, after 1895 by 19/3/1898

(1) reputedly not entirely successful as a loco and converted to drive a pump in the quarry.

(2) s/s; possibly tdt: Upper Glynrhonwy Quarry "CATHERINE FANNY".

(3) the 25/4/1916 auction catalogue lists four locos: "LOUISA 6"x8" by Hunslet; DeWinton vertical boiler 6" cylinders [presumed to be WELLINGTON]; Two old locomotives to be sold as scrap [no details]".

In J/MM/7.7.1916 R. White & Sons, dealers, Widnes, Lancs, were advertising "for sale: 2 gauge loco by Hunslet 6"x8" four wheel coupled, and 2ft gauge coffeepot loco". These could be WELLINGTON? and LOUISA - but see also 'Glanrafon Slate Quarry' entry. It has been suggested (but as yet no proof) that LOUISA was sold to the Upper (Premier Glynrhonwy Quarry in 1916.

Locomotives: Gauge 4'8½" (Construction of Depot for Air Ministry)

1940 - 1941 : **JOHN MOWLEM & CO LTD**, contractors.

STAINES	0-6-0ST	IC	HC	1513	1924	(ma)	(m1)
YEOVIL	0-6-0ST	IC	HC	1529	1924	(ma)	(m2)

(ma) here by 7/1941 - YEOVIL was noted on a lorry at Betws-y-Coed on 23-24/4/194. (perhaps en-route to Llanberis). Both locos wfw: Badnall Wharf Royal Ordnance Factory Contract, Swynnerton, Staffs. (STAINES until 21/12/1940 at least; YEOVIL until 16/4/1941 at least).

(m1) wlw(tdt?): War Department, WD 69, 1941 (after 8/1941)
(m2) wlw(tdt?): War Department, WD 68, 1941 (after 8/1941)

Locomotives: Gauge 2ft (Air Ministry Bomb Store Railway)

At least two locomotives (almost certainly 4wDM RH) here by 2/1941; such locos reputedly still here until c1956 but details unknown.

Locomotives: Gauge 4'8½" (Air Ministry sidings)

The siding connections were closed by British Railways 31/12/1956 and track subsequently lifted. Two-road (four-loco) shed in use as bus depot by 1988.

No.186		4wDM	88hp RH	198324	1940	New 7/40	(A1)
No.187		4wDM	88hp RH	198325	1940	(Aa)	(A2)
No.237		4wDM	88hp RH	210478	1942	New 9/42	(A3)
		0-4-0DM	JF			(Ab)	s/s

(Aa) tdx: Air Ministry, Harpurhill, Derbyshire, c5/1941 (by 7/6/1941)
(Ab) observed from a passing train 8/1948 and 8/1951; the Air Ministry had many such locos.

(A1) tdt: Air Ministry, Harpurhill, Derbyshire, c12/1940
      tdx: Air Ministry, Harpurhill, c5/1942 (by 15/7/1942)
      tdt: Air Ministry, Harpurhill, c3/1943 (after 10/9/1942)
(A2) tdt: Air Ministry, Broadheath, Cheshire, c1951 (after 13/11/1950)
(A3) wlw(tdt?): Eccles Slag Co Ltd, Scunthorpe, Lincs, by 16/3/1961

LLANDDULAS LIMEWORKS and QUARRIES   L10
                                                                  (Cd/GR:below)

LLANDDULAS (CRAIG) LIMESTONE QUARRY   (GR:900783)
       by 1870 -   c1905   : Llanddulas Quarry Co (Giles & Fazakerley)
       c1905 -   : Llanddulas Quarry Co Ltd (reg.24/11/1904 £5K)
                              : Kneeshaw Lupton & Co Ltd - with below:-

PENTRE'R-GWYDDEL QUARRY and (old) LLYSFAEN LIMEWORKS   (GR:897783)
       by 1820   : open
       by 1848   : Tomkinson, Raynes, Lupton, Kneeshaw and Brassey
       by 5/1860   : Raynes, Lupton & Co
                              : Kneeshaw Lupton & Co Ltd
                              : (subsidiary of William Robertson Ltd)
       by 2/1986   : A.R.C.(Powell Duffryn) Ltd

Originally two adjacent but separate quarries, each having a tramroad incline passing under the LNWR (PR/7) to a pier; Craig Pier at GR:902787 and Pentre Pier at GR:897787. Later the two quarries were combined, and Craig incline and pier were removed. Locomotives were first used within the quarries in 1906. Most of the narrow gauge track was replaced by road vehicles and conveyor belts in 1956, other than a portion retained at the Brick Plant until c1970.
Sidings off PR/7 served the limeworks area, the wagons being moved by cable-haulage apart from a few years from 1968 when a loco was used. Sidings later closed, and tracks removed in 1981.

Locomotives: Gauge 2'10½"

MINNIE		0-4-0 IT	OC	WB	1426	1894	(a)	(1)
POWERFUL	*	0-4-0ST	OC	WB	1901	1911	New	Scr/1958
		4wPM	20hp	HU	32145	1927	New	(2)
		4wDM	48hp	RH	283869	1949	New	(3)

*   Modified at quarry between 1935 and 1942; chimney, cab and footplate lowered to suit tunnel. This considerably altered the appearance of this loco.

Locomotives: Gauge 4'8½"

In 4/1942 a visitor was told that there were three overhead-wire electric locos at the works [perhaps self-propelled transfer cars ?] He was unable to investigate.

No.2		0-4-0DM	80hp	AB	349	1941	(b)	(4)

(a)   arrived after 11/1903 by 7/1907 - wfw(tdx?): Newcastle & Gateshead Water Co [? Catcleugh Reservoir (1889-1905) Contract].
       [Loco may have come to Llanddulas per/via Snowball & Co, dealers, who were the original purchasers of this loco, and may have hired it out on Tyneside, rather than sold it there.]
(b)   tdx: Haunchwood Brick & Tile Co Ltd, Warwickshire, 6/1968

(1) tdt: WB, Stafford, in part-exchange (allowance £30) against new loco WB 1901, 1911
(2) still here 4/1942; gone by 3/1951; no further trace.
(3) tdt: Snowdon Mountain Railway (PR/58), per Colwyn Model Railway Club, 27/8/197?
(4) tdt: Mr D.G.Owen, private store Llandudno, after 10/1973 by 11/1974
    wlw: Colne Valley Railway, Castle Hedingham, Essex.

LLANDUDNO JUNCTION BRICKWORKS   L12
(Gc/GR:below)

There were two separate brickworks in close proximity:

HILL'S BRICKWORKS   (GR:801774)
by 7/1905   -   : Arthur Hill
           after 1914   : closed, demolished, track removed.

There were narrow gauge tracks in the clay-pit, and a c300 yard long tramroad from the works to a siding on the LNWR coastal loop line (the original PR/23 route).

LEWIS' BRICKWORKS   (GR:797775)
by 11/1890 -   : P.& H.Lewis Ltd
after 1948 -   9/1957 : Hartley & Partners Ltd
                   9/1957 : closed; remained derelict; site later occupied by H.L.Motors as car scrap yard.
                   1970s   : works demolished, rail tracks buried or removed.

Narrow gauge railway in clay pit with incline to works, which was also served by a siding of the LNWR/LMS coastal loop line, near Llandudno Junction loco shed.

Locomotives: Gauge 2'0" - LEWIS' BRICKWORKS

No.11   4wDM 11hp   OK   4372   (a)   (1)

(a) arrived c1954. Reputed tdx: Ruby Brickworks, Rhydymwyn, but not remembered at that location. Ruby was then another Hartley & Partners site [? which perhaps dealt with correspondence].
No previous owner yet known for this loco.

(1) lay disused for many years - indeed, may never have been put to work here. Last seen 4/1971; gone by 5/1972; undoubtedly scrapped.

LANDUDNO PIER REPAIR CONTRACT 1968-1969   L14
(Gc/GR:784830)

NORWEST CONSTRUCTION CO LTD, contractors.

Pier built by Llandudno Pier Co Ltd (reg.11/11/1875 £25K). Contract 1968 for construction of new berthing facilities at pier head for pier owners Fortes (Holdings) Ltd. To transport Piles and other materials, a 420 yard long 2ft gauge "portable" railway was laid along the pier 10/1968 and remained in use until 24/6/1969, after which the track was removed. A locomotive was delivered for use on this railway but was not in fact used, all traffic being hand-worked.

Locomotive: **Gauge 2'0"**

DL 461   4wDM 20hp   FH [?   2523 c1941] (a)   (1)

(a)   arrived during first week of 11/1968, most probably from Norwest Construction plant pool. Loco had a FH works-plate, but the space for the number on this plate was blank. Loco was one of the "1939 class" (similar to OK loco design) hence one of series FH 2513-2572. The most likely loco otherwise unaccounted for in this series is FH 2523 which wfw: Christiani & Neilson Ltd, contractors (and was used originally on a Contract in Mozambique, Africa).

(1)   left site late in 11/1968; probably tdt: Norwest Construction Co Ltd, Bootle Plant Depot, Liverpool (noted there 3/7/1970).
      wlw: Rossendale Forest Railway Society.
      wlw: South Tynedale Railway, Alston, Cumbria.

LLANERCH-Y-MOR SMELTING WORKS   L16
(Cf/GR:176792)

c1755		: opened (lead smelting works)
by 1825		: Kyrke & Eyton
c1840		: Eyton & Co
-	6/1886	: Adam Eyton & Son (who formed:-)
6/1886		: Adam Eyton Ltd (reg.19/6/1886)
by 1891		: Llanerch-y-Mor Lead Works Ltd
by 1903		: Heaths Dee Collieries Ltd
by 1908		: J.P.Eyton & Others
c1940 -	1955	: Ministry of Supply - ferro-manganese production unit operated by Darwen & Mostyn Iron Co Ltd
	1955	: closed; demolished; site used for light industry.

There was a 4'8½" gauge siding off PR/7 into this works prior to 1870, and probably from 1857-58 when the LNWR installed a siding "at Llanerch y Mor". Date siding removed not known, but probably 1955. Between 1870 and 1900 a narrow-gauge tramroad was laid from the works to a wharf on the river Dee; this line passed under PR/7 and later became a footpath ["Tramway (disused)" on OS/6"/1914.]

Locomotives : **Gauge narrow**

No record of any locos here other than that a mysterious narrow-gauge petrol/diesel loco was in use within the Ministry of Supply factory in 1942. This loco had then recently been built for the job at Mostyn Ironworks. No further trace.

LLANGOLLEN DISTRICT FORESTRY RAILWAYS, VIVOD L18
(Cd/GR: below)

c1915 - 1918 : **Board of Trade, Home Grown Timber Supply Dept. Canadian Forestry Corps.**
c1940 - c1944 : **Ministry of Supply**, Forestry Control.

During WW1, a temporary railway was laid from (GR:188418) roadside near Bryn Newydd up valley to GR:c172409. During WW2 a temporary railway was laid from a roadside loading dock (GR:196400) near Rhos Pengwern, up valley to GR:c182396; this line was lifted c1944 and relaid on approximate route of WW1 line above. During WW2, repairs to the MR locos were handled by local motor mechanics Jones Bros (Llangollen) Ltd, to whom MR supplied spare parts frequently from 9/1942 to 3/1944, and in 2/1948 (though this latter could have been for repairs to a loco at Chirk Forestry Depot (which see)).

Locomotives: Gauge 2'0"

0-4-0PM	10hp	Bg	649	1918	New 9/18 (a)	s/s
4wPM	20hp	MR	7093	1940	New 7/40 (b)	(1)
4wPM	20hp	MR	7094	1940	New 7/40 (b)	(2)

(a) despatched New to "Llangollen".
(b) despatched New to Mr Humphries, Timber Control, Vivod,, via GWR Whitehurst Station.

(1) wlw: G.W.Bungey Ltd, dealer, Hayes, Middlesex
    wlw: J.& A.Jackson Ltd, brickworks, Stockport, Cheshire.
(2) tdt: Ministry of Supply Forestry, Llanwddyn, Vyrnwy [Powys], 1943.

LLANRWST TRANSPORT MUSEUM L20
(Gc/GR:794623)

	1976	: established
1976 -	1978	: **Llanrwst Transport Group**
1978 -	1980	: **Conwy & Llanrwst Railway Society**
	1980	: closed; site cleared.

Located in the goods-yard at Llanrwst station (PR/23), this scheme did not come to fruition.

Locomotives: Gauge 4'8½"

4007	4wDM	FH	3147	1947	(a)	(1)
900348	2w-2PMr	Wkm	509	1932	(b)	(2)
965051	2w-2PMr	Wkm [?	7574	1956]	(b)	(3)

(a) tdx: Lowton Metals Ltd, Haydock, Lancashire, 21/1/1978
    wfw: Canning Town Glass Works Ltd, London E.16
(b) tdx: store at Welsh Highland Railway (PR/44), 1978
    wfw: British Railways (platelayers trolleys).

(1) tdt: Mr D.C.Owen, private store at Llandudno, 1980 by 11/8/1980
    wlw: Colne Valley Railway, Castle Hedingham, Essex (ex Llandudno on 22/2/1982)
(2) tdt: Talycafn Transport Museum, c8/1980
(3) tdt: Mr Ian Jolly (see Section 1) 10/5/1980

LLAY HALL COLLIERY & BRICKWORKS L22
and LLAY BANK FIRECLAY MINE, CEFN-Y-BEDD (Cd/GR:315552)

```
              1866    : a brickworks existed by this date.
 5/1866  -   c1872    : North Wales Coal, Iron & Firebrick Co Ltd (reg.5/1866)
  c1872              : colliery sinking started and abandoned.
 4/1873  -   c1876    : Llay Hall Coal, Iron & Brick Co Ltd
 4/1873  -   2/1877   : colliery sinking - John Fidler (of Chesterfield)
  c1876  -    1881    : Llay Hall Coal, Iron & Firebrick Co Ltd
              3/1877  : first coal winning.
   1881  -    1885    : Llay Hall Coal & Clay Works Co Ltd
                       (reg.16/7/1881  £100K  liq.3/1885-8/1887)
   1885  -    1900    : Llay Hall Coal & Iron Co     - E.Stanley Clarke
   1900  -            :                              - E.Stuart Clarke
              by 1913 : Exors of E.S.Clarke
   1915  -   c1980    : Llay Hall Brick Co Ltd [rebuilt the brickworks]
   1915  -    1928    : Llay Hall Colliery Co Ltd [colliery only]
   1928  -  12/1946   : Llay Hall Colliery Co Ltd (reg.25/10/1928 £100K)
  1/1947  -   c1957   : National Coal Board
             25/11/1949 : coal winding ceased; site retained as store.
              c1954   : rail traffic ceased.
              c1957   : track lifted (after 5/1956)
              c1980   : brickworks closed.
```

On 6/1/1874 the Llay Hall Coal, Iron & Brick Co Ltd obtained permission from Flintshire Quarter Sessions to divert a road and erect an iron bridge for the construction of "a railroad" from the colliery. The contractors building the 1.1/4 mile private railway in 4/1874 were "Messrs Edwards". [J/CDH/2.5.1874/7]

This railway opened 9/1877 from Llay Colliery Junction (on PR/28), and served both brickworks and colliery. Clay for the bricks was obtained both from the colliery, from the LLAY BANK DRIFT MINE (1923-1926), and from a small quarry, served by a short narrow-gauge line, behind the brickworks. During the 1980s the site became a light-industry area though many original buildings survive [1989].

John Fidler, the sinking contractor, settled in the area and his descendants held prominent positions here (colliery engineer, brickworks manager, etc.).

[Read: J/CG/7.4.1899/610; B/107]

Locomotives: Gauge 4'8½"

NOTE: Cudworth & Johnson used this site as a store for their locomotives from time to time the most recent being DEPTFORD in the 1950s. For details see C&J in Section 1.

	THORNHILL	0-6-0ST	IC	MW	101	1864	(a)	(1)
No.2		0-6-0ST	IC	MW	664	1878	New 5/78	(2)
	THE WELSHMAN	0-6-0ST	IC	MW	1207	1890	New 1/91	
			rebuilt	MW		1908		(3)
	-	4wPM	45hp	MR	4623	1932	(b)	(4)

(a) here by 2/1878, and probably by 9/1877 when railway opened.
   wfw(tdx?): Barnes & Beckett, contractors, Rochdale, Lancs.
(b) tdx: Point of Ayr Colliery, after 7/1953 by 7/6/1954

(1) wlw(tdt?): W.& H.Chambers, contractors; and possibly used on GWR Wrexham-Rho (PR/59: 1899-1901) Contract.
(2) still here 3/1899 and probably some years thereafter - but no further trace.
(3) tdt: Llay Main Colliery, between 1949 and 10/1950
   tdx: Llay Main Colliery, after 1/1952 by 6/1952
   tdt: Llay Main Colliery, after 8/1952 by 4/1953
(4) tdt: Llay Main Workshops, after 9/1956 by 4/1957 (and Scr 6/1970).

LLAY HALL GRAVEL PITS, CEFN-Y-BEDD L24
(Cd/GR:317555)

: A.Monk & Co Ltd (contractors of Warrington).

Pits worked for many years by Monks to obtain materials for use on their work elsewhere. A "portable" railway connected the digging area to screens until c1955 (after 6/1954), when it was replaced by road vehicles.

Locomotives: Gauge 2'0"

	4wDM	20hp	RH			(a)	(1)
L.13	4wDM	20hp	RH	194776	1939	(a)	(2)

(a) tdx: Monk plant pool at Padgate Yard, Warrington.

(1) tdt: Monk plant pool at Padgate Yard, Warrington, by 6/1954
(2) tdt: Monk plant pool at Padgate Yard, Warrington, c1955; Scr 9/1959

LLAY MAIN COLLIERY & NCB WORKSHOPS, LLAY L26
(Cd/GR:327565)

	1913	: new colliery on greenfield site.
8/1913 - 12/1946		: **Llay Main Collieries Ltd** (reg.7/8/1913 £250K) a joint venture of Rea Ltd, and Hickleton Main Colliery Co Ltd (a "Markham" company). From 1/1926 the Hickleton interest was purchased by Carlton Main Colliery Co Ltd
7/1914 -	1922	: Sinking 2715ft - see below. First Winning 1922.
1/1947 -	1968	: **National Coal Board**
	11/3/1966	: seams abandoned.
-	1968	: boiler house retained to generate electricity for Gresford Colliery.
1966 -	1970	: colliery dismantled. Railway lifted by George Cohen, Sons & Co Ltd, between mid-1966 and 7/1967. Site later occupied by light industry.

The colliery was connected by a 1 mile LNER/BR branch from Llay Colliery Junction - see PR/28 for details. This branch was normally worked by LNER/BR locos, though colliery locos were permitted to be, and often were, used. In c1912 the GWR surveyed a direct line, from the colliery to PR/5, but it was not built.

A "model village" was built at Llay to house colliery workers, and Roberts & Sloss, contractors (of Liverpool) built 275 houses 5/1920 to 1923; a narrow gauge rail system may have been used.

[Read: J/Colliery Engineering/6.1925/272; B/107A]

COLLIERY SINKING 1914-1922

7/1914 -	8/1914	: **Rheinisch West Falische Co** [of Germany]
8/1914 -	12/1914	: work suspended due to War
12/1914 -	c1922	: **Simon Carves Ltd** (of Manchester) - this work was also suspended 4/1917 to 4/1/1919

Locomotive: Gauge 2ft

	0-4-0WT	OC	OK [?	6915	1914] (a)	(1)

COLLIERY OPERATION 1923-1966

Locomotives: Gauge 4'8½"

NOTE: In addition to the locomotives listed, there is an unconfirmed report that loco BEATTY 0-4-0ST OC MW 1902/1916 was hired c1921 from Bullcroft Colliery, Yorkshire. Also, "main-line" locos were hired from time to time; 68727 was here 13/4/1957; 68714 here 2/3/1958.

	TEES VALLEY	0-6-0ST	IC	MW	1594	1903	(b)	(2)
R1	DAVID	0-6-0ST	OC	AE	1868	1921	New Scr c5/1964	
	ROBERT	0-6-0ST	OC	AE	1951	1924	New 11/24	(3)
	BRITISH No.1	0-4-0ST	OC	P	976	1903	(c)	(4)
	HAFOD	0-6-0ST	IC	P	775	1899	(d)	(5)
	SIR JOSEPH	0-6-0ST	OC	HC	1196	1916	(e)	(6)
B17C		0-4-0ST	OC	HL	2466	1900	(f)	(7)

R2	GWYNETH	0-6-0ST	IC	RSH	7135	1944	(g)	(8)
	FRANCES VALERIE	0-6-0ST	IC	HE	3700	1950	New 12/50	(9)
	THE WELSHMAN	0-6-0ST	IC	MW	1207	1890		
			rebuilt MW			1908	(h)	(10)

Locomotives: Gauge 2'0" Surface Stockyard System.

-	4wDM	31hp	RH	375701	1954	New 7/54	(11)
-	4wDM	31hp	RH	375700	1954	(i)	(12)

Locomotives: Gauge 2'0" Underground System.

	4wBE		?			(j)	(13)
	4wBE	Bg 3379+		EE 1960	1954	New	(14)
	4wBE	Bg 3380+		EE 1961	1954	New	(15)
	4wBE	Bg 3381+		EE 1963	1954	New	(16)
	4wBE	Bg 3382+		EE 1962	1954	New	(17)
	4wBE	Bg 3537+		EE 2697	1954	New	(18)
5	4wDM	48hp	RH	497549	1963	New 7/63	(19)
6	4wDM	48hp	RH	497758	1963	New 7/63	(20)
7	4wDM	48hp	RH	497759	1963	New 8/63	(21)
14	4wDM	48hp	RH	506496	1964	(k)	(22)
1	4wDM	48hp	RH	481551	1962	(m)	(23)

NOTE: The DIRECT RETURN TRANSFER of any loco to AND from Area Workshops (at Llay o Walkden), being a common occurrence for routine overhauls, is not recorded in this list Transfers to/from Area Workshops are noted only when the loco was concurrently transferred to/from another colliery.

(a) OK 6915 was supplied New to "Hickleton Main Colliery", but there is no record of it having worked there (Yorkshire). As Hickleton were the prime owners of Llay Main, OK 6915 could be the loco of this type which appears in photographs of Llay Main sinking activity.
(b) tdx: Chas.Baker & Sons, contractors, Llay Main Branch Railway (PR/28) Contract, c1915
(c) hired from Cudworth & Johnson, dealers, Wrexham, c1928
(d) tdx: Hafod Colliery, 8/1933
(e) hired from Cudworth & Johnson, Wrexham, 1938
(f) hired from Cudworth & Johnson - tdx: previous "hired at" site (Joseph Perrin & Sons Ltd, Birkenhead) after 7/1944 by 11/1944
(g) tdx: War Department, WD 75185, 6/1947 - ex Calais, France.
(h) tdx: Llay Hall Colliery, between 1949 and 10/1950
 tdt: Llay Hall Colliery, after 1/1952 by 6/1952
 tdx: Llay Hall Colliery, after 8/1952 by 4/1953
 tdt: Gresford Colliery, after 4/1953 by 5/1953
 tdx: Gresford Colliery, after 8/1954 by 3/1955
(i) tdx: Gresford Colliery, 6/11/1964
(j) this loco was on loan in 1953 during construction of the underground loco line. May have belonged to a contractor.
(k) tdx: Llay Main Workshops (New loco), 30/7/1964
(m) tdx: Llay Main Workshops, 15/2/1965
 wfw: Point of Ayr Colliery.

1) Llay Main Collieries Ltd were advertising surplus plant for sale, at the colliery, in 1926 [J/CG/4.1926/708]; the list included a 2ft gauge loco by OK, 4w 20hp 6x10¾ 1'10"dw 3'11"wb - presumably this same loco. No further trace.
(2) wlw(tdt?): Markham & Co Ltd, Chesterfield, Derbyshire.
(3) scrapped at Llay Main by Mee & Cocker Ltd (of Chequerbent, Lancs) 1/1967
(4) returned to Cudworth & Johnson, off hire, c1928
(5) not at Llay Main 5/1942; no further trace.
(6) tdt: Cudworth & Johnson, off hire, [c1939] by 22/3/1940
(7) tdt: Joseph Perrin & Sons Ltd, Birkenhead, 11/1944 per C&J (hire).
(8) tdt: Llay Main Workshops c1966 (by 6/3/1966); thence:-
    tdt: Gresford Colliery, after 6/3/1966 by 4/1966
(9) tdt: Hafod Colliery, 2/1951
(10) tdt: Hafod Colliery, after 11/1959 by 1/1960
(11) tdt: Walkden Workshops, Lancashire, 1966
    wlw: Gresford Colliery, by 9/1967
(12) scrapped at Llay Main by I.Hayward Ltd (of Wrexham), c5/1969
(13) see footnote (h); returned off loan c1954
(14) tdt: Murton Colliery, Co.Durham, 2/1964
(15) tdt: South Hetton Colliery, Co.Durham, 2/1964
(16) tdt: EEV works 2/1964 and thence to Bg works 11/1964
    wlw: Parkside Colliery, Lancashire.
(17) tdt: Bg works c1955; re-gauged to 2'3".
    wlw: Bold Colliery, Lancashire, c1955
(18) tdt: Bg works, 11/1964; re-gauged to 2'6".
    wlw: Parkside Colliery, Lancashire, 4/1965
(19) tdt: Llay Main Workshops, 7/4/1966
    wlw: Point of Ayr Colliery
(20) tdt: Walkden Workshops, Lancs, after 23/11/1967 by 8/7/1968
    wlw: Point of Ayr Colliery
(21) tdt: Parsonage Colliery, Lancashire, by 23/11/1967
    wlw: Point of Ayr Colliery
(22) tdt: Walkden Workshops, Lancashire, 11/3/1966
    wlw: Gresford Colliery
(23) tdt: Llay Main Workshops, 28/9/1965
    wlw: Point of Ayr Colliery

AREA CENTRAL WORKSHOPS, LLAY MAIN

The National Coal Board established a central repair workshops at the eastern end of the Llay Main colliery premises, for the repair of machinery, including locomotives, from all North Wales (and Ifton, Salop) collieries. Visitors to Llay Main sometimes reported locomotives seen at these workshops as if they were at the colliery, and this has to be borne in mind when considering details of loco transfers. Within this book, transfers to/from these workshops are dealt with within the transfer footnotes of the colliery which despatched the loco to, or received the loco from, central workshops; and routine visits of locos to the workshops, coming from and returning to the SAME colliery, are not recorded at all. The only "long term" resident loco here was MR 4623, received from Llay Hall Colliery c1956, then standing disused in the yard until scrapped 6/1970.

Llay Main Workshops closed 12/1965; some work was transferred to Llay Main Colliery fitting-shop until this closed 29/12/1967. Thereafter, the (hitherto) Lancashire Area Workshops at Walkden was used for servicing North Wales equipment.

LLECHWEDD SLATE QUARRY & TOURIST CAVERNS   L28
BLAENAU FFESTINIOG
(Gm/GR:702469 etc)

c1846	- 11/1900	: J.W.Greaves & Sons
11/1900	-	: J.W.Greaves & Sons Ltd (reg.22/11/1900 £250K)
by 1990	-	: Greaves Welsh Slate Co Ltd
ALSO 1971	-	: Quarry Tours Ltd

Most slate was obtained from underground workings, the lowest level (floor I) being 900ft below surface. Internal railways were apparently used from the outset, an incline being opened to the Ffestiniog Railway (PR/3) in 1848. This remained in use, latterly to reach a BR (PR/23) siding and lorry loading yard, until 8/1965. Whilst locomotives were used through tunnels to reach workings and inclines on the upper floors, they do not seem to have been used in the deep mine. The principal surface lines on Floors 5 and 7 were fitted with overhead wire electrification but this was never extensive. After 1976 work was concentrated on upper levels, often using opencasting techniques with road transport, resulting in the elimination of rail transport from the Quarry Section by 1981.

In 1972 a section of the underground workings was opened to visitors using rail transport, becoming a major tourist attraction. Facilities extended in 1979 by reopening an old incline to convey visitors deeper into the mine, using a cable-operated passenger car. Various items of quarry railway equipment, including locomotives, are on view within the Tours Section of the premises.

[Read: B/279; B/281; B/282; B/283; J/IRR/No.126/315]

Locomotives: Gauge 2ft

Many questions are unresolved. Initially there were three known vertical boilered locos, followed by three known Bagnalls. However, in 9/1902 Bagnall repaired a locomotive called MAX for J.W.Greaves of which nothing else is known.

In 1920 it was decided to make maximum use of electric power; this was described in a booklet [B/279] by Capt.M.I.Williams-Ellis which was published (undated) in 1927/28. From this we read that there were two 2hp BEV battery locos "in operation close on seven years" yet, according to BEV makers' records, the second known loco (BEV 323) was not delivered until 1926. If this was a third loco, why is it not mentioned in the book ? If it was a replacement loco, why is the second original one not in BEV records ?

An inventory [DRO/Z/DBE/3522] of 9/1933 lists (inter alia):
    Three battery locos value £50 each; one ditto, broken frame, value £20; 3 trolley locos 250v value £100 each; 1 steam loco value £20.
However, another 9/1933 inventory of electric MOTORS lists those in the 3 trolley locos, but only 2 in battery locos "308" and "323". As regards the "trolley" (overhead-wire) electric locos, BEV 640 and THE COALITION present no problems - that the latter is a rebuild of EDITH is proved by its chassis having wheels inside the frames. THE ECLIPSE, however, could be a rebuild of either MARGARET or DOROTHY, and what has been available for examination of these two locos since 1954 is insufficient to clinch the argument. However, B/279 states that No.4 loco was reconstructed at Llechwedd..."been in operation 12 months...converted from a steam loco almost thirty years old...". This seems to point to DOROTHY, the 1899 loco, though as not all Bagnall locos carried dated plates, he could have been confused as to the true age of either loco.

In 6/1945 Llechwedd wrote to Edison Accumulators Ltd saying they had purchased a battery loco from Maenofferen Quarry - and the loco had Edison batteries (serial number quoted). Edison replied that they had sold the batteries to Maenofferen 1/1936. This confirms WR

918, which was of a different design to the BEVs, having a single battery box with end platform for the driver.

In 1970/71, a private consortium proposed to lease a disused part of the Llechwedd Mine and develop it as a tourist facility. Work started but, prior to opening in 1972, the venture was largely taken over by Greaves and, for all practical purposes, the tourist area (operated by subsidiary company Quarry Tours Ltd) is a section of the quarry complex. To operate the tourist trains, three WR "BEV type" locos were obtained, two being used and the third broken up for spares. A fourth similar loco was subsequently obtained, becoming (the second) No.3. All four were devoid of worksplates, and have defied identification. They soon lost their running numbers and became known by their different colours, though as the colours (white, orange, green, blue, red, yellow) have changed, these are not a positive guide to identity. More permanent and obvious points of difference are the direction of the 'rails' on which the battery-box sits (side to side, or front to rear), and the quantity, size and position of the various holes drilled in the driver's end buffer-beam. The situation currently [1990] is as follows:-

No.1, latterly (at least) painted blue, has front-to-rear batterybox rails, and a plain bufferbeam (no buffer) at driver's end.
No.2, latterly red, has front-to-rear batterybox rails, and driver's end buffer has a pin-plate BELOW it, plus a large hole in the buffer beam each side of the buffer. A brass plate under the power controller reads "241/345".
No.3, latterly yellow, has side-to-side batterybox rails, and the driver's end buffer has a pin-plate ABOVE it.
The two 1963-built locos have higher-sided driving-cabs, and:-
Loco (LE/12/64) originally ran with that number clearly visible on the driver's end cab sheet but this was later removed. Loco was fitted (inside the cab) with worksplate WR 6807 (in error). Driver's end buffer has pin-plate ABOVE it. Loco is painted green (1990).
Loco (LE/12/65) also ran with visible number, and had worksplate WR 6766 in cab. Driver's end buffer has pin-plate BELOW it, and loco painted orange (1990).
In all cases, the colour refers to the chassis; battery-boxes, being interchangeable, are no guide to identity.

In 1975 the neighbouring Maenofferen Mine was taken over by Llechwedd resulting in some transfers of locomotives with that site.

Quarry Section Locomotive List

	-	0-4-0VBT	VC	DeW		1878	New (a)	Scr/c	1898
	FREDA	0-4-0VBT	VC	DeW		1880	New		(1)
	-	0-4-0VBT	VC	FE		1882	New (b)		s/s
	EDITH	0-4-0 IT	OC	WB	1278	1890	New 8/90		(2)
	MARGARET	0-4-0ST	OC	WB	1445	1895	New 10/95		(3)
	DOROTHY	0-4-0ST	OC	WB	1568	1899	New 10/99		(3)
(No.1)		4wBE	2hp	BEV	308	1921	New 1/21	Ø	OOU
(No.2)		4wBE	2hp	BEV		1921	New (c)		s/s
(No.2)		4wBE	2hp	BEV	323	1921	(d)	Ø	OOU
(3)		4wBE	2hp	BEV			(e)	Scr	10/1973
"No.3"	WELSH PONY	4wWE	10hp	BEV	640	1926	New 6/26		(4)
No.4	THE ECLIPSE	0-4-0WE	15hp	Llechwedd		1927	New	Ø	OOU
	THE COALITION	0-4-0WE	15hp	Llechwedd		1930	New	Ø	OOU
	-	4wBE		WR	918	1936	(f)		(5)
	-	2-2wPM		Llechwedd		c1936	New (g)	Ø	OOU
	-	4wDM	21hp	RH	174542	1935	(h) *		OOU

Tours Section Locomotive List

(No.1)	4wBE		WR			(j)
(No.2)	4wBE		WR			(j)
"No.3"	4wBE		WR			(j)	Scr/1972
MBS 387	4wBE		LMM	1053	1950	(k)	± OOU
MBS 236	4wBE		LMM	1066	1950	(m)	± OOU
(No.3)	4wBE		WR			(n)	(6)
(LE/12/64)	4wBE	4hp	WR	6765	1963	(o)
(LE/12/65)	4wBE	4hp	WR	6766	1963	(o)

- Ø : transferred from Quarry Section to Tours Section, between 1978 and 1981, for static display.
- * : stored since arrival, in Quarry Section.
- ± : obtained for Tours Section use but unsuitable; placed on static display.

(a) arrived 13/6/1878 via Ffestiniog Railway (PR/3).
(b) possibly supplied per Spooner & Co (who feature in FE customer list, whilst Greaves and Llechwedd do not).
(c) the existence of this loco has yet to be confirmed.
(d) tdx: BEV, 1/1926.
    wfw: Southport Corporation, Lancashire.
(e) here by 9/1933 per inventory; seen 31/8/1951 and thereafter, stored in electricians workshop on Floor 5. May POSSIBLY be same loco as (the first) "(No.2)" listed above.
(f) tdx: Maenofferen Slate Quarry, 6/1945
(g) consists of cab, engine and gearbox of Morris Car No.323414, mounted onto a rail chassis with steerable front axle. Disused by 5/1968.
(h) tdx: Maenofferen Slate Quarry 1/1978, for storage only.
(j) arrived c11/1971; two at least being from M.R.Q.Construction Ltd, contractors (of Oldham, Lancashire).
(k) tdx: Mitchell Bros, Sons & Co Ltd, contractors, Tickhill Depot, Doncaster, after 2/1972 by 4/1972.
    wfw: Trap Brickworks, Buckley.
(m) tdx: Mitchell Bros, Sons & Co Ltd, contractors, Tickhill Depot, Doncaster, after 2/1972 by 4/1972.
    wfw: Edmund Nuttall Ltd, contractors.
(n) tdx: Thyssen (Great Britain) Ltd, contractors, Llanelli, by 4/1972;
    (last used at Mount Washington Mine, Cornwall).
(o) tdx: Marchlyn Mawr Reservoir Contract
    (note: WR 6765 fitted with incorrect worksplate WR 6807).

(1) wlw(tdt?): Tonfanau Granite Quarry, after 1/1898 by 9/1898;
    possibly per/via Owen, Isaac & Owen, dealers, Union Iron Works, Porthmadog.
(2) Chassis and cab used in manufacture of THE COALITION in 1930.
(3) Chassis and cab of one of these used 1927 in the manufacture of THE ECLIPSE; the other was dismantled with intention of making another electric loco, but never completed. This frame, cab-sides and saddle-tank remained stored until:
    tdt: Mr R.P.Morris (private store) 12/1972
    wlw: Gloddfa Ganol - see "Oakeley Slate Quarry".
(4) stored disused by 8/1951
    tdt: Mr P.D.Nicholson (private store) 20/7/1976
    wlw: Gloddfa Ganol - see "Oakeley Slate Quarry".
(5) tdt: Maenofferen Slate Quarry, c7/1981
(6) tdt: Maenofferen Slate Quarry, c1987 (by 2/1988).

LLYN CELYN RESERVOIR CONSTRUCTION, near BALA   L30
(Gm/GR:855405)

1963 - 1965 : **Tarmac Construction Ltd**, contractors (of Wolverhampton) For Liverpool Corporation.

Whilst the majority of the construction work was undertaken using road vehicles, monorail and "portable" railway equipment was used on some areas of soft ground.

Locomotives: Gauge 2'0"

At least three "Simplex" locos were seen here, including:

                      4wDM   20hp   MR   8600   1940   (a)   (1)

(a)   here by 31/7/1965; owned by Tarmac Ltd since 11/1955
      wfw: Diesel Loco Hirers Ltd, Bedford.

(1)   wlw: preserved by private owner Mr D.Turner at Wychbold, Worcs.

LLYSFAEN LIMEWORKS & QUARRIES, LLYSFAEN   L32
(Cd/GR:890782 etc)

1860 -   : **Brundrit & Whiteway**
1873 -   1920   : **Raynes & Co** (James T.Raynes)
1920 - 10/1931 : **Raynes & Co Ltd** (reg.1920 vol.liq.25/11/1931)

From c1921 was subsidiary of United Alkali Co Ltd, thus in 1927 becoming a subsidiary of The Buxton Lime Firms Co Ltd - which was controlled by Imperial Chemical Industries Ltd through Brunner Mond & Co Ltd.

10/1931 - 12/1943 : **I.C.I.Lime Ltd** (reg.10/1931 vol.liq.31/12/1943)
1/1944 -   : **Imperial Chemical Industries Ltd, Lime Division**.
          c1952   : ceased to use railways within the quarry.

The quarry remained in use; by 2/1986 was owned by RMC North West Aggregates Ltd.

Stone was first quarried at this site in a small way by local men, and loaded into barges on the nearby beach. First pier built after 1860, and quarry opened on two levels between the (then) main road and the L&NWRly (PR/7). A tramroad incline connected the two quarry levels and, from the bottom level the tramroad crossed over PR/7 before descending another incline to the pier. After 1873, Raynes erected a Hoffman (rotary burning) Kiln on the second quarry level, and a crushing Mill - the latter fed from a third, higher, level, reached by a new incline. From this third level, a tunnel was driven under the main road in 1875 to open up a new quarry (Merllyn Quarry) on the south side of the road. In c1901, a second tunnel was driven under the road, connecting the Hoffman Kiln level to a lower level in Merllyn.

The quarry railway system was 3ft gauge; the top level line from Merllyn to Crushing Mill was worked by the Sentinel loco, its shed being located at GR:8903 7834. When New, this loco was numbered '2', suggesting maybe the existence of a loco '1' of which nothing is yet known. Overburden was stripped from above the working face and originally taken by a tramroad, of unknown gauge, which crossed the main road to a tip to the east of the works.

In the 1930s this was replaced by a 2ft gauge line worked by locomotives; this line bridged over the main road to the west of the works to enable spoil to be tipped into the original (bottom level) quarry north of the road. The 2ft gauge loco shed was at GR:8862 783. Towards the end of the 1940s the 3ft gauge system was replaced by road vehicles and conveyor belts; the 2ft gauge remained in use to c1952.

No evidence has been found of industrial locos being used on the 4'8½" gauge sidings at Llysfaen.

Locomotives: Gauge 3ft

Rail system on quarry floor, to kilns, and via incline to pier. The track gauge was shown in official returns as 2'11½", to avoid the more stringent regulations that applied to quarry railways of "three foot gauge and over".

According to ICI records, four locomotives were rebuilt at the ICI South Central Workshops at Tunstead, Derbyshire, for use at Llysfaen, and the records suggest all four (RS39, RS40, RS54, RS60) thus rebuilt were then 3ft gauge machines. It is known, however, that RS54 definitely operated on the 2ft gauge "overburden" line hence the ICI records are, perhaps, suspect. However, it is certain that at least one petrol loco (believed to be RS60) did work with the Sentinel on the 3ft gauge. Pending further data, we give the ICI records the benefit of the doubt in respect of RS39, RS40 and RS60 (which, apparently, were not actually observed by visitors on either line); and this seems reasonable, as all three arrived in one lot at Bungey's, doubtless consequent on cessation of loco haulage on the 3ft lines at Llysfaen. The gauge of the locos as received by Bungey's does not seem to have been recorded.

RS28	(formerly 2)	4wTG	VB	S		6901	1927 New	(1)
RS39		4wPM	40hp	MR	[* 1301		1918]	
				rebuilt SCW			1930 (a)	(2)
RS40		4wPM	20hp	MR	[± 1259		1919]	
				rebuilt SCW			1931 (b)	(2)
RS60		4wPM	20hp	MR				
				rebuilt SCW			1937 (c)	(2)

* Per ICI records, RS39 was rebuilt from RS17 MR 1301, but when seen at Bungey's 12/1950 the loco was plated "Honeywill Bros 1302".
Perhaps, therefore, it was in fact MR 1302, or even FH (KC&E) 1302.
Neither MR nor FH records assist in this problem. Also, in 12/1950 it carried plate LR2912 - presumably on an engine casing exchanged with RS30 below.

± Per MR records, no loco was built numbered MR 1259. Per ICI records RS40 (exRS14) was MR 1259. This could be an error, or again could be a FH (KC&E) number. Many KC&E locos were, in fact, overhauled MR locos and thus virtually indistinguishable.

Locomotives: Gauge 2ft

Rail system above, and inland of, the quarry, for removal of overburden. Rail traffic ceased 1952.

RS54	LR2370	4wPM	20hp	MR	[# 1649	1918]			
			rebuilt SCW			1935	(d)		(3)
RS44		4wDM	30hp	MR	5655	1934	(e)		(4)
RS30	LR2912	4wPM	20hp	MR	1191	1918	(f)		(5)
RS49		4wDM	30hp	MR	5680	1935	(g)		(6)
RS58		4wDM	30hp	MR	5692	1937	(h)		(6)
RS35		4wDM	30hp	MR	5642	1933	(j)		(6)

\# Per ICI records, RS18 (no MR number recorded) was rebuilt as RS54 for Llysfaen. At Llysfaen, RS54 carried (WD) plate LR2370 but no MR plate. LR2370 was originally MR 1649/1918. Per ICI records, RS26 (a Hindlow Quarry loco) was MR 1649. Perhaps ICI records are faulty or perhaps RS54 "inherited" the LR2370 plate from MR 1649. Per MR records, MR 1649 was with Brunner Mond Ltd (an ICI constituent) in 10/1922 - thus apparently confirming its presence in the ICI fleet.

(a) arrived c9/1930.   wfw: Hindlow Quarry, Derbyshire, RS17.
(b) arrived c2/1931.   wfw: Hoffmans Works, Derbyshire, RS14.
(c) arrived 1937.   wfw: Tunstead Quarry, Derbyshire, RS31.
(d) arrived c8/1935.   wfw: Cowdale Quarry, Derbyshire, RS18.
(e) arrived by 2/1938.   wfw: Cowdale Quarry, to 3/1934 at least.
(f) arrived by 30/4/1942. wfw: Buxton Central Cheadle Works.
(g) arrived after 3/1944. wfw: Cowdale Quarry, Derbyshire.
(h) arrived after 3/1944. wfw: Tunstead Quarry, Derbyshire.
(j) arrived after 5/1947. wfw: Tunstead Quarry, Derbyshire.

(1) s/s, after 3/1944
(2) three locos numbered RS39, RS40, RS60 were seen at G.W.Bungey Ltd, dealer, Hayes, Middlesex, on 2/12/1950, recently arrived, apparently direct from Llysfaen. They were subsequently scrapped.
(3) left here after 3/1944; per ICI records it was scrapped (still a petrol loco) in 1945 - but an unidentified MR loco numbered RS54 was reported 7/1958 lying at Buxton Central Quarry, Cheedale; though another report of 1960 lists the locos at Cheedale as RS36/RS38/RS56 so maybe the 1958 report of RS54 is an error.
(4) left here after 5/3/1944 - no further trace.
(5) left here after 5/3/1944 - reputedly scrapped at Buxton Central Quarry, Cheedale, Derbyshire.
(6) Per ICI records, sold as scrap 4/1953 "probably to Vernon & Roberts of Stalybridge". However, RS49 and RS58 turned up at G.W.Bungey Ltd, dealer, Hayes, Middlesex, where they were overhauled and sold to "Stillfontein" [? South Africa] by 10/1953. Of RS35 there is no further trace - but the probability is that all three went direct to Bungey's from Llysfaen.

MAENOFFEREN SLATE MINE, BLAENAU FFESTINIOG M2
(Gm/GR:714466 etc)

c1800 -	1848	: various local men
1848 -	1852	: Shelton & Greaves
1859 -	1861	: David Jones & Co
1861 -	1975	: Maen Offeren Slate Quarry Co Ltd (inc.12/6/1861 £50K)
1975 -		: J.W.Greaves & Sons Ltd [of Llechwedd Quarry]

Original opencast workings developed into deep mine, with inclined shaft access from M area (GR:714466) connected by siding to "second incline summit" level of the "Rhiwbach Tramway" (PR/13). After closure of PR/13 to Cwt-y-Bugail, Maenofferen became sole use of PR/13 (including its No.1 and No.2 Inclines) down to Duffws (Blaenau Ffestiniog). No. Incline was last used 7/1962; subsequently No.2 Incline used to lower output to a landsal yard beside the Maenofferen Office (GR:707465). After 1975 a roadway was driven up th mountainside from the Office to the Mill, and No.2 Incline - the last remnant of PR/13 - wa then abandoned. Use of rail transport was then restricted to the Mill area, the access drif and the extensive underground galleries within the mine.

[Read: B/378; B/169]

Locomotives: Gauge 2ft

	SANFORD		0-4-0ST	OC	WB	1571	1900	(a)	(1)
	SKINNER		0-4-0ST	OC	WB	1766	1906	New 1/07	(2)
	-	[A]	4wPM	20hp	MR	1904	1920	New 1/20	(3)
	-	[B]	4wPM		MH	?	1925	(b)	(4)
	-		4wPM		LAdB				(5)
	-	[C]	4wDM	30hp	MR	5506	1929	New 7/29	(6)
	-	[D]	4wPM	20hp	FH	1821	1933	New 5/33	(3)
	-		4wBE		WR	918	1936	New (c)	
	-		4wDM	12hp	RH	174535	1936	New 5/36	(7)
(3)	-		4wDM	12hp	RH	174536	1936	New 5/36 OOU/1989	
	-		4wDM	12hp	RH	177642	1936	New 8/36	(7)
	-		4wDM	13hp	RH	191674	1938	New 4/38 Scr/1966	
	-		4wDM	13hp	RH	200762	1942	New 7/42	(8)
	-		4wDM	21hp	RH	175127	1935	(d)	OOU/1989
	-		4wDM	21hp	RH	174542	1935	(e)	(9)
	-		4wPM	10hp	FH	1929	1935	(f)	(10)
	-		4wDM	20hp	MR	20073	1950	(g)	(11)
	-		4wDM	21hp	RH	175138	1935	(h)	(12)
	-		4wDM	12hp	RH	177638	1936	(h)	(13)
	-		4wBE		CE	5688/2	1969	(i)	
	-		4wBE		WR			(j)	

NOTES:
[A] worked for many years on Rhiwbach Tramway (PR/13) - transferred between 8/1951 and 8/1953 to Maenofferen Tip Railway.
[B] for discussion re the builder of this loco (which was - from c1948 at least - used for shunting around the BR goods yards at Blaenau Ffestiniog) see entry "Rhiwbach Slate Quarry".
[C] fitted with special overall cab for use on the (very exposed) Maenofferen Tip Railway - where it replaced the steam locos.

[D] not truly a "new" loco, but a rebuild by FH of an older (and unidentified) MR loco. Modified by FH to suit Maenofferen specification: "top speed increase to 10mph....to haul 15 tons up 1 in 70 gradient". Apparently intended for use on Rhiwbach Tramway (PR/13) and may have been so used. By 8/1951 was used for working Maenofferen Office Level section of PR/13, from top of Incline No.1 to foot of Incline No.2

(a) New 7/1900; purchased via Owen, Isaac & Owen, dealers, Union Iron Works, Porthmadog.
(b) taken over with Rhiwbach Quarry (and PR/13) in 1928.
(c) tdt: Llechwedd Slate Quarry 6/1945
 tdx: Llechwedd Slate Quarry c7/1981
(d) arived after 7/1939 by 2/1946
 wfw: Gardden (Lodge) Brick Works, Ruabon
(e) wfw: Bergerat Dutry SA, Brussels, Belgium
(f) wfw: Whitley Bros, contractors, Wrexham. Apparently still with Whitley Bros until 9/1946, then "lost"; next seen 15/4/1954 lying off track by ex-GWR Goods Shed in Blaenau Ffestiniog station yard, and reputedly then the property of Maen Offeren Quarry but this not proven.
(g) tdf: MR, Bedford, 8/12/1961
 wfw: Birmingham Corporation Water Department, Knighton, Radnor
(h) tdf: Votty & Bowydd Slate Quarry, /1963
(i) tdf: ? , c7/1980
 wfw: Wheal Jane Ltd, Cornwall
(j) tdf: Llechwedd Quarry (Tours Section) c1987 (by 2/1988)

(1) tdt: Penrhyn Slate Quarries 7/1929
(2) tdt: Penrhyn Slate Quarries 8/1929
(3) scrapped after 8/1965 by 8/1966
(4) scrapped after 7/1964 by 7/1965 by T.Glyn Williams, Blaenau Ffestiniog
(5) derelict near Maenofferen Office 5/12/1941; s/s by 8/1951
(6) disused by 10/1953; scrapped by 6/1964
(7) tdt: Mr J.Crosskey, c/o Brockham Museum, Surrey, 20/10/1975
(8) dismantled by 9/1960; parts used to repair other locos;
 chassis scrapped after 4/1974 by 4/1975.
(9) tdt: Llechwedd Slate Quarry 1/1978
(10) still lying by Goods Shed 12/7/1954; no further trace.
(11) tdt: Mr J.Crosskey, c/o Brockham Museum, Surrey, 4/1975
(12) ran away down Incline No.2 (to Office level) in 1965;
 remains were scrapped after 6/1969.
(13) dismantled after 4/1965; parts used to repair other locos;
 chassis scrapped after 7/1969 by 4/1975.

MANOD (BWLCH-Y-SLATER) SLATE QUARRY M4
near FFESTINIOG (Gm/GR:732455)

		1805	:	started
4/1805	-		:	**O.A.Poole**
7/1813	-		:	**F.Webster** et al
5/1824	-	1866	:	**J.Pritchard** et al

```
     1866   -      1883     : Bwlch y Slater Slate Co
     1883   -   1/1909 +    : Bwlch-y-Slater Quarry Co Ltd [Agents: Rch.Bowton]
                              (reg.11/12/1883  £50K)
       by 1911  -           : Manod Quarries Ltd
       by 1937  -           : Manod Slate Quarries Ltd
       by 6/1967  -         : Cwt-y-Bugail Slate Quarries Ltd
       from c1971  -        :  subsidiary of Ffestiniog Slate Quarry Co Ltd
```

In early years there were, it seems, two opencast workings here, known as "Manod" "Bwlch Slaters"; one probably being reached by the old incline up from the eastern end of latter-day Mill area. The developed workings, however, were underground; and during W some of the chambers were occupied by the Ministry of Works (later the Ministry of Pu Building & Works; later the Department of the Environment) and used as a store for Nati Gallery paintings. For fuller details see J/FRS/No.104/33. During this period, slate extracted only from workings in the nearby Craig Ddu Quarry, reached by a tunnel f Manod. The DoE vacated in 1983, and mining restarted using road transport. The qu was connected to the Rhiwbach railway (PR/13) from c1860 to 1953; otherwise ou travelled via the mountain road to Llan Ffestiniog.

[Read: J/FRS/No.104/33-36; 'The Civil Engineer in War, Volume 3, Inst.C.E, 1948, pp264-

Locomotives: Gauge 2ft

```
                        4wBE   3hp     BE   16303  [1917?](a)      (
                        4wBE   3hp     BE   16306  [1917?](a)      (
        116             4wDM   20hp    HE   [?1965  1939 ] (b)     (
```

NOTE: The BE numbers 16303/6 are "engine identity numbers", not "works numbe (latter apparently not allocated to this type of loco by BE).
Loco 116 - the HE works plate was missing by 1954 and no earlier observation yet been located. The suggested identity HE 1965 is based on the engine num (Ailsa Craig 4127) and presumes this to be the original engine.
A similar loco, HE 2024, was temporarily stored at Manod 1974-1976. It was used here. For details see entry "Cwt-y-Bugail Slate Quarry".

(a)   reputedly tdx: W.O.Williams, dealer, Harlech, in the 1920s.
      These locos were of a batch built for the Ministry of Munitions during WW Some of the batch were used at Queensferry Government Depot, and auctioned th until 1925 (at least), hence this is a possible source.
(b)   brought here c1940 by Ministry of Works for store depot construction
            and, if HE 1965 - wfw: G.Wimpey & Sons Ltd, contractors, in 1940.

(1)   used for slate haulage until 1979.
            tdt: Gloddfa Ganol (see OAKELEY QUARRIES), after 5/1981 by 2/1982
(2)   dismantled for spares; perhaps never put to work here. By 1954 only the b bodywork survived - which was later:-
            tdt: Mr M.A.G.Jacob, private store, 30/10/1973
            wlw: Gloddfa Ganol (see OAKELEY QUARRIES) from 19/7/1978
(3)   lay disused here, on tips, for many years until scrapped 1974 after 15/4/1974.

MARCHLYN MAWR RESERVOIR and SLATE QUARRY   M6
(Reservoir Gc/(GR:617624)
(Quarry Gc/GR:602628)

RESERVOIR: Constructed in 1930s; a narrow-gauge horse- and hand-worked railway was laid to the site from the upper levels of the Penrhyn Slate Quarry. Locomotives were obtained by PSQ in 1936 for use on this line, but were not in fact so used. They later became CEGIN, OGWEN and MARCHLYN in the Penrhyn Quarry fleet. Railway removed c1940.

QUARRY: Operated by Dinorwic Quarry Company spasmodically from 1931 to 1958; some short 2ft gauge railways installed but no locos used. Redeveloped from 6/1961 using road vehicles, but site abandoned 7/1969 and equipment removed.

BOTH SITES: Taken over by Central Electricity Generating Board in 1974; reservoir enlarged by building up dam using stone from the quarry, thus forming the top lake of the Dinorwic Pumped Storage Hydro-Electric Generating Station. A rail system was used for construction of spillway tunnel at the eastern end of the dam.

Spillway Tunnel Construction - mid 1976 to late 1977.
Contractor   : **"MBZ"** (McAlpine/Brand/Zschokke consortium).

The locomotives used were supplied by Brand.
(Charles Brand & Son Ltd; a member of the French Kier Group of companies)

Locomotives: Gauge 2'0"

(E8-12/79)	4wBE		WR	7556	1972	(a)	(1)
LE/12/64	4wBE	*	WR	6765	1963	(b)	(2)
LE/12/65	4wBE		WR	6766	1963	(b)	(2)

*   Because of an exchange of components during repairs at Kings Lynn, this loco carried plate WR 6807 (off Kier loco - plant No.17271) whilst at Marchlyn.

(a)   tdx: Kiers Ltd, Setch, Kings Lynn, Norfolk, 20/4/1976
(b)   tdx: Kiers Ltd, Setch, Kings Lynn, Norfolk, 15/6/1976

(1)   auctioned at Marchlyn 19/6/1980;
      sold to Track Supplies & Services Ltd, Wolverton, Bucks;
      wlw: WR for rebuild - renumbered WR 10114
      wlw: Clogau St.Davids Gold Mine, Bontddu
(2)   auctioned at Marchlyn 19/6/1980;
      tdt: Llechwedd Slate Quarry (Tours Section) 7/1980

MARFORD SAND & GRAVEL QUARRY, ROSSETT   M8
(Cfd/GR:357562)

1927	-	1948	: Rossett Sand & Gravels Ltd
1942	-	1943	: closed
1948	-	c1954	: closed
c1954	-		: United Gravel Co Ltd [using road vehicles only]

Sidings into this quarry off the GWR main line (PR/5) were laid in under Agreements c 11/2/1927 and 25/2/1928. About this time, Nott, Brodie & Co Ltd, contractors, wer working on their "Rossett Siding Contract" - perhaps this was the sidings at this quarry. Th quarry temporarily closed during 1942-1943, and lay derelict from 1948 until the track wa lifted in 1952.

Locomotives: Gauge 4'8½"

PAT	0-4-0ST	OC	HC	276	1885		
		rebuilt	HC		1922	(a)	(1)
GORDON	0-4-0ST	OC	P	600	1895	(b)	(2)
[? SWANSEA	0-4-0ST	OC	HE	648	1897	(c)	(3)]
NETHERTON	0-6-0ST	IC	MW	1603	1903	(d)	Scr 6/1952

(a) arrived here after 9/1927 by 7/1928
    wfw(tdx?): Taf Fechan Water Supply Board, Pontsticill Reservoir (1921-1927) Contract
(b) here by 1/1930
    wfw(tdx?): Lever Bros.Ltd, Gossage Works, Widnes, Lancs, until c1928
(c) not confirmed here, but reputed:-
    hired from Cudworth & Johnson, dealer, Wrexham, c1941
(d) arrived after 15/7/1943 by 30/7/1944
    In early 1940s was owned by Sir Lindsay Parkinson & Co Ltd, and c1943 was seer standing at their Winwick Quay Plant Yard, Warrington, Lancs. Cudworth & Johnson may have had this loco in 8/1943 when they approached RSH for spare parts - or they may then have been repairing it at or for Marford Quarry

(1) tdt: Cudworth & Johnson, dealer, Wrexham, by 10/1936
(2) tdt: Cudworth & Johnson, dealer, Wrexham, after 21/8/1942 by 4/1943
    wlw: hire to W.J.Lee, Seacombe, Cheshire, by 4/1943
(3) if loco was here, then:-
    tdt: Cudworth & Johnson, Wrexham, off loan, by 8/1942

MINERA LEAD and ZINC MINES   M10
(Cd/GR:below)

The study of lead mining at Minera is a specialist subject which cannot be adequately dealt with in a book of this nature. Many small mines have been worked since Roman times, and those that existed in the 1800s would almost all have railways of some sort. The most important mining zone was between the Minera Limeworks (say GR:255520) and New Brighton (GR:274508) - a series of shafts between these points dropping into workings which were eventually to become one vast united labyrinth. All the mines were plagued by flooding and, as water passed from mine to mine through fissures in the rocks, amalgamation was the only possible solution to provide drainage for all. Deep adits were then driven, and pumping then restricted to cope only with workings below adit level. Pumping ceased in 1909, subsequent mining being in the upper altitudes only.

The mines in this zone that are known to have been working since 1800 are listed below. There were other mines in the surrounding area (Park, South Minera, etc) which were a little further from rail transport.

[Read: B/199/19/109 (etc); B/211; B/270; B/352]

MINERA EISTEDDFOD GROUP - listed west to east.
                    Most sites visible today [1991].

TOP EISTEDDFOD MINE (GR:246525)
            -     7/1865   : **Rock Mining Co Ltd**

TWELVE APOSTLES MINE (GR:251525)
            -     7/1865   : **Rock Mining Co Ltd**
                  1884   : working

MINERA UNION MINE (GR:253525; later 260520 new shaft)
            -     1873   : **Minera Union Mine Co Ltd** (vol.liq.8/8/1873)
                  1877   : **Union Mine Co**
                  1888   : working

WEST MINERA MINE (GR:254525)
            -     7/1865   : **Rock Mining Co Ltd**
                  1882   : working

CENTRAL MINERA MINE, GWYNFRYN (GR:259524)
            no details

ALSO: in 1877 the following Companies were active within this Group:
    Minera Boundary Company
    Charles F.Gibbons
    George Wynn & Co
    Hush Eisteddfod Minera Lead Mining Co Ltd

MINERA LIMEWORKS AREA GROUP - listed west to east.
                    Most sites have been lost due to quarrying.

RAGMAN MINE   (GR:255522)
MAESYFFYNNON MINE
CORNISH MINE   (GR:260518)
MORGANS MINE   (GR:261519)
DAVIES MINE   (GR:261518)
        The last three listed mines eventually formed the (relatively unimportant) western extremity of the United Mine.

OTHER MINES IN THE AREA not yet located are:
   DEANS MINE (working 1907)
   GRAIGPOETH MINE (working 1887)
   GREAT MELBOURNE MINE (working 1883)
   LLYWELLYN MINE (working 1887)

MINERA UNITED MINE GROUP - listed west to east.
Most sites visible today [1991].

WESTERN GROUP:
   BOUNDARY SHAFT   (GR:261518)
   BUSY BEE SHAFT   (GR:262518)
   GRAND TURK (TOPPINGS WEST END) SHAFT   (GR:263517)
   ROYLES SHAFT   (GR:264516)
   REIDS SHAFT   (GR:265516)
   ELLERTONS SHAFT   (GR:266514)
   ST.ANDREWS SHAFT   (GR:268514)

EASTERN GROUP:
   LLOYDS SHAFT   (GR:269513)
   TAYLORS SHAFT   (GR:271511)
   ROYS SHAFT   (GR:272510)
   MEADOW (CITY) SHAFT   (GR:275509) - 1220 ft deep.
   BURTONS (NEW MINERA) SHAFT   (GR:278508)
   NANT MINERA MINE   (GR:275505)
   Adit portals: Upper adit   GR:265518
                 Park adit   GR:271516
                 Deep adit   GR:288502

In addition to the shafts listed, there were various other minor shafts sunk for exploration and ventilation, some (though not all) of which had names. Railways are only likely to have existed at and around the listed shafts that were used for winding. The early editions of OS/6" and 25" maps show many "tramways" in the area.

The names of operators of the various shafts changed frequently, but prior to 1850 the major operators were Hunt, Noble & Co; J.Wilkinson & R.Kyrke; J.Burton & R.Kyrke. In the late 1840s [the exact date varies with each source, but perhaps the process was gradual] John Taylor & Sons took over eleven leases to gain control of the western end of the Eastern Group, thus leading the way to final amalgamation.

ROYS, TAYLORS and MEADOW
   c1847 -   : **Minera Mining Co** - John Taylor & Sons
   1850   -   1877   : **Minera Mining Co Ltd** [John Taylor et al]
   1877   -   1897   : **Minera Mining Co Ltd** (liq.1895)

BURTONS
   1889   -   1897   : **New Minera Mining Co Ltd** (reg.1887 vol.liq. 12/1896-1898)

CITY
   by 5/1865 -   : **Great Minera Mining Co**

ALL EXISTING SHAFTS
1897 -   1914 : **United Minera Mining Co Ltd** (reg. 4/6/1897)
           1914 : closed. Dispersal auction 25-26/11/1914.

BOUNDARY SHAFT
1919 -   1933 : small scale operations by local men.

With amalgamation, a 4'8½" gauge railway was constructed c1850 between the Minera Limeworks and City Shaft - though who built the line is not yet known. It was initially horse-worked; from 1868 the Limeworks loco worked some (if not all) of the traffic, until 1897 when the United company obtained their own locomotives. The track was lifted in 1915, after closure of the Mines, but in 1930 it was relaid and extended by the GWR (see Section 2 PR/6 - for details).

Locomotives: Gauge 4'8½" - Minera United Mines

HENRIETTA	0-6-0ST	IC	MW	[? 21	1861]		
		rebuilt	HL	by	1897	(a)	(1)
SIR THEODORE	0-4-0ST	OC	AE	1397	1899	New 4/99	(2)

(a)   almost certainly MW 21, a loco to which more than its fair share of incorrect historical data has been attributed:

From details recorded in the Minute Book of the United Minera Mining Co Ltd, and a surviving photograph, we know that a HENRIETTA was at Minera by 2/1899 "in poor condition", and that it carried a HL (not a MW) plate at that time.   MW 21 was supplied New to Charlesworths' Rothwell Haigh Colliery, Yorkshire, and "named" J & J CHARLESWORTH. Apparently subsequently sold as "Green Engine 21" to the East & West Yorkshire Union Railways Co (possibly moving via Whitaker Bros, the contractors, then building on that railway).   The next owners (circa 1888) were Meakin & Dean, contractors of "Birkenhead", Cheshire [per the MW Engine Book]. In fact, Meakin & Dean were around that time working on parts of the Wirral Railway [J/IRR/Vol.5/236]; but they were also among the promoters of the Broughton & Plas Power Coal Co Ltd, shareholders in other Clwyd companies, constructors of railways in North Wales - and close associates of Henry Robertson who had a daughter named Henrietta. After being 'rebuilt' by HL, the loco apparently passed to United Minera - probably in 1897 when this company started (though perhaps it came earlier, to the Minera Mining Co Ltd). Apart from work at Gatewen Colliery and PR/47 (which see), we do not yet know of any other job handled by Meakin & Dean in the 1890s. A photograph of this loco at Minera shows it with an oval [? HL Rebuild] rather than rectangular [MW 1860s era] works-plate.

(1)   A loco HENRIETTA (presumably this same loco) was still at Minera in 4/1899 (but had gone by 1903). It is very likely that AE took it in part exchange for AE 1397 (delivered 4/1899).

By 25/7/1900 it was receiving extensive repairs at AE Works (job No.1132) for new owner Herbert Weldon, contractor (of Birmingham).   AE recorded the loco as '11 inch Loco HENRIETTA by Hawthorn & Co, Newcastle'. Despatched by AE late in 9/1900 to Weldon's Congresbury-Blagdon (Wrington Vale Light) Railway (1899-1901) Contract; it received further repairs by AE at Congresbury during 10-11/1900 (job 1146) and during 1-9/1901 (job 1162),

with more spares supplied to Weldon at Congresbury in 23/12/1901. [No evidence whatsoever can be found to support claims made elsewhere that Meakin & Dean used this loco at Blagdon Reservoir; this Contract was actually handled by Pethick Bros in 1891-190 using - apparently - only horse haulage.]
Apparently then returned to HL for a second "rebuild" - from 5/1903 to 10/1904 Weldon wa advertising for sale "11 inch 6wc MW just rebuilt by HL" - in 1907 it arrived at the Hundred of Manhood & Selsey Tramway, where it was named SIDLESHAM and recorded as "rebuil HL 1907"; suggesting perhaps that it had remained unsold at HL since the "1903 rebuild" and was sent to Selsey with plates dated 1907. Photographs taken at Selsey show the visible outline of a previous nameplate which apparently coincides with the HENRIETTA plate in the Minera photograph; also both Minera and some Selsey photographs show a loco (which the evidence as related above strongly suggests to be the same loco) with an unusual flat topped steam dome not of MW normal design.

(2)   for sale 25/11/1914 and tdt: Gresford Colliery.

MINERA LIMEWORKS and QUARRY   M12
(Cd/GR:256520)

Early workings at the head of the Minera valley developed into two main ventures, which combined in 1899 to work as one unit. Prior to the 1850s operations were mostly small scale; archives refer to "Campbell & Co" and "Burton & Kyrke". There were 17 kilns here by 1852.

[Read: B/352]

LESTER'S WORKS (North side of valley)
    1857   -   7/1887   : **William Lester**
    7/1887 -   1899   : **Lester's Limeworks** (Evan Morris)
    1899   -   : combined with Minera Works [below]

MINERA WORKS (South side of valley; South & North from 1899)
    1852   -   7/1865   : **Minera Lime Co** [Robertson, Darby et al]
    7/1865 -   1954   : **Minera Lime Co Ltd**
    1954   -   12/1954 : closed
    12/1954 -   : reopened as stone quarry only
    12/1954 -   1959   : **M.F.Freeman** (on behalf of Lythgoe Bros Ltd)
    1959   -   c1968   : **Lythgoe Bros Ltd**
    c1968   -   : **Tarmac Roadstone Holdings Ltd**

The quarries and kilns on both sides of the valley had 2ft gauge internal rail systems from an early date which, with horse haulage and gravity inclines, remained in use until 1954. Locomotives were introduced on one route, quarry to kilns, on the North (Lester) side in 1938. After 1954 the quarries were worked by road vehicles only, the 2ft gauge tracks being abandoned and mostly removed.

The 4'8½" gauge reached the quarries 7/1847 when PR/6 from Brymbo was opened and, when the Lead Mines railway was constructed towards New Brighton, rail tracks in the area became complicated with the individual ownerships difficult to define. From c1968 all shunting was performed by BR locos or gravity; rail traffic ceased in 1971 and almost all of the rails were removed in 1972.

Locomotives: Gauge 4'8½" - Minera Works.

MINERA	0-4-0ST	OC	BP	810	1868	New	Scr/1910
OLWEN	0-4-0ST	OC	BP	5408	1910	New	Scr 12/1964
SWANSEA	0-4-0ST	OC	HE	648	1897	(a)	(1)
-	4wDM	48hp	RH	224338	1944	(b)	Scr 2/1971

Because it worked over PR/6 tracks at Minera, OLWEN was registered by BR-WR No.278/1949.

Locomotives: Gauge 2'0"

-	4wPM	10hp	L	10020	1938	New 2/38	(2)
No.1	4wDM	20hp	RH	202979	1940	New 11/40	(3)
-	4wDM	20hp	RH	235704	1945	New 10/45	(4)

(a) tdx: Cudworth & Johnson, dealer, Wrexham, loan, 1942
(b) tdx: F.Watkins (Engineering) Ltd, dealers, Coleford, Glos, 4/1963
    wfw: H.J.Heinz Co Ltd, Standish, Lancashire

(1) tdt: Cudworth & Johnson, dealer, Wrexham, off loan, c1942
(2) disused by 4/1953; stored in smithy to 1963 at least; later s/s.
(3) tdt: Dinorwic Slate Quarries 22/6/1956
(4) tdt: Dinorwic Slate Quarries 20/6/1956

MOELFERNA & DEE SIDE SLATE QUARRIES & TRAMROAD,   M14
GLYNDYFRDWY
(Cm/GR:below)

DEE SIDE QUARRY:
-     1875   : Dee Side Slate & Slab Quarry Co Ltd
                    (vol.liq.1/1875)

MOELFERNA QUARRY:
-     1876   : ?

COMBINED BUSINESS:
    1876 - c9/1948   : **Moelferna & Dee Side Slate & Slab Quarries Co Ltd** (reg.1876)
            1923   : Dee Side Quarry abandoned
   c9/1948 -   1960   : **Moelferna Quarries Ltd**
           9/7/1960   : Moelferna Quarry closed.
        2/11/1960 : Dispersal Sale 2/11/1960

Early working developed at Dee Side Quarry (GR:137405), and a wooden-railed tramroad was built (c1852 ?) 1¼ miles long to connect this quarry to the water-powered Mill (GR:148416) near Glyndyfrdwy. This tramroad, of 2'7" nominal gauge, together with "nine large and eight small trucks" was included in the sale of Dee Side Quarry 24/9/1875 [J/CDH/18.9.1875]. A report of 29/2/1876 includes: "I am told [the tramroad] was laid out and designed to be worked by one of Thompson's patent engines, but the gradients are so very bad - 1 in 13 and in some places 1 in 6 or 8 - it would be very expensive to work it even by engine power......always supposing an engine could be got to work it safely". As far as we know the original tramroad and the later extensions were always worked by a combination of horses and gravity.

Under the combined ownership from 1876, the Moelferna Quarry (GR:125398), hitherto a small almost exploratory working, was considerably enlarged and, (apparently in the 1890s the tramroad was extended, using conventional track, from Dee Side Quarry to Moelferna and from Dee Side Mill down to the GWR (PR/18) - this latter section being mostly a self acting incline. The lower terminus of the tramroad was then at a loading platform in the GWR goods yard.

The tramroad remained in use until 1947. The track was advertised [J/CJ/15.12.1948] for sale in 12/1948, and was subsequently lifted as scrap; but the timber-built sections remained virtually intact into the 1970s, and some sections can be seen today [1986]. A short length of 2'7" track, with a few wagons, remained in use at the GWR yard until 1955, and a transporter incline at Moelferna Quarry was retained until 1960 to connect the different working levels. The tramroad was replaced by road vehicles, using a rough mountain road.

At Dee Side Quarry (a relatively small opencast) there were short 2ft gauge lines for conveying waste and overburden to tips. Moelferna "Quarry" was a Mine; adits on different levels giving access to (ultimately) 25 chambers. Track in the Mine and around the Moelferna Mill was 2ft gauge, mostly hand-worked though one locomotive was used. The Quarry was dismantled, tracks removed and adits blocked, in 1961.

[Read: J/IRR/Vol.7/303]

Locomotives: Gauge 2'0" - Moelferna Quarry

                        4wDM 10hp   RH   171905   1935   New 4/35   (1)

(1)   auctioned 2/11/1960. No further trace.

MOEL TRYFAN SLATE QUARRY, MOEL TRYFAN   M16
                                                                               (Gc/GR:514557)

[For the avoidance of confusion, note that the Moel Tryfan Crown Slate Co (Ltd) operated Hafodywern Quarry, Betws Garmon; and not Moel Tryfan Quarry.]

	c1800	:	opened
c1800	- 1853	:	quarry site included in Crown "Braichrhydd" lease, which was held by the lessees of Cilgwyn Quarry, who did not do much work at Moel Tryfan
5/1853	- 12/1854	:	John Hayward et al
12/1854	-	:	Moel Tryfan Slate Co (Ellis Williams et al)
	- 10/1861	:	Sir Charles Kennaway
10/1861	- 10/1876	:	Charles Pearson
10/1876	-	:	Griffith Williams & Hugh Pugh, who formed:-
	- c1899	:	Moel Tryfan Slate & Slab Quarry Co Ltd
c1899	-	:	Moel Tryfan Slate Quarry Co (Roberts & Davies)
3/1914	- 10/1917	:	Moel Tryfan Quarry Co (wound up 18/2/1918)
7/1918	- 10/1918	:	Moel Tryfan Slate & Slab Co Ltd; which joined:-

10/1918	-	1928	: Amalgamated Slate Association Ltd
			(reg.1918 £50K vol.liq.3/1/1931)
1928	-	1932	: closed
1932	-		: Carnarvonshire Crown Slate Quarries Co Ltd
1959	-	c1984	: limited operations by various lessees
		c1984	: closed: most buildings then demolished.

In the early years, slabs from the quarry were lowered down an incline then taken by steeply-graded tramroad [see J/NG/No.128/25] to a water-powered Mill at Glandwr (GR:503558). This Mill and tramroad were closed and dismantled when a new Mill was constructed at the quarry. The new Mill was connected to the quarry by a small-bore tunnel through which the special "low-height" design Hunslet steam locomotives (and later the RH diesel) worked. From the Mill a new incline descended directly to within a few yards of the head of the Bryngwyn Incline (PR/44, closed 6/1937). After the 1918 amalgamation of the Crown Land quarries, one - maybe both - of the HE locos was used from time to time on the other lines radiating from Bryngwyn Drumhead - see entry BRAICH/OLD BRAICH SLATE QUARRY for further comment. After the 1934 closure of ALEXANDRA QUARRY, the Moel Tryfan operations were extended directly into that quarry. Other than for a few yards of track at the Mill, rail operations at Moel Tryfan ceased 9/1966 in favour of road vehicles; all tracks were later removed.

[Read: B/182; B/174; J/NG/No.128/25]

Locomotives: Gauge 1'11"

	0-4-0VBTG	SVC	DeW		c1870	(a)	(1)
TRYFAN	0-4-0ST	OC	HE	781	1902	New 2/02	(2)
CADFAN	0-4-0ST	OC	HE	848	1904	New 5/04	(2)
-	4wDM	20hp	RH	175414	1936	(b)	(3)

(a) reputed to have been a single-cylinder loco and used on the tramroad to Glandwr; however, the existence of this loco has not been positively confirmed. [See J/NG/No.128/25].

(b) tdx: Cilgwyn Slate Quarry, after 3/1938 by 11/1940

(1) Disposal not known - if indeed it was here. However, an inventory [CRO/XD/35/436] of Moel Tryfan Quarry 11/9/1916 includes "old engine frame and cylinder £5" in "loco house No.2" (perhaps "cylinder" -singular- is truly significant).

(2) insured and in use 1/1940; scrapped after 2/1941.

(3) tdt: Welsh Highland Railway (PR/44), 5/1974.

MOELYGEST GRANITE QUARRY, PORTHMADOG M18
(Gc/GR:554390)

	mid 1870s	:	opened
by 1876	- c1896	:	**Moel y Gest Sett Quarry Co**
	by 1896	:	closed
1899	- 6/1900	:	**Portmadoc Granite Quarries Ltd**
			(reg.21/4/1899; liq.16/8/1901)
6/1900	- 1903	:	**Carnarvonshire Granite Quarries Ltd**
			(reg.16/6/1900; sale 8/1903; liq. 21/12/1904)
c6/1903	- 7/1904	:	closed
7/1904	- 1907	:	**Moel y Gest Granite Co** [L.Sommerfeld]
by 8/1907	- c1919	:	closed
c1920	-	:	**Carnarvon Granite Co** [54 High Street, Runcorn]
	by 1950	:	closed and dismantled

Quarry situated on northern slope of Moel-y-Gest, with rope-worked incline to foot of mountain (GR:556392) from where the line was extended c1880 to Cam.Rys. (PR/3) station; further extended c1903 to Porthmadog Harbour via part of route of Gorsedda Railway (PR/4) plus running powers over parts of Croesor Tramway (PR/25) and of the Ffestiniog Railway (PR/3). Line closed in 1907; track later removed. The Quarry incline (only) was re-laid in 1919 (new winding drum supplied by Britannia Foundry, Porthmadog), and a 4'8½" gauge siding laid direct to foot of incline from the GWR (PR/32) goods yard.
[There may have been a 4'8½" gauge siding prior to 1906, as "mixed gauge track" over part of the route is mentioned in B/101/98.]

[Read : J/IRR/No.126/310]

Locomotive: Gauge 2ft

0-4-0VBT   VC   FE   1883   (a)   (1)

(a)   tdx: Oakeley Slate Quarry, Blaenau Ffestiniog, 1904

(1)   tdt: Oakeley Slate Quarry, Blaenau Ffestiniog, 1906 or 1907 [probably 1906 and by 10/1906]

MOLD GAS WORKS M20
(Cf/GR:243634)

1847	- 4/1949	:	**Mold Gas & Water Company** (Act: 1847)
5/1949	-	:	**Wales Gas Board**

Gasworks served by private siding (which existed by 1882) branching off the sidings entering Bromfield Colliery. Siding noted in use 9/1952, when a road tractor was pulling the wagons, but subsequently closed. Track removed c1960.

Locomotives: Gauge 4'8½"

[? LLIEDI	tank loco				(a)	s/s
DEE	0-4-0ST OC AB	1179	1910			
	rebuilt KS		1924	(b)		(1)

Note: AB 1179 built for stock in 1909. Completed 21/10/1909. Sold 18/4/1910 as a New loco with plate dated 1910.

a) reputed to have been here prior to AB 1179, but neither identified nor confirmed. Name LLIEDI from oral source - ? mis-spelled.
b) wfw: I.C.I.Ltd, Billingham Works, Teesside, until 3/1930 at least.

1) withdrawn from use by 1948; scrapped 5/1950.

MOSTYN COLLIERIES, IRONWORKS and DOCKS M22
(Cf/GR:156811 etc)

The history of industrial activity at Mostyn is very much a subject for specialist study, somewhat beyond the scope of this Handbook. It is on record that Sir Roger Mostyn had a coal shaft-mine in production in 1640, when an explosion occurred, and later there were some twenty mines within a small area. These were operated by various lessees, and changed hands fairly frequently. By 1800 the principal collieries were known as BYCHTON, HANMER, BRIDGE, EYTON, SOUTH MOSTYN (LLETTY), and MOSTYN. When the Chester & Holyhead Railway (PR/7) was built in 1845, arrangements were made to "cross on the level the existing railways at Mostyn and Lletty" which connected "Eytons' collieries and ironworks to wharves on the River Dee". ["Lletty" - Lletty Gonest - The Honest Man (public) house GR:161803).] When Hanmer Colliery was auctioned 25/1/1871 its assets included a 'tramway from the colliery to the shipping place" in the "Llanerch y Mor Gutter" [J/CDH/14+21.1.1871/1]. The first ironworks apparently dated from c1800, but the latter-day ironworks was founded in 1871. Mostyn Colliery was flooded-out 22/7/1884; this then flooded Eyton Pit, and seems to have marked the end of mining other than for Hanmer Colliery which continued for a few years as Hanmer Coal Co. A Mostyn Collieries Recovery Syndicate Ltd (reg.31/5/1906; liq.10/6/1910) apparently failed to reopen any of the mines.

Of the principal collieries, Bridge Pit was at GR:162804; Eyton Pit was GR:159806; Mostyn Pit GR:155811. The title "Mostyn Colliery" was adopted c1900 by the Bychton Hall Colliery - [and "West Mostyn Colliery" was an early title for Point of Ayr Colliery - which see]. Hanmer (Pwll Hanmer) Colliery was later buried by the Ironworks slag bank, and in due course became the site of Mostyn Magnetite Works (which see).

[Read: J/FHS/1969/86]

	by 1843	: Eyton & Co "Mostyn Collieries" "Mostyn Ironworks"
1850 -	1859	: James Thomas Cookney "Mostyn Colliery"
	in 1851	: J.Stanley "Standard Mine, Mostyn"
1854 -	1863	: Eyton et al "South Mostyn Colliery"
1860 -	1861	: Exors of J.T.Cookney "Mostyn Colliery"
1862		: Eyton & Elliot "Mostyn Coal Co"
c1871 -	c1874	: Lancaster, Taylor et al "Mostyn Ironworks"
by 1875 -	1879	: Mostyn Coal & Iron Co Ltd (vol.liq.1879)
-	4/1887	: Mostyn Coal & Iron Co (Stoney & Lancaster)
4/1887 -	1951	: Darwen & Mostyn Iron Co Ltd (reg.30/4/1887 £240K)
1951 -	3/1959	: British Steel Corporation
4/1959 -	7/1963	: Barrow Haematite Steel Co Ltd
1/1963 -	7/1963	: ironworks idle

7/1963	-	3/1964	: Barrow Haematite Steel Co Ltd as subsidiary of:- General & Engineering Industries Ltd
		9/1964	: for sale
1965			: Thos.W.Ward Ltd - Ironworks demolished but Dock retained, trading as:- : Mostyn Docks & Trading Co
	-	c1983	: Mostyn Docks & Trading Ltd
c1983	-		: Mostyn Docks Ltd

Locomotives: Gauge 4'8½"

The works, including "locomotives", was advertised for sale 5/1879 by private treaty - "app" to the solicitors of H.E.Taylor at the works". H.E.Taylor, also the proprietor of Sandycro Foundry, had been offering a FJ loco (of apparently the same dimensions as FJ 114) for sa at Sandycroft since 7/1877. The assets of "Mostyn Coal & Iron Co in voluntary liquidation including Mostyn Pits, Eyton Pits, Ironworks, 116 railway wagons and 2 tank locomotiv engines" - were auctioned 7/8/1879.

In 1906, Lingford, Gardiner & Co Ltd, locomotive engineers of Bishop Auckland, supplied "new" 0-4-0ST OC 12x18 3'3" wheels loco to North Bitchburn Coal Co Ltd, Randolp Colliery, Co.Durham. This "new" loco was probably a rebuild of an older loco and, as it wa named MOSTYN, it may possibly have originated at Mostyn Ironworks.

In the 1960s, Thos.W.Ward Ltd used part of the Mostyn premises for the scrapping c withdrawn British Railways steam locos.

-		0-4-0ST	OC	FJ	114	1873	New 3/73	(1)
No.1	FORWARD	0-4-0ST	OC	[?Bs	216	1874]		(2)
No.2		0-4-0ST	OC	MW	346	1871	(a)	s/s by 5/42
	[?	0-4-0ST	OC	HC	304	1888	(b)	(3)]
No.3		0-4-0ST	OC	MW	444	1873	(c)	s/s by 5/42
4	(AVONSIDE)	0-4-0ST	OC	AE	1408	1899	(d)	(4)
5		0-4-0ST	OC	HC	1204	1917	New 5/17	(5)
6		0-4-0ST	OC	HC	1360	1919	New 7/19	(6)
2	"MEDLOCK"	0-6-0ST	IC	HC	314	1888		
			rebuilt	HC		1926	(e)	(7)
3		0-4-0ST	OC	HE	622	1895	(f)	(8)
(7)	DIAMOND	0-4-0ST	OC	HE	829	1903	(g)	(9)
(8)	WINSTON CHURCHILL	0-4-0ST	OC	HC	1743	1946	New 5/46	(9)
-		4wTG	VB	S	9575	1954	(h)	(10)
-		0-6-0DE	260hp	YE	2604	1955	(j)	(11)
1		0-4-0DE	200hp	YE	2627	1957	New 2/57	
2		0-4-0DE	220hp	YE	2819	1960	New 8/60	

Also within the Ironworks a 4'8½" gauge electrified line (overhead wire pick-up) on which operated two large self-propelled wagons built (date not known) by Wilfrid Marley, Hawkeshead Works, Workington, Cumberland. These vehicles were scrapped in 1966 during demolition of the Ironworks by Thos.W.Ward Ltd.

(a) here by 1887.
     wfw: S.C.Ridley, contractor, LNWR Kings Langley-Bletchley Widening (c1871-1876) Contract - where two locos were for sale 10/1874.

b) there is yet no definite confirmation if or when this loco was at Mostyn. One of a pair of locos HC 304 and HC 305 supplied New to T.A.Walker, contractor, Manchester Ship Canal Contract. The HC records are confused, but suggest that spares were supplied to Mostyn at unknown date. The two locos were originally named HULME (304) and CHEADLE (305), but one HC archive notes an exchange of names and has 304 named CHEADLE located at the Cliffe Hill Granite Quarries, Leics (in/by 10/1935); and 305 as HULME one-time at the Horrocksford Lime Co Ltd, Clitheroe. However, T.Mitchell & Sons Ltd, dealers, Bolton, Lancs, bought a loco from Horrocksford Lime on 1/3/1912; Mitchells (from their on-site visual inspection) recorded this loco as HULME HC 304/1888. It thus appears certain that the HC records are incorrect. [Mitchell apparently resold this loco in 1914 but details of the purchaser are not in their surviving books.]
c) here by 1914; [? arrived c1904]
   wfw(tdx?): Thos.Bolton & Sons Ltd, Widnes
d) New 12/1899; per Ratcliffe & Sons, dealers, Hawarden [see Section 1]
e) wfw(tdx?): Darwen Ironworks, Lancashire - arrived c1926 [either from Darwen or perhaps from HC after rebuild]
f) arrived by 26/5/1944, per or via G.Cohen Sons & Co Ltd, dealers.
   wfw: Lofthouse Colliery, Yorkshire WR.
g) tdx: G.Cohen Sons & Co Ltd, dealers, Stanningley, Leeds, 1946
   wfw: Pope & Pearson Ltd, West Riding Colliery, Yorks, until 1945
h) arrived 1955, by 19/7/1955 - on demonstration only.
j) tdx: Brymbo Steelworks, 5/11/1955 - on demonstration only.

1) No further trace after 1870s sale references detailed above.
   Per one source - still here in 1914; but this may be an error arising from a presumption that FJ 114 was Mostyn 'No.1', whereas it is now known that FORWARD was 'No.1' by 1916 definite, and probably earlier.
2) s/s after 3/1916 by 5/1942. Darwen & Mostyn Iron Co Ltd ordered spare parts for "12 inch loco No.1 FORWARD works number 216" from AB in 3/1916. The Mostyn loco is very unlikely to have been AB 216 (the history of which is almost certainly established) hence it is possible that FORWARD was built Barclays & Co number 216 - a loco for which no positive details seem to be known.
3) if ever here, then no further trace.
   As related in footnote (b) above, HULME HC 304 has not been found since sale by Mitchell in 1914 - though if at Mostyn very much earlier, it could have been at Horrocksford after Mostyn.
   Per HC records, HC 304 CHEADLE was with Cliffe Hill Granite Co Ltd, Leics, by 10/1935 - though Cliffe Hill have denied ever owning it.
4) disused by 1949.
   tdt: Mostyn Wagon Works (Crump) for scrap, 1957; Scr c4/1957
5) scrapped on site by C.C.Crump & Co, c1960 after 7/1960
6) scrapped on site by C.C.Crump & Co, 7/1960
7) scrapped on site by C.C.Crump & Co, c1960 after 10/1959
8) disused by 1955.
   tdt: Mostyn Wagon Works (Crump) for scrap, 1957; Scr c4/1957
9) scrapped on site by Thos.W.Ward Ltd, 2/1966
10) tdt: Ribblesdale Cement Co Ltd, Houghton in Ribblesdale, 8/8/1955
11) tdt: Bowaters Paper Mill, Ellesmere Port, Cheshire (on demonstration), 14/11/1955
    wlw: Brymbo Steelworks (permanent stock), ESMOND.

MOSTYN MAGNETITE later TARMACADAM WORKS M24
(Cf/GR:160806)

by 5/1897	-		: G.H.Skelsey
	-	1906	: Magnetite Sewage & Water Purification Co Ltd
by 1914	-		: Mostyn Magnetite Co
by 1921	-	c1938	: Tarmacadam Roads Ltd
by 1965			: Slag Reduction Co Ltd

Works existed by 1865 and was served by sidings within the Mostyn Ironworks & Collieries complex. By 1897 a new connection 626 yards long existed direct to LNWR (PR/7) at Eyton Sidings (GR:165802). Converted to a Tarmacadam Plant by 1921 with a 2ft gauge rail system used from c1920 to c1938. Derelict factory demolished early 1960s.

Locomotives: Gauge 2'0"

		0-4-0WT OC HC	1034 1913	(a)	(1)
		Petrol loco		(b)	(2)
		Petrol/Diesel loco		(b)	s/s

(a) here by 1928.
    wfw: W.Jones [? Wm.Jones, dealer], London, in 1923
    wfw: Ilford Gas Co, Ilford, in 1919
    wfw: Holloway Brothers, contractors [? at Rosyth] in 1917
    wfw: W.Alban Richards & Co, contractors [? at Ministry of Munitions Stratton Contract] in 1917
    wfw: Garden Suburb Builders Ltd, Hampstead, London, MIDGE.
(b) replaced the steam loco, but further details not yet known.
    Local resident recalled two internal combustion locos in use here prior to WW2.

(1) here until 1934 at least; gone by 1942 (by which time no track remained here) - no further trace.
(2) "went with the plant" [whatever that may mean] - per "old man".

MOSTYN WAGON REPAIR WORKS M26
(Cf/GR:162804)

by 1957 - c1968 : **C.C.Crump & Co**
                : track removed, site redeveloped.

Modern works located on the site of former Mostyn Collieries "Bridge Pit". The sidings were probably shunted by Ironworks locos prior to arrival of NELLIE.

Locomotive: Gauge 4'8½"

| NELLIE | 4wDM 50hp | FH | 2346 | 1940 | (a) | (1) |

(a) here by 19/10/1964.
    wfw(tdx ?): Imperial Chemical Industries Ltd, Runcorn Engineering Works, Cheshire

(1) tdt: Connah's Quay Wagon Works, after 12/2/1966 by 27/9/1967 [and possibly on 14/8/1967].

NANTLLE VALE DRAINAGE SCHEMES N2
(Gc)

Slate quarries, particularly Dorothea and Talysarn, in the lower-lying areas of the Nantlle Valley, were continually damaged by flooding from the River Llyfni which meandered through the area. The river then flowed via two lakes (the Upper and Lower Llyn Nantlle) which, to some extent, regulated the flow of water in the river but, in times of heavy rain, had only limited effect. Coincidentally, the quarries were troubled by a lack of sites for the dumping of waste rock. A "grand scheme" was prepared which included a drainage pipe from the valley to the sea, and a railway to carry waste to dump in the sea: this, presented to Parliament 1/2/1880 as the NANTLLE VALE DRAINAGE & TRAMWAY BILL, did not receive Assent. On 30/12/1884 the river again flooded Dorothea Quarry, with fatal results; a Committee of local interests was then formed to promote a lesser scheme, to construct a new canalised river some 2 miles long, the depth to be 8 feet below current river level. A shallow side-cut would partially drain the lakes, hopefully to increase their floodwater capacity. This work was undertaken 1893-1895 as detailed below; the contract included three new road bridges over the river.

Unfortunately the work was not entirely successful, possibly (as later surveys showed) because the new river had not been cut as deeply as planned. The Dorothea Quarry Company undertook additional works between 1896 and 1901 which resulted in the complete draining of the lower lake, and the extension of the new river direct to the upper lake, with the intent of draining that lake too. With the loss of reservoir capacity, the new river was unable to cope with heavy rainfall, and flooding remained a considerable problem throughout the life of the quarries.

Read: B/175/67,/68,/229 (contains errors); J/NWC/9.9.1893 article]

NEW RIVER CONTRACT 1893-1895 - 2 mile cut plus 3 bridges; c£10K.

    Wm.Winnard & Chas.Braddock, contractors [of Wigan]
    L.H.Moorson MICE [of Manchester] - Engineer.   First Sod: 2/9/1893

Locomotive: Gauge 4'8½"

                0-4-0ST   OC   MW   (1)

(1)   for sale here 29/5/1895 on behalf of Wm.Winnard. No further trace.

NERQUIS RAILWAY & COLLIERIES, NERCWYS, near MOLD N4
(Cf/GR:below)

1856	-	1868	: **Nerquis Colliery Co**
1868	-	1876+	: **Nerquis Coal & Cannel Co**
		in 1912	: [Cannel Colliery] siding in use by "**Griffiths**"
by 1923	-	8/1930	: [Cannel Colliery] **Nerquis Colliery Co Ltd**

The Nerquis Colliery Co built [? c1850] the private 4'8½" gauge "Nerquis Railway" from Nercwys to Coed Talon. From Nerquis [Main] Colliery (GR:237602) the railway descended a rope-worked incline to the river valley (GR:243600), where there was a large pumping station and a 30ft x 20ft single-road 4'8½" gauge loco shed. The line then ran southerly arc easterly to head for Coed Talon. Partway around this arc, a short branch ran westerly Nerquis Cannel Colliery (GR:242696 - a small drift mine).

The Nerquis Railway was taken over by the LNWR 13/5/1868, much of the route being incorporated into PR/39 (the Mold-Brymbo line). When PR/39 was built, it followed a new route around the "Nerquis arc", leaving the original Nerquis Railway route (now the LNWR Nerquis Colliery Branch) on its own parallel arc to serve the collieries. The two lines joined Nerquis Colliery Junction (GR:247598).

The tracks between the Cannel Colliery and the foot of Nerquis Incline were removed by the LNWR 2/1911; the connection to PR/39 was removed 9/1913, but reinstated in 1923 to serve a siding for the revived Cannel Colliery.

Locomotives: Gauge 4'8½"

No information has been discovered regarding Nerquis Railway locos, though the existence of the loco shed at Nerquis Incline Foot, prior to the LNWR take-over, is significant. And it possible that the colliery retained a loco at Incline Foot until closure [? c1911], though as the LNWR had purchased the railway, perhaps all shunting duties became its responsibility.

NEW ROAD (PANT FARM etc) GRAVEL PITS, LLAY N6
(Cd/GR:333547)

: United Gravel Co Ltd

Extensive sand and gravel pits have been worked on the west side of the B5425 "New Road" south of Llay, by United Gravel and the associated companies Sir Robert McAlpine & Son (Midlands) Ltd, and (later) Sir Alfred McAlpine & Son Ltd. Pant Farm, and perhaps other, pits were worked by narrow-gauge railways between the digging area and lorry-loading points. Later diggings used road transport only.

Locomotives: Gauge 2'0"

R 10	4wDM	32hp	MR	7710	1939	New 6/39	(1)
R 11	4wDM	32hp	MR	7711	1939	New 6/39	(2)
R 13	4wDM	20hp	MR	7479	1940	New 4/40	(3)
	4wDM	32hp	MR	7932	1941	New 10/41	(4)
	4wDM	32hp	MR	7933	1941	New 10/41	(4)

(1) wlw: Derbyshire Stone Quarries Ltd, Hopton, Derbyshire
(2) wlw: Sir Alfred McAlpine & Son Ltd, Ellesmere Port plant depot, Cheshire, by 5/1954; to 1/1955 at least
     wlw: Derbyshire Stone Quarries Ltd, Hopton, Derbyshire
(3) wlw: Sir Alfred McAlpine & Son Ltd, Ellesmere Port plant depot, Cheshire, by 5/1954; later s/s.
(4) wlw: G.W.Bungey, dealer.
     wlw: Leighton Buzzard Light Railway, Beds, by 22/10/1956

OAKELEY SLATE QUARRIES, BLAENAU FFESTINIOG   O2
(Gm/GR: below)

The latter-day workings consisted of an amalgamation of three former properties:

LOWER (PALMERSTON) QUARRY   (GR:692472)
```
 1819   -  3/1825  : Samuel Holland (formal lease from 25/3/1821)
3/1825  -  6/1838  : Welsh Slate, Copper & Lead Mining Co
                     [Palmerston, Homfray et al; which became:-]
6/1838  - 10/1884  : Welsh Slate Co
 1883   -   1888   :  closed due to collapse of mountain into workings
 1888   -          : Oakeley Slate Quarries Co Ltd (reg.13/7/1882)
```

UPPER (CESAIL/HOLLANDS) QUARRY   (GR:691468)
```
1/1826  -   1877   : Samuel Holland [Senior; Junior]
 1877   -  7/1882  : Oakeley Slate Co [W.E.Oakeley]
7/1882  -          : Oakeley Slate Quarries Co Ltd
```

MIDDLE (RHIWBRYFDIR/MATTHEWS) QUARRY - GLODDFA GANOL (GR:693469)
```
 1833   -   1840   : N.Matthews & G.Huddart
 1840   - 12/1877  : Rhiwbryfdir Slate Co
12/1877 -  7/1882  : Oakeley Slate Co [W.E.Oakeley]
7/1882  -          : Oakeley Slate Quarries Co Ltd
```

COMBINED QUARRIES   (GR:692472 - main pit, to underground)
```
        - 10/1970  : Oakeley Slate Quarries Co Ltd
                      (reg.13/7/1882; re-reg. same title 17/5/1933)
           5/1969  :  deep mine closed
10/1970 -   1971   :  closed; partially dismantled
  1971  -          : Ffestiniog Slate Quarry Co Ltd [no railway used]
```

GLODDFA GANOL TOURIST CENTRE   (GR:693469)
```
  1974  -          : Ffestiniog Mountain Tourist Centre Ltd
```

Since 1974 the Tourist Centre and Slate Production activities have intermingled. By arrangement, Narrow Gauge Enterprises [Mr Rich. Morris et al] established a collection of locomotives and rolling stock on display within the Tourist Area.

Originally each quarry had its own incline connection down to the Ffestiniog Railway (PR/3); that from the Lower Quarry was in use by 10/1838, and from Upper Quarry in 1839. Another main outlet was by way of a level "horse tunnel" from the floor (later Floor DE) of the Lower Quarry to Glanydon. After the closure of the inconvenient exchange sidings (removed by LMSR 6/1941) close by the tunnel mouth, and the closure of Ffestiniog Railway (PR/3) in 1946, the Glanydon route became the only rail outlet, with a short incline down to a direct connection to the LMSR goods yard at Blaenau.

[Read: B/182; B/168; B/169; B/317; B/319; B/320; B/378; J/IRR/No.126/310]

Locomotives: Gauge 2ft - Slate Quarries

Per J/CDH/22.2.1873 there was then, at the Welsh Slate Co quarry, a "small locomotive running along their lines". No other reference to this loco has been found but, coincidentally an undated photograph exists of a rather peculiar machine, named MOLE, which from the surroundings visible is almost certainly standing on the wharf occupied by the Welsh Slate Co at Porthmadog. The builders of MOLE are unknown, but components of the loco are lettered "J.H.Wilson & Co Ltd" - a firm from Sandhills, Liverpool, who built a variety of ship auxiliaries, quarrying equipment such as steam diggers for the ironstone industry, and a winches; and a few of the latter - perhaps also coincidentally - survived at Oakeley Quarries until at least 1970. The popular hypothesis is that MOLE arrived at Porthmadog by sea, was photographed on the quay then transferred to the quarry, was noticed there in 1873 as per reference above; and was most probably used through the "horse tunnel" - which certainly existed by 1854 - to Glanydon Mill. MOLE is therefore included in our list on the unproved presumption that it and the 1873 loco are one and the same. Subsequent locos listed, as operated by the Combined Quarries, are much better documented in surviving records.

	Name	Type		Builder	Works No	Date	Notes	Ref
	MOLE	0-4-0TG	OC	[? Wilson]		c1872	(a)	(1)
	MARY OAKELEY	0-4-0VBT	VC	FE		1883	New	(2)
	WILLIAM	0-4-0T	OC	DA	292	1885	New	(3)
	EDWARD	0-4-0T	OC	DA		1886	New	(3)
	MARY CAROLINE	0-4-0T	OC	DA	346	1888	New	(3)
	ALGERNON	0-4-0T	OC	DA		1890	New	(3)
	CHARLES	0-4-0T	OC	DA		1890	New	(3)
	SNOWDON	0-4-0ST	OC	WB	1569	1899	New 12/99	(4)
	HILDA	4wTG					(b)	(5)
[	ROSA ?]	0-4-0PM	20hp	Bg	[? 777]	1919	(c)	Wdn/37,Scr
	EILEEN	0-4-0ST	OC	WB	2045	1918	(d)	(6)
	CLIFFORD	0-4-0WT	OC	HC	1142	1915	(e)	(7)
	DIANA	0-4-0T	OC	KS	1158	1917	(f)	(8)
	-	0-4-0PM	10hp	Bg	[? 708]	1917	(g)	(9)
	CLIFFORD	0-4-0PM	20hp	Bg	774	1919	(h)	(10)
	ALGERNON	0-4-0WT	OC	OK	1028	1903	(i)	(11)
	-	4wPM	28hp	Dtz			(j)	(12)
	KIDBROOKE	0-4-0ST	OC	WB	2043	1917	(k)	(13)
	-	4wPM	10hp	RP	51901	1917	(m)	(14)
	-	4wDM	32hp	RH	174139	1935	New 2/35	(15)
	-	4wDM	32hp	RH	175986	1935	New 9/35	(16)
	-	4wDM	21hp	RH	175405	1935	New 11/35	(17)
	-	4wDM	12hp	RH	177638	1936	New 7/36	(18)
	-	4wDM	20hp	RH	182137	1936	New 11/36	(19)
	-	4wDM	32hp	RH	177598	1935	(n)	(20)
	-	4wDM	21hp	RH	174540	1935	(o)	(16)
	-	4wDM	31hp	RH	432652	1959	(p)	(21)
	-	4wDM	13hp	RH	264252	1952	(q)	(22)

(a) a loco was here by 2/1873 and is presumed to be MOLE but see notes at head of list. Incidentally, a narrow-gauge loco, named MOLE (but otherwise unidentified), reputedly worked on the Blea Moor Tunnel (1872-1876?) Contract, Settle & Carlisle Railway.
(b) tdx: Arthur Koppel, London, c6/1905; Hydroleum loco, on trial.
(c) purchased at Pennal (between Machynlleth and Aberdovey) for £385 in 8/1920. Loco almost certainly one of Bg 774-779 series built for Board of Trade, Timber Supply Department. Of these, Bg 777, sent New 22/2/1919 to Kerry, Montgomeryshire [and possibly later moved to forestry work at Pennal] seems the most likely candidate.
(d) purchased "at Newport" in 1923. WB 2045 was originally New 3/1918 to "Ministry of Munitions Air Board", and spares supplied 5/1918 and 9/1918 to Air Ministry, National Shipyards HQ, Pill, Chepstow, Mon. An auction 1-3/11/1921 at Ministry of Munitions, CSD Beachley, Chepstow, included a 2ft 4wc WB loco and, in 11/1921, A.R.Adams, dealer, Newport had various locos for sale, apparently ex CSD Beachley, including a 2ft 6x10 0-4-0 [? perhaps WB 2045].
(e) purchased "at Nottingham" in 1924; note, it carried Hudson, not HC, plates. Trent Concrete Ltd, Netherfield, Notts, had a "small Hudson 2ft gauge loco" for sale 8/1923. R.S.Davies, dealer, Mold, unsuccessfully offered Hudson 1142 to Flintshire County Council in 1921 - its location at that time is unknown.
(f) tdx: E.Longhurst & Sons Ltd, Kerry Sawmills, Mont., 12/1925
(g) tdx: Thos.W.Ward Ltd, dealer, Sheffield, £120, 11/1926
wfw: War Department, Calais, France [WDLR 253, if Bg 708]
(h) tdx: Baguley, Burton on Trent, 1/1927; per J.C.Oliver & Co, dealer, Leeds, £365.
[? wfw: Hendre-ddu Forestry Railway, Aberangell - which see]
(i) purchased from A.R.Adams & Co, dealers, Newport, Mon, 4/8/1927.
No previous history known since delivery New to the OK Agency in London 2/1903.
(j) purchased second-hand in "London, early in 1929".
(k) tdx: Geo.Wimpey & Co Ltd, contractors, Hammersmith Depot, London, between 10/1928 and 5/1929
[Originally ordered by Air Board, Kidbrooke. Frequently reported as having worked there, this is unlikely to be true. Loco was New ex WB 17/12/1917, and in 1/1918 & 7/1918 spares supplied to Marske-on-Sea Aerodrome Contract (J.Gerrard & Son, contractors). Loco sold as Government Surplus at Lemington-on-Tyne 5/1920, and subsequently used by Gerrards (again), J.H.Bentham & Co (in Durham) and J.H.Waddell in North Yorkshire and Devon before passing to Geo. Wimpey Aller Vale (1925) Contract, near Newton Abbott.]
(m) despatched to Oakeley 29/11/1933 by Henry H.Gardam & Co Ltd, Staines, Middlesex (after overhaul); sale and overhaul having been arranged by Capt. R.G.Davison, dealer, Ellesmere Port, Cheshire.
Loco originally built as 1'6" gauge for Royal Gunpowder Factory, Enfield Lock, Middlesex, and was probably one of four similar locos sold from Enfield Lock to E.T.Pugsley, dealer, Abbey Wood - per or via "Giddy of Golders Green" in 1924-1925.
(n) tdx: RH, Lincoln, 11/1937
wfw: RH at Royal Agricultural Show, Cairo, Egypt, 2-3/1936
(o) here by 3/1945
wfw(tdx?): General Plant Reconstruction Ltd, contractors, Cardiff, until 1/1943 at least (and had been used by them at eg. ROF Glascoed in 1939.
(p) New; per or via R.S.Davies, dealer, Mold, c2/1959
(q) tdx: Votty & Bowydd Slate Quarries, after 5/1963 by 5/1966

(1) either s/s c1885, or possibly taken into Oakeley stock in 1888 and subsequently s/s.
(2) tdt: Moelygest Granite Quarry, 1904
     tdx: Moelygest Granite Quarry 1906/1907 (probably by 10/1906)
     Subsequently little or perhaps not used, until scrapped c1920.
(3) The name ALGERNON was transferred to OK 1028 by 10/1927 "named after old loco now taken off list". There are many "lists" of the loco stock in the Oakeley Archives at Dolgellau Record Office [DgRO] but, because locos disappear and later reappear throughout the lists, many questions remain. It seems these DA locos were gradually withdrawn, but remained stored or dismantled for some years.
     An inventory [DgRO/Z/DBE/3584] 21/10/1933 includes CHARLES ("£45, poor") but not MARY CAROLINE, whilst a list [DgRO/Z/DAF/366] 26/9/1933 includes MARY CAROLINE but not CHARLES. List [DgRO/Z/DAF/361] 2/8/1933 includes both, plus "one loco as scrap" at the "Upper Quarry Shed"; whilst another list [DgRO/Z/DAF/362] 18/10/1933 has "one loco steam, one loco scrap, one old scrapped loco" at this same shed.
     These DA locos subsequently faded away, though some components did survive for many years. [See also J/IRR/No.110/137; No.120/80.]
(4) the last recorded boiler test was 9/5/1935 - loco not in list dated 9/1935, and gone by 8/1937. Hence s/s c1936, probably scrapped.
(5) tdt: Arthur Koppel, dealer, London, c12/1905
(6) scrapped after 9/1935 by 8/1937
(7) scrapped after 11/1936 by 8/1937
(8) sold 31/3/1942 to W.O.Williams, dealer, Harlech
     wlw: Penyrorsedd Slate Quarry, Nantlle.
(9) still here 10/1933; subsequently [? c1937] s/s
(10) disused from 1939.
     tdt: Mr C.R.Weaver, private store, 24/6/1968
     wlw: Gloddfa Ganol - see entry below.
(11) still here 8/1937 "in poor condition"; later scrapped.
(12) disused by 8/1951 (in "horse tunnel" shed); scrapped 1964.
(13) tdt: Mr R.Hilton c11/1961; to store on Ffestiniog Railway (PR/3).
(14) sold to [tdt ?]: W.O.Williams, dealer, Harlech, 2/1941
     wlw: R.S.Davies, dealer, Mold, by 1/9/1952
(15) tdt: Foraky Ltd, contractors, Colwick, Nottingham, after 10/1971 by 7/1972.
     wlw: Nobels Explosives Ltd, Roburite Works, Wigan, Lancs, in 1977.
(16) disused by 1964; s/s after 1/1970 by 9/1970.
(17) tdt: Fraser Bros Ltd, Peat Works, Entwistle, Lancs, after 8/1969 by 1/1970
(18) tdt: Votty & Bowydd Slate Quarries, after 8/1953 by 8/1960
(19) tdt: Glynceiriog Private Railway, after 13/8/1969 by 26/10/1969
     wlw: Bala Lake Railway (PR/66)
(20) tdt: Glynceiriog Private Railway, after 6/1968 by 7/1969
(21) tdt: Bala Lake Railway, after 4/1971 by 8/1971
(22) tdt: Foraky Ltd, contractors, Colwick, Nottingham, after 10/1971 by 7/1972
     wlw: Mr H.Frampton-Jones, c/o Surrey Light Railway.

Here we also mention that a Mr Wm.J.Williams, resident of one of the cottages near the Middle Quarry Mill, converted "for fun" a vintage motor-cycle to run on the railtracks on that level. For further details see entry "Welsh Slate Centre, Llanberis".

Locomotives: Gauge 2'0" - Gloddfa Ganol Tourist Railway

Line, commencing near the car park, opened 28/7/1987.

87025	4wDM	40hp	MR	22238	1965	(ga)
87028	4wDM	40hp	MR	40s308	1967	(ga)
87032	4wDM	40hp	MR	40s412	1972	(ga)

(ga) tdx: Severn Trent Water Authority, Newstead Works, Staffs. after 9/1986 by 5/1987

Locomotives - Gloddfa Ganol Static Display

A large collection of locomotives has been assembled here, initially by "Narrow Gauge Enterprises" (a group of enthusiasts) but later of mixed NGE/FMTC ownership. The situation has proved to be rather fluid, some locos having been passed on to other sites, with others never being restored or placed on formal display. In some instances the site has been used for locos in "private store" only. As none of the locos has actually operated here, virtually all of the movements are of no historical significance. In this Handbook, therefore, the listing is confined to those locos which have a positive "North Wales" connection. A complete list of locos currently on site is maintained and published in the frequently revised "Handbook EL".
After leaving their industrial (etc) locations, many of the locos listed here have passed through "private stores" - including at Penyrorsedd Quarry, where the NGE exhibition was originally intended to be set up. Source footnotes for these are thus given in the form "wfw" rather than "tdx".
Most of the locos listed are of the 2ft group of gauges; those that are not are detailed in the footnotes. Some locos at Gloddfa Ganol helpfully display their "works number" as an identity number, with sometimes the addition of a name indicating their source or their present location. These are not specifically listed, as some have proved temporary, and their meaning is self-evident.

	4wBE	3hp	BE	16303	[1917?]	(na)	
	4wBE	3hp	BE	16306	[1917?]	(na)	(n1)
WELSH PONY	4wWE	10hp	BEV	640	1926	(nb)	
	0-4-0PM	20hp	Bg	774	1919	(nc)	
KATHLEEN	0-4-0VBT	VC	DeW		1877	(nd)	
LLANFAIR	0-4-0VBT	VC	DeW		1895	(ne)	
	2-2-0PM	10hp	FRSociety		1974	(nf)	
	4wDM	20hp	HE	2024	1940	(ng)	
	4wDM	20hp	HE	2207	1941	(nh)	*
	4wDM	20hp	HE	2209	1941	(ni)	**
	0-4-0ST	OC	KS	3114	1918	(nj)	
	4wPM	6hp	L	3916	1931	(nk)	
WHIPPIT QUICK	0-4w-4DM		Fairbourne		1962	(nm)	
	4wDM	40hp	RH	198297	1939	(nn)	
	4wDM	20hp	RH	213834	1942	(no)	
	4wDM	20hp	RH	235711	1945	(np)	
	4wDM	48hp	RH	235729	1944	(nq)	
	4wDM	31hp	RH	398102	1956	(nr)	***
	2-2-0PM		Rhiwbach	[? c1935]		(ns)	(n2)
DOROTHY	0-4-0ST	OC	WB	[?1568	1899]	(nt)	
	4wDM	13hp	RH	209430	1942	(nu)	

	On display at Blaenau Ffestiniog (LNW, later Central) stations (PR/23) since 14/7/1979
*	
**	On display at Dolwyddelen station (PR/23) since 7/7/1979
***	On display at Corris Craft Centre (see BRAICH GOCH) since 4/1983.

(na) wfw: Manod Slate Quarry (16306 being incomplete)
(nb) wfw: Llechwedd Slate Quarry
(nc) wfw: Oakeley Slate Quarry
(nd) wfw: Penrhyn Slate Quarries
(ne) wfw: Penmaenmawr Granite Quarries 3'0" gauge
(nf) wfw: Ffestiniog Railway (PR/3), "5628 MONSTER"
(ng) wfw: Cwt-y-Bugail Slate Quarry and Trefor Granite Quarry
(nh) wfw: Trefor Granite Quarry
(ni) tdx: NCB Haig Colliery, Whitehaven, Cumbria, 14/1/1977, initially to private store at Blaenau Ffestiniog. 2'6" gauge
(nj) wfw: Mr P.Beard, Hill Farm, Brockamin, Worcs, until 1961; first to private store in Kent; arrived Gloddfa Ganol 24/6/1978
(nk) wfw: Dorothea Slate Quarry
(nm) wfw: Fairbourne Railway (PR/53) 1'3" gauge
        A rebuild of 4wPM L 6902/1935.
(nn) tdx: Croesor Slate Quarry, 19/11/1979
(no) wfw: Dinas River Authority Depot, Caernarfon
(np) wfw: Pen-yr-Orsedd Slate Quarry
(nq) tdx: store at Bala Lake Railway (PR/66), 8/1985 2'6" gauge
(nr) wfw: Carlisle Plaster & Cement Co Ltd 2'4" gauge
(ns) wfw: Rhiwbach Slate Quarry (loco incomplete).
(nt) wfw: Llechwedd Slate Quarry (loco incomplete)
(nu) tdx: Bala Lake Railway (PR/66) enthusiasts collection, /1987

(n1) tdt: Mr F.Stapleton, near Newbury, Berkshire, /1988
(n2) tdt: Surrey Light Railway, 2/12/1979

OLD BROUGHTON (BROUGHTON/BROUGHTON HALL) COLLIERY 04
(Cd/GR:below)

1835	-	1853	: John Pearce & Richard Gough [of Southsea Colly]
9/1855	-	1881	: Broughton Coal Co [Robertson & Darby]
1/1881	-	1890	: Broughton & Plas Power Coal Co Ltd
		1890	: closed: retained as pumping shaft for Plas Power Colly.

The history of this colliery is confused due to there being two sites (in effect, two collieries) physically separated by PR/21 (the Wrexham-Brymbo direct railway). The 9/1855 takeover is recorded as including "the Lodge and Broughton Hall estates, including the old Southsea Colliery". The colliery to the west of PR/21 (at GR:303524) was drowned-out in 1878, but later used for pumping. The other site (GR:304523) adjacent to Broughton Hall was abandoned in 1890, work being transferred to the nearby Plas Power Colliery. It is believed that the Old Broughton Colliery locos also shunted the Broughton Forge sidings - see notes under Plas Power entry.

By 1985 the sites of both Old Broughton pits had been landscaped.

[New Broughton Colliery (GR:308513) was another site nearby; opened in 1883 by Thomas Clayton (of Brynmally Colliery - which see) - and hence known locally as "Clayton's Pit"; becoming New Broughton Colliery Co Ltd in 1899; closed 1910; dispersal sale 16/5/1911. Situated on the "island" between the loop of PR/47 and PR/21, it was quite a large colliery with sidings to both GWR and GCR, but no records of any locomotives here have been discovered. Much of the site remains [1991] as semi-derelict land.]
[Read: B/107]

Locomotives: Gauge 4'8½"

SARAH	0-4-0T	OC	BP	91	1857	New 8/57	(1)
COLLIER	0-4-0ST	OC	AB	179	1876	New 12/76	(2)

(1) some BP records suggest this was originally a 0-4-0 tender loco, but the early BP listings are not entirely reliable on such matters.
BP records also quote cylinder size as 11x16.
In 2/1878 the Broughton Coal Co advertised for sale a 4wc 11x15 BP tank loco; perhaps this was BP 91.
Maybe it was not sold, but transferred to Bersham Colliery, where there was an early loco named SARAH.
Note: Edward Ratcliffe (Section 1) advertised a loco of this type in 8/1879.
(2) tdt: Plas Power or Gatewen Colliery by 2/1891 - see entry "Gatewen Colliery".

PADESWOOD and NANT MAWR COLLIERIES, BUCKLEY   P2

(Cf/GR:below)

NOTE: some early references quote "Nant Mawr Colliery, Mold". Nant Mawr Colliery, though near Buckley, was in the Bistre district and within the Parish of Mold.

NANT MAWR COLLIERY   (GR:276632)
   by 1854 -   1856 : Hancock & Co
                 1856 : closed
   by 1860 -   1864 : Nant Mawr Coal Co
     1865   -   1869 : Nant Mawr Coal Co Ltd
   by 1871 -   1874 : Padeswood United Cannel Coal & Iron Co Ltd
     1875   -   : Padeswood United Coal & Cannel Co Ltd
          by 1886 : closed

PADESWOOD COLLIERY   (GR:276625)
   by 1865 -   1866+ : Wm.Fidler & Co   *
   by 1871   : A.C.King   *
   by 1876 -   1889+ : Padeswood United Coal & Cannel Co Ltd
   by 1894 -   : Padeswood Cannel & Coal Co Ltd
          by 1898 : closed and dismantled

* possibly another site nearby.

Nant Mawr Colliery had a 4'8½" gauge private railway over ½ mile long running southwards from the Pit to join PR/9 at "Padeswood Colliery Junction" (a few yards east of the PR/10 Ffrith Junction). This private railway was dismantled by the 1890s and, if OS/25" of 1898 is accurate, the quite substantial earthworks of the line were also removed. There is very little trace of the line today [1985]. However, the southernmost section of this line was utilised in the mid 1870s to serve the new Padeswood Colliery; though it did not have a long life. This part of the route can still [1985] be seen.

By 1902, George Watkinson & Sons Ltd were filing returns for their "Nant Mawr Colliery"; location uncertain, perhaps a re-working of this site ? If so, no significant railways seem to have been used.

Locomotives: Gauge 4'8½" - Nant Mawr

A sale "In Chancery [re] Nant Coal Company (Limited)....Nant Colliery, 3 miles from Mold....Mold branch of [LNWR] runs through the centre of the property and the pits are connected with it by a private Locomotive Branch nearly a thousand yards long [including] a tank locomotive engine nearly new...." was scheduled for 13/3/1867 but soon deferred to 17/4/1867 [J/CG/16.2.1867/164 to 13.4.1867/356]. What then happened is not clear, but three years later another auction of "Nant Colliery plant (near Padeswood Station, Mold)" on 22/5/1871 - and again postponed, to 22/7/1871 - included one tank loco with 10x18 cylinders [J/CG/1871/478]. This may, or may not, have been the same loco as that for sale in 1867. One source has stated this loco (or one of these locos) as being a Lewin loco. But the earliest documented Lewin was built in 1874, hence 1871 - and 1867 more so - seems rather early for this builder.

Of possible related interest is an advert [J/CG/1.1871/80] for sale, a 10x18 tank loco, 180 brass tubes, apply T.B.Forwood, Thornton Manor in Cheshire. Forwood had previously worked on the Neath & Brecon Railway (after John Dickson, contractor) where an 11/1868 sale had included a 10x18 tank loco NEATH by BP; and a 10x16 tank loco by Neilson variously quoted named BUCKLEY or BULKELEY. Whilst the latter name is appropriate to Anglesey (and perhaps Dickson's PR/26 Contract), the name BUCKLEY could perhaps be appropriate to Padeswood.

Locomotive: Gauge 4'8½" - Nant Colliery

Mystery loco or locos in 1867 and 1871 - see notes above   s/s

Locomotive: Gauge 4'8½" - Padeswood

0-4-0ST   OC   VF   792   1876   New   s/s

PADESWOOD CEMENT WORKS, near BUCKLEY   P4
(Cf/GR:292622)

```
                1946    : new factory. First production in 1950.
    1946    -           : Tunnel Portland Cement Co Ltd
                        : Tunnel Cement Ltd
by 10/1984  -  10/1986  : Tunnel Cement (North Western) Ltd
    11/1986 -           : Castle Cement (Padeswood) Ltd
```

Factory served by sidings off PR/28 between Hope Exchange and Buckley Junction. Limestone brought to factory by road, mainly from Cefn Mawr Quarry (GR:200635), near Gwernaffield, Mold. Rail traffic ceased c4/1991; wagons cleared from sidings 7/5/1991.

Locomotives: Gauge 4'8½"

Note: British Railways class 02 diesel shunter D.2867 was hired for some months during 1970 ex Allerton (Liverpool) Depot.

```
1                       0-4-0DM 165hp RH    248439   1946  New 1/47   (1)
2                       0-4-0DM 165hp RH    252687   1949  New 7/49   (2)
-                       0-4-0DE 165hp  RH   418596   1957  (a)        (3)
2                       0-6-0DM 204hp HE      4208   1948  (b)        (4)
3                       0-6-0DM 204hp HE      3526   1947  (c)        (5)
(TPC) 7   (f.No.7)      4wDH           S     10276   1967  (d)        OOU
(TPC) 6   (f.No.6)      4wDH           S     10235   1965  (e)        OOU
-                       0-4-0DE 220hp  YE     2854   1961  (f)        (6)
```

(a) tdx: Thos.W.Ward Ltd, dealers, Templeborough Works, Sheffield, 1969 by 12/7/1969
    wfw: I.C.I.Ltd, Fleetwood, Lancs.
(b) tdx: Shotton Steelworks, after 3/1970 by 4/1971
(c) tdx: Shotton Steelworks, after 4/1971 by 5/1972
(d) tdx: West Thurrock Cement Works, Essex, c9/1976 by 20/10/1976
(e) tdx: West Thurrock Cement Works, Essex, 27/10/1976
(f) tdx: Pitstone Cement Works, Bucks, 10/10/1980

(1) scrapped at Padeswood, after 8/1971 by 5/1972
(2) tdt: West Thurrock Cement Works, Essex, /1961
(3) tdt: Tilsley & Lovatt Ltd, dealers, Stoke-on-Trent, after 5/1972 by 12/1972
    wlw: Patent Shaft Steel Works Ltd, Wednesbury, Staffs.
(4) tdt: West Thurrock Cement Works, Essex, 11/1976
    wlw: Kent & East Sussex Railway.
(5) tdt: Cambrian Railways Society, Oswestry, Shropshire, 7/7/1978
(6) tdt: Llangollen Railway (PR/68), 18/10/1991

PANTDREINIOG SLATE QUARRY, BETHESDA P6
(Gc/GR:623671)

		c1820	:	started
		1856	:	for sale
by 1858	-		:	"The Proprietors of the Pantdrainiog [sic] Quarry"
1873	-		:	Bangor & Pantdreiniog Slate Co Ltd
11/1895	-	7/1903	:	W.J.Parry; W.J.Parry & Lloyd George [who formed:]
8/1903	-	1911	:	North Wales Quarries Ltd (reg.7/1903 liq.11/1911)
		29/4/1911	:	dispersal auction
by 1918	-	c1920	:	Pantdreiniog Slate Quarry Co Ltd, jointly with:
				North Wales Development Co Ltd (reg.7/1919 £150K liq.1925
		c1920	:	closed

The quarry developed as a large pit ("sinc") from which wagons were lifted by Blondin ropeways to the Mill and tips at ground level. The 1903 Company was an attempt to operate three local quarries on "co-operative" principles (the others being Tanybwlch and Moel Faban), to alleviate hardship caused by the Penrhyn Quarry 1900-1903 strike. Pantdreiniog was virtually closed from 1909.
The 1918 activity was principally an effort to process slate waste, and soon failed. The derelict site was landscaped in the 1970s and little of archaeological interest now remains.

Locomotives: Gauge 2'0"

| RICHARD BELL | 0-4-0ST | OC | WB | 1726 | 1903 | New 10/03 | (1) |
| J.C.GRAY | 0-4-0ST | OC | WB | 1863 | 1907 | New 11/07 | (2) |

(1) wlw(tdt?): Henry Boot & Sons (London) Ltd, contractors. Loco was sent by Boots to WB, Stafford for overhaul during (or by) 10/1920, subsequently used on Boots A226 Gravesend-Strood Road (1921-1923) Contract, and Boots A41 Watford Way Road (1924-) Contract [and possibly other jobs too].
wlw: Orpington Ballast Co, St.Mary Cray, Kent, in 1930.

(2) wlw(tdt?): Henry Boot & Sons (London) Ltd, contractors, who had spare parts sent to them at 42 Law Street, West Bromwich, Staffs, 9/1920 [perhaps loco then in use on one of Boots council-housing estates then in hand in the Birmingham area]. Loco later used by Boots on A226 and A41 Contracts (with WB 1726 above) until after 7/1925. Loco was renamed SUGWORTH; in 1920 Charles Boot lived at Sugworth Hall, near Sheffield.
wlw: E.J.Rice & Co, Friars Wash Sand & Gravel Pits, Flampstead, near Redbourn, Bedfordshire, by 12/1928 until 5/1929 at least.

NOTE: It seems possible that both these locos were not sold in the 1911 auction at Pantdreiniog, but perhaps remained until c1920 closure as [UCNW/KF/149/116928] one loco at least was still here when WW1 started. They have not been located with Boots prior to 1920 - they could perhaps be the two 2ft gauge WB saddle tank locos offered for sale by Wm.Rowlands, Bangor Road, Conwy, in J/MM/19.3.1920.

PANT GLAS COMPENSATION RESERVOIR CONSTRUCTION   P8
NANT-Y-CROGFRIN, near PENYCAE, WREXHAM   (Cd/GR:265470)

1935 -   1939 : Wrexham & East Denbighshire Water Co
                      (direct labour contract).

A temporary railway was used on this site during the construction period. Track removed in 1939; no obvious traces found in 1982

Locomotive: Gauge 2'0"

4wDM	20hp	RH	187045	1937	New 9/37	(1)

(1) tdt: Lehane, McKenzie & Shand Ltd, contractors [of Matlock, Derbys] 6/1940. Used by LMcK&S; at Barrasford Reservoir Contract in 11/1940 [at least] and possibly elsewhere.
wlw: George Cohen, Sons & Co Ltd, dealers, c8/1955

PARC (GWYDYR PARK CONSOLS/D'ERESBY MOUNTAIN) LEAD MINE
NANT BWLCH-YR-HAIARN, near LLANRWST   P10
(Gc/GR:788602)

1855 -	1875	: Gwydyr Parc Consols
1888 -		: D'Eresby Mountain Lead Mining Co Ltd
1894 -	1913	: Parc Lead & Zinc Mining Co Ltd
1919 -	1920	: Llanrwst Consolidated Mines Ltd
1936 -	1939	: (working)
1951 -	1958	: Johannesburg Consolidated Investment Co Ltd; trading as Llanrwst Lead Mines Ltd
2/1962 -	3/1963	: Hawkswick Investments Ltd
1963 -	c1966	: mine and railway disused; crusher used by Pengwern & Gwydyr Quarries Ltd
	1967	: mine abandoned; surface equipment scrapped.

An adit mine, with entrance near to crusher at GR quoted. Original railway into mine was c20" gauge, worked by ponies. After 1919 the Parc adit was extended to enter the workings of Hafna, Llanrwst and Cyffty Mines - all thus becoming one mine. The adit was modernised in the 1950s and the locomotive railway installed, much ore being found but quality too low for commercial success. Reopening in 1962 was for experiments in automated mining methods rather than seeking to win ore. Most surface rail tracks removed 1964, and site landscaped in 1970s. By 1984 only the gated adit remained.

[Read: B/199/23/65; J/NMRS/No.4; B/270]

Locomotives: Gauge 2'0"

4wDM	20hp	RH	260734	1951	New	Scr 4/1967	
4wDM	20hp	RH	323547	1951	New	Scr 4/1967	
4wBE	5hp	GB	2473	1953	New 10/53		(1)
4wDM	20hp	RH	226292	1944	(a)		(2)

(a) purchased 26/4/1956 for £185 and delivered to Parc Mine 5-6/1956. Supplier not known. Built originally for Ministry of Supply; not as a 'mines' loco, but exhaust treatment equipment was on loco prior to 1956 hence had probably been used in mine or tunnel elsewhere.

(1) G.W.Madoc Jones, dealer, Denbigh, handled the disposal of plant at this mine, and this is probably his 6/1965 advertised "Greenwood & Batley 24 inch gauge battery loco lying in Caernarvonshire".
No further trace.
(2) tdt: Wm.Latimer & Co Ltd, Dolgarrog [see "Dolgarrog Railways"], loan [? per G.W.Madoc Jones, dealer], 4/1965.
Returned to Parc from Dolgarrog c7/1965 after 24/6/1965.
Scrapped at Parc Mine 4/1967.

PARYS MOUNTAIN COPPER MINES, AMLWCH P12
(Ga/GR:443903)

: Anglesey Mining plc

Shaft sunk 1989; first winning (of zinc) early 1990 [J/MM/12.4.1990].

Parys Mountain has been exploited for metals from Roman times, and was extensively worked over a large area particularly in the 1800s. Today it is largely a total confusion of the remains of workings and re-workings, with some ruined buildings of considerable interest. An excellent book [B/274] is available for those interested in its history.

Recent activity is confined to a corner of the area, where a shaft has been sunk to explore the minerals at depth.

[Read: B/274; B/270; B/199/23; B/199/30]

Locomotives: Gauge 2'0"

                        4wBE   CE   (a)

(a) tdx: Gwynfynydd Gold Mine, after 17/5/1990 by 14/9/1990

PENMACHNO (RHIWFACHNO/CWM-MACHNO) SLATE QUARRIES P14
(Gm/GR:752470)

                c1838 : opened
by 1882   : **Penmachno Slate Co Ltd**
by 1948 -   1962 : **Cwm-Machno Slate Quarries Ltd**
                1962 : closed; dismantled 1963-1964

There were inclines at this quarry by 1853 [CRO/X/Plans/R/21]. The workings subsequently developed, by galleries and further inclines, up the head of the Machno valley, and to underground chambers by inclines down from floor of quarry pit (sinc) at valley level.

During or soon afer WW2, a new "Foel Tramway" was built up the south-east side of the valley to new workings at GR:756466.

The locomotive was used around the main Mill GR:752471; this area has been partially destroyed by a reclamation scheme, but otherwise the quarry and its layout are clearly visible 1988].

Locomotive: Gauge 2'0"

                              4wPM   20hp   MR   2102   1921 (a)   (1)

(a)   wfw(tdx?): Glynceiriog Slate Quarry. This loco was auctioned at Glynceiriog 14/7/1948, and is believed to have come direct to Cwm Machno from that sale.

(1)   still here 6/1963; gone by 2/1964. Probably scrapped.

PENMAENMAWR GRANITE QUARRIES   P16
(Gc/GR: below)

OLD (GR:716753) and **GRAIGLWYD** (GR:713756) **QUARRIES**

1834	-	1840	: Thomas Brassey & John Tomkinson - joined 1840 by:-
1840	-	2/1848	: J.T.Raynes, Richard Kneeshaw, Wm.Lupton
2/1848	-	1870s	: Brassey, Raynes, Kneeshaw, Lupton (as above)
1870s	-	12/1877	: closed and partly dismantled
1/1878	-	6/1890	: Darbishires & Co
6/1890	-	1/1911	: Darbishires Ltd (liq.4/4/1911)
1/1911	-		: Penmaenmawr & Welsh Granite Co Ltd

PENMAEN EAST (GR:700758) and **PENMAEN WEST** (GR:695755) **QUARRIES**

1832	-	1873	: Dennis Brundrit & Philip Whiteway
1873	-	9/1897	: Brundrit & Co
9/1897	-	1/1911	: Brundrit & Co Ltd
1/1911	-		: Penmaenmawr & Welsh Granite Co Ltd

COMBINED QUARRIES

	-	1965	: Penmaenmawr & Welsh Granite Co Ltd (reg.21/1/1911)
	from 7/1963		: subsidiary of Bath & Portland Stone Firms Ltd
1965	-	12/1985	: Kingston Minerals Ltd
		6/1967	: last regular use of locomotives
1/1986	-		: A.R.C.Western Ltd

Originally two separate 3'0" gauge rail systems connected the quarries to piers, and to sidings beside the LNWR (PR/7). After the 1911 amalgamation the two 3'0" gauge systems were connected, and by the 1930s quarrying was concentrated at the summit of Penmaenmawr Mountain in an extension of the Penmaen East Quarry, though stone processing and despatch was mainly via the Graiglwyd Quarry inclines. In 1932 mechanical

loading was introduced at the quarry face, with a 4'8½" gauge system to transport sto
from the face to the primary Mill. The 4'8½" gauge was moved down to a lower level in
early 1940s as the summit was quarried away. Road dumpers were introduced c1950 a
had replaced the 4'8½" gauge completely by 1956. The 3'0" gauge system was gradua
replaced by conveyor belts and road vehicles.

[Read: for a good general history see J/CHS/1974/27; for the inclines see J/IRR/No.86/17
See also B/177/162.]

Locomotives: Gauge 3'0"

[B] - locos originally Brundrit & Co quarries
[D] - locos originally Darbishires quarries

[B]		MONA	0-4-0VBT		HVF			New		(1
[B]		PENMAEN	0-4-0VBT	VC	DeW		1878	New	OOU by 194	
[D]		LILIAN	0-4-0VBT	VC	DeW		1891	New		(2
[D]		LOUISA	0-4-0VBT	VC	DeW		1892	New		(2
[D]		ADA	0-4-0VBT	VC	DeW		1892	New		(2
[B]		PUFFIN	0-4-0VBT	VC	DeW		1893	New		(2
[D]		WATKIN	0-4-0VBT	VC	DeW		1893	New		(3
[D]		HAROLD	0-4-0VBT	VC	DeW		1894	New		(4
[B]		LLANFAIR	0-4-0VBT	VC	DeW		1895	New		(5
[D]		HUGHIE **	0-4-0ST	OC	HE	706	1899	New 1/90		(6
[B]		TIGER	0-4-0ST	IC	HE	764	1902	New 4/02		(6
[D]		STEPHEN	0-4-0ST	OC	HE	771	1902	New 3/02		(6
[D]		SINGAPORE	0-4-0ST	OC	HE	798	1903	New 3/03		(6
[D]		DONALD **	0-4-0ST	OC	HE	866	1905	New 6/05		(7
[B]		DUTCHMAN	0-4-0WT	OC	OK	2464	1907	New	Scr/1932	
		-	0-4-0BE		PWG			New	s/s c1930	
		(COED) #	4wDM f.4wPM	20hp	MR5024	1929	New 8/29			(8
		-	4wDM 20hp		MR	5611	1931	New 5/31		(9
		NANT	4wDM f.4wPM	20hp	MR5513	1930	(a)			(8
		(LLWYD)	4wDM 42hp		MR	5905	1933	New 7/33		(8
		ALICE	0-4-0DE 60hp		AW	D53	1935	New	Scr 6/1969	
		(MARIAN)	4wDM 42hp		MR	5941	1936	New 5/36		(8
		HAROLD	4wDM 42hp		MR	5950	1938	New 2/38		(8
14		LLWYD (f.STEPHEN)	4wDM 42hp		MR	5951	1938	New		
		VIXEN	0-4-0DM 88hp	HE		3129	1944	New	Scr 7/1969	
		(WELLS)	4wDM 20hp		RH	202989	1941	(b)	Scr/1968	
		TAFF	4wDM 37hp		HE	1770	1935	(c)	Scr 6/1969	
		(CRIMEA)	4wDM 20hp		RH	202987	1941	(d)		(10)

** The saddletank with nameplates of HE 706 was fitted to loco HE 866 by 4/1942, thu
HE 866 thenceforth carried name HUGHIE.
The saddletank with DONALD nameplates may have been fitted to HE 771 for a perio
around the early 1940s.

Re-engined mark 2HW diesel, 2/1935.

Locomotives: Gauge 4'8½"

	KIMBERLEY	0-4-0DM	80hp	AE	2062	1932	New 2/32	(11)
	ATTIC	0-4-0DM	80hp	AE	2063	1932	New 2/32	(11)
(11245)	VIXEN	0-4-0ST	OC	Hor	1099	1910	(e)	(12)
	PUFFIN II	4wDM		MR			(f)	(13)
	FOX	0-4-0DM	77hp	HE	2069	1940	New 10/40	(14)
	HEATHER	0-4-0DM	77hp	HE	2070	1940	New 10/40	(15)
	PUFFIN II	4wDM	40hp	MR	1928	1919	(g)	Scr/c1958
	NEWRY	0-4-0DM	100hp	HE	3513	1948	New 1/48	(16)

(a) tdx: Trefor Granite Quarry 1933 by 6/1933; altered from 2'0" gauge.
    20/28hp diesel engine fitted 5/1934.
(b) tdx: B.C.S.(Engineers & Contractors) Ltd, dealers, Taffs Well, Glam, 8/1947.
    wfw: Balfour Beatty & Co Ltd, contractors, Orkney.
(c) tdx: B.C.S.(Engineers & Contractors) Ltd, dealers, Taffs Well, Glam, 12/1947.
    wfw: Balfour Beatty & Co Ltd, contractors, Orkney.
(d) tdx: B.C.S.(Engineers & Contractors) Ltd, dealers, Taffs Well, Glam, 3/1948
    wfw: Balfour Beatty & Co Ltd, contractors, Orkney.
(e) tdx: LMS Railway, 1/1933.
(f) here by 8/1934.
(g) purchased 1946.
    wfw(tdx?): British Oil & Cake Mills Ltd, Greenock, Renfrewshire.
    Received as a petrol loco, re-engined diesel at Penmaenmawr.

(1) tdt: DeWinton & Co, Caernarfon, c1878 (and, reputedly, wlw: Little Orme Limestone Quarry - which see for further comment).
(2) noted as withdrawn from use 1931 (ADA), 1933 (LILIAN), 1934 (PUFFIN), and 1936 (LOUISA). Later, four frames of DeW locos (which by deduction seem to be these locos) were used as chassis for mobile concrete blocks which tensioned the conveyors on Graiglwyd Pier. These were scrapped 1/1984 whilst the Pier was being demolished.
(3) disused by 1944. tdt: Mr Hughes, 2/1966 (and subsequently Mrs Williams), private stores at Llanrwst; then:
    tdt: Penrhyn Castle Railway Museum, Bangor, 24/5/1971.
(4) disused by 1938; virtually intact less wheels 8/1948; frame later re-used as a wagon (which was scrapped in 1967).
(5) disused by 1940. tdt: Mr Hughes, private store at Llanrwst, 2/1966
    Later to Walcroft Brothers, Pershore; to Mr P.Nicholson, Brockham;
    wlw: Gloddfa Ganol Tourist Centre - see OAKELEY SLATE QUARRIES.
(6) disused by 4/1942 - SINGAPORE then intact, the others partially dismantled. Most of the surviving components were scrapped 1951.
(7) in use 4/1942 (name HUGHIE, see note ** above) but disused in 1943.
    Still virtually intact 6/1950; scrapped 1951.
(8) scrapped on site by B.& Z.Transport Ltd (of Wellington, Salop), after 11/1967 by 1/1968.
(9) dismantled by 9/1949; scrapped [? 1951].
(10) virtually disused, on quay, from 1965;
    tdt: Mr R.Watson-Jones, private store in Penmaenmawr, 4/1986.
(11) tdt: Pittrail Ltd (contractors of Aldridge, Staffs), 1956;
    per James N.Connell Ltd, dealers.

(12) wlw(tdt?): Doughty-Goole Fertilisers Ltd, Lincoln.
Had left Penmaenmawr by 1946 certain, and recalled at Lincoln as having arriv
there by 1940.
(13) gone by 2/1953; disposal unknown.
(14) tdt: H.Lees & Sons Ltd, Oldham, Lancs, 1956;
per James N.Connell Ltd, dealers.
(15) tdt: Northampton Corporation Highways Department, 8/1956;
per James N.Connell Ltd, dealers.
(16) tdt: William Denny & Bros Ltd, Dumbarton, Scotland, 1956;
per James N.Connell Ltd, dealers.

PENMON PARK (BULKELEY PARK & DEER PARK) MARBLE QUARRIES
PENMON, near BEAUMARIS P18

(Ga/GR:628805

	in 1834	: William Thomas
	- 12/1875	: Samuel Blatchford Tucker
12/1875	-	: Anglesea (Penmon) Marble Quarries Co Ltd
		(reg.7/1875 by Spargo)
	- 3/1886	: Public Works & Contract Co Ltd (reg.13/6/1883 liq.1890)
3/1886	- 1890	: Penmon Quarries Ltd (reg.27/3/1886 liq.1890-91)
1900	- 1911	: John Harold Hope
	1911	: closed and dismantled

Quarry developed on two levels or galleries, the upper being known as Bulkeley Park Quarr
and that below it being Deer Park Quarry. A self-acting incline from the upper level, an
having a turnout to the lower gallery, ran down to pass under the road to reach the stackin
ground and quay. This incline and associated railways existed by 1875. After 190
J.H.Hope introduced more machinery, including the locomotive, though little work wa
actually done.

Locomotives: Gauge 3'6"

[VIOLET ?] 0-4-0ST OC HE 348 1884 (a) (1)

(a) per HE records, purchased by J.H.Hope in or by 1904; and probably purchased fron
J.Wardell, dealer, London, who was advertising what was apparently this loco for sal
from 1/1902 to 8/1902 (at least).
wfw: T.Oliver, contractor, Green Withens Reservoir (1894-1899) Contract, Rishworth,
Yorkshire, (named VIOLET); for sale at Green Withens 3/1899 [J/CJ/1.3.1899].

(1) auction sale at Penmon 14-15/6/1911 included "plant, machinery, 50 tons steei rails
tip waggons, trollies, locomotive engine".
No further trace.

PENRHYN CASTLE RAILWAY MUSEUM, LLANDEGAI, BANGOR   P20
(Gc/GR:602719)

1963 -   : The National Trust.

The Museum contains a general collection of locomotives, rolling stock, track-samples, photographs and models, mostly related to industrial railways though not all are connected with North Wales history. Those locomotives which did work at North Wales sites, plus the diesel loco used for demonstration operation at this Museum, are listed below. A complete list of locos currently on site is published in the frequently revised Handbook EL. The steam locos are not currently [1991] operational, though restoration of HUGH NAPIER is in hand.

Locomotives: Gauge various

10¾"	CHARLES	0-4-0ST	OC	HE	283	1882	(a)
8½"	VESTA	0-6-0T	IC	HC	1223	1916	(b)
10¾"	HUGH NAPIER	0-4-0ST	OC	HE	855	1904	(c)
'0"	FIRE QUEEN	0-4-0	OC	AH		1848	(d)
'0"	WATKIN	0-4-0VBT	VC	DeW		1893	(e)
'0"		4wDM	20hp	RH	327904	1951	(f)

a) tdx: Penrhyn Slate Quarries, 21/5/1963
b) tdx: Shotton Steelworks, 3/12/1963
c) tdx: Penrhyn Slate Quarries, 11/11/1966
d) tdx: Dinorwic Slate Quarries, 17/12/1969
e) tdx: private store at Llanrwst, 24/5/1971
   wfw: Penmaenmawr Granite Quarries
f) tdx: Mr R.G.Honeychurch, private store, Kinnerley, Salop, 12/7/1984
   wfw: Wenlock Stone & Concrete Products Ltd, Much Wenlock, Salop.

PENRHYN SLATE QUARRIES, BETHESDA   P22
PENRHYN RAILROAD; PENRHYN RAILWAY   (Gc)
PORT PENRHYN HARBOUR, BANGOR

1580 -	1768	: various lessees
1768 -	1782	: Warburton & Pennant
1782 -	11/1951	: Penrhyn Slate Quarries [Pennant; becoming from 1783 the Lords Penrhyn]
11/1951 -	1964	: Penrhyn Quarries Ltd [Lord Penrhyn]
1964 -		: subsidiary of Marchwiel Holdings Ltd;
		: Sir Alfred McAlpine & Son Ltd
		: McAlpine Quarries Ltd.

Primitive railways existed in the quarry by 1775. Work commenced on 2/9/1800 on the construction of the 6¼ mile Penrhyn Railroad, a horse- and gravity-operated line from the quarry to the coast at Abercegin, where slates were loaded for shipment. Railroad first used 25/6/1801. Track gauge 2ft (centre-to-centre of rails - the wagons having double-flanged wheels). Route included three inclines. Abercegin harbour was improved and renamed Port Penrhyn.

In 1874 the upper section of the Railroad, from the Quarry to the head of the first (Tynyclwt) incline, was improved, and a locomotive (GEORGE SHOLTO) introduced 12/1875. The improved Railroad was extended, partly on new formation to avoid Tynyclwt incline, to Dinas Incline Top, and loco working extended to Dinas 10/1876. Concurrently, other locos were introduced at the Port and within the Quarry.

Between 3/1878 and 10/1879 a new Railway was built between Dinas Incline Top and the Port enabling locomotives to work throughout; the superseded section of Railroad was then closed and dismantled. Passenger trains for quarrymen were operated over the new Railway until 9/2/1951; the last slate train ran on 24/7/1962; the track was sold to the Ffestiniog Railway (PR/3) and lifted in 1965 for re-use. Rail traffic ceased at the Port 8/1962 but continued on a lesser scale within the Quarry until c1965 - the last tipping gallery railway closing on 29/3/1965.

[Read: B/182; B/201; B/204; B/176; B/147; B/148; B/118; B/151; etc]

Locomotive: Gauge 2ft - Railway Construction

    RICHARD PARRY, contractor [of Menai Bridge].

    COETMOR   0-4-0VBT   [HVF ?]   (c1)

(c1) sold to Penrhyn Slate Quarries 12/1880.
    Parry had advertised "loco engine for sale, suitable for two feet railway, equal to new" 12/1879 [J/CDH/27.12.1879]; presumably, though not definitely, this loco.

Locomotives: Gauge 1'10¾" - Quarries, Port and Railway

No.3	GEORGE SHOLTO	0-4-0UT	OC	FE(HH)		1875	New ±	Scr
No.1	LORD PENRHYN	0-4-0VBT	VC	DeW		1876	New	Scr 1/1909
No.2	LADY PENRHYN	0-4-0VBT	VC	DeW		1876	New	Scr *
No.4	EDWARD SHOLTO	0-4-0ST	IC	DeW		1876	New	Scr c1907
	GEORGE HENRY	0-4-0VBT	VC	DeW		1877	New	(1)
	ALICE	0-4-0VBT	VC	DeW		1877	New	Scr #
	KATHLEEN(f.KATIE)	0-4-0VBT	VC	DeW		1877	New	(2)
	GEORGINA	0-4-0VBT	VC	DeW		1877	New	Scr 1/1904
	HILDA	0-4-0T	IC	DeW		1878	New	Scr #
	INA	0-4-0VBT	VC	DeW		1878	New	Scr #
	VIOLET	0-4-0T	IC	DeW		1879	New	Scr 1/1902
	BRONLLWYD (f.COETMOR)	0-4-0VBT		[HVF ?]		(a)		Scr/1906
	CHARLES	0-4-0ST	OC	HE	283	1882	New 5/82	(3)
	GWYNEDD	0-4-0ST	OC	HE	316	1883	New 7/83	(4)
	LILIAN	0-4-0ST	OC	HE	317	1883	New 8/83	(5)
	WINIFRED	0-4-0ST	OC	HE	364	1885	New 4/85	(6)
	BLANCHE	0-4-0ST	OC	HE	589	1893	New 6/93	(7)
	LINDA	0-4-0ST	OC	HE	590	1893	New 6/93	(8)
	MARGARET	0-4-0ST	OC	HE	605	1894	New 5/94	(9)
	ALAN GEORGE	0-4-0ST	OC	HE	606	1894	New 5/94	(10)
	NESTA	0-4-0ST	OC	HE	704	1899	New 12/98	(6)
	ELIN	0-4-0ST	OC	HE	705	1899	New 12/89	
		rebuilt Bethesda Ø				1938		(11)
	HUGH NAPIER	0-4-0ST	OC	HE	855	1904	New 8/04	(12)

	Name	Wheel	Cyl	Builder	No.	Year	Note	Ref
	PAMELA	0-4-0ST	OC	HE	920	1906	New 11/06	
		rebuilt	Bethesda Ø			1951		(13)
	SYBIL MARY	0-4-0ST	OC	HE	921	1906	New 11/06	(14)
	GEORGE SHOLTO	0-4-0ST	OC	HE	994	1909	New 5/09	(15)
	GERTRUDE	0-4-0ST	OC	HE	995	1909	New 5/09	(16)
	EDWARD SHOLTO	0-4-0ST	OC	HE	996	1909	New 5/09	(17)
	SGT.MURPHY	0-6-0T	OC	KS	3117	1918	(b)	
		rebuilt	Bethesda Ø			1932		(18)
o.1	LLANDEGAI	2-6-2PT	OC	BLW	47143	1917	(c)	(19)
o.2	FELIN HEN	2-6-2PT	OC	BLW	46828	1917	(c)	(20)
o.3	TREGARTH	2-6-2PT	OC	BLW	46764	1917	(c)	(19)
	JUBILEE 1897	0-4-0ST	OC	MW	1382	1897	(d)	(21)
	LILLA	0-4-0ST	OC	HE	554	1891	(d)	(22)
	EIGIAU	0-4-0WT	OC	OK	5668	1913	(e)	
		rebuilt	Bethesda Ø			1930		(23)
	SANFORD	0-4-0ST	OC	WB	1571	1900	(f)	(24)
	SKINNER	0-4-0ST	OC	WB	1766	1906	(g)	(25)

[Construction of petrol locomotives now commenced; for convenience these are presented in the list below.]

	Name	Wheel	Cyl	Builder	No.	Year	Note	Ref
	BRONLLWYD	0-6-0WT	OC	HC	1643	1930	(h)	(26)
	STANHOPE	0-4-2ST	OC	KS	2395	1917	(i)	(27)
	CEGIN	0-4-0WT	OC	AB	1991	1931	(j)	(6)
	OGWEN	0-4-0T	OC	AE	2066	1933	(j)	(6)
	MARCHLYN	0-4-0T	OC	AE	2067	1933	(j)	(6)
	GLYDER	0-4-0WT	OC	AB	1994	1931	(k)	(6)

±   arrived 12/1875; supplied per John Beatson, dealer, Derby.

*   usually quoted as Scr/1911, but per J/LM/15.5.1917 it was still [ie. c1916] in occasional use as a spare loco.

\#   usually quoted as Scr/1911, but in fact scrapped at some date AFTER 1/1911 [perhaps some years after; as, apparently, was LADY PENRHYN - note * above].

♪   locos rebuilt with clearly visible alterations:-
- ELIN : Higher pitched (Marshall No.83501) boiler fitted 11/1938
- PAMELA : Boiler from 0-6-0T BRONLLWYD fitted 5/1951
- SGT.MURPHY : Boiler and tanks lowered by 7½" in 10/1932
- EIGIAU : Cab height reduced 3"; new chimney fitted; side bunkers converted to water tanks (0-4-0TWT) in 1930

From 1932 a series of 18 four-wheeled PETROL LOCOMOTIVES was assembled at the Quarry Workshops, by mounting motor cars onto rail chassis. Surviving records detail 40 cars purchased between 1929 and 1940; mostly Morris but also Austin, Rover and Wolseley. Probably some of the locos were 'renewed' from time to time, resulting in some altered appearances. The descriptive details given in the following list are based on actual observations and photographs.

No.	built/rebuilt	Frame	Engine	Radiator	Status
No.1	built 1932	LCF	Rover 14hp		
	rebuilt by 1940	PF			
	rebuilt 1941		Wolseley	FR	XX
No.2		LCF	Morris	RR	in use 9/1949
No.3		HCF	Morris	FR	in use 1964
No.4		HCF	Morris	FR	fo 8/1949; 7/1952
No.5		HCF	Morris	RR	fo 8/1949; 7/1952
No.6		HCF			fo 8/1949; 7/1952
No.7		HCF	Morris	RR	fo 8/1949; 7/1952
No.8		PF	Morris	RR	in stock 1950
No.9		PF			fo 7/1952
No.10	built by 7/1934	PF	Morris	FR	OOU/1949; fo 7/1952
No.11		PF			fo 9/1949
No.12		PF	Morris	FR	
	rebuilt by 1942		Morris	RR	in stock 1950; 7/1952
No.13		PF		FR Ø	OOU/1949; fo 7/1952
No.14		PF	Morris	FR	in use 7/1945
No.15		PF	Morris	FR	OOU/1950
No.16		PF	Morris	FR	OOU/1950
No.17		PF	Morris	FR	XX
No.18	built by 5/1940	PF	Morris	FR	OOU/1949; fo 7/1952

LCF: Light Channel Frame, unsprung
HCF: Heavy Channel Frame, sprung
PF: Heavy Plate Frame, sprung
FR: Flat fronted Radiator
RR: Rounded Radiator

fo: frame (only) on site
Ø: in use 7/1945

XX These locos have not yet been reported since the early 1940s. Two PF chassis were used (1946, 1949) in the construction of diesel locos 1 and 17 (below) - whilst it is possible that No.1 Petrol became No.1 Diesel, it would be very remarkable if No.17 Petrol were to be rebuilt as Diesel on a date that ensured it entering service between the arrival of diesel locos No.16 and No.18.

The bottom edges of the frame side-plates of the chassis used for the diesel conversions, were modified; apparently to provide more visibility in the event of derailment.

The axleboxes and spring units from another plate-frame Petrol loco were used in a new chassis for a brake-van, c1947.

Any of the above locos or chassis that survived to 1968 were then removed as scrap.

Around 1942 parts of the quarry estate were leased by the Ministry of Supply and occupied by the Ministry of Aircraft Production in association with the Saunders-Roe sea-plane assembly plant at Beaumaris (Ynys Mon/Anglesey). Aeroplane components were manufactured and a diesel loco (RH 198292) was employed by 2/1943 (and possibly earlier). This locomotive later joined the quarry fleet and is detailed in the list below.

1		4wDM		Bethesda	1946	New (m)	(28)
2		4wDM	40hp	RH 198292	1939	(n)	(29)
3		4wDM	40hp	RH 218033	1943	(o)	(28)
4		4wDM	20hp	RH 218011	1943	(o)	(29)
5		4wDM	20hp	RH 222072	1943	(o)	(28)

6	4wDM	20hp	RH	223674	1943	(o)	(28)
7	4wDM	20hp	RH	223680	1943	(o)	(28)
8	4wDM	20hp	RH	187084	1937	(p)	(28)
9	4wDM	20hp	RH	183763	1937	(q)	(28)
10	4wDM	20hp	RH	181818	1936	(r)	(30)
11	4wDM	20hp	RH	189994	1938	(r)	(28)
12	4wDM	20hp	RH	181812	1936	(r)	(28)
13	4wDM	20hp	RH	211596	1941	(s)	(29)
14	4wDM	20hp	RH	211605	1941	(t)	(28)
15	4wDM	20hp	RH	202976	1940	(u)	(28)
16	4wDM	20hp	RH	211640	1941	(v)	(29)
17	4wDM	20hp	Bethesda		1949	New (w)	(28)
18	4wDM	20hp	RH	223685	1944	(x)	(28)
19	4wDM	20hp	RH	223701	1944	(x)	(28)
20	4wDM	20hp	RH	223753	1944	(x)	(28)
21	4wDM	20hp	RH	226297	1944	(x)	(28)
22	4wDM	20hp	RH	226302	1944	(x)	(31)
23	4wDM	20hp	RH	229651	1944	(x)	(28)
24	4wDM	40hp	RH	382820	1955	New 5/55	(32)

(a)   purchased from Richard Parry, contractor, Menai Bridge, COETMOR, by agreement of 22/12/1880
(b)   tdx: Admiralty, Beachley Dock, Chepstow, Monmouthshire;
          per C.D.Phillips Jnr, auctioneer, £820, 10/1920
(c)   tdx: ? , 9/1924; purchased from Hardinge & Co, dealers, London.
       wfw: United States Army Transportation Corps, France; 5159, 5104, and 5096 respectively.
(d)   tdx: Cilgwyn Slate Quarry 21/5/1928
(e)   tdx: Dolgarrog (see "Dolgarrog Railways") 18/7/1929
(f)   tdx: Maenofferen Slate Quarry 15/7/1929
(g)   tdx: Maenofferen Slate Quarry 15/8/1929
(h)   tdx: Surrey County Council, Guildford, CP39, 12/1934
(i)   tdx: Durham County Water Board, Burnhope Reservoir, 12/1934
       per: H.Stephenson & Sons, dealers.
(j)   tdx: Durham County Water Board, Burnhope Reservoir, 10/1936
(k)   tdx: Durham County Water Board, Burnhope Reservoir, 19/1/1938
(m)   New: loco built at Penrhyn Quarry incorporating plate-frame of a petrol loco, plus [Lister ?] diesel engine number 388036 and two-speed OK gearbox.
(n)   tdx: Ministry of Supply Depot within Penrhyn Quarry, 11/1946.
       Prior to arriving at Penrhyn by 2/1943, wfw: Charles Brand & Son Ltd, contractors, Royal Edward Dock Extension Contract, Avonmouth.
(o)   tdx: ? , 4/1947
       wfw: RAF Works Squadron, Mill Green, Hatfield, Herts., in 1943
(p)   tdx: [? Ministry of Supply, Swansea], 1/1948
       wfw: John Mowlem & Co Ltd, contractors, Staines Reservoir, in 1941
(q)   tdx: [? Ministry of Supply, Swansea], 1/1948
       wfw: [? wfw: War Department, Corsham, Wiltshire].
(r)   wfw: War Department, Corsham, Wiltshire
(s)   tdx: ? , 4/1949; per/via G.W.Bungey, dealer, Hayes, Middlesex
       wfw: Army, RAOC, Worksop (1942-43) and Retford (1943), Notts.
(t)   tdx: ? , 4/1949; per/via G.W.Bungey, dealer, Hayes, Middlesex
       wfw: Ministry of Supply, 'Bottisford', in 12/1947

(u) tdx: ? , 4/1949; per/via G.W.Bungey, dealer, Hayes, Middlesex
     wfw: WD (Army), Long Marston, Warwicks, in 6/1946
(v) tdx: ? , 4/1949; per/via G.W.Bungey, dealer, Hayes, Middlesex
     wfw: Ministry of Supply
(w) New: loco built at Penrhyn Quarry incorporating plate-frame from a petrol loco, plus RH Lister engine number 390080 and RH gearbox.
(x) tdx: ? , by 8/1951
     wfw: Ministry of Supply

(1) last used 12/1934;
     tdt: Tywyn Railway Museum 18/5/1956
(2) last used 2/1934;
     tdt: Mr R.P.Morris, Longfield, Kent, 12/1/1965
     wlw: Gloddfa Ganol - see "Oakeley Slate Quarries"
(3) last used 1/1956;
     tdt: Penrhyn Castle Museum 21/5/1963
(4) last used 8/1954;
     tdt: Mr J.M.Hutchings (private store) 6/5/1965
     wlw: Bressingham Gardens, Diss, Norfolk
(5) last used 1958;
     tdt: Mr N.Bowman & Mr T.Gibson (private stores at Llanddona, Anglesey and later Guildford, Surrey) 12/1965
     wlw: Launceston Steam Railway, Cornwall
(6) tdt: Mr C.B.Arnette, Murfreesboro, Tennessee, USA, 7/1965
     wlw: WINIFRED - Early Wheels Museum, Terre Haute, Indiana, USA, by 1975 - still here 1991
     NESTA - Mr R.Johnson, Rossville, Georgia, USA, by 1991
     CEGIN - Mr H.Hoover, Birmingham, Alabama, USA, by 1977; Mr R.Johnson, Rossville, Georgia, USA, by 1991
     MARCHLYN - Lake Winna Pesuaka Amusement Park, Rossville, Georgia, USA - still here 1991
     OGWEN - Early Wheels Museum, Terre Haute, Indiana, USA, by 1991
     GLYDER - Early Wheels Museum, Terre Haute, Indiana, USA, by 1991
(7) tdt: Ffestiniog Railway (PR/3) 17/12/1963
(8) tdt: Ffestiniog Railway (PR/3) 13/7/1962
(9) last used 11/1950;
     tdt: Messrs Boston & Pealling, Cadeby, Leics, 17/5/1968
(10) last used 11/1953;
     tdt: Mr J.Buckler, Howdenclough Light Railway, near Leeds, 17/8/1965
     wlw: Vale of Teifi Railway, Henllan, Dyfed, 7/1982
(11) last used 11/1954;
     tdt: Mr J.R.Burdett, Louth, Lincs, 8/1962
     wlw: Lincolnshire Coast Light Railway, 11/1969
(12) last used 11/1954;
     tdt: Penrhyn Castle Museum 18/11/1966
(13) last used 3/1958;
     tdt: Mr J.Vernon, Newbold Verdon, Leics, per Cornish Traction Preservation Society, 9/10/1966
     wlw: Mr J.Crosskey, Old Kiln Light Railway, Surrey, by 1985
(14) last used 2/1955;
     tdt: Mr C.Pealling c/o Mr J.Vernon, Newbold Verdon, Leics, 15/4/1966
     wlw: Lynton & Barnstaple Railway Association, Landkey, Devon, from 30/4/1988

15) last used 1947;
    tdt: Bressingham Gardens, Diss, Norfolk, 2/1966
16) last used 2/1955;
    tdt: Messrs Lamb, Bromsgrove, Worcs, 9/1960
    wlw: Mr C.Mathews, Thornhill, Ontario, Canada
    wlw: Centennial Centre of Science & Technology, Don Mills, Ontario, Canada
          - loco sectionalised and on display from 1966
17) tdt: Mr C.Mathews, Thornhill, Ontario, Canada, 10/1961
    wlw: Andrew Merrilees Ltd, Toronto, Canada - for sale there 10/1979
    wlw: J.Johnson, Garden Prairie, Illinois, USA, by 1991
18) tdt: Messrs Pealling & Weaver (private store, Staffs) 25/7/1964
    wlw: Betws-y-Coed Railway Museum
19) last used 15/11/1927 (LLANDEGAI) and 24/4/1929 (TREGARTH); both scrapped at Port Penrhyn by Howards of Warrington, 1/1940
20) last used 29/6/1927;
    tdt: Fairymead Sugar Co Ltd, Bundaberg, Queensland, Australia, 10/3/1940
21) last used 1/1/1955;
    tdt: Tywyn Railway Museum 4/12/1963
22) last used 3/1957;
    tdt: Mr J.B.Latham, Woking, Surrey, 12/12/1963
23) last used 9/1953;
    tdt: Mr G.J.Mullis, Droitwich, Worcs (dismantled and moved 26/1/1963-9/2/1963)
    wlw: Hills & Bailey Ltd, Llanberis - see PR/65
24) last used 1936; dismantled 1956; chassis used 7/1956 for the construction of a brake-van and, as such, scrapped 7/1968
25) disused by 1954; dismantled by 1954; chassis and most surviving components scrapped 21/6/1968
26) last used 1949; dismantled and boiler fitted to PAMELA 5/1951;
          chassis only tdt: Bressingham Gardens, Diss, Norfolk, 1/1966
27) last used 1947; cylinders and valve-gear to Talyllyn Railway (PR/27) in 1953.
          Boiler and chassis (dismantled) later:
    tdt: Bressingham Gardens, Diss, Norfolk, 24/11/1966-6/12/1966 and
          boiler later fitted to chassis of 0-6-0T BRONLLWYD.
          chassis only wlw: Lynton & Barnstaple Railway Association.
28) tdt: GFM, New Haden Works, Draycott Road, Cheadle, near Stoke-on-Trent, Staffs, for scrap, c3/1968
29) tdt: GFM, New Haden Works, Draycott Road, Cheadle, near Stoke-on-Trent, Staffs, for scrap, 28/3/1968
30) ran away down incline 2/10/1957 and severely damaged; remains stored in "Baldwin" shed until cut up as scrap in 1968.
31) tdt: Mr G.J.Mullis, Wychbold, Worcs,, 3/1967
    wlw: Mr J.Crosskey, Old Kiln Light Railway, Surrey
32) tdt: Sir Alfred McAlpine & Son Ltd, contractors, Deanhead Reservoir, Yorkshire WR, 13/1/1967
    tdx: Deanhead Reservoir by 7/1967
    tdt: GFM, New Haden Works, Draycott Road, Cheadle, near Stoke-on-Trent, Staffs, c3/1968
    wlw: Foxfield Railway Society, Staffs
    wlw: Mr J.Crosskey, Old Kiln Light Railway, Surrey, by 1985

PENYBONT BRICKWORKS, NEWBRIDGE, near CEFN MAWR   P24
(Cd/GR:292415)

```
            c1865  :  established
c1865   -          :  J.C.Edwards
                   :  J.C.Edwards (Ruabon) Ltd
            1960   :  closed (by 7/1960)
1962    -          :  Castle Fire Brick Co Ltd (but remained closed).
                      Track lifted and much of works demolished.
```

Clay was obtained from a quarry on the northern side of the Works, using a system of hand-worked and incline railways of 2'0" and 2'8" gauges. From earliest times, output from the Works was taken by narrow [? 2'8"] gauge tramroad which ran generally beside the main road south-westwards, across the GWR (PR/8) main line by the road bridge, to reach a canal wharf at GR:286408. On 26/6/1881 Edwards opened a new steeply-graded (1 in 38) 4'8½" gauge line from the Works to PR/8; the locomotives listed below worked on this line. Map OS/6"/1898 indicates both the tramroad and the 4'8½" gauge line coexisting; OS/6"/1909 indicates one half of the tramroad removed - perhaps track was being lifted c1907 whilst the OS surveyors were in the area. The 4'8½" gauge line was removed 5/1961.
[Read: J/DHS/Vol.20/248]

Locomotives: Gauge 4'8½"

```
  [ ?  MILTWIN        0-6-0tank                      (a)   Scr/cWW1 ]
       THE FLY        0-6-0ST   IC   MW   1111  1889 (b)             (1)
                      0-4-0ST   OC                   (c)             s/s
       -              4wPM  40hp  MR       1922 1919 New 7/19        (2)
       -              4wTG  VB    S        5734 1925 New             (3)
```

(a)   this loco apparently recalled by old employee, but not proven.
(b)   tdx: Black Park Colliery, loan, c1910.
(c)   reputed to have arrived here c1910; [if here, perhaps this was MILTWIN if memory erred about its number of wheels].

(1)   tdt: Black Park Colliery, off loan, c1910.
(2)   scrapped at Penybont after 3/12/1960 by 5/1961.
(3)   scrapped in 1953, c5/1953. It is of interest to note that this loco was ordered to have a special low cab, maximum height 10'7" above the rails; this distinctive feature is visible in photographs (reduced space between windows and roof). This was probably to pass beneath the loading dock at Penybont Works. However, a Sentinel publicity photograph, clearly taken at Penybont, shows a similar loco but with a full height cab. Maybe S 5734 was altered after delivery, or is this a photograph of a different loco, perhaps here on a demonstration visit.
Sentinel announced in 1925 that Edwards had purchased their loco "to replace a 40hp petrol loco". Perhaps Edwards had two such petrol locos, or MR 1922 outlived expectations.

PENYBRYN (CLODDFA'RLON) SLATE QUARRY, NANTLLE   P26

(Gc/GR:505537)

```
           c1770    : opened
1808  -             : Wm.Turner, Rich.Garnons, Hugh Jones, Wm.Wynne
      -    1839     : Rich.Garnons (and -1841, Cloddfa'rlon Pit only)
1839  -    1841     : Penybryn Slate Co [Henry English]
1848  -             : Bronyfoel Co [David & Chaloner Smith]
         by 3/1856  : Cloddfa'rlon Slate Co
      -    2/1882   : Penybryn Slate Co
2/1882 -   1891     : Penybryn Slate Quarry Co Ltd (reg.25/2/1882 liq.1891)
           1889     :   closed; dispersal auctions 24/8/1891, 21/4/1892
                    : later re-worked on small scale by Dorothea Qy.
```

Originally four individual small quarries (Cloddfa'rlon, Dew's, Herbert's and Penybryn) combined as one property from 1882. Both Chaloner Smith, and Dew & Co [of London], were involved in formation of the 1882 Company.
Served by 3'6" (centre) gauge inclines from PR/2, with 2ft gauge tracks between quarries, mill and tips.

[Read: B/175; B/182]

Locomotives: Gauge 2ft

RHYMNEY	0-4-0VBT	VC	DeW	1875 New 9/75	(1)
CHALONER	0-4-0VBT	VC	DeW	1877 [New ?]	(2)
JAMES DEW	[? 0-4-0ST	OC]			(3)

An advertisement for the 11/12/1888 auction of surplus plant listed a "hooded locomotive steam engine" with two cylinders 5½x9; also "another capital locomotive with horizontal boiler". The term "hooded", apparently applied to CHALONER, is not now understood. Loco RHYMNEY is mentioned by name in the later sales catalogue here.

(1)   for sale in 1891 and 1892 auctions.
       tdt: Penyrorsedd Slate Quarry.
(2)   tdt: Penyrorsedd Slate Quarry, £150, 12/1888.
(3)   for sale in 1891 and 1892 auctions, but not described in catalogues [24/8/1891 - HRO/D/DM/244/82] other than as "JAMES DEW"; but it is probably the same item as the "steam engine with horizontal boiler" listed in an 1888 auction of surplus equipment here.
       An old man recalled JAMES DEW as a horizontal boiler saddle tank loco at Penybryn Quarry. It is possible that JAMES DEW moved to Talysarn Quarry 4/1892, where a "normal" type loco - but not the name JAMES DEW - was later recalled.

PENYCLIP ROADWORKS & TUNNELS, LLANFAIRFECHAN P28
(Gc/GR:700762)

1930 - 1936 : **M.A.Boswell**, contractor [of Wolverhampton]
for Carnarvonshire County Council.

Contract for construction of new section of main coast road (A55), including a viaduct an
two tunnels through Penmaenmawr headland.
A temporary railway system was used around the site.

Locomotives: Gauge 2'0"

4wPM 20hp	MR	5054	1930	New 2/30 Ø	(1)
[? 4wPM 20hp	MR	5072	1930	New 4/30 *	(2)]
[? 4wPM 20hp	MR	5080	1930	New 6/30 *	s/s]

(1)   wlw: A.E.Farr Ltd, contractors, Winchester, by 12/2/1937
(2)   wlw(tdt?): Aled Reservoir construction, Denbigh Moor, by 8/1935

Ø   ordered by Carnarvonshire County Council and delivered Penyclip.

*   ordered by M.A.Boswell, delivery location not recorded; but in view of dates very likel
to this site.

Advertisements [J/CJ, J/MM] by Boswell for sale of equipment at end of contract refer to tw
Simplex locos "in yard at Penmaenmawr" 6/1936; also a Simplex loco (apparently) taken t
Boswells' yard at Wolverhampton by 1/1936. Boswell continued to order MR spare part
until 20/4/1940.

Williams, Needham & Simm Ltd, of Sheffield, were also offering "Simplex locos new 1931/3.
ex Penyclip diversion scheme" in 1/1935; dealers perhaps, or another contractor here ?

PEN-YR-ORSEDD SLATE QUARRY, NANTLLE P30
(Gc/GR:508540 etc)

1816	-	1848	: Wm.Turner; Turner & Morgan; Wm.Turner & Co
1848	-	1859	: John Lloyd Jones; Owen & Jones; Wm.Owen & Co
1859	-	1862	: W.A.Darbishire & Co
1862	-	2/1979	: Penyrorsedd Slate Quarry Co Ltd (reg.19/9/1862)
3/1979	-		: Ffestiniog Slate Quarries Co Ltd
			t/a **Nantlle Slate Quarry Co Ltd**

Located on northern slope of Nantlle valley, this quarry eventually comprised of four main pit
(Ellen, Eureka, two others) with Mills on three levels. Wagons were lifted out of the pits by
Blondin ropeways onto the internal 2ft gauge rail system connecting to the Mills and tips
3'6" (centre) gauge was used for product despatch via the Nantlle Tramway (PR/2), which
was reached down a series of inclines. Use of wider gauge wagons was very limited afte
PR/2 closed in 1963. Loco haulage ceased c10/1970 but some hand pushing and road
tractor haulage continued until 1979. By 7/1986 almost all track had been lifted.

1976 proposals to open a railway museum on part of the site resulted in the arrival of many locomotives and other items, but a change of plans caused removal of these, in 1978, to Gloddfa Ganol Tourist Centre. For further details see entry "Oakeley Slate Quarries, Blaenau Ffestiniog".

[Read: B/175; B/182]

Locomotives: Gauge 2ft

		BALADEULYN	0-4-0VBT	SVC	DeW			[New ?]		(1)
		STARSTON	0-4-0VBT	SVC	DeW			[New ?]		(2)
		INVERLOCHY	0-4-0VBT	VC	DeW		1877	[New ?]		(**)
		KELSO	0-4-0T	OC	VF	[? 832	1878]	(a)	Scr/1916	(**)
		GLYNLLIFON	0-4-0VBT	VC	DeW		1880	[New ?]	(*)	(3)
		CHALONER	0-4-0VBT	VC	DeW		1877	(b)		(4)
		RHYMNEY	0-4-0VBT	VC	DeW		1875	(c)		(**)
		GELLI	0-4-0VBT	VC	DeW		1893	New		(5)
		PENDYFFRYN	0-4-0VBT	VC	DeW		1894	New		(6)
		ARTHUR	0-4-0VBT	VC	DeW		1895	New		(7)
		VICTORIA	0-4-0VBT	VC	DeW	201	1897	New		(7)
		BRITOMART	0-4-0ST	OC	HE	707	1899	New	1/00	(8)
		SYBIL	0-4-0ST	OC	HE	827	1903	New	10/03	(9)
		UNA	0-4-0ST	OC	HE	873	1905	New	6/05	(10)
		DIANA	0-4-0T	OC	KS	1158	1917	(d)		(11)
-			0-4-0PM		PyO			(e)		(12)
No.2	(f.No.1)		4wDM	20hp	RH	235711	1945	New	10/45	(13)
No.1	(f.No.2)		4wDM	20hp	RH	235712	1945	New	10/45	(14)
No.3			4wDM	20hp	RH	226298	1944	(f)		(14)
No.4			4wDM	20hp	RH	226264	1944	(f)		(14)

(*) A new loco was purchased during the half-year ending 12/1879 [CRO/PyO/1873]. This presumably refers to the Order for GLYNLLIFON.

(**) INVERLOCHY last used 15/1/1938; stored in workshops, subsequently scrapped.
RHYMNEY last used in 1933; in 12/1933 company decided "to scrap", but frame, boiler and bunker still survived as a unit to 6/1935 at least.
KELSO sold for £150 [CRO/PyO/Add 2059] which was not a "scrap value" price. However, it has been recalled as having been broken up; and there is no known further trace of it.

(a) Penyrorsedd archives [CRO/PYO/1873/p.299,p.301 etc] confirm that, during the six months ended 3/1878, the quarry ordered a loco direct from VF, £406, to a Spooner & Co specification, and KELSO, which certainly was at Penyrorsedd, is presumed to be the outcome of that order. However, VF records do not confirm Penyrorsedd as a purchaser, though their records are rather imperfect in connection with the "Kelso" type locos. [For further comment see entry "Fron Slate Quarry".]
(b) tdx: Penybryn Slate Quarry, £150, 12/1888
(c) tdx: Penybryn Slate Quarry, 4/1892
(d) purchased from W.O.Williams, dealer, Harlech (? /1945) by 16/7/1946
    wfw: Oakeley Slate Quarries, Blaenau Ffestiniog
(e) construction in progress at Penyrorsedd Quarry 6/1942; Morris Cowley car engine plus substantial chassis with jackshaft drive. Reputedly never completed; seen 1949 with no engine fitted, chassis in use as a wagon.

(f)   tdx: Railway Mine & Plantation Equipment Co, ex store at W.G.Allen Ltd, Tipton
      Staffs, c1956 (by 8/1956) - in New condition; built for Ministry of Supply but not used

(1)   tdt: Glynrhonwy Quarry (see "Llanberis West"), £55, 10/1893
(2)   gone by 1895 [perhaps tdt: Glynrhonwy Quarry - which see - c1894]
      Old Men recalled locally that a loco fell over the end of a tip and was left where it lay
      This may have been STARSTON; and of course it may have been salvaged in fact.
      Loco name has also been quoted as "Starstone", but a director of the Company reside
      at Starston Hall, hence this is probable correct spelling for name of loco.
(3)   disused from 1/1923; scrapped 9/1933
(4)   disused from 1952
      tdt: Mr A.R.Fisher, private store, Hertfordshire
      wlw: Leighton Buzzard Light Railway, Bedfordshire
(5)   working 6/1942; disused by 7/1945; scrapped by 8/1949
(6)   disused 9/1949
      tdt: Mr A.J.Hills, private store, Bickenhill, Warwicks, 1/5/1965
      wlw: Hills & Bailey Ltd, Llanberis (see PR/65)
(7)   disused by 6/1942; scrapped c1956
(8)   tdt: private owners c/o Ffestiniog Railway (PR/3), 6/1965
(9)   tdt: Mr A.J.Hills, private store, Bickenhill, Warwicks, 23/9/1963
      wlw: Hills & Bailey Ltd, Llanberis (see PR/65)
(10) tdt: Mr G.J.Mullis, Salwarpe, Worcs, 8/5/1965
      wlw: Hills & Bailey Ltd, Llanberis (see PR/65)
(11) tdt: Mr G.J.Mullis, Salwarpe, Worcs, 21/8/1964
      wlw: Hills & Bailey Ltd, Llanberis (see PR/65)
(12) tdt: Mr J.Marshall, Hockley Heath, Warwicks, after 6/1968 by 6/1969
(13) tdt: Menai Bridge Rebuilding Contract (see PR/7), /1971 (by 9/1971)
(14) tdt: John S.Allen & Sons Ltd, dealers, London SW19, c4/1973
      wlw: exported to Singapore 6/1973

PLAS MAWR PRIVATE RAILWAY, PENMAENMAWR   P32
(Gc/GR:712762)

9/1905 -   1921   : Mr C.S.Darbishire

Railway, laid c1905 in the gardens of this house, was c200 yards long in simple "end-to-end" layout. Although operated purely for pleasure, it was recorded on the larger scale OS maps. Dismantled 1921 when Mr Darbishire moved to Trefor.

Locomotive: Gauge 2'0"

| | REDSTONE | 2-2-0VBT VC | Redstone | * | 1905 | New 9/05 | (1) |

*   constructed at the engineering workshops of Darbishires' Quarry at Penmaenmawr by
     Mr Redstone; design loosely based on the 3ft gauge DeWinton locos at that quarry -
     but only one axle driven, and the basic dimensions reduced approximately 2:3.

(1) tdt: Trefor Granite Quarry, with Mr Darbishire, c1921

PLAS POWER COLLIERY, SOUTHSEA, BROUGHTON   P34
(Cd/GR:299519)

3/1874 -		: Fitzhugh lease to **Plas Power Coal Co**: (J.W.Dean, H.Robertson, A.T.A.Sherriff, T.E.Jones)
9/1875 -		: sinking by (unknown) contractor
	c9/1877	: first winning
-	1880	: **Plas Power Coal Co**
1/1881 -	1938	: **Broughton & Plas Power Coal Co Ltd** (reg.1/1/1881 £200K)
	from 1936	: subsidiary of Lancashire Steel Corporation Ltd
	7/1938	: closed

, large colliery with extensive sidings connected to PR/21 and PR/47. The latter WM&CQJRly) line was, from 8/1882 to 12/1887, used and operated almost exclusively by initially Gatewen and later additionally Plas Power Collieries, both in the same ownership. By 1985 the colliery site was mostly derelict apart from some light industry on the site.

Read: B/107]

Locomotives: Gauge 4'8½"

Locomotives were used here, but due to frequent interchange with Gatewen Colliery it is not possible to prepare a list from the fragments of information available. The locos are therefore listed together in the GATEWEN COLLIERY entry.

"The Broughton & Plas Power Colliery Company's engine is, by arrangement, allowed to work over the G.W. Main lines between Broughton Forge and Broughton Level Crossing Signal Boxes and between Broughton Solvay Coke Works Inlet Siding and Plas Power Colliery, under the block telegraph regulations." [GWR Chester Division Appendix to Working Timetable 1/1/1935 page 154.]

POINT OF AYR COLLIERY, TALACRE   P36
(Cf/GR:127837)

	1865	: **Lord Mostyn** (first trial drillings)
	1866	: **Prestatyn Coal Co** [little or no work done]
6/1873 -	1876+	: **West Mostyn Coal & Iron Co Ltd** [G.Batters et al] [still sinking in 1876 but later abandoned]
1885 -	12/1946	: **Point of Ayr Collieries Ltd** [Batters et al] (reg.5/2/1885 £50K)
1/1947 -	4/1986	: **National Coal Board**
4/1986 -		: **British Coal Corporation**

From 1885 to 1907 (at least) the landsale output from this colliery was taken by 2'0" gauge railway to a yard (GR:123829) beside the main road near Tanlan. This railway, which ran along what is today [1992] the access road to the colliery, was constructed in 1885 at the same time that a shipping quay was constructed alongside the colliery J/CDH/7.11.1885/5c6]. Of related interest: opposite Tanlan Yard, a self-acting incline railway, built after 1870 and dismantled by 1910, ran up the hillside to Picton Yard. Some say it was used to lower coal from small pits near Picton, though a local resident claimed 3/1948) that it was used to carry lime, from a quarry near Glan-yr-Afon. And the 1851

Tithe Map shows another old line, marked as "Crockford's Tramway", commencing ne Tanlan and, roughly following a course parallel to the (later) colliery railway, runni northwards to a riverside wharf.

In 1907 a new 2'0" gauge, double-track cable-operated, railway was built westwards fro the colliery to a transfer dock beside newly-installed sidings off the LNWR (PR/7). Th colliery had its own 4'8½" gauge loco working at these sidings - possibly from 1907.

Between 1950 and 1953 this 2'0" gauge line was replaced by new 4'8½" gauge sidings la direct into the colliery. MGR ("Merry Go Round") haulage of trains was introduced in 198 worked by British Rail locos.

Locomotives: Gauge 2'0" - Railway to Tanlan

BATTERS	0-4-0tk		WB	434	1885 (a)	(1)

Locomotives: Gauge 4'8½"

In 12/1907, W.G.Bagnall of Stafford supplied spares to Point of Ayr Collieries Ltd for "loc 648". The identity of this loco is not yet known - WB 648 is not shown as a railway loco i the WB product numbering series. See also comments in footnote (a).
Obviously, however, the date (12/1907) does coincide with the introduction of 4'8½" gaug sidings at Point of Ayr.

[?	MERMAID	0-4-0ST	OC	MW	1380	1898	(b)	(2)]
		4wPM	45hp	MR	4623	1932	New 5/32	(3)
		4wDM	88hp	RH	326068	1953	New 2/53	(4)
63.000.328		0-6-0DM	325hp	HE	6664	1969	(c)	(5)
63.000.370		0-6-0DM	400hp	HE	7040	1971	(d)	(6)
		4wDH	230hp	S	10097	1962	(e)	(7)

Locomotives: Gauge 2'0" - Underground. Loco roadways first built 1955.

-	0-4-0DM	75hp	RH	379096	1955	New	s/s by 9/67
-	0-4-0DM	75hp	RH	379097	1955	New	s/s by 9/67
-	0-4-0DM	75hp	RH	379099	1955	New	s/s by 9/67
-	0-4-0DM	75hp	RH	427857	1959	New	s/s by 9/67
1	4wDM	48hp	RH	481551	1962	(f)	
9	4wDM	48hp	RH	497762	1963	(g)	
11	4wDM	48hp	RH	504628	1963	(h)	(8)
15	4wDM	48hp	RH	506914	1964	(i)	
8	4wDM	48hp	RH	497761	1963	(j)	(9)
13	4wDM	48hp	RH	506495	1964	(k)	
5	4wDM	48hp	RH	497549	1963	(m)	(10)
3	4wDM	48hp	RH	481553	1962	(n)	
2	4wDM	48hp	RH	481552	1962	(o)	(11)
6	4wDM	48hp	RH	497758	1963	(p)	(12)
7	4wDM	48hp	RH	497759	1963	(q)	
14	4wDM	48hp	RH	506496	1964	(r)	
-	4wDM	48hp	RH	203032	1942	(s)	(13)
-	4wDM	48hp	RH	200803	1941	(s)	(13)

0-4-0DM	66hp	HE	7374	1973 New
0-4-0DM	66hp	HE	7375	1973 New
0-4-0DM	66hp	HE	7376	1973 New
0-4-0DM	66hp	HE	7379	1974 New
4wDM	48hp	RH	497547	1963 (t)

NOTE: The DIRECT RETURN TRANSFER of any loco TO AND FROM NCB/BCC Area Workshops, being a common occurrence for routine overhauls, is not recorded in this list. Visits to Area Workshops are noted when a transfer of the loco to/from another colliery also took place.

(a) the history of this loco is unclear. Per WB records WB 434 ordered by "J.H.Riddell" 3/1882, but not despatched by WB until 9/1885.
Perhaps it had become one of the three 5" cylinder locos for sale by WB [J/CG] 8/5/1885. It could be the "new 4 wheel tank loco 5" cylinders 2'0" gauge" for sale [in J/TE, J/MM] 3/1892-2/1893 by John H.Riddel, dealer, Glasgow.
Point of Ayr Colliery ordered spare parts for [what WB recorded as] 434 BATTERS 12/9/1894, and again ordered spares 17/2/1900 but for an unspecified loco [though presumed to be 434].
[And it is possible that the spares supplied by WB for loco 648 in 12/1907 were for this loco. In 1892-93 Riddel applied reference numbers to his goods for sale (J/MM/5.1892 has eg. locos refenced 564, 581, 613)].
(b) this loco not confirmed at Point of Ayr.
wfw: Monks Ferry Wharf, Birkenhead, Cheshire until 1/1929 at least.
(c) tdx: Bersham Colliery 4/3/1980
(d) tdx: Walkden Workshops 7/1981
wfw: Hem Heath Colliery, Staffordshire
(e) tdx: William Pit Shed, Whitehaven, Cumberland, c1982
(f) delivered New here.
tdt: Llay Main Workshops 29/5/1964; wlw: Llay Main Colliery
tdx: Llay Main Workshops 28/1/1966
(g) tdx: Llay Main Workshops (New loco) 20/11/1963
tdt: Llay Main Workshops 22/12/1964; wlw: Gresford Colliery
tdx: Walkden Workshops 9/1972
(h) tdx: Llay Main Workshops (New loco) 16/12/1963
(i) tdx: Llay Main Workshops (New loco) 27/8/1964
(j) tdx: Llay Main Workshops 1/12/1964
wfw: Gresford Colliery
(k) tdx: Llay Main Workshops 16/9/1965
tdt: Walkden Workshops c1972; wlw: Cronton Colliery, Lancashire.
tdx: Walkden Workshops 12/1975
(m) tdx: Llay Main Workshops 26/4/1966
wfw: Llay Main Colliery
(n) tdx: Walkden Workshops 12/1966; wfw: Gresford Colliery
(o) tdx: Gresford Colliery, after 11/1967 by 1973
(p) tdx: Walkden Workshops c1969; wfw: Llay Main Colliery
(q) tdx: Walkden Workshops 7/1972; wfw: Parsonage Colliery, Lancs
wfw: Llay Main Colliery
(r) tdx: Gresford Colliery [c1973 ?]

(s) Air Ministry locos purchased by EEV(RH) from J.G.Ashurst & Co Ltd, dealers, Newton le-Willows, Lancs; and overhauled for sale to NCB; delivered to Point of Ayr c1973 but not put to work.
(t) tdx: Bersham Colliery, after 2/1984 by 4/1986

(1) presumably made redundant in 1907 by the new cable-operated line. No further trace However, Bagnall records suggest that loco 434 was called MENDIP with Riddel, prior to becoming BATTERS; though it is difficult to tell whether or not the name MENDIP has been added to the records at a later date. Thus the name MENDIP has led to the suggestion that 434 was the (as-yet unidentified) WB loco of similar type that worked for Somerset Mineral Syndicate Ltd; who ordered spares for unspecified "2 ft gauge loco has been used for tunnel work in quarry" on 30/9/1907. [Note this is prior to the 12/1907 spares order for Point of Ayr loco "648"; though this may be quite irrelevant !]
(2) if ever here, then probably disposed of c1932 when MR 4623 came. No further trace.
(3) tdt: Llay Hall Colliery, after 7/1953 by 6/1954
(4) tdt: Bersham Colliery 3/1980
(5) tdt: Marple & Gillott Ltd, Sheffield, 21/3/1985, and scrapped 4/1985
(6) tdt: Marple & Gillott Ltd, Sheffield, 13/3/1985, and scrapped 4/1985
(7) tdt: Sutton Manor Colliery, Lancashire, 9/6/1982
(8) tdt: Llay Main Workshops 16/9/1965
    wlw: Gresford Colliery
(9) tdt: Walkden Workshops c1977
    wlw: Hem Heath Colliery, Staffordshire
(10) tdt: Gresford Colliery 30/4/1966
(11) tdt: Walkden Workshops c1973
    wlw: Gresford Colliery
(12) tdt: Walkden Workshops 8/1972
    wlw: Hem Heath Colliery, Staffordshire
(13) tdt: Walkden Workshops c1973
    wlw: Cronton Colliery, Lancashire, by 7/1973

QUEENSFERRY CHEMICAL & TAR WORKS　　　　　　　　　　　　Q2
(Cf/GR:324683)

[in 1862	: Queensferry Alkali Co - on this site ?]
by 12/1871	: Joseph Turner
10/1884 -	: Joseph Turner & Co Ltd (reg.21/10/1884 £30K)
after 1921 by 1935	: Midland Tar Distillers Ltd (reg.1923)

Works connected to Dundas Sidings of PR/7 by short branch line operated by locomotives listed below. The loco shed was located mid-way along this branch.
In 1862-63 the LNWR laid in a connection to "Queensferry Alkali Co" which was apparently this same site. Joseph Turner did take over an existing "chemical works" here [J/MJ/2.12.1871]
Rail traffic ceased c1962; track in works lifted c1965 but branch to PR/7 not removed until after 3/1968.

Locomotives: Gauge 4'8½"

TARTAR		0-4-0ST	OC	AE	1407	1899	New 11/99 (*)	(1)
		0-4-0ST	OC	P	1649	1924	(a)	(2)
JOSIAH HARDMAN LTD		0-4-0ST	OC	YE	1011	1908		
			rebuilt	WB		1934	(b)	Scr/1955
-		4wPM	40hp	MR	2025	1920	(c)	Scr c8/1965

* supplied per Ratcliffe & Sons, Hawarden [see Section 1]

(a) tdx: Bettisfield Colliery, Bagillt, 11/4/1934
　　　　per Thos.W.Ward Ltd, dealers, loan.
(b) tdx: Chesterton Tar Works, Staffs, after 1934 by 25/8/1942.
(c) tdx: Oldbury Tar Works, Staffs; c12/1949; after 29/11/1949 by 8/1950

(1) tdt: War Department, 1941 - [possibly Queensferry Depot]
　　wlw: GWR, Stafford Road Works, Wolverhampton (for repair) 11/1941
　　wlw: Queensferry Government Depot
(2) tdt: Thos.W.Ward Ltd, Charlton Works, Sheffield, off loan, after 22/5/1934 by 6/1934.
　　wlw: Fison, Packard & Prentice Ltd (of Ipswich), 5/1935

QUEENSFERRY GOVERNMENT FACTORY ESTATE　　　　　　　　Q4
(Cf/GR:324682-335675)

An Engineering or Boiler Works (both descriptions have been used) was established in 1900 by Willans & Robinson Ltd at Queensferry, occupying land (centred on GR:328680) between the LNWR (PR/7) and the (canalised) River Dee. The Company already had a Works at Rugby and soon abandoned Queensferry; offered for sale 1907 [J/GH/20/4/1907]; closed in 1908, there were auctions of the premises on 15/7/1908, 16/9/1908 and 3/11/1908 but no buyer was found. By 10/1909 the contents had been sold, though the Company was still in ownership of the empty buildings to 10/1911 at least. In 1915 the premises were taken by the Government, firstly as a Prisoner of War depot but then as the nucleus of an explosives factory, which soon occupied all the land, between PR/7 and the River, eastwards to Sandycroft Station.

After 1919, sections of the Estate were taken over by various Companies for civilian trade, though the Government retained part of the land as a Central Stores Depot - CSD 473 - until 1931 when this too was put up for sale. By 1939 much of the area was disused, and again the Government took possession of the land for military purposes. After WW2 this use declined, until by the mid-1950s only a small store depot - 81 CESD - remained, at the Sandycroft end of the Estate. From c1960 shunting at this store depot was performed by the Wagon Repair Works loco, until 10/1967 when an Army road tractor took over. Rail traffic subsequently ceased the final rails being lifted c1975. The original Willans & Robinson area at the western end became occupied by a number of small businesses not using rail transport.

ENGINEERING WORKS: 1900-c1911 **Willans & Robinson Ltd**

Locomotives: Gauge 1'6"

In 1901, W.G.Bagnall of Stafford supplied on hire "to Willans & Robinson" (no destination recorded) an "18 inch gauge loco of usual contractors type". And in 8/1901 Bagnall hired to Willans & Robinson some 18 inch gauge wagons. As these wagons were despatched to Queensferry, it seems likely the loco was too.
No further details.

Locomotives: Gauge 4'8½"

	NICLAUSSE	0-4-0ST	OC	P	882	1901	New 12/01	(E1)

(E1) for sale here in 11/1908 auction [J/GH/10.10.1908]; sold then or by 10/1909.
    wlw: Steel, Peach & Tozer Ltd, Rotherham, Yorks WR

GOVERNMENT WORKS CONSTRUCTION 1915-1917

Locomotives: Gauge 4'8½" - WILSON LOVATT & SONS LTD, contractors

2	(f. No.5 (*))	0-6-0ST	IC	HE	152	1876	(La)	(L1)
18	WIGSTON	0-6-0ST	IC	HE	719	1900	(Lb)	(L2)
	DEVONSHIRE	0-6-0ST	IC	MW	996	1886	(Lc)	(L3)
	CATHERALL	0-6-0ST	IC	MW	1560	1902	(Ld)	(L3)
7	WINDSOR	0-4-0ST	OC	MW	993	1887	(Lc)	(L4)
	[NIPPER	0-4-0ST		MW			(Le)	]
	[TERRIER	0-4-0ST		MW			(Le)	]
	[HAXEY	0-6-0ST	IC	MW	1507	1901	(Lf)	]

(*) loco was numbered 2 by 1/1916.

La) here by 23/11/1915, "No.5".
     wfw: Henry Lovatt Ltd, GWR Avonmouth-Filton (1907-1910) Contract.
Lb) wfw: Lovatt, GWR Ealing-Shepherds Bush (c1912-1917) Contract until 22/7/1913 at least.
Lc) wfw: Lovatt, MSLR East Leake-Aylestone (1894-1898) Contract
Ld) with Lovatt since c1906 but no location known before Queensferry.
     wfw: Mitchell Bros, contractors, GSWR Dumfries-Moniaive (1901-1905) Contract.
Le) locos recalled here by old employees, but not traced or proven.
Lf) this loco indeed owned by Lovatt at this time, but report that it was here has not been proven.

L1) here until 6/1916 at least.
     wlw: Wilson Lovatt & Sons Ltd, Wolverhampton Depot, by 3/12/1917; and
          at Bromborough (Cheshire) Margarine Factory Contract by 6/1919
L2) tdt: Holland & Hannen and Cubitts Ltd (this site - below) by 6/1916
L3) tdt: Ministry of Munitions (this site - below).
L4) tdt: ?; spares for this loco were supplied to unknown customer until 1/1925 (at least).
          A pencil note in the MW records reads "Thomas Miller, Son & Clarke" but no such firm has yet been traced.

Locomotives: Gauge 4'8½" - HOLLAND & HANNEN AND CUBITTS LTD, contractors

| 18 | | 0-6-0ST | IC | HE | 719 | 1900 | (Ha) | (H1) |

Ha) tdx: Wilson Lovatt & Sons Ltd (this site) by 24/1/1916.

H1) tdt: Ministry of Munitions (this site - below) by 8/8/1918.

GOVERNMENT WORKS OPERATION & STORES - Ministry of Munitions CSD 473 Store Depot

A large number of surplus locomotives, mostly of "main line" type, were stored 1919-1920 in the "Dundas Sidings" adjacent to this site.
These are not included in the list below.

Locomotives: Gauge 4'8½"

H.M.FACTORY No.1	0-4-0ST	OC	MW	1888	1915	New 10/15	(M1)
2	0-6-0ST	IC	MW	996	1886	(Ma)	(M2)
H.M.FACTORY No.3	0-4-0F	OC	AB	1434	1916	New 2/16	(M3)
H.M.FACTORY No.4	0-4-0F	OC	AB	1435	1916	New 2/16	(M4)
H.M.FACTORY No.5	0-4-0F	OC	AB	1437	1916	New 4/16	(M5)
H.M.FACTORY No.6	0-4-0F	OC	AB	1438	1916	(Mb)	(M6)
7	0-6-0ST	IC	HE	719	1900	(Mc)	(M7)
H.M.FACTORY No.10	0-4-0F	OC	AB	1572	1918	New 1/18	(M8)
	0-6-0ST	IC	MW	1560	1902	(Ma)	(M9)
DUDDON	0-4-0ST	OC	HL	3261	1917	(Md)	(M10)
	0-4-0ST		MW				(M11)

(Ma) tdx: Wilson Lovatt & Sons Ltd (this site).
(Mb) tdx: Asiatic Petroleum Depot (this site - below), 6/1918.
(Mc) tdx: Holland & Hannen and Cubitts Ltd (this site), by 8/8/1918.
(Md) wfw: Ministry of Munitions, NFF13, Morecambe, Lancs, until 1/1923 at least.

(M1) for sale here 9/1919.
       wlw: Mersey Power Company, Runcorn, Cheshire, by 8/1928.
(M2) wlw: Shanks & McEwan Ltd, contractors, Mossend, Lanarks, in 1920s.
(M3) for sale here 9/1922.
       wlw: John Dickinson & Co Ltd, Croxley Green, Herts, by 2/1924.
(M4) wlw(tdt?): Carr & Co Ltd, Carlisle, who purchased it in 1924.
(M5) for sale here 9/1922.
       wlw: Shell Chemicals Ltd, Stanlow, Cheshire.
(M6) tdt: Power Station (this site - below) [on date unknown].
(M7) for sale in a Cohen, dealers, catalogue 9/1924.
       wlw: Shanks & McEwan, contractors, by 2/1926 - and at their Shieldhall Dock (1924-
       1931) Contract, Glasgow, by 8/1926.
(M8) tdt: Planters Margarine Co Ltd, Bromborough, Cheshire, by 3/1920.
(M9) for sale here by Cohen & Armstrong Disposal & Liquidating Committee in 9/1926.
       tdt: Sir Robert McAlpine & Sons Ltd, contractors, No.53, 10/1926.
(M10) sold 20/4/1927 to George Cohen, Sons & Co Ltd, dealers, and
       tdt: Shire Oaks Colliery Co, Notts, 14/5/1927.
(M11) for sale here 9/1925; no further trace. [Was possibly MW 1888 listed above ?]

Locomotives: Gauge 2'0"

An unknown number of 4wBE locos by Brush (BE) were used here.
The two locos of this type (BE engine numbers 16303 and 16306 built c1917) later used at Manod Slate Quarry almost certainly originated at a sale at this depot.

One battery loco was included in an auction here 31/3/1925.

On 8/6/1925 Fuller Horsey auctioned items from various depots including Queensferry; the sale included 2'0" gauge Edison electric trolley locos. These were, in fact, self-propelled flat wagons of about 5hp. The Votty & Bowydd Slate Quarry purchased one such vehicle from Fuller Horsey in 6/1925, and this could suggest that Queensferry was the source.

Of related interest, J/Surplus/12.1921 offered 222 "Bisulphate trucks" of 2'6" gauge built by Kerr Stuart, for sale at this Depot. These may have been brought here from elsewhere for sale, or they may have originated here. "Surplus" contained many typographical errors, and the gauge could be an error for 2'0".

PETROLEUM DEPOT - Asiatic Petroleum Co Ltd

Company registered 29/6/1903 to market petrol from Russia and the Dutch East Indies.
The Depot, at the Sandycroft end of the Estate, was constructed c1915 and remained (nominally ?) independent until absorbed into the MoM plant 6/1918.
The MoM provided Asiatic Petroleum with a loco as follows.

Locomotive: Gauge 4'8½"

                                0-4-0F   OC   AB   1438   1916 (Aa)   (A1)

(Aa) New 4/1916, per Ministry of Munitions.

(A1) absorbed into Government Works fleet (see above) 6/1918.

ELECTRICITY GENERATING STATION - GR:327682

The Government Works included a coal-fired generating plant, subsequently operated for civilian supply.

    c1919 - 3/1948 : City of Chester Electric Power Company
    4/1948 - 3/1955 : British Electricity Authority
    4/1955 -   : Central Electricity Authority
                   1955 : closed

Locomotive: Gauge 4'8½"

        -                 0-4-0F   OC   AB   1438   1916 (Pa)   (P1)

(Pa) tdx: Government Works (see above).

(P1) disused by 5/1955; stored on site.
        tdt: Clarence Dock Power Station, Liverpool, 1957

SMOKELESS FUEL PLANT - Stellite Ltd

Locomotive: Gauge 4'8½"

        SHEPPERTON   0-6-0ST   OC   P   1616   1923 (Sa)   (S1)

(Sa) tdx: Willys Overland Crossley Ltd, Heaton Chapel, Stockport, Cheshire, after 4/1934
        by 12/1/1935.

(S1) departed after 25/2/1938; advertised for sale by George Cohen, Sons & Co Ltd, dealers, 1938.
        wlw(tdt?): Tyne Improvement Commissioners, Percy Main, North Shields, Northumberland, by 6/4/1939.

WAGON REPAIR WORKS -   GR:326660

    by 1942 - 10/1955 : North Wales Wagon Co Ltd
    10/1955 -   : Central Wagon Co Ltd
    by 10/1967   : Central Wagon (Engineering)) Ltd
                 10/1967 : closed

Apparently shunted by Power Station loco until 2/1953 when own loco obtained; this was initially kept in Power Station shed but later stabled in the Wagon Works. The North Wales Wagon Co Ltd is in a list of Companies who cut up ex-BR locos, but this may have been at their Llanymynech (Salop) Depot.

Locomotive: Gauge 4'8½"

-		4wDM	48hp	RH	349032	1953 New 2/53	(W1)

(W1) tdt: Thompson & Co (Ince) Ltd, Lower Ince, Lancashire, 10/1967.

OTHER MAJOR COMPANIES who took premises on the Estate include:

Electrical Metallurgical Co Ltd, who took over the acid section in 1919 to produce lead, silver and acids from spelter, but do not appear to have survived long. No railway use or locos known.

Scientific Roads Ltd; road surfacing contractors who remained during WW2 and up to the 1970s. Their premises were adjacent to the WD loco shed, which led to some incorrect reports concerning this Company having locomotives.

GOVERNMENT STORE DEPOT - No.81 CESD   c1941-c1975
   Ministry of Defence   - War Department
                         - Army Department.

Locomotives: Gauge 4'8½"

No.	Name	Type	hp	Builder	Works No.	Date	Notes	Ref
236		0-6-0ST	IC	HC	845	1909	(Ga)	(G1)
70202	(f. 202 TARTAR)	0-4-0ST	OC	AE	1407	1899	(Gb)	(G2)
59	AUSSIE	0-6-0ST	IC	HE	1705	1937	(Gc) Ø	(G3)
44		0-4-0DM	153hp	AB	359	1941	(Gd)	(G4)
45		0-4-0DM	153hp	AB	360	1941	(Ge)	(G5)
4584	DOUGLAS	0-4-0ST	OC	P	820	1900	(Gf)	(G6)
75153		0-6-0ST	IC	WB	2741	1944	(Gg)	(G7)
75179		0-6-0ST	IC	WB	2767	1945 New 2/45	(G8)
808	(72215 to /52)	4wDM	48hp	RH	224347	1945	(Gh)	(G9)
850	(75520 to /52)	0-4-0DM	153hp	HE	2068	1940	(Gi)	(G10)
852	(70028 to /52)	0-4-0DM	150hp	JF	22889	1939		
		rebuilt		JF		1949	(Gj)	(G11)
839		0-4-0DM	150hp	VF	* 5266	1945	(Gk)	(G12)

* loco has dual identity - is also DC 2185/1945.
Ø doubt exists as to whether AUSSIE was Government Depot stock, or working here for owners Sir Lindsay Parkinson Ltd, contractors - or even on hire to WD from SLP. AUSSIE visited Queensferry at least twice - see footnotes.

[ANZAC   0-6-0ST IC HE   1856 1937 property of SLP
   is also reputed to have been here c1944 but this is not proven.]

(Ga) arrived [c1940 ?] - after 1937 before 7/1941.
     wfw: South Wales Coalite Ltd, Wern Tarw.

Gb) [? tdx: Queensferry Tar Works /1941]
was at GWR Wolverhampton Stafford Road Works for repair 11/1941;
thence tdt: WD, Kinnerley, Salop, 2/1942;
later to Eastleigh SR Works - then [again ?] at Queensferry:-
tdx: Eastleigh S.Rly. Works, Hampshire, 2/1943
Gc) apparently here by 8/1941 - certainly here 25/8/1942 - though see note 'Ø' above.
wfw: ROF Chorley construction Contract, Lancs, in 6/1940 at least.
Later in 1942 (or early 1943) apparently at U.S.A. Munitions Depot Contract, Moreton-on Lugg, Oxon
Seen 13/3/1943 travelling through Birmingham en route back to Queensferry, where it had arrived by 20/3/1943
Gd) tdx: WD, Kinnerley, Salop, 1942 by 25/8/1942.
Ge) tdx: WD, Kinnerley, Salop, after 8/1942 by 7/1943.
Gf) tdx: WD, RE Workshops, Bramley, Hants, 1944 after 19/6/1944.
wfw: James Pain Ltd, Glendon East Quarries, Kettering, Northants.
Gg) tdx: WD, Bramley, Hants, c1945 by 4/1945
Gh) tdx: WD, Kinnerley, Salop, after 3/1945 by 12/1945
Gi) here in 1947.
wfw: WD, Corsham, Wilts, in 2/1946.
Gj) tdx: JF 2/1950 (despatched from Leeds 22/2/1950).
Gk) tdx: WD, Moreton-on-Lugg, Herefords, after 10/1955 by 6/1956.

G1) wlw: WD, Shoeburyness, Essex, by 7/1941.
G2) wlw: WD, Dillichip, Dunbartonshire, by 1946.
G3) still here 8/1943.
wlw: Sir Lindsay Parkinson, contractor, Abercynon Plant Depot [by 12/1943 ?].
wlw: Powell Duffryn Ltd, Phoenix Works, Port Talbot, by 6/1946
G4) tdt: WD, Longmoor, Hants, 12/1943.
G6) wlw: WD, Weedon, Northants, in 1947.
G7) tdt: LNER, 8019, 8/1946.
G8) tdt: WD, Long Marston, Warwicks, after 5/1949 by 4/1951.
G9) tdt: WD, Bicester, Oxon, after 10/1955 by 6/1956.
G10) gone away by 6/1953.
wlw: Mays By Products, Bourne, Lincs.
G11) tdt: WD, Kinnerley, Salop, 8/1951.
tdx: ? [Kinnerley ?] by 9/1952.
tdt: WD, Bicester, Oxon, 30/7/1957.
G12) tdt: WD, Honeybourne, Worcs, 17/7/1957

QUEENSFERRY LEISURE CENTRE   Q6
(Cf/GR:315684)
: Alyn & Deeside District Council

Locomotive: Gauge 4'8½" - On Static Display

41		0-4-0DM 107hpHC	D1020	1956	(a)	OOU

a) wfw: Shotton Steelworks - loco first placed at Steelworks Sports Ground close to Shotton (PR/7) station; and moved to Leisure Centre in 1986

QUEENSFERRY SHIPBUILDING & ENGINEERING YARD Q8
(Cf/GR:323685)

by 1914 : **Isaac J.Abdela & Mitchell Ltd** (reg.4/1901 £10K)
[office: Manchester]

Shipyard was connected by a short private branch line to the Dundas Sidings of LNWR (PR/7); branch was also a connection to the Aston Hall Colliery Railway. The site was ultimately lost beneath the A494 Queensferry By-Pass road.

Locomotives: Gauge 4'8½"

0-6-0ST	IC	HE	457	1888	(a)	(1)

(a) obtained by 7/1926, perhaps from Cohen & Armstrong Disposal Corporation (selling on behalf of the War Department) c3/1925.
HE 457 may have been WD MCR (Military Camp Railways) number 82 or 89 which were for sale 1922 at Tuxford Engine Sheds, GER Dukeries Station [J/Surplus/1.5-1.7.1922].
Originally T.A.Walker, contractor, Manchester Ship Canal Contract.

(1) Nothing yet known to prove this loco worked at Queensferry (though there was sufficient track to suggest a loco would be useful).
It may have only been repaired here. Apparently this loco was for sale by Capt.R.G.Davison, dealer, Ellesmere Port, Cheshire, 9/1926 (though he probably did not own it). No further trace.

RHIW MANGANESE MINES R2
(Gc/GR:below)

BENALLT MINE (GR:222282 etc)
by 1881 - 1895 : **Benallt Mining Co** (Isaac Roberts & Owen Williams)
    1895 - 1904 : closed
    1904 - 1925 : **North Wales Iron & Manganese Co Ltd**
                                 (reg.8/8/1903 £55K liq.27/8/1925)
    1925 - 1939 : closed
    1939 - 1941 : **Prys & Co**
    1941 - 12/1945 : **Ministry of Supply**
           31/12/1945 : closed; dismantled.

RHIW MINE (GR:223283 etc)
              1886 : opened
    1886 - 1893 : small scale activity, various lessees, intermittent working.
    1903 - 8/1906 : **British Manganese Co Ltd**
                               (reg.15/7/1903 £130K liq.4/8/1906)

```
   4/1907  -    5/1913    : British Manganese Co Ltd
                            (reg.24/4/1907  £10K  liq.17/12/1918)
                 1911     : closed
   c1916  -    c1920      : Rhiw Manganese Mines Ltd
        from 12/1919      : subsid.of Hudson Consolidated
              by 1/1921   : closed
   1941  -    12/1945     : Ministry of Supply
            31/12/1945    : closed; dismantled.
```

NANT (TYNLLAN) MINE, LLANFAELRHYS (GR:209266)

```
   in 1894                : Tynllan Manganese Co
   1902  -    c1903       : Frederick Hall
   1904  -    1925        : as for Benallt Mine; then closed.
```

TYDDYN MEIRION MINE (GR:223277)

```
              1906        : opened; H.J.Wright [of Llanbedr]
       -      1920        : intermittent operation, various lessees
   c1916  -  c1920        : as for Rhiw Mine
   1941  -   12/1945      : as for Benallt Mine; then closed.
```

TY CANOL MINE (GR:221278)

```
              1907        : opened; H.J.Wright [of Llanbedr]
       -      1920        : intermittent operation, various lessees
   c1916  -  c1920        : as for Rhiw Mine
   1941  -   12/1945      : as for Benallt Mine; then closed.
```

Read: for explanations of this complicated mining area, where the territory of the adjacent mines is inter-related and confused, see J/NMRS/No.14 and J/CHS/1989; also brief details and map in B/175/260.]

Although there was some opencasting, most of the mining was underground, reached by shafts and adits, with tramroads thus largely out of sght. At Rhiw Mine, a surface incline climbed up to a ropeway terminal; the ropeway, built 1903-04, carried the ore to a pier (GR:238274) at Porth Neigwl (Hell's Mouth Bay). At Nant Mine, 1'8" and later 2'0" gauge lines emerged from adits to reach the nearby Rhiw beach, later Rhiw Pier (GR:208263).

Benallt Mine built a c2 mile 3ft gauge railway overland from the Mine to Rhiw Pier. Construction of this line commenced in 1904, the contractor being I.Phoenix of Crewe - it is not known whether he employed any locos on the job, which he did not complete; the work being finished by Benallt Mine direct labour.

From a drumhead (GR:221283) a double-track gravity incline fell, via a level crossing (GR:219282) to Bodwyddog (GR:215279); thence by locomotive operated roadside route to inclines dropping direct to pier. Most of this route is visible today (1989), including rails at level crossing on incline, some remains of all inclines and of loco shed at Pier end of route. From c1914, mining was largely concentrated at Nant Mine, and the railway was little used after this date. The track was apparently removed c1920.

During the WW2 Ministry of Supply activity, all surface transport was by road, but doubtless rail vehicles would be used then below ground.

Locomotives: Gauge 3'0"

	JEANNIE	0-4-0T(WT?)					(a)	s/s
	RHIW	0-4-0ST	OC	WB	1820	1907	New (b)	(1

(a) tdx ? [reputed Thos W.Ward Ltd, dealers, Liverpool] c1905
(b) ordered 9/4/1907 by H.B.Smith, Mersey Chambers, Liverpool, "loco to be name RHIW". The Registered Office of NWI&M Co Ltd was in Liverpool.

(1) final spare parts order by NWI&M Co Ltd (c/o Pwllheli Station) was in 1/1921. N further trace. Loco reputed to have been scrapped "by T.Williams of Llanbedr c1922 T.O.Williams, father of W.O.Williams, dealer, Harlech (see Section 1), lived at Llanbe in the 1920s - he was manager of Llanfair Slate Quarry, Harlech, in 9/1927.

RHIWBACH SLATE QUARRY, RHIWBACH R4
near FFESTINIOG
(Gc/GR:743462)

```
        1812   -    1852   : various lessees
   by 12/1852               : Rhiw Bach Slate Quarries Co
   by   1855   -    2/1856 : Cambrian Slate Quarrying Co
        2/1856 -    7/1858 : Manchester & Ffestiniog Slate & Slab Co Ltd
        7/1858 -    1877   : Ffestiniog Slate Quarry Co Ltd (reg.    £100K)
        1877   -    1890   : Festiniog Slate Co Ltd  (reg.24/4/1877)
   by   1906   -    1913   : H.Humphris - t/a "Rhiwbach Slate Quarry Owners"
        1913   -    1920   :  closed
        1920   -    1928   : Festiniog Slate Quarries Co Ltd
        1928   -    1975   : owned by Maen Offeren Slate Quarry Co Ltd BUT:-
    in 1931                :     t/a Rhiwbach Slate Quarry Co
               -    1953   :     t/a Rhiwbach Quarries Ltd
                    1953   :  closed; machinery and railways later removed.
        1975   -           : Owners of Llechwedd Slate Quarry (not worked).
```

An extensive quarry and mine in a remote location, having its own village and school. From the mine, a drainage tunnel containing a railway ran east to the third level of the Penmachno Quarry, but the outlet from Rhiwbach Mill was up an incline to the terminus of the "Rhiwbach Tramway" (PR/13). Construction of this railway was proposed in the prospectus of the 1858 Company [J/MJ/19.11.1859/798]. It was owned and operated by the Owners of Rhiwbach Quarry, and served other quarries en route.

An auction of the "Rhiw Bach Slate Quarry" 6/7/1894 included "3½ miles of railway" [J/GH/2.6.1894]. It is likely that the first two locomotives listed below were obtained to operate PR/13. The duties of the third loco are unknown.

[Read: B/182; B/169/460; B/185/94]

Locomotives: Gauge 2ft

```
                    0-4-0PM  10hp  Bg      731   1918    (a)      Scr/c1937
                    4wPM     20hp  MH            ?1925   (b)           (1)
                    2-2-0PM   7hp  *            [c1935]  New           (2)
```

* apparently constructed at Rhiwbach; an Austin 7 car engine and gearbox mounted on a steel skip-wagon chassis, with chain drive to one axle only.

(a) arrived 4/1921.
    wfw: Air Ministry, Bicester Aerodrome, Oxon.
(b) purchased 12/1925 - possibly New. Apparently one of a batch, made and marketed in the early 1920s by Muir Hill (Engineers) Ltd, consisting of a purpose-made chassis onto which was mounted the engine and gearbox of a standard Fordson farm tractor. These locos pre-dated the "proper" locos built by Muir Hill (from 1926, and from 1931 by their successors E.Boydell & Co) which were allocated works-numbers.
    [A similar early Muir Hill loco is known to have operated on the Cowlyd Railway (see 'Dolgarrog Railways') and which ran trials on the Ffestiniog Railway (PR/3) in 1924; it was available for disposal thereafter, and this circumstantial evidence suggests the possibility that the Rhiwbach loco could have originated at Cowlyd, though no records have been found to support this theory.]

(1) ownership passed to Maenofferen Quarry in 1928 and loco absorbed later into Maenofferen stock.
(2) disused at Rhiwbach Quarry 1953 and remained derelict (originally in boiler house) until:-
    tdt: temporary store at Gloddfa Ganol (Oakeley Quarry) 9/1976
    wlw: Mr J.Crosskey, Surrey Light Railway.

RHOS and MOEL SIABOD SLATE QUARRIES   R6
near CAPEL CURIG
(Gc/GR: below)

MOEL SIABOD QUARRY   (Gc/GR:717555)

```
        1798  -    1857    : small activities
        1861  -            : Trewydir Slate & Slab Co
  by    1873                : Robert Williams
              -    c1885   : Moel Siabod Slate & Slab Works Co
  by    1901                : Owen J.Owen
                   1902    : closed
```

RHOS QUARRY   (Gc/GR:730563)

```
        1861  -            : Samuel Clift [of Manchester]
        1869  -            : Rhos Slate & Slab Quarry Co Ltd
        1872  -    1882    : Capel Curig Slate & Slab Quarry Co Ltd
                             (reg.29/2/1872 liq.1882)
        1883  -    4/1891  : Capel Curig Slate Co Ltd (reg.7/2/1883 £20K liq.1890-91)
        1893  -    1901    : P.& H.Lewis et al [of Conwy]
```

1903 -   1904 : **Frederick Kitchen** [of Trefriw]
1906 -   1951 : **Rhos Slate Quarry Co (Capel Curig) Ltd** [Riley's]
           1951 : closed

A 2ft gauge railway 1½ miles long was built 1862 from a slate mill (GR:734570) near Pont Cyfyng to the Moel Siabod Quarry. From the mill, the railway climbed by three steep self acting inclines and a fourth longer but not so steep incline to reach GR:727563, beyond which the line was horse and gravity operated for c1 mile to the foot of the final incline into Moel Siabod Quarry. The mill at Pont Cyfyng was subsequently abandoned, and the first incline closed. A road transhipment dock was created at the foot of the second (ie, now the first) incline. Approximately half-way up the (original) fourth incline, at GR:730565 connection was made to a short branch line running southwards to Rhos Quarry and, perhaps after closure of Moel Siabod Quarry, a winding-drum was built over the incline at this junction. Thus, 2½ inclines of the original railway remained in use until Rhos Quarry closed. The railways and machinery at Rhos were removed in 1955, the line to Moel Siabod very much earlier. Nevertheless, much is easily traceable today [1990] though Rhos Quarry is on private property, and cannot be visited without permission of Mr Gwilym Jones at Rhos Farm. Such permission is usually readily given.

Rhos Quarry used locomotives on the main (Mill) level [one loco shed intact 1990], and also through the lower adit (entrance marked by stonework of a large waterwheel). The wagons used for product output had, unusually, single-flanged wheels and side dumb-buffers.

[Read: B/177/187; B/290]

Locomotives: Gauge 1'11" - Rhos Quarry

```
              0-4-0VBT VC   DeW                    (a)           (1)
              4wDM  10hp    RH    171902  1934  New 9/34         (2)
              4wPM   8hp    Dtz    49051  c1911   (b)            (3)
```

(a) reputedly arrived c1896, possibly second-hand.
(b) arrived late 1935, reputedly from Nottingham. [Thus possibly is the 8hp Deutz of 1911 from Cafferata & Co Ltd, Barton Gypsum Mines, Notts (which was replaced at Barton by a new RH loco in 1935).]

(1) still here in early 1940s but had been disused for some time.
     Reputedly sold as scrap, but also thought locally to have been buried on site when the shed in which it stood was lost due to land subsidence.
(2) tdt: either "a dealer [? Will Rowlands], Conwy Wharf" [? Conwy Morfa] - or to
           W.O.Williams, dealer, Harlech (who dismantled Rhos Quarry); 1955.
     wlw: Votty & Bowydd Slate Quarry, Blaenau Ffestiniog.
(3) not used after 1941; scrapped 1955 by W.O.Williams whilst he dismantled the quarry.

RHYD-DDU FORESTRY RAILWAY, near BEDDGELERT   R8
(Gc/GR: below)

1914 - c1920 : Thomas Parry & Co, timber merchants [of Mold].

During WW1 the Canadian Forestry Corps were felling timber over an extensive area west of the main (A4085) road between Pitts Head and Beddgelert. A sawmill was established at Rhyd-ddu. The North Wales Narrow Gauge Railway (PR/44) had been partially constructed southwards from Rhyd-ddu and northwards from Beddgelert, but the two sections had not been joined - these incomplete lines, however, were put to use for timber extraction during this period. Both were extended by temporary branch-lines into the forest, the branch lines being worked by horse, gravity and winch power. The only locomotive known to have been used is listed below; this worked for Parry on the route up to Rhyd-ddu Sawmill. The extraction area was later replanted by the Forestry Commission, and it is unlikely that any traces of the temporary branch-lines survive.

Locomotive: Gauge 2ft

    MURIEL   0-4-0VBT VC   DeW   [? c1879] (a)   s/s c1920

(a)   tdx: Glanrafon Slate Quarry c1914

RHYDYMWYN GOVERNMENT DEPOT   R10
ex LEAD MINE and FOUNDRY
(Cf/GR:207665)

PENYFRON (BRYN CELYN WEST) LEAD MINE Tramroad Adit   GR:197663
    by 1796 -   1823   : Richard Ingleby
        1823 -   1845   : John Taylor "Mold Mines" (joint with Rhydymwyn,
                                    Llynypandy, Pantymwyn and Pantybuarth Mines)
        1892 -   1913   : South Halkyn & Rhydymwyn Mining Co Ltd (reg. 5/8/1890)

RHYDYMWYN (BRYN CELYN EAST) LEAD MINE Davey's Shaft   GR:203664
                                   : Bryn Celyn East Mines Co
        1823 -   1913   : (as for Penyfron above).

RHYDYMWYN FOUNDRY; site later **GOVERNMENT STORE DEPOT**
        1837 -   1862   : John Taylor
        1890 -   : South Halkyn & Rhydymwyn Mining Co Ltd
       c1940 -   : Ministry of Supply Explosives Store, operated by
                                   Imperial Chemical Industries (Castner Kellner)
     by 1957   : Ministry of Public Buildings & Works

The Bryn Celyn mineral lode courses east-west a little way south of Rhydymwyn Station, and has been exploited from GR:197663 to GR:209665 by a series of 12 shafts, plus adits. The four shafts to the west formed Penyfron Mine, the easterly shafts being Bryn Celyn East Mine. Work eventually ceased when the ore descended below the level of economic pumping. When the Halkyn Drainage Tunnel reached the area the two mines were re-worked as one and, via a secondary drain tunnel, work extended into the Garreg Boeth lode farther north (near Hendre). During this period, the principal winding shaft was Davey's, from which a self-acting 2ft gauge incline railway descended to the valley and foundry. The route of this incline, with bridge under minor road, can still [1986] be seen.

The foundry, which served many mines in the area, was closed by John Taylor in 1862 when he opened his new Sandycroft Foundry. One of the declared intentions of the South Halkyn (1890) Company, however, was to work the Rhydymwyn Foundry; though whether they did so is not known. Mining ceased in 1913; in 1928 the Company joined Halkyn District United Mines and, when the Sea Level (Milwr) tunnel reached the area, in the 1930s, mining resumed at depth. [See the "Halkyn District Mines Drainage Tunnels" entry for details.]

During WW2 the site of Rhydymwyn Foundry and adjoining land was developed as a munitions store, with sidings installed off PR/37. Explosives were stored in various local mine workings, including the Bryn Celyn lode and the nearby North Hendre area. It has been stated that there were tunnels direct from the foundry area into the upper mine workings, and that diesel locos worked 2ft gauge railways in these tunnels, but this is not confirmed. Deeper chambers were reached along the Milwr Tunnel Railway via Olwyn Goch Shaft at Hendre.

[Read: B/199/19/66,80,143; B/270/17; J/NMRS/OP7/69]

Locomotives: Gauge 4'8½" - Depot sidings; track lifted c1960.

No.5	0-4-0DM 80hp	JF	22906	1940	New 9/40	(1)
No.8	0-4-0ST OC	AB	2095	1940	New 11/40	(2)

Locomotive: Gauge 1'10½" - Milwr Tunnel Railway.

4wDM 20hp	RH	217972	1942	New 11/42	(3)

(1) tdt: Ministry of Supply, Chelford Depot, Cheshire, c6/1960 after 12/4/1960
(2) tdt: I.C.I.Ltd, Wigg Works, Bank Quay, Runcorn, Cheshire, 5/1949
(3) tdt: ? , c1953
   wlw(tdt?): G.W.Bungey Ltd, dealer, Middlesex, by 5/8/1954

RHYL to GRONANT ROAD CONSTRUCTION CONTRACT   R12
(Cf)

1921 -   1923 : **Flintshire County Council** - Direct Labour.

Four miles of road built in two sections, from Glanant to Prestatyn (Bodnant Bridge), and from Prestatyn to Rhyl. 2ft gauge "portable railway" equipment was used throughout the four miles, mostly using horse-haulage; only one locomotive is recorded.

[Read: J/ILS/No.35/228]

Locomotive: Gauge 2'0"

NANCY   0-4-0ST   OC   WB   2079   1918   (a)   (1)

(a) wfw(tdx?): J.Lyons & Co Ltd, Greenford, Middlesex;
    per or via R.H.Mansell, dealer, Slough, Bucks, 3-4/1922

(1) tdt: R.H.Neal & Co Ltd, dealer, Ealing, Middlesex, 1/1924
    wlw: Concrete Aggregates Ltd, Chiswick, by 8/1924

RIVER DEE CANALISATION   R14
and LAND RECLAMATION SCHEMES   (Cf)

The original course of the River Dee is virtually defined by the present England/Wales boundary as between Burton Point and Chester. Since the 1730s, various schemes have created the canalised river channel from Flint to Chester, and much land has been reclaimed. Contracts continued into the 1890s, and doubtless railways were used for many of these works, though few details of these have yet been discovered.
[Read: J/FHS/1967/35]

         1700 -   1707 : **City of Chester**, Act 1700. Little work done.
         1732 -   1737 : **Nathaniel Kinderley & Co**, Act of 1732 created:-
                           The Company of Proprietors of the Undertaking for
                           Recovering and Preserving the Navigation of the River
                           Dee.
       4/1733 - 4/1737 : New 8 mile channel cut - **Kinderley & Co**, contractors.
         1744 -   1889 : **RIVER DEE COMPANY** (Joint Stock Company)

Many Acts obtained to reclaim marsh, mostly on the north side of the new river:-
         1744 : Blacon Embankment (breached, replaced by:-)
         1754 : Blacon New Embankment
         1763 : Sealand Embankment
         1769 : Act - reclaim land near Blacon
         1790 : Act - reclaim land south of Saughall
         1826 : Act - reclaim land west of Saughall
         1833 : Act - reclaim land Sealand South
         1857 : Act - reclaim land Sealand North [later Air Force Depot etc. area]
         1865 -   1866 : Embankment on north side of new river extended 1200 yards
                           seaward from (opposite) Connah's Quay.
                           Brassey, Field & Meakin, contractors.
         1869 -   1877 : Act - 2 mile embankment from opposite Connah's Quay,
                           northward to Burton Point [to reclaim the area later occupied
                           by Shotton Steelworks]. Breached 1877; repairs attempted
                           [? using loco] but work abandoned [later completed by John
                           Summers & Sons].

As constructed (1733-1737) the new river had an embankment on the north side only allowing land on the south (Welsh) side to flood at high tides. Reclamation on this south side was undertaken by a series of individual efforts.

        1778 - 1780 : Saltney Marsh Act. Embankment built Chester to Shotton, and subsequently held by the **Hawarden Embankment Trustees**. (Acts for minor works had previously been obtained by landowners in 1740, 1742 and 1753).
                    1790 : Act - Embankment, Shotton (Wepre)-Connah's Quay.
        1885 - c1887 : Straightening and deepening channel from Chester
                            to the sea, including "huge embankments", one being 4 miles
                            long - **River Dee Co**. [J/BET/10.10.1885]
                            [J/MM/2.1886; J/BWR/6.8.1886 - vast work,
                               rapidly proceeding].
                            Other work seaward of Connah's Quay was done as required by local industrialists - Flint Chemical Works, Mostyn Collieries, Holyhead (PR/7) Railway, etc.
        1889 - 1934 : **Dee Conservancy Board**
        1934 -   : **River Dee Catchment Board**
       by 1967 -   : **Dee & Clwyd River Board**

Locomotive: Gauge 3'0" - River Dee Company [? Burton Point Embankment 1878]

    DEE [? ERNEST *]   0-4-0 IT   IC   WB   138   1878 (a)   (1)

*   The name DEE, as carried by the loco at the Bristol Show, would logically be carried during its use at the River. However, the name ERNEST appears in Bagnall archives [but could perhaps refer to the loco under subsequent ownership - the method of recording names in early Bagnall records is not precise].

(a)   ordered 11/1877, delivered 3/1878. Loco (named DEE) was exhibited by WB at the 1878 Royal Agricultural Society Exhibition, Bristol

(1)   apparently returned to WB in 1878 [? when embankment abandoned]. Was probably the "new 3'0" gauge loco, ordered by a firm but not now required" in a WB sale advert [J/TE/17.1.1879].
Exhibited by WB at Royal Agricultural Society Exhibition, Kilburn, 1879.
Was probably the "3'0" gauge 5"x7½" cylinders 1'6" wheels loco by Bagnall £200" for sale in J/PMR 7/1882 and 4/1883.
No further trace.

ROYAL WELSH SHOW, ABERGELE   R16
(Cd)

Ruston & Hornsby Ltd displayed their 2'0" gauge 4wDM RH 235663 at this show held in July 1950. This loco was then, in fact, their "show" loco, having been displayed at Dublin 4/1947, York 6/1948, Shrewsbury 6/1949, Paisley 6/1950. Many years later, the loco turned up at Dyserth Limestone Quarry.

RUABON (BRANDIE/RUABON OLD) COLLIERY & COKE OVENS   R18
and PARK PIT, near PANT, RUABON
(Cd/GR:below)

RUABON BRANDIE COLLIERY (GR:298457)
          1846 : (No.6 Pit drowned out)
         - 1856 : **Henry Robertson**
  1856 -   : **Ruabon Coal Co** [Sir Daniel Gooch et al]
          1870 : **Ruabon Coal Co Ltd**
          1871 : dismantled

Note: J/MS ("Mineral Statistics") lists Gomar Roberts of Ruabon as operator of "RHOS or BRANDY" colliery in 1873-74, and of "BRANDY" Colliery in 1875-76. [? This site, or elsewhere.]

RUABON BRANDIE (BRANDY) COKE OVENS (GR:299457)
        - 1870 : **Ruabon Coal Co Ltd**
  1871 - 7/1880 : **North Wales Coke Co Ltd**
  7/1880 -   : **Ruabon Coal & Coke Co Ltd** (reg.14/7/1880 £30K)
     after 1890 : closed; dismantled
[by 1874 - after 1890 : Patent Mineral Carbon Co Ltd, Brandy Works, was perhaps a subsidiary company on same site]

PARK PIT (GR:293456)

This is probably the "Park Farm Colliery" listed in J/MS/1858-1860 with no owner quoted. "Park Shaft" ("Park Pit" on OS/1874) was, for a period at least, the No.1 Shaft of Ruabon (Brandie) Colliery.

Since the 1600s, coal has been won from many small shafts in the compact tract of land between Pant village (in the west) and the Moreton Inn (at GR:301456); the Brandie Pits being the centre of activity since c1850.
Both the 1840 and 1867 editions of OS/1" show a "Rail Road" running from the Moreton Inn north-east to a wharf near the (later) Johnstown & Hafod GWR station [the route of this - presumably narrow-gauge - Railroad is now built over] whilst OS/6"+25"/c1874 indicate a trackbed of what could have been a short branch line from Brandie direct to the GWR main line (PR/5) at GR:304451, near Vauxhall Colliery Sidings. [Another railway plan notes this as "New Tramway or Branch to Ponkey Branch"]. After 1861 the then new "Ponciau Branch" (PR/17) bisected Brandie, thus providing direct connection to the GWR. By 1870 - and probably in the 1850s - a line from Brandie ran westwards to Park Pit. From 1867 production was gradually transferred to Hafod ("Ruabon New") Colliery. Since WW2 much of the area has been disturbed by opencast mining, and some parts redeveloped.

[Read: B/107; B/276; B/301]

Locomotives: Gauge 4'8½"

No specific information regarding locomotives has come to light, though the extensive trackage (eg.OS/25"/1874) suggests a possible need. In view of the GWR involvement with the Company, perhaps GWR locos were used. Wrexham Loco Shed was well known for its fleet of 0-4-0 tank locos suitable for such work, and there is a known history of GWR locos being used at Hafod (Ruabon New) Colliery.

RUTHIN (CRAIG-Y-DDYWART) LIMESTONE QUARRY R20
(Cd/GR:111592)

by	1860	: Frederick Richard West
by	1889	: Ruthin Lime Co
by	1920	: Ruthin Lime & Limestone Co Ltd
by	1948	: Ruthin & Denbigh Tar Macadam Co Ltd
	c1960	: closed [by 4/1964]

Quarry connected to PR/20 by own railway over half-mile long - the original siding Agreement was 30/11/1860 hence quarry rail traffic probably commenced when PR/20 opened in 1862. Within the quarry a narrow-gauge line linked the working-face with the kilns, and a separate 2ft gauge handworked system ran from below the kilns to the shipment dock. 4'8½" gauge track was lifted between 4/1964 and 11/1965 (except for a short length [in-situ 1989] near the kilns.

[Whilst the site has been partly re-used, much remains (with prior permission) to be seen today [1989], including the uncompleted embankment and cutting of PR/46 - the narrow gauge line to Cerrig - visible between quarry land and main road a few yards northwards of the former 4'8½" gauge level crossing.]

Locomotives: Gauge 4'8½"

	0-4-0VBT OC			(a)	Scr/c1920	
*	4wPM 40hp	MR	2021	1920	New 6/20	(1)

* re-engined Diesel in 1956.

(a) here during WW1 [say c1916 ?] - [J/ME/11.2.1943/143]
   [wfw: Trevor Silica Brickworks ? - which see]

(1) still here, disused, 4/1964; gone by 11/1965 [presumably scrapped].

SALTNEY QUAY SHIPYARD later SCRAPYARD S2
(Cf/GR:386653)

by 1913	-	1928+	: J.Crichton & Co Ltd, Shipbuilders
by 1969			: Spencer Bros (Chester) Ltd, Metal Merchants
			: closed; site cleared.

The GWR (PR/5) freight branch from Saltney Dee Junction to Saltney Riverside (1844-1970) served numerous industries during its life, Spencers being the final user. During the late 1960s, Spencers obtained a large number of wagons from the Mersey Docks & Harbour Board; the loco listed was retained for shunting these within the yard during scrapping.

Locomotives: Gauge 4'8½"

-	0-4-0DM 66hp	JF	22872	1940	(a)	Scr 2/1971

(a)   tdx: Fred'k.Braby & Co Ltd, Aintree, Lancs, 1969 by 7/1969

SANDYCROFT FOUNDRY, SANDYCROFT S4
(Cf/GR:338676)

```
              7/1847   : Sandycroft Premises of Hawarden Iron Works for sale
                         - see 'Ratcliffes' in Section 1.
              7/1853   : Sandycroft (Machinery & Ship) Works for sale or to Let.
[Perhaps the above were on the site of the new Sandycroft Foundry ? :-]
              1862     : opened by John Taylor
   by  1877 - 1900     : Sandycroft Foundry & Engine Works Co Ltd
       1900 - 1912     : Sandycroft Foundry Co Ltd
       1912 - c1927    : Sandycroft Ltd  (reg.7/1912 £50K)
              c1927    : closed. Dispersal auction 11/10/1927
   by  1942            : International Electroplate Co Ltd
   by  1967            : rail connection intact but disused
              1970s    : track removed
```

John Taylor operated a foundry at Rhydymwyn [see 'Rhydymwyn Government Depot'] to produce equipment for the Flintshire lead mines and, in 1862, the business was transferred to his "new" foundry at Sandycroft; which was connected to the LNWR (PR/7) by a half-mile roadside railway - this remained in use until after WW2, though by 1942 the wagons were being hauled along it by a lorry running on the adjacent roadway.

Business at the foundry included loco repairs and some dealing in locos. Advertisements in various journals 7/1877 offered "for sale a four wheel coupled loco, overhauled and repainted, 10"x20" cylinders, 3'0" (3'4" in some issues) wheels, 4'8½" gauge, by Fletcher Jennings. Can be inspected at Sandycroft Foundry". This is very probably FJ 114 of Mostyn Ironworks [in which H.E.Taylor had an interest]. The WM&CQ Rly viewed a small loco here in 12/1877 with a view to using it at Connah's Quay docks. Price asked was £665 and it was said to be "five years old". FJ 114 was built in 1873 and thus some 4 to 5 years old. WM&CQR declined to purchase.

Henry E.Taylor, 15 Newgate Street, Chester [an office address], supplied six narrow-gauge 0-4-0T locos to J.B.White's cement works at Swanscombe, Kent, between 1877 and 1882. These locos were then apparently new; it is very likely they were built at Sandycroft.

Sandycroft Foundry advertisements around 1900 sometimes included a drawing of an electric loco for underground use in mines. It seems unknown whether any such locos were built, but the Foundry was very much involved in the manufacture of electrical machinery for mines in the 1890s and later.

Locomotives: Gauge 4'8½"

It does seem likely, though proof is lacking, that a loco would have been used on the line between the foundry and PR/7. In 1968 Mr Reg. Appleton met an elderly resident who vaguely recalled "the Foundry loco" of the early 1920s. The 11/10/1927 dispersal auction included a 9" cylinder four-wheel steam loco - though this could have been a loco "in stock" rather than one used on the site.

A photograph exists of an unidentified 0-4-0ST OC loco named SANDYCROFT, at an unknown location.
The original copy of this photo was not discovered in Clwyd.

SEALAND (ex SHOTWICK) AERODROME & AIR FORCE DEPOT   S6
(Cf/GR:337700)

10/1917 -	1924	: Air Ministry, SHOTWICK aerodrome & depot.
1924 -	1957	: Air Ministry, SEALAND aerodrome & depot.
1957 -		: Royal Air Force Maintenance Unit.

Shotwick Aerodrome established during WW1 north of LNER Hawarden Bridge to Chester line, west of A550 road, with an adjacent "Acceptance Park" Depot on the south side of the LNER. Both locations were served by sidings at Welsh Road (later Sealand) station, those into the Depot area being installed (or remodelled) by 1933, under an Agreement of 16/12/1930 between LNER and Air Ministry. A loco shed within this Depot area was at GR:333698.
From 1935, the aerodrome was expanded north of the LNER east of the A550; additional sidings were connected to serve this area, with a second loco shed at GR:337700.
Rail traffic ceased c1971; most of track removed c1975.

CONSTRUCTION CONTRACTS

8/1917-1918 SIR ROBERT McALPINE & SONS

McAlpine records show that an extensive system of railway sidings was laid down to facilitate construction. It is likely that a number of locomotives were employed here, but only the following has yet been identified.

Locomotives: Gauge 4'8½" - McAlpine

No.4		0-4-0ST OC HC	589	1901	(Ma)		(M1)

(Ma) arrived here 1918
   Loco originally McAlpine No.3, but renumbered No.4 by 1918.
   wfw: McAlpine, GNR Cuffley (1912-1916) Contract.

(M1) departed 20/1/1919 (as Plant No.1485). Another McAlpine record has Plant No.1485 as at "Ministry Queensferry" until 5/3/1919 but this entry has, at some time, been crossed out. Hence, probably moved direct from Sealand to Ellesmere Port (Great Stanney) Plant Depot, though possibly hired to Queensferry Government Factory for a period.
   wlw: McAlpine, Blandford Aerodrome (1919) Contract.

Locomotives: Gauge 4'8½" - Air Ministry Shunting.

No.121 TORCROSS	0-4-0ST OC MW	1036	1887	(a)	(1)
AMW No.149	0-4-0DM 150hp JF	22496	1938	New 10/38	(2)
AMW No.170	0-4-0DM 150hp JF	22879	1939	New 11/39	(3)
No.238	4wDM 88hp RH	210479	1942	New 1/43	(4)
AMW No.223	0-4-0DM 150hp JF	22970	1942	(b)	(5)
AMW No.245	0-4-0DM 150hp JF	23002	1943	(c)	(5)

(a) here in 1937.
 wfw(tdx?): Air Ministry, Kidbrooke, London.
(b) here by 7/1969.
 wfw(tdx?): Air Ministry, Burtonwood, Lancs.
(c) arrived after 7/1969 by 6/1972.
 wfw(tdx?): Air Ministry, Burtonwood, Lancs.

(1) still here 20/3/1943; gone by 1952; no further trace.
(2) wlw: Air Ministry, Burtonwood, Lancs (by 7/1968).
(3) tdt: Connah's Quay Wagon Works, after 10/1970 by 10/1971.
(4) tdt: Air Ministry, Broadheath Maintenance Unit, Cheshire [? for repair only] by 4/1943; returned to Sealand by 12/1944.
 still at Sealand 10/1955.
 wlw(tdt?): Chas.Jones (Aldridge) Ltd, dealer, Aldridge, Staffs.
 wlw: William Gray & Co Ltd, West Hartlepool, Co.Durham, c1958.
 wlw: West Somerset Railway.
(5) tdt: Connah's Quay Wagon Works, 13/1/1973.

SEALAND TRADING ESTATE S8
(Cf/GR:31x71x)

Following the decline and contraction of Shotton Steelworks and the Sealand Aerodrome, many new factories have been established on and near these sites. Two of these use rail sidings, each using "road-rail convertible" tractors for moving wagons.

DEESIDE TITANIUM LTD (Cf/GR:313716)

New factory, opened 10/1982. Within the factory there is also a short length of 6'3" gauge track, used by a 4wBE flask-carrying vehicle, built Sharebex Ltd, Dudley, No.771 of 1982. By 6/1988 this vehicle was non-powered, being moved as required by a road tractor.

    4wDM 60hp   Unilok   2186   1982   New 6/82

SHOTTON PAPER CO plc (Cf/GR:303717)
(formerly Shotton Paper Ltd)

	4wDM	Unimog				(1)
D682NWX	4wDM	Unimog	1145	1986	(a)	(2)
F612VFR	4wDM	Unimog	4241261W150799	1989	New	

(a) tdx: Euro Trac Ltd, Wetherby, c5/1988

(1) damaged in accident c5/1988; sent away for possible repair, but scrapped.
(2) tdt: Euro Trac Ltd, Wetherby. 1989 after 14/6/1988.

SEIONT BRICKWORKS, CAERNARFON S10
(Gc/GR:488613)

		9/1878	: first lease, to **Wm.Hayward**
11/1880	-		: **Samuel Sargeant & Sydney Toms**
	-	1930	: **Carnarvon Brickworks Ltd**
1930	-		: **Castle Firebrick Co Ltd**
	-	3/1970	: **Castle Brick Co Ltd**
3/1970	-	c5/1972	: **British Steel Corporation**
c5/1972	-		: **Butterley Brick Ltd**

The Works was served by a siding - "Seiont Siding" - off PR/35, and a narrow-gauge railway connected the Works to the clay pit on the opposite side of the river. This railway, which was worked by both horses and a locomotive, was replaced by road vehicles soon afer WW2. In the 1970s the original Works was demolished, replaced by a modern brick factory on an adjacent site.

Locomotive: Gauge narrow

Reputedly only one 4wDM loco, no longer here by 1948.
An "old man" at Castle Brickworks, Ewloe, recalled bringing this loco to Caernarfon. He said it was of foreign manufacture, but not built by OK (as were the locos he knew at Ewloe).
No further details known.

SHOTTON (HAWARDEN BRIDGE) STEELWORKS   S12
(Cf/GR:30x70x)

	1895	:	works founded
	1896	:	production commenced
1895 -	3/1898	:	John Summers & Sons
3/1898 -	3/1970	:	John Summers & Sons Ltd
3/1970 -		:	British Steel Corporation
		:	British Steel plc

A large Works, built mainly on land reclaimed from the River Dee. Steel making ceased in the 1970s; Works subsequently reduced in size and production confined to the treatment of steel strip produced elsewhere.
[Read: B/249]

Locomotives: Gauge 4'8½" - General shunting and furnace charging.

No information known re any locomotives prior to 1900, though works was in production from 1896.

NUMBERING OF DIESEL LOCOMOTIVES: Initially, locos were numbered progressively from '1' virtually in order of receipt and probably in sequence of the orders placed for them. From c1955 the 204hp HE locos were altered into a series from '12' (which eventually reached '28'); the small furnace-charging locos were renumbered into series '37' (to '45'); series '1' to '9' was then used for "miscellaneous" locos. When the "second generation" locos were introduced in 1970, these were numbered from '10' upwards and any surviving earlier locos obstructing this series were then renumbered onto the end of the '12' to '28' series (eg, Hunslet '18' became '29', etc). Three-figure numbers (106 etc) were East Moors, not Shotton, numbers - and were not altered at Shotton.

Many of the "first generation" diesels (and indeed some steam locos) were withdrawn from service, dismantled, and the chassis used as heavy-duty wagons, for some years prior to final scrapping. In this listing, the scrapping date is given as when the locomotive was dismantled, and NOT the final scrapping date of its wagon-chassis. Fleet numbers sometimes allocated to such wagons are ignored.

Two diesel multiple-unit railcar vehicles ex British Rail were obtained, and used as mobile work-vans by the track maintenance staff within the steelworks. These vehicles (M51691, M51692 both built by Cravens in 1960) were not self-propelled, the engines having been removed, and therefore do not qualify for listing here. They were last noted, derelict on site, 22/9/1982.

SEALAND	0-4-0ST	OC	HC	563	1900	(a)		(1)
MACK	0-4-0ST	OC	HC	619	1902	New 7/02		(2)
SIEMENS	0-4-0ST	OC	HC	627	1902	New 12/02		(3)
VULCAN	0-4-0ST	OC	HC	703	1904	New 6/04	Scr/1950	
WINDMILL	0-4-0ST	OC	HC	738	1905	New 9/05		(4)
SHOTTON	0-4-0ST	OC	HC	786	1906	New 1/07		(5)
VENUS	0-4-0ST	OC	HC	901	1909	New 12/09		(5)
JUPITER	0-4-0ST	OC	HC	902	1910	New 1/10	Scr/1955	
NEPTUNE	0-6-0T	IC	HC	926	1911	New	Scr 7/1962	
SATURN	0-6-0T	IC	HC	967	1912	New	Scr/c1959	
MARS	0-6-0T	IC	HC	968	1912	New	Scr/c1960	

No.	Later	Name	Type			Works No.	Built	New/Notes	Scr/Notes
		JUNO	0-6-0T	IC	HC	1021	1913	New	Scr/c1959
		DIANA	0-6-0T	IC	HC	1117	1916	New 7/16	(6)
		VESTA	0-6-0T	IC	HC	1223	1916	New 8/16	(7)
		MINERVA	0-6-0T	IC	HC	1241	1917	New 5/17	(8)
		REMUS	0-4-0ST	OC	HC	1399	1920	New 3/20	(9)
		ROMULUS	0-6-0T	IC	HC	1425	1921	New 2/21	Scr/c1959
		PLANET	0-4-0ST	OC	HC	720	1905		
			rebuilt HC				1920	(b)	Scr/1950
1	later 12		0-6-0DM 204hp HE			3526	1947	New 7/47	(10)
2	later 13		0-6-0DM 204hp HE			4208	1948	New 12/48	(11)
		THOR	0-6-0T	OC	HC	1819	1949	New	Scr 4/1966
		TITAN	0-6-0T	OC	HC	1820	1949	New	Scr 4/1964
3	later 14		0-6-0DM 204hp HE			4209	1950	New 9/50	(12)
4	later 15		0-6-0DM 204hp HE			4210	1950	New 10/50	Scr/1973
7	later 37		0-4-0DM 107hp HC			D762	1952	New 4/52	Scr/1982
8	later 38		0-4-0DM 107hp HC			D763	1952	New 4/52	Scr/1982
9	later 39		0-4-0DM 107hp HC			D764	1952	New 5/52	
			rebuilt 0-4-0DH HB				1972		Scr/1982
6			0-6-0DE 400hp YE			2527	1953	New	Scr/1979
5			0-6-0DH NB			27402	1954	New	Scr/1977
7			0-6-0DM 500hp HE			4003	1954	(c)	Scr/1976
2			0-6-0DH NB			27411	1954	New	Scr/1982
3			0-6-0DH NB			27412	1954	New	Scr/1979
10	later 40		0-4-0DM 107hp HC			D927	1955	New 5/55	
			rebuilt 0-4-0DH HB				1972		Scr/1982
16			0-6-0DM 204hp HE			4975	1955	New 7/55	Scr/1972
17			0-6-0DM 204hp HE			4985	1956	New 2/56	Scr/c1973
41			0-4-0DM 107hp HC			D1020	1956	New 10/56	
			rebuilt 0-4-0DH HB				1972		(13)
1			0-6-0DH NB			27649	1956	New	Scr/1979
4			0-6-0DH NB			27749	1957	New	Scr/1979
18	later 29		0-6-0DM 204hp HE			5132	1957	New 3/57	(14)
19			0-6-0DM 204hp HE			5139	1957	New 7/57	(15)
20	later 31		0-6-0DM 204hp HE			5140	1957	New 9/57	Scr/1977
21			0-6-0DM 204hp HE			5141	1957	New	Scr/c1975
22			0-6-0DM 204hp HE			5142	1957	New 12/57	Scr/1976
23			0-6-0DM 204hp HE			5143	1958	New 1/58	Scr/1977
24			0-6-0DM 204hp HE			5144	1958	New 2/58	(16)
25			0-6-0DM 204hp HE			5300	1958	New 3/58	Scr/1977
26			0-6-0DM 204hp HE			5301	1958	New 6/58	(17)
27			0-6-0DM 204hp HE			5671	1960	New 5/60	(14)
28			0-6-0DM 204hp HE			5672	1960	New 6/60	(18)
8			0-6-0DH NB			28034	1960	New	Scr/1979
9			0-6-0DH NB			27098	1954	(d)	Scr/c1975
42			0-4-0DM 107hp HC			D1409	1969	New	Scr/1982
10			0-6-0DH 500hp EEV			3985	1970	New	Scr/1982
11			0-6-0DH 500hp EEV			3986	1970	New	(19)
13			0-6-0DH 500hp EEV			3998	1970	New	(20)
14			0-6-0DH 500hp EEV			3999	1970	New	Scr/1982
12			0-6-0DH 500hp EEV			5352	1971	(e)	
15			0-6-0DH 500hp EEV			5353	1971	(e)	s/s by 5/88

16			0-6-0DH	500hp	GECT	5391	1973	New	
17			0-6-0DH	500hp	GECT	5392	1974	New	
18			0-6-0DH	500hp	GECT	5396	1975	New	(20)
19			0-6-0DH	500hp	GECT	5397	1975	New	Scr/1982
20			0-6-0DH	500hp	GECT	5398	1975	New	s/s by 5/88
21			0-6-0DH	500hp	GECT	5399	1975	New	s/s by 5/88
22			0-6-0DH	500hp	GECT	5400	1975	New	s/s by 5/88
23			0-6-0DH	500hp	GECT	5401	1975	New	(20)
24			0-6-0DH	500hp	GECT	5402	1975	New	
106			0-6-0DH		NB	27768	1959	(f)	Scr/1982
109			0-6-0DH		NB	27870	1960	(f)	Scr/1982
117		**	0-6-0DH	440hp	AB	507	1966	(f)	Scr/1982
118			0-6-0DH	440hp	AB	508	1966	(f)	Scr/1982
111			0-6-0DH		NB	28045	1961	(g)	Scr/1982
112			0-6-0DH		NB	28046	1962	(g)	Scr/1982
43			0-4-0DH	165hp	GECT	5575	1979	New 4/79	(21)
44			0-4-0DH	165hp	GECT	5576	1979	New 4/79	(21)
45			0-4-0DH	165hp	GECT	5577	1979	New 4/79	(21)
115			0-6-0DH	440hp	AB	489	1964	(h)	OOU 9/1982

** : Loco 117, AB 507, carried worksplates NB 27934 (ex another loco).

Locomotives: Gauge 4'8½" - at Coke Ovens - Closed 1981 (GR:305710)

-		0-4-0WE	80hp	GB	2374	1952	New	Scr/1973
2		0-4-0WE	80hp	GB	2373	1952	New	Scr/c1974
3		0-4-0WE	80hp	GB	2563	1954	New	Scr/c1974
1		0-4-0WE		EE	5360	1971	New	(22)
2		0-4-0WE		EE	5361	1971	New	(22)

Locomotives: Gauge 2'6" - at Cold Strip Mill (GR:305705, 307707)

(B)		4wBE	20hp	GB	2186	1949	New 5/49	
A		4wBE	20hp	GB	2187	1949	New	Dsmt/1979
F		4wBE	20hp	GB	2188	1949	New	Dsmt/1979
E		4wBE	20hp	GB	2643	1955	New	OOU/1979
D		4wBE	20hp	GB	2973	1959	New	OOU/1979
C		4wBE	20hp	GB	2974	1959	New	Dsmt/1979
(G)		4wBE	20hp	GB	6114	1965	New	Dsmt/1979
H	6	4wBE	20hp	GB	420155	1968	New	Dsmt/1979
A	No.1	4wBE	24hp	GB	420330/1	1972	New 11/72	
	No.2	4wBE	24hp	GB	420330/2	1972	New	Dsmt/1979
	No.3	4wBE		WR	7628	1976	New 7/76	
	4	4wBE		WR	7807	1976	New 7/76	
	No.5	4wBE		WR	7808	1976	New 7/76	
	6	4wBE		WR	7809	1976	New 7/76	
No.1		4wDH		HE		c1985	New	
No.2		4wDH		HE		c1985	New	

Locomotives: Gauge 2'6" - at Hot Strip Mill (GR:303704)

48	0-6-0DM 120hp HC	D1417	1971	New 10/71
49	0-6-0DM 120hp HC	D1419	1971	New 11/71
50	0-6-0DM 120hp HC	D1418	1971	New 12/71
51	0-6-0DM HC	D1447	1981	
	HE	8847	1981	New

Locomotive: Gauge 2'0"

Components of 4wDM 12hp RH 182144/1937 were noted within the steelworks in 1956 but there is no evidence that this loco was ever used here, and it possibly arrived as scrap metal. The last known owner was Bowmaker (Plant) Ltd, to whom spares were despatched at Willenhall, Staffs, on 8/1/1943. Prior to this, wfw: F.Parker Ltd, Viaduct Works, Leicester

(a) ordered for delivery to Summers' Stalybridge Works, Cheshire, but believed delivered 'New' to Shotton.
(b) tdx: HC, despatched 30/3/1920.
 wfw: Granville Colliery Co Ltd, Derbyshire, until 1914; from 11/1914 to 2/1920 was used by HC as a 'hire loco', named CODFORD, and used (inter alia) by Sir John Jackson, contractor; Macdonald Gibbs & Co, contractor; WD Fovant Military Railway; Partington Iron & Steel Co, Lancs; Rowland Owen & Sons, Seacombe, Cheshire.
(c) tdx: National Coal Board, Walkden Yard, Lancs, per HE (on trial), 14/4/1954; possibly remained at Shotton until purchased by Summers 19/5/1954.
(d) tdx: Shelton Steelworks, Staffs, /1961.
(e) New to Shotton. tdt: Workington Works, Cumbs, (for repair) c3/1979;
 tdx: Workington Works, Cumbs, by 8/1979.
(f) tdx: East Moors Works, Cardiff, c6/1978.
(g) tdx: East Moors Works, Cardiff, c1/1979.
(h) tdx: East Moors Works, Cardiff, c7/1979.

(1) tdt: Elm Colliery Yard (see BUCKLEY COLLIERIES RAILWAY), by 4/1943
 tdx: Elm Colliery Yard by 8/1948; Scr/1950.
(2) tdt: Stalybridge Works, Cheshire, 17/2/1956;
 tdx: Stalybridge Works, 27/11/1956;
 tdt: Stalybridge Works, c1957.
(3) believed loaned at some time to Buckley Collieries Railway (which see); Scrapped at Shotton c1963.
(4) tdt: Wolverhampton Corrugated Iron Co Ltd, Ellesmere Port, Cheshire, c1935; returned c1935; Scr/1950.
(5) SHOTTON HC 786 was withdrawn and dismantled in 1953. Some parts were used to repair VENUS HC 901, which then worked carrying plates VENUS HC 786. Loco VENUS and remaining parts of HC 786 were all scrapped in 1955.
(6) DIANA was withdrawn from service c1960, then used as a stationary boiler for some years, after which it was dumped until scrapped 5/1974.
(7) tdt: Penrhyn Castle Railway Museum, 3/12/1963.
(8) reputedly hired to Brymbo Steelworks "at some time"; Scr c1959.
(9) tdt: Wolverhampton Corrugated Iron Co Ltd, Ellesmere Port, c1948.
(10) tdt: Padeswood Cement Works, c1972 by 5/1972.
(11) tdt: Padeswood Cement Works, c1971 by 10/4/1971.

(12) Dismantled by 4/1971; Scr c1973.
(13) tdt: "preservation", initially at steelworks' sportsfield near to Shotton station c6/1981 (by 8/1981); then tdt: Queensferry Leisure Centre, 1986.
(14) tdt: A.Allsop, metal merchant, Bagillt (see BETTISFIELD COLLIERY), for scrap, 1982; Scrapped 1982.
(15) Wdn by 10/1975; allocated number 30 but this not carried.
 tdt: ?, scrap dealer, Buckley, for scrap, 7/5/1976.
(16) Dismantled by 10/1975
 tdt: ?, scrap dealer, Buckley, for scrap, 7/5/1976.
(17) sold for scrap, 14/5/1976.
(18) tdt: ?, scrap dealer, Buckley, for scrap, 1978.
(19) tdt: Thomas Hill (Rotherham) Ltd, 24/3/1981
 wlw: U.K.Fertilisers Ltd, Ince, Cheshire.
(20) tdt: Ribblesdale Cement Ltd, Clitheroe, Lancs, 8/5/1982.
(21) tdt: BSC, Clydesdale Steelworks, Lanarkshire, 3/1982.
(22) tdt: Andrew Barclay, Sons & Co Ltd, Kilmarnock, Scotland, after 4/1981 by 1/8/1981. Rebuilt AB 6082/1983, 6083/1983 respectively, and:
 wlw: BSC, Ravenscraig Works, Lanarks, by 5/1983.

STABLA CABLE-LAYING CONTRACT, near LLANRUG S14
(Gc/GR:551634)

10/1977 - 9/1979 : **Arclive Construction Co Ltd**, contractors, for
Central Electricity Generating Board.

Contract for laying power cables along a section of route of former Padarn Railway [see 'Dinorwic Slate Quarries'] approximately ¾ mile long. Due to restricted width of route, road vehicles could not be used. Rail track, ex Marchlyn Mawr Reservoir Contract, laid by Arclive; rolling stock supplied by CEGB, locos hired as below.
Track lifted on completion of Contract.

Locomotives: Gauge 1'11½"

| No.10 | YR ENFYS | 4wDM 40hp | RH | 297030 | 1952 | (a) | (1) |
| No.12 | MÔR LEIDR | 4wDM 40hp | RH | 375316 | 1954 | (a) | (1) |

(a) tdx: Llanberis Lake Railway (PR/65), 20/1/1978

(1) tdt: Llanberis Lake Railway (PR/65), 10/8/1979

TALYCAFN TRAMWAY MUSEUM, TALYCAFN T2
(Gc/GR:787716)

```
              c1980   : founded
  c1980   -   3/1985  : North Wales Tramway Museum Association; AND:-
  c1980   -   3/1985  : Llandudno Tramway Society; AMALGAMATED AS:-
  3/1985  -           : Llandudno & Colwyn Bay Electric Railway Society.
```

An accumulation of road and rail vehicles located in the former goods-yard of Talycafn (PR/23) station. The collection includes the body of Northampton tramcar No.21, and three vehicles from the Southend Pier Railway (3'6" gauge) - closed cars No.7 and No.21 and Flat car maintenance vehicle.

Locomotive: Gauge 4'8½" - stored on site.

2w-2PMr   Wkm   509   1932 (a)   (1)

Locomotive: Gauge 1'3" - short operational line.

4wPM   L   20886   1943 (b)

(a) tdx: Llanrwst Transport Museum, c8/1980
(b) tdx: Fairbourne Railway (PR/53), 12/1985

(1) tdt: ? , after 4/1985 by 7/1986

TALYSARN SLATE QUARRY, NANTLLE T4
(Gc/GR:495534)

```
  1802    -   1857     : Talysarn Slate Co (John Evans & Partners; and subsequently
                         other operators/lessees)
  1857    -   1859     : Thomas Harvey, Bennett, & Co - who sold to:-
  1859    -   1860     : Talysarn Slate Co Ltd
                         (reg.18/6/1859; flooded out; liq.1882)
  2/1867  -   11/1871  : Carnarvon & Bangor Slate Co Ltd
                         (reg.1/2/1867 - which changed name to:-)
  11/1871 -   1874     : Talysarn Slate Co Ltd
                         (reg:8/11/1871; liq.8/1873-12/1876)
  1874    -   c1897    : John Robinson
  c1897   -   8/1904   : Thomas Robinson
  8/1904  -   c1929    : Talysarn Slate Quarries Ltd  (reg.1904; liq.5/1930)
          c1930        :  closed. Lease taken by Dorothea Quarry but site not worked
                         again. Dismantled.
```

The operators of Talysarn Quarry, particularly during the Robinson era (1867-1904), worked from time to time other nearby quarries, under the general title of "Talysarn Quarries". Such quarries include BRAICH, CLODDFA'RCOED, TAN'RALLT, and TY MAWR WEST. When studying archival references to "Talysarn" it is sometimes difficult to be certain as to which quarry (and Company) is at issue.

The "true" Talysarn Quarry consisted mainly of a large pit (sinc) immediately north of, and on the same level as, the Nantlle Tramroad (PR/2), together with tips and Mills to the south of that line. The quarries and Mills were connected by a higher-level railway which passed over PR/2 by a tall, slender, stone bridge, known as Pont-Fawr. Much, but not all, of the area was destroyed in a 1970s reclamation scheme.

[Read: B/182; B/175]

Locomotives: Gauge 2ft

The use of locomotives here was apparently not popular, horses being preferred. Documentary evidence of locomotives is virtually non-existent, and only two (DeWinton VRON, and a "horizontal boilered loco") can be tabled with any certainty. There must, however, have been at least one more, as it is recorded that a loco fell off Pont-Fawr 1/1879 and a boy was killed. Just what sort of loco it was we do not know, though an old man once recalled it as having a vertical boiler on a normal 0-4-0 OC chassis. [A loco of this description, named VIOLET, is illustrated in B/419 - it is clearly not a DeWinton, and the location of the photograph is apparently not known (despite the erroneous caption in the book).] The remains of the Pont Fawr loco are reputed to have been sold (then or later) to E.H.Owen, Vulcan Foundry, Caernarfon, where it was repaired before seeing further use at GLANRAFON SLATE QUARRY - where it was variously recalled as being both an "ordinary loco", perhaps with a big dome, and as a VB loco, perhaps named MURIEL. It has also been recalled that Talysarn may have had two VB locos - presumably VRON, and either the Pont-Fawr casualty or another loco. Apparently no locos survived the WW1 period at Talysarn.

```
        VRON              0-4-0VBT  VC   DeW       c1878   (a)              (1)
    [? JAMES DEW ]        0-4-0[ST  OC ?]                  (b)              (2)
```

a) possibly New here; possibly tdx: Fron Quarry c1880; possibly 3'4½" gauge. See entry for Fron Quarry for explanation.
b) If indeed JAMES DEW, then - wfw(tdx ?): Penybryn Slate Quarry (was for sale there 24/8/1891).

1) reputedly scrapped during WW1.
2) reputedly scrapped during WW1. A loco-type boiler was sold by Talysarn Quarry to Oakeley Slate Quarry 11/1920 and there fitted to loco SNOWDON WB 1569. If "JAMES DEW ?" was the source of this boiler, perhaps it was a similar sort of loco.

TANYGRISIAU POWER STATION CONSTRUCTION T6
near BLAENAU FFESTINIOG
(Gm/GR:679445)

1958 - 1961 : Cementation Co Ltd, contractors.
1958 - 1961 : Sir Alfred McAlpine & Son Ltd, contractors.

Temporary railways, used during construction of tunnels, reservoirs and ancillary works fo Central Electricity Generating Board Pump-storage Power Station.

Locomotives: Gauge 3'0" - CEMENTATION; tunnel works.

70401		0-4-0DM	75hp	RH	374457	1955	(a)		s/s
70402		0-4-0DM	75hp	RH	379092	1955	(a)		s/s
		0-4-0DM	75hp	RH	427855	1958	New 6/58		s/s
		4wDM	44hp	RH	435393	1959	New 6/59		(1)

Locomotives: Gauge 2'0" - CEMENTATION; tunnel & Stwlan Dam.

| 970297 (f. A.85.18) | 4wDM | 32hp | MR | 10349 | 1953 | (b) | (2) |
| 970298 (f. A.85.19) | 4wDM | 32hp | MR | 10350 | 1953 | (b) | (2) |

Locomotives: Gauge 2'0" - MCALPINE; tunnel works

| R 9 | 4wDM | 20hp | MR | 7184 | 1937 | (c) | (3) |

(a) wfw: a Cementation Contract elsewhere (details not known).
      [delivered New to Cementation, Bentley Works, Doncaster]
(b) arrived after 5/1957 by 4/1958.
      wfw: Cementation Co Ltd, Lawers Contract, Killin, Scotland.
(c) tdx: McAlpine Ellesmere Port Plant Depot, Cheshire, 1957 by 25/5/1957

(1) tdt: G.W.Bungey Ltd, dealer, c1961.
      wlw: North Devon Clay Co Ltd, Peters Marland, Devon, 7/1965.
(2) still here 9/1960; subsequently no further trace.
(3) tdt: McAlpine Plant Depot, Ellesmere Port, after 5/1957 by 4/1958.

TONFANAU GRANITE QUARRIES, near TYWYN T8
(Gm/GR:572033)

	-	c1906	: John Corbett
c1906	-	7/1920	: Tonfanau Granite Quarries
7/1920	-		: Tonfanau Granite Quarries Ltd (reg.3/7/1920)
	-	1965	: subsid.of Penmaenmawr & Welsh Granite Co Ltd
1965	-	8/1981	: Kingston Minerals Ltd
8/1981	-		: Mr G.C.Evans [of Aberllefenni]

Quarry connected to wharf alongside Cambrian Coast Line (PR/24) by 2ft gauge railway c½ mile long. This was replaced, c1906, by a 4'8½" gauge "long siding", worked by Cam.Rys. locos. By 1970 this line was intact but disused; it was later dismantled. The quarry itself extended to four levels; 2ft gauge rail tracks on the lowest level served the mill directly, and were connected to the railway by an incline. The three upper levels had isolated 2ft gauge rail systems, from which stone reached the Mill via a system of chutes. Later the top level was connected direct to the Mill by an aerial ropeway. All rail systems were eventually replaced by road vehicles.

Locomotives: Gauge 2ft.

[? FREDA]		0-4-0VBT	VC	DeW	1880 (a)	(1)

(a) wfw(tdx?): Llechwedd Slate Quarry, Blaenau Ffestiniog; , possibly transferred per or via Owen, Isaac & Owen, dealers, Union Iron Works, Porthmadog, after 1/1898 by 9/1898.

(1) left here c1906; disposal uncertain.
Reputedly taken away by Cam.Rys. goods train for use at another quarry - perhaps near Llandrindod Wells.

TRAP BRICKWORKS, BUCKLEY T10
(Cf/GR:279653)

		-	1936	: Catherall & Co Ltd
	1936	-		: Castle Fire Brick Co Ltd
				(subsidiary of John Summers & Sons Ltd)
by	1970	-		: Castle Brick Co Ltd
				: British Steel Corporation
	1972	-		: Butterley Brick Ltd
		-	11/1985	: Butterley Building Materials Ltd
		28/11/1985	:	closed; redeveloped as Pinfold Industrial Est.

Works originally connected by narrow-gauge tramroad to a siding on the LNER (PR/22). Between WW1 and WW2 this was replaced by road transport. During 1961-1962 the Works was rebuilt and modernised; a 2ft gauge locomotive railway was installed within the Works c1964 but soon abandoned.

Locomotives: Gauge 2'0"

		4wBE	LMM	1049	1950	(a)	(1)
		4wBE	LMM	1053	1950	(a)	(2)

(a) tdx: R.S.Davies & Co Ltd, dealer, Mold, c1964
wfw: E.Nuttall, Sons & Co Ltd, contractors.

(1) tdt: M.E.Engineering Ltd, dealers, London, 2/4/1968
wlw: Mitchell Bros, Sons & Co Ltd, contractors, Tilbury Contract.

(2) tdt: M.E.Engineering Ltd, dealers, London, 2/4/1968
wlw: Llechwedd Slate Quarry (Tours Section), Blaenau Ffestiniog.

TRAWSFYNYDD RESERVOIR CONSTRUCTION and EXTENSION CONTRACTS

T12
(Gm/GR:675376 etc)

Natural lake converted into reservoir 1925-1928 to supply Maentwrog Power Station (o North Wales Power Co Ltd).

5/1924: "a large railway siding, on the GWR, between Maentwrog Road and Trawsfynydd [PR/49] is being erected".

4/1925: "the contractors have constructed the various temporary buildings and railroads required for the works".

A former loco driver here recalled that the 3'0" gauge ran from the GWR to the dam, and that both petrol and steam locos were used.

The reservoir was enlarged 1954-1956 to additionally supply the Trawsfynydd Nuclear Power Station; temporary 2'0" gauge railways were used during this work.

RESERVOIR CONSTRUCTION 1925-1928 - SIR ROBERT MCALPINE & SONS

Locomotives: Gauge 3'0"

[No.14 ?]	0-4-0ST	OC	HC	538	1899		(1)
			rebuilt HC		1924	(a)	
No.28	0-4-0ST	OC	HC	998	1912	(b)	(1)
No.12	0-4-0ST	OC	HC	1037	1913	(c)	(2)
No.38	0-4-0ST	OC	HC	1506	1923	(d)	(3)
No.37	0-4-0ST	OC	HC	1533	1924	(e)	(4)
No.50	0-4-0ST	OC	HC	1535	1924	(f)	(5)
	4wPM					(g)	s/s

RESERVOIR ENLARGEMENT 1954-1956 - JOHN LAING & SONS LTD

Locomotives: Gauge 2'0"

3	4wDM	20hp	RH	371545	1954	New 10/54	(6)
4	4wDM	20hp	RH	375349	1954	New 11/54	(6)
2	4wDM	20hp	RH	375354	1954	New 11/54	s/s
12	4wDM	30hp	RH	392102	1955	New 8/55	(7)

(a) 4'8½" gauge loco converted to 3'0" gauge by HC in 1924 and perhaps delivered direct from HC to Trawsfynydd.
   wfw: McAlpine, Slough WD Contract until c1919.
(b) wfw: McAlpine, Great Stanney Depot, Cheshire, on 31/10/1921
   wfw: McAlpine, National Spelter Avonmouth Contract, 1918-28/10/1919
(c) wfw: McAlpine, Stornaway (Lewis & Harris) Contract, 1919-3/1923
(d) [probably tdx: McAlpine, Great Stanney Depot, Cheshire: no previous history known]
(e) delivered New 5/1924 to McAlpine at Shieldhall, Glasgow.
(f) tdx: Dolgarrog Housing Contract [see 'Dolgarrog Railways'].
(g) "petrol locos" were employed, but not known how many. McAlpine had many such locos at this time.

(1) tdt: Great Stanney Depot; eventually sold as scrap in 1937.
(2) after leaving this site, was converted to 3'6" gauge and by 8/1928 was at McAlpine Wimbledon-Sutton Railway Contract (still as No.12 but later became No.34).
(3) tdt: Great Stanney Depot.
(4) after leaving this site, was converted to 3'6" gauge, and used on McAlpine Wimbledon-Sutton Railway Contract.
(5) tdt: Great Stanney Depot [in 1928 ?]
wlw: McAlpine, Royal Victoria Dock Extension Contract, London, 8/37
(6) wlw: Rickmansworth Gravel Co Ltd, Herts, by 1964.
(7) tdt: Dolgarrog (Coedty Leets) Contract [c1956]; after 6/1956.

TREFOR (YR EIFL) GRANITE QUARRY T14
(Gc/GR:below)

1850	-		: Samuel Holland
1855	-	1864	: Welsh Granite Co (Hutton & Roscoe)
1864	-	1/1911	: Welsh Granite Co Ltd (reg.9/11/1864:liq.1911-12)
1/1911	-	1965	: Penmaenmawr & Welsh Granite Co Ltd (reg.21/1/11)
	from 7/1963		: subsidiary of Bath & Portland Stone Firms Ltd
1965	-	1971	: Kingston Minerals Co Ltd
2/1972	-		: Gwaith Brics (Trefor) Ltd

The quarry developed as a number of levels with interconnecting inclines; from the lowest quarry level (GR:365463) two long inclines down to workshops, loco shed, etc at (GR:370468) Trefor village, thence a level railway to the Pier (GR:376474). This latter line was worked by steam locos; later these were replaced by petrol and diesel locos, which were also put to work within the quarry. Railways within quarry replaced by road vehicles and chutes from 1951 to 1961; inclines from quarry and railway to pier replaced by road vehicles in 1959. Railway on Pier replaced by conveyors 1962. Quarrying ceased 1971; premises subsequently used for manufacture of bricks from waste, using road vehicles only. Pier demolished in 1980s.

[Read: B/355; B/175/268]

Locomotives: Gauge 2ft

When the Welsh Granite Co Ltd took over in 11/1864, it was noted that the valuation of assets of the Welsh Granite Co excluded "loco engine not yet delivered". This suggests an early loco of which we know no more, intended either for Trefor, or perhaps Gwylwyr (also owned by Welsh Granite Co), Quarry.

It is not yet possible to prepare a definitive list of the early non-steam locos at this location. These were Petrol engined, and of "Simplex" design, but not necessarily of MR source - FH supplied spare parts for a loco here in 12/1929. Of course, early FH "Simplex" locos were almost always FH rebuilds of MR locos of WW1 origin, and trying to trace their true identity is extremely difficult. Also, MR supplied Trefor with a new 20hp loco frame (only) 11/1924 - whether this was for the repair of an existing loco, or formed the basis of a "new" loco, is not yet known.

	-	0-4-0VBT	VC	DeW		1873	New	Scr by 1914	
	-	0-4-0VBT	VC	DeW		1876	New	Scr by 1914	
	ISABEL	0-4-0ST	OC	WB	1614	1900	New	11/00 Scr/1930	
	BETTY	0-4-0ST	OC	HE	1101	1912	New (a)		(1)
	REDSTONE	0-4-0VBT	VC	Redstone		± 1905	(b)		(2)
	MICHAEL	0-4-2ST	OC	KS	2494	1917	(c)		(3)
	MARK	4-6-0T	OC	HE	1323	1918			
		Rebuilt		KS	4213	1921	New (*)		(4)
[1	?]	4wPM	40hp	MR	1378	1918	(d)		(5)
2		4wDM f.4wPM	20hp	MR	1078	1918	(e)		(6)
[3	?]	4wPM	20hp	MR	3736	1925	New (f)		(7)
[4	?]	4wPM		[MR/FH ?]			(g)	s/s by 9/52	
5		4wPM		[MR/FH ?]			(h)	s/s by 9/52	
6	later 4 by 9/52	4wDM f.4wPM	20hp	MR	5025	1929	New 8/29		(8)
[7	?]	4wPM	20hp	MR	5513	1930	New 6/30		(9)
1		4wDM	20hp	MR	5609	1931	New 5/31		(10)
2		4wDM	42hp	MR	5949	1937	New	s/s after 7/54	
3		4wDM	20hp	MR	7221	1938	New 3/38		(8)
5		4wDM	20hp	HE	2207	1941	New 3/41		(12)
6		4wDM	20hp	HE	2208	1941	New 3/41		(13)
7		4wDM	20hp	RH	189953	1938	(j)		(14)
8		4wDM	20hp	MR	8570	1940	(k)		(11)
9		4wDM	20hp	HE	2024	1940	(m)		(15)
10		4wDM	20hp	HE	2025	1940	(n)		(13)
11		4wDM	20hp	HE	c1940		(o)		(16)
12		4wDM	30hp	RH	200480	1940	(p)	Scr c/1960	

± built by Mr Redstone, foreman fitter at Penmaenmawr (Darbishires') Granite Quarries, as 0-2-2VBT. Altered to 0-4-0VBT and used at Trefor.

(*) built by Hunslet, HE 1323/1918, for War Department, WDLR 2351.
For sale at WD Purfleet, Essex, after WW1, and bought by KS for "rebuilding"; re-plated KS 4213/1921.

In 1937 there were five (only) petrol locos at Trefor - recorded only by their running numbers 1, 2, 3, 5 and 6.
In 1947 eight of the locos here were of "Simplex" (MR or FH) type:
 1 5609; 2 1078; 3 [7221 ?]; 3 [3736 ?]; 5; [6 ?] 5025; 8 8570;
 and one other without any visible identity.

(a) New ex HE 5/6/1912 apparently consigned to Penmaenmawr; doubtless forwarded immediately to Trefor.
(b) tdx: home of Mr C.S.Darbishire, Penmaenmawr, 1921 (or thereabouts; Mr Darbishire quoted different dates from time to time).
(c) for sale at WD, CSD 18, Swindon, Wilts, 5/1920 and perhaps came to Trefor around this time. Was at Trefor in late 1920s.
(d) wfw: War Department, WDLR 3099.
(e) wfw: War Department, WDLR 2799.

(f) per MR records, it appears that MR 3736 was a MR rebuild of an older loco which was apparently sent to MR per or by Penmaenmawr & Welsh Granite for repair. MR recorded the older loco as "Old 1030 LR 2438" However, WDLR 2438 was MR 1717/1918 and not MR 1030/1918; thus the identity and source of this "older loco" is open to doubt.
(g) not in official stocklist 1937; seen here 6/1947.
(h) in 1937 stocklist, and seen here 6/1947. Perhaps this was the loco for which FH supplied spare parts to Trefor in 12/1929.
(j) here by 6/1947.
  wfw: Mearns Sawmills, Laurencekirk, Kincardine-shire, Scotland, until 4/1946 at least.
(k) here by 6/1947.
  wfw: Admiralty (from New, at unknown location).
(m) arrived after 6/1947 by 9/1952.
  wfw: Forestry Commission, Newcastleton, Roxburghshire, Scotland.
(n) arrived after 6/1947 by 9/1952.
  wfw: Forestry Commission, Selkirk, Scotland.
(o) arrived after 6/1947 by 9/1952.
(p) arrived after 6/1947 by 10/1947.
  wfw: Ministry of Supply, Home Grown Timber Products Department, Fyvie,
    Aberdeenshire, Scotland, until 11/1942 at least.

(1) sold to Thos.W.Ward Ltd, dealers, 15/6/1940, who resold same day to Brymbo Steel Co Ltd, Brymbo. Loco probably went to Brymbo Steelworks for overhaul; subsequently delivered to their Hook Norton ironstone pits, Oxon, 9/1942.
(2) tdt: home of Mr C.S.Darbishire, Trefor, c1922 (private store only).
  wlw: Hills & Bailey Ltd, Llanberis (see under PR/65).
(3) spare parts were purchased 7/1931, but by 6/1932 loco officially "has been scrapped" (perhaps meaning "withdrawn from use"). s/s.
(4) not a success at Trefor. Could be the loco of this type advertised for sale by Cudworth & Johnson, dealers, Wrexham, in 1929-1930.
  Probably later scrapped at Trefor, as some components were found in the stores there in 1971.
(5) wlw: Tarmac (South Wales) Ltd, contractors, Dowlais, Glam.
(6) scrapped after 6/1947 by 9/1952.
(7) s/s by 9/1952 (if it was number 3, was s/s after 6/1947 by 9/1952)
(8) tdt: Dyserth Limestone Quarry, 1/1964.
(9) tdt: Penmaenmawr Granite Quarries, 1933 (c6/1933).
(10) tdt: Mr C.Pealling, c/o Cadeby Rectory, Leics, 3/4/1967.
(11) s/s after 9/1960.
(12) tdt: Mr B.Goodchild, Weston under Wetherley, Warwicks, 5/1965;
  wlw: Gloddfa Ganol - see OAKELEY SLATE QUARRIES.
(13) tdt: Thakeham Tiles Ltd, Storrington, Sussex, 26/9/1967;
  per Madoc Jones, dealer, Denbigh.
(14) tdt: Mordale Ltd, Little Woolden, Lancashire, 5/1962;
  per Madoc Jones, dealer, Denbigh.
(15) tdt: Cwt-y-Bugail Slate Quarry, c1962 by 6/1964.
(16) tdt: Pwllheli Plant Hire Ltd, c1964; loco taken to their yard and engine removed for use in road vehicle. Wheels etc sold to Mr C.Pealling 4/1965, and remainder disposed of as scrap.

TREVOR (GARTH) SILICA BRICKWORKS & MINES, TREVOR   T16
(Cd/GR:265426)

by 5/1885 - 7/1921 : **Roberts & Maginnis**
    7/1921 - : **Roberts & Maginnis Ltd** (reg.7/1921 £20K)
by   1943 :   subsidiary of J.C.Edwards (Ruabon) Ltd
by   1980 (after 1970) : **Romag Ltd**
       by 3/1985 : brickworks closed; later mostly demolished.

Brickworks beside main road at Trevor served by siding off PR/18 with level crossing over main road. Rail traffic ceased 1966; most of track removed in 1967. From 1913 to 1938 (at least), the Works obtained material from the adjacent "Garth Ganister & Clay Mine" also operated by Roberts & Maginnis.

Locomotives: Gauge 4'8½"

```
    [                      0-4-0VBT OC                        (a)          (1)]
    [ CLARA                0-4-0tank                          (b)          s/s]
      F.W.COOPER           0-4-0ST  OC  MW   [? 983  1886]    (c)          (2)
    [ PAT                  0-4-0ST  OC  HC      276  1885
                           rebuilt HC                  1922   (d)         (3)]
    ( CORONATION)          0-4-0ST  OC  P      1255   1911
                           rebuilt A.R.Adams           1937   (e)          (4)
    [ MELSONBY No.3        0-4-0ST  OC  MW     1681   1906    (f)         (3)]
      MALCOLM              0-4-0ST  OC  P       447   1886
                           rebuilt A.R.Adams           1948   (g)          (5)
       -                   0-4-0DM  80hp JF  4110012   1951   New 2/51     (6)
```

(a) from 11/1898 to 1/1901 (at least) Roberts & Maginnis were advertising "wanted - small coffeepot loco, standard gauge"; and it is reputed that they did obtain one, also that it was later sold to a "quarry beyond Corwen". Thus is perhaps the loco listed herein at Ruthin Limeworks. But none of this is yet confirmed.
(b) recalled by old employee that the coffepot engine was replaced by a loco called CLARA - but such a loco has not yet been traced nor can its existence yet be confirmed.
(c) here by 1/1930, and perhaps arrived here 1919. Suggested identity is based on circumstantial evidence.
MW 983 wfw: Wm.Jones & Sons, contractors, [LNWR/GWR Joint, Brynmawr-Nantyglo (c1903-1905) Contract ?] and then "lost".
(d) reputed to have been here on short term loan from Cudworth & Johnson, Wrexham - but not proven. If true, it would refer to the mid 1930s period.
(e) tdx: A.R.Adams, dealer, Newport, Monmouth, 1937
wfw: Victoria Petroleum Co, Penarth.
(f) reputed to have been here on short term loan from Cudworth & Johnson, Wrexham - but not proven. If true, it would refer to the 1947-1948 period.
(g) tdx: A.R.Adams, dealer, Newport, Monmouth; on loan; by 2/1951

(1) perhaps to Ruthin - see footnote (a).
(2) by 4/1944 no longer here - possibly scrapped.
(3) if here, then returned to Cudworth & Johnson off loan, by 5/1949
(4) tdt: A.R.Adams, dealer, Newport, Mon, 1951 by 6/1951.
(5) tdt: A.R.Adams, dealer, Newport, Mon, off loan, after 2/1951
(6) tdt: Connah's Quay Wagon Works, 7/1967.

TYDDYN HYWEL & TANYGRAIG GRANITE QUARRIES, CLYNNOG T18
(Gc/GR:below)

Originally two small sett quarries (Williams No.1 Quarry GR:393467 and Hugh Evans No.2 Quarry GR:394468) each with short 2ft gauge incline railways down to nearest roadway; plus Aberaven (later Tyddyn Hywel) Quarry GR:399471 with long railway including four inclines connecting quarry to pier GR:389479.
[Read: B/175/265-266]

TANYGRAIG No.1 QUARRY
```
    1864  -    1866   : Tan-y-Graig Sett Quarry Co Ltd (liq.1866)
    1877  -    1882   : North Wales Granite Quarry Co [J.H.White]
             6/1882   : dispersal auction
    1901  -    1915   : British Grey Granite Co Ltd (liq.1915)
  6/1916  -           : as Tyddyn Hywel Quarry [below]
```

TANYGRAIG No.2 QUARRY
```
    1877  -    1879   : lease held by Edmund Spargo & Sir.Ll.Turner
    1879  -           : National Granite Paving Sett Co Ltd
    1879  -    1886   : New Tan-y-Graig Sett Quarry Co Ltd (liq.1886)
    1901  -    1904   : Tan-y-Graig Granite Co Ltd (liq.1904))
    1905  -           : as Tanygraig No.1 [British Grey, etc - above]
```

TYDDYN HYWEL QUARRY (ABERAVEN; later ABERAVEN plus the TANYGRAIGs)
```
    1877  -    1879   : Aberaven Granite Co [Spargo & Turner]
          -  10/1904  : Carnarvonshire Granite Co [Grace, Grace, Robson]
 10/1904  -   3/1915  : Grace & Robson Ltd (reg.1/10/1904 which became:]
  3/1915  -    1928   : Enderby (Welsh) Granite Co Ltd  (reg.12/3/1915
                         liq.1928-1932)
  8/1930  -   c1947   : Thos.W.Ward Ltd [of Sheffield]
    c1947             : closed. Dismantled c1958.
```

A railway connection was installed, via incline and level track, from Tanygraig No.2 Quarry area to join the Aberaven railway at GR:397473. From c1905 all Tanygraig area was reworked as a macadam quarry, with new incline railway to own pier GR:382472. From 1916 all these quarries were in common ownership, output being concentrated via the Tyddyn Hywel/Aberaven rail system, the lower section [between main-road and sea] of which was replaced by an aerial ropeway to a new "hopper pier" c1922. This system was still in use 9/1943 but closed after WW2; equipment still intact 6/1957 but soon stripped thereafter.
Apparently the locomotive was only used on the short level section of railway which passed beneath the main [A489] road and to the head of the next incline down [drum close to minor road nearer the coast]. From c1922 this drumhead area was converted into ropeway loading terminal, the ropeway passing beneath the minor road to lower the buckets beneath the level of the rail wagons.

Locomotives: Gauge 2'0" - (locoshed GR:393476)

```
        LESTER           0-4-0ST    OC   WB    1618   1900   New 12/00       (1)
```

(1) tdt: Enderby & Stoney Stanton Granite Co Ltd, Leicestershire
[The date of transfer is unknown - 1924 per some sources; but loco recalled locally as still at Clynnog to late 1920s. Spare parts were purchased on many occasions from 6/1908 to 9/1932 (at least), though the last specific delivery to Clynnog was in 9/1912; later orders being amalgamated with deliveries of spares to other Enderby Company quarries for subsequent re-delivery to Wales. Next known confirmed locations are Enderby Quarry [J/RO/10.1935/187], and seen at Earl Shilton Quarry, Leics, 19/6/1937.]

TY MAWR RESERVOIR CONSTRUCTION, RHOSLLANERCHRUGOG   T20
(Cd/GR:277480)

1903 -   1911 : **Wrexham & East Denbighshire Water Company**
(inc.Act 1864 as Wrexham Waterworks Co; name changed 1902)
Direct Labour Contract.

Materials were conveyed to the site by a specially constructed 2'0" gauge railway one mile long, from Llwyneinion Sidings on PR/59. Reservoir completed 1906; railway retained until 1910 for ancillary works, maintenance and access. Local people were allowed to travel as passengers on the train for a fare of 3d. Track removed 1911; little or no trace survives.
[Read: J/IRR/Vol.2/146; J/IL/No.62/41]

Locomotives: Gauge 2'0"

According to the W.& E.D.W.Co records, loco GLADYS was sold in 1906 to a 'Mr.Roberts'. This cannot be a reference to either loco listed below as the fates of both are well documented. If true, it must be a reference to a third loco of which we know nothing more. The association of the name 'Gladys' with this reputed third loco could be an error.

GLADYS	0-4-0ST	OC	WB	1724	1903	New 10/03	(1)
GLADYS	0-4-0ST	OC	WB	1740	1903	New 10/03	(2)

(1) returned to WB 10/1903 (exchanged for larger loco WB 1740).
Resold by WB to Blackbrook Colliery Co Ltd, St.Helens, Lancashire, 4/11/1903.
Returned from Blackbrook to WB by 1/1905
wlw: Blackburn Corporation from 5/1905 [? used on construction of sewage works; ? near Hoddlesden] and apparently was the "nearly new" 2ft WB steam loco for sale by Blackburn Corpn. 4/1909 [J/CJ/21.4.1909]
wlw: Wm.Underwood & Brother, contractors [of Dukinfield, Cheshire] by 10/1909
wlw: James Johnson & Sons, contractors, by 5/1914; still with them at Egremont, Cumberland, 3/1916
No further trace
(2) For sale here by W&EDWCo 5-6/1911.
wlw (tdt?): Dick, Kerr & Co Ltd, contractors, by 5/1912; latterly (at least) at their Hackney Marshes - National Projectile Factory (-1916) Contract (until 12/1915 at least).
wlw: John Mowlem & Co Ltd, contractors, National Filling Factory Contract, Hereford (by 9/1916 to 12/1916 at least).
No further trace.

[Cudworth & Johnson, dealers, Wrexham; advertisements in J/MM/21.10.1910 to 4.11.1910 - for sale: Loco 6½x10 150.lbs; 1 mile portable railway 2ft gauge, wagons, points etc "all by Bagnall" - would seem to refer to the Ty Mawr Reservoir Railway.]

TYWYN RAILWAY MUSEUM, WHARF STATION, TYWYN   T22
(Gm/GR:586004)

Located at the terminus of the Talyllyn Railway (PR/27), the Museum contains a general collection of locomotives, wagons, samples of track, notices, photographs and small items relating to narrow-gauge railways throughout Britain. Locomotives here, which have been used within North Wales, are listed below. A full list of the locos currently on site is maintained and published in the frequently revised "Handbook EL".
[Read: B/287]

Locomotives: Gauge 2ft

RUSSELL	2-6-2T	OC	HE	901	1906	(a)	(1)
GEORGE HENRY	0-4-0VBT	VC	DeW		1877	(b)	
JUBILEE 1897	0-4-0ST	OC	MW	1382	1897	(c)	
ROUGH PUP	0-4-0ST	OC	HE	541	1891	(d)	

(a) tdx: Pike Bros, Fayle & Co Ltd, Corfe, Dorset, 9/1955
     wfw: Welsh Highland Railway (PR/44)
(b) tdx: Penrhyn Slate Quarries, 18/5/1956
(c) tdx: Penrhyn Slate Quarries, 4/12/1963
(d) tdx: Dinorwic Slate Quarries, 15/6/1968

(1) tdt: private store at Kinnerley, Shropshire, 12/4/1965
     wlw: Welsh Highland Railway (PR/44)

Note: the bare frame of 1'3" gauge KATIE 0-4-0T, from Fairbourne Railway (PR/53), was also stored and on view here from 12/1970, until c5/1982 when it was transferred to Ravenglass station, Cumbria, for further display.

VOTTY & BOWYDD SLATE QUARRIES, BLAENAU FFESTINIOG   V2
(Gm/GR:706462)

Initially two separate sites, which came under common ownership from 1846 and were subsequently worked as a single unit.

VOTTY (Fotty/Hafodty) QUARRY
```
c1834  -    1846   :  local men
1846   -           :  F.S.Percival [therafter with Bowydd, below:]
```

BOWYDD (Lords/Percivals) QUARRY
```
by 1801   -              :  open
[1823                    :  purchased rails - first quarry railway in area]
1828   -    1833         :  John Roberts [of Caernarfon]
1834   -    1846         :  J.W.Greaves & E.Shelton
1846   -    1870         :  Percival & Co [F.S.Percival]
1870   -    1962         :  Votty & Bowydd Slate Quarries Co Ltd
1933   -    1962         :     subsidiary of Oakeley Slate Quarries Co Ltd
            5/10/1962    :     workings abandoned
            11/1962      :     final load of slate sent down incline to Duffws
1963   -    1964         :  dismantled, track removed, machinery scrapped.
```

The workings at Votty and Bowydd were almost entirely underground, though both started by working surface outcrops; the initial Votty quarry (GR:708468 etc) was abandoned at an early date, the site was then used for a waste-tip and as a reservoir. As the workings went deeper, the Bowydd outcrop area was largely abandoned other than as a tip; it remains [1990] as a derelict zone between the Maenoffern and Diphwys Casson quarry areas. Latterly, access to V&B was by (part only of) the bottom Bowydd/Casson [ie, Newborough Estate Quarries] incline up from Duffws Station (Ffestiniog Railway - PR/3); from a turn-out on this incline wagons reached the V&B Main Mill level, with its adit entrance to the mine.

DIPHWYS CASSON QUARRY is not known to have used locomotives but, in the 1950s, a diesel loco from Oakeley Quarry was taken there for demolition work on Diphwys Floor 6. The identity of this loco, and duration of the work, is not known.

[Read: B/168; B/169; B/182; B/378; J/FRS/No.103/22]

Locomotives: Gauge 2ft

	Name	Type	Cyl	Builder	No.	Date	Notes	Ref
	TAFFY	0-4-0T	OC	VF	[? 810	1878]	(a)	(1)
	MEIRION	0-4-0ST	OC	MW	487	1874	(b)	(2)
		4wPM 12hp		Dtz	1105	1912	New	(3)
		4wPM 10hp		Dtz	1325	1913	New	(4)
	WENDY	0-4-0ST	OC	WB	2091	1919	New 8/19	(5)
		4wBE 6hp		EAV	662		(c)	s/s after 1933
		4wBE 5hp		EAV			(d)	s/s
		4wBE 10hp		BE		c1917	(e)	s/s
		4wBE 10hp		BE		c1917	(f) #	(6)
No.9		4wBE 6hp		EAV	667		(f)	s/s after 1933
		4wPM 20hp		Dtz	68179	[1916?]	(g)	(7)
		4wPM 20hp		Dtz	92972	[1916?]	(h)	(8)
		4wDM 8hp		WB	2499	1934	New 3/34 (j)	(9)

No.8	4wDM	21hp	RH	175`38	1935	New 9/35	(10)
	4wDM	12hp	RH	182141	1936	New	Scr/c1964
	4wDM	20hp	RH	194773	1939	New 1/39	Scr/1963
	4wBE	5hp	Votty		c1939	New (k)	(6)
	4wBE		Votty			New (m)	Scr
	4wDM	13hp	RH	264252	1952	(n)	(11)
	4wDM	10hp	RH	171902	1934	(o)	(12)
	4wDM	12hp	RH	177638	1936	(p)	(13)

\# in later years (at least), fitted with electric motor 7C36

The details listed above for Battery and Deutz locomotives are based on surviving Votty records [DgRO/Z/DAG; /DBE/3523] (which are incomplete) plus some information from quarry employees, reports of visitors, and scraps of data from elsewhere. It is apparent that interchange of battery-loco components took place over the years; precise details cannot be ascertained. Some Deutz serial numbers quoted are probably engine, not loco, numbers. [See also J/IRR/No.49/72.]

(a) the V&B Minute Book for 1880 reports "the new engine works well"; apparently a reference to this loco. For earlier history see 'Fron Slate Quarry'.
(b) arrived after 7/1886 and probably c1900.
  wfw: Locke & Co, St John's Colliery, Normanton, near Leeds.
(c) purchased from R.J.Winder, dealer, Belgrave Works, Leeds, 2/1925.
(d) purchased from Fuller, Horsey Son & Cassell, auctioneers (at sale on behalf of Cohen & Armstrong Disposal Corporation), 6/1925.
(e) purchased from George Cohen, Sons & Co Ltd, dealers, 7/1925
(f) purchased from B.E.White, dealers, 8/1925
(g) purchased (second-hand), 1926
(h) purchased (second-hand), after 1926 by 2/1932 - V&B sent this loco to WB, Stafford, for repairs, 2/1932.
(j) purchased new by parent company Oakeley Slate Quarry; but delivered direct to V&B. Known at V&B as a 'Deutz' - it having an engine of that make. Not a popular loco, it did little work.
(k) built on a chassis that incorporated parts of the frame of the VF steam loco TAFFY. It had Stellite electric motor No.4089.
(m) built on frame of a Deutz petrol loco, very likely Dtz 1325.
(n) tdx: R.S.Davies, dealer, Mold, after 9/1952 by 5/1953.
(o) tdx: EITHER a dealer [Wil Rowlands ?] at "Conwy Wharf" [maybe Conwy Morfa ?], c1958 by 9/1960
  OR W.O.Williams, dealer, Harlech, c1958 by 9/1960
  wfw: Rhos Slate Quarry, Capel Curig.
(p) tdx: Oakeley Slate Quarry, after 8/1953 by 8/1960.

(1) disused for many years until dismantled in late 1930s; parts from frames used in construction of battery loco No.8. The fate of the boiler is not known. Most other components [5/12/1941: smokebox front with door, dome cover, side tanks - green, lined yellow/black with painted name TAFFY - cab sides, cab front, buffers] dumped on upper tip at quarry. The side tanks survived there for many years.
(2) repaired at Boston Lodge Works (PR/3) in 1915, but reputedly not used after 1916; later scrapped.

(3)   this loco (though possibly Dtz 1325) lying disused in shed behind upper level Mil 8/1953; scrapped [where it lay] c12/1963.
(4)   this loco (though possibly Dtz 1105) dismantled, and frame used in construction o battery loco [footnote (m)].
(5)   advertised for sale here 8/1923
        tdt: Dorothea Slate Quarry 5/1930
(6)   tdt: Aberllefenni Slate Quarry, Corris, 8/1963.
(7)   tdt: Dorothea Slate Quarry, Nantlle.
(8)   disused by 8/1953; later scrapped.
(9)   tdt: WB, Stafford, for repairs, 4/1937
        tdx: WB, 29/5/1937; spares last purchased 10/1945. Wheels reputedly later used fo a battery loco, otherwise loco still intact 8/1953 but gradually dismantled; frame scrapped after 9/1960 by 6/1964.
(10)   tdt: Maenofferen Slate Quarry, after 9/1960 by 8/1964.
(11)   tdt: Oakeley Slate Quarry, after 5/1963 by 5/1966.
(12)   retained on site for demolition work; scrapped 8/1964.
(13)   tdt: Maenofferen Slate Quarry, after 8/1960 by 9/1963.

VRON COLLIERY & BRICKWORKS, near BRYMBO   V4
also OFFA'S DYKE COLLIERY   (Cd/GR:293522)

		c1806	:	first sinking - Mr Rogers
by	1854	-	6/1872	: **Vron Colliery Co** (Maurice & Lowe)
	6/1872	-	c1880	: **Vron Colliery Co Ltd**
			1884	(reg.6/1872 £100K liq.c1880-c1885) : shafts enlarged and deepened
	c1884	-	8/1887	: **Vron Colliery Co** (W.F.Butler & Co)
	8/1887	-	1/1905	: **Vron Colliery Co Ltd** [Hyde & Co] (reg.9.8.1887)
	1/1905	-	1933	: **Broughton & Plas Power Coal Co Ltd**
	1905	-	1913	: pumping only
	1914	-5/12/1930		: mining
	12/1930	-	3/1933	: pumping only.
	by 1938	-	1943	: an adit at Vron was reopened by Mr John Houghton and named **OFFA'S DYKE COLLIERY**
			1943	: closed

By 1845 a narrow-gauge incline ran eastwards from the colliery, down the hill to Tanyfron. From 1847 Vron had a standard-gauge outlet via a branch (initially horse-worked, apparently until c1863) of PR/6 from Brymbo and, from 8/10/1888 an alternative outlet via PR/47.

The brickworks (GR:290522), slightly to the west of the colliery, opened in 1873 and was served by a short branch-line, from the colliery, which crossed Llewelyn Road on the level. About 1890 a narrow-gauge incline railway c½ mile long was built south-west to Talwrn Colliery, Coed Poeth; this colliery was then also operated by Vron Colliery Co and provided ventilation to some Vron seams. This Talwrn incline was a single-track route, worked by an endless chain powered by a stationary steam engine.

In 1986 the Talwrn incline route was clearly visible, the Vron colliery area was derelict land, and tips in the brickworks area were being worked by Slag Reduction Co Ltd. No railtracks remain.

[Read: J/CG/3.2.1893/214; B/107]

Locomotives: Gauge 4'8½"

BERTHA - an old loco, disused by 1/1873, and purchased by Thos. Mitchell, dealer, Bolton, Lancs, 7/1873. No further details known. (1)

VRON	0-6-0T(ST?)	LNWR	1865	(a)	s/s

(a)   tdx: LNWR, (number) 1804, £1000, 11/1872.
      This loco was an LNWR rebuild of 0-6-0 IC tender loco RS 622/1848.

(1)   Mitchell advertised for sale a "tank loco, 7.3/4" cylinders, 4ft 8.1/2in gauge by Adamson & Co, in good condition", in 7/1873 [J/CG/Vol.25(1873)/734] which is probably not BERTHA as the latter is unlikely to have been in "good condition". Later in 1873 he advertised 4wc tank 10x24 "equal to new, first class maker" [J/CG/Vol.26(1873)/94], and 6wc tank 3'0"dw 12x18 by MW [J/CG/Vol.26(1873)/356]. Perhaps more likely is the 4wc tank 10¼x24 13¼ tons, no condition stated, which lingered on in his advertisements from 3/1874 to 1/1875 [J/CG]. But this is all just muse, and no proof whatsoever.

WELSH SLATE CENTRE, GILFACH DDU, LLANBERIS   W2
                                                (Gc/GR:586603)

1972 -   : National Museum of Wales

Initially known as the North Wales Quarry Museum; located within the former engineering workshops of the Dinorwic Slate Quarries.
The railway tracks within the Museum were connected to the Llanberis Lake Railway (PR/65) on 16/12/1982 allowing subsequent interchange of some locomotives and rolling stock. Such transfers, generally of short duration, are not recorded here.
[Read: B/289; B/177]

Locomotives: Gauge 1'11½"

SYBIL	0-4-0ST	OC	HE	827	1903	(a)	(1)
UNA	0-4-0ST	OC	HE	873	1905	(b)
-	2-2wPMr		*			(c)
	4wBE		BE	# c1917		(d)

*   this machine consists of a vintage motor-cycle mounted on a rail chassis; it was constructed by Mr W.J.Williams at the Oakeley Slate Quarry, Blaenau Ffestiniog.

fitted with electric motor 7036

(a) tdx: Hills & Bailey Ltd (see PR/65), loan, 13/6/1974
(b) tdx: Hills & Bailey Ltd (see PR/65), 15/12/1977
(c) tdx: private store, Dinorwic village, 29/6/1982
     wfw: store on Llanberis Lake Railway (PR/65)
(d) tdx: Aberllefenni Slate Quarry, Corris, 20/4/1963

(1) tdt: Betws-y-Coed Railway Museum, per Hills & Bailey Ltd, 13/2/1976

WEST BUCKLEY COLLIERY, ALLTAMI   W4
(Cf/GR:266654)

in 1874	: West Buckley Colliery Co Ltd
1875 -	: North Buckley Coal Co Ltd
by 1902 -	: Joseph Ellis & Co
- 1909	: West Buckley Colliery Co
1909 -	: West Buckley Colliery Co Ltd (reg.21/1/1909 £5K)

Small colliery, having two shafts and a drift, connected to the South Buckley Brickworks [see 'Buckley Colliery Railway' entry] by a narrow-gauge railway c¾ mile long. Colliery site and much of railway route visible [1969] with aid of OS/6"/1914.

Locomotive: Gauge 1'9"

    HAMPSTEAD   0-4-0ST   OC   WB   1728   1903 (a)   (1)

(a) delivered new 28/11/1903 1'9" gauge named HAMPSTEAD, to Price & Reeves contractors, Charing Cross, Euston & Hampstead Underground Railway (1903-1907). Contract. For sale by Price & Reeves 12/1907 but perhaps not sold, as 3/1909 sale at Lower Shadwell of material used by Price & Reeves on Rotherhithe Road Tunnel (c1905-1909) Contract included 0-4-0 1'9" gauge 6" cylinder loco [thus possibly WB 1728]. However, J.F.Wake, dealer, ordered spares for WB 1728 in 2/1909 and 4/1909 - as 2/1909 pre-dates the Rotherhithe Sale, either Wake purchased the loco in advance of the Sale, or, the loco at Rotherhithe was not in fact this loco. Wake advertised for sale 21" gauge loco [J/CJ/24.3.1909]; and 21" WB 6x9 £145/£140 [J/MM/25.6.1909-22.7.1910]. And, J/PMR/7.1909 to 6.1910 offered HAMPSTEAD 4wc ST WB 6x8 1'9" £145/£150 - possibly this advert was also placed by Wake.
West Buckley Colliery ordered spares for WB 1728 in 7/1910, having presumably purchased the loco from Wake 6-7/1910.

(1) still here 4/1912 [and probably to c6/1915].
    wlw(tdt?): Kinmel Camp Construction Contract - W.Alban Richards & Co; who sent this loco to WB, Stafford, 7/1915, for alteration to 2'0" gauge.

WHIXALL and FENN'S MOSS PEAT RAILWAYS, MAELOR   W6
(Cfd/GR: below)

FENN'S BANK SYSTEM
c1890 -	:
by 1919 -	: Whixall Moss Litter Co [J.E.Allmark]
by 1968 -	: L.S.Beckett Ltd [Allmarks]

BETTISFIELD SYSTEM
? c1915 - 1919	: Government
1919 -	: Midland Peat Products Ltd
by 1967 -	: North Western Peat Products [Allmarks]

After closure of the railway, but before its disposal, the Allmark interests became a subsidiary of Croxden Horticultural Products Ltd. In 1990 ownership of the Moss passed to the Nature Conservancy Council, and peat cutting ceased.

A large area of natural bog-land, roughly centred around GR:49x37x, which has been a source of peat for very many years. It is today bounded by the Shropshire Union Canal to the south, and by the route of the Cambrian Railways Whitchurch-Ellesmere line, between Fenn's Bank and Bettisfield stations, to the north.

OS/1872 shows no railways on the Moss, but OS/1899 indicates a narrow-gauge line running south from an exchange siding at Fenn's Bank (GR:508389) to a "Peat Litter Moss Works" (GR:504367) near Moss Cottages, thence running westerly to GR:c495367. On OS/1910 this line is further extended, southward to GR:c490363. Loco MR 1934 was delivered New to "J.E.Allmark" at "their siding, Fenns Bank station".

A second railway system was later established based on Bettisfield Peat Mill which was located close to, and served by a siding off, the Cam.Rys. line at GR:478367. A clue to the origins of the Bettisfield system may lie in the advertisement J/CJ/25.6.1919 "Auction sale for Disposal Board of plant at Bettisfield Peat Moss Works, including Decauville track and trucks for same". No locos are mentioned; the term "Disposal Board" indicates a Government wartime activity.

Subsequently all activities were controlled by the Allmark family. Milling was concentrated on the Bettisfield Mill, the Mill at 504367 was demolished, the railway thence to Fenn's Bank lifted and the remainder of this system, from Moss Cottages westwards, was connected by rail across the Moss to the Bettisfield system. These changes occurred prior to 8/1945.

After closure of the Cam.Rys. line 27/3/1965 peat from the '478367' Mill was taken by train to Moss Cottages for transfer to road vehicles; later the route of the Cam,Rys. was converted to a rough road. This Mill was later abandoned; cut peat then being taken direct to Moss Cottages for transfer by road to a smaller Mill at Whixall Manor House. By 1971 all digging was concentrated at the eastern end of the Moss, with tractors and trailers carrying the peat direct from the workings to the Manor Mill, and the railway fell into disuse; though the equipment remained for almost 20 years before being removed.

Locomotives: Gauge 2'0"

4wPM 20hp	MR	1934	1919	New 10/19	(1)
4wPM 20hp	MR	4023	1926	(a) Ø	(1)
4wDM 10hp	RH	171901	1934	(b)	(1)
4wDM 13hp	RH	191679	1938	(c) *	(2)

    Ø   rebuilt 1967 at Whixall 22hp Armstrong Siddeley diesel engine.
    *   rebuilt c1966 at Nash Rocks with air-cooled Lister diesel engine.

(a) tdx: ? , by 16/5/1964
    wfw: A.M.Cochrane & Co, Parkhead, Glasgow, in 5/1928
(b) tdx: Dowlow Lime & Stone Co Ltd, Dowlow, Derbyshire, c1/1968 by 4/4/1968.
    2'3" gauge loco, altered to 2'0" gauge at Whixall.
(c) tdx: Nash Rocks Stone & Lime Co Ltd, Dolyhir, Radnor, after 2/9/1968 by 26/9/1968.

(1) tdt: Mr G.Fairhurst, private store, 17/3/1990
(2) tdt: Mr R.Fuller, Limekiln Wharf Industrial Railway, Canalside, Stone, Staffordshire, 11/1990

WILLOUGHBY LEAD MINE, MYNYDD BWLCH-YR-HAIARN   W8
near LLANRWST   (Gc/GR:767601)
Alias: FOXDALE / WELSH FOXDALE / WELSH CROWN / PANDORA / NEW PANDORA STANDARD / THE EAGLE

		by 1853	: closed (Willoughby Mine)
c10/1853	-		: open
1871	-	1882	: **Pandora Lead Mining Co** (Pine & Murchison)
1888	-	1889	: **Welsh Foxdale Mine Syndicate**
1889	-		: **Thomas Gilbert**, 31 Lombard St, London EC
1894	-	1897	: **Welsh Foxdale Mine Ltd**
1899	-	1907	: **Welsh Crown Spelter Co Ltd**
			(reg.1899 liq.2/1905-1907) (sale 18-19/7/1907)
1909	-	1911	: **New Pandora Mining Syndicate Ltd**
			(reg.10/12/1908) (sale 3/1912)
8/1919	-	c1920	: **Western Development Co Ltd** (New Pandora)(£25K)
c1920	-	1922	: **Crafnant & Devon Mining Syndicate Ltd**
			(reg.8/1918 - a fraud - liq.1932)
1930s			: Eagle Mine [? prospecting only]

This mine, like many others in the Llanrwst area, had a chequered existence consisting of short bursts of activity punctuated by periods of virtual dereliction, the surface equipment (at least) usually being sold-off each time the mine closed. The earlier editions of the OS map indicate short surface tramroads (in different positions on each map) between the Mine and an area of ground (GR:765598) at the nearby road. Later, probably c1900, a long railway was constructed from the Mine to Llyn Geirionydd, thence along the shore of the lake, and beyond, to a point (GR:767621) on the hillside above the Klondyke Mine Mill. From this point, an aerial ropeway spanned the gap down to the Mill (GR:765621) which was then to be used to process the Willoughby ore.

This railway would appear to have survived until 1912 at least; the OS of 1911 shows track in situ, and the Mill as "New Pandora Lead Works" hence suggesting it was used by the 1909-1911 activity, during which time both lead and zinc were produced. The route is well preserved today (1990) including some fine stone-wall embankments. The "New Pandora" period seems related to the loco LILY (HC 621 of 1902). For further details of this, see the Eigiau Reservoir Construction section of entry DOLGARROG RAILWAYS.

[Read: B/199/23/68; B/211; B/177/175]

Locomotives: Gauge 1'10" - Welsh Crown Spelter Co Ltd

                0-4-0PM 25hp   KS   861   1904   New 4/04   (1)

(1)   included in auction sale 7/1907; no further trace.

WREXHAM INDUSTRIAL ESTATE former ORDNANCE FACTORY   W10
(Cd/GR: below)

11/1939	-	c1941	: Holland & Hannen and Cubitts Ltd, contractors.
12/1939	-	c1942	: Pauling & Co Ltd, contractors.
1940	-	2/1946	: Ministry of Supply: Royal Ordnance Factory No.34
2/1946	-	4/1960	: Wales & Monmouthshire Industrial Estates Ltd
4/1960	-		: Industrial Estates Management Corp'n for Wales
		c1960	: Rail traffic ceased.

An extensive depot covering some 4 square miles of 'green-field' site 3 miles east of Wrexham. The internal rail system extended from a junction (GR:375475) with PR/57 thence via a circuitous route in a generally northerly direction to the main station and loco shed (GR:383507), and continuing south-easterly to GR:393493. Various depots were served by sidings en-route; a passenger service was operated, calling at various Halts along the line, some trains running through to Wrexham along PR/57. Wartime ROF traffic was such that the normal civilian services on PR/57 were withdrawn, to keep the line clear. After the War, new factories were built on the ROF land, the railway being retained to serve these.

By 1960 rail traffic had ceased, other than the first ½ mile from PR/57 to Maelor Gasworks, which was worked as a long siding by BR. This too was disused by 5/1964, though the track was subsequently renewed, and reopened 9/1965. The remainder of the track through the industrial estate was removed shortly prior to 4/1967; the line to the Gasworks being lifted when PR/57 was cut back to Abenbury.

Locomotives: Gauge 4'8½" - PAULING & CO LTD construction work.

15	MOMBASA	0-6-0ST	OC	WB	2167	1921	(a)	(1)
85	THIKA	0-6-0ST	OC	WB	2197	1922	(b)	(2)
		4wVBT	ICG	AtW	113	1928	(c)	(3)
P.237	VICTORY	[?0-4-0ST	OC	N	420	c1859]	(d)	(4)

Locomotives: Gauge 2'0" - PAULING & CO LTD construction work.

P.203	4wDM	25hp	HE	1977	1939	New 12/39	(5)
	4wDM	25hp	HE	1978	1940	New 1/40	s/s
P.201	4wDM	25hp	HE	1979	1940	New 1/40	(5)
P.204	4wDM	25hp	HE	1980	1940	New 1/40	(5)
	4wDM	30hp	RH	192858	1939	(e)	(6)

Locomotives: Gauge 4'8½" - Factory Fleet

No.2	0-4-0DM	153hp HE	2121	1940	New 12/40	(7)
No.3	0-4-0DM	153hp HE	2122	1940	New 12/40	(8)
No.1	0-4-0DM	153hp AB	345	1941	New 2/41	(9)
No.4	0-4-0DM	HL	3949	1939	(f)	(10)
No.5	0-4-0DM	HL	3950	1939	(f)	(11)
	0-4-0ST	OC HL	2686	1907	(g)	(12)

Locomotives: Gauge 2'6" - Factory Fleet

An auction on 5-12/7/1948 at "MoS Depot 162, ROF Wrexham" included "two BEV electric locomotives 2'6" gauge and 1½ miles of track".

In 1988, extensive traces of a 2'6" gauge system, including lengths of track set in concrete, were visible, on a part of the ROF that had not been re-developed, near to the Courtauld factory.

The following BEV type locos, of uncertain gauge, were delivered New to "ROF Wrexham":

4wBE	WR	1898	1941	New 11/41	s/s
4wBE	WR	2308	1942	New 2/42	s/s
4wBE	WR	2333	1942	New 11/42	s/s
4wBE	WR	2334	1942	New 11/42	s/s

(a) arrived here after 3/1940 by 4/1940
 wfw: Pauling & Co Ltd, Park Royal Depot, London, in 1939
(b) arrived here after 22/4/1940 by 10/7/1940
 wfw: Pauling & Co Ltd, ROF Walsall, Staffs.
(c) tdx: J.W.Leask, dealer, Glasgow, on hire, c1940
 wfw: Blaxters Ltd, Elsdon Freestone Quarries, Northumberland.
(d) The history of this locomotive is confused. In 7/1941 Paulings at ROF Wrexham ordered spare parts from Bagnall of Stafford "for Neilson loco VICTORY No.P237" which suggests the loco then carried a Neilson plate, and that P237 was a Pauling plant number perhaps.
 J/RCTS/RO/Supplement No.5/5.1952 lists WD.234 as built by Dick & Stevenson 1880?, Coltness Ironworks No.5; to WD 1940; then named VICTORY. IRS/Handbook N & Bulletins, re Coltness Ironworks, lists No.5 as N 420/c1859 scrapped; replaced by second No.5 built by Sharp Henderson which became WD 234. However, Sharp Henderson seem to have only rebuilt (and not built) locos; they were active c1870 to c1890. On balance, therefore, WD234 VICTORY could be N 420, re-built Sharp Henderson - rather than built Dick & Stevenson - c1880.
(e) arrived by 1/1941. wfw(tdx?): Pauling & Nuttall Consortium, Royal Naval Armament Depot Contract, Trecwn, Pembrokeshire.
(f) arrived c9/1941. wfw(tdx?): ROF Chorley, Lancashire.
(g) tdx: George Cohen, Sons & Co Ltd, dealers, 1942
 wfw: Wallsend & Hebburn Coal Co Ltd, Northumberland.

(1) still here 11/1941; in 3/1942 spares sent to Pauling & Co Ltd at Paradise, Coven, Staffs [ie, ROF Featherstone Contract].
 wlw: Ministry of Fuel & Power, Awsworth Opencast Coal Site, Derbyshire, by 1943.
(2) still here 21/2/1941
 wlw: Pauling, ROF Featherstone, by 7/4/1941.
 wlw: Board of Trade Mines Department, Cambois, Northumberland.
(3) tdt: J.W.Leask, Glasgow, off hire, c1941
 wlw: Tottenham Gasworks, 6/1942
(4) In 1942 an unidentified loco named VICTORY was repaired by Pecketts in Bristol, and despatched 7/9/1942 to the Ministry of Works Store Depot at Shrawardine, Shropshire. This seems to tie-in with the RCTS listing, which places WD234 VICTORY on the Shropshire & Montgomeryshire Rly c1942. (Shrawardine being on that railway).
 wlw: Northfleet Deep Water Wharf, Kent, until 3/1943
 wlw: WD, Queniborough Depot, Rearsby, Leicestershire
 wlw: Longmoor Military Railway in 10/1945 - as WD 70234
 scrapped 4/1947 at Steel Breaking & Dismantling Co, Chesterfield.

(5) tdt: ? , c1941
    wlw: Pauling & Co Ltd, Park Royal Depot, London, in 4/1951
(6) tdt: ? , c1941
    wlw: Sevenoaks Brickworks Ltd, Kent - who ordered spare parts in 1/1945 for delivery to Standard Brick & Sand Co Ltd, Redhill.
(7) tdt: Thos.W.Ward Ltd, dealers, Sheffield, 1962 after 5/1962
    wlw: Duncan Logan (Plant) Ltd
(8) tdt: Thomas Mitchell & Sons Ltd, dealers, Bolton, Lancs, 3/1956
    wlw: Rea Ltd, Birkenhead, Cheshire (hire from 10/1959).
(9) tdt: Wales Gas Board, Grangetown, Cardiff, 8/1963
(10) wlw: Ministry of Supply, ROF Ranskill, Notts.
(11) wlw: Ministry of Supply, ROF Dalmuir, Scotland.
(12) wlw: Ministry of Supply, ROF Risley, Lancashire, by c9/1945

WYNNSTAY (Pit C/Green Pit) COLLIERY, RUABON   W12
(Cd/GR:294433)

1856	:	sinking
1856 - 11/1883	:	New British Iron Co
11/1883 - 1886	:	New British Iron Co Ltd (reg.28/11/1883 £600K)
1886 - 1889	:	Exors of N.B.I.Co Ltd in liquidation
6/1889 - 1927	:	Wynnstay Collieries Ltd (reg.28/6/1889 £60K)
6/9/1927	:	coal winding ceased. Closed; dismantled.

Originally sunk as part of the "Acrefair Ironworks" conglomerate; connected to Acrefair by the NBI railway system via a line which, after 1886, became GWR (PR/19). Colliery also connected by siding directly to adjacent (PR/8) main line. Waste material from the colliery was taken by a narrow-gauge line, via bridge over PR/8, to land on the west of PR/8. In 1893 this line was worked by endless chain powered by a stationary steam engine.
After closure the colliery site was used by light industry; in the 1970s it was cut through by road works; some original buildings remain [1992].
Read: J/CG/17.3.1893/485; B/107]

Locomotives: Gauge 4'8½"

Prior to 1889 the colliery was shunted by locos based at, or pooled with, Acrefair Ironworks.

	WELD BLUNDELL	0-4-0ST	OC	MW	802	1882	(a)		(1)
	HALIFAX	0-6-0ST	IC	MW	604	1877	(b)		s/s
	WEEDON	0-6-0ST	IC	MW	976	1886	(c)		(2)
[?		0-6-0ST	IC	MW	1145	1890	(d)		(3)]
	WYNNSTAY	0-6-0ST	IC	MW	1646	1905	New		(4)
	DAISY	0-4-0ST	OC	P	581	1894			
			rebuilt	P		1904			
			rebuilt	P		1915	(e)		(5)

(a) almost certainly obtained by New British Iron Co Ltd c1886 - see under "Acrefair Ironworks" - and transferred to Wynnstay stock by liquidators of NBI Co. Loco suffered a minor explosion at Wynnstay 24/8/1906, prior to which it had been overhauled by MW.
wfw: J.P.Edwards, contractor, Aintree-Southport CLC (1882) Contract
(b) per MW records this loco was here and possibly in/by early 1890s.
wfw: J.D.Nowell, contractor, [? LYR Manchester Victoria Station Extension (1881-1884) Contract] and [? LYR Halifax Station Enlargement (1885-1886) Contract] and [? Manchester Central Station (1889-1892) Contract]; it may have been the 13" 6wc MW for sale at Levenshulme 11/1892 ex Manchester Central Contract. [Perhaps, therefore, it came to Wynnstay late 1892 - maybe per/via H.Croom Johnson (see Section 1) who purchased other locos from this source.]
(c) tdx: Davies Bros, contractors, Wrexham-Ellesmere (PR/57) Contract [6/1897; assuming this was the 12" 6wc MW then on sale there].
(d) not confirmed at Wynnstay, though one source reputes it was here.
wfw: T.Oliver & Son, contractors, Rugby MSLR (1894-1898) Contract. [and perhaps Neasden-Northolt GCR (1902-1905) Contract].
(e) despatched by Peckett Bristol, to Wynnstay 2/11/1922, after repair.
wfw: Greyfield Colliery Co Ltd, Clutton, Bristol (to 3/1916 at least, and was probably the 14x20 0-4-0 for sale there 10/1921).
[Perhaps purchased ex Greyfield by Wynnstay and sent to Peckett for repair; or purchased ex Greyfield by Peckett and repaired for sale.]

(1) tdt: [W.Y.Craig & Sons Ltd ?], Ifton Colliery, Shropshire, c1919
[Perhaps owned by contractor building Ifton railway, rather than owned by Craig.]
(2) wlw(tdt?): A.Kellett, contractor, [? c1900].
[Probably used by A.Kellett on Birmingham Corporation Waterworks Frankley Reservoir (1897-1903) Contract.]
(3) wlw(tdt?): Wolverhampton Corrugated Iron Co Ltd, Ellesmere Port, Cheshire.
(4) In J/MM/16.9.1927 Marple & Gillott Ltd, dealers, Sheffield, had for sale a 16x22 6wc MW/1905 - almost definitely this loco.
Loco still at Wynnstay 1/1928.
wlw: Perry & Co (Bow) Ltd, contractors, Bromborough Dock Construction (1927-1931) Contract, Cheshire, by 7/1928.
(5) For sale in J/PMR 4/1929-9/1929; loco then owned by C.D.Phillips but not located at their depot. Definitely owned by Cudworth & Johnson, dealers, Wrexham, by 3/1932. Also, a 14" 4wc P for sale 2/1930-9/1930 by Cudworth & Johnson, dealers, Wrexham, could be DAISY; and if so it would appear that C&J may have purchased from Phillips "as and where lying" at Wynnstay - but this is not proven.
wlw: Amalgamated Anthracite Collieries Ltd, Gwaun-cae-Gurwen, Glam.

INDEXES

LOCOMOTIVES	IDENTITIES	424
LOCOMOTIVES	NAMES	479
LOCATIONS, OWNERS, OPERATORS		487

INDEX OF LOCOMOTIVES - IDENTITIES

AB - ANDREW BARCLAY, CALEDONIA WORKS, KILMARNOCK.
    First locomotive built 1859
    1859 -   : Andrew Barclay
         -1886   : Andrew Barclay & Son
    1886 -1892   : Andrew Barclay, Son & Co
    1892 -   : Andrew Barclay, Sons & Co Ltd (reg.20.7.1892)
    1972   : subsidiary of Hunslet Holdings Ltd
                    : Hunslet Barclay Ltd

Worksnumb	Ex.Works	Gauge	Type	wheels	cyl	size	engine/notes	pages
176	4.10.1876	4' 8½"	0-4-0 ST		OC	12x20		196
179	21.12.1876	4' 8½"	0-4-0 ST	3' 7"	OC	12x20		266, 347
643	22. 5.1889	4' 8½"	0-4-0 ST	3' 7"	OC	13x20		194, 207, 279
659	22. 3.1890	4' 8½"	0-4-0 ST		OC	13x20		256
783	6. 4.1897	4' 8½"	0-4-0 ST	2' 9"	OC	11x16		42
820	6.1898	4' 8½"	0-4-0 ST	3' 2"	OC	10x18		36
821	6.1899	4' 8½"	0-4-0 ST	3' 0"	OC	10x18		40, 233
875	1. 9.1900	4' 8½"	0-4-0 ST	3' 0"	OC	10x18		287
1179	18. 4.1910	4' 8½"	0-4-0 ST	3' 0"	OC	10x18		334
1232	20.12.1912	4' 8½"	0-4-0 ST	3' 7"	OC	16x24		273, 279
1304	15.11.1912	4' 8½"	0-4-0 ST	3' 2"	OC	12x18		42, 194
1431	21. 2.1918	2' 0"	0-4-0 WT	1'10"	OC	6¾x10¾		108
1434	17. 2.1916	4' 8½"	0-4-0 F	3' 0"	OC	15x20		375
1435	17. 2.1916	4' 8½"	0-4-0 F	3' 0"	OC	15x20		375
1437	1. 4.1916	4' 8½"	0-4-0 F	3' 0"	OC	15x20		375
1438	1. 4.1916	4' 8½"	0-4-0 F	3' 0"	OC	15x20		375, 377
1572	5. 1.1918	4' 8½"	0-6-0 F	3' 0"	OC	14½x18		375
1584	5. 9.1917	4' 8½"	0-4-0 ST	3' 0"	OC	10x18		292
1761	21. 2.1922	4' 8½"	0-4-0 ST	3' 0"	OC	10x18		189
1831	22.11.1924	4' 8½"	0-4-0 ST	3' 2"	OC	12x20		194, 266
1991	14. 7.1931	2' 0"	0-4-0 WT	1'10"	OC	7x11	class E	359
1994	8.10.1931	2' 0"	0-4-0 WT	1'10"	OC	7x11	class E	359
1995	30.11.1931	2' 0"	0-4-0 WT	1'10"	OC	7x11	class E	236
2095	11.11.1940	4' 8½"	0-4-0 ST	3' 8"	OC	16x24		386
2232	26. 2.1948	4' 8½"	0-6-0 F	3' 0"	OC	17x18		224
2263	29. 4.1949	3' 0"	0-4-0 WT	2' 0"	OC	8½x12		108
345	30. 1.1941	4' 8½"	0-4-0 DM			153hp	Grd:	419
349	25. 1.1941	4' 8½"	0-4-0 DM			80hp	Grd:	307
359	13.12.1941	4' 8½"	0-4-0 DM			153hp	Grd:	378
360	3.12.1941	4' 8½"	0-4-0 DM			153hp		378
394	23. 8.1955	4' 8½"	0-4-0 DM	3' 2"		204hp		96
396	17. 1.1956	4' 8½"	0-4-0 DM			153hp	Grd:6L3:	292
397	10. 2.1956	4' 8½"	0-4-0 DM			153hp	Grd:6L3:	292
489	3. 4.1964	4' 8½"	0-6-0 DH			440hp	MAN:	397
507	18. 4.1966	4' 8½"	0-6-0 DH			440hp	MAN:	397
508	18. 4.1966	4' 8½"	0-6-0 DH			440hp	MAN:	397
# 632								138
# 775								153

\# - Dual Identity locomotives.
    For AB 632 see HE 8518;   For AB 775 see HE 9305

AD - AUSTRO DAIMLER, WIENER NEUSTADT, AUSTRIA.

Worksnumb	Ex.Works	Gauge	Type	wheels	cyl	size	engine/notes	pages
		2ft	4w PM			c20hp		70

AE - AVONSIDE ENGINE WORKS, BRISTOL.
First locomotive built in 1841
1841 -1856   : Stothert, Slaughter & Co
1856 -1866   : Slaughter, Gruning & Co
1866 -   : Avonside Engine Co Ltd (reg.1864; vol.liq.1879)
     -1934   : Avonside Engine Co Ltd
Closed 11/1934   ; Goodwill etc bought by Hunslet 'HE'.

Worksnumb	Ex.Works	Gauge	Type	wheels	cyl	size	engine/notes	pages
929/930	1872	1'11½"	0-4-4-0T	2' 8"	4OC	8½x14	Fairlie	68
1397	12. 4.1899	4' 8½"	0-4-0 ST	3' 3"	OC	14x20	class SS	41, 273, 279, 329
1407	2.11.1899	4' 8½"	0-4-0 ST	3' 3"	OC	14x20	class SS	52, 225, 373, 378
1408	19.12.1899	4' 8½"	0-4-0 ST	3' 3"	OC	14x20	class SS	52, 336
1432	1902	4' 8½"	0-6-0 ST	3' 3"	OC	14x20	special	297
1472	1904	4' 8½"	0-6-0 ST	3' 3"	OC	14x20	class B2	37
1603	1912	4' 8½"	0-6-0 ST	3' 3"	OC	14x22	class B3	45, 279
1604	1912	4' 8½"	0-6-0 ST	3' 3"	OC	14x22	class B3	37, 198, 273
1770	1917	4' 8½"	0-6-0 ST	3' 3"	OC	14x20	class B3	205, 273
1796	27. 2.1918	4' 8½"	0-4-0 ST	3' 6"	OC	14x20	class SS3	44
1868	7. 6.1921	4' 8½"	0-6-0 ST	3' 3"	OC	14½x20	class B5	313
1876	8. 2.1921	4' 8½"	0-4-0 ST	2'11"	OC	12x18	Std 12x18	44
1913	24. 4.1923	4' 8½"	0-4-0 ST	2'11"	OC	12x18	Std 12x18	230
1923	31. 5.1923	4' 8½"	0-6-0 ST	3' 3"	OC	14x20	class B3	297
1951	13.11.1924	4' 8½"	0-6-0 ST	3' 3"	OC	15x20	class B5	313
2062	27. 2.1932	4' 8½"	0-4-0 DM	2'9½"		80hp	Grd:6L2:	355
2063	27. 2.1932	4' 8½"	0-4-0 DM	2'9½"		80hp	Grd:6L2:	355
2066	7. 4.1933	2' 0"	0-4-0 T	2' 0"	OC	7x12		359
2067	7. 4.1933	2' 0"	0-4-0 T	2' 0"	OC	7x12		359
2071	28. 6.1933	2' 0"	0-4-0 T	2' 0"	OC	7½x12		236

AH - A.HORLOCK & CO, NORTH FLEET IRON WORKS, NORTHFLEET, KENT.

Worksnumb	Ex.Works	Gauge	Type	wheels	cyl	size	engine/notes	pages
	8.1848	4' 0"	0-4-0 tdr	4' 6"	OC	13x22		235, 357
	1848	4' 0"	0-4-0 tdr	4' 6"	OC	13x22		235

ALCo - AMERICAN LOCOMOTIVE COMPANY, COOKE WORKS, PATERSON NJ, U.S.A.

Worksnumb	Ex.Works	Gauge	Type	wheels	cyl	size	engine/notes	pages
57156	c5.1917	600mm	2-6-2 T	2' 3"	OC	9x14		68

AP - AVELING & PORTER LTD, ROCHESTER, KENT.
(built about 130 locomotives between 1864 and 1926).

Worksnumb	Ex.Works	Gauge	Type	wheels	cyl	size	engine/notes	pages
221	17. 9.1866	4' 8½"	4w	WT	SC		6hp	95
235	23.10.1866	4' 8½"	4w	WT	SC		10hp	95

AtW - ATKINSON WALKER WAGGONS LTD, FRENCHWOOD WORKS, PRESTON.
(built c20 locomotives c1926-c1931).

Worksnumb	Ex.Works	Gauge	Type	wheels	cyl	size	engine/notes	pages
113	1928	4' 8½"	4w	VBT	2' 6"	ICG 7x10	class C	419

AW - SIR W.G.ARMSTRONG WHITWORTH & CO (ENGINEERS) LTD, SCOTSWOOD WORKS, NEWCASTLE ON TYNE.
1847 -   : W.G.Armstrong & Co
      -1937   : Sir W.G.Armstrong Whitworth & Co (Engineers) Ltd
After WW1, AW factories at Openshaw (Manchester) and Elswick were used also, for locomotive repair work (only).

Worksnumb	Ex.Works	Gauge	Type	wheels	cyl	size	engine/notes	pages
D.53	6.1935	3' 0"	0-4-0 DE	2' 3"			60hp ASr:4BOD:	354

Barber - TREVOR BARBER & ALAN KEEF, BEDFORD.
(One loco built).

Worksnumb	Ex.Works	Gauge	Type	wheels	cyl	size	engine/notes	pages
TRIXIE	1974	2ft	0-4-0 ST	1' 8"	OC	6x9		170, 172

Barnes - A.BARNES & CO, ALBION WORKS, RHYL.

Worksnumb	Ex.Works	Gauge	Type	wheels	cyl	size	engine/notes	pages
101	1920	1' 3"	4-4-2 tdr	1' 8"	OC	4¼x7		163
[102]	? 1921	1' 3"	4-4-2 tdr	1' 8"	OC	4¼x7		163
103	1921	1' 3"	4-4-2 tdr	1' 8"	OC	4¼x7		163
[104]	? 1927	1' 3"	4-4-2 tdr	1' 8"	OC	4¼x7		163
105	? 1928	1' 3"	4-4-2 tdr	1' 8"	OC	4¼x7		163
[106]	? 1934	1' 3"	4-4-2 tdr	1' 8"	OC	4¼x7		163

BE - BRUSH (FALCON) LOCOMOTIVE WORKS, LOUGHBOROUGH.
1889 -1951   : Brush Electrical Engineering Co Ltd
1951 -1956   : Brush Bagnall Traction Ltd
1956 -   : Brush Electrical Machines Ltd, Traction Division.
Brush took over the Falcon Works (see 'FE') in 1889. The Falcon loco number series was continued, and Falcon Works-plates fitted until (including) No.275 of 1898. However, the battery-locos as listed below were entered in an 'Order No.' series.

Worksnumb	Ex.Works	Gauge	Type	wheels	cyl	size	engine/notes	pages
16303	c1917	2ft	4w	BE		c8hp		324, 345, 376
16306	c1917	2ft	4w	BE		c8hp		324, 345, 376
	c1917	2ft	4w	BE		c8hp	Votty	412
	c1917	2ft	4w	BE		10hp	7036	184, 412, 415
	c1917	2ft	4w	BE			Q'ferry	376
		2ft	4w	BE			Williams	57
		2ft	4w	BE			Williams	57

For BE [BT] 102 of 1958, see BP 7859 (page 96 -dual identity loco).

BEV - BRITISH ELECTRIC VEHICLES LTD, SOUTHPORT, LANCASHIRE.
    (closed 1926; business purchased by Wingrove & Rogers - see 'WR').

Worksnumb	Ex.Works	Gauge	Type	wheels	cyl	size	engine/notes	pages
308	19. 1.1921	1'11½"	4w	BE		2hp	No.1 type	317
323	8. 2.1921	2ft	4w	BE		2hp	No.1 type	317
?	1921	2ft	4w	BE		2hp	Llechwedd No.2	317
?		2ft	4w	BE		2hp	Llechwedd 3	317
603	28. 5.1925	2ft	4w	BE			No.2 type	248
604	11. 6.1925	2ft	4w	BE			No.2 type	248
640	18. 6.1926	2ft	4w	WE		10hp	No.3 Trolley	317, 345

Bg - BAGULEY LOCOMOTIVES & RAILCARS.
1911 -1923 : Baguley Cars Ltd, Shobnall Road, Burton on Trent
1923 -1931 : Baguley (Engineers) Ltd
1932 -1967 : E.E.Baguley Ltd, Uxbridge Street, Burton on Trent
1967 - : Baguley-Drewry Ltd.
Always closely associated with Drewry ('DC').
In 1913 purchased Goodwill etc. of McEwan Pratt & Co Ltd (of Wickford, Essex) and for some years thereafter, Bg built locos using the McEwan Pratt name.

Worksnumb	Ex.Works	Gauge	Type	wheels	cyl	size	engine/notes	pages
553	1914	4' 8½"	4w	PMr		20hp		291
649	30. 9.1918	600mm	0-4-0	PM		10hp		310
708	24.11.1917	600mm	0-4-0	PM		10hp		342
731	22. 2.1918	600mm	0-4-0	PM		10hp		383
774	5. 3.1919	2ft	0-4-0	PM		20hp	Bg:4cyl:4120cc	285, 342, 345
[777 ?]	1919	2ft	0-4-0	PM	1'8½"	20hp	Bg:4cyl:	342
1442	31. 3.1925	4' 8½"	0-4-0	PM		35hp		259
3003	1937	4' 8½"	4w	DM				225
#3379	1954	2' 0"	4w	BE		EM2A1	flameproof	314
#3380	1954	2' 0"	4w	BE		EM2A1	flameproof	314
#3381	1954	2' 0"	4w	BE		EM2A1	flameproof	314
#3382	1954	2' 0"	4w	BE		EM2A1	flameproof	314
#3537	1959	2' 0"	4w	BE		EM2A1	flameproof	314
3767	5.1985	600mm	0-6-0	DH				70

Ø : these locos built jointly with English Electric Co Ltd, hence
dual identities :- Bg 3379 = EE 1960; Bg 3380 = EE 1961;
Bg 3381 = EE 1963; Bg 3382 = EE 1962; Bg 3537 = EE 2697.

BH - BLACK, HAWTHORN LOCOMOTIVE WORKS, GATESHEAD ON TYNE.
1865 -1892 : Black, Hawthorn & Co, Gateshead on Tyne
1892 -1896 : Black, Hawthorn & Co Ltd
In 1865 took over the loco building business of R.Coulthard & Co.
Closed 1896; purchased by Chapman & Furneaux who continued same number series (from 1144) until closure in 1902. Goodwill etc. purchased by 'HL'.

Worksnumb	Ex.Works	Gauge	Type	wheels	cyl	size	engine/notes	pages
21	1867	4' 8½"	0-4-0 ST	3' 3"	OC	12x20		35
1014	1890	4' 8½"	0-6-0 ST	3' 3"	OC	15x20		205
1038	1891	4' 8½"	0-4-0 ST	3' 2"	OC	12x19		44
1059	1892	4' 8½"	0-4-0 ST	3' 3"	OC	12x19		35, 52
1116	1896	4' 8½"	0-6-0 ST	3'0½"	IC	12x18		45
1125	1895	3' 0"	0-4-0 ST	2' 3"	OC	9x16		188, 247

BL - W.J.BASSETT LOWKE LTD, NORTHAMPTON.

Worksnumb	Ex.Works	Gauge	Type	wheels	cyl	size	engine/notes	pages
15	7.1909	1' 3"	4-4-2 tdr	1' 6"	OC	3½x6	class 10	163
18	1911	1' 3"	4-4-2 tdr	1' 6"	OC	3½x6	class 10	163
22	1915	1' 3"	4-4-2 tdr	1' 6"	OC	3½x6	class 20	146
32	1924	1' 3"	4-4-2 tdr	1' 8"	OC	4x6¾	class 30	146

BLW - BALDWIN LOCOMOTIVE WORKS, PHILADELPHIA, U.S.A.

Worksnumb	Ex.Works	Gauge	Type	wheels	cyl	size	engine/notes	pages
15511	10.1897	600mm	2-6-0 tdr		OC		class 8-18	70
45172	3.1917	2' 0"	4-6-0 PT	1'11½	OC	9x12	class 10-12-D	136
45221	3.1917	2' 0"	4-6-0 PT	1'11½"	OC	9x12	class 10-12-D	129
46764	10.1917	2' 0"	2-6-2 PT	2' 0"	OC	9x12	class 10-12-D5	359
46828	1917	2' 0"	2-6-2 PT	2' 0"	OC	9x12	class 10-12-D5	359
47143	1917	2' 0"	2-6-2 PT	2' 0"	OC	9x12	class 10-12-D5	359
? 49604	8.1918	600mm	0-4-0 PM	2' 6"		45hp	PME:class 4-50	68
61269	3.1930	2' 0"	4-6-2 tdr	3' 0"	OC	13½x18		169

E.BOYDELL & CO - see 'MH'.

BP - BEYER PEACOCK LOCO WORKS, GORTON, MANCHESTER.
```
1854 -1883    : Beyer, Peacock & Co
1853 -1902    : Beyer, Peacock & Co Ltd
1902 -1923    : Beyer, Peacock & Co (1902) Ltd
1923 -1966    : Beyer, Peacock & Co Ltd
```
A joint company, Beyer Peacock (Hymek) Ltd, was set up to build diesel locos within the same Works.
Last loco left the Works 7/1966 - Works then closed.

Worksnumb	Ex.Works	Gauge	Type	wheels	cyl	size	engine/notes	pages
68	29. 7.1857	4' 8½"	? 0-4-0 ST	4' 0"	IC	14x20		185
91	31. 8.1857	4' 8½"	0-4-0 T	3' 0"	OC	11x16		194, 347
92	20. 9.1858	4' 8½"	0-4-0 T	3' 0"	OC	11x16		205
810	22. 5.1868	4' 8½"	0-4-0 ST	3'0½"	OC	11x16		331
811	15. 9.1868	4' 8½"	0-4-0 ST	3'0½"	OC	11x16		194, 205
1878	1879	4' 8½"	4-4-0 T	5' 9"	OC	17x24		227
2157	22. 5.1882	4' 8½"	0-6-0 ST	4' 0"	IC	16x24		110, 266
2465	1884	4' 8½"	2-4-0 T		?			295
2649	1885	4' 8½"	0-6-2 ST	4' 3"	IC	18x24		110
2650	1886	4' 8½"	0-6-2 ST	4' 3"	IC	18x24		110
2962	1888	4' 8½"	0-6-2 ST	4' 3"	IC	18x24		110
2963	1888	4' 8½"	0-6-2 ST	4' 3"	IC	18x24		110

2969	17.10.1888	2' 4½"	0-4-2 T	2' 6"	OC	10½x16		129
2970	11. 4.1889	2' 4½"	0-4-2 T	2' 6"	OC	10½x16		129
3500	23. 5.1892	2' 4½"	0-4-2 T	2' 6"	OC	10½x16		129
3866	1896	4' 8½"	0-6-2 T	5' 1"	IC	18x26		110
3867	1896	4' 8½"	0-6-2 T	5' 1"	IC	18x26		110
5292	1909	2' 0"	0-4-4-0T	2'7½"	4OC	11x16	Garret	68
5408	26. 9.1910	4' 8½"	0-4-0 ST	3'0½"	OC	12x18		331
#7859	1958	4' 8½"	0-4-0 DE					96
8039	1965	4' 8½"	4w+4w	DE				173

- dual identity loco; is also BE 102 of 1958.

Bs - BARCLAYS & CO, RIVERBANK WORKS, KILMARNOCK.
    Opened 1871 - a separate business operated by relatives of Andrew Barclay (see 'AB'). Closed 1/1886, and business amalgamated into the AB Caledonia Works. Around 1890, 'AB' re-opened the Riverbank Works as an out-station of the Caledonia Works, but the Riverbank Works closed again 11/1892.

Worksnumb	Ex.Works	Gauge	Type	wheels	cyl	size	engine/notes	pages
216	1874	4' 8½"	0-4-0 ST		OC	12x		336
?	?1875		0-6-0 ST	3' 0"	OC	12x20	FERNHILL	128

Bton - BRIGHTON LOCOMOTIVE WORKS, SUSSEX.
    1852 -1922   : London, Brighton & South Coast Rly Co
    1923 -1947   : Southern Rly Co
    1948 -1957   : British Railways.

Worksnumb	Ex.Works	Gauge	Type	wheels	cyl	size	engine/notes	pages
BR 32640	1878	4' 8½"	0-6-0 T	4' 1"	IC	12x20	Terrier	211

Bury - BURY LOCO WORKS, CLARENCE FOUNDRY, LOVE LANE, LIVERPOOL.
    c1825 -1842   : Edward Bury & Co - first loco built 1830.
    1842 -1851   : Bury, Curtis & Kennedy
           1851   : closed.

Worksnumb	Ex.Works	Gauge	Type	wheels	cyl	size	engine/notes	pages
	1839	4' 8½"	0-4-0 tdr	5' 0"	?		E.Preston	102
	?1846	4' 8½"	0-6-0 tdr	4' 6"	?	14½x	CHANCELLOR	109
	8.1847	4' 8½"	2-2-2 tdr	5' 6"	IC	15x20	S&CR No.11	75
	9.1847	4' 8½"	2-2-2 tdr	5' 6"	IC	15x20	S&CR No.12	75
	11.1847	4' 8½"	0-4-0 ST	4' 0"	IC	15x20	S&CR No.15	76
	7.1848	4' 8½"	0-4-2 tdr	5' 0"	IC	16x24	S&CR No.17	76
	8.1848	4' 8½"	0-4-2 tdr	5' 0"	IC	16x24	S&CR No.18	76
	9.1848	4' 8½"	2-2-2 tdr	5' 6"	IC	15x20	S&CR No.19	76
	9.1848	4' 8½"	2-2-2 tdr	5' 6"	IC	15x20	S&CR No.20	76

CE - CLAYTON LOCOMOTIVE WORKS, HATTON, DERBYSHIRE.
Clayton Equipment Co Ltd.
Clarke Chapman Ltd, Clayton Works, by 1975.

Worksnumb	Ex.Works	Gauge	Type	wheels	cyl size	engine/notes	pages
5370	1967	2' 0"	4w	BE			277, ?352
5667	8.1969	2' 0"	4w	BE			288
5667	8.1969	2' 0"	4w	BE			288
5667	8.1969	2' 0"	4w	BE			288
5688/2	1969	2ft	4w	BE			322
5885	1971	1' 6"	4w	BE			277, ?352
B0457	1974	2' 3"	4w	BE			184

Ch - CHAPLIN PATENT VERTICAL BOILERED LOCOMOTIVES.
1849 -   : Alexander Chaplin & Co, Anderson, Glasgow
    -1930 : Alexander Chaplin & Co Ltd
Originally located at Cranstonhill Engine Works, Port Street, Anderson; relocated to Helen Street, Govan, Glasgow in c1890.
Locomotives were built from 1860s to early 1900s.
Closed 1930; assets sold 4/1932.

Worksnumb	Ex.Works	Gauge	Type	wheels	cyl size	engine/notes	pages
? 153	c1860	4' 8½"	0-4-0 VBT	VC		PR/12 (?)	88
1685	1874	3' 0"	0-4-0 VBT	VC	7x11	MONA (?)	300
?	? pre.1875	4' 8½"	0-4-0 VBT	VC		PR/12 (maybe)	88

Chance - CHANCE MANUFACTURING CO INC, WICHITA, KANSAS, U.S.A.

Worksnumb	Ex.Works	Gauge	Type	wheels	cyl size	engine/notes	pages
31	1964	2' 0"	4w-2-4w PM				211
157	1978	2' 0"	4w-2-4w PM			Ford 2820cc	211

Cilgwyn - CILGWYN SLATE QUARRY, NANTLLE.
For details of petrol locomotive see Location listing "Cilgwyn Quarry" page 218..

CoedTalon - COED TALON COLLIERY CO, COED TALON, CLWYD.

Worksnumb	Ex.Works	Gauge	Type	wheels	cyl size	engine/notes	pages
	1874	4' 8½"	4w TG	SC	9x12		221

Cromford - CROMFORD & HIGH PEAK RLY CO, CROMFORD WORKS, DERBYSHIRE.

Worksnumb	Ex.Works	Gauge	Type	wheels	cyl	size	engine/notes	pages
	1859	4' 8½"	0-6-0 ST	3' 0"	OC	10x12		103

Cross - JAMES CROSS & CO, SUTTON ENGINE WORKS, St.HELENS.
Founded 1864; built c60 locomotives before ceasing trading c1869.
Part of premises became LNWR Sutton Oak loco shed c1872.

Worksnumb	Ex.Works	Gauge	Type	wheels	cyl	size	engine/notes	pages
	1866	4' 8½"	0-4-4-0T	4' 0"	4OC	10x16	Dble. Fairlie	106

Cwe - CREWE LOCOMOTIVE WORKS, CREWE, CHESHIRE.
```
1843 -1846    : Grand Junction Rly Co
1846 -1922    : London & North Western Rly Co
1923 -1947    : London, Midland & Scottish Rly Co
1948 -        : British Railways.
```

Worksnumb	Ex.Works	Gauge	Type	wheels	cyl	size	engine/notes	pages
253	1935	4' 8½"	4-6-2 tdr	6' 6"	4C	16¼x28		211
(46443)	1950	4'8½"	2-6-0 tdr	5' 0"	OC	16x24		174

DA - DANIEL ADAMSON & CO, NEWTON MOOR WORKS, DUKINFIELD, MANCHESTER.
Locomotives built from 1866 to 1896.

Worksnumb	Ex.Works	Gauge	Type	wheels	cyl	size	engine/notes	pages
292	1885	1'11½"	0-4-0 T	1' 8"	OC	6x10		342
	1886	1'11½"	0-4-0 T	1' 8"	OC	6x10	EDWARD	342
346	1888	1'11½"	0-4-0 T	1' 8"	OC	6x10		342
	1890	1'11½"	0-4-0 T	1' 8"	OC	6x10	ALGERNON	342
	1890	1'11½"	0-4-0 T	1' 8"	OC	6x10	CHARLES	342

DB - SIR ARTHUR P.HEYWOOD, DUFFIELD BANK, DERBYSHIRE.

Worksnumb	Ex.Works	Gauge	Type	wheels	cyl	size	engine/notes	pages
4	8.1896	1' 3"	0-4-0 T	1' 3"	OC	4¾x7		146, 411

DC - DREWRY CAR CO LTD, LONDON.

Although Drewry locos and railcars were numbered in a 'DC' series, they were largely manufactured by others - particularly 'Bg' - under contract.

Worksnumb	Ex.Works	Gauge	Type	wheels	cyl size	engine/notes	pages
1818	1935	4' 8½"	4w PMr				291

DC 2185 - dual identity of VF 5266 - which see, p.378.

DCL - DAVID CURWEN LTD, DEVIZES, WILTSHIRE.

Worksnumb	Ex.Works	Gauge	Type	wheels	cyl size	engine/notes	pages
	10.1952	2' 3"	4w PM		20hp	Ford	108

Derby - DERBY LOCOMOTIVE WORKS.

- 1840 -1844 : North Midland Rly Co
- 1844 -1922 : Midland Rly Co
- 1923 -1947 : London, Midland & Scottish Rly Co
- 1948 -   : British Railways.

Worksnumb	Ex.Works	Gauge	Type	wheels	cyl size	engine/notes	pages
(08195)	1956	4' 8½"	0-6-0 DE	4' 6"	350hp		173
(25313)	1966	4' 8½"	4w+4w DE	3' 9"	1250hp		173
(51618)	1959	4' 8½"	4w+4 DMr				173

DeW - DeWINTON & CO, UNION IRON WORKS, CAERNARFON.

Locos built from c1867 to c1898.

Worksnumb	Ex.Works	Gauge	Type	wheels	cyl size	engine/notes	pages
[A]	c1869	2ft	0-4-0 VBT	SVCG		LwrGlynrhonwy	305
[A]	c1870	2ft	0-4-0 VBT	SVCG		Dorothea	252
[A]	c1870	2ft	0-4-0 VBT	SVCG		Moeltryfan	333
[A]	by 1873	2ft	+0-4-0 VBT	SVCG		LwrGlynrhonwy	305
[? A]	?	2ft	+0-4-0 VBT	VC		CATH.FANNY	304
[B]	?	2ft	0-4-0 VBT	SVC		PADARN	305
[B]	?	2ft	0-4-0 VBT	SVC		BALADEULYN	305, 367
[B]	?	2ft	0-4-0 VBT	SVC		STARSTON	367
[B]	?	2ft	0-4-0 VBT	SVC		New Braich	200
[?C ?A]	14. 7.1873	2ft	0-4-0 VBT	VC		Dorothea	252
[C]	10.1873	1'11½"	0-4-0 VBT	VC	5½x10	Trefor	406
[C]	5.1874	2ft	0-4-0 VBT	VC	6x10	GLYN	252
[C]	10. 7.1874	2ft	#0-4-0 VBT	VC	6x12	PERT	74
[? C]	?c1874	2ft	#0-4-0 VBT	VC		Coedmadoc	220
[C]	9.1875	2ft	0-4-0 VBT	VC	6x10	RHYMNEY	365, 367
[C]	3.1876	2ft	0-4-0 VBT	VC	6x12	Trefor	406

[C]	11. 5.1876	2ft	0-4-0 VBT	1' 8"	VC	6x10	LORD PENRHYN	358
[D]	c6.1876	2ft	0-4-0 VBT		VC	6x10	C'VON CASTLE	302
[D]	3.10.1876	2ft	0-4-0 VBT	1' 8"	VC	6x10	LADY PENRHYN	358
[H]	12.1876	1'10¾"	0-4-0 ST		IC	8x12	EDWARD SHOLTO	358
[D]	1876	2ft	0-4-0 VBT		VC	6x10	ADDA	187
[D]	? 1876	2ft	0-4-0 VBT		VC	6x10	LIZZIE	218
[D]	5.1877	2ft	0-4-0 VBT	1' 8"	VC	6x12	GEORGE HENRY	358, 411
[D]	c6.1877	2ft	0-4-0 VBT	1' 8"	VC	6x10	ALICE	358
[D]	6.1877	2ft	0-4-0 VBT	1' 8"	VC	6x12	KATHLEEN	345, 358
[D]	1.10.1877	2ft	0-4-0 VBT	1' 8"	VC	6x12	GEORGINA	258
[D]	c11.1877	2ft	¢ 0-4-0 VBT		VC	6x10	GERTRUDE	218, 220
[? D]	?	2ft	¢ 0-4-0 VBT		VC		Coedmadoc	220
[D]	1877	2ft	0-4-0 VBT		VC	6x10	INVERLOCHY	367
[D]	1877	2ft	0-4-0 VBT		VC	6x10	WELLINGTON	235, 305
[D]	1877	2ft	0-4-0 VBT	1' 8"	VC	6x10	CHALONER	365, 367
[D]	1877	2ft	0-4-0 VBT		VC	6x10	EVA	187
[** D]	1877	2ft	0-4-0 VBT		VC		FLORINDA	187
[D]	6.1878	1'11½"	0-4-0 VBT		VC	6x10	Llechwedd	317
[H]	9.1878	1'10¾"	0-4-0 T		IC	9½x	HILDA	358
[D]	10.1878	2ft	0-4-0 VBT	1' 8"	VC	6x12	INA	358
[D]	1878	3' 0"	0-4-0 VBT	1' 8"	VC	5¾x10	PENMAEN	354
[D]	c1878	3½ft ?	0-4-0 VBT		VC		VRON	263, 401
[H]	8.1879	1'10¾"	0-4-0 T		IC		VIOLET	358
[D]	c1879	2ft	0-4-0 VBT		VC		MURIEL	268, 385
[D]	? 5.1880	2ft	0-4-0 VBT		VC	6x10	FREDA	317, 403
[D]	1880	2ft	0-4-0 VBT		VC	6x10	MADGE	218
[D]	1880	2ft	0-4-0 VBT		VC	6x10	GLYNLLIFON	367
[D]	1880	2ft	0-4-0 VBT		VC	6x10	MOELEILIA	220
[D]	1891	3' 0"	0-4-0 VBT	1' 8"	VC	5¾x10	LILIAN	354
[D]	1892	3' 0"	0-4-0 VBT	1' 8"	VC	5¾x10	LOUISA	354
[D]	1892	3' 0"	0-4-0 VBT	1' 8"	VC	5¾x10	ADA	354
[D]	7.1893	2ft	0-4-0 VBT		VC	5¾x10	GELLI	367
[D]	1893	3' 0"	0-4-0 VBT	1' 8"	VC	5¾x10	PUFFIN	354
[D]	1893	3' 0"	0-4-0 VBT	1' 8"	VC	7x12	WATKIN	354, 357
[D]	1894	3' 0"	0-4-0 VBT		VC	7x12	HAROLD	354
[D]	1894	2ft	0-4-0 VBT		VC	5¾x10	PENDYFFRYN	169, 367
[F]	1895	2ft	0-4-0 VBT		VC	7x12	ARTHUR	367
[D]	1895	3' 0"	0-4-0 VBT	1' 8"	VC	7x12	LLANFAIR	345, 354
[D]	c1895	2ft	0-4-0 VBT		VC	5¾x10	EMILY	304
201 [E]	1897	2ft	0-4-0 VBT	1' 8"	VC	5¾x10	VICTORIA	367
[D]	?	2ft	* 0-4-0 VBT		VC		Rhos	384

Original DeWinton records are "lost" - this list reconstructed from many sources. Some cylinder dimensions are nominal. "2ft" gauge indicates approximate as opposed to 2'0" gauge.

'Types' are not official, and are shown for guidance only.

```
   + +   possibly same loco.        Types:  [A] Single cylinder Geared drive
   # #   possibly same loco.                [B] Single cylinder Direct drive
   ¢ ¢   possibly same loco.                [C] 2VC; Chimney over cylinders
    *    possibly a loco already            [D] 2VC; Chimney over boiler
         included in this list.             [E] type D [?converted ex type C]
   **    existence not confirmed.           [F] Jackshaft Drive
                                            [H] Horizontal Boiler
```

DK - DICK, KERR & CO, BRITANNIA WORKS, KILMARNOCK.
         Locomotives built c1884 to ?? .
Company with a complicated history - various "Kerr" companies traded in Glasgow and
London from early 1870s, becoming sellers of locomotives built by others - particularly those
of Barr, Morrison & Co, and Hartley & Arnoux - some of which were fitted with 'DK' plates.
Were instrumental in creation of 'KS' (which see).
  1883 -1890   : Dick, Kerr & Co
  1890 -1918   : Dick, Kerr & Co Ltd
Became a constituent of English Electric Co Ltd, reg.14/12/1918.

Worksnumb	Ex.Works	Gauge	Type	wheels	cyl	size	engine/notes	pages
			0-4-2 T	2' 1"	OC	7x12	MORFA	226

Dodds - DODDS & SON, HOLMES ENGINE WORKS, ROTHERHAM.
         Locomotives built from 1849 to 1868. Closed 1868.

Worksnumb	Ex.Works	Gauge	Type	wheels	cyl	size	engine/notes	pages
	8.1854	4' 8½"	? 0-4-2 tdr	4' 6"	IC	14x20	WMCQR 14	110, 207

Dtz - DEUTZ ("OTTO" etc.) LOCOMOTIVES, GERMANY.
by1896 -1930   : Gasmoteren Fabrik Deutz, Cologne.
   1930 -1936   : Humboldt Deutz
   1936 -   : Magirus Humboldt Deutz
by1964 -   : Klockner-Humboldt-Deutz A.G.

Worksnumb	Ex.Works	Gauge	Type	wheels	cyl	size	engine/notes	pages
1105	1912	2ft	4w PM			10hp		412
1325	1913	2ft	4w PM			8hp		412
49051	? c1911	2ft	4w PM					384
68179	? 1916	2ft	4w PM			20hp		252, 412
92972	? 1916	2ft	4w PM			20hp		412
?	?	2ft	4w PM			28hp	Oakeley	342

Dub - DUBS LOCOMOTIVE WORKS, POLMADIE (LITTLE GOVAN), GLASGOW.
  1865 -   : Dubs & Co
        -1903   : Dubs & Co Ltd
Amalgamated in 1903 with 'NR' and 'SS' to form 'NB', the Dubs Works becoming the
Queens Park Works of NB.

Worksnumb	Ex.Works	Gauge	Type	wheels	cyl	size	engine/notes	pages
2064	1884	4' 8½"	0-4-0 CT	3' 4"	OC	12x22		205

EAV - EDISON ACCUMULATOR VEHICLES, 15 UPPER GEORGE STREET, LONDON W.1.
    Apparently a division of Edison Accumulators Ltd, registered 1913 (as a branch of Edison U.S.A.) to sell battery electric locomotives having motors and mechanical parts made by Automatic Transportation Co, Buffalo NY, USA. and Edison batteries. An identical or similar product was sold by H.C.Slingsby Ltd as the "Slingsby-Automatic Electric Truck". Edison Accumulators Ltd was re-registered as Britannia Batteries Ltd 1/1929 and liquidated in 1948-1949.

Worksnumb	Ex.Works	Gauge	Type	wheels	cyl	size	engine/notes	pages
662		2ft	4w BE				AA-AA4 loco	412
667		2ft	4w BE				class AA loco	412
?		2ft	4w BE				Platform Truck	412

EBW - E.B.WILSON RAILWAY FOUNDRY, LEEDS.
    1840 -1844   : Shepherd & Todd
    1845 -1846   : Shepherd & [E.B.] Wilson
    1846 -1847   : Fenton, Craven & Co
    1847 -1858   : E.B.Wilson & Co
Closed 1858; Goodwill and part of premises purchased by 'MW'; other parts of premises purchased by 'HC'.

Worksnumb	Ex.Works	Gauge	Type	wheels	cyl	size	engine/notes	pages
	1856	4' 8½"	2-4-0 tdr	5' 6"	OC	15½x20	Savin/DR&CRly	54, 98
301/601?	by 2.1859	4' 8½"	0-6-0 T	3' 0"	?C	11x18		53, 114

EE - ENGLISH ELECTRIC CO LTD.
    EES -   Stephenson Works, Darlington (ex 'RSH').
    EEV -   Vulcan Foundry, Newton-le-Willows (ex 'VF')
        Became G.E.C.Traction Ltd - see 'GECT'.

Worksnumb	Ex.Works	Gauge	Type	wheels	cyl	size	engine/notes	pages
3985-V	1970	4' 8½"	0-6-0 DH			500hp	Dmn:8QT	396
3986-V	1970	4' 8½"	0-6-0 DH			500hp	Dmn:8QT	396
3998-V	1970	4' 8½"	0-6-0 DH			500hp	Dmn:8QT	396
3999-V	1971	4' 8½"	0-6-0 DH			500hp	Dmn:8QT	396
5352-V	1971	4' 8½"	0-6-0 DH			500hp	Dmn:8QT	396
5353-V	1971	4' 8½"	0-6-0 DH			500hp	Dmn:8QT	396
5360-	1971	4' 8½"	0-4-0 WE				Coke Ovens	397
5361-	1971	4' 8½"	0-4-0 WE				Coke Ovens	397

Also EE 1960 to EE 1963, EE 2697 (p.314): dual identities of Bg 3379-3382, 3537, which see.

Ellis - H.& J.ELLIS, IRWELL WORKS, SALFORD, LANCASHIRE.

Worksnumb	Ex.Works	Gauge	Type	wheels	cyl	size	engine/notes	pages
		2' 3"	0-4-0 VBT		?C			182

FAIRLIE ENGINE & STEAM CARRIAGE CO - see 'GE'

Fbn - WILLIAM FAIRBAIRN & SONS, CANAL STREET WORKS, MANCHESTER.
Locos built from 1839 until business sold to 'SS' in 1863.

Worksnumb	Ex.Works	Gauge	Type	wheels	cyl	size	engine/notes	pages
	1839	4' 8½"	0-4-0 tdr	5' 0"	IC	12x18		185

FE - FALCON ENGINE WORKS, LOUGHBOROUGH.
by 1861 -   : Hughes & March, Falcon Works.
c 1865 -1877 : Henry Hughes & Co
   1877 -1881 : Hughes Locomotive & Tramway Engine Works Ltd
4/1882 -1888 : Falcon Engine & Car Works Co Ltd
Hughes & March advertised "cheap contractors locomotives" for sale in 1861 but perhaps built none. Henry Hughes built first loco c1865.
Falcon Works taken over by Brush in 8/1889 - see 'BE'.

Worksnumb	Ex.Works	Gauge	Type	wheels	cyl	size	engine/notes	pages
HH&Co	1867	4' 8½"	0-4-0 ST		?C		12 ton	120, 121
? HH&Co	c1875	2ft	0-4-0 VBT		VC		PERIS	235
HH&Co	12.1875	2ft	0-4-0 UT		OC	7x	GEORGE SHOLTO	358
HH&Co	? 1877	?	? 0-4-0 ST	2'7½"	OC	12x15	BELMONT	128
HH&Co	?	4' 8½"	?				Grange Qys	271
322-HLT	11.1878	2' 3"	0-4-0 ST	2' 6"	OC	7x12	Corris	92
323-HLT	11.1878	2' 3"	0-4-0 ST	2' 6"	OC	7x12	Corris	92, 108
324-HLT	11.1878	2' 3"	0-4-0 ST	2' 6"	OC	7x12	Corris	92
FE&CW	1882	2ft	0-4-0 VBT		VC		Llechwedd	317
FE&CW	8.1883	2ft	0-4-0 VBT		VC		MARY OAKELEY	334, 342

FENTON, CRAVEN & CO - see 'EBW'

FH - "PLANET" LOCOMOTIVES.

1922 -1927 : Kent Construction & Engineering Co Ltd. Ashford, Kent.
(Honeywill Bros.Ltd, Ashford, sales agents for KC&E,
sometimes fitted their own plates to locos.)
1927 -1963 : F.C.Hibberd & Co Ltd, Park Royal, London.
1963 - : subsidiary of Butterley Co Ltd, Ripley, Derbyshire.
Some or all locos 1927-1932 built for FCH by Stableford & Co, Coalville, Leics., and by Bedford Engineering Ltd.

Worksnumb	Ex.Works	Gauge	Type	wheels	cyl size	engine/notes	pages
?	c1925	2ft	4w PM	1' 3"	10hp	Dmn: 4cyl	56
1596			See FH 1929				56
1617	6.1929	2' 0"	4w PM		11hp	Med:	269
1653			See FH 1828				56
1666	4.1930	2' 0"	4w PM		20hp	Med:2008	56
1677	c1931	2ft	4w PM		40hp		137
1678	c1931	2ft	4w PM		40hp		137
1708	1930	2' 0"	4w DM	1'5¾"	20hp	L:CS.855 4ton	193
1725	c1930	2' 0"	4w PM		20hp	Dmn:2JO	193
1779	27.10.1931	2ft	4w PM		40hp		137
1799	8.1932	3' 0"	4w PM	1'5¾"	20hp	Dmn:2JO/17511	232, 257
1821	10. 5.1933	1'11½"	4w PM	2' 0"	20hp	Dmn:2JO.	322
1838	28.10.1933	2' 6"	4w PM	1'5¾"	20hp	Dmn:2JO.7418	213
1847	8. 2.1934	3' 0"	4w TG	1'11" 2C		Foden 11320	232
1913/4 ?	1935	2'11"	4w DM	1'5¾"	20hp	Nat:46284/93	253
1928	1. 6.1935	2' 0"	4w PM	1' 3"	10hp	Med:4EC/12766	56
1929	1. 6.1935	2' 0"	4w PM	1' 3"	10hp	Med:4EC/12486	56, 322
1930	10. 7.1935	2' 0"	4w PM	1' 3"	10hp	Med:4EC/6377	56
1931	c1935	2' 0"	4w PM	1' 3"	8hp	Ford:Y.102066	56
1932	22. 7.1935	2' 0"	4w PM	1' 3"	8hp	Ford:Y.105742	56
1961	c1936	2' 0"	4w DM	1'5¾"	20hp	Nat:2D.46534	271
1962	c1936	2' 0"	4w DM	1'5¾"	20hp	Nat:2D.46536	271
1988	16. 6.1936	2' 0"	4w PM	1'5¾"	20hp	Dmn:2JO.166[?]	245, 250
2346	12.1940	4' 8½"	4w DM	3'1½"	50hp	McL:MR2.25203	225, 338
Ø 2401	c1940	600mm	4w DM	1'5¾"	20hp	Nat:2D.54768	213
2523	c1941	2' 0"	4w DM				309
2544	1942	600mm	4w DM	1'5¾"	20hp	Nat:56018	171
2782	1.1944	600mm	4w DM	1'5¾"	20hp	Nat:2D.56894	236
2791	2.1944	600mm	4w DM	1'5¾"	20hp	Nat:2D.57400	236
2792	2.1944	600mm	4w DM	1'5¾"	20hp	Nat:2D.57406	236
3147	31. 3.1947	4' 8½"	4w DM	3'1½"		Nat:DA.58161	311
3307	15. 7.1948	2' 0"	4w DM	1' 6"	50hp	Perk:3024378	70
3687	22.11.1954	2' 6"	4w DM	2' 0"	102hp	Fodn:FD6.2636	68
3831	28. 3.1958	2' 6"	4w DM	2' 0"	77hp	Dmn:4DL3.66069	68
3953	1960	4'8½"	4w DM				174

Ø : 2401 - details given as New to War Department. Loco later reconditioned by FH, altered to 2'6" gauge, fitted Engine Nat:DA2C.56059 and ex-works 1.10.1949 "New" to CarregyLlam Quarry.

FJ - LOWCA WORKS, WHITEHAVEN.

1830 -1854	: Tulk & Ley	
1857 -1884	: Fletcher, Jennings & Co	
1884 -1905	: Lowca Engineering Co Ltd	
1905 -1912	: New Lowca Engineering Co Ltd	
1912	: closed.	

Worksnumb	Ex.Works	Gauge	Type	wheels	cyl	size	engine/notes	pages
42	24.9.1864	2' 3"	0-4-0 ST	2' 4"	OC	8x16	class 'C'	108
63	1866	2' 3"	0-4-0 WT	2' 4"	OC	8x16	class 'Bb'	108
114	7. 3.1873	4' 8½"	0-4-0 ST		OC	10x20	10" patent	336, 391

FRCo - FESTINIOG RAILWAY COMPANY, PORTHMADOG, GWYNEDD.

Worksnumb	Ex.Works	Gauge	Type	wheels	cyl	size	engine/notes	pages
	21. 7.1879	1'11½"	0-4-4-0T	2'9¼"	4OC	9x14	Dble.Fairlie	68
	6.1886	1'11½"	0-4-4-0T	2'9¼"	4OC	9x14	Dble.Fairlie	68
	22. 1.1955	1'11½"	2-2-0 PMr				BUSTA	70
	5.1974	1'11½"	0-2-2 PMr			10hp	MONSTER	70, 345
	12. 6.1979	1'11½"	0-4-4-0T	2'9¼"	4OC	9x14	Dble.Fairlie	68

FW - FOX, WALKER & Co, ATLAS ENGINE WORKS, BRISTOL.
Locomotives built 1864-1880; taken over by 'P'.

Worksnumb	Ex.Works	Gauge	Type	wheels	cyl	size	engine/notes	pages
29	c1865	4' 8½"	0-6-0 tnk		?C	13½x	PENWYLLT	151
167	1872	4' 8½"	0-6-0 ST		OC	13x20	class B	192
?	?	4' 8½"	?		?		Aston Hall	192
253	1874	4' 8½"	0-4-0 ST		OC	10x18	class D	271
287	15.11.1875	4' 8½"	0-6-0 ST	3' 6"	OC	13x20	class B1	279
291	2.1876	4' 8½"	0-6-0 ST	3' 6"	OC	13x20	class B1	205
318	c1876	4' 8½"	0-6-0 ST		OC	13x20	class: B1	206

GB - GREENWOOD & BATLEY LTD, ALBION WORKS, LEEDS.
built electric locomotives from 1927 to 1980.
Absorbed by 'HE' in 1980.

Worksnumb	Ex.Works	Gauge	Type	wheels	cyl	size	engine/notes	pages
2186	5. 5.1949	2' 6"	4w BE			20hp		397
2187	5. 5.1949	2' 6"	4w BE			20hp		397
2188	5. 5.1949	2' 6"	4w BE			20hp		397
2373	30. 6.1952	4' 8½"	0-4-0 WE			80hp	cokeoven	397
2374	18. 7.1952	4' 8½"	0-4-0 WE			80hp	cokeoven	397
2473	14.10.1953	2' 0"	4w BE			5hp	DWD trammer	351

2563	30. 7.1954	4' 8½"	0-4-0	WE	3'1½"	80hp	cokeoven	397
2643	10.10.1955	2' 6"	4w	BE		20hp	(built by LMM)	397
2973	19.10.1959	2' 6"	4w	BE		20hp	(built by LMM)	397
2974	19.10.1959	2' 6"	4w	BE		20hp	(built by LMM)	397
6114	1. 3.1965	2' 6"	4w	BE		20hp		397
420155	12.1968	2' 6"	4w	BE		20hp		397
420330/1	11.1972	2' 6"	4w	BE		24hp		397
420330/2	11.1972	2' 6"	4w	BE		24hp		397

GE - GEORGE ENGLAND & CO, HATCHAM IRONWORKS, NEW CROSS, LONDON.

c1839 -1869 : George England & Co
1869 -1872 : Fairlie Engine & Steam Carriage Co
Locomotives built from c1850 to 1872; the manufacturing rights for Fairlie locomotives passed to 'AE' in 1871.

Worksnumb	Ex.Works	Gauge	Type	wheels	cyl	size	engine/notes	pages
? 199	7.1863	1'11½"	0-4-0 Tt	2' 0"	OC	8x12	MOUNTAINEER	68
? 200	7.1863	1'11½"	0-4-0 Tt	2' 0"	OC	8x12	PRINCESS	68
? 201	c12.1863	1'11½"	0-4-0 Tt	2' 0"	OC	8x12	PALMERSTON	68, 135
? 202	1864	1'11½"	0-4-0 Tt	2' 0"	OC	8x12	PRINCE	68
234	1867	1'11½"	0-4-0 STt	2' 2"	OC	8x12	WELSH PONY	68
235	1867	1'11½"	0-4-0 STt	2' 2"	OC	8x12	LITTLE GIANT	68
	8.1869	1'11½"	0-4-4-0T	2' 4"	4OC	8¼x13	Dble Fairlie	68

GECT - G.E.C.TRACTION Ltd, VULCAN WORKS, NEWTON-LE-WILLOWS.

Direct successor of 'EEV' - see under 'EE'.
Also traded as GEC Industrial Locomotives Ltd.

Worksnumb	Ex.Works	Gauge	Type	wheels	cyl	size	engine/notes	pages
5391	1973	4' 8½"	0-6-0 DH			500hp	Dmn:8QT	397
5392	1974	4' 8½"	0-6-0 DH			500hp	Dmn:8QT	397
5396	1975	4' 8½"	0-6-0 DH			500hp	Dmn:8QT	397
5397	1975	4' 8½"	0-6-0 DH			500hp	Dmn:8QT	397
5398	1975	4' 8½"	0-6-0 DH			500hp	Dmn:8QT	397
5399	1975	4' 8½"	0-6-0 DH			500hp	Dmn:8QT	397
5400	1975	4' 8½"	0-6-0 DH			500hp	Dmn:8QT	397
5401	1975	4' 8½"	0-6-0 DH			500hp	Dmn:8QT	397
5402	1975	4' 8½"	0-6-0 DH			500hp	Dmn:8QT	397
5575	4.1979	4' 8½"	0-4-0 DH			165hp	Grd:6LX	397
5576	4.1979	4' 8½"	0-4-0 DH			165hp	Grd:6LX	397
5577	4.1979	4' 8½"	0-4-0 DH			165hp	Grd:6LX	397

GUEST - GUEST ENGINEERING WORKS, STOURBRIDGE, WORCESTERSHIRE.
by 1946   : G.& S.Light Engineering Co Ltd
by 1963   : Guest Engineering & Maintenance Co Ltd.

Worksnumb	Ex.Works	Gauge	Type	wheels	cyl	size	engine/notes	pages
9	1946	1' 3"	4-6-0 tdr	1' 8"	OC	5x8	PRINCE CHARLES	146
10	1949	1' 3"	4-6-2 tdr	1' 8"	OC	5x8	E W TWINING	146
13	1954	1' 3"	2-4-2 tdr	1' 8"	OC	5x8	KATIE	146
14	1961	1' 3"	4w+4w PH				SYLVIA	146
15	1959	1' 3"	0-6-0 PM				RACHEL	146
-	1961	1' 3"	0-4-2 DM				CLARA	163
18	1963	1' 3"	2-4-2 tdr	1' 8"	OC	5x8	SIAN	146
20	9.1964	1' 3"	2-6-2 PH				TRACY JO	146

HARTLEY, ARNOUX & FANNING - see 'KS'.

HUDSWELL BADGER LTD - see 'HC'.

HC - THE RAILWAY FOUNDRY, LEEDS.
1861 -1870   : Hudswell & Clarke
1870 -1880   : Hudswell, Clarke & Rodgers
1880 -1889   : Hudswell, Clarke & Co
1899 -   : Hudswell, Clarke & Co Ltd
by 1971   : Hudswell Badger Ltd
                : closed; Goodwill bought by 'HE'.
Hudswell & Clarke took over part of premises of 'EBW' in 1861, including the title "The Railway Foundry".

Worksnumb	Ex.Works	Gauge	Type	wheels	cyl	size	engine/notes	pages
2	16. 4.1861	4' 8½"	0-6-0 ST	4' 0"	IC	15x24		101, 109
3	16. 4.1861	4' 8½"	0-6-0 ST	4' 0"	IC	15x24		101, 109
63	30.11.1865	4' 8½"	0-6-0 ST	4' 0"	IC	15½x24		101, 109
64	30.12.1865	4' 8½"	0-6-0 ST	4' 0"	IC	15½x24		101, 109
119	28. 3.1872	4' 8½"	0-4-0 ST	3' 6"	OC	13x20		110
133	28. 1.1873	4' 8½"	0-4-0 ST	3' 0"	OC	12x18		210
179	18. 9.1876	4' 8½"	0-4-0 ST	3' 3"	OC	13x20		210
189	13. 3.1876	4' 8½"	0-4-0 ST	3' 3"	OC	13x20		110
213	1. 9.1882	4' 8½"	0-4-0 ST	2' 3"	OC	12x19		35, 256, 299
224	28.10.1880	4' 8½"	4-4-0 T	4' 6"	OC	14x20		295
232	31.10.1881	4' 8½"	4-4-0 T	4' 6"	OC	14x20		295
276	28. 4.1885	4' 8½"	0-4-0 ST	3' 0"	OC	12x18		37, 273, 326, 408
278	30. 5.1885	4' 8½"	0-4-0 ST	3'6½"	OC	15x20		110
303	29. 2.1888	4' 8½"	0-4-0 ST	2' 9"	OC	11x16		199
304	18. 5.1888	4' 8½"	0-4-0 ST	2' 9"	OC	10x16		336

314	23.10.1888	4' 8½"	0-6-0 ST	3' 3"	IC	13x20	336
451	3.12.1895	4' 8½"	0-4-0 ST	3' 0"	OC	13x20	42
521	29. 3.1899	4' 8½"	0-4-0 ST	2' 9"	OC	9x15	247
538	31.10.1899	4' 8½"	0-4-0 ST	2' 9"	OC	9x15	404
539	31.10.1899	4' 8½"	0-6-0 ST	3' 0"	IC	12x18	295
560	20. 3.1900	4' 8½"	0-6-0 ST	3' 3"	IC	13x20	82
563	31. 5.1900	4' 8½"	0-4-0 ST	3' 3"	OC	14x20	210, 395
589	21. 3.1901	4' 8½"	0-4-0 ST	2' 9"	OC	9x15	392
619	30. 6.1902	4' 8½"	0-4-0 ST	3' 3"	OC	14x20	395
621	3. 6.1902	4' 8½"	0-6-0 ST	3' 1"	IC	12x18	243
627	15.12.1902	4' 8½"	0-4-0 ST	3' 3"	OC	14x20	210, 395
657	11. 9.1903	4' 8½"	0-4-0 ST	2'9½"	OC	10x16	82
676	18. 1.1904	4' 8½"	0-4-0 ST	2'9½"	OC	10x16	230
703	27. 6.1904	4' 8½"	0-4-0 ST	3' 3"	OC	14x20	395
720	26. 1.1905	4' 8½"	0-4-0 ST	3' 7"	OC	14x20	396
738	26. 9.1905	4' 8½"	0-4-0 ST	3' 3"	OC	14x20	395
786	28.12.1906	4' 8½"	0-4-0 ST	3' 3"	OC	14x20	395
812	4.12.1907	4' 8½"	0-4-0 ST	3'3½"	OC	14x20	40
833	18. 2.1910	4' 8½"	0-6-0 ST	3' 1"	IC	12x18	291
845	26. 5.1909	4' 8½"	0-6-0 ST	3'3½"	IC	14x20	378
901	22.12.1909	4' 8½"	0-4-0 ST	3' 3"	OC	14x20	395
902	26. 1.1910	4' 8½"	0-4-0 ST	3' 3"	OC	14x20	395
926	8. 3.1911	4' 8½"	0-6-0 T	3' 4"	IC	15½x20	395
967	17. 1.1912	4' 8½"	0-6-0 T	3' 4"	IC	15½x20	395
968	23. 9.1912	4' 8½"	0-6-0 T	3' 4"	IC	15½x20	395
998	13. 6.1912	3' 0"	0-4-0 ST	2'0½"	OC	8x12	188, 404
999	13. 6.1912	3' 0"	0-4-0 ST	2'0½"	OC	8x12	188
1021	30. 7.1913	4' 8½"	0-6-0 T	3' 4"	IC	15½x20	396
1028	14. 5.1913	4' 8½"	0-6-0 ST	3' 1"	IC	12x18	247
1034	7. 6.1913	2' 0"	0-4-0 WT	1' 8"	OC	5x8	338
1037	25. 6.1913	3' 0"	0-4-0 ST	2'6½"	OC	9x15	404
1109	26. 1.1915	2' 0"	0-4-0 WT	1' 8"	OC	5x8	304
1117	7. 7.1916	4' 8½"	0-6-0 T	3' 4"	IC	15½x20	396
1129	6. 5.1915	2' 0"	0-4-0 WT	1' 8"	OC	5x8	294
1142	13. 5.1915	2' 0"	0-4-0 WT	1' 8"	OC	5x8	46, 342
1196	4. 5.1916	4' 8½"	0-6-0 ST	3' 7"	OC	14x20	38, 313
1204	25. 5.1917	4' 8½"	0-4-0 ST	3'3½"	OC	14x20	336
1223	21. 8.1916	4' 8½"	0-6-0 T	3' 4"	IC	15½x20	357, 396
1241	9. 5.1917	4' 8½"	0-6-0 T	3' 4"	IC	15½x20	206, 396
1243	8.1917	4' 8½"	0-6-0 T	3' 9"	OC	16x24	174, 273
1305	30.11.1917	4' 8½"	0-6-0 ST	3' 7"	OC	14x20	38
1360	22. 7.1919	4' 8½"	0-4-0 ST	3'3½"	OC	14x20	336
1399	25. 3.1920	4' 8½"	0-4-0 ST	3'3½"	OC	14x20	44, 396
1425	18. 2.1921	4' 8½"	0-6-0 T	3'4½"	IC	15½x20	396
1452	2. 3.1921	3' 0"	0-4-0 ST	2'6½"	OC	9x15	56
1506	30. 6.1923	3' 0"	0-4-0 ST	2'6½"	OC	9x15	404
1513	20. 3.1924	4' 8½"	0-6-0 ST	3'3½"	IC	13x20	306
1525	11. 4.1924	4' 8½"	0-6-0 ST	3'1½"	IC	12x18	249
1529	2. 6.1924	4' 8½"	0-6-0 ST	3'3½"	IC	13x20	283, 306
1533	24. 5.1924	3' 0"	0-4-0 ST	2'6½"	OC	9x15	404
1535	2. 7.1924	3' 0"	0-4-0 ST	2'6½"	OC	9x15	249, 404
1641	3. 9.1929	600mm	0-6-0 WT	1'11"	OC	6½x12	262
1642	6. 9.1929	600mm	0-6-0 WT	1'11"	OC	6½x12	262
1643	23.10.1930	2' 0"	0-6-0 WT	1'11"	OC	6½x12	359

1743	25. 5.1946	4' 8½"	0-4-0 ST	3' 9"	OC	16x24		336
1798	30. 4.1947	4' 8½"	0-4-0 ST	3'3½"	OC	14x22		45
1819	7. 3.1949	4' 8½"	0-6-0 ST	3' 9"	OC	17x24		396
1820	1. 4.1949	4' 8½"	0-6-0 ST	3' 9"	OC	17x24		396
1864	27.10.1952	4' 8½"	0-6-0 T	3' 9"	OC	16x24		222
P 252	8. 3.1926	2' 0"	4w PM			25hp		248
D 611	29. 4.1938	1' 9"	4-6-2 DM	2' 9"		32½hp	Dorman	211
D 612	29. 4.1938	1' 9"	4-6-2 DM	2' 9"		32½hp	Dorman	211
D 762	4. 4.1952	4' 8½"	0-4-0 DM	3' 0"		107hp	G:6L3.89734	396
D 763	28. 4.1952	4' 8½"	0-4-0 DM	3' 0"		107hp	G:6L3.89735	396
D 764	8. 5.1952	4' 8½"	0-4-0 DM	3' 0"		107hp	G:6L3.89561	396
D 927	25. 5.1955	4' 8½"	0-4-0 DM	3' 0"		107hp	G:6LW.103641	396
D 1012	24. 9.1956	4' 8½"	0-4-0 DM	3' 0"		107hp	G:6LW.109379	174
D 1020	3.10.1956	4' 8½"	0-4-0 DM	3' 0"		107hp	G:6LW.109764	379, 396
D 1031	27.10.1956	4' 8½"	0-4-0 DM	2'9½"		128hp	Nat:M4A5.90780	297
DM1082	29.11.1957	2' 6"	0-4-0 DM	2' 2½"		68hp	G:4LW.115482	278
DM1083	29.11.1957	2' 6"	0-4-0 DM	2' 2½"		68hp	G:4LW.115485	278
D 1189	25. 2.1960	4' 8½"	0-6-0 DM	3' 4½"		204hp	G:8L3.123135	288
DM1227	3.10.1960	2' 6"	0-4-0 DM	2' 2½"		68hp	G:4LW.126132	278
D 1409	3.12.1969	4' 8½"	0-4-0 DM	3' 0"		107hp	G:6LW.169307	396
D 1417	25.10.1971	2' 6"	0-6-0 DM	2' 2½"		120hp	G:6LW.179617	398
D 1418	8.11.1971	2' 6"	0-6-0 DM	2' 2½"		120hp	G:6LW.178331	398
D 1419	15.12.1971	2' 6"	0-6-0 DM	2' 2½"		120hp	G:6LW.179618	398

Loco D.1447 - dual identity of HE 8847 (page 398), which see.

HE - HUNSLET ENGINE WORKS, HUNSLET, LEEDS.
 1864 -1902   : Hunslet Engine Co
 1902 -   : Hunslet Engine Co Ltd
              : Hunslet Holdings Ltd
 1972 -   : Hunslet Barclay Ltd

Works constructed on part of site of 'EBW'. First loco completed 1865.
From 1927 expanded into part of 'MW' site. Took over Goodwill of 'KS' in 1930, 'AE' in 1935, 'K' with 'MW' from 'RSH' in 1960, and 'HC' in 1971.
Amalgamated with 'AB' in 1972. Absorbed 'GB' in 1980.

Worksnumb	Ex.Works	Gauge	Type	wheels	cyl	size	engine/notes	pages
42	28. 2.1870	4' 8½"	0-4-0 ST	2' 9"	OC	10x15		260
51	15.10.1870	1'10¾"	0-4-0 ST	2' 0"	OC	7½x14		235
152	10. 2.1876	4' 8½"	0-6-0 ST	3' 1"	IC	12x18		374
184	4. 4.1877	1'10¾"	0-4-0 ST	2' 0"	OC	7½x14		235
195	20.11.1877	1'10¾"	0-4-0 ST	1' 6"	OC	5x8		235, 305
206	26. 7.1878	1'11¼"	0-6-4 ST	2' 6"	OC	10x16		132
283	27. 5.1882	1'10¾"	0-4-0 ST	2' 1"	OC	10x12		357, 358
302	15.12.1882	4' 0"	0-6-0 T	3' 6"	OC	12½x20		235
304	10. 1.1883	4' 8½"	0-4-0 ST	2' 4"	OC	9x14		225
316	6. 7.1883	1'10¾"	0-4-0 ST	1' 8"	OC	7x10	Port	358
317	21. 8.1883	1'10¾"	0-4-0 ST	1' 8"	OC	7x10	Port	358
348	30. 7.1884	3' 3"	0-4-0 ST	2'4½"	OC	9x14		356
364	9. 4.1885	1'10¾"	0-4-0 ST	1' 8"	OC	7x10	Port	358

365	18. 9.1885	4' 8½"	0-4-0 ST	2' 9"	OC	10x15		158
404	23. 6.1886	3' 0"	0-4-0 ST	2' 6"	OC	9½x14		188
409	9.10.1886	1'10¾"	0-4-0 ST	1' 8"	OC	7x10		235
410	6.11.1886	4' 0"	0-6-0 T	3' 6"	OC	12½x20		235
411	18.10.1886	4' 8½"	0-4-0 ST	3' 1"	OC	13x18		43
425	11.11.1887	4' 8½"	0-4-0 ST	2' 9"	OC	10x15		244
449	30. 3.1888	4' 8½"	0-6-0 ST	3' 1"	IC	12x18		205
457	8. 6.1888	4' 8½"	0-6-0 ST	3' 1"	IC	13x18		380
492	28.10.1889	1'10¾"	0-4-0 ST	1' 8"	OC	7x10		235
493	12.11.1889	1'10¾"	0-4-0 ST	1' 8"	OC	7x10		166, 235
541	8. 6.1891	1'10¾"	0-4-0 ST	1' 8"	OC	7x10		235, 411
542	21. 8.1891	1'10¾"	0-4-0 ST	1' 8"	OC	7x10		235
554	5.11.1891	1'11½"	0-4-0 ST	2' 2"	OC	8½x14		218, 359
579	16. 6.1893	4' 8½"	0-6-0 ST	3' 1"	IC	13x18		82
589	22. 6.1893	1'10¾"	0-4-0 ST	2' 1"	OC	10½x12	Mainline	68, 358
590	29. 6.1893	1'10¾"	0-4-0 ST	2' 1"	OC	10½x12	Mainline	68, 358
601	29. 1.1894	1'11½"	0-4-0 ST	1'6½"	OC	6x8		268
605	7. 5.1894	1'10¾"	0-4-0 ST	1' 8"	OC	7x10	Small	358
606	7. 5.1894	1'10¾"	0-4-0 ST	1' 8"	OC	7x10	Small	358
622	8. 1.1895	4' 8½"	0-4-0 ST	3' 1"	OC	13x18		336
627	21. 6.1895	4' 8½"	0-6-0 ST	3' 1"	IC	13x18		293
631	11. 7.1895	4' 0"	0-6-0 T	3' 6"	OC	12½x20		235
638	20. 9.1895	1'10¾"	0-4-0 ST	2' 2"	OC	8½x14	Mills	236
648	4. 7.1898	4' 8½"	0-4-0 ST	2'10"	OC	10x15		39, 207, 326, 331
652	22. 5.1896	2' 0"	0-4-0 ST	1'8¼"	OC	7x10		236
671	11. 5.1898	1'10¾"	0-4-0 ST	2' 2"	OC	8½x14	Mills	236
678	20. 8.1898	1'10¾"	0-4-0 ST	1' 8"	OC	7x10		170, 236
679	26.11.1898	1'10¾"	0-4-0 ST	1' 8"	OC	7x10		236
680	17.10.1898	1'10¾"	0-4-0 ST	1' 8"	OC	7x10		236
704	8.12.1899	1'10¾"	0-4-0 ST	1' 8"	OC	7x10	Small	358
705	8.12.1899	1'10¾"	0-4-0 ST	1' 8"	OC	7x10	Small	358
706	30.12.1899	3' 0"	0-4-0 ST	1' 8"	OC	7x10		354
707	29.12.1899	1'11½"	0-4-0 ST	1' 8"	OC	7x10		70, 367
719	13. 3.1900	4' 8½"	0-6-0 ST	3'2½"	IC	12x18		374, 375
761	26. 2.1902	4' 8½"	0-6-0 ST	3'2½"	IC	12x18		244, 245
763	17.10.1901	1'11½"	0-4-0 ST	1' 8"	OC	7x10		169, 252
764	4. 4.1902	3' 0"	0-4-0 ST	2' 0"	IC	6½x10		354
771	5. 3.1902	3' 0"	0-4-0 ST	1' 8"	OC	7x10		354
779	29. 5.1902	1'10¾"	0-4-0 ST	1' 8"	OC	7x10		170, 236
780	16. 6.1902	1'10¾"	0-4-0 ST	1' 8"	OC	7x10		171, 236
781	30. 5.1902	1'11"	0-4-0 ST	1' 8"	OC	7x10		333
798	24. 3.1903	3' 0"	0-4-0 ST	1' 8"	OC	7x10		354
822	2.10.1903	1'10¾"	0-4-0 ST	1' 8"	OC	7x10		167, 170, 236
823	30.10.1903	1'10¾"	0-4-0 ST	1' 8"	OC	7x10		236
827	26.10.1903	1'11½"	0-4-0 ST	1' 8"	OC	7x10		169, 196, 367, 415
829	31.10.1903	4' 8½"	0-4-0 ST	3' 7"	OC	15x20		336
832	8.12.1903	3' 0"	0-4-0 ST	2' 6"	OC	9½x14		188
848	14. 5.1904	1'11"	0-4-0 ST	1' 8"	OC	7x10		333
849	13. 6.1904	1'10¾"	0-4-0 ST	1' 8"	OC	7x10		166, 236
855	29. 8.1904	1'10¾"	0-4-0 ST	1'8¼"	OC	7½x10	Large	357, 358
866	14. 6.1905	3' 0"	0-4-0 ST	1' 8"	OC	7x10		354
873	1. 6.1905	1'11½"	0-4-0 ST	1' 8"	OC	7x10		169, 367, 415
901	29. 5.1906	1'11¼"	2-6-2 T	2' 4"	OC	10¾x15		132, 136, 138, 169, 411

No.	Date	Gauge	Wheels	Type	Cyl1	Type2	Cyl2	Notes	Page
920	17.11.1906	1'10¾"	0-4-0	ST	1'8¼"	OC	7½x10	Large	359
921	17.11.1906	1'10¾"	0-4-0	ST	1'8¼"	OC	7½x10	Large	70, 359
979	3. 9.1908	1'11¼"	0-6-4	T	2' 4"	OC	9½x14	Fairlie	132
994	11. 5.1909	1'10¾"	0-4-0	ST	1'8¼"	OC	7½x10	Large	359
995	27. 5.1909	1'10¾"	0-4-0	ST	1'8¼"	OC	7½x10	Large	359
996	27. 5.1909	1'10¾"	0-4-0	ST	1'8¼"	OC	7½x10	Large	359
1101	5. 6.1912	1'11½"	0-4-0	ST	1'8¼"	OC	7½x10		406
1167	19. 8.1914	4' 8½"	0-6-0	ST	3'2½"	IC	13x18		112
1323	2.12.1918	600mm	4-6-0	T	2' 0"	OC	9½x12	WDLR	406
1429	1. 8.1922	1'10¾"	0-4-0	ST	1' 8"	OC	7x10		236
1430	11. 8.1922	1'10¾"	0-4-0	ST	1' 8"	OC	7x10		166, 236
1436	24.10.1922	3' 0"	0-4-0	ST	2' 6"	OC	9x14		56
1437	1.11.1922	3' 0"	0-4-0	ST	2' 6"	OC	9x14		56
1439	19. 3.1923	4' 8½"	0-6-0	ST	3' 7"	IC	15x20		273
1463	29.10.1924	4' 8½"	0-6-0	T	4' 7"	IC	18x26	Jinty	173
1705	3. 3.1937	4' 8½"	0-6-0	ST	3' 0"	IC	12x18		378
1709	27. 9.1932	1'10¾"	0-4-0	ST	1' 8"	OC	7x10		236
1770	14. 3.1935	1000mm	4w	DM	2' 0"		37hp	McL:	354
1856	29.10.1937	4' 8½"	0-6-0	ST	3' 0"	IC	12x18		378
1858	27. 9.1937	4' 8½"	0-4-0	DM	2' 9"		40hp	JF:4B.M705	283
1965	c7.1939	2' 0"	4w	DM	1' 6"		20hp	AC:CF2/4127	324
1974	17.11.1939	2' 0"	4w	DM	1' 6"		20hp	AC:RF2/4308	171
1977	14.12.1939	2' 0"	4w	DM	1' 6"		20hp	AC:RF2/4187	419
1978	1. 1.1940	2' 0"	4w	DM	1' 6"		20hp	AC:RF2/4262	419
1979	1. 1.1940	2' 0"	4w	DM	1' 6"		20hp	AC:RF2/4307	419
1980	9. 1.1940	2' 0"	4w	DM	1' 6"		20hp	AC:RF2/4373	419
2024	31. 1.1940	2' 0"	4w	DM	1' 6"		20hp	AC:4282	229, 345, 406
2025	31. 1.1940	2' 0"	4w	DM	1' 6"		20hp	AC:4299	406
2036	14. 2.1940	600mm	4w	DM	1' 6"		20hp	AC:4330	46
2068	8. 7.1940	4' 8½"	0-4-0	DM	3' 4"		153hp	Grd:49298	378
2069	3.10.1940	4' 8½"	0-4-0	DM	2' 9"		70hp	Grd:6L2:49377	355
2070	8.10.1940	4' 8½"	0-4-0	DM	2' 9"		70hp	Grd:6L2:49376	355
2121	5.12.1940	4' 8½"	0-4-0	DM	3' 4"		153hp	Grd:50510	419
2122	21.12.1940	4' 8½"	0-4-0	DM	3' 4"		153hp	Grd:6L3:50509	419
2207	25. 3.1941	2' 0"	4w	DM	1' 6"		20hp	AC:4665	345, 406
2208	25. 3.1941	2' 0"	4w	DM	1' 6"		20hp	AC:4663	406
2209	31. 3.1941	750mm	4w	DM	1' 6"		20hp	AC:4693	345
2290	31. 5.1941	600mm	4w	DM	1' 6"		30hp	McL:LMR2:25132	70
2975	7. 9.1944	600mm	4w	DM	1' 6"		20hp	AC:	46
3129	19.10.1944	3' 0"	0-4-0	DM	2' 4"		80hp	McL:30090	354
3163	24. 4.1944	4' 8½"	0-6-0	ST	4' 3"	IC	18x26	Austerity	273
3187	28. 9.1944	4' 8½"	0-6-0	ST	4' 3"	IC	18x26	Austerity	280
3206	26. 2.1945	4' 8½"	0-6-0	ST	4' 3"	IC	18x26	Austerity	273, 280
3513	5. 1.1948	4' 8½"	0-4-0	DM	2' 0"		100hp	Grd:	355
3526	21. 7.1947	4' 8½"	0-6-0	DM	3' 4"		200hp	Grd:8L3:	349, 396
3700	28.11.1950	4' 8½"	0-6-0	ST	4' 3"	IC	18x26	Austerity	279, 314
3783	30. 9.1953	4' 8½"	0-6-0	ST	3' 9"	IC	16x22		173
3793	3. 2.1953	4' 8½"	0-6-0	ST	4' 3"	IC	18x26	Austerity	174
3885	30. 4.1965							see HE 3163	273
4003	19. 5.1954	4' 8½"	0-6-0	DM	4' 0"		500hp	Pax:	396
4113	28. 2.1955	2' 0½"	0-4-0	DM			70hp	Med:602071	70
4135	1950	2' 3"	0-4-0	DM			65hp		108
4136	1950	2' 3"	0-4-0	DM			65hp		108

4208	29.11.1948	4' 8½"	0-6-0	DM	3' 4"	204hp	Grd:8L3:	349, 396
4209	22. 9.1950	4' 8½"	0-6-0	DM	3' 4"	204hp	Grd:8L3:	396
4210	25.10.1950	4' 8½"	0-6-0	DM	3' 4"	204hp	Grd:8L3:	396
4975	25. 7.1955	4' 8½"	0-6-0	DM	3' 4"	204hp	Grd:8L3:	396
4985	17. 2.1956	4' 8½"	0-6-0	DM	3' 4"	204hp	Grd:8L3:	396
5132	20. 3.1957	4' 8½"	0-6-0	DM	3' 4"	204hp	Grd:8L3:	396
5139	16. 7.1957	4' 8½"	0-6-0	DM	3' 4"	204hp	Grd:8L3:	396
5140	16. 9.1957	4' 8½"	0-6-0	DM	3' 4"	204hp	Grd:8L3:	396
5141	18.12.1957	4' 8½"	0-6-0	DM	3' 4"	204hp	Grd:8L3:	396
5142	27.12.1957	4' 8½"	0-6-0	DM	3' 4"	204hp	Grd:8L3:	396
5143	23. 1.1958	4' 8½"	0-6-0	DM	3' 4"	204hp	Grd:8L3:	396
5144	5. 2.1958	4' 8½"	0-6-0	DM	3' 4"	204hp	Grd:8L3:	396
5300	17. 3.1958	4' 8½"	0-6-0	DM	3' 4"	204hp	Grd:8L3:	396
5301	29. 5.1958	4' 8½"	0-6-0	DM	3' 4"	204hp	Grd:8L3:	396
5671	17. 5.1960	4' 8½"	0-6-0	DM	3' 4"	204hp	Grd:8L3:	396
5672	30. 5.1960	4' 8½"	0-6-0	DM	3' 4"	204hp	Grd:8L3:	396
6285	1968		4w	DM		40hp		138
6292	1967	3' 0"	4w	DM				108
6663	1969	4' 8½"	0-6-0	DM		325hp		194
6664	1969	4' 8½"	0-6-0	DM		325hp		194, 370
7018	1971	4' 8½"	0-6-0	DM		400hp		194
7040	1971	4' 8½"	0-6-0	DM		400hp		370
7183	21. 1.1972	4' 8½"	0-4-0	DH		252hp		288
7374	1973	2' 0"	0-4-0	DM		66hp	flameproof	371
7375	1973	2' 0"	0-4-0	DM		66hp	flameproof	371
7376	1973	2' 0"	0-4-0	DM		66hp	flameproof	371
7379	1974	2' 0"	0-4-0	DM		66hp	flameproof	371
7460	1977	4' 8½"	0-4-0	DH				190
7535	1977	2' 0"	4w	DH				138
# 8518	1977		4w	DM			WHRly	138
# 8847	1981	2' 6"	0-6-0	DM				398
8901			See	HC	D.1189			288
?	c1985	2' 6"	4w	DH			Shotton No.1	397
?	c1985	2' 6"	4w	DH			Shotton No.2	397
9249	4.1986	2' 7½"	0-4-0	DH		320hp	RR:	153
9250	4.1986	2' 7½"	0-4-0	DH		320hp	RR:	153
# 9305	1991	2' 7½"	0-4-0	DH		320hp	RR:	153
?	c1940	2ft	4w	DM		20hp		406
?	c1940	2ft	4w	DM		20hp		57

- locos with dual identity:
    HE 8518 - AB 632; HE 8847 - HC D1447; HE 9305 - AB 775.

HEN   - HENSCHEL & SOHN G.M.B.H., KASSEL, GERMANY.

Worksnumb	Ex.Works	Gauge	Type	wheels	cyl	size	engine/notes	pages
28035	1948	600mm	0-4-0 WT		OC		Reisa class	167, 170

HICK - HICK LOCOMOTIVES, SOHO IRONWORKS, BOLTON, LANCS.
   1833 -c1840   : Benjamin Hick
   c1840 - 1850   : Hick, Hargreaves & Co
c100 locomotives were built in the 1833-1850 period, the Company then concentrating on other work - becoming Hick, Hargreaves & Co Ltd in 1889.

Worksnumb	Ex.Works	Gauge	Type	wheels	cyl	size	engine/notes	pages
	3.1849	4' 8½"	0-6-0 tdr	5' 0"	IC	16x24	11 BIRKENHEAD	76
	3.1849	4' 8½"	0-6-0 tdr	5' 0"	IC	16x24	12 CHESTER	76
	3.1849	4' 8½"	0-6-0 tdr	5' 0"	IC	16x24	13 MERSEY	76
	3.1849	4' 8½"	0-6-0 tdr	5' 0"	IC	16x24	14 DEE	76

HL - HAWTHORN and HAWTHORN LESLIE, NEWCASTLE-ON-TYNE.
   1820 -1886   : R.& W.Hawthorn
   1886 -1937   : R.& W.Hawthorn, Leslie & Co Ltd
Locomotives were constructed from c1831.
Amalgamated with 'RS' 27/9/1937 to form 'RSH' - which see.

Worksnumb	Ex.Works	Gauge	Type	wheels	cyl	size	engine/notes	pages
2034	26. 6.1885	4' 8½"	0-4-0 ST	3' 6"	OC	14x20		42
2466	18. 7.1900	4' 8½"	0-4-0 ST	3' 6"	OC	14x20		40, 313
2623	2.11.1905	4' 8½"	0-4-0 ST	3' 6"	OC	14x22		194, 198
2646	2. 5.1906	4' 8½"	0-4-0 ST	3' 6"	OC	14x22		202
2686	13. 6.1907	4' 8½"	0-4-0 ST	3' 9"	OC	15x22		419
2878	29. 7.1911	4' 8½"	0-6-2 T	3' 6"	OC	14x22		295
2879	29. 7.1911	4' 8½"	0-6-2 T	3' 6"	OC	14x22		36, 295
3027	25.11.1914	4' 8½"	0-6-0 T	3'10"	OC	16x24		295
3072	25.11.1914	4' 8½"	0-4-0 ST	3' 6"	OC	14x22		36, 194, 279
3088	22. 4.1915	4' 8½"	0-6-2 T	4' 0"	OC	16x24		295
3214	6. 1.1917	4' 8½"	0-6-0 ST	3'10"	OC	16x24		205
3261	9.10.1917	4' 8½"	0-4-0 ST	3' 6"	OC	14x22		375
3589	5.12.1924	4' 8½"	0-4-0 ST	3' 6"	OC	14x22		44
3949	5. 1.1939	4' 8½"	0-4-0 DM	3' 3"				419
3950	5. 1.1939	4' 8½"	0-4-0 DM	3' 3"				419

HL 4267 was a rebuild of MW 1570 (page 196) - which see.

HoL - HAWTHORNS & CO, LEITH ENGINE WORKS, LEITH
   1846 -c1852   : R.& W.Hawthorn ('HL')
   c1852 - 1900s : Hawthorns & Co
Works originally started as a branch of the 'HL' works at Newcastle, but sold 1852 to become an independant builder of locos. New locos built until 1880s, with rebuilding and repair work being carried out for many years thereafter.

Worksnumb	Ex.Works	Gauge	Type	wheels	cyl	size	engine/notes	pages
284	6.1862	4' 8½"	0-6-0 WT	3' 6"	OC	15x21		106

Hor - HORWICH LOCOMOTIVE WORKS, HORWICH, LANCASHIRE.
1887 -1922   : Lancashire & Yorkshire Rly Co
1923 -1947   : London, Midland & Scottish Rly Co
1948 -   : British Railways.

Worksnumb	Ex.Works	Gauge	Type	wheels	cyl	size	engine/notes	pages
1099	1910	4' 8½"	0-4-0 ST	3' 0"	OC	13x18	L&YR class 21	355
1105	1910	4' 8½"	0-4-0 ST	3' 0"	OC	13x18	L&YR class 21	227
(47006)	11.1953	4' 8½"	0-4-0 ST	3'10"	OC	15½x30	BR class OF	194

HRM - HARDY RAIL MOTORS LTD, SLOUGH.
       (subsidiary of Four Wheel Drive Lorry Co Ltd).
Constructed petrol locomotives and railcars from 1923-1931, using standard lorry components. Company taken over c1930 by Associated Equipment Co Ltd, who from 1933 produced a series of streamlined bogie railcars for the Great Western Railway. [J/IL/No.56/162]

Worksnumb	Ex.Works	Gauge	Type	wheels	cyl	size	engine/notes	pages
954	1925	4' 0"	4w PM	2'9½"				235

HU - ROBERT HUDSON LTD, LEEDS.
       Long-established Company manufacturing and dealing in a wide range of light railway equipment, particularly for narrow-gauge "portable" lines. Most "Hudson" locomotives were manufactured by others, though often fitted with 'Hudson' plates. From c1923 to c1933 a design of 20hp Petrol/Paraffin loco was apparently built on Hudsons' premises.

Worksnumb	Ex.Works	Gauge	Type	wheels	cyl	size	engine/notes	pages
32145	17. 2.1927	2'10½"	4w PM			20hp		307
38384	23. 1.1930	2' 0"	4w PM			45hp	Go-Go class	171

HUGHES & MARCH; HENRY HUGHES; HUGHES LOCO & TRAMWAY ENGINE WORKS LTD.
       For details see listing 'FE'.

HVF - OWEN HUGHES, VALLEY FOUNDRY, VALLEY, near HOLYHEAD.
       Reputed to have built two locomotives, though one at least may only have been a rebuild, or repair, of a loco built by others.

Worksnumb	Ex.Works	Gauge	Type	wheels	cyl	size	engine/notes	pages
		3' 0"	0-4-0 VBT		2VC		MONA	300, 354
		2ft	0-4-0 VBT		2VC		BRONLLWYD	358

Hz - HOHENZOLLERN A.G. fur LOKOMOTIVBAU, DUSSELDORF, GERMANY.

Worksnumb	Ex.Works	Gauge	Type	wheels	cyl	size	engine/notes	pages
4311	1925	4' 8½"	0-4-0 F		OC			43

IWB - ISAAC WATT BOULTON, DEALER, ASHTON-UNDER-LYNE.
Bought, sold, hired, repaired, rebuilt, and built locos 1858-1894.

Worksnumb	Ex.Works	Gauge	Type	wheels	cyl	size	engine/notes	pages
	9.1874	4' 8½"	0-6-0 ST	3' 0"	IC	12x18	ARIADNE	198
	c1875	4' 8½"	0-4-0 ST	4' 0"	IC	13¼x20	BRYMBO	205

JF - JOHN FOWLER LOCO & STEAM PLOUGH WORKS, LEEDS.
1850 -1886   : John Fowler & Co
1886 -   : John Fowler & Co (Leeds) Ltd
Locomotives built from 1866 to 1968; loco business Goodwill sold to 'AB'.

Worksnumb	Ex.Works	Gauge	Type	wheels/cyl	size	engine/notes	pages
923	1.1868	4' 8½"	2-2-0 TG	SC	convertible		259
17305	6.1927	4' 8½"	0-4-0 PM		40hp	Waukesha	259
21999	7.1937	4' 8½"	0-4-0 DM		40hp	JF: 4B	203
22288	28. 2.1938	4' 8½"	0-4-0 DM		40hp	JF: 4B	99
22496	24.10.1938	4' 8½"	0-4-0 DM		150hp	JF: 4C	392
22500	7.1938	4' 8½"	0-4-0 DM		60hp	Sanders 6B	283
22753	26.10.1939	4' 8½"	0-4-0 DM		40hp	JF: 4B.M1282	174, 203
22872	3.1940	4' 8½"	0-4-0 DM		66hp	JF: 6B	390
22879	20.11.1939	4' 8½"	0-4-0 DM		150hp	JF: 4C.2290	225, 392
22882	10.11.1939	4' 8½"	0-4-0 DM		150hp	JF: 4C	225
22889	12. 9.1939	4' 8½"	0-4-0 DM		150hp	JF: 4C.1675	283, 378
22906	3. 9.1940	4' 8½"	0-4-0 DM		80hp	JF: 6A.3024	386
22970	1.1942	4' 8½"	0-4-0 DM		150hp	JF: 4C	225, 392
22992	31.12.1942	4' 8½"	0-4-0 DM		150hp	JF: 4C.5036	224
23002	6.1943	4' 8½"	0-4-0 DM		150hp	JF: 4C	225, 392
3900011	24. 3.1947	3' 0"	4w DM	2' 0"	40hp	JF: 4B.2420122	232
4000007	4.1947	4' 8½"	0-4-0 DM		60hp	JF: 6B	174
4110006	8.1950	4' 8½"	0-4-0 DM		80hp	McL	83
4110012	14. 2.1951	4' 8½"	0-4-0 DM		80hp	McL:MR3.30548B	225, 408
4200045	11. 7.1949	4' 8½"	0-4-0 DM		150hp	JF: 4C.3220048	292
4210001	6.1949	4' 8½"	0-4-0 DM		150hp	McL:	224
4210069	3.1952	4' 8½"	0-4-0 DM		150hp	McL	224
4210077	8. 7.1952	4' 8½"	0-4-0 DM		150hp	McL: M6.60245	224
4210090	24. 2.1954	4' 8½"	0-4-0 DM		150hp	McL: M6.60256	224
4210144	29. 8.1958	4' 8½"	0-4-0 DM		150hp	McL:	225
?	?	4' 8½"	0-4-0 DM		150hp?		306

Jones - JONES LOCO BUILDERS, NEWTON-LE-WILLOWS later LIVERPOOL.
c1837 -c1844   : Jones, Turner & Evans, Viaduct Foundry, Newton-le-Willows.
c1844 - 1852   : Jones & Potts, Viaduct Foundry.
c1853 -   : John Jones, William Street, Liverpool.
      - 1863   : John Jones & Son, William Street.
Locos built at Newton had works numbers up to c290; those built at Liverpool being numbers c291 to 342. Business then closed.

Worksnumb	Ex.Works	Gauge	Type	wheels	cyl	size	engine/notes	pages
1846		4' 8½"	2-4-0 tdr	5' 6"	OC	15x24	S&CR No.7	75
1847		4' 8½"	2-4-0 tdr	5' 6"	OC	15x24	S&CR Mo.8	75
c1848		4' 8½"	2-2-2 tdr	6' 6"	IC	15½x20	S&CR No.32	76
? 1853		4' 8½"	2-4-0 tdr	5' 6"	?C	15x20	DR&CR No.4	54, 98

Jung - ARN. JUNG LOKOMOTIVFABRIK GMBH, JUNGENTHAL, GERMANY.

Worksnumb	Ex.Works	Gauge	Type	wheels	cyl	size	engine/notes	pages
1261	21. 8.1908	600mm	0-6-2 WTt	2' 1"	OC	8½x12		169
7509	30. 9.1937	600mm	0-4-0 WT	2' 1"	OC	9½x12		166

Kellow - MOSES KELLOW, CROESOR SLATE QUARRY, GWYNEDD.

Worksnumb	Ex.Works	Gauge	Type	wheels	cyl	size	engine/notes	pages
	c1904	2ft	4w WE				30hp	228

KENT CONSTRUCTION & ENGINEERING CO LTD - see 'FH'.

Kirtley - KIRTLEY & CO, DALLAM FOUNDRY, WARRINGTON, LANCASHIRE.
Locomotives built from 1837 to 1841.

Worksnumb	Ex.Works	Gauge	Type	wheels	cyl	size	engine/notes	pages
	10.1841	4' 8½"	0-4-2 tdr	5' 0"	IC	13x20		205

Kit - KITSON LOCOMOTIVES, AIREDALE FOUNDRY, LEEDS.
```
1838              : Todd, Kitson & Laird.
1838    -c1842    : Kitson & Laird.
c1842   - 1858    : Kitson, Thompson & Hewitson.
1858    -c1863    : Kitson & Hewitson
c1863   -         : Kitson & Co
        - 1938    : Kitson & Co Ltd.
```
First loco built in 1838; bought Goodwill of 'MW' in 1927. Closed down in 1938; Goodwill (including that of 'MW') bought by 'RSH'.

Worksnumb	Ex.Works	Gauge	Type	wheels	cyl	size	engine/notes	pages
1251	10.1865	4' 8½"	0-6-0 tdr	4' 6"	IC	16x24		98
? T.109	? 1884	4' 8½"	0-4-0 WT	3' 0"	OC	8x12		43
5459	1932	4' 8½"	0-6-0 ST		IC			173

KS - CALIFORNIA ENGINE WORKS, STOKE-ON-TRENT.
```
  ?    -1886     : Hartley & Arnoux Bros
1886   -1893     : Hartley, Arnoux & Fanning
1893   -1930     : Kerr, Stuart & Co Ltd
1930             : closed.
```
Locomotive construction commenced in 1891, the early history being tied up with Glasgow dealers James Kerr & Co, and Kerr, Stuart & Co, who were involved with 'DK', and had "Kerr Staurt" locos made for them by 'JF', 'FE', Hartley, Arnoux & Fanning, etc., prior to the takeover of the latter by 'KS'.
In 1930, Goodwill purchased by 'HE'.

Worksnumb	Ex.Works	Gauge	Type	wheels	cyl	size	engine/notes	pages
639	29. 8.1898	2' 0"	0-4-0 T		OC	6x10		265
861	2. 4.1904	1'10"	0-4-0 PM	1' 6"		25hp	Grd:	418
1158	14. 4.1917	2' 0"	0-4-0 T	2' 0"	OC	6x10	Sirdar	57, 169, 342, 367
1255	17. 5.1912	3' 0"	0-4-2 ST	2' 6"	OC	9x15	Brazil class	300
1257	9. 6.1914	3' 0"	0-4-2 ST	2' 6"	OC	9x15	Brazil class	300
1265	5.12.1914	2' 0"	0-4-2 ST	2' 0"	OC	7x12	Tattoo class	265
2395	23. 2.1917	2' 0"	0-4-2 ST	2' 0"	OC	7x12	Tattoo class	359
2419	12. 6.1915	2' 0"	0-4-0 ST	1' 8"	OC	6x9	Wren class	304
2460	23. 8.1915	2' 0"	0-4-0 ST	1' 8"	OC	6x9	New Wren class	214
2473	2.10.1916	2' 0"	0-4-0 ST	1' 8"	OC	6x9	Wren class	214
2494	19. 6.1917	2' 0"	0-4-2 ST	2' 3"	OC	8x12	Darwin class	406
3092	4. 6.1918	3' 0"	0-4-2 ST	2' 6"	OC	9x15	Brazil class	300
3114	1. 5.1918	2' 0"	0-4-0 ST	1' 8"	OC	6x9	New Wren class	170, 345
3117	3.12.1918	2' 0"	0-6-0 T	1'11½	OC	8½x11	Haig class	196, 359
4005	31.12.1918	2' 0"	0-4-0 ST	1' 8"	OC	6x9	Wren class	214
4047	10. 6.1921	2' 3"	0-4-2 ST	2' 0"	OC	7x12	Tattoo special	92, 108
4213	12.11.1921	2' 0"	4-6-0 T	2' 0"	OC	9½x12	(ex HE 1323)	406
4415	1928	600mm	6w DM	2' 0"		60hp	McL:	70, 136
4450	29. 4.1930	4' 8½"	0-6-0 PT	4'7½"	IC	17½x24	GWR 57XX	174

L - LISTER LOCOMOTIVES.
R.& A.Lister & Co Ltd, Dursley, Glos.
Lister Blackstone Rail Traction Ltd, Dursley.

Worksnumb	Ex.Works	Gauge	Type	wheels	cyl	size	engine/notes	pages
3742	28. 2.1931	2' 0"	PM	4w		6hp	JAP: 600cc	229, 276
3804	31. 3.1931	1'11½"	PM	4w		6hp	JAP: 600cc	46, 298
3916	19. 6.1931	2' 0"	PM	4w		6hp	JAP: 600cc	252, 345
3950	1. 7.1931		PM	4w		6hp	JAP: 600cc	252
4472	29. 6.1932	1'11½"	PM	4w		6hp	JAP: 600cc	30
6502	4. 5.1935	1' 3"	PM	4w		9hp	JAP: 980cc	146
10020	18. 2.1938	2' 0"	PM	4w		9hp	JAP: 980cc	331
20886	18. 1.1943	2' 0"	PM	4w		6hp	JAP:	146, 400
28068	18. 1.1946	1'10¾"	PM	4w		9hp	JAP: 980cc	236
29890	1946	2' 0"	DM	4w				70
30233	1946	1'11½"	PM	4w				48
33527	22. 4.1949	2ft	PM	4w		6hp	JAP: 600cc	252
34025	1949		DM	4w				171
34521	1949	2ft	DM	4w				70
35588	1. 6.1950		PM	4w				272
35589	12. 6.1950		PM	4w				272
41545	1955		PM	4w		6hp	JAP: 600cc	70
44052	1958	2ft	DM	4w				171

LAdB - LES ATELIERS DE BONDY.

Worksnumb	Ex.Works	Gauge	Type	wheels	cyl	size	engine/notes	pages
?		? 2ft	icM	4w			Maenofferen	322

Lane - CLAUDE W.LANE (LANCASTER ELECTRICAL CO, BARNET, HERTS).

Worksnumb	Ex.Works	Gauge	Type	wheels	cyl	size	engine/notes	pages
	1948	1' 3"	WE	8w			tram 23	165
	1950	1' 3"	WE	8w			tram 225	165
	1952	1' 3"	WE	4w			tram 3	165
	1953	1' 3"	WE	8w			tram 6	165

LIL - LILLESHALL IRON WORKS, OAKENGATES, SHROPSHIRE.
by 1862 -1880 : Lilleshall Iron Co
1880 - : Lilleshall Co Ltd
Built locomotives from 1862 to c1890, both for sale and own use.

Worksnumb	Ex.Works	Gauge	Type	wheels	cyl	size	engine/notes	pages
	1862	4' 8½"	0-4-0 ST	3' 0"	OC	13x20	Savin	54, 198
	? 1869		0-4-0 T		OC		Ceiriog	215

Llechwedd - LLECHWEDD SLATE QUARRIES, BLAENAU FFESTINIOG, GWYNEDD.
  J.W.Greaves & Sons Ltd.

Worksnumb	Ex.Works	Gauge	Type	wheels	cyl	size	engine/notes	pages
	1927	2ft	0-4-0 WE			15hp		317
	1930	2ft	0-4-0 WE					317
	c1936	2ft	2-2-0 PM				Morris 323414	317

LMM - LOGAN MINING MACHINERY CO LTD, DUNDEE.
  Manufactured battery locomotives until closed on 17.2.1978.

Worksnumb	Ex.Works	Gauge	Type	wheels	cyl	size	engine/notes	pages
1049	1950	2' 0"	4w BE					46, 403
1053	1950	2' 0"	4w BE					46, 318, 403
1066	1950	2' 0"	4w BE					318
		2' 0"	4w BE				Dolgarrog	250
		2' 3"?	4w BE				Braichgoch	184, 202, 276

LOWCA ENGINEERING CO LTD - see 'FJ'

McEWAN, PRATT & CO LTD - see 'Bg'

MH - MUIR HILL LOCOMOTIVES, OLD TRAFFORD, MANCHESTER.
by1920 -c1929   : Muir Hill (Engineers) Ltd
  c1929 -   : E.Boydell & Co

Worksnumb	Ex.Works	Gauge	Type	wheels	cyl	size	engine/notes	pages
	c1922	2ft	4w PM	1' 8"		20hp	Fordson 4cyl	70, 245
	? 1925	2ft	4w PM			20hp	Fordson 4cyl	322, 383
5	1926	2' 0"	4w PM					212

MR - MOTOR-RAIL SIMPLEX WORKS, BEDFORD.
by 1916 -1931 : Motor Rail & Tram Car Co Ltd
1931 -1972 : Motor Rail Ltd
1972 - : Simplex Mechanical Handling Ltd
(subsidiary of Motor Rail Ltd).

Worksnumb	Ex.Works	Gauge	Type	wheels	size	engine/notes	pages
264	c 12.1916	600mm	4w PM		20hp	Dmn: 2JO.	48
596	1917	600mm	4w PM	1' 6"	40hp	Dmn: 4JO.6247	68
985			See MR	3831			250
992			See MR	2199			135
997	1918	600mm	4w PM		20hp	Drm: 2JO.	48, 171
1030			See MR	3736			406
1073	8.11.1918	600mm	4w PM		20hp	Dmn: 2JO.	255
1078	12.11.1918	600mm	4w PM		20hp	Dmn: 2JO.	406
1111	1918	600mm	4w PM		20hp	Dmn: 2JO.	48
1191	1918	600mm	4w PM		20hp	Dmn: 2JO.	321
* 1259		600mm	4w PM				320
1301	1918	600mm	4w PM		40hp	Dmn: 4JO.	320
1320	10. 9.1918	600mm	4w PM		40hp	Dmn: 4JO.	48
1378	17.12.1918	600mm	4w PM		40hp	Dmn: 4JO.	406
* 1552	by 1924		4w PM		20hp	Dmn: 2JO	258
1649	7. 5.1918	600mm	4w PM		20hp		321
1684			See MR	2193			135
1739			See MR	2192			135
1895	1919		See MR	3694			70
1904	27. 1.1920	1'11½"	4w PM		20hp	Dmn: 2JO.	322
1922	28. 7.1919	4' 8½"	4w PM		40hp	Dmn: 4JO.	364
1928	16.10.1919	4' 8½"	4w PM		40hp	Dmn: 4JO	355
1934	8.10.1919	2' 0"	4w PM		20hp	Dmn: 2JO.8450	417
1944	8.12.1919	4' 8½"	4w PM		40hp	Dmn: 4JO.7398	48, 189, 261
2021	16. 6.1920	4' 8½"	4w PM		40hp	Dmn: 4JO.8400	390
2025	26. 8.1920	4' 8½"	4w PM		40hp	Dmn: 4JO.8788	373
2033	3.12.1920	4' 8½"	4w PM		40hp	Dmn: 4JO.8853	189
2059	7. 1.1921	1' 11"	4w PM		20hp	Dmn: 2JO.8302	285
2102	21. 3.1921	2' 0"	4w PM		20hp	Dmn: 2JO.8309	269, 353
2179	31. 5.1922	600mm	4w PM		20hp	Dmn: 2JO.8423	135
2192	2. 9.1922	600mm	4w PM		20hp	Dmn: 2JO.6829	135
2193	2.10.1922	600mm	4w PM		20hp	Dmn: 2JO.6583	135
2197	c10.1.1923	600mm	4w PM		20hp	Dmn: 2JO.6825?	135
2199	28. 2.1923	600mm	4w PM		20hp	Dmn: 2JO.6802	135
3694	9. 9.1924	2' 0"	4w PM		20hp	Dmn: 2JO.10136	70
3730	16. 3.1925	4' 8½"	4w PM		40hp	Dmn: 4JO.	99, 227
3736	30. 5.1925	600mm	4w PM		20hp	Dmn: 2JO.	406
3831	19. 4.1926	600mm	4w PM		20hp	Dmn: 2JO.	250
4023	3. 2.1926	600mm	4w PM		20hp	Dmn: 2JO.10296	417
4623	29. 4.1932	4' 8½"	4w PM		40hp	Dmn: 4JO.15096	312, 370
4803	3.12.1934	2' 0"	4w PM		20hp		48
5024	2. 8.1929	3' 0"	4w PM		20hp	Dmn: 2JO.15024	354
5025	31. 7.1929	2' 0"	4w PM		20hp	Dmn: 2JO.15025	48, 253, 406
5054	12. 2.1930	2' 0"	4w PM		20hp		366

5061	29. 3.1930	600mm	4w	PM	20hp		250
5072	26. 4.1930	2' 0"	4w	PM	20hp		186, 366
5080	6.1930	2' 0"	4w	PM	20hp		366
5236	13.11.1930	2' 0"	4w	PM	35hp	Dmn:4MRX.19035	232
5297	7. 4.1931	2ft	4w	PM	35hp	Dmn:4MRX.19095	48
5342	15. 8.1931	2' 0"	4w	PM	35hp		232
5461	31. 3.1937	3' 0"	4w	PM	35hp		232
5506	17. 7.1929	600mm	4w	DM	30hp	McL:35475	322
5513	2. 6.1930	2' 0"	4w	PM	20hp	. :57341	354, 406
5609	5. 5.1931	2' 0"	4w	DM	20hp	Dmn: 2RB.24759	406
5611	26. 5.1931	3' 0"	4w	DM	20hp	Dmn: 2RB.24758	354
5642	12. 5.1933	2' 0"	4w	DM	30hp	Dmn: 2RB.26160	321
5655	20. 6.1934	2' 0"	4w	DM	30hp	Dmn: 2RB.26621	321
5680	1935	2' 0"	4w	DM	30hp	Dmn: 2RB.28593	321
5692	18. 2.1937	2' 0"	4w	DM	30hp	Dmn: 2RB.30388	321
5821	4.10.1934	2ft	4w	DM	20hp	AC: RFS2.3313	171
5852	18.10.1933	2' 0"	4w	DM	28hp	Dmn: 2HW.26814	48
5859	13.7.1934	2 '0"	4w	DM	28hp	Dmn: 2HW.26810	48
5861	10. 5.1934	2' 0"	4w	DM	28hp	Dmn: 2HW.26816	166
5905	20. 7.1933	3' 0"	4w	DM	42hp	Dmn:2RBL.26396	354
5941	5.1936	3' 0"	4w	DM	42hp	Dmn:2RBL.29715	354
5949	c8.1937	600mm	4w	DM	42hp	Dmn:2RBL.30159	406
5950	11. 2.1938	3' 0"	4w	DM	42hp	Dmn:2RBL.30258	354
5951	c2.1938	3' 0"	4w	DM	42hp	Dmn:2RBL.30259	354
6013	1. 1.1931	2ft	4w	PM	20hp	. :4MVR.24488	48
7093	4. 7.1940	2' 0"	4w	PM	26hp	Dmn: 2JO.32609	310
7094	11. 7.1940	2' 0"	4w	PM	26hp	Dmn: 2JO.32610	310
7097	18. 2.1941	2' 0"	4w	PM	26hp	Dmn: 2JO.33616	216, 286
7135	27. 8.1936	2' 0"	4w	DM	28hp	Dmn: 2HW.29665	262
7140	12.11.1936	2' 0"	4w	DM	28hp	Dmn: 2HW.29678	262
7184	6.1937	2' 0"	4w	DM	28hp	Dmn: 2HW.29983	402
7201	20.10.1937	2' 0"	4w	DM	20hp		48
7221	3.1938	2' 0"	4w	DM	28hp	Dmn: 2HW.30565	253, 406
7479	13. 4.1940	2' 0"	4w	DM	28hp	Dmn:2DWD.33041	340
7710	9. 6.1939	2' 0"	4w	DM	42hp	Dmn: 2DL.31352	340
7711	16. 6.1939	2' 0"	4w	DM	42hp	Dmn: 2DL.31405	340
7902	1939	2' 0"	4w	DM	42hp	Dmn: 2DL.31406	166
7927	12. 3.1941	2' 0"	4w	DM	42hp	Dmn: 2DL.33889	166
7932	29.10.1941	2' 0"	4w	DM	42hp	Dmn: 2DL.33898	340
7933	31.10.1941	2' 0"	4w	DM	42hp	Dmn: 2DL.33899	340
8565	27. 9.1940	2' 0"	4w	DM	28hp	Dmn:2DWD.33141	70
8570	30.10.1940	2ft	4w	DM	28hp	Dmn:2DWD.33144	406
8600	13.12.1940	2' 0"	4w	DM	28hp	Dmn:2DWD.33517	319
8603	13. 1.1941	2' 0"	4w	DM	28hp	Dmn:2DWD.	199
8604	17. 1.1941	2' 0"	4w	DM	28hp	Dmn:2DWD.	199
8703	31.12.1941	2' 0"	4w	DM	28hp	Dmn:2DWD.34749	138
8720	21. 3.1941	2' 0"	4w	DM	28hp	Dmn:2DWD.33833	269
8723	3. 4.1941	2' 0"	4w	DM	28hp	Dmn:2DWD.	48
8729	1.10.1941	2' 0"	4w	DM	28hp	Dmn:2DWD.34360	211
8786	10. 9.1942	2' 3"	4w	DM	28hp	Dmn:2DWD.35762	202
8788	26. 3.1943	600mm	4w	DM	28hp	Dmn:2DWD.35768	70, 168
9215	20. 6.1946	3' 0"	4w	DM	28hp	. 37883	232
9547	28.11.1950	600mm	4w	DM	28hp	. 51269	48, 138
10130	16. 8.1949	2' 0"	4w	DM	42hp	Dmn: 2DL.48190	288

10349	20. 2.1953	600mm	4w	DM		42hp	Dmn: 2DL.56462	402
10350	20. 2.1953	600mm	4w	DM		42hp	Dmn: 2DL.56474	402
11102	18. 2.1959	2' 0"	4w	DM		50hp	Dmn: 3LA.66384	138
11177	31. 7.1961	600mm	4w	DM		50hp	Dmn: 3LB.73095	167
20073	19.10.1950	2' 0"	4w	DM		28hp	Dmn:2DWD.51254	322
20558	11. 1.1955	600mm	4w	DM		28hp	Dmn:2DWD.61151	48
21282	10. 2.1959	2' 0"	4w	DM		28hp	Dmn:2DWD.68193	172
21513	24. 8.1955	600mm	4w	DM		28hp	Dmn:2DWD.61269	166
21579	1. 1.1957	600mm	4w	DM		28hp	Dmn:2DWD.64839	70
21615	11. 9.1957	600mm	4w	DM		28hp	Dmn:2DWD.66447	70
22119	26. 4.1961	600mm	4w	DM	1' 6"	28hp	Dmn: 2LB.72852	70
22154	29. 6.1962	600mm	4w	DM	1' 6"	28hp	Dmn: 2LB.75840	167, 245
22238	13. 7.1965	2' 0"	4w	DM		40hp	Dmn: 2LB.80842	345
22258	20.10.1965	2' 0"	4w	DM	1' 6"	40hp	Dmn: 2LB.81123	93
40s308	29.12.1967	2' 0"	4w	DM		40hp	Dmn: 2LB.88788	345
40s412	27. 2.1972	2' 0"	4w	DM		40hp	1272/130	345
60s333	23. 9.1966	2' 0"	4w	DM		60hp	Dmn: 3LB.85596	138
60s363	28. 6.1968	2' 0"	4w	DM		60hp	Dmn: 3LB.88748	138
?	?	4' 8½"	4w	?PM			PUFFIN II	355
?	?	2ft	4w	PM		20hp	PR/44 - No.14	137
?	?	2ft	4w	?PM		20hp	Trefor 4?	406
?	?	2ft	4w	?PM		20hp	Trefor 5	406
?	?	2ft	4w			20hp	Arnold 21	48
?	?	?2ft	4w	PM		20hp	Finnie	48
?	?	2' 0"	4w	PM			ICI RS60	320
?	?	2' 0"	4w	DM		20hp	Chirk Forestry	216

* - MR1259 : is recorded in ICI records as being ICI loco RS14 which was rebuilt by ICI to become ICI RS40. However, MR records show that no MR loco 1259 was built (the 12XX batch finishing at MR1255). "1259" could be an 'FH' number, or an error.

* - MR1552 : again, MR records show that no such MR loco was built; yet Courtaulds successfully ordered spares from MR for "1552" from 1924 to 1939. Maybe it was an engine number, or perhaps an "FH" number ('FH' sold many reconditioned MR locos as 'Planet' locos).

MW - MANNING WARDLE LOCOMOTIVES, BOYNE ENGINE WORKS, LEEDS.
1858 -   : Manning Wardle & Co
     -1927 : Manning Wardle & Co Ltd
Liquidated 1927; Goodwill sold to 'Kit', part of premises occupied by 'HE'.

Worksnumb	Ex.Works	Gauge	Type	wheels	cyl	size	engine/notes	pages
19	26.10.1860	4' 8½"	0-4-0 tdr	4' 0"	OC	14x18	cl:LordWard	53, 98
21	22. 1.1861	4' 8½"	0-6-0 ST	3'1¼"	IC	11x17	class: I old	329
35	14.12.1861	4' 8½"	0-6-0 ST	3'1½"	IC	12x17	cl: I old	53, 114, 117
36	29. 1.1862	4' 8½"	0-6-0 ST	3'1½"	IC	12x17	class: I old	53
41	30. 6.1862	4' 8½"	0-6-0 tdr	4' 6"	IC	16x22	Special Goods	54
45	30. 4.1862	4' 8½"	0-6-0 ST	3'1½"	IC	12x17	class: I old	54, 98
49	27. 5.1862	4' 8½"	0-6-0 ST	3'1½"	IC	12x17	class: I old	54
52	2. 8.1862	4' 8½"	0-6-0 ST	3'1½"	IC	12x17	class: I old	54, 207
55	17.10.1862	4' 8½"	0-6-0 ST	3'1½"	IC	12x17	class: I old	54, 114
58	11.12.1862	4' 8½"	0-6-0 ST	3'1½"	IC	12x17	class: I old	54
62	21.11.1862	4' 8½"	0-4-0 ST	2' 9"	OC	9½x14	Class: E	260
63	22.12.1862	4' 8½"	0-4-0 ST	2'11½"	OC	9½x14	Class: E altd.	54
66	30. 1.1863	4' 8½"	0-6-0 ST	3'1½"	IC	12x17	Class: I old	54
81	30. 6.1863	4' 8½"	0-6-0 ST	3'1½"	IC	12x17	class: I old	58
83	3. 8.1863	4' 8½"	0-6-0 ST	3'1½"	IC	12x17	class: I old	266
93	27.10.1863	4' 8½"	0-6-0 ST	3'1½"	IC	12x17	class: I old	198
101	23. 1.1864	4' 8½"	0-6-0 ST	3'1½"	IC	12x17	class: I old	154, 312
126	30. 6.1864	4' 8½"	0-6-0 ST	3' 0"	IC	12x17	Class: K	51
140	23.11.1864	4' 8½"	0-6-0 ST	3' 0"	IC	12x17	Class: K	116, 123
155	28. 7.1865	4' 8½"	0-6-0 ST	3'1½"	IC	11x17	class: I old	95
171	2.10.1865	4' 8½"	0-6-0 ST	3' 0"	IC	12x17	Class: K	144
259	27. 8.1868	1'11¼"	0-4-2 ST	2' 3"	OC	8½x14	special	119, 278
260	23. 9.1868	1'11¼"	0-4-2 ST	2' 3"	OC	8½x14	special	119, 278
264	29. 9.1868	4' 8½"	0-4-0 ST	3' 0"	OC	12x18	Class: H	259
268	10. 2.1869	4' 8½"	0-6-0 ST	3' 0"	IC	13x18	Class: M	116
346	27. 7.1871	4' 8½"	0-4-0 ST	3' 0"	OC	12x18	Class: H	336
351	28. 9.1871	4' 8½"	0-4-0 ST	2' 9"	OC	10x16	Class: F	259
373	27.11.1871	4' 8½"	0-6-0 ST	3'1½"	IC	12x17	Class: K	158
380	3.11.1871	4' 8½"	0-4-0 ST	2' 6"	OC	9x14	Class: E spl	273
444	9. 6.1873	4' 8½"	0-4-0 ST	3' 0"	OC	12x18	Class: H	51, 336
478	17.10.1873	3' 0"	0-4-0 ST	2' 6"	OC	6x12	Class: B	300
487	12. 5.1874	2' 0"	0-4-0 ST	1' 8"	OC	6x8	special	412
502	8. 8.1874	4' 8½"	0-4-0 ST	2' 11	OC	13x18	Class: I	259
510	21. 9.1874	4' 8½"	0-6-0 ST	3' 0"	IC	13x18	Class: M	196
553	26. 8.1875	4' 8½"	0-4-0 ST	3' 0"	OC	10x16	Class: F	80
575	9. 8.1876	4' 8½"	0-4-0 ST	3' 0"	OC	12x18	Class: H	120
577	8.11.1875	4' 8½"	0-4-0 ST	2' 8"	OC	8x14	Class: D	287
592	31. 3.1877	4' 8½"	0-4-0 ST	3' 0"	OC	12x18	Class: H	81
604	4. 1.1877	4' 8½"	0-6-0 ST	3' 0"	IC	13x18	Class: M	421
634	2. 2.1877	4' 8½"	0-4-0 ST	2' 9"	OC	10x16	Class: F	243
664	13. 5.1878	4' 8½"	0-6-0 ST	3' 0"	IC	13x18	Class: M	312
684	21. 2.1878	4' 8½"	0-6-0 ST	3'1¼"	IC	12x17	Class: K	244
778	24. 1.1881	4' 8½"	0-4-0 ST	3' 0"	OC	12x18	Class: H	259
802	15. 9.1882	4' 8½"	0-4-0 ST	2' 9"	OC	10x16	Class: F	185, 421
818	24. 3.1882	4' 8½"	0-6-0 ST	3'1¼"	IC	12x17	Class: K	47
976	6. 8.1886	4' 8½"	0-6-0 ST	3'1½"	IC	12x17	Class: K	151, 421
977	19. 4.1886	4' 8½"	0-4-0 ST	2' 8"	OC	8x14	Class: D	151

983	8. 6.1886	4' 8½"	0-4-0 ST	2' 9"	OC	10x16	Class: F	408
991	11. 3.1887	4' 8½"	0-4-0 ST	2'10"	OC	9x14	Class: E spl	51, 58
993	4. 3.1887	4' 8½"	0-4-0 ST	2' 9"	OC	10x16	Class: F	374
996	29.10.1886	4' 8½"	0-6-0 ST	3' 1"	IC	12x17	Class: K spl	374, 375
1005	15. 6.1887	4' 8½"	0-6-0 T	2'11¼	IC	13x18	Class: M alt'd	38
1036	3.11.1887	4' 8½"	0-4-0 ST	2' 9"	OC	10x16	Class: F alt'd	392
1098	1.10.1888	4' 8½"	0-6-0 T	3' 0"	IC	13x18	Class: M spl	244
1105	20. 8.1889	4' 8½"	0-6-0 ST	3' 6"	IC	14x20	Class: Q	47, 110
1106	20. 9.1888	4' 8½"	0-4-0 ST	3' 6"	OC	14x18	Class: P	193
1111	11. 1.1889	4' 8½"	0-6-0 ST	3' 0"	IC	12x17	Class: K	198, 364
1145	27. 6.1890	4' 8½"	0-6-0 ST	3' 1"	IC	12x17	Class: K	421
1207	30.12.1990	4' 8½"	0-6-0 ST	3' 6"	IC	15x22	Special	273, 279, 312, 314
1229	4.1.1895	4' 8½"	0-4-0 ST	2' 9"	OC	9x14	Class: E	279
1237	20. 6.1892	4' 8½"	0-6-0 ST	3' 0"	IC	12x17	Class: K	41
1295	23.8.1895	4' 8½"	0-6-0 ST	3' 6"	IC	14x20	Class: Q	279
1380	2.11.1898	4' 8½"	0-4-0 ST	2' 9"	OC	9x14	Class: E	370
1382	16. 7.1897	1'11½"	0-4-0 ST	2' 2"	OC	9x14	Special	218, 359, 411
1384	29. 3.1898	4' 8½"	0-4-0 ST	2'10"	OC	10x16	Class: F	291, 292
1481	12.3.1900	4' 8½"	0-6-0 ST	3' 0"	IC	12x18	Class: L	30
1507	13. 2.1901	4' 8½"	0-6-0 ST	3' 0"	IC	12x17	Class: K	41, 245, 374
1560	16. 5.1902	4' 8½"	0-6-0 ST	3' 0"	IC	12x18	Class: L	374, 375
1570	16. 3.1903	4' 8½"	0-6-0 ST	3' 0"	IC	13x18	Class: M	196
1576	26. 1.1903	4' 8½"	0-6-0 ST	3' 1"	IC	12x17	Class: K	158
1593	22.12.1902	4' 8½"	0-6-0 ST	2'10"	IC	12x18	Class: L spl	112
1594	25. 2.1903	4' 8½"	0-6-0 ST	3' 0"	IC	12x18	Class: L	112, 313
1595	6. 3.1903	4' 8½"	0-6-0 ST	3' 0"	IC	12x18	Class: L	112
1598	18. 6.1903	4' 8½"	0-6-0 ST	3' 0"	IC	12x18	Class: L	112
1603	16. 4.1903	4' 8½"	0-6-0 ST	3' 1"	IC	12x17	Class: K	30, 40, 326
1605	14. 8.1903	4' 8½"	0-6-0 ST	3' 1"	IC	12x17	Class: K	158
1617	10.12.1903	4' 8½"	0-6-0 ST	3' 1"	IC	12x17	Class: K	158
1646	27. 2.1905	4' 8½"	0-6-0 ST	3' 9"	IC	16x22	Special	45, 421
1681	31. 1.1906	4' 8½"	0-4-0 ST	3' 0"	OC	14x18	Class: P	41, 408
1726	9. 1.1908	4' 8½"	0-6-0 ST	3' 0"	IC	13x18	Class: M	39
1728	28. 2.1908	4' 8½"	0-4-0 ST	3' 0"	OC	14x18	Class: P	41
1744	6. 6.1909	4' 8½"	0-6-0 ST	3' 0"	IC	12x18	Class: L spl	293
1888	7.10.1915	4' 8½"	0-4-0 ST	3' 8"	OC	16x24	Special	375
1902	24. 7.1916	4' 8½"	0-4-0 ST	3' 1"	OC	14x20	Special	313
1922	29.12.1916	4' 8½"	0-4-0 ST	3' 1"	OC	14x20	Special	194
1984	5.11.1919	4' 8½"	0-4-0 ST	3' 0"	OC	12x18	Special	258, 259
?		4' 8½"	0-4-0 ST		?C		NIPPER	374
?		4' 8½"	0-4-0 ST		?C		TERRIER	374
?	?	4' 8½"	0-4-0 ST		?C		Winnard	339

N - NEILSON LOCOMOTIVES, GLASGOW.

by1840 -1845 : Kerr, Neilson & Co; first loco built in 1843
1845 -1855   : Neilson & Mitchell
1855 -1898   : Neilson & Co
1898 -1903   : Neilson, Reid & Co

Works at Hyde Park Street, Glasgow, to 1861; thereafter at Hyde Park Works, Springburn, Glasgow.
In 1903 became part of North British Loco Co - see 'NB'.

Worksnumb	Ex.Works	Gauge	Type	wheels	cyl	size	engine/notes	pages
[? 420	c1859]	4' 8½"	0-4-0 ST		OC	14" ?	VICTORY	419
697	1862	7' 0"	? 0-4-0 ?T		IC	12x18		290
978	1863	7' 0"	0-4-0 ST	4' 0"	OC	12x18		290
3788	1888	4' 8½"	0-4-0 ST	3' 0"	OC	12x20		35
?	? c1866	4' 8½"	? ?T	3' 6"	?	10x16	BULKELEY	348

NB - NORTH BRITISH LOCOMOTIVE CO LTD, GLASGOW.

1903 -1962   : North British Locomotive Co Ltd.
       1962 : Closed.

Company formed by amalgamation of 'Dub', 'N', and 'SS', retaining all three Works. Atlas Works (ex 'SS') closed 1927.
Goodwill bought in 1962 by 'AB'.

Worksnumb	Ex.Works	Gauge	Type	wheels	cyl	size	engine/notes	pages
21521	1917	4' 8½"	0-6-0 T	4' 2"	OC	17x22	G&SWR/LMS	279
24042	1930	4' 8½"	0-6-0 PT	4' 7½"	IC	17½x24	GWR 57XX	174
24048	1930	4' 8½"	0-6-0 PT	4'7½"	IC	17½x24	GWR 57XX	174
27098	1954	4' 8½"	0-6-0 DH					396
27402	1954	4' 8½"	0-6-0 DH					396
27411	1954	4' 8½"	0-6-0 DH					396
27412	1954	4' 8½"	0-6-0 DH					396
27649	11.1956	4' 8½"	0-6-0 DH					396
27734	1958	4' 8½"	0-4-0 DH				225hp	174
27749	1957	4' 8½"	0-6-0 DH					396
27768	1959	4' 8½"	0-6-0 DH					397
27870	1960	4' 8½"	0-6-0 DH					397
28034	1960	4' 8½"	0-6-0 DH					396
28045	1961	4' 8½"	0-6-0 DH					397
28046	1962	4' 8½"	0-6-0 DH					397

NBICo - NEW BRITISH IRON CO, ACREFAIR IRONWORKS, CLWYD.

Worksnumb	Ex.Works	Gauge	Type	wheels	cyl	size	engine/notes	pages
	by 11.1886	4' 8½"	0-4-0 VBT		?C		Geared. 8 tons	185

OK - ORENSTEIN & KOPPEL A.G., GERMANY.

Worksnumb	Ex.Works	Gauge	Type	wheels	cyl	size	engine/notes	pages
1028	2.1903	610mm	0-4-0 WT		OC		20hp	342
2464	11.1907	914mm	0-4-0 WT		OC		20hp	354
4372		2ft	4w DM	1' 6"		llhp	class: RL1A	308
5668	4.1913	600mm	0-4-0 WT	1' 7½	OC		30hp	169, 245, 359
5675		2ft	4w DM					214
6915	13. 7.1914	600mm	0-4-0 WT		OC		20hp	313
7733	c 1938	2ft	4w DM	1' 6"		14hp	class: RL1C	214
9239	6.1921	600mm	0-6-0 WT		OC		40hp	138
10808	1924	600mm	0-6-0 WT		OC			138
12518	8.1934	600mm	0-8-0 tdr	2'1½"	OC	12¾x12	180hp	70
12722	3.1936	600mm	0-4-0 WT		OC		50hp	169, 196
?	?	2ft	0-4-0 ?T		?C		not proven	269

P - PECKETT LOCOMOTIVES, ATLAS WORKS, BRISTOL.

1880 - : Peckett & Sons
    -1958 : Peckett & Sons Ltd
    1958 : Closed.

Peckett took over the 'FW' Works in 1880, continuing the FW series of loco numbers with, initially, a similar product range.

Worksnumb	Ex.Works	Gauge	Type	wheels	cyl	size	engine/notes	pages
447	23. 3.1886	4' 8½"	0-4-0 ST	3' 2"	OC	14x20	class: W4	408
458	18. 1.1887	4' 8½"	0-4-0 ST	3' 2"	OC	14x20	class: W4	43
502	20. 1.1890	4' 8½"	0-4-0 ST	2' 6"	OC	10x14	class: M4	259
503	13. 4.1892	4' 8½"	0-4-0 ST	2' 6"	OC	10x14	class: M4	39
581	28.12.1894	4' 8½"	0-4-0 ST	3' 2"	OC	14x20	class: W4	37, 421
600	24. 9.1895	4' 8½"	0-4-0 ST	3' 2"	OC	14x20	class: W4	40, 326
644	9.11.1896	4' 8½"	0-4-0 ST	2' 6"	OC	10x14	class: M4 dwarf	36
775	6. 3.1899	4' 8½"	0-6-0 ST	3'10"	IC	16x20		279, 313
820	14. 9.1900	4' 8½"	0-4-0 ST	2' 6"	OC	10x14	class: M4	378
882	2.12.1901	4' 8½"	0-4-0 ST	3' 2"	OC	14x20	class: W4	374
897	11.11.1901	4' 8½"	0-4-0 ST	3' 2"	OC	14x20	class: W4	42
976	28. 9.1903	4' 8½"	0-4-0 ST	3'0½"	OC	12x18	class: R1	36, 313
1044	15. 3.1905	4' 8½"	0-4-0 ST	2' 6"	OC	10x14	class: M4	258, 259
1079	18.12.1906	4' 8½"	0-4-0 ST	2' 9"	OC	10x15	class: M5	36
1116	25. 9.1907	4' 8½"	0-4-0 ST	3'2½"	OC	14x20	class: W5	39
1255	4. 5.1911	4' 8½"	0-4-0 ST	2' 9"	OC	10x15	class: M5	408
1297	7. 3.1913	4' 8½"	0-4-0 ST	3'2½"	OC	14x20	class: W5	37, 273
1327	16. 5.1913	2' 0"	0-6-0 ST	1' 8"	OC	7x10	class: 7x10	169
1567	21. 6.1920	4' 8½"	0-6-0 ST	3'10"	IC	16x22	class: X2	174
1616	27. 4.1923	4' 8½"	0-6-0 ST	3' 7"	OC	14x20	class: B2	377
1649	10. 1.1924	4' 8½"	0-4-0 ST	3'0½"	OC	12x18	class: R2	196, 373
1810	28. 4.1930	4' 8½"	0-4-0 ST	3'10"	OC	16x24	class: OY	259
1873	18. 6.1934	4' 8½"	0-4-0 ST	2' 9"	OC	10x15	class: M5	292
1892	10. 7.1935	4' 8½"	0-4-0 ST	3'10"	OC	16x24	class: OY	272
1900	31.12.1935	4' 8½"	0-4-0 T	2' 0"	OC	8x12	Spl 5'9" high	272
1935	8.11.1937	4' 8½"	0-4-0 ST	3'2½"	OC	14x22	W6 Spl	194, 198

1947	15. 8.1938	4' 8½"	0-4-0 ST	3'10"	OC	16x24	class: OY	272
2024	26. 6.1942	2' 0"	0-4-2 T	2'6½"	OC	10x15	class: M5 Spl	138
2050	22. 2.1944	2' 0"	0-6-0 ST	2'3½"	OC	9½x14	class: 9½" Spl	68
2084	31. 3.1948	4' 8½"	0-4-0 ST	3'10"	OC	16x24	OY1 Spl 83, 174,	272
2085	23. 2.1948	4' 8½"	0-4-0 ST	3'10"	OC	16x24	OY1 Spl	259
2087	16. 6.1948	4' 8½"	0-4-0 ST	3'10"	OC	16x24	OY1 Spl	259
2115	16.10.1950	4' 8½"	0-6-0 ST	3' 7"	OC	14x22	class: B3	205, 266

Penrhyn - PENRHYN SLATE QUARRIES, BETHESDA.
For details of petrol and diesel locomotives built at the Penrhyn Slate Quarries see Location Listing of that title, pp 360-361.

PWG - PENMAENMAWR & WELSH GRANITE CO LTD.
For details of battery loco built by Penmaenmawr & Welsh Granite Co Ltd, see Location listing "Penmaenmawr Quarries" page 354.

PyO - PEN-YR-ORSEDD SLATE QUARRY, NANTLLE.
For details of petrol locomotive built by Pen-yr-Orsedd Slate Qy Co Ltd, see Location listing "PenyrOrsedd Quarry" page 367.

R&R - RANSOMES & RAPIER LTD, IPSWICH.

Worksnumb	Ex.Works	Gauge	Type	wheels	cyl	size	engine/notes	pages
93		2ft	4w DM					57, 212

RBL - R.B.LONGRIDGE & CO, BEDLINGTON, NORTHUMBERLAND.
Built more than 200 locomotives, between 1837 and 1852.

Worksnumb	Ex.Works	Gauge	Type	wheels	cyl	size	engine/notes	pages
	1845	4' 8½"	0-6-0 tdr	4' 9"	IC	15x24	S&CR No.1	75
	1845	4' 8½"	2-4-0 tdr	4' 9"	IC	15x24	S&CR No.2	75
	1845	4' 8½"	2-2-2 tdr	5' 9"	?C	15x24	S&CR No.3	75
	1845	4' 8½"	2-4-0 tdr	4' 9"	IC	15x24	S&CR No.4	75
	1846	4' 8½"	2-4-0 tdr	5' 0"	IC	14½x24	S&CR No.5	75
	1.1847	4' 8½"	2-4-0 tdr	5' 0"	IC	14½x24	S&CR No.6	75
	3.1849	4' 8½"	0-6-0 tdr	4' 9"	IC	15x24	S&CR No.25	76
309	1852	7' 0"	0-4-0 WT	3' 2"	IC	10¼x18	PRINCE ALBERT	290
	? 1852	7' 0"	0-4-0 WT	3' 2"	IC	10¼x18	(Azores)	290
	c1852	7' 0"	0-4-0 WT	3' 2"	IC	10¼x18	CAMBRIA	290
	c1852	7' 0"	0-4-0 WT	3' 2"	IC	10¼x18	HOLYHEAD	290
	c1852	7' 0"	0-4-0 WT	3' 2"	IC	10¼x18	LONDON	290
	c1852	7' 0"	0-4-0 WT	3' 2"	IC	10¼x18	QUEEN ?	290

Redstone - Mr REDSTONE, FITTER at PENMAENMAWR GRANITE QUARRIES.

Worksnumb	Ex.Works	Gauge	Type	wheels	cyl	size	engine/notes	pages
	9.1905	2ft	0-2-2 VBT	11"	2VC	4x6		169, 368, 406

RH - RUSTON LOCOMOTIVES, LINCOLN.
1851 -1880   : Richard Hornsby & Sons
1880 -1918   : Richard Hornsby & Sons Ltd
             [amalgamated with 'RP' (Ruston Proctor) 11/9/1918 :-]
1918 -1966   : Ruston & Hornsby Ltd
             [first R&H loco built in 1931].
             [acquired by English Electric Co Ltd 10/1966]
Last loco despatched from Lincoln 19/2/1969.

Worksnumb	Ex.Works	Gauge	Type		size	engine/notes	pages
166031	28. 1.1933	2ft	4w	DM	10hp	L:CS.5019	218
171901	27. 7.1934	2' 3"	4w	DM	10hp	L:CS.10687	417
171902	10. 9.1934	1'11"	4w	DM	10hp	L:CS.10685	384, 413
171905	23. 4.1935	2' 0"	4w	DM	10hp	L:CS.11304	332
174139	11. 2.1935	2' 0"	4w	DM	27/32	L:3JP.503118	342
174529	6. 1.1936	2' 0"	4w	DM	10hp	L:CS.14602	253, 297
174535	7. 5.1936	600mm	4w	DM	12hp	L:CS.17513	322
174536	7. 5.1936	600mm	4w	DM	12hp	L:CS.17508	322
174540	9. 3.1935	2' 0"	4w	DM	18/21	L:CS.14151	342
174542	20. 3.1935	600mm	4w	DM	18/21	L:CS.14147	317, 322
175127	22. 5.1935	2' 0"	4w	DM	18/21	L:CS.14528	264, 322
175138	24. 9.1935	600mm	4w	DM	18/21	L:CS.15038	322, 413
175405	20.11.1935	600mm	4w	DM	18/21	L:CS.16448	342
175414	7. 2.1936	600mm	4w	DM	18/21	L:CS.15830	138, 218, 333
175986	24. 9.1935	600mm	4w	DM	27/32	L:3JP.50-3529	342
175987	7.10.1935	1'10¾"	4w	DM	27/32	L:3JP.50-3926	236
177598	16.12.1935	600mm	4w	DM	27/32	L:3JP.50-3934	269, 342
177638	30. 6.1936	600mm	4w	DM	12hp	L:CS.17507	322, 342, 413
177642	14. 8.1936	600mm	4w	DM	12hp	L:CS.17503	322
181807	2.12.1936	1'10¾"	4w	DM	27/32	L:3JP.181783	236
181812	22.10.1936	2' 0"	4w	DM	20hp	L:CS.20258	361
181818	11.1936	2' 0"	4w	DM	20hp	L:CS.20268	361
182137	25.11.1936	600mm	4w	DM	20hp	L:CS.21038	170, 269, 342
182138	21.11.1936	1'10½"	4w	DM	20hp	L:CS.21044	282
182141	19.11.1936	600mm	4w	DM	12hp	L:CS.21091	413
182144	12. 1.1937	2' 0"	4w	DM	12hp	L:CS.21469	398
183727	12. 3.1937	1'10½"	4w	DM	20hp	L:CS.21975	282
183763	5. 5.1937	2' 0"	4w	DM	16/20	RH:2VSO.183325	361
186322	26. 6.1937	2' 0"	4w	DM	16/20	RH:2VSO.183333	236
186339	12. 8.1937	2' 0"	4w	DM	33/40	RH:3VRO.184134	103
186342	8.1937	2' 0"	4w	DM	16/20	RH:2VSO.186299	236
187045	16. 9.1937	2' 0"	4w	DM	16/20	RH:2VSO.187456	351
187084	4.11.1937	2' 0"	4w	DM	16/20	RH:2VSO.188002	361
189953	14. 1.1938	2' 0"	4w	DM	16/20	RH:2VSO.188027	406
189962	4.3.1939	2' 0"	4w	DM	33/40	RH:3VRO.186740	228

189968	22. 4.1939	2' 0"	4w	DM	44/48	RH:4VRO.186204	108
189972	28.3.1938	2' 0"	4w	DM	11/13	RH:2VTO.190461	171
189994	14. 3.1938	2' 0"	4w	DM	16/20	RH:2VSO.188019	361
191645	14. 3.1938	2' 0"	4w	DM	16/20	RH:2VSO.188039	236
191658	20. 4.1938	2' 0"	4w	DM	25/30	RH:3VSO.191821	138
191661	7. 4.1938	2' 0"	4w	DM	16/20	RH:2VSO.188025	236
191674	27. 4.1938	600mm	4w	DM	11/13	RH:2VTO.190465	322
191679	3.11.1938	2' 0"	4w	DM	11/13	RH:2VTO.190478	417
192844	4.10.1938	2' 0"	4w	DM	16/20	RH:2VSO.192188	230
192858	19. 1.1939	2' 0"	4w	DM	25/30	RH:3VSO.191830	419
193971	2.12.1938	2' 0"	4w	DM	16/20	RH:2VSO.192210	253
193984	5.1939	2' 0"	4w	DM	11/13	RH:2VTO.190479	70
194771	28. 1.1939	2' 0"	4w	DM	33/40	RH:3VRO.186742	170
194773	25. 1.1939	2' 0"	4w	DM	16/20	RH.2VSO.194406	413
194776	25. 2.1939	2' 0"	4w	DM	16/20	RH:2VSO.194407	312
198286	12. 3.1940	2' 0"	4w	DM	44/48	RH:4VRO.201804	167
198292	20.11.1939	2' 0"	4w	DM	33/40	RH:3VRO.190169	360
198297	19.12.1939	2' 0"	4w	DM	33/40	RH:3VRO.190166	228, 345
198324	30. 7.1940	4' 8½"	4w	DM	80/88	RH:4VPO.202724	306
198325	26.12.1940	4' 8½"	4w	DM	80/88	RH:4VPO.204986	306
200480	13. 5.1940	2' 0"	4w	DM	25/30	RH:3VSO.201409	406
200744	27. 7.1940	2' 0"	4w	DM	33/40	RH:3VRO.201931	171
200748	12.1940	2' 0"	4w	DM	33/40	RH:3VRO.202151	166, 171
200762	14. 7.1942	600mm	4w	DM	11/13	RH:2VTO.213869	322
200792	8. 2.1941	2'6½"	4w	DM	44/48	RH:4VRO.202307	108
200800	1. 4.1941	2' 0"	4w	DM	44/48	RH:4VRO.202311	108
200803	9.10.1941	2' 0"	4w	DM	44/48	RH:4VRO.201813	370
201970	6. 5.1940	2' 0"	4w	DM	11/13	RH:2VTO.200090	70
202976	19.12.1940	600mm	4w	DM	16/20	RH:2VSO.200579	361
202979	8.11.1940	2' 0"	4w	DM	16/20	RH:2VSO.200573	236, 331
202987	8.10.1941	3' 0"	4w	DM	16/20	RH.2VSO.212031	354
202989	10.10.1941	3' 0"	4w	DM	16/20	RH:2VSO.212038	354
203001	20. 2.1941	600mm	4w	DM	16/20	RH:2VSO.206359	57, 212
203009	17. 3.1941	600mm	4w	DM	16/20	RH:2VSO.206368	236
203031	21. 5.1942	2' 0"	4w	DM	44/48	RH:4VRO.208129	167
203032	23. 7.1942	2' 0"	4w	DM	44/48	RH:4VRO.208130	370
209430	22. 6.1942	500mm	4w	DM	11/13	RH:2VTO.213867	171, 345
210478	26. 9.1942	4' 8½"	4w	DM	80/88	RH:4VPO.205005	306
210473	31.12.1942	4' 8½"	4w	DM	80/88	RH:4VPO.205006	392
210955	28. 3.1941	600mm	4w	DM	16/20	RH:2VSO.206373	57, 70, 212
211596	26. 4.1941	600mm	4w	DM	16/20	RH:2VSO.206595	361
211598	10. 5.1941	600mm	4w	DM	16/20	RH:2VSO.206387	236
211605	21. 5.1941	600mm	4w	DM	16/20	RH:2VSO.206604	361
211620	12. 7.1941	600mm	4w	DM	16/20	RH:2VSO.212027	236
211625	6.10.1941	2' 0"	4w	DM	16/20	RH:2VSO.212020	228
211640	16.12.1941	600mm	4w	DM	16/20	RH:2VSO.212060	361
213834	23. 6.1942	2' 0"	4w	DM	16/20	RH:2VSO.213894	168, 231, 345
217972	26.11.1942	600mm	4w	DM	16/20	RH:2VSO.222413	386
218011	10. 3.1943	2' 0"	4w	DM	16/20	RH:2VSO.224167	360
218033	12. 3.1943	2' 0"	4w	DM	33/40	RH:3VRO.218908	360
218049	30. 3.1943	4' 8½"	4w	DM	44/48	RH:4VRO.218080	283
221593	28. 4.1943	600mm	4w	DM	16/20	RH:2VSO.224922	282
221605	26. 5.1943	600mm	4w	DM	16/20	RH:2VSO.225885	236
222072	13. 8.1943	2' 0"	4w	DM	16/20	RH:2VSO.226716	360

222081	11.10.1943	600mm	4w	DM	16/20	RH:2VSO.226798	236
223674	3.11.1943	2' 0"	4w	DM	16/20	RH:2VSO.228837	361
223680	12.11.1943	2' 0"	4w	DM	16/20	RH:2VSO.228835	361
223685	13. 1.1944	600mm	4w	DM	16/20	RH:2VSO.228809	361
223687	5. 1.1944	600mm	4w	DM	16/20	RH:2VSO.229697	229
223701	5. 2.1944	600mm	4w	DM	16/20	RH:2VSO.230031	361
223753	6. 4.1944	600mm	4w	DM	16/20	RH:2VSO.233717	361
224338	3. 6.1944	4' 8½"	4w	DM	48DS	RH:4VRO.234646	331
224347	6. 3.1945	4' 8½"	4w	DM	48DS	RH:4VRO.232328	378
226264	8. 6.1944	600mm	4w	DM	20DL	RH:2VSO.234281	367
226292	21. 8.1944	600mm	4w	DM	20DL	RH:2VSO.234309	251, 351
226297	24. 8.1944	600mm	4w	DM	20DL	RH:2VSO.234311	361
226298	30. 8.1944	600mm	4w	DM	20DL	RH:2VSO.234314	367
226302	8. 9.1944	600mm	4w	DM	20DL	RH:2VSO.234322	361
226309	16. 6.1944	600mm	4w	DM	20DL	RH:2VSO.234289	282
229651	18.12.1944	600mm	4w	DM	20DL	RH:2VSH.234768	361
235652	3. 4.1945	600mm	4w	DM	20DL	RH:2VSH.238026	251
235663	10. 4.1947	2ft	4w	DM	20DL	RH:2VSH.239815	253, 388
235704	25.10.1945	2' 0"	4w	DM	20DL	RH:2VSH.239842	236, 331
235711	26.10.1945	600mm	4w	DM	20DL	RH:2VSH.240642	83, 168, 345, 367
235712	26.10.1945	600mm	4w	DM	20DL	RH:2VSH.240643	367
235729	7.12.1944	2' 6"	4w	DM	48DL	RH:4VRO.234967	171, 345
237914	7. 5.1946	2' 0"	4w	DM	30DL	RH:3VSH.244678	138
244487	17.10.1946	2' 0"	4w	DM	48DL	RH:4VRO.236963	214
246809	3. 3.1947	1'10¾"	4w	DM	30DL	RH:3VSH.252634	236
248439	30.12.1946	4' 8½"	0-4-0	DM	165DS	RH:6VPH.242264	349
252687	27. 7.1949	4' 8½"	0-4-0	DM	165DS	RH:6VPH.266217	349
252799	1. 4.1947	1'10¾"	4w	DM	30DL	RH:3VSH.253199	236
260734	23. 2.1951	2' 0"	4w	DM	20DLU	RH:2VSH.260925	351
264252	5. 3.1952	2' 0"	4w	DM	13DL	RH:2VTH.255185	46, 342, 413
268878	10. 1.1956	2' 6"	4w	DM	48DLZ	RH:4VRH.388640	167
273854	1. 7.1949	1'10¾"	4w	DM	30DL	RH:3VSH.266742	236
277265	25. 4.1949	1'10¾"	4w	DM	30DL	RH:3VSO.281557	166, 236
277269	1. 7.1949	1'10¾"	4w	DM	30DL	RH:3VSH.281556	236
283512	22. 8.1949	2' 0"	4w	DM	30DL	RH:3VSH.284635	171
283869	2. 9.1949	2'10½"	4w	DM	48DL	RH:4VRH.272425	153, 168, 307
287664	24. 1.1952	2' 0"	4w	DM	40DL	RH:3VRH.276062	168
296091	22.12.1949	2' 4¼"	4w	DM	20DL	RH:2VSH.273680	253
297030	12. 2.1952	2' 0"	4w	DM	40DL	RH:3VRH.295530	138, 167, 399
313394	29. 8.1952	4' 8½"	0-4-0	DM	165DS	RH:6VPH.332648	190
319284	17.12.1952	4' 8½"	0-4-0	DM	165DS	RH:6VPH.339139	190
321727	15. 4.1952	4' 8½"	4w	DM	88DS	RH:4VPH.335640	190
323547	21. 8.1951	2' 0"	4w	DM	20DLU	RH:2VSH.321864	351
326068	2. 2.1953	4' 8½"	4w	DM	88DS	RH:4VPH.344209	194, 370
327904	4.12.1951	2' 0"	4w	DM	20DL	RH:2VSH.325720	357
331250	1.10.1952	1'10½"	4w	DM	20DLU	RH:2VSH.327326	282
339209	8.12.1952	2' 0"	4w	DM	30DLU	RH:3VSH.339893	269
349032	6. 2.1953	4' 8½"	4w	DM	48DS	RH:4VRH.349319	378
354029	19.10.1953	1'10½"	4w	DM	20DLU	RH:2VSH.362828	282
354068	10.1953	2' 0"	4w	DM	40DL	RH:3VRH.361812	138
370555	8. 9.1953	2' 0"	4w	DM	48DL	RH:4VRH.349490	138
371545	19.10.1954	2' 0"	4w	DM	20LAT	RH:2VSH.369995	404
374457	12. 1.1955	3' 0"	0-4-0	DM	75LHU	RH: 4TE.386406	402

375316	15. 4.1954	2' 0"	4w	DM	40DL	RH:3VRH.369749	167, 399
375349	10.11.1954	2' 0"	4w	DM	20LAT	RH:2VSH.370169	404
375354	5.11.1954	2' 0"	4w	DM	20LAT	RH:2VSH.380991	404
375362	1. 2.1955	2' 0"	4w	DM	20LAT	RH:2VSH.381147	250
375700	28. 7.1954	2' 0"	4w	DM	31LBT	RH:3VSH.379588	273, 314
375701	28. 7.1954	2' 0"	4w	DM	31LBT	RH:3VSH.379577	273, 314
375702	11. 8.1954	2' 0"	4w	DM	31LBT	RH:3VSH.379530	103
379092	1. 2.1955	3' 0"	0-4-0	DM	75LHU	RH: 4YE.386422	402
379096	25. 4.1955	2' 0"	0-4-0	DM	75LHG	RH: 4YE.386474	370
379097	26. 4.1955	2' 0"	0-4-0	DM	75LHG	RH: 4YE.386490	370
379099	28. 4.1955	2' 0"	0-4-0	DM	75LHG	RH: 4YE.387998	370
382820	13. 5.1955	1'11"	4w	DM	40DL	RH:3VRH.388520	361
384143	30.12.1955	3' 6"	0-6-0	DE	165DE	RH:6VPH.395262	232
387819	10. 6.1955	2' 0"	4w	DM	31LBT	RH:3VSH.393453	250
387820	10. 6.1955	2' 0"	4w	DM	31LBT	RH:3VSH.393474	250
390775	27. 3.1956	3' 6"	0-6-0	DM	165DS	RH:6VPH.395249	232
392102	24. 8.1955	2' 0"	4w	DM	31LBT	RH:3VSH.393539	250, 404
398102	13. 8.1956	2' 4"	4w	DM	31LBU	RH:3VSH.398185	345
416207	9. 9.1957	4' 8½"	0-4-0	DE	165DE	RH:6VPH.416580	174
416213	11.11.1957	4' 8½"	0-4-0	DE	165DE	RH:6VPH.416589	174
418596	26.11.1957	4' 8½"	0-4-0	DE	165DE	RH:6VPH.421703	349
425796	5. 9.1958	2' 0"	4w	DM	48DLZ	RH:4VRH.425461	168
427855	6. 6.1958	3' 0"	0-4-0	DM	75LHU	RH: 4YE.422486	402
427857	13. 4.1959	2' 0"	0-4-0	DM	75LHG	RH: 4YE.431861	370
432652	20. 2.1959	2' 0"	4w	DM	31LBT	RH:2YDA.431987	170, 342
435393	29. 6.1959	3' 0"	4w	DM	48DLU	RH: 4YC.441503	402
441427	13.10.1961	2' 6"	4w	DM	48DLZ	RH:4VRH.466603	167
444207	28. 3.1961	2' 0"	4w	DM	48DLU	RH: 4YC.459901	169
451901	28. 7.1961	2' 9"	4w	DM	48DLG	RH:4VRH.433385	166
476108	10.12.1964	3' 0"	4w	DH	48LFT	RH:3YDA.363/8	108
476109	10.12.1964	3' 0"	4w	DH	48LFT	RH:3YDA.663/11	108
481551	25. 9.1962	2' 0"	4w	DM	48DLG	RH:4VRH.485076	314, 370
481552	28. 9.1962	2' 0"	4w	DM	48DLG	RH:4VRH.485077	138, 273, 370
481553	25.10.1962	2' 0"	4w	DM	48DLG	RH:4VRH.485078	273, 370
487963	27. 3.1963	2' 0"	4w	DM	48DL	RH: 4YC.467132	211
497547	28. 3.1963	2' 0"	4w	DM	48DLG	RH:4VRH.485081	194, 273, 371
497549	17. 7.1963	2' 0"	4w	DM	48DLG	RH:4VRH.497714	273, 314, 370
497758	25. 7.1963	2' 0"	4w	DM	48DLG	RH:4VRH.497715	314, 370
497759	1. 8.1963	2' 0"	4w	DM	48DLG	RH:4VRH.497716	314, 370
497761	1.10.1963	2' 0"	4w	DM	48DLG	RH:4VRH.499511	273, 370
497762	29.10.1963	2' 0"	4w	DM	48DLG	RH:4VRH.499513	273, 370
497763	18.11.1963	2' 0"	4w	DM	48DLG	RH:4VRH.499512	273
504628	4.12.1963	2' 0"	4w	DM	48DLG	RH:4VRH.499514	273, 370
506494	8. 5.1964	2' 0"	4w	DM	48DLG	RH:4VRH.499515	273
506495	8. 5.1964	2' 0"	4w	DM	48DLG	RH:4VRH.499516	273, 370
506496	25. 6.1964	2' 0"	4w	DM	48DLG	RH:4VRH.504548	273, 314, 370
506914	20. 7.1964	2' 0"	4w	DM	48DLG	RH:4VRH.504549	370
518493	16. 3.1966	2' 6"	4w	DH	48LFT	RH:3YDA.266-24	93

Rhiwbach - **RHIWBACH SLATE QUARRY Co, near FFESTINIOG.**

Worksnumb	Ex.Works	Gauge	Type	wheels	cyl	size	engine/notes	pages
-	? c1935	2ft	2-2-0 PM	1' 0"		7hp	Austin	345, 383

RP - RUSTON, PROCTOR & CO, SHEAF IRONWORKS, LINCOLN.
1857 -1899   : Ruston Proctor & Co
1899 -1918   : Ruston Proctor & Co Ltd.
11/9/1918   : Amalgamated with Richard Hornsby & Sons Ltd to form R&H - see 'RH'.
RP built locomotives - first steam, later petrol - from 1866.

Worksnumb	Ex.Works	Gauge	Type	wheels	cyl	size	engine/notes	pages
51901	28. 9.1917	1' 6"	4w PM			10hp		46, 57, 342

ROLLS ROYCE LTD, SHREWSBURY - See 'S' list.

RS - ROBERT STEPHENSON & CO, NEWCASTLE & DARLINGTON.
- first loco built in 1824
  Forth Street Works, Newcastle on Tyne, 1823-1902
  Darlington Works   1902-1937
  Amalgamated with 'HL' in 1937 to become 'RSH'

Worksnumb	Ex.Works	Gauge	Type	wheels	cyl	size	engine/notes	pages
622	6.1848	4' 8½"	0-6-0 tdr	4' 6"	IC	15x24		415
716	4.1849	4' 8½"	0-6-0 tdr	4' 9"	IC	15x24		76
774	2.1851	4' 8½"	0-6-0 tdr	5'0¾"	IC	18x24		110

RSH - ROBERT STEPHENSON & HAWTHORNS LTD.
formed 1/1937 by amalgamation of 'RS' and 'HL'
Loco construction continued at both Newcastle (HL) and Darlington (RS) Works.
Controlled by Vulcan Foundry Ltd ('VF') from 1944
Became English Electric Co Ltd (with 'VF' etc) 3/1955.
Newcastle Works closed 1960

Worksnumb	Ex.Works	Gauge	Type	wheels	cyl	size	engine/notes	pages
7026	2. 7.1941	4' 8½"	0-6-0 ST	3' 8"	OC	16x24		205
7074	8. 1.1943	4' 8½"	0-6-0 ST	3' 1"	OC	12x20		245
7088	1943	4' 8½"	0-6-0 ST	4' 3"	IC	18x26	Austerity	273
7096	1943	4' 8½"	0-6-0 ST	4' 3"	IC	18x26	Austerity	280
7103	1943	4' 8½"	0-6-0 ST	4' 3"	IC	18x26	Austerity	279

Worksnumb	Ex.Works	Gauge	Type	wheels	cyl	size	engine/notes	pages
7135	1944	4' 8½"	0-6-0 ST	4' 3"	IC	18x26	Austerity	273, 314
7141	1944	4' 8½"	0-6-0 ST	4' 3"	IC	18x26	Austerity	283
7162	1944	4' 8½"	0-6-0 ST	4' 3"	IC	18x26	Austerity	266
7335	3. 1.1947	4' 8½"	0-4-0 ST	3' 8"	OC	16x24		272

RSP - REGENT STREET POLYTECHNIC, LONDON.

Worksnumb	Ex.Works	Gauge	Type	wheels	cyl	size	engine/notes	pages
	1898	1' 6"	4-2-2 tdr	2' 6"	OC	4x6		146

S - SENTINEL LOCOMOTIVES, BATTLEFIELD, SHREWSBURY.

```
1918 -1920       : Sentinel Waggon Works Ltd
                   (reg.1918, vol.liq.24/3/1920)
1920 -1925       : Sentinel Waggon Works (1920) Ltd (reg.1920; became :-)
1925 -1936       : Sentinel Waggon Works Ltd (reg.9/3/1925; became :-)
1936 -           : Sentinel Waggon Works (1936) Ltd (which became :-)
     -1957       : Sentinel (Shrewsbury) Ltd
1957 -           : Rolls Royce Ltd, Oil Engine Division.
                 : loco production ceased.
```
Also, 1925-1928 locos part manufactured and assembled at Saltney, Chester, by subsidiary - Sentinel Industrial Locos (England) Ltd.

Worksnumb	Ex.Works	Gauge	Type	wheels	cyl	size	engine/notes	pages
5734	1925	4' 8½"	4w VBT	2' 6"	2VC	6¾x9	class: CE	364
6255	1927	3' 0"	4w VBT	1' 8"	2VC	6¾x9	80hp	300
6256	1927	3' 0"	4w VBT	1' 8"	2VC	6¾x9	80hp	300
6257	1927	3' 0"	4w VBT	1' 8"	2VC	6¾x9	80hp	300
6897	1927	3' 0"	4w VBT	1' 8"	2VC	6¾x9	class: BE	56
6898	1927	3' 0"	4w VBT	1' 8"	2VC	6¾x9	class: BE	56
6901	1927	2'11½"	4w VBT	1' 8"	2VC	6¾x9	class: BE	320
8085	11.12.1929	3' 0"	4w VBT	1' 8"	2VC	6¾x9	class: BE	232
9575	1954	4' 8½"	4w VBT		4VC	6¾x9	200hp	336
9596	24. 6.1955	4' 8½"	4w VBT	2' 6"	2VC	6¾x9	100hp	259
10097	1962	4' 8½"	4w DH				230hp	370
10231	1965	4' 8½"	4w DH					272
10235	1965	4' 8½"	4w DH					349
10251	1966	4' 8½"	4w DH				255hp	272
10252	1966	4' 8½"	4w DH				255hp	272
10254	1967	4' 8½"	0-4-0 DE					205
10276	1967	4' 8½"	4w DH					349

SB - SHARP LOCOMOTIVES, MANCHESTER.
1828 -1843   : Sharp, Roberts & Co, Atlas Works, Manchester.
             (first loco built in 1833). Company re-named:-
1843 -1852   : Sharp Brothers, Atlas Works, Manchester.
             became Sharp, Stewart & Co in 1852 - see 'SS'.

Worksnumb	Ex.Works	Gauge	Type	wheels	cyl	size	engine/notes	pages
55	10.1839	4' 8½"	2-2-2 tdr		IC		DOVE	53
348	1846	4' 8½"	0-6-0 tdr	4' 6"	IC	18x24		110
400	2.1847	4' 8½"	2-2-2 tdr	5' 0"	IC	15x20		75
405	3.1847	4' 8½"	2-2-2 tdr	5' 6"	IC	15x20		75
441	9.1847	4' 8½"	2-2-2 tdr	5' 6"	IC	15x20		75
[? 521]	7.1848	4' 8½"	2-2-2 tdr	5' 0"	IC	14x20		75
[? 524]	7.1848	4' 8½"	2-2-2 tdr	5' 6"	IC	15x20		76
555	11.1848	4' 8½"	2-2-2 tdr	5' 6"	IC	15x20		76
580	5.1849	4' 8½"	0-4-0 WT	4' 6"	IC	15x22		76
[? 589]	7.1849	4' 8½"	2-2-2 tdr	5' 6"	IC	15x20		76
663	1850	4' 8½"	0-4-0 tk	3' 9"	?	13x18		65, 80, 221

Sdn - SWINDON WORKS, WILTSHIRE.
Great Western Railway to 1947
British Railways from 1/1/1948

Worksnumb	Ex.Works	Gauge	Type	wheels	cyl	size	engine/notes	pages
GW 2859	1918	4' 8½"	2-8-0 OC	4'7½"	OC	18½x30	class: 28XX	174
GW 4566	10.1924	4' 8½"	2-6-2 T	4'7½"	OC	17x24	class: 45XX	174
GW 5532	1928	4' 8½"	2-6-2 T	4'7½"	OC	17x24	class: 4575	174
GW 5538	1928	4' 8½"	2-6-2 T	4'7½"	OC	17x24	class: 4575	174
GW 5572	2.1929	4' 8½"	2-6-2 T	4'7½"	OC	17x24	class: 4575	174
GW 5199	1934	4' 8½"	2-6-2 T	5' 8"	OC	18x30	class: 5101	174
GW 5952	1935	4' 8½"	4-6-0 tdr	6' 0"	OC	18½x30	class: 49XX	174
GW 1466	2.1936	4' 8½"	0-4-2 T	5' 2"	IC	16x24	class: 14XX	174
BR 7821	1950	4' 8½"	4-6-0 OC	5' 8"	OC	18x30	class: 78XX	174
BR 7822	1950	4' 8½"	4-6-0 tdr	5' 8"	OC	18x30	class: 78XX	173
BR 7828	1950	4' 8½"	4-6-0 tdr	5' 8"	OC	18x30	class: 78XX	174
BR D2148	1960	4' 8½"	0-6-0 DM	3' 7"		204hp		266
BR D2162	1960	4' 8½"	0-6-0 DM	3' 7"		204hp		173
BR D2182	1962	4' 8½"	0-6-0 DM	3' 7"		204hp		266
BR D9500	1964	4' 8½"	0-6-0 DH	4' 0"		650hp		174
BR D9502	1964	4' 8½"	0-6-0 DH	4' 0"		650hp		173

SG - STOTHERT SLAUGHTER & SLAUGHTER GRUNING, BRISTOL.

1837	-1841	: Henry Stothert & Co, became:-
1841	-1856	: Stothert, Slaughter & Co
		First locomotive built 1841. Company became:-
1856	-1866	: Slaughter, Gruning & Co
	1866	: became Avonside Engine Co - see 'AE'.

Worksnumb	Ex.Works	Gauge	Type	wheels	cyl	size	engine/notes	pages
[? 358]	1857	4' 8½"	0-6-0 tdr	4' 6"	IC	16x24	ANTELOPE	53
[? 359]	1858	4' 8½"	0-6-0 tdr	4' 6"	IC	16x24	ELEPHANT	53

SHEPHERD & TODD; SHEPHERD & WILSON - see 'EBW'

SIG - SCHWEIZERISCHE INDUSTRIE GESELLSCHAFT, NEUHAUSEN, SWITZERLAND.

Worksnumb	Ex.Works	Gauge	Type	wheels	cyl	size	engine/notes	pages
706-716	1976	750mm	4w BE					234
706-717	1976	750mm	4w BE					234

SIMPLEX MECHANICAL HANDLING LTD - see 'MR'

SL - SEVERN LAMB LTD, STRATFORD ON AVON.

Worksnumb	Ex.Works	Gauge	Type	wheels	cyl	size	engine/notes	pages
22	1973	1'11½"	4w+4w	DH		100hp	Leyland	170

SLM - SCHWEIZERISCHE LOKOMOTIV & MASCHINENFABRIK, WINTERTHUR, SWITZERLAND.

Worksnumb	Ex.Works	Gauge	Type	wheels	cyl	size	engine/notes	pages
923	1895	800mm	0-4-2 T	rack	OC	cyls:-	300x600mm	153
924	1895	800mm	0-4-2 T	rack	OC	cyls:-	300x600mm	153
925	1895	800mm	0-4-2 T	rack	OC	cyls:-	300x600mm	153
988	1896	800mm	0-4-2 T	rack	OC	cyls:-	300x600mm	153
989	1896	800mm	0-4-2 T	rack	OC	cyls:-	300x600mm	153
2838	1922	800mm	0-4-2 T	rack	OC	cyls:-	300x600mm	153
2869	1923	800mm	0-4-2 T	rack	OC	cyls:-	300x600mm	153
2870	1923	800mm	0-4-2 T	rack	OC	cyls:-	300x600mm	153

SS - SHARP, STEWART & CO, MANCHESTER & GLASGOW.

1852 -1864 : Sharp, Stewart & Co, Atlas Works, Manchester.
direct successors to 'SB'.
1864 -1903 : Sharp, Stewart & Co Ltd
Company removed to Glasgow in 1888 to occupy the premises
of the Clyde Locomotive Co Ltd.
The Glasgow Clyde Works was then renamed Atlas Works.
1903 : 'SS' became a constituent of 'NB' (which see).

Worksnumb	Ex.Works	Gauge	Type	wheels	cyl	size	engine/notes	pages
743	10.1853	4' 8½"	2-2-2 tdr	5' 6"	IC	14½x20		76
744	10.1853	4' 8½"	2-2-2 tdr	5' 6"	IC	14½x20		76
1079	1858	4' 8½"	0-4-2 ST	4' 9"	IC	14x20		91
1080	1858	4' 8½"	0-4-2 ST	4' 9"	IC	14x20		91
1123	3.1859	4' 8½"	0-4-2 ST	4' 9"	IC	14x20		53
1136	1859	4' 8½"	0-4-2 ST	4' 9"	IC	14x20		91
1146	10.1859	4' 8½"	0-4-2 tdr	5' 0"	IC	15½x22		53
1147	10.1859	4' 8½"	0-4-2 tdr	5' 0"	IC	15½x22		53
1148	11.1859	4' 8½"	0-4-2 tdr	5' 0"	IC	15½x22		53
1224	12.1860	4' 8½"	0-4-2 tdr	5' 0"	IC	15½x22		53, 98, 114
1225	12.1860	4' 8½"	0-4-2 tdr	5' 0"	IC	15½x22		53
1226	12.1860	4' 8½"	0-4-2 tdr	5' 0"	IC	15½x22		53, 114
1301	12.1861	4' 8½"	0-6-0 tdr	4' 6"	IC	16x24		53
1302	12.1861	4' 8½"	0-6-0 tdr	4' 6"	IC	16x24		53
1310	12.1861	4' 8½"	0-6-0 tdr	4' 6"	IC	16x24		54
1311	12.1861	4' 8½"	0-6-0 tdr	4' 6"	IC	16x24		54, 114
1341	11.1862	4' 8½"	0-6-0 tdr	4' 6"	IC	16x24		54
1342	11.1862	4' 8½"	0-6-0 tdr	4' 6"	IC	16x24		54
1343	2.1863	4' 8½"	0-6-0 tdr	4' 6"	IC	16x24		54
1344	2.1863	4' 8½"	0-6-0 tdr	4' 6"	IC	16x24		54
1400	3.1863	4' 8½"	2-4-0 tdr	5' 6"	IC	16x20		54
1401	3.1863	4' 8½"	2-4-0 tdr	5' 6"	IC	16x20		54
1408	3.1863	4' 8½"	0-6-0 tdr	5' 0"	IC	16½x24		54
1409	3.1863	4' 8½"	0-6-0 tdr	5' 0"	IC	16½x24		54
1412	3.1863	4' 8½"	2-4-0 tdr	5' 6"	IC	16x20		54
1413	3.1863	4' 8½"	2-4-0 tdr	5' 6"	IC	16x20		54
1431	6.1863	4' 8½"	0-4-0 ST	4' 0"	IC	14x20		54
1432	6.1863	4' 8½"	0-4-0 ST	4' 0"	IC	14x20		54
1433	6.1863	4' 8½"	0-4-0 ST	4' 0"	IC	14x20		54
1445	6.1863	4' 8½"	0-6-0 tdr	4' 6"	IC	16x24		54
1446	6.1863	4' 8½"	0-6-0 tdr	4' 6"	IC	16x24		54
1485	3.1864	4' 8½"	2-4-0 tdr	5' 6"	IC	16x20		54
1486	3.1864	4' 8½"	2-4-0 tdr	5' 6"	IC	16x20		54
1487	3.1864	4' 8½"	2-4-0 tdr	5' 6"	IC	16x20		54
1488	3.1864	4' 8½"	2-4-0 tdr	5' 6"	IC	16x20		54
1530	8.1864	4' 8½"	0-6-0 tdr	4' 6"	IC	16x24		54
1531	8.1864	4' 8½"	0-6-0 tdr	4' 6"	IC	16x24		54
1579	4.1865	4' 8½"	2-4-0 tdr	5' 6"	IC	16x20		54
1580	4.1865	4' 8½"	2-4-0 tdr	5' 6"	IC	16x20		54
1587	4.1865	4' 8½"	0-6-0 tdr	4' 6"	IC	16x24		54
1588	4.1865	4' 8½"	0-6-0 tdr	4' 6"	IC	16x24		54
1590	4.1865	4' 8½"	0-6-0 tdr	4' 6"	IC	16x24		54
1597	5.1865	4' 8½"	0-6-0 tdr	4' 6"	IC	16x24		54

Worksnumb	Ex.Works	Gauge	Type	wheels		cyl	size	engine/notes	pages
1632	10.1865	4' 8½"	2-4-0	tdr	5' 6"	IC	16x20		54
1633	10.1865	4' 8½"	2-4-0	tdr	5' 6"	IC	16x20		54
1655	12.1865	4' 8½"	2-4-0	tdr	5' 6"	IC	16x20		54
1656	12.1865	4' 8½"	2-4-0	tdr	5' 6"	IC	16x20		54
1683	5.1866	4' 8½"	2-4-0	T	4' 6"	IC	14x20		114
1757	? c5.1867	4' 8½"	2-4-0	tdr	5' 6"	IC	16x20		114
1859	1868	4' 8½"	0-6-0	ST	4' 0"	IC	15x22		185
1899	12.1868	4' 8½"	2-4-0	tdr	5' 6"	IC	16x20		114
2510	9.1875	4' 8½"	0-6-0	tdr	4' 6"	IC	16x24		98
2932	1880	4' 8½"	0-6-0	T	4' 3"	IC	18x24		110
3419	1888	4' 8½"	0-4-0	ST	2' 9"	OC	12x18		38, 273
3471	1888	4' 8½"	0-6-0	T	3' 0"	IC	13x20		266
3475	1888	4' 8½"	0-6-0	T	3' 0"	IC	13x20		192, 298
4056	1895	4' 8½"	2-4-0	T	5' 3"	IC	17x24		295

T&G - THWAITES & GARBUTT, VULCAN WORKS, THORNTON ROAD, BRADFORD.
  (became Thwaites Bros; Thwaites Bros Ltd; in 1880s)
  T&G were general engineers who built a few locos.

Worksnumb	Ex.Works	Gauge	Type	wheels	cyl	size	engine/notes	pages
	?c1850	4' 8½"	0-6-0 tdr	5' 6"	IC	15x24		110

CHARLES TAYLEUR & CO   - see 'VF'.

TODD, KITSON & LAIRD - see 'Kit'.

TRCo - TALYLLYN RAILWAY CO & PRESERVATION SOCIETY.
  Machines built for own use on PR/27.

Worksnumb	Ex.Works	Gauge	Type	wheels	cyl	size	engine/notes	pages
	1954	2' 3"	4-2-0 PM				Mercury	108
	12.1954	2' 3"	2-2-0 PMr	1' 0"		7hp	Austin	108
	1991	2' 3"	0-4-2 T	2' 0"	OC	8½x12	TOM ROLT	108

TULK & LEY - see 'FJ'

Unilok - UNILOK ROAD-RAIL TRACTORS.
Unilok "road/rail" multipurpose tractors, built by:-
Hugo Aeckerle, of Hamburg (Germany) and Ireland (South).

Worksnumb	Ex.Works	Gauge	Type	wheels	cyl	size	engine/notes	pages
2005	1972	4' 8½"	4w	DM				266
2186	1982	4' 8½"	4w	DM			60hp Perkins	393

Unimog - MERCEDES BENZ GMBH, GERMANY.
Road/Rail multipurpose tractors.

Worksnumb	Ex.Works	Gauge	Type	wheels	cyl	size	engine/notes	pages
?	?	4' 8½"	4w	DM				393
1145	1986	4' 8½"	4w	DM				393
150799	1989	4' 8½"	4w	DM				393

VF - VULCAN FOUNDRY, NEWTON-LE-WILLOWS, LANCASHIRE.
1830 -1847   : Charles Tayleur & Co,
1847 -1864   : Vulcan Foundry Co,
1864 -1897   : Vulcan Foundry Co Ltd
1898 -1955   : Vulcan Foundry Ltd
Taken over (with 'RSH' etc) by English Electric Co Ltd in 1955.
For later history see 'EE'.

Worksnumb	Ex.Works	Gauge	Type	wheels	cyl	size	engine/notes	pages
231 to 233	1845	4' 8½"	4-2-0 tdr	6' 0"	OC	15x22	(note Ø below)	80
263 to 268	1847	4' 8½"	4-2-0 tdr	6' 0"	OC	15x22	(note Ø below)	80
316	1848	4' 8½"	0-4-0 tdr	5' 3"	IC	16x24		76, 84
317	1848	4' 8½"	0-4-0 tdr	5' 3"	IC	16x24		76, 84
[? 319]	1848	4' 8½"	0-4-2 tdr	4' 7"	OC	16x18		185
342	7.1853	4' 8½"	0-4-2 tdr	5' 0"	IC	16x24		76
343	8.1853	4' 8½"	0-4-2 tdr	5' 0"	IC	16x24		76
344	9.1853	4' 8½"	0-4-2 tdr	5' 0"	IC	16x24		76
345	9.1853	4' 8½"	0-4-2 tdr	5' 0"	IC	16x24		76
738	1875	2ft	0-6-4 T	2' 6"	OC	8½x14	Fairlie	132
739	1875	2ft	0-6-4 T	2' 6"	OC	8½x14	Fairlie	68, 132, 136
791	8.1876	1'11½"	0-4-4 T	2' 8"	OC	9x14	Fairlie	68
792	1876	4' 8½"	0-4-0 ST	3' 0"	OC	11x17		348
805	5.1877	1'11½"	0-4-0 T	1' 9"	OC	7x12		187
810	1878	1'11½"	0-4-0 T	1' 8"	OC	7x12		263, 412
832	1878	1'11½"	0-4-0 T		OC	6x10		263, 367
5266	1945	4' 8½"	0-4-0 DM	3' 3"			150hp DC 2185	378

Ø - ordered and built for the Chester & Holyhead Rly (PR/7) but apparently not delivered; resold to other customers and/or taken direct into L&NW Rly stock.

Votty - VOTTY & BOWYDD SLATE QUARRY, BLAENAU FFESTINIOG, GWYNEDD.

Worksnumb	Ex.Works	Gauge	Type	wheels	cyl	size	engine/notes	pages
	?	2ft	4w	BE			ex Dtz diesel	413
	c1939	2ft	4w	BE		5hp	ex VF steam	184, 413

W&M - WILKINS & MITCHELL, DARLASTON, STAFFORDSHIRE.

Worksnumb	Ex.Works	Gauge	Type	wheels	cyl	size	engine/notes	pages
	1951	1' 3"	4w+4w	PM			Daimler	146

WB - W.G.BAGNALL, CASTLE ENGINE WORKS, STAFFORD.
1875 -1887 : W.G.Bagnall
1887 -1951 : W.G.Bagnall Ltd
1951 -1961 : Brush Bagnall Traction Ltd
1961 -   : English Electric Co Ltd - work transferred to 'RSH' and last WB loco built Stafford 1962.

Worksnumb	Ex.Works	Gauge	Type	wheels	cyl	size	engine/notes	pages
138	3.1878	3' 0"	0-4-0 IT	1' 6"	IC	5x7½		388
272	12.1879	2' 7"	0-4-0 IT	1' 0"	IC	3½x5¼		223
358	1881	2' 4"	0-4-0 IT	1' 3"	OC	4½x7½		128
434	9.1885	2' 0"	0-4-0 tk		?	5x7½		370
930	10.1887	1'11½"	0-4-0 IT		OC	7x10½		218
1278	8.1890	1'11½"	0-4-0 IT		OC	6x9		317
1426	24. 2.1894	3' 0"	0-4-0 IT	2' 0"	OC	8x12		307
1445	15.10.1895	1'11½"	0-4-0 ST	1' 6"	OC	6x9		317
1568	30. 9.1899	1'11½"	0-4-0 ST	1' 7"	OC	6x9		317, 345
1569	9.12.1899	1'11½"	0-4-0 ST	1' 7"	OC	6x9		342
1571	20. 7.1900	1'11½"	0-4-0 ST	1' 7"	OC	6x9		322, 359
1614	31.10.1900	1'11½"	0-4-0 ST	1'9½"	OC	7x12		406
1618	30.11.1900	2' 0"	0-4-0 ST	1'9½"	OC	7x12		409
1655	17. 9.1901	2' 6"	0-4-0 ST	1'9½"	OC	7x12		158
1668	30. 4.1903	2' 0"	0-4-0 ST	1'6¾"	OC	6x9		191
1724	9.10.1903	2' 0"	0-4-0 ST	1'6¾"	OC	6x9		410
1726	6.10.1903	2' 0"	0-4-0 ST	1'6¾"	OC	6x9		350
1728	28.11.1903	1' 9"	0-4-0 ST	1'6¾"	OC	6x9		294, 416
1731	14. 7.1904	1'11½"	0-4-0 ST	1'6¾"	OC	6x9		133
1740	10.10.1903	2' 0"	0-4-0 ST	1'9½"	OC	6½x10½		410
1760	25. 5.1906	1'10¾"	0-4-0 ST	1'9½"	OC	7x12		236
1761	2. 8.1905	3' 0"	0-4-0 T	2'3½"	OC	9x14		188
1766	11. 1.1907	1'11½"	0-4-0 ST	1' 7"	OC	6x9		322, 359
1820	4. 7.1907	3' 0"	0-4-0 ST	1'9½"	OC	7x12		382
1863	21.11.1907	2' 0"	0-4-0 ST	1' 7"	OC	6½x10		350
1901	19.10.1911	2'10½"	0-4-0 ST	1'9½"	OC	7x12		307
1916	29.10.1910	1'11½"	0-4-0 ST	1'3¼"	OC	5x7½	dwarfed	46, 269
2037	1915	2' 0"	0-4-0 ST	1' 7"	OC	6x9		214

Worksnumb	Ex.Works	Gauge	Type	wheels	cyl	size	engine/notes	pages
2043	17.12.1917	2' 0"	0-4-0 ST	1' 7"	OC	6x9		70, 342
2045	21. 3.1918	2' 0"	0-4-0 ST	1' 7"	OC	6x9		342
2075	27. 9.1918	2' 0"	0-4-0 ST	1' 7"	OC	6x9		214
2079	13.11.1918	2' 0"	0-4-0 ST	1' 7"	OC	6x9		387
2080	20.11.1918	2' 0"	0-4-0 ST	1' 7"	OC	6x9		135, 247, 248
2091	20. 8.1919	1'11½"	0-4-0 ST	1' 7"	OC	6x9		252, 412
2167	24.12.1921	4' 8½"	0-6-0 ST	2'9¼"	OC	13x18		419
2197	9.12.1922	4' 8½"	0-6-0 ST	2'9¼"	OC	13x18		419
2498	23. 3.1934	1'10½"	0-4-4-0DM	1' 4"		24hp	Deutz 2-cylndr	282
2499	29. 3.1934	1'11½"	4w DM	1' 2"		8½hp	Deutz 1-cylndr	412
2741	6.1944	4' 8½"	0-6-0 ST	4' 3"	IC	18x26	Austerity	378
2767	13. 2.1945	4' 8½"	0-6-0 ST	4' 3"	IC	18x26	Austerity	378
2963	5.10.1950	4' 8½"	0-4-0 ST	3'6½"	OC	14½x22		272
3023	27. 3.1953	2' 0"	0-4-2 T	2'3½"	OC	9x14		138
3050	27. 3.1953	2' 0"	0-4-2 T	2'3½"	OC	9x14		138

WCI - WIGAN COAL & IRON CO, KIRKLESS WORKSHOPS, WIGAN.

Worksnumb	Ex.Works	Gauge	Type	wheels	cyl	size	engine/notes	pages
Lindsay	1887	4' 8½"	0-6-0 ST	4' 4"	IC	16x26		279

Wilson - J.H.WILSON & CO LTD, SANDHILLS, LIVERPOOL.

Worksnumb	Ex.Works	Gauge	Type	wheels	cyl	size	engine/notes	pages
?	c1872	2ft	0-4-0 T		OC		MOLE	342

WJW - Wm.J.WILLIAMS, TAI GANOL OAKELEY, BLAENAU FFESTINIOG, GWYNEDD.

Worksnumb	Ex.Works	Gauge	Type	wheels	cyl	size	engine/notes	pages
	?	1'11½"	2-2-0 PMr					168, 344, 415

WkB - WALKERS, PAGEFIELD IRONWORKS, WIGAN.
by 1873 -c1880   : J.Scarisbrick Walker & Bro, Globe Foundry
c1880 -   : Walker Bros. (Wigan) Ltd

Worksnumb	Ex.Works	Gauge	Type	wheels	cyl	size	engine/notes	pages
412	? 1873	4' 8½"	0-4-0 ST		IC	14x	GRAHAM	210
861	1874	4' 8½"	0-4-0 ST		OC	14x	BRINSOP HALL	298
890 ?	1875 ?	4' 8½"	0-6-0 ?ST ?		IC ?		DOCTOR ?	192
1017	c1876	4' 8½"	0-4-0 ST		IC	13x20		198
[WkB ??]	?	2' 6"?	0-4-0? tk	?	?	?	GLADSTONE	223

WkM - D.WICKHAM & CO LTD, WARE. HERTFORDSHIRE.

Worksnumb	Ex.Works	Gauge	Type	wheels	cyl	size	engine/notes	pages
509	1932	4' 8½"	2w-2	PMr				311, 400
1543	1934	4' 8½"	2w-2	PMr				70
3030	1943	600mm	2w-2	PMr			Target trolley	48
4132	1947	4' 8½"	2w-2	PMr				48
6901	1954	4' 8½"	2w-2	PMr				48, 174
7516	1956	4' 8½"	2w-2	PMr				291
[? 7574	1956?]	4' 8½"	2w-2	PMr				48, 311
7692	1957	4' 8½"	2w-2	PMr				291
8196	1958	4' 8½"	2w-2	PMr				48

WMCQ - WREXHAM, MOLD & CONNAH'S QUAY RAILWAY CO.
Rhosddu Workshops, Wrexham.

Worksnumb	Ex.Works	Gauge	Type	wheels	cyl	size	engine/notes	pages
	1901	4' 8½"	2-6-0 T	4' 8"	IC	18x24		110

Worsdell - THOMAS WORSDELL, BERKELEY STREET, BIRMINGHAM.
By 1869 had become R.C.Gibbons & Co.

Worksnumb	Ex.Works	Gauge	Type	wheels	cyl	size	engine/notes	pages
3.	1862	4' 8½"	0-4-0 ST	3' 0"	OC	9x15		53

WR - WINGROVE & ROGERS LTD, LIVERPOOL.

In 1926 purchased the business of British Electric Vehicles Ltd, of Southport - see 'BEV' - and continued production of BEV type locomotives etc. at Liverpool.
From 1961, Works Numbers remained in one series but were prefixed by a letter indicating year of construction (A = 1961, B = 1962, etc). These prefixes are unimportant and, for clarity, ignored.
From 1979 a new numbering system collected different types of loco into different numeric series, all pre-fixed 'L' (L.10xx = WR5, L.20xx = WR8, etc). From 1986, unique six-digit numbers were introduced. Rebuilt locos were not necessarily numbered in accordance with these schemes.

Worksnumb	Ex.Works	Gauge	Type	wheels	cyl	engine/notes	pages
667	20.11.1926	2' 0"	4w	BE		class: BEV No2	248
668	9.12.1926	2' 0"	4w	BE		class: BEV No2	248
744	12. 8.1929	1'10½"	4w	BE		class: W.127	282
773	10. 4.1930	1'10½"	4w	BE		class: W.127	282
898	5. 7.1935	1'10½"	4w	BE		class: W.227	282
899	5. 7.1935	1'10½"	4w	BE		class: W.227	282
918	29. 1.1936	1'11½"	4w	BE		class: W.417	317, 322

Worksnumb	Ex.Works	Gauge	Type	wheels		pages
1080	17. 9.1937	1'10½"	0-4-0	BE	class: W.217	282
1277	25. 8.1938	2' 0"	4w	BE	class: W.417	277
1898	25.11.1941	?	4w	BE	class: W.117	420
2308	10. 2.1942	?	4w	BE	class: W.117	420
2333	11.11.1942	?	4w	BE	class: W.117	420
2334	11.11.1942	?	4w	BE	class: W.117	420
5311	22. 9.1955	1'10½"	0-4-0	BE	class: W.217	282
5537	26. 1.1956	2' 0"	4w	BE	class: W.417	70, 277
6765	17.12.1963	2' 0"	4w	BE	class: W.227	318, 325
6766	17.12.1963	2' 0"	4w	BE	class: W.227	318, 325
7556	16. 3.1972	2' 0"	4w	BE	class: W.227	325
7628	30. 7.1976	2' 6"	4w	BE	class: W.128	397
7661	23. 8.1974	2' 0"	0-4-0	BE	class: WR5	48, 288
7807	30. 7.1976	2' 6"	4w	BE	class: W.128	397
7808	30. 7.1976	2' 6"	4w	BE	class: W.128	397
7809	30. 7.1976	2' 6"	4w	BE	class: W.128	397
L.1009	1979	2' 0"	0-4-0	BE	class: WR.5	219
10114	c9.1984	2' 0"	4w	BE	WR7556 rebuilt	219
?	?	2ft	4w	BE	Q.Tours (No.1)	318
?	?	2ft	4w	BE	Q.Tours (No.2)	318
?	?	2ft	4w	BE	Q.Tours "No.3"	318
?	?	2ft	4w	BE	Q.Tours (No.3)	318, 322

YE - YORKSHIRE ENGINE CO LTD, MEADOWHALL WORKS, SHEFFIELD.

1865	-	: Yorkshire Engine Co
		: Yorkshire Engine Co Ltd
1948	-1965	: subsidiary of United Steel Companies Ltd
1965		: Rolls Royce Ltd; closed, work transferred to Sentinel Works ('S') at Shrewsbury.

Worksnumb	Ex.Works	Gauge	Type	wheels	cyl	size	engine/notes	pages
1011	28.12.1908	4' 8½"	0-4-0 ST	3' 3"	OC	14x20	class: J	373
2527	25.11.1953	4' 8½"	0-6-0 DE	3' 8"		400hp	class: DE4	396
2604	27.10.1955	4' 8½"	0-6-0 DE			200hp		205, 336
2623	1956	4' 8½"	0-4-0 DE					205
2627	4. 2.1957	4' 8½"	0-4-0 DE			200hp		336
2632	14. 3.1957	4' 8½"	0-6-0 DE			200hp		205
2658	7.10.1957	4' 8½"	0-6-0 DE			200hp		205
2659	4.10.1957	4' 8½"	0-6-0 DE			200hp		205
2669	11. 4.1958	4' 8½"	0-6-0 DE			400hp	class: Janus	173
2722	15.11.1958	4' 8½"	0-6-0 DE			400hp	class: Janus	205
2732	2. 9.1959	4' 8½"	0-4-0 DE			200hp		225
2752	3. 7.1959	4' 8½"	0-4-0 DE			400hp	class: Janus	205
2782	7. 4.1960	4' 8½"	0-4-0 DE			200hp		173
2792	20. 2.1961	4' 8½"	0-6-0 DE			440hp		205
2800	13. 3.1962	4' 8½"	0-6-0 DE			440hp	class: Janus	205
2819	30. 8.1960	4' 8½"	0-4-0 DE			220hp		336
2853	5. 5.1961	4' 8½"	0-4-0 DE			220hp		205
2854	5. 5.1961	4' 8½"	0-4-0 DE			220hp		173, 349
2855	11. 5.1961	4' 8½"	0-4-0 DE			220hp		205
2858	9. 6.1961	4' 8½"	0-4-0 DE			220hp		205

2867	20. 3.1962	4' 8½"	0-6-0	DE		440hp	class: Janus	205
2870	1.10.1962	4' 8½"	0-4-0	DE		220hp		205
2884	13.11.1962	4' 8½"	0-6-0	DE		440hp		205
2942	12. 2.1965	4' 8½"	0-6-0	DE		220hp		205

ZZ - LOCOS BY BUILDERS AS YET UNKNOWN.

This list includes only those locomotives for which a name - being a positive identifying feature - is known. Other mystery locomotives, about which very little is known, are mentioned in some Location entries of this book.

Worksnumb	Ex.Works	Gauge	Type		wheels	cyl	size	engine/notes	pages
	pre-1864	4' 8½"	? 0-4-0 tk?			?		ANNA MARIA	109
	pre-1873	4' 8½"	?	?	?	?	?	BERTHA	415
	pre-1895	4' 8½"	0-4-0	ST	?	OC	10x14	CYMRO #	35
	pre-1865	4' 8½"	?	tdr	?	?	?	DART	53
	by 1864	4' 8½"	?	?	?	?	?	DIRECTOR	106
	pre-1865	4' 8½"	?	tdr	?	?	?	FAIRY	53
	c1874	1'10¾"	0-4-0?	VBT	1'8"?	VC?	?	HARRIET	235
	pre-1890	2ft	0-4-0?	ST?	?	OC?	?	JAMES DEW	365, 401
	pre-1905	3ft	0-4-0	WT?	?	OC	?	JEANNIE	382
	pre-1865	4' 8½"	?	?	?	?	?	LEON	53
	pre-1861	4' 8½"	?	?	?	?	?	LLANIDLOES	53
	pre-1859	4' 8½"	?	?	?	?	?	LLEWELYN	53
	c1875	1'10½"	0-4-0	VBT	?	VC	?	PERIS #	235
	pre-1865	4' 8½"	?	?	?	?	?	STAG	53
	pre-1858	4' 8½"	?	?	?	?	?	SQUIRREL	53
	c1876	1'10¾"	0-4-0?	VB?	?	?	?	VICTORIA	235
	pre-1867	4' 8½"	?	?	?	?	?	WELLINGTON	106
	pre-1947	4' 8½"	4w	PM	?		Guy	HARLECH EXPRES	283

: CYMRO - reputed by some to have been built or assembled by C&J but this may not be true if it had a prior history (at, for example, Green's Foundry - as has been suggested).
  PERIS - possibly built by Henry Hughes, but proof is lacking.

INDEX OF LOCOMOTIVE NAMES

A

A.H.WORTH	48	ANGLESEA	106
ACKTON HALL	174	ANGLESEY	80
ACTIVE	196	ANNA MARIA	109
ACTON	65	ANNIE	30
ADA	354	ANT	198
ADDA	187	ANTELOPE	53
ALAN GEORGE	358	ANZAC	205, 378
ALAN MEADEN	93	ARENIG	205, 273
ALBION	54	ARIADNE	198
ALEXANDRA	54	ARKAYAR	199
ALF	108	ARTHUR	367
ALGERNON	342	ASHOVER	70, 170
ALICE	171, 235, 236, 354, 358	ASTON	223
ALISON	273	ATTIC	355
ALISTAIR	70	AUSSIE	378
ALISTER	171	AUSTIN	205
ALYN	116, 123	AUSTIN No.1	173
ALYNVA	189	AVON	38
AMALTHAEA	235	AVONSIDE	336
AMY	47	AYLWIN	153
ANDREW	70		

B

B17C	40, 313	BIDDY	56
BABY	265	BILLY	163
BABY SENIOR	265	BLANCHE	68, 358
BALA	273	BOBS	205
BALADEULYN	305, 367	BOOTLE	40
BANTAM	151, 182	BORTH	54
BARBY	56	BRAICH	166, 167
BARTON No.2	41	BRECKNOCK	54
BASIC	205	BRIAN	44
BATTERS	370	BRITANNIA	197
BEAR	269	BRITISH No.1	36, 313
BEATTY	313	BRITOMART	70, 367
BEDDGELERT	132	BROMFIELD	202
BEE	198	BRONLLWYD	358, 359
BELMONT	128	BRYMBO	205
BERNSTEIN	236	BUCKLEY	348
BERTHA	415	BULKELEY	106, 348
BERWYN	205, 266, 273	BURTONWOOD BREWER	173
BERYL	273	BUSTER	70
BETTY	206, 406		

C

C.P.HUNTINGTON	211
CACKLER	236
CADBURY	174
CADER IDRIS	54
CADFAN	333
CAERLEON	54
CAERPHILLY	54
CAMBRIA	54, 290
CARDIGAN	54, 104, 114
CARNARVON CASTLE	302
CASTELL CONWY	69
CASTELL DEUDRAETH	54, 114
CASTELL HARLECH	70
CATHERALL	374
CATHERINE FANNY	304
CEGIN	359
CERNYW	166, 171
CHALONER	365, 367
CHAMPION	279
CHANCELLOR	109
CHARLES	205, 342, 357, 358
CHARLES BAKER	112
CHARLIE	210, 235
CHARLOTTE	77
CHAROLETTE	77
CHILMARK	170
CILGWYN	138
CLARA	163, 408
CLIFFORD	342
CLOISTER	235
CLWYD	91
CNICHT	138
COED	354
COETMOR	358
COGAN HALL	174
COLLIER	266, 347
COLWALL	266
CONWAY	227
CONWAY CASTLE	68
COOLMORE	188
CORA	70
CORONATION	408
CORRIS No.6	93
COUNT LOUIS	146
COUNTESS VANE	54
COURTAULDS LTD	258, 259
COVERTCOAT	236
CRIMEA	354
CROWHURST	291, 292
CYCLOPS	42
CYFRONYDD	54
CYMRO	35, 151

D

D	103
D.ARTIS	224
DAFYDD	259
DAISY	37, 421
DANBY LODGE	112
DARFIELD No.1	173
DART	53
DAVID	313
DAVID PAYNE	83
DE WINTON	54
DEE	110, 334, 388
DENNIS	129
DEPTFORD	44
DEVONSHIRE	374
DIAMOND	80, 221, 336
DIANA	57, 70, 169, 342, 367, 396
DIKE	56
DILLICHIP	225
DINGO	146
DINORWIC	235
DIRECTOR	106
DISRAELI	116
DITCHEAT MANOR	174
DIXON	35, 299
DOCTOR	192
DOLBADARN	166, 236
DOLGARROG	41, 167, 245
DOLGARROG No.1	245
DOLGOCH	108
DONALD	354
DOROTHEA	169, 252
DOROTHY	151, 317, 345
DOUGLAS	108, 378
DOVE	53
DUDDON	375
DUKE	110
DUTCHMAN	354
DWARF	53
DYNEVOR	39

E

EARL OF MERIONETH	68, 69	ELLEN	51
EASTWOOD	42, 194	ELLESMERE	300
EDITH	317	ELWY	91
EDWARD	342	EMILY	110, 266, 304
EDWARD SHOLTO	358, 359	EMRYS	205
EDWARD THOMAS	108	ENID	153, 235
EIGIAU	169, 245, 247, 359	ENTERPRISE	53, 114
EILEEN	342	ERNEST	388
ELEANOR	297	ERNEST W.TWINING	146
ELEPHANT	53	ERYRI	153
ELIDIR	166, 236	ESMOND	205
ELIN	358	EVA	187
ELISEG	174	EVE	295
ELISIG	174	EXPRESS	221

F

F.W.COOPER	408	FOJO	138
FAIRY	53	FORWARD	336
FELIN HEN	359	FOX	355
FERNHILL	128	FOXCOTE MANOR	173
FIRE QUEEN	235, 357	FRANCES VALERIE	279, 314
FIREFLY	222	FREDA	317, 403
FLORINDA	187		

G

GALLTFAENAN	91	GLANMOR	42
GARRET	166, 167	GLANSEVERN	53
GARTH	300	GLASLYN	138
GELERT	138	GLYDER	359
GELLI	367	GLYN	129, 252
GEORGE	235	GLYNLLIFON	367
GEORGE B	236	GLYNLLYFNI	114
GEORGE HENRY	358, 411	GLYNNE	192, 252
GEORGE SHOLTO	28, 358, 359	GORDON	40, 244, 326
GEORGE THE FIFTH	163	GOWRIE	132
GEORGINA	358	GRAHAM	210
GERTRUDE	218, 220, 359	GREEN DRAGON	53
GINETTE MARIE	166	GWEN	287
GLADSTONE	54, 223, 230	GWRIL	146
GLADYS	410	GWYNEDD	205, 358
GLANDOVEY	54	GWYNETH	273, 314

H

H.M.FACTORY	375	HARLECH CASTLE	70
HAFOD	279, 313	HAROLD	354
HALIFAX	421	HARRIET	235
HAMPSTEAD	294, 416	HAXEY	374
HANNAH	188, 247	HEATHER	355
HARLECH	54	HELEN KATHRYN	167, 170

HENRY DAWSON	38		HOMEPRIDE	44
HERCULES	54, 110		HOPE	205
HEREFORD	54		HORNET	194, 198
HILDA	342, 358		HOWARD	232
HOLLINS	56		HUGH NAPIER	357, 358
HOLY WAR	170, 236		HUGHIE	354
HOLYHEAD	290			

I

IARLL MEIRIONYDD	69		INVERLOCHY	367
INA	358		IRISH MAIL	236
INCE	244		IRISH PETE	108
INDIAN RUNNER	171		ISABEL	406
INFLEXIBLE	120			

J

J.C.GRAY	350		JENNY LIND	235
J.STRACHAN No.3	158		JERRY M	236
J.STRACHAN No.5	158		JESSIE	39
J.STRACHAN No.6	158		JOAN	163
J.STRACHAN No.7	158		JOHN	163, 205
J.STRACHAN No.9	158		JONATHAN	138, 170
J.STRACHAN No.10	158		JOSIAH HARDMAN LTD	373
JACOBITE	247		JUBILEE	51, 58
JAMES DEW	365, 401		JUBILEE 1897	218, 359, 411
JAMES HALL	194, 266		JUMBO	208
JAMES SPOONER	68		JUNO	396
JANE	70		JUPITER	395
JEANNIE	382			

K

KAREN	138		KIDBROOKE	70, 342
KATHERINE	138		KIMBERLEY	355
KATHLEEN	187, 201, 345, 358		KING OF THE SCARLETS	235
KATIE	146, 358, 411		KINNERLEY	138
KELSO	201, 263, 367		KINROSS	273, 279
KELVINSIDE	45		KNUTSFORD	266
KENYON	101, 109			

L

L.A.D.A.S.	153		LILIAN	82, 354, 358
LADY JOAN	236		LILIAN WALTER	147
LADY MADCAP	236		LILLA	218, 359
LADY PENRHYN	358		LILLESHALL	54, 198
LADY STEVENSON No.7	196		LILY	243
LADYSMITH No.18	82		LINCOLN	259
LEIGH	273		LINDA	68, 358
LEIGHTON	53		LINDSAY	279
LEON	53		LITTLE GIANT	68
LESTER	409		LITTLE ORME	300

LITTLE USK	54	LLOYD GEORGE	230
LITTLE WONDER	68	LLWYD	354
LIVINGSTON THOMPSON	68	LMS	279
LIZZIE	218	LONDON	290
LLANDEGAI	359	LORD PENRHYN	358
LLANELLI	166	LORD RICHARD	101, 109
LLANERCHYDOL	53, 98, 114	LORD WEASTE	36
LLANFAIR	345, 354	LOUGHOR	293
LLANIDLOES	53	LOUISA	235, 305, 354
LLEWELYN	53	LOUISE	163
LLIEDI	334	LUCERO	244

M

MABEL	259	MERSEYSIDER	108
MACK	395	MESOZOIC	169
MADGE	218	MICHAEL	163, 236, 406
MAESTEG	293	MIDDLESBORO	112
MAID MARIAN	166, 170, 236	MIDLANDER	108
MALCOLM	408	MILFORD	53, 104
MARCHLYN	359	MILLENNIUM	36
MARGARET	297, 317, 358	MILTWIN	364
MARIAN	354	MINERA	331
MARIE	225	MINERALS	191
MARK	173, 406	MINERVA	54, 206, 396
MARS	395	MINNIE	307
MARY ANN	68	MOEL HEBOG	70
MARY CAROLINE	342	MOEL SIABOD	153
MARY OAKELEY	342	MOEL TRYFAN	68, 132, 136
MAWDDWY	116	MOELEILIA	220
MAX	259, 316	MOELWYN	68
MAYFLOWER	43	MOLE	342
MAZEPPA	54	MOMBASA	419
MEDLOCK	336	MONA,	300, 354
MEIRION	104, 412	MONARCH	39
MEIRIONNYDD	170	MONSTER	70
MELSONBY No.3	41, 408	MONTGOMERY	53
MEMNON	80	MOR LEIDR	167, 399
MERDDIN EMRYS	68	MORFA	226
MERION	54	MOSTYN	336
MERLEN GYMRAEG	69	MOUNTAINEER	54, 68, 106
MERMAID	370	MURIEL	268, 385
MERSEY	35, 52		

N

NANCY	387	NETHERTON	30, 40, 326
NANT	354	NEVILLE	205
NANTCLWYD	54, 98	NEWRY	355
NANTMOR	138	NICLAUSSE	374
NEATH	106, 348	NINIAN	153
NELLIE	225, 338	NIPPER	119, 374
NEPTUNE	194, 395	NORTHUMBRIA	295
NESTA	358		

O

ODNEY MANOR	174	OLD SPARKY	211
OGDEN	188	OLWEN	331
OGWEN	359		

P

P L A 37	42	PLASFYNNON	54
PADARN	153, 305	PLYNLIMON	54
PALMERSTON	54, 68, 135	PORT DINORWIC	236
PAMELA	359	POWERFUL	307
PANDORA	235	PREMIER	110
PAT	37, 273, 326, 408	PRETORIA	108
PEDEMOURA	138	PRINCE	68
PEGASUS	54	PRINCE ALBERT	290
PENDYFFRYN	169, 367	PRINCE CHARLES	146
PENMAEN	354	PRINCE EDWARD OF WALES	146, 163
PENRHYN	300	PRINCE OF WALES	53, 75
PENWYLLT	151	PRINCESS	68
PERIS	235	PRINCESS ELIZABETH	211
PERT	74	PRINCESS MARGARET ROSE	211
PERTHEL KOLN 5	46	PROGRESS	106, 133, 298
PETER SAM	108	PROMETHEUS	54
PIERCY	148	PUFFIN	354
PILKINGTON	173	PUFFIN II	355
PIONEER	53, 114, 117	PYRAMUS	295
PIRAEUS	194, 207, 279	PYTHON	205
PLANET	396		

Q

QUEEN	53, 110, 290	QUEENIE	28, 218
QUEEN ELIZABETH	211		

R

RACHEL	146	RICHARD BELL	350
RAILWAY QUEEN	163	RICHARD BORRETT	173
RALPH	153	RICHBORO	174, 273
RALPH SADLER	153	ROBERT	313
RED DAMSEL	235	ROBERTSON	205
REDSTONE	169, 368, 406	ROLAND	259
REMUS	44, 396	ROMULUS	396
RHEIDOL	54	ROSA	342
RHIEWPORT	54	ROUGH PUP	235, 411
RHIW	382	RUSSELL	132, 136, 138, 169, 206, 411
RHYDYCHEN	167	RUTHIN	53, 98
RHYMNEY	365, 367	RYE	295

S

SAMSON	223	SKINNER	322, 359
SANDRA	70	SLUDGE	70
SANDYCROFT	391	SNOWDON	54, 153, 194, 205, 342
SANFORD	322, 359	SNOWDON RANGER	132
SARAH	194, 347	SPENCER	205
SATURN	395	SPIDER	194, 198, 279
SCORCHER	119	SPRITE	96
SCOTIA	256	SQUIRREL	53
SEAHAM	114	ST.SEIRIOL	155
SEALAND	210, 395	ST.SILIO	155
SGT.MURPHY	196, 359	ST.TRILLO	155
SHAKESPEARE	36, 194, 279	ST.TUDNO	155
SHAMROCK	43	STAFFORD	256
SHEPPERTON	377	STAFFORD VERNON	292
SHON	146	STAG	53
SHOTTON	395	STAINES	306
SIAN	146	STALYBRIDGE	192, 298
SIEMENS	210, 395	STANHOPE	359
SILURIAN	268	STANLEY	47
SINGAPORE	354	STARSTON	305, 367
SIR HARMOOD	153	STEPHEN	354
SIR HAYDN	108	STOCKS	56
SIR HENRY	205	STONEYWAY	95
SIR JOHN FRENCH	295	SWANSEA	39, 207, 326, 331
SIR JOSEPH	38, 313	SYBIL	169, 196, 236, 367, 415
SIR MAX	259	SYBIL MARY	70, 359
SIR STEPHEN	101, 110	SYDNEY	147
SIR THEODORE	41, 129, 273, 279	SYLVIA	146
SIR WATKIN	54	SYMONDS	210

T

TAFF	354	THIKA	419
TAFFY	185, 412	THISBE	295
TALERDDIG	54	THOMAS BACH	166
TALIESIN	68	THOR	396
TALYLLYN	108	THORNHILL	154, 312
TARTAR	225, 373, 378	TIGER	354
TEES VALLEY	112, 313	TINY	54
TERRIER	374	TITAN	396
THE COALITION	317	TOBY	108
THE COLONEL	70	TOM ROLT	108
THE ECLIPSE	317	TORCROSS	392
THE FIRST	236	TOWYN	54
THE FLORISTON FLYER	103	TRACY JO	146
THE FLY	198, 364	TREFLACH	54
THE GROGAN	70	TREGARTH	359
THE HARLECH EXPRESS	283	TRIXIE	170, 172
THE LADY DIANA	70	TRYFAN	333
THE PRINCE	69	TUBAL CAIN	54
THE PRINCESS	69	TUNIS	128
THE SECOND	236	TUXFORD	82
THE WELSHMAN	273, 279, 312, 314	TWLL COED	167

TYKE	70	TYNESIDER	43, 45
TYNE	112		

U

UNA	169, 367, 415	USK	54
UPNOR CASTLE	68	UXBRIDGE	244-245

V

VELINHELI	235	VIOLET	220, 356, 358, 401
VENUS	395	VIXEN	354, 355
VESTA	357, 396	VOLUNTEER	53, 114
VICTORIA	235, 367	VRON	263, 401, 415
VICTORIA & ALBERT	76	VULCAN	38, 54, 273, 395
VICTORY	419		

W

W.G.ELLERY	42	WHITTINGTON	54
W.K.WILLIAMS	166	WHIXALL	53
WALTER SCOTT	41	WIGSTON	374
WARWICK	35, 148, 256, 299	WILD ASTER	167, 236
WATKIN	354, 357	WILLIAM	205, 342
WATKINSON	210	WINDMILL	395
WATKINSON No.2	210	WINDSOR	374
WEEDON	151, 421	WINIFRED	35, 358
WELD BLUNDELL	185, 421	WINNINGTON	174
WELLINGTON	106, 235, 236, 305	WINSTON	205
WELLS	354	WINSTON CHURCHILL	336
WELSH PONY	68, 317, 345	WREKIN	76, 205
WENDY	252, 412	WREXHAM	58
WEST YORKSHIRE	51	WYDDFA	153
WHEATLEY	101, 109	WYE	54
WHIPPIT QUICK	146, 345	WYNNSTAY	45, 53, 421

Y

YEOVIL	283, 306	YORKE	279
YETI	153	YR ENFYS	167, 399
YORK	279		

LOCATIONS, OWNERS AND OPERATORS

This index refers main headings, and lists of operators/owners (except for latter-day main-line railway companies common throughout Section 2), plus the more important references in the descriptive texts. Items in locomotive footnotes are not indexed.

The index is comprehensive but has been compressed. If the precise title sought is not found, refer to the most similar entry. For example, for "Abenbury Firebrick Co Ltd" try "Abenbury Brickworks".

A

A.R.C.(Powell Duffryn) Ltd	307
A.R.C.Western Ltd	212, 353
Abbey, Dolgarrog & Trefriw Light Rly	241
Abdela & Mitchell Ltd	380
Abenbury Brickworks	182
Aber Works, Flint	257
Aberangell	284
Aberaven Granite Co	409
Aberconwy Borough Council	155
Abercwmeiddaw Slate Quarry	182
Aberdovey Slate Co	107
Aberllefeni Slate Quarries	183
Aberystwith & Welsh Coast Rly	104, 117
Acrefair (Ruabon New) Ironworks	184
Acton Grange Colliery	272
Admiralty	289
Afonwen Branch Rly	113
Air Ministry	199, 305, 392
Air Products Ltd	184
Aled Reservoirs	186
Alexandra Slate Quarry	186
Alletson, G.H.	214
Allied Cement Manufacturers	299
Allied Portland Cement	264
Allmark, J.E.	416
Allsopp's Plant Hire	195
Aluminium Corporation	243, 245
Alwen Reservoir	187
Alyn & Deeside District Council	379
Alyn Steel Tinplate Co	189
Alyn Works, Mold	189
Amalgamated Roadstone Corpn	190, 213
Amalgamated Slate Assn	186, 200, 217, 333
Amlwch Branch Rly	106
Amlwch Light Railway	107, 190
Amlwch (Octel) Chemical Wks	190
Andrews [Solomon] & Son	149, 150
Anglesea Central Railway	106
Anglesea (Penmon) Marble Quarries	356
Anglesey Aluminium	288
Anglesey Mining plc	352
Anwell, Isaac	226
Arclive Construction Co Ltd	399
Ardda Iron-Sulphide Mine	240
Area Central Workshops (NCB), Llay	315
Arenig Granite	190
Army Department	378
Arrol, Sir Wm.	203
Arthog Tramway	150
Ash Colliery	209
Asiatic Petroleum Co	376
Associated Ethyl Co	190
Associated Octel Co	190
Associated Portland Cement	264, 299
Aston Hall Coal & Brick Co	191, 298
Aston Hall Colliery	191
Aston Hall Railway	148, 191

B

Bache, Trevor	29
Bagillt Coal Co Ltd	195
Baird [William] & Co	257
Baker [Chas.] & Sons	112
Bala & Dolgelley Railway	94
Bala & Festiniog Railway	143
Bala & Festiniog Rly Co	119, 143
Bala Lake Railway	170
Baldry, Yerburgh & Hutchinson	293
Baldwins Ltd	203
Bangor & Carnarvon Railway	87
Bangor & Pantdreiniog Slate Co	350
Bangor & Portmadoc Slate & Slab Co	73
Bangor Slate Quarry Ltd	200
Barde, Henry	212
Barmouth Sea Defences	193
Barmouth Urban District Council	193
Barnes & Co	193
Barrow Haematite Steel Co Ltd	335
Barry, J.D.	301

Bateson, Bateson, McConnell	186
Bath & Portland Stone Firms	353, 405
Batters, G.	369
Beckett, L.S.	416
Beddgelert Railway Company	115
Benallt Mining Co	380
Bersham Colliery	193
Bethesda Branch Rly	144
Bettis, George	219
Bettisfield Colliery	195
Bettisfield Peat Moss Works	417
Betts, Edward Ladd	79, 85
Betts, William	75, 203
Betws-y-Coed Railway Museum	196
Biggs, Jacob	222
Birkenhead Corporation	187
Birmingham & Liverpool Canal	64
Black Diamond Colliery	221
Black Park Colliery	197
Blaenau Ffestiniog	275 (et al)
Blaenau Ffestiniog station	346
Blaikie, Mr	217
Blakemore, G.	30
Blakewell, Mr	207
Board of Trade	285, 289, 310
Bodfari Casting-Sand Pits	199
Bontddu	219
Borras Airfield	199
Boswell, M.A.	366
Bott & Stennett	243
Bow Slate & Enamel Co	183
Bowers, Edward	260
Bowley's Quarries	285
Bowydd Slate Quarries	412
Boys, J.	131
Braddock & Matthews	28
Bradwell, Jacob	285
Braich & Coed Madoc Slate	200, 219
Braich Goch Slate & Slab	201
Braich (New Braich) Slate Quarry	200
Braich (Old Braich) Slate Quarry	201
Braichrhydd Slate Quarry	200
Brand [Charles] & Son Ltd	325
Brandie (Brandy) Coke Ovens	389
Brandie Colliery	389
Brassey & Field	95
Brassey, Field & Meakin	387
Brassey, Mackenzie & Stephenson	84
Brassey, Thomas	75, 77, 95, 307, 353
Brewer & Alleyn	301
Brewer, Gordon & Liddell	301
Britannia Bridge	83
Britannia Foundry	28, 29
British Coal Corporation	193, 369
British Electric Traction Co	130
British Electricity Authority	224, 243, 377
British Glanzstoff Manufacturing	257
British Grey Granite Co	409
British Iron Co	184
British Manganese Co	380
British Quarrying Co	215
British Railways	289
British Railway Engineers Dept	103
British Slate Co	242, 243, 262
British Steel Corpn	204, 335, 394, 395, 403
British Steel Smelters	303
Brodie & Hunt	240
Bromfield Colliery	202
Bronyfoel Co	365
Brookes Ltd	226
Broughton & Plas Power	141, 193, 265, 346, 369, 414
Broughton Aircraft Factory	203
Broughton Coal Co	265, 346
Broughton Engineering Works	51
Broughton (Hall) Colliery	346
Broughton Solvay Coke Works	369
Brown [Wm] & Sons	257
Brundrit & Co	353
Brundrit & Whiteway	319
Brundrit, Dennis	353
Brunner Mond & Co Ltd	319
Brymbo Branch Rly	99, 140
Brymbo Colliery & Ironworks	203
Brymbo Mineral & Railway Co	77, 203
Brymbo Steelworks Ltd	204
Brym Celyn Lead Mine	385
Brynkinallt Colliery	207
Brynmally Colliery Co	208, 254
Brynmawr Slate Quarry	301
Buckley Collieries Railway	209
Buckley Colliery Co	209
Buckley Railway	100
Buckley, Sir Edmund	285
Bugail Slate Co Ltd	229
Bugbird, Thomas	80, 81, 240
Bulgin & Partners	303
Bulkeley Park Quarries	356
Burr	254
Burton & Kyrke	328
Burton Point Embankment	388
Butler [W.F.] & Co	414
Butlins, Pwllheli	211
Butterley Brick Ltd	394, 403
Buxton Lime Firms Co	230, 319
Bwlch y Groes Slate Co	301
Bwlch y Slater Slate Co	324

C

Caedryn Slate Quarry	243
Caello Brickworks	204
Caerglaw Granite Quarry	212
Caerhun Slate Co	242
Caermeinciau Quarry	301
Caernant (Rivals) Granite Quarry	212
Caernarfon Branch Rly	87
Caernarfon Town Rly	121
Cambrian Coast Line	104, 117
Cambrian Granite Co	212
Cambrian Railways	53 (et al)
Cambrian Slate Companies	268, 301, 303, 382
Campbell, Col.A.H.	70
Campbell, J.T.	301
Canadian Forestry Corps	310, 385
Capel Curig Slate Co Ltd	383
Carder's Stone-Lino Ltd	226
Carlton Main Colliery Co	278
Carnarvon & Bangor Slate Co	262, 400
Carnarvon & Llanberis Railway	120
Carnarvon Brickworks Ltd	394
Carnarvon Corporation	29
Carnarvon Granite Co	334
Carnarvon Mining Co Ltd	219
Carnarvonshire County Council	366
Carnarvonshire Crown Slate Qys	186, 217, 333
Carnarvonshire Electric Traction Synd	155
Carnarvonshire Granite Co	409
Carnarvonshire Granite Quarries Ltd	334
Carnarvonshire Railway Co	66, 113
Carreg-y-Llam Quarries	213
Carves [Simon] Ltd	313
Castle Brick Cos	214, 298, 364, 394, 403
Castle Brickworks	214
Castle Cement (Padeswood) Ltd	349
Castner Kellner	385
Catherall & Co Ltd	403
Cawood Wharton Group	231
Cefn Tramway	64
Cefn-y-Bedd	256 (et al)
Cefndu Slate Co, Cilgwyn &	217
Cefndu Slate Quarry Co	302
Ceiriog Granite	127, 215
Cementation Co Ltd	402
Central Electricity Authority	224, 243, 377
Central Electricity Gen. Board	224, 243, 399
Central Wagon Co Ltd	377
Chambers, Walter & Herbert	154
Charlwood, G.W.	254
Chester & Holyhead Rly	79, 85, 86, 87
Chester, C.H.	82
Chester, Thomas W.	88
Chirk Castle Estate	84
Chirk Forestry Plant Depot	216
Chwarel Fawr Slate	303
Chwarel y Parson	303
Cilcen Limespar Co	287
Cilgwyn & Cefndu Slate Co	303
Cilgwyn Slate Quarries	217
City of Chester Electric Power Co	377
Clarke, E.S.	311
Clayton, Thomas	208
Cleveland Bridge & Engineering	83
Clift, Samuel	383
Climie [? Daniel], Mr	100
Cloddfa Turner Slate Quarry	251
Cloddfa'r Glai Slate Quarry	219
Cloddfa'rlon Slate Quarry	365
Clogau St.Davids Gold Mine	219
Cobden & Bright	287
Coed Hendre	287
Coed Talon Collieries	220, 221
Coed-y-Chwarel Quarry	285
Coedmadoc Slate Quarry	219
Coedty (etc) Leats	248, 250
Coedty Reservoir	248
Cohen [George] & Sons	67, 93, 121, 137, 313
Colman, L.M. & D.M.	276
Colwyn Bay & Rhos-on-Sea Sea Wall	222
Colwyn Bay District Council	222
Colwyn Bay Station "Platform Three"	222
Coneybeare, Henry	104, 117
Connah's Quay Alkali	223
Connah's Quay Marsh Drainage	223
Connah's Quay Power Station	224
Connah's Quay Wagon Works	224
Connell [James N.] Ltd	159
Conway & Colwyn Bay Joint Water Bd	240
Conway & Llanrwst Railway	101
Conway Corporation	29
Conway Stone Quarries	226
Conway Valley Light Railway	241
Conwy & Llanrwst Railway Society	310
Conwy Gasworks & Scrapyard	225
Conwy Penmaenbach Quarries	226
Conwy Valley Line	101
Conwy Valley Railway Museum	196
Cook & Ddol Slate Quarries	303

Cooke's Explosives Ltd	228
Cookney, James Thomas	335
Cooper & Croft	303
Cooper & Tullis	148
Corbett, John	402
Corris Craft Centre	201, 346
Corris Railway	92
Cors-y-Bryniau Slate Quarry	186
Corwen & Bala Railway	94
Courtaulds Ltd	257, 258, 271
Cousens, Mr	27, 81
Cowlyd Pipeline Construction	250
Cowlyd Reservoir & Railway	245, 246
Crafnant & Devon Mining Syndicate	418
Craig-Lelo Quarry	227
Craig [W.Y.] & Sons	207
Craig-y-Ddywart Limestone Quarry	390
Criccieth Urban District Council	30
Crichton & Co	390
Crockford's Tramway	370
Croesor & Port Madoc Railway	105
Croesor Fawr Slate Quarry Co	227
Croesor New Slate Co	228
Croesor Slate Mine	227
Croesor Tramway	105
Croesor United Slate Co	228
Croft Granite, Brick & Concrete	212
Crompton, Rev.B.	202
Croxden Horticultural Products	417
Crump & Co, C.C.	224, 338
CSD 444 Government Store	294
CSD 473 Government Store	375
Cudworth & Johnson	34
Cudworth, Arthur	34
Curling, Charles	200
Cwm Eigia Quarry	242
Cwm-Machno Slate Quarries	352
Cwt-y-Bugail Slate Quarries	229, 324
Cymdeithas Rheilffordd Llyn Llanberis	166

D

Dalescroft Nurseries	31
Dalrymple & Finlay	120
Darbishire & Co	353, 366
Darbishire, C.S.	368
Darbishire, W.A.	243
Darby	203, 346
Darwen & Mostyn Iron Co	309, 335
Davies Brothers	100, 151, 182
Davies, David	52
Davies, E.J.	263
Davies, J.P.	208
Davies, R.S.	46, 202
Davies, T.Llewelyn	29
Dean, John W.	148, 369
Dee & Clwyd River Board	388
Dee Conservancy Board	388
Dee Side Slate & Slab Quarry	331
Deer Park Quarries	356
Deeside Colliery Co	260
Deeside Mill	258
Deeside Titanium Ltd	393
DeHaviland Aircraft Co	203
Demolition & Construction Co Ltd	193
Denbigh Graig Quarry	230
Denbigh Lime & Stone Co	230
Denbigh Quarries Ltd	230
Denbigh, Ruthin & Corwen Rly	98
Dennis, Henry	93
Dennis Ruabon Ltd	264
Dentith's Sidings Wagon Works	224
Department of the Environment	324
D'Eresby Mountain Lead Mining Co	351
Dick, Kerr & Co Ltd	130
Dickin, John	197
Dickson & Russell	106
Dickson, John	106, 348
Dinas Llanwnda River Authority Depot	231
Dinmor Park Quarries	231
Dinmor Quarries Ltd	231, 257
Dinorben (Tan Dinas) Quarries	233
Dinorwic Power Station	233
Dinorwic Slate Quarries	234
Diphwys Casson Quarries	412
Dobbins (Chester) Ltd	83
Dolgarrog Aluminium Works	240
Dolgarrog Dam Disaster	249
Dolgarrog Light Railway	241
Dolgarrog Power Station	243
Dolgarrog Village Development	249
Dolwyddelen station	346
Donenlas Slate Co Ltd	301
Dorothea Slate Quarry	251
Dove, Ken	159
Drake & Gorham Electric Power & Traction	130
Dundas Tramroad	191
Dutton Massey & Co	208, 254
Dyserth Branch Rly	122
Dyserth Limeworks & Quarry	253

E

Eachus, John T.	118, 270	Ellesmere & Glyn Valley Railway	127
Eagle Foundry, Wrexham	34	Ellesmere Canal Company	64
Eagle Mine	418	Ellis & Co, Joseph	416
Eagre Construction Co	30	Elm Colliery	209
Eddy [Walter] & Co	207	Enderby (Welsh) Granite Co	409
Edwards, contractors	311	English, Henry	365
Edwards, J.C.	96, 364, 408	Entam Leisure Ltd	159
Edwards, J.P.	80, 119	Evan Evans & Partners	270
Edwards, Johnson	256	Evans, Captain Robert	217
Edwards Private Siding	96	Evans, G.C.	402
Eifl, yr, Granite Quarry	405	Evans, John	79, 217, 262, 303, 400
Eigiau Reservoir	243	Eve [J.L.] Construction Co	250
Eigiau to Cowlyd Tunnel	248	Eyton & Co	309, 335
Electrical Metallurgical Co	378	Eyton Brothers	260

F

Fairbourne Railway	146	Flint Aber Works	257
Fenn's Moss Peat Railway	416	Flint Castle Works	258
Festiniog & Blaenau Railway	119	Flint Coal & Cannel Co	260
Festiniog Granite	275	Flint Colliery	260
Festiniog Railway	67	Flint Marsh Colliery	260
Festiniog Slate Co	89, 382	Flint Paper Mill	261
Ffestiniog	229	Flintshire County Council	386
Ffestiniog Extension Railway	89	Flookersbrook Foundry	27
Ffestiniog Mountain Tourist Centre	341	Fogg, Nathaniel B.	126
Ffestiniog Slate Qy Co	228, 324, 341, 366, 382	Forestry Commission	216, 286
Ffridd Glyn Quarries	301	Forshaw, W.H.	262
Ffrith Colliery	254	Fortes Ltd	159
Ffrith Fireclay	254	Forwood, T.B.	348
Ffrith Lime	255	Foryd River Diversion	261
Ffrith Roadstone	255	Fothergill Bros	30
Ffrwd Collieries & Iromworks	256	Foulkes, Robert	230
Fiddler, E.	299	France, R.S.	116, 123
Fidler, John	311	Francis, Absalom	281
Fidler, Wm.	347	Freeman, M.F.	277, 330
Firth [Thomas] & John Brown	203	French Kier Group	325
Fishponds Branch Rly	141	Fron & Old Braich Slate	262
Flagstaff Limestone Quarry	257	Fron Branch Rly	84
Flint	223	Fron Slate Quarry	262
Flint & Deeside Railway	173	Fryer, James B.	140

G

Gamble, W.	28	Garth Ganister & Clay Mine	408
Ganllwyd	277	Garth Shale Quarry, Mochdre	264
Ganz & Co	134	Garth (Trevor) Silica Brickworks	408
Gardden Hall (Moreton) Pits	264	Gartheiniog Slate	285
Gardden Lodge (New) Colliery	263	Gates & Thomas	82
Garden Lodge Old) Colliery	264	Gatewen Colliery & Opencast CDP	265
Gardner	226	General & Engineering Industries Ltd	336
Garnons, Richard	365	Geochemical Remining	277

Gilbert, Thomas	418
Giles & Fazakerley	307
Giles, George	80
GKN Steel Co Ltd	203
Glanrafon Slate Quarry	267
Glascoed Adit	254
Glascoed Colliery	254
Gloddfa Ganol	345
Gloddfa Ganol Tourist Centre	341
Glyn Canol Mill	304
Glyn Ceiriog Granite	215
Glyn Quarries Ltd	268
Glyn Quarry Enterprises	268
Glyn Quarry Museum	268
Glyn Slate Co Ltd	268
Glyn Valley Tramway	127
Glynceiriog Private Railway	269
Glynceiriog Quarries	268
Glynne (Sir John) & Mr George Berks	298
Glynrhonwy Quarries (etc)	304, 305
Gooch, Sir Daniel	389
Goodman's Quarry	303
Gorsedda Junction & Portmadoc Rly	73
Gorst & Sons	30
Grace & Robson Ltd	409
Graig (Denbigh) Quarry	230
Graiglwyd Quarries	353
Grange Cavern Military Museum	270
Grange Quarries & Tramway	270
Granite, Lime & Clinker Ltd	212
Great Ash Colliery	209
Great Minera Mining Co	328
Great Oak Colliery	209
Great Orme Railway	155
Greaves & Shelton	304, 322, 412
Greaves & Sons, J.W.	316, 322
Greaves Welsh Slate Co Ltd	316
Green, James	119
Green Lane Pits	197
Green Pit Colliery	421
Greenfield	270
Greenfield (Courtaulds) Factory	271
Gregory, Mr	229
Gregson	79
Gresford (Acton Grange) Colliery	272
Griffith, Elias	127
Griffith, Owen	200
Griffiths, Rch.	243
Groby Granite Quarry	275
Groesddwyafon Slate Quarries	276
Groeslon (Tudor) Slate Works	276
Guest Keen & Nettlefolds	204
Gunn, Mrs & Mr Bob	219
Gwaith Brics (Trefor) Ltd	405
Gwaith-y-Coed Colliery	260
Gwalchmai (Caerglaw) Quarry	212
Gwyddelwern	227
Gwydyr Parc Consols	351
Gwynedd Quarries Ltd	230
Gwynedd River Board	231
Gwynfynydd & Beddcoedwr Gold	277

H

Hafod Opencast CDP	280
Hafodlas & Coedmadog Welsh Slate	219
Hafodty Quarry	412
Hafod(ybwch) Colliery	278
Halkyn & Hendre Lime Co	287
Halkyn District Drainage Tunnels	281
Halkyn District United Mines	281
Hall, Frederick	381
Hancock & Co	347
Hancocks' Lane End Brickworks	298
Harding & John Cropper	79
Harlech Beach Tramways	139
Harlech Military Railway	283
Hartley & Partners Ltd	308
Harvey	81
Harvey, Bennett, & Co	400
Haswell, W.D.	221
Hawarden Bridge Steelworks	395
Hawarden Collieries Co	298
Hawarden Embankment Trustees	388
Hawarden Iron Works	50, 391
Hawarden Loop Line	148
Hawker Siddeley Aviation	203
Hawkswick Investments Ltd	351
Haworth & Thompson	192
Hayward, John	217, 332
Hayward, William	217, 394
Hazeldine, William	64
Heaths Dee Collieries Ltd	309
Hendre Ddu Slate	285
Hendre Lead & Lime	286, 287
Hendre Meredydd Quarry	285
Hendre Spar Mine	287
Henshaw, Owen &	226
Hewitt & Rhodes	155
Hibbert & Son Ltd	302
Hickman Ltd, Alfred	303
Higginbottom & Co	221
Higginbottom, S.W.	195
Hill, Arthur	308

Hills & Bailey	169	Hope, John Harold	356
Hill's Brickworks	308	Hopley, C.P.	47
Hobbs (Dyserth) Ltd	253	Houghton, Thomas	260
Holland & Hannen and Cubitts	375, 419	Howard [John] & Co Ltd	232
Holland, Samuel	139, 243, 303, 341, 405	Howl, S.	221
		Hudson Consolidated	381
Holland's Quarry	341	Hughes & Lancaster	184
Holme & King	28, 152	Hughes, H.L.	46
Holyhead Aluminium	288	Hughes, H.W.E.	29
Holyhead, Extensions at	80	Hughes, J.O. & G.J.	303
Holyhead Harbour	289	Hughes, Shone	225
Holywell	270	Hughes, W.H.	28
Holywell-Halkyn Mining Co	281	Humphreys, E.Noel	182
Holywell Junction	271	Humphris, H.	382
Holywell Lime & Cement	118, 270	Hunt, Noble & Co	328
Holywell Railway & Limestone	270	Hutton & Roscoe	405
Holywell Railway Company	118	Hyde & Co	414
Home Grown Timber Supply Dept.	310		

I

Imperial Chemical Industries	228, 319, 385	Ingleby, Richard	385
Imperial Tramways Co	92	International Electroplate Co	391
Industrial Estates Management Corp'n	419	Ireland, R.	222

J

Jackson, Thomas	79	Johnstown	278, 280
James, Brian	268	Jolly, Ian	48
Jardine & Son	118, 191	Jones & Co, David	322
Jeffrey, W.B.	302	Jones & Ingham	276
Jegon, Trew.	303	Jones & Sons, Walter	30
Jenkins, John	285	Jones, Gethin Owen	89
Jenks Brickworks	263	Jones, Griffith	200
Johannesburg Consolidated Investment Co	351	Jones [Inigo] & Co	276
		Jones, John	262
John Summers & Sons	395	Jones, John Lloyd	262
Johnson, Bryan	27	Jones M.& Luck P.	276
Johnson, H.Croom	47, 101, 128, 148, 192	Jones, Owain Gethin	102
		Jones, William	102

K

Keef Railways Ltd	159	Kitchen, Frederick	384
Kennaway, Sir Charles	332	Kleeneezi Quarry	226
Kinderley & Co, Nathaniel	387	Kneeshaw Lupton & Co Ltd	307
King, A.C.	347	Kneeshaw, Richard	353
Kingdon, F.B.	29	Krauss & Co	133
Kingston Minerals Ltd	212, 353, 402, 405	Kyrke & Eyton	309
Kinmel Park Military Camp	293	Kyrke, Richard	256
Kirk, Richard	208		

L

Laing [John] & Sons Ltd	250, 404
Lancashire Steel Corpn	193, 199, 369
Lancaster Electrical Co	165
Lancaster, Taylor et al	335
Lane, C.W.	165
Lane End Colliery	101
Lane End Colliery Co	298
Latimer [Wm] & Co Ltd	251
Law & Ward	253
Lea, George	131
Ledward, E.H.	212
Lee, Gwalia Forge	30
LeFeuvre, W.H.	115
Leslie Leisure Ltd	159
Lester's Limeworks	330
Level Fawr	204, 254
Lewis' Brickworks	308
Lewis, P.& H.	308, 383
Lime Firms Ltd	293
Limestone Products Ltd	253, 293
Lindley Plant Ltd	265
Little Mountain Colliery	298
Little Orme's Head Limestone Co	299
Liverpool Corporation	319
Llan Ffestiniog	276
Llanberis	234
Llanberis Branch Rly	120
Llanberis Lake Railway	166
Llanberis Quarries	235
Llanberis River Tunnel	233
Llanberis Slate Co Ltd	301, 302, 303
Llanberis West Quarrires	300
Llanddonna	233
Llanddulas (Craig) Quarries	307
Llandudno & Colwyn Bay Electric Rly	155
Llandudno & Colwyn Bay Elect.Rly.Society	400
Llandudno Branch Rly	90
Llandudno Junction Brickworks	308
Llandudno Pier Contract	309
Llandudno Tramway Society	400
Llandudno Urban District Council	155
Llanerch-y-Mor Lead Works	309
Llanfynydd Branch	86
Llangollen & Corwen Railway	94
Llangollen District Forestry Railways	310
Llangollen, Peckett at	29
Llangollen Steam Railway	173
Llanrwst Consolidated Mines Ltd	351
Llanrwst Lead Mines Ltd	351
Llanrwst Transport Museum	310
Llay Bank Fireclay Mine	311
Llay Hall Brick Works	311
Llay Hall Colliery	311
Llay Hall Gravel Pits	312
Llay Main Colliery	313
Llay Main Colliery Railway	112
Llechwedd Slate Quarry	316, 382
Lloyd & Griffith	186
Lloyd's Spar Quarries	287
Llyn Celyn Reservoir	319
Llyn Cowlyd	240
Llysfaen Limeworks	319
Llysfaen (Old) Limeworks	307
Lomax, Henry	254
London, Midland & Scottish Railway	293
Lord Penrhyn	357
Lord's Slate Quarry	412
Lovatt & Sons Ltd, Wilson	374
Lupton, Wm.	353
Lythgoe Bros Ltd	330

M

Mackenzie, Brassey & Stephenson	79
Mackenzie, William	79
Maen Offeren Slate Qy Co	89, 322, 382
Maentwrog Power Station	404
Maes-y-Gamfa Quarry	285
Magnetite Sewage & Water Purification Co	338
Makin, J.J.	261
Manchester & Ffestiniog Slate & Slab Co	382
Manod Slate Quarries Ltd	324
Marchlyn Mawr Reservoir	325
Marchwiel Holdings Ltd	357
Marford Sand & Gravel Quarry	326
Marples, Ridgeway & Partners	190
Marr, Lawrence	257
Masson	212
Matthews & Huddart	341
Maurice & Low	414
Mawddwy Railway	116
"MBZ" (McAlpine/Brand/Zschokke)	233, 325
McAlpine Quarries Ltd	357
McAlpine, Sir Alfred	67, 199, 265, 340, 357, 402
McAlpine, Sir Robert	135, 187, 246, 248, 249, 340, 392, 404
McAlpine-Brand-Zschokke	233, 325
McCormick & Holme	87
McDougall	146

McKenzie, D.	119	Moel Tryfan, lessees of	262
McKie, Hugh Unsworth	131	Moel Tryfan Slate Quarry	332
Meakin	84	Moel y Gest Sett Quarry	334
Meakin & Dean	140, 143, 266	Moelferna Quarries	331
Meirion Mill Railway	172	Mold & Denbigh Junction Railway	123
Melville, Dundas & Whitsun	271	Mold & Treiddyn Railway	125
Menzies, John	212	Mold Collieries Ltd	195, 202
Mersey Docks & Harbour Board	233	Mold Gas & Water Co	334
Metallic Salvage & Supply	272	Mold Railway	85
Midland Peat Products Ltd	416	Mold Railway Company	86
Midland Tar Distillers Ltd	373	Mold Tinplate Co	189
Military Railways	293	Monk & Newell	103
Milwr Tunnel	281	Monk [A] & Co Ltd	312
Milwr Tunnel Railway	386	Moreton Pits	264
Minera Lead & Zinc Mines	326	Morgan [of Old Braich]	251
Minera Lime Co	330	Morris, D.	254
Minera Mining Co Ltd	328	Morris, George	217
Minerals Concentration Co	231	Morris, Owen	102
Ministry of Aircraft Production	360	Morrish, A.E.	156
Ministry of Defence	378	Morton, Godfrey	139
Ministry of Fuel & Power	280	Moss Valley Branch Rly	142
Ministry of Munitions	375	Mostyn Collieries	335
Ministry of Public Building & Works	324, 385	Mostyn Docks & Trading Co	336
		Mostyn Ironworks	335
Ministry of Supply	189, 201, 228, 270, 309, 360, 380, 385, 419	Mostyn, Lord	369
		Mostyn Magnetite Co	338
Ministry of Supply, Forestry Control	310	Mostyn Wagon Repair Works	338
Ministry of Transport	289	Mountain Colliery	210
Ministry of Works	324	Mowddwy Railway Co	116
Minshall, T.E.	49	Mowlem [John] & Co Ltd	283, 306
Mochdre Shale Quarry	264	Muskett, George	217
Modern Electric Tramways Ltd	165	Muspratt Bros. & Huntley	258
Moel Siabod Slate & Slab	383		

N

Nant Mawr Coal Co	347	NCB Workshops, Llay	313
Nant Mine	381	Nelson [Thomas] & Co	144
Nantlle	251	Nerquis Colliery & Railway	339
Nantlle Branch Rly	126	New Ash Colliery	209
Nantlle Railway Co	66, 113	New Braich Slate Quarries	200
Nantlle Slate Quarry Co	366	New British Iron Co	184, 421
Nantlle Vale Drainage	339	New Brynmally Colliery Co	208
Narrow Gauge Enterprises	341	New Cambrian Slate Co	268
Narrow Gauge Railways Ltd	146, 159	New Flint Colliery	260
National Co-operative Quarries Ltd	303	New Minera Mining Co Ltd	328
National Coal Board	193, 197, 272, 278, 311, 313, 369	New Pandora Mining Syndicate	243, 418
		New Prince of Wales Slate Co	73
National Coal Board Opencast	280	New Road Gravel Pits	340
National Granite Paving Sett Co	409	New Tan-y-Graig Sett Quarry Co	409
National Museum of Wales	415	New Welsh Slate Co	229
National Trust	357	Newborough Estate	304
National Welsh Slate Quarries	285	Newmarket Extension Railway	144
Nationwide Slate Products	276	Newton, Robert	212

Newtown, Flint	29
North & South Buckley Colliery	210
North Buckley Coal Co	416
North Hendre Lead	286
North Wales Coal, Iron & Firebrick	311
North Wales Coke Co	389
North Wales Construction Co	212
North Wales Development Co	350
North Wales Granite Co	226
North Wales Granite Quarry Co	409
North Wales Iron & Manganese Co	380
North Wales Mineral Extension Rly	75
North Wales Mineral Railway	75, 77
North Wales Narrow Gauge Rly	131, 146
North Wales Paper Co	261
North Wales Power & Traction	243
North Wales Power Co	404
North Wales Quarries Ltd	350
North Wales Quarry Museum	415
North Wales Tarred Macadam Co	230
North Wales Tramway Museum Assn	400
North Wales Wagon Co Ltd	377
North West Wales River Authority	231
North Western Peat Products	416
Northern Welsh Slate Co Ltd	303
Norwest Construction Co Ltd	309
Nott, Louis P.	82
Nowell, Hemmingway & Pearson	79
Nowell, James & George	125

O

Oak Colliery	209
Oak Pits Colly Co	202
Oakeley, Edward	221
Oakeley Slate Quarries	341
Oakeley Slate Quarries Co	412
Oakeley, W.E.	341
Oakenholt Mill	261
Offa's Dyke Colliery	414
Old Broughton Colliery	346
Old Kilgwyn	217
Olwyn Goch Mine	281
Opencast Coal Disposal Point	265
Ordish, R.M.	115
Ormiston, John	260
Oughtibridge Silica Firebrick Co	182
Owen & Co	66
Owen & Co, Wm.	366
Owen, E.H.	267
Owen, Owen J.	383
Owen, Thomas & John	155
Owen, William	276

P

Padarn Railway	235
Padeswood Cannel & Coal Co	347
Padeswood Cement Works	349
Padeswood United Cannel Coal & Iron	347
Padeswood United Coal & Cannel Co	347
Palmerston Quarry	341
Pandora Lead Mining Co	418
Pant Farm Gravel Pits	340
Pant Glas Reservoir	351
Pant Glas Slate & Slab	268
Pantdreiniog Slate Quarry	350
Parc Lead & Zinc Mining Co	351
Parc [Park] & Croesor Estate	105
Park & Croesor Slate Quarries Co	228
Park Farm Colliery	389
Park Pit	389
Parkinson, Sir Lindsay	261, 378
Parry & Co	260
Parry & Co, Thomas	385
Parry & Collingwood	102
Parry, Edward	66
Parry, Richard	358
Parry, S.	90
Parry, W.J.	350
Partington Iron & Steel Co	199
Parys Mountain Mines	352
Patent Mineral Carbon Co	389
Pauling & Co Ltd	419
Pearce & Gough	346
Pearson	219
Pearson, Charles	332
Pearson, E.	242
Pearson, George	200
Pearson, John	200
Pearson [S] & Son Ltd	290
Peebles, Bruce	134, 155
Pen-ychain Holiday Camp	211
Pengwern & Gwydyr Quarries Ltd	351
Penmachno Slate Co	352
Penmaen East & West Quarries	353
Penmaenbach Stone Quarries	226
Penmaenmawr & Welsh Granite	212, 353, 402, 405
Penmaenmawr Granite Quarries	353

Penmon	231, 257, 356	Plasmadoc Railways	184
Penmon Park Quarries	356	Pochin, H.D.	144
Penmon Quarries Ltd	356	Point of Ayr Colliery	369
Penrhos Colliery	204	Ponkey [Ponciau] Branch Rly	93
Penrhyn Castle Museum	357	Pontcysyllte Branch Rly	96
Penrhyn, Lord	86	Pontybodkin Colliery Co	202
Penrhyn Railway	357	Poole, O.A.	323
Penrhyn Slate Quarries	357	Pope, Samuel	228
Pentre Ffwrndan Alkali Works	223	Port Dinorwic	86, 87, 234, 235
Pentre'r-Gwyddel Quarry	307	Port Penrhyn	86, 357
Pentrobin Hall Colliery	192	Portmadoc, Beddgelert &	
Penybont Brickworks	364	South Snowdon Rly	105, 131
Penybryn Mine	281	Portmadoc, Croesor & Beddgelert	
Penybryn Slate Co	365	Tram Rly	105
Penyclip Roadworks & Tunnels	366	Portmadoc Granite Quarries Ltd	334
Penyfron Lead Mine	385	Powell, Frank R.	50
Penyrorsedd Slate Quarry Co	366	Pratt, Alan	196
Percival, F.S.	412	Premier Glynrhonwy Slate Quarry Ltd	304
Perkins, John	222	Prestatyn Coal Co	369
Peto & Betts	85	Preston, Edward	66, 102
Peto, Samuel Morton	90	Prince of Wales Colliery	278
Phillips, Melvin	269	Pritchard & Gregory	105
Phoenix, I.	381	Pritchard & Stephens	302
Phoenix Wagon Works	51	Pritchard et al, J.	323
Piercy & Robertson	141	Providence Iron Works	51
Piercy, Benjamin	109, 111, 141	Prys & Co	380
Piercy, Exors of Benjamin	148	Public Works & Contract Co	356
Pine & Murchison	418	Pullen & Crane	301
Plas Mawr Railway	368	Pwllheli Corporation	150
Plas Power Coal Co	369	Pwllheli, Tramways at	149
Plaskynaston Foundry	28	Pwllycrochan Estate	222
Plasmadoc Branch Rly	96		

Q

Quarry Tours Ltd	316	Queensferry Petroleum Depot	376
Queen's Ferry Coal Co	192	Queensferry Power Station	377
Queensferry Alkali Co	373	Queensferry Shipbuilding Yard	380
Queensferry Colliery	192	Queensferry Tar Works	373
Queensferry Government Factory	373	Queensferry Wagon Works	377
Queensferry Leisure Centre	379		

R

R.A.F. Wrexham	199	Rheilffordd Llyn Tegid	170
R.O.F. Wrexham	419	Rheinisch West Falische Co	313
Ratcliffes of Hawarden	50	Rhiw Manganese Mines	380
Raynes & Co (James T.Raynes)	319	Rhiw Manganese Mines Ltd	381
Raynes, J.T.	353	Rhiwbach Slate Quarries	382
Raynes, Lupton & Co	307	Rhiwbach Slate Quarry	89
Red Wharf Bay Branch	158	Rhiwbach Tramroad	89
Reid, Campbell & McDougall	203	Rhiwbryfdir Slate Co	341
Renshaw & Sons	257	Rhiwfachno Slate Quarry	352
Rheilffordd Llyn Padarn Cyf	166	Rhodes of Sheffield	116

Rhos Branch	154
Rhos Limestone Quarry	299
Rhos Slate & Slab Quarry Co	383
Rhuddlan Borough Council	159
Rhyd-Ddu	267
Rhyd-Ddu Forestry Railway	385
Rhydymwyn	286
Rhydymwyn Foundry	385
Rhydymwyn Government Depot	385
Rhyl	261
Rhyl Amusements Ltd	159
Rhyl Electric Tramway	165
Rhyl Lime & Quarrying Co	253
Rhyl Miniature Railway	159
Rhyl to Gronant Road	386
Rhyl Urban District Council	186
Richard Thomas & Co	189
Richards, W.Alban	293
Richardson, Henry.	200
Ridley & Seckham	120
Ridley, S.C.	120, 121, 126
Rigby & Hancock	298
Rigby, J.& C.	80, 289
Rigby, James	242
Riley's	384
Rival Granite Quarries	212
River Dee Company	387
Roberts & Maginnis Ltd	408
Roberts & Sloss	313
Roberts, Hugh Beaver	105, 200, 260
Roberts, J.R.	263
Roberts, John	412

Roberts, Owen	212
Robertson & Darby	265, 346
Robertson, Henry	75, 77, 84, 95, 141, 203, 369, 389
Robinson, John	124, 400
Robinson, Thomas	400
Roe & James Venables	208
Romag Ltd	408
Rose, Thomas	298
Roskell, George	258
Ross, A.M.	203
Rossett Sand & Gravels Ltd	326
Rowland & Geo.Homfray	184
Rowland, E.Ll.	184
Rowlands, Wm.	29
Roy, Robert	203
Royal Air Force	392
Royal Welsh Show	388
Ruabon	263
Ruabon Brandie Colliery	389
Ruabon Brick & Terra-Cotta	264
Ruabon Brook Tramroad	64
Ruabon Coal & Coke Co	278, 389
Ruabon Coal Co	278, 389
Ruabon Iron Co	184
Ruabon New Colliery	278
Ruabon New Ironworks	184
Ruabon Old Colliery	389
Ruthin & Cerrigydruidion Railway	140
Ruthin & Denbigh Tar Macadam Co	230, 390
Ruthin Lime & Limestone Co	230, 390

S

Saltney Quay Scrapyard	390
Saltney Quay Shipyard	390
Sandycroft Foundry	391
Sandycroft (Machinery & Ship) Works	391
Sargeant & Toms	394
Savin	52, 66, 98
Savin & Co	104, 109, 113, 115, 117
Savin, Davies &	91
Scientific Roads Ltd	378
Scott & Edwards	80, 122, 123
Scott, John	80
Sealand Aerodrome	392
Sealand Trading Estate	393
Seddon, E.& J.	28
Seddon, J.B.	27-28
Seiont Brickworks	394
Sharpe, Edmund	102
Ship Canal Portland Cement	264, 299
Shotton	223

Shotton Paper Co	393
Shotton Steelworks	395
Shotwick Aerodrome	392
Shrewsbury & Chester Rly	75, 77, 84
Shrewsbury, Oswestry & Chester Junction Rly	84
Shropshire Union Railway & Canal Company	127
Shropshire Union Railways	64
Skelsey, G.H.	338
Slag Reduction Co Ltd	338, 414
Smelt Colliery	204
Smelt Lead Works	204
Smelters Union	303
Smith, James	67
Smith, Wm.	102
Snowdon Mountain Tramroad	152
Sommerfeld, L.	334
South Buckley Colliery	210

South Halkyn & Rhydymwyn Mining	385	Stacey, J.		119
South Mostyn Colliery	335	Standard Mine, Mostyn		335
Southall, Wm.	202	Stanley, J.		335
Spanish & General Corporation	213	Stanlow Works Estates Ltd	264,	299
Spargo & Turner	409	Stellite Ltd		377
Spargo, Edmund	212, 213	Stoney & Lancaster		335
Sparrow & Poole	256	Stott-Milne [John] & Co		197
Sparrow, James	256	Strachan, Exors of John		158
Sparrow, Pearson & Co	256	Strachan, John		158
Spencer Bros (Chester) Ltd	390	Strutton, George		303
Spooner & Co	187	Stubbs, Berks & Co		298
Spooner, C.E.	113	Stubbs Brothers		223
Spooner, James Swinton	107	Sullivan, H.E.		242
St Georges Harbour & Railway	90	Summers [John] & Sons	209,	214
St.George Limeworks	293	Synthite Ltd		189
Stabla Cable-Laying Contract	399			

T

Tal-Y-Mieryn Quarry	285	Tilcon (Tilling Construction)	253
Talwrn Colliery	414	Tomkinson, John	353
Talycafn Tramway Museum	400	Tonfanau Granite Quarries	402
Talyllyn Railway	107	Tram-Railway Company	74
Talysarn	219	Trap Brickworks	403
Talysarn Slate Co	400	Trawsfynydd Reservoir	404
Tan Dinas Quarries	233	Trefor Granite Quarry	405
Tan-y-Graig Granite Co Ltd	409	Tremadog Ironstone Mines	73
Tan-y-Graig Sett Quarry Co	409	Trevor Silica Brickworks	408
Tanygraig Granite Quarries	409	Trewydir Slate & Slab Co	383
Tanygrisiau Power Station	402	Trimley Hall Roadstone	255
Tarmac Construction Ltd	319	Trust House Forte Leisure	159
Tarmac Ltd	255, 280	Tucker, Samuel Blatchford	356
Tarmac Roadstone Holdings Ltd	330	Tudor Slate Works	276
Tarmac Roadstone (Northern) Ltd	230	Tunnel Portland Cement Co	349
Tarmacadam Roads Ltd	338	Turner & Morgan	366
Taylor & Sons, John	328	Turner, Joseph	373
Taylor, Captain J.H.	305	Turner [of Parkia]	251
Taylor, Henry E.	391	Turner, Sir Ll.	213
Taylor, James	116	Turner, Wm.	365
Taylor, John	385, 391	Twigdons	165
Taylor Woodrow Construction	288	Twll Goch Quarry	303
Thomas Botfield	298	Ty Canol Mine	381
Thomas, William	356	Ty Mawr Reservoir Construction	410
Thompson, Fred	192	Tyddyn Hywel Quarry	409
Thompson, Isaac	192	Tyddyn Meirion Mine	381
Thompson, John	192, 256	Tynllan Manganese Co	381
Thompson, John & James	203	Tywyn Railway Museum	411
Tilcon Ltd	287		

U

Underwood [Wm] & Brother	222, 241	United Minera Mining Co Ltd	329
United Alkali Co	258, 319	United Westminster & Wrexham Colls	272
United Engineering Steels Ltd	204	Upper Croesor Slate Quarry Co	227
United Gravel Co Ltd	287, 326, 340	Upper Glynrhonwy Slate Co	304

V

Vale of Clwyd Railway	91, 98
Vale of Llangollen Railway	94
Vaynol Estate	87
Veingoch	217
Vereinigte Glanzstoff-Fabriken	257
Vickers-Armstrongs	203
Voryd Park Electric Tramway	165
Votty & Bowydd Slate Quarries Co	412
Vron & Old Braich Welsh Slate	262
Vron & Talysarn Tramroad	124
Vron Colliery Co	414
Vron Mineral Branch	141
Vron Welsh Slate	262
Vron WMCQR Branch	140

W

Wales & Monmouthshire Ind. Estates	419
Wales Gas Board	334
Walkinshaw, E.	202
Walton, Major	285
War Department	283, 293, 378
Warburton & Pennant	357
Ward, Alex	192
Ward, T.E.	197
Ward, [Thos.W.] Ltd	96, 304, 336, 409
Warton & Warden	79
Watkinson [George] & Sons	209
Webster et al, F.	323
Welsh Crown Spelter Co	418
Welsh Foxdale Mine Syndicate	418
Welsh Granite Co	405
Welsh Highland Railway	131
Welsh National Water Development Authority	231
Welsh Slate Centre	415
Welsh Slate Co	341
Wepre Chemical Works	223
West Buckley Colliery Co	416
West, Frederick Richard	390
West Mostyn Coal & Iron Co	369
West Nant Granite Co	213
Western Development Co	418
Westminster, Duke of	281
Wheldon, Chas	254
Wheldon, Edward	28, 255
White, J.H.	409
White [Richard] & Sons	155
Whiteway, Philip	353
Whitley Brothers	56
Whitwham, F.G.	111
Whixall Moss Litter Co	416
Whixall Moss Peat Railway	416
Wilkinson & R.Kyrke	328
Wilkinson, John	203
Willans & Robinson Ltd	374
William Carpenter	200
William Wild & Sons	290
Williams & Son, J.H.	28, 29
Williams & Sons, R.	224
Williams, E.	254
Williams, Ellis	332
Williams, Isaac	119
Williams, James	285
Williams [John] & Co	251
Williams, Martin	73
Williams, Needham & Simm Ltd	366
Williams, Pugh, Davies	262
Williams, Richard	27
Williams, Robert	200, 383
Williams, T.Glyn	285
Williams, W.O.	57, 93, 137
Williams, Wm.J.	344
Willoughby Lead Mine	418
Willow Colliery	209
Wills, C.J.	82
Wilson, Edward	95
Wilson [J] & Sons	258
Winberg, M.	277
Wincilate Group	201
Wincilate Ltd	183
Winnard & Braddock	339
Wonder Pit	204
Woolley, John	58, 141, 145, 148
Wrexham & East Denbighshire Water Co	351, 410
Wrexham & Ellesmere Railway	151
Wrexham & Minera Extension Railway	126
Wrexham & Minera Railway	99
Wrexham District Tramways	130
Wrexham Industrial Estate	419
Wrexham, Mold & Connah's Quay Rly	100, 109, 140, 145, 148
Wrexham Steel Works Ltd	203
Wright, H.J.	212, 213, 381
Wright, Messrs	264
Wynne, Edward	268
Wynne Slate Quarry	268
Wynnstay Collieries Ltd	421

Although the rail system at Castle Brickworks (p.214) survived until 1950, it was only possible to see the three Kerr Stuart 'Wrens' intact together prior to 1940. Hence taken in the late 1930s, this rare view shows, left to right, KS 2473, KS 2460 and KS 4005.
[collection I.Jolly]

BASIC was the only Dubs loco, and the only crane-tank, known to have worked in North Wales, yet it served the Brymbo Steelworks (p.205) well for over 70 years.
[G.Alliez: 20/5/1951]

Motor Rail Simplex 2033 at Alyn Works, Mold (p.189), retained its Lancashire & Yorkshire Railway numberplate '3' firmly rivetted to its sideframe, despite having passed through various ownerships in its life. [collection I.Jolly]

Hybrid battery locomotive constructed at Votty & Bowydd Quarry (p.412) incorporating the frames of Vulcan Foundry steam loco TAFFY, and seen here at Aberllefenni Quarry (p.183), Corris, in the 1960s. [A.F.Leleux]

The unidentified Logan battery loco about to enter the adit at Braich Goch Quarry, Upper Corris (p.201); this loco is now on public display at Inigo Jones Tudor Slate Mill, Groeslon (p.276). [P.Hindley: 19/10/1967]

Cudworth & Johnson (p.44) made good use of many locos, but Avonside 1876 was probably an exception. It remained stored for some years, as seen here, beneath the ex-GWR main line at Wrexham, then disappeared without trace.[G.P.Roberts: 3/4/1953]

As far as is known, Hudswell Clarke 303 of 1888 was the only loco that ever worked at the Bodfari Sand Sidings (p.199) during their ten years life. Its unusual name, ARKAYAR, originated in the initials of its first owner, one Robert K.Roberts of Bury, Lancashire. [R.G.Pratt: 1929]

NETHERTON, Manning Wardle 1603 of 1903, was a familiar sight for several years, standing knee-deep in mud beside the GWR main line at the foot of Gresford Bank. It had shunted Marford Sand Sidings (p.326) during the latter years of World War 2 before being abandoned. [R.T.Russell: 1/5/1949]

Locomotives designed for passenger train duties do not make ideal quarry shunters; one can only presume that this former Metropolitan Railway Beyer Peacock came to the Conwy Stone Quarries (p.226) at a bargain price. Named CONWAY it, sadly, did not remain long. [collection F.Jones]

Narrow-gauge Ruston diesels became very popular in the slate industry, the Blaenau Ffestiniog quarries being first to purchase fleets. Newly-arrived RH 174139 shunting Oakeley (p.341) traffic in the LMS yard at Blaenau, admired by PALMERSTON of the Ffestiniog Railway (p.67). [RH Publicity: 6/3/1935]

With many operators the popularity has not waned; Ruston 297030 has been re-bodied, re-engined and air-braked and, named GLASLYN, is still capable of useful work on the Welsh Highland Railway (p.138). [V.J.Bradley: 5/1987]

Hunslet turned out many 20hp 2ft-gauge diesels for Government use in World War 2; they were usually sold via agents Robert Hudson Ltd, as "Hudson-Hunslets". Two, however, went direct to Trefor Quarry (p.405), as simple "Hunslets" - this is HE 2208 of 1941, Trefor '6', on the line to the pier. [P.Hindley: 21/6/1964]

Hibberd "Planet-Simplex" 1821 of 1933 was a rebuild of a Motor Rail Simplex of probably First World War origin; Hibberds modified it to increase its top speed, probably for use on the Rhiwbach Tramroad (p.89). Seen here at Maenofferen office level (p.322). [V.J.Bradley: 15/4/1954]

Very few industrial locos remain in service yet Anglesey still has three, two of these being at Amlwch Factory (p.190). The more modern of this pair, Hunslet 7460 of 1977, is seen here shunting at the terminus of the Amlwch Light Railway.

[P.Hindley: 25/7/1980]

Locos are still used at Connah's Quay Wagon Works (p.224) in Clwyd, often having been purchased for scrapping but found to have useful life left in them. This is MARIE, Fowler 22882, which came here from Shell Refinery at Ellesmere Port in 1970.

[P.Hindley: 5/6/1976]

In the aftermath of the Beeching cuts, British Railways sold hundreds of diesel shunters in virtually un-used condition; many found their way into industrial service. Gatewen Opencast Coal Depot (p.266), near Wrexham, made use of Swindon-built ex-D.2182 for several years. [P.Hindley: 3/3/1977]

Shotton Steelworks (p.395) had the largest stock of industrial locos in North Wales, and was the first major steelworks in Britain to fully dieselise its fleet. This imposing North British six-wheeler (NB 28034) had hydraulic transmission; it came new in 1960, but was scrapped in 1979 as the works was gradually closed. [P.Hindley: 17/10/1964]

No book about North Wales quarry locos would be complete without an illustration of a DeWinton loco, which were designed and built near to the castle in Caernarfon. This is LLANFAIR, a fairly typical example though on the 3ft gauge at Penmaenmawr (p.353); the majority were 2ft gauge machines in fact. [G.Shuttleworth: 29/8/1949]

Other examples of local endeavour were the eighteen "motor-car" locos built at Penrhyn Slate Quarry (p.357). No.3 is seen here in original condition, complete with circular thermometer on the radiator cap, and squeeze-bulb horn. [collection B.Roberts]

The '7x10' cylindered Hunslets were popular workhorses in many quarries, and most that survived until after World War 2 have been saved for preservation or tourist railway operation. This is WILD ASTER, a Dinorwic Quarry (p.234) loco now in service on the Llanberis Lake Railway (p.166). [V.J.Bradley: 8/1988]

Despite being built from similar major components, not all the '7x10' locos were the same; indeed, most were modified to suit specific conditions at the different quarries. With low-profile cabs and miniature chimneys, TRYFAN and CADFAN at Moeltryfan Quarry (p.332) appeared very small indeed. [collection: R.Wm.Jones]

Manufactured in Shrewsbury, the Sentinel vertical-boilered loco could perhaps be regarded as a much-modernised DeWinton; it sold well throughout the world, but not extensively in North Wales. Little Orme Quarry (p.299) obtained three of 3ft gauge, of which this is number 2, Sentinel 6255, in its later days. [G.Alliez: 15/4/1938]

There were standard gauge Sentinels too, and a mystery surrounds that at Penybont Brickworks, Cefn (p.364) where this photo was taken. In immaculate condition, and obviously brand new, it has a high cab - unlike the loco ordered for this site. Hence the identity of this loco is in doubt. [Sentinel Magazine, 10/1925]

The railway to Red Wharf Bay (p.158) was the last main-line branch to be built in North Wales, and one of the few for which photographs of construction locos can be found. Seen here is J.STRACHAN No.7 (MW 1576 of 1903), thought to be near Red Wharf in the autumn of 1908. [collection V.J.Bradley]

The Kinmel Railway (p.293) ran for miles across the flat Rhuddlan marsh and, in later years, was operated by the St.George Limestone Quarry (p.297) which alone it then served. The regular loco was an Avonside called MARGARET, but here we see her twin, AE 1432, known as "ELEANOR", approaching a level crossing with the daily run. [F.Boughey: 4/1950]

Formerly number 16379 in the LMS 'main-line' fleet, this substantial six-wheeler was a popular performer at Hafod Colliery (p.278) for some 25 years before being withdrawn - it was subsequently preserved in Glasgow. It was overhauled in 1957, and the colliery staff painted the letters "L M S" back onto its sidetanks.   [V.J.Bradley: 13/4/1958]

Other ex-main line locos used in North Wales included some 4-4-0 tanks, from the Midland & Great Northern Railway, which saw service at Kinmel Camp (p.293). Four locos were involved, but which came to Kinmel is uncertain - see p.295. '8', Hudswell Clarke 209 of 1878, is a typical example of the batch, seen here in later years at Edinburgh Collieries.   [collection: J. Peden]

Wartime 'austerity' locos were used widely in industry, and particularly in the coal industry, towards the end of the steam era. This example (RSH 7162) shunted at Gatewen Opencast Coal Depot (p.266) and was probably the last Alfred McAlpine loco in service anywhere. [V.J.Bradley: 16/11/1958]

PIRAEUS was a small Barclay loco, originally intended for service in Greece but which ended its days at Hafod Colliery, Johnstown (p.278). It was AB 643 of 1889, and carried an early pattern rectangular worksplate stating it was built at "Kilmarnock N.B." - the initials standing for 'North Britain'. [F.Jones: 6/1955]

The earliest internal-combustion locos to be used underground in the slate quarries were built by Deutz in Cologne, Germany. A fairly typical example is seen here c1935 at Oakeley Quarry (p.341), near to the viaduct that spanned the Conwy Valley line.
[collection A.Neale]

Before standardising on Rustons, the Oakeley (p.341) fleet, both steam and non-steam, contained considerable variety; it included three of the unusual Baguley petrol locos of the type favoured by WW1 forestry systems. Bg 774 is seen here prior to removal for preservation; it has since returned to the Gloddfa Ganol display at Oakeley.
[V.J.Bradley: 14/6/1968]

Small Bagnall locos were quite numerous in the area, though not every location mastered the art of handling the unusual circular fireboxes with which many were fitted. SANFORD was the first loco at Maenofferen (p.322), but was soon laid aside; eventually it found a new home at Penrhyn Quarries (p.357) where it is seen here in the 1930s. [collection R.T.Russell]

Llechwedd Quarries (p.317) solved their Bagnall problems in a different way, by converting them into electric locos. Twin trolley poles collected current from a fearsome tangle of sagging copper conductors. THE ECLIPSE had its origins in Bagnall MARGARET - or was it DOROTHY ? [P.Hindley: 14/8/1976]

Kneeshaw Lupton at Llanddulas (p.307) used rope-haulage to shunt their standard gauge sidings for over a century, except for some five years when this small 80hp Barclay diesel (AB 349) was utilised. Traffic declined; it was sold for preservation, later reaching the Colne Valley Railway in Essex. [P.Hindley: 7/1969]

NELLIE was a 50hp 'Planet' diesel which saw limited use at Crump's Mostyn Wagon Works (p.338) before transfer to their Connah's Quay Works (p.224). Here too it was found underpowered, and did not last long. Photo taken at Mostyn Works.
[P.Hindley: 19/10/1964]

Beyer Peacock of Manchester primarily built 'main-line' locos, though they did have some success in selling shunters as well. The Wrexham area had a few, of which MINERA, BP 810 of 1868, was a typical example, new to Minera Limeworks (p.330)
[BP Official]

CYMRO, popularly regarded as being a product of Cudworth & Johnson's (p.34) own staff, though the true origin of this hotch-potch of assorted components is shrouded in mystery. It was subsequently used on construction of the Wrexham to Ellesmere line (p.151), then faded into obscurity once again. [collection G.Alliez]

Hudswell Clarke 1535, a typical 3ft-gauge contractor's shunter, was owned by McAlpine. It first ran along the streets of Dolgarrog assisting in the construction of new houses (p.249), then later transferred to operate on the temporary railway from Maentwrog Road station to the Trawsfynydd Reservoir (p.404). A few years later it was working in London docks, as seen here. [G.Alliez: 7/8/1937]

Hudwell Clarke 1642 was another design for contract work, but a 6-wheeler for 2ft-gauge, and is seen here standing on the beach at Rhyl whilst engaged on the cutting of a new river channel at Foryd (p.261). A twin sister, HC 1643, was used at Penrhyn Quarries (p.357). [B.D.Stoyel: 22/9/1936]